The Complete Words of Wall Street

of Wall Street

The Professional's Guide
to Investment Literacy

The Complete Words of Wall Street

of Wall Street

The Professional's Guide to Investment Literacy

Allan H. Pessin
Joseph A. Ross

BUSINESS ONE IRWIN
Homewood, Illinois 60430

Sponsoring editor: Amy Hollands
Project editor: Karen Nelson
Production manager: Bette K. Ittersagen
Jacket design: Image House
Compositor: Precision Typographers
Typeface: 10/12 Century Schoolbook
Printer: R. R. Donnelley & Sons Company

Library of Congress Cataloging-in-Publication Data

Pessin, Allan H.
    The complete words of Wall Street : the professional's guide to
investment literacy / by Allan H. Pessin and Joseph A. Ross.
        p.   cm.
    ISBN 1-55623-330-2
    1. Investments—Dictionaries.   2. Securities—Dictionaries.
3. Finance—Dictionaries.   I. Ross, Joseph A.   II. Title.
HG4513.P46   1991
332.6′03—dc20   90–19290

Printed in the United States of America
1 2 3 4 5 6 7 8 9 0 DOC 8 7 6 5 4 3 2 1

To my wife Linda for her interest in financial terminology and her patience while proofreading this book

A.H.P.

Preface

This edition of the *Complete Words of Wall Street* has taken more than 10 years to write.

The book first started with the initial concepts of Allan Pessin who felt that Wall Street terminology deserved a dictionary. Ralph Rieves of BUSINESS ONE IRWIN fostered this idea and brought Joseph Ross, another long-time Wall Street teacher, into the loop. This gave birth to *Words of Wall Street* in 1983.

Then in 1986, the co-authors wrote *More Words of Wall Street*—and in 1990 *Still More Words of Wall Street.*

In the preface of each of these three volumes, the authors asked the readers to send in words that exemplify the current usage of the terminology of Wall Street.

The authors want to repeat that invitation. The "words of Wall Street" are made by you, the daily users of such words. Scarcely a day goes by without the members of the investment community, the daily newspapers who report their activities, and the evening TV news inventing a new word to describe this or that event. Again, we invite you to send in words from the insurance, banking, and brokerage business that should be included in future editions of this work. We would like the subsequent editions of the *Complete Words of Wall Street* to be "complete."

Nowhere is this previous concept better stated than in the preface by Samuel Johnson to his dictionary (1755):

"I am not so lost in lexicography as to forget that words are the daughters of earth, and that things are the sons of heaven. . . ."

The "daughters of earth" have indeed been busy on Wall Street. This book is the evidence of their fertility.

The authors want to thank their readers—and their publishers—for their continued support. We will wager that 10 years from now this volume will be twice its present size.

Allan H. Pessin
Joseph A. Ross

The Complete Words of Wall Street

A

A

First letter of the English alphabet, used:
1. Lowercase in newspaper stock transaction tables after dividend report to designate extra cash dividends in that year; for example, 2.40a. Formerly used in option transaction tables to designate no trades that day.
2. Uppercase in corporate newspaper reports to designate that the American Stock Exchange is the principal marketplace for a security; for example, Atlas Van (A).
3. In NASDAQ market system as the fifth letter of a stock symbol if there are various classes of common stock outstanding; for example, BISHA to designate Biscayne Holdings Class A common stock.
4. Uppercase to designate American Medical Buildings, Inc., common stock. This stock is traded on the American Stock Exchange.

ABANDONMENT

The failure of an owner to claim property that is rightfully his or hers over a long period. Such property then becomes subject to escheat (pronounced ess–cheet) laws of the individual states or country. For example, a brokerage client has on deposit with the broker 100 shares of fully paid stock and fails to claim that stock or to communicate with the broker over a prestated time period. In such a case, the property may be considered abandoned and reverts to the state.

ABC

See AGENCY BACKED COMPOUNDER SECURITIES.

ABC AGREEMENT

New York Stock Exchange term to designate this situation: a member uses borrowed funds to purchase an exchange seat. So called because the

1

exchange-approved agreement has three provisions: the member may (1) retain the seat and purchase another seat for a designee of the lender's choice, (2) sell the seat and remit the proceeds to the lender, (3) transfer the seat, at a nominal consideration, to another person in the employ of the lending member firm.

ABOUT-AMOUNT TRADE
In the English marketplace, customer orders may be entered for an amount in pounds, rather than for a specific number of shares. Thus, an order for shares of an English insurance company stock for 5,000 pounds sterling can be accepted. When the share price is set, the actual number of shares will be determined accordingly. The English marketplace gives marketmakers flexibility in accommodating such customer instructions.

ABOVE THE MARKET
Identification of an order to sell a security at a price that is greater than the present lowest offering price for that security in a particular marketplace. For example, if the present lowest offering price for a security is $45 per share, an offer at $47 is above the market.

See also AWAY FROM THE MARKET.

ABS
The Automated Bond System (ABS) is a subscription service whereby member firms can be linked to the bond trading floor of the NYSE. This automated system replaced the inactive (cabinet) bond crowd formerly in use. Through ABS, previously entered limit orders to buy or sell can be automatically paired off and reported to subscribing members.

ABS AGREEMENT
ABS is an acronym for Associated Broker Service. The agreement is a contract between Trans Canada Options, Inc., and a U.S. broker/dealer with membership in the Options Clearing Corporation or an exchange on which equity options are traded. The agreement provides for daily and periodic reports by TCO to the U.S. firm and for clearance and settlement of Canadian options transactions.

ABUSIVE TAX SHELTER
Popular name for an investment without economic merit. Such an investment, for example, would be one that provides subscribers with tax deductions of questionable applicability with little or no probability of profit on the enterprise.

The Tax Reform Act of 1986 (TRA 86) permits the IRS to challenge the tax deductions on abusive tax shelters.

ACAPULCO SPREAD
Tongue-in-cheek expression for a long and short option position which, when closed, automatically creates four commissions for the broker. Although the customer may profit, the broker always will enjoy risk-free commission income. Theoretically, the broker will use the money to vacation in sunny Acapulco, Mexico.

Also called "Cadillac spread."

ACAT
See AUTOMATED CUSTOMER ACCOUNT TRANSFER SERVICE.

ACCELERATED DEPRECIATION
Accounting procedure whereby the cost of a fixed asset is amortized over the period of the useful life of the asset. Acceleration means that more revenues are set aside in the earlier years than in later years, thus reducing tax liabilities on income received by the corporation.

See also DOUBLE DECLINING BALANCE and SUM-OF-THE-YEARS'-DIGITS.

ACCEPTANCE, WAIVER, AND CONSENT AGREEMENT
See AWC.

ACCOUNT
General industry term for:
1. The bookkeeping record of a client's transactions and credit or debit balances of either cash or securities with the member firm. The term also is used of the conduct of such business relationships. For example, "Our firm emphasizes accounts productive to the firm and to clients."
2. The books of an investment syndicate that indicate contractual relationships, the securities owned and sold, and the final financial balance between a participant in a syndicate and the syndicate itself.

ACCOUNT DAY
In England, the day on which securities transactions arranged during the preceding two-week period (the account) are due for settlement. Account day is usually seven business days after the end of the account period.

Also called "SETTLEMENT DAY."

ACCOUNT EXECUTIVE
Commonly used term for an employee of a broker/dealer who has been registered with the NASD or one of the exchanges, or both. Such employ-

ees are permitted to solicit buy and sell orders for securities and, in general, to handle client accounts.

Technically, the term applies to a registered representative (RR), although some member firms use other designations for registered employees.

See also REGISTERED REPRESENTATIVE."

ACCOUNT STATEMENT

General name for the periodic statement that gives the status of a client's account with a broker/dealer. Such statements, which must be sent at least quarterly to clients with open accounts, give a summary of all transactions during the previous period, plus a recounting of debits, credits, and long and short positions.

In practice, most broker/dealers send account statements monthly if the client has bought or sold during the previous month.

Also used of the option agreement that must be signed when a client opens an options account.

ACCREDITED INVESTOR

SEC term from Regulation D. In general, a person whose wealth or investment sophistication is such that he or she is not included in the enumeration of the 35 persons that forms the upper limit on an unregistered offering of securities.

Regulation D lists eight categories. Here are three examples of accredited investors:
1. A person with a net worth exceeding $1 million.
2. A person with income of at least $200,000 in the current year as well as in the last two years.
3. A person who is a senior official of the issuer.

ACCRETION

Technical term for the upward adjustment of the cost of acquisition of a bond purchased at an original issue discount. Internal Revenue Service rules adopted in July 1982 give precise provisions for this upward adjustment. The difference between the adjusted cost basis in successive tax years is considered interest income for the tax year in which the adjustment is made.

ACCRUAL BASIS

Designation of an accounting procedure whereby debits and credits are entered in the books of the company on the date they are incurred, rather than on the date they are paid or received. For example, ABC Corporation sells an item worth $20 on credit. It would debit inventory and credit accounts receivable by $20. Then, when the $20 is actually received, it will credit cash and debit accounts receivable.

ACCRUAL BOND
See Z-BOND.

ACCRUED INTEREST
Term designating the interest due on a bond or other fixed-income security that must be paid by the buyer of a security to its seller. Usual computation: coupon rate of interest times elapsed days from prior interest payment date (i.e., coupon date) up to but not including settlement date. Principal exceptions: money market securities that are sold at a discount do not have accrued interest.

Antonym: flat (i.e., without accrued interest).

Synonym: and interest (used as a qualifier). Example: "The trade was made and interest" (i.e., the accrued interest must be added to the contract price).

ACCUMULATION AREA
Term used by technical analysts if the market price of a security tends to move sideways. The term implies that buyers are willing to purchase at present prices.

Because prices tend to reflect the accumulated decisions of buyers and sellers, it is difficult to tell in practice whether a sideways price movement results from buying (accumulation) or from selling (distribution).

See also DISTRIBUTION AREA.

ACCUMULATION UNITS
Term used of annuities if a person buys an annuity, either fixed or variable, through a lump-sum purchase for future payout or by periodic purchases (i.e., accumulation). When the purchaser elects a payout method, these units will be converted to annuity units.

Basic concept: accumulation units remain the property of the purchaser; upon election of a payout method, the annuitant surrenders the property and, in exchange, receives a right to future payments from the insurance company. These payments are fixed if the annuity is a fixed annuity; variable if the annuity is variable.

ACE
An acronym for:
1. American Commodities Exchange. This is a corporate affiliate of the American Stock Exchange where certain futures contracts for interest-rate sensitive financial instruments are traded.

2. The cooperative confirmation, comparison, and settlement systems initiated by *A*IBD, *C*edel, and *E*uroclear, three independent associations that specialize in the handling of non-U.S. securities transactions.
3. "Approximate certainty equivalent," which is a portfolio valuation concept. ACE measures and anticipates changes in the risk premium associated with equity portfolios as changes in the economy's interest-rate environment occur. Generally, the more stable a company's earnings, the greater its ACE predictability.

ACES

Acronym for Advanced Computerized Execution System. This is an NASD market system that enables dealers to execute both proprietary and customer orders in quantities in excess of 1,000 shares, which is the upper limit on the Small Order Execution System (SOES).

Through ACES, preapproved members or customers can trade electronically and immediately with the marketmaker whose quotations and sizes are displayed on the CRT screen. In this way, the marketmaker can control its market risk exposure.

ACH

See AUTOMATED CLEARINGHOUSE.

ACHA

Acronym for Associate Clearing House of Amsterdam, a wholly owned subsidiary of the European Stock Options Clearing Corporation. ACHA acts as an intermediary clearing point for OCC in the comparison and settlement of XMI options trading on the European Options Exchange.

ACID-TEST RATIO

A measurement of corporate liquidity. Accepted measurement: subtract inventory from current assets; divide the remainder by current liabilities. For example, a company has current assets of $10 million and inventory of $3 million. Net: $7 million. It has current liabilities of $3.5 million. Its acid-test ratio is:

$$\frac{\$7 \text{ million}}{\$3.5 \text{ million}} = \frac{2}{1}$$

Ratios below 1 to 1 are considered low. However, ratios that are extremely high may indicate that a company is not using assets effectively, may be cash rich, and is subject to a takeover by other companies.

See also LIQUIDITY RATIO.

ACKNOWLEDGMENT

Term used to designate the signature verification on a certificate or on an assignment and power of substitution form. To transfer ownership of a certificate (stock or registered bond), or to transfer an account from one broker to another, the owner must have his or her signature validated (guaranteed, or acknowledged) by a recognized broker/dealer or a commercial bank.

Popular synonym: signature guarantee.

ACQ

Abbreviation used on the consolidated tape for a transaction that represents an exchange acquisition (i.e., a block trade initiated by a buyer with all transaction costs paid by a purchaser). Such transactions are infrequent.

ACQUISITION DATE

The calendar day, for legal and tax purposes, on which someone commits to the purchase of an asset.

Note: For assets received as a gift, the recipient normally uses the acquisition date on which the donor acquired the asset (so long as the donor has a "paper profit"). Assets received as the result of a bequest are considered as acquired on the day of death of the previous owner.

ACROSS THE BOARD

Used to describe all stocks (bonds) in the same industry or with similar credit characteristics. For example, "Tobacco stocks were up across the board following a favorable ruling by a New York District Court," or "Long corporate bonds were down sharply across the board as the yield curve flattened this week."

ACRS

See MACRS.

ACTING IN CONCERT

Basic concept: two or more persons who, either collectively or through a common agent, endeavor to achieve an investment goal.

Basic restrictions against acting in concert: such persons may not (1) exceed the position and exercise limits set by the options exchanges, (2) work to change the management of a registered corporation without filing with the SEC, (3) accumulate a control position in the security of a corporation without reporting to the SEC, (4) manipulate the price of a security. Each of these restrictions also applies to individuals.

ACTIVE BOND CROWD
New York Stock Exchange term for the combination of these two ideas: (1) the bond floor members who (2) most frequently trade in actively traded bonds.

Antonym: the can, or cabinet crowd.

In practice, all NYSE members who trade on the bond floor act as agents. Therefore, the distinction between active-crowd and can-crowd brokers refers more to the securities traded than to the designation of the NYSE members who trade on the bond floor. For example, if you were to trade bond A you could be in the can crowd, and if you trade bond B you could be in the active crowd.

See also CABINET CROWD.

ACTIVE BOX
Jargon for location of securities, held in the vault of a broker/dealer, that are eligible for use as collateral for broker or customer account financing. To be eligible for broker financing, the securities must be owned by the broker/dealer. To be eligible for customer account financing, the securities must be customer owned but held as a pledge for a margin loan made by the broker to the customer.

ACTIVE MARKET
Term used to describe either a marketplace or the buying and selling of an individual security that is so marked by: (1) frequent transactions with (2) reasonable volume and (3) relatively narrow spreads between the bids-offers that successive transactions are made at moderate price changes.

The term is relative; thus, no precise definition can be given. In practice, what is active for security A may be inactive for security B.

Often used to abbreviate advance(s) versus decline(s) in a particular marketplace or of equity securities in general.

See also ADVANCE DECLINE THEORY.

ACT SYSTEM
See AUTOMATED CONFIRMATION TRANSACTION.

ACTUAL VALUE OF REAL ESTATE
This is the dollar value placed on property by the economic forces of supply and demand. Accordingly, this value is volatile and generally is not used as a basis for property taxes.

See also ASSESSED VALUATION.

A-DAY
English designation of Authorization Day. This was the specific day in 1988 when the 1986 Financial Services Act became fully operative in the United Kingdom. On that date, as determined by the Department of Trade and Industry (DTI), any firm or person intent on doing business in the financial industry in the UK must have been licensed by the Securities Investment Board (SIB) or by one of the self-regulatory organizations (SROs) empowered to grant such licenses.

ADB
See ASIAN DEVELOPMENT BANK and ADJUSTED DEBIT BALANCE.

AD HOC
Latin: for this purpose. Commonly used of an action that is taken to solve a particular problem. For example, "Let's appoint an ad hoc committee." Or, "Joe, this is an ad hoc solution." The term may imply a permanent or a temporary solution. For example, "This is a very complex situation, but—ad hoc—let's concentrate on the financial effects of Plan A."

ADJUSTABLE RATE CONVERTIBLE NOTE
Debt security issued at a substantial premium over its redemption value at maturity. However, the note is exchangeable for a number of shares of common stock whose market value upon conversion is equal to the original issue price of the note; thus, it makes conversion economically more attractive than redemption.
   Popular abbreviation: ARCN.

ADJUSTABLE RATE PREFERRED STOCK (ARP)
An equity security that pays dividends at rates which change monthly or quarterly and are set at the highest of the then-prevailing rates for 90-day Treasury bills, 10-year Treasury notes, or 20-year Treasury bonds.
   Also called "floating-rate preferred stock."

ADJUSTABLE TENDER SECURITY
See ATS.

ADJUSTED DEBIT BALANCE (ADB)
The ledger debit balance (i.e., the dollar amount a client owes a broker) plus any available special memorandum account (SMA) balance adjusted by any paper profits on short accounts. The ADB determines whether a client's margin account is subject to the retention requirement.

In practice, following the Regulation-T adjustments made in February 1982, the term *adjusted debit balance* is meaningless, with this exception: withdrawals of cash or securities based on the SMA entries are not permitted if the client's account would thereby be in violation of margin maintenance requirements.

ADJUSTED EXERCISE PRICE
Term used of GNMA put and call options. Contract is for $100,000 unpaid principal balance on a GNMA pass-through security with an 8% nominal coupon. If GNMA pass-throughs with higher coupon rates are delivered, the exercise (strike) price will be so adjusted that the yield is the same. For example, the strike price on a GNMA call is 56. The yield will be 11%. If the call is exercised and the writer delivers a GNMA pass-through with an 11% coupon, the adjusted exercise price will be par, or 100.

ADJUSTED GROSS INCOME (AGI)
The bottom line of the front page of Form 1040 for individual taxpayers.

AGI includes all forms of taxable income—including net items from Schedules B, C, D, and E—minus contributions to IRA (deductible) and Keogh plans, and alimony paid.

AGI, except for personal exemptions and deductions (either standard or itemized), is the main determinant of the taxpayer's bracket and ultimate tax obligation.

It is the goal of tax-free and tax-deferred investing to keep items off the front page of Form 1040.

ADJUSTED NET CAPITAL
See ANC.

ADJUSTED TRADING
An NASD term used to designate a broker/dealer swap with a customer at prices not reasonably related to the current market value of the securities; that is, a purchase at a price above the current market, and a sale below the current market. Such transactions may impact the customer's tax liability and represent a fraud.

Also called "linked transactions."

ADJUSTMENT BOND
Bond, issued in exchange for other bonds, that promises to pay interest only if earned or to the extent earned. Authorization for the exchange must come from the bondholders who accept the adjustment bonds. Normally, the exchange will be made only if the company will otherwise be

bankrupt—and bondholders give their authorization in an endeavor to avoid liquidation of the company.

Also called INCOME BOND.

ADMINISTRATOR
1. Person responsible for the supervision of state securities laws.
2. Court-appointed person to oversee the distribution of the estate of a person who dies intestate.

The feminine term *administratrix* is occasionally used.

ADMINISTRATRIX
This is a seldom used but legal term for a female who has been appointed by a court to liquidate the estate of a deceased person who left no valid Will or qualified executor.

See also ADMINISTRATOR.

ADR
See AMERICAN DEPOSITORY RECEIPT.

ADR INDEX OPTION
See INTERNATIONAL MARKET INDEX.

ADS
Acronym for American Depository Shares.

ADS differs from ADR in that ADS are shares created for the American market by the issuer. ADRs, in turn, are created by a commercial bank as receipts for the underlying shares.

Both ADRs and ADSs facilitate the sale and transfer of foreign security ownership.

See also AMERICAN DEPOSITORY RECEIPT.

A/D THEORY
Often used to abbreviate advance(s) versus decline(s) in a particular marketplace or of equity securities in general.

See ADVANCE DECLINE THEORY.

AD VALOREM
Latin: according to the value. Used both of the assessed valuation of property and of the tax on such property. For example, the Township of Southhold has an ad valorem tax of 76 mills ($.076) per dollar of assessed valuation.

See also ASSESSED VALUATION.

ADVANCED COMPUTERIZED EXECUTION SYSTEM
See ACES.

ADVANCE DECLINE THEORY
Often used as a measurement of market sentiment (i.e., relative bullishness or bearishness of the stock market).

One frequently used formula: divide number of advancing issues by number of declining issues on a market day. For example, if 900 issues advance and 450 decline on a market day, the A/D index is 2. Numbers greater than 1 are bullish, numbers less than 1 are bearish.

Another formula: divide number of advances plus one half of stocks unchanged by number of issues traded. Numbers above 50% are bullish, numbers less than 50% are bearish.

ADVANCE REFUNDING
Term used to describe this situation: A municipality has outstanding bonds that are not yet callable (e.g., the earliest call date is 1998). If general interest rates drop, the municipality may find it advantageous to issue new bonds at a lower rate. The proceeds are invested in government securities that will mature in 1998, at which time the money will be used to call the earlier issue.

Also called "prerefunding."

ADVERTISEMENT
In securities industry usage, any material for use in a newspaper or magazine, or on radio or television, or with another public medium. Substantially identical letters to 10 or more people are considered advertisements.

Industry rules require: truthfulness and good taste; approval by a designated person within the issuing firm; and adequate recordkeeping of all advertisements. Also, the National Association of Securities Dealers requires that advertising copy be filed with the association within ten days of use (prior approval if the advertisement pertains to options or tax shelter securities).

ADVICE
1. A written acknowledgment by a broker/dealer or bank of receipt or delivery of money, or the transaction of securities business in a customer's account.

   In practice, a broker/dealer confirmation is an advice, and a statement is a summary of advices during an accounting period.
2. A recommendation by a salesperson, security analyst, or portfolio manager to buy, sell, or hold one or more specific securities issues.

AFBD
Acronym for Association of Futures Brokers and Dealers. AFBD is a SRO in the United Kingdom. It is authorized to regulate firms dealing or brokering in futures or options or who provide advice or management about this business.

AFFIDAVIT
A written statement of facts submitted voluntarily before a governing, judicial, or regulatory body. Affidavits must be signed in the presence of a court officer, notary public, or other designated person. For example, an executor of an estate files an affidavit of domicile of the decedent with an issuer's transfer agent to make a decedent's security certificate negotiable for sale.

AFFIDAVIT OF DOMICILE
Statement by executor or administrator of an estate attesting to the domicile of a decedent at the time of death. The affidavit is important for the transfer of securities from an estate because it, together with the tax waiver from the state of domicile, shows that no tax liens are outstanding against the securities about to be transferred.

AFFILIATED CORPORATION
1. In the United States, a term similar in meaning to affiliated person, as used in the Investment Company Act of 1940. In general, any officer, director, employee, or partner of an investment company or its advisor. It also includes anyone who holds 5% or more of the voting stock of such companies, or who is controlled by anyone who holds 5% or more of the voting stock.
2. In Japan, because of interlocking corporate relationships, this term applies only to institutions that control 20% or more of a corporation's stock. Such companies are "insiders" and may not buy equity securities of the issuer controlling them during the announcement and stabilization periods preceding financings.

AFFILIATED PERSON
General name for a person who can influence the management decisions of a corporation. Although legal advice may be needed in specific situations, the term includes: holders of 10% or more of the outstanding stock of a corporation, directors, elected officers (chairman, president, vice presidents, secretary, and treasurer), and members of their immediate family.

Also called "control person."

AFT
See AGENCY FACILITATION TRADER.

AFTERMARKET
General name for the trading activity in a security during the period of its initial offering to the public, and immediately thereafter, until the syndicate account is closed.

More popular name: secondary market.

AFTERTAX BASIS
Used to identify an investor's average rate of return on a bond purchased at a discount (i.e., the return after federal tax on the income and on the capital gain). Normally based on a corporate holder paying the maximum corporate tax on income and capital gains.

Often given by government bond dealers on their offer sheets so prospective purchasers can compare directly the aftertax yield with the nontaxable yield on municipal bonds selling at par.

AG
See ATTORNEY GENERAL.

AGED FAIL
Industry jargon for a contract between two broker/dealers that remains unsettled after 30 days from the time that delivery and payment should have been completed. Term is important because aged fails severely affect the capital of the affected firm, in that an aged fail may no longer be considered an asset because the chances of its successful completion are negligible.

AGENCY
1. A security, almost always debt, issued by a corporation sponsored by the U.S. government. Examples: bonds of the Federal Intermediate Credit Banks (FICB) or the Tennessee Valley Authority. Agency securities are exempt from registration under the Securities Act of 1933.
2. The act of buying or selling for the account and risk for another person.
   See also BROKER.

AGENCY BACKED COMPOUNDER SECURITIES
Trademark of Kidder Peabody & Co., for zero-coupon bonds backed by Ginnie Mae and Fannie Mae securities. Sold at a discount from face value, ABCs pay no current interest. The difference between purchase

price and redemption value at maturity represents compound interest at a rate prevailing at the time of purchase.

Popular abbreviation: ABC.

AGENCY FACILITATION TRADER (AFT)

A new category of NYSE member expected to satisfy the balance of a large stock trade when it cannot be completed by other members (such as the specialist) on the exchange. Obligated to trade between 100 and 5,000 shares at the prevailing quotation the AFT provides liquidity for block customers and is therefore allowed to initiate "on-floor" orders.

AGENCY FOR INTERNATIONAL DEVELOPMENT (AID)

AID is a U.S. governmental entity organized to assist developing countries in financing low-cost housing. Bonds issued under the sponsorship of AID are backed by the full faith and credit of the U.S. government. These bonds are exempt from registration, have maturities as long as 30 years, and are taxable as foreign-source income to U.S. investors.

AGENCY NOTE

One- to two-year obligation offered at a discount from par by U.S. government agencies, such as the Federal National Mortgage Association, the Federal Home Administration, and the Farm Credit System. Such notes generally represent interim financing prior to the issuance of long-term bonds.

AGENT

1. A person who buys or sells for the account and risk of another. Generally, an agent takes no financial risk and charges a commission for his services.
2. In state securities law, any person who represents an issuer or a broker/dealer in the purchase or sale of securities to, or for, a person domiciled in that state.

AGENT BANK

A commercial bank that acts as an intermediary between a customer and the customer's broker/dealer. For example, an agent bank may serve the customer by settling securities transactions with the broker/dealer, by acting as a custodian of securities purchased, by entering orders to buy or sell, and by acting as an investment adviser to the customer.

AGENTS DE CHANGE

French title for brokerage firm. Until 1992, these firms have a government authorized monopoly to conduct a securities business in France.

Only *agents de change* are authorized to become members of the Paris Bourse. All *agents de change* in France must be specifically approved by the French Ministry of Finance.

AGE OF MAJORITY
Age at which a person may legally contract. Depending on state law, the age of majority is from 18 to 21.

AGGREGATE EXERCISE PRICE
Term in security options: the exercise (strike) price times the number of securities involved in the contract. For example, a call is purchased at 50 for 100 shares. The aggregate exercise price is $5,000. Exception: GNMA options and T-bill, T-note, and T-bond options, in which the aggregate exercise price is the strike price times the face value of the underlying contract. For example, a GNMA call at 68 is 68% times $100,000, the face value of the underlying contract.
   See ADJUSTED EXERCISE PRICE.

AGGREGATE INDEBTEDNESS (AI)
Term used by the SEC in the computation of broker/dealer compliance with the SEC's net capital requirements. Best definition: the total of the broker/dealer's indebtedness to customers. For example, a broker/dealer owes $200,000: $50,000 is owed to a partner in the business and $150,000 is owed to customers for their credit balances in their accounts. The broker/dealer's aggregate indebtedness is the $150,000 owed to customers.

AGGRIEVED PARTY
Industry term for:
1. A person who accuses a member or a person associated with a member of a trade practice complaint under the National Association of Securities Dealers' (NASDs') Rules of Fair Practice.
2. A person who requests arbitration of a controversy between himself or herself and a member through the arbitration facilities provided by the NASD, the Municipal Securities Rulemaking Board (MSRB), or any of the exchanges.

AGI
See ADJUSTED GROSS INCOME.

AGM
In Japan, an acronym for a corporation's annual general meeting. Such meetings are required under Japanese law. Anyone holding 1,000 or

more shares may attend and participate in the annual discussion of corporate affairs and objectives.

AGREEMENT AMONG UNDERWRITERS
The formal contract between the members of an underwriting, or syndicate, account.

In general, the agreement among underwriters appoints one or more syndicate managers, defines the powers of the manager(s), and sets the rules for the conduct of the account.

AI
See AGGREGATE INDEBTEDNESS.

AIBD
See ASSOCIATION OF INTERNATIONAL BOND DEALERS.

AIBDQ
Acronym for Association of International Bond Dealers Quotations. AIBDQ is a computerized CRT system for trading Eurodollar debt issues among its European members. The system is designed to provide trade and market information among dealers. Some members of AIBD fear that AIBDQ provides too much information to competitors and customers and thus gives them an advantage over dealers.

AICPA
Acronym for American Institute of Certified Public Accountants. AICPA is a trade association for members of the accounting profession. Its purpose is to represent the business interests of its members, to serve for the exchange of ideas and information, and to improve the accounting skills of its members.

AID
See AGENCY FOR INTERNATIONAL DEVELOPMENT.

AID AND ABET
Legal term: to help, encourage, and incite. The term often is used in the statement of charges brought against someone who is alleged to have facilitated a violation of federal securities law.

AID CALL
See ANY-INTEREST-DATE CALL.

AIM

Acronym for Amsterdam Interprofessional Market. AIM is an experimental block trading system for equities listed on the Amsterdam Stock Exchange. The system consists of 40 video display terminals distributed to members and institutional investors. Timely quotations and trade reports are displayed. Those who use the terminals for executions receive lower than usual commission rates.

AIR

See ANTICIPATED INVESTMENT RETURN.

AIR POCKET

Term used if a stock, or the market, suffers a sudden and precipitous drop. Term is an analogy based on the sudden drop when an airplane hits an air pocket (a down current). The term itself describes the fact, but not the reason, for the drop.

Similar terms: *downward spike, freefall.*

A/K/A

Abbreviation: also known as. Often used in securities brokerage offices to identify short titles of customer accounts maintained by that firm.

Synonym: an alias.

Note: A/K/A is a different name for a person or entity. D/B/A is used if a person does business under a different name. For example, William Smith A/K/A Bill Smiley, as opposed to William Smith D/B/A Scimitar Company. Both sets of letters often are used lowercase.

ALFRED BERG NORDIC INDEX

A daily index of performance of the Swedish, Norwegian, Finnish, and Danish stock markets. Named after a Swedish brokerage firm, this index is comprised of 136 issues, with each country weighted according to marking capitalization. In effect, the Alfred Berg Nordic Index tracks Scandinavian market performance.

ALLIED MEMBER

New York Stock Exchange term for a senior officer of a member firm who is not a member of the exchange. For example, the chairman, the president, or a vice president of a NYSE member firm is not a member of the exchange; such a person is an allied member. Allied members must register with the NYSE, must pass a special examination, and are bound by the rules of the exchange.

ALLIGATOR SPREAD
Slang for an option spread position that offers more in commission dollars to an account executive than to a client who accepts the risks of the spread. In effect, the client's potential profit on the position is eaten up by the cost of the transaction.

ALL IN
Trader's slang for "all included." The term is used to give the issuer's interest cost after all other costs; for example, commissions, are included. Thus, an issuer's bonds may be offered at 8.30%, but after the payment of expenses its all-in cost may be 8.375%.

ALL OR ANY PART
Order instruction sometimes given by a customer for the execution of a block transaction, either a purchase or sale. With this instruction, the trader is advised to execute when, and as, offers or bids become available, regardless of quantity provided. The original parameters of the order as established by the customer are observed.
  Abbreviation: AOAP.

ALL ORDINARIES INDEX
An index of 85% of the domestic issues traded on the floors of the Australia Stock Exchange.
  See AUSTRALIA STOCK EXCHANGE.

ALL OR NONE
1. Used of an underwritten offering: it is conditional to a total subscription of the shares offered. If every share is not subscribed, issuer has the right to cancel the offering. For example, the Women's Bank offered shares on an all-or-none basis.
2. Used of an order ticket by a buying or selling customer: buy or sell the entire amount on a single transaction. Do not execute a partial transaction. Order entry symbol: AON. All-or-none instructions that require immediate execution must be marked fill or kill (FOK). Thus, AON restricts the size but not necessarily the time of the transaction.

ALLOTMENT LETTER
In England, a term for a temporary stock certificate issued to persons entitled to a stock dividend or stock split. The notification of the allotment of the stock dividend or split is in the form of a letter; hence, the name.

ALL-SAVER CERTIFICATE
Name used of special one-year CD that was exempt from federal taxation if the deposit was made between September 1981 and the end of December 1982. Up to $1,000 of interest income was exempt.

All-saver certificates have been discontinued.

ALL SUBSEQUENT COUPONS ATTACHED
This characteristic, popularly initiated as ASCA or simply SCA, means that a bearer municipal bond has the current and all subsequent coupons attached. If the bond has been in default, the initial passed coupon is listed and ASCA follows. For example, the Highland County Sewer Revenue Bonds, 7 5/8s due 5/1/09, with coupon #4 and ASCA.

ALL THE EIGHTHS
Order room and exchange floor slang for orders and transactions at 7/8ths; that is, with all the eighths before a new digit is used.

ALL YOUR MARKET
Jargon in the over-the-counter market. Situation: An OTC broker/dealer asks another dealer for a quote. The response: "It's all your market." Meaning: The only interest in the security seems to be localized in the area from where the dealer in Little Rock calls a dealer in Chicago for a quote on the stock of a bank in Fayetteville, Arkansas. Response: "It's all your market."

ALL YOURS
See ALL YOUR MARKET

ALPHABET STOCK
Slang for any of the variously lettered stock introduced by General Motors as it acquired different companies. These shares have different voting features and varying dividends that are dependent on the financial success of the acquired companies. Thus, there is General Motors "E" stock issued to acquire Electronic Data Systems, and General Motors "H" stock issued to acquire Hughes Aircraft.

ALPHA (COEFFICIENT)
The calculation of a (alpha in Greek) in the formula for the slope of a line: $a + bx = y$. If b (beta in Greek) is set at zero, thereby eliminating market price volatility, alpha will measure the investment return for a particular security when compared to the baseline of the Standard & Poor's Index.

Alpha measurements that are positive (e.g., plus 10) mean that the particular stock will yield dividend returns 10% greater than the average of the S&P. An alpha of 0 is equal to the S&P dividend return; an alpha of minus 5 is 5% lower than the S&P. Thus, alpha measures investment return and beta measures price volatility of individual stocks versus a commonly accepted baseline. These concepts are extensively used.

ALTERNATIVE MINIMUM TAX (AMT)
An alternative tax computation method (minimum tax = 24% as of 1991) whereby certain taxpayers who have lowered their tax by the use of certain "preference items" must pay the larger tax. About 1% of U.S. taxpayers are subject to AMT.

Preference items include the appreciation on charitable gifts, the bargain element on incentive stock options, certain deductible losses from passive investments, certain deductions from amortization and depletion, itemized deductions of state and local taxes, and the like. Tax advice is needed. Of particular importance is the fact that the interest income on some private activity bonds is considered preference income.

ALTERNATE NET CAPITAL REQUIREMENT
The SEC has established net capital requirements for broker/dealers. The formulas are complex. The alternate net capital requirement is particularly appealing for U.S. broker/dealers who maintain proprietary accounts (trading positions). Here, the net capital must be equal to the greater of $100,000 or 2% of the aggregate debit items as computed in the SEC's Rule 15c3-3 formula for customer protection.

ALTERNATIVE ORDER
Exchange order that combines a limit with a stop order for the same security. Because limit orders and stop orders are entered on opposite sides of the market (e.g., a buy limit should be below the current market, and a buy stop above), the execution of one side of the alternative order requires the cancellation of the other side of the order. Alternative orders may not combine a buy with a sell order for the same security.

Also called an "either-or order."

AMBAC
See AMERICAN MUNICIPAL BOND ASSURANCE CORPORATION

AMBULANCE STOCK
Tongue-in-cheek term, used primarily in Japan, to describe stock that is about to be manipulated upward—thus, an advantage to those who buy before the upward movement. Allusion: if you are losing money in the market, this stock will make you well—financially speaking—in a hurry.

AMERICAN COMMODITIES EXCHANCE
See ACE.

AMERICAN DEPOSITORY RECEIPT (ADR)
Negotiable receipt, registered in the name of the owner, for shares of a foreign corporation held in the vault of a foreign branch of an American bank. The receipt may or may not be on a share-for-share basis with the underlying security. ADRs, if sold in the United States, are subject to the securities laws of the United States, and many foreign corporations sell their securities in the United States in the form of ADRs. Because of ease of transfer and resale, ADRs are a popular form of domestic equity ownership of foreign corporations.

AMERICAN DEPOSITORY SHARES
See ADS.

AMERICAN INSTITUTE OF CERTIFIED PUBLIC ACCOUNTANTS
See AICPA.

AMERICAN MUNICIPAL BOND ASSURANCE CORPORATION
This insuror guarantees payment of principal and interest on insured municipal bonds. The insurance premium is paid by the issuer of the bonds.

AMBAC-insured bonds generally are rated AAA by Standard & Poor's.

AMERICAN OPTION
Term used of a put or call if it is necessary to distinguish from a European option, many of which do not have the same exercise privileges during the life of the option.

AMERICAN STOCK EXCHANGE
Located in New York City, the American Stock Exchange is the second largest of the securities exchanges in the United States. Prior to 1921, the exchange was known as the New York Curb Exchange—hence its popular name as the Curb.

Both ASE and AMEX are commonly used as abbreviations for the American Stock Exchange. Listed stocks, bonds, and options are traded on the AMEX.

AMERICAN STOCK EXCHANGE MARKET VALUE INDEX
This is a market index for all common stocks listed on the American Stock Exchange. It is prepared daily, and often within the day. Subgroupings are by geography and industrial categories.

AMERICAN-STYLE EXERCISE

Quality of most listed option contracts traded in the United States. If an option permits American-Style Exercise, the option holder may exercise the option at anytime during its effective life.

Antonym: European-Style Exercise. Some index options may only be exercised in a short period before their expiration.

AMERICUS TRUST

A five-year unit investment trust into which holders of American Telephone & Telegraph common stock could deposit their shares. Upon divestiture of AT&T in 1984, the trust held the original shares and the shares of the old AT&T subsidiaries. Unit holders also had the option to split their interest in the trust into two components: The PRIME component was to receive all dividends; the SCORE component was to receive all capital gains over $75 per share based on the original telephone stock.

AMEX

See AMERICAN STOCK EXCHANGE.

AMEX OPTIONS SWITCHING SYSTEM

See AMOS.

AMICUS CURIAE

Latin: friend of the court. Term used of briefs filed by parties who are interested in a court trial but who are not participants in the trial. For example, there is a trial between the United States and a company that imports pianos, with the government charging that the importer is violating import laws. Another manufacturer of pianos files an amicus curiae brief to show that the importing of pianos does violate certain U.S. laws.

AMORTIZE

Accounting method whereby the cost of acquisition of an asset gradually is reduced to reflect the theoretical resale value of the asset.

As a noun: method is amortization.

Uses:
1. A company purchases a fixed asset that, over time, decreases in value because of use or obsolescence.
2. An investor purchases a security at a premium over its par (or redemption) value. For example, an investor buys a municipal bond at a premium over its redemption value.

Tax advice is needed if government or corporate securities, purchased at a premium, are amortized.

See also DEPRECIATION.

AMORTIZED LOSSES
Accounting technique used by banks if they sell debt instruments at a loss. The technique permits the bank to prorate the loss over what would have been the remaining life of the instrument, thereby reducing taxable income over that period.

AMOS
Acronym for Amex Options Switching System. A computerized options order-routing system that will transmit incoming options orders to the appropriate trading posts and—if the orders are executed—report the executions to the member who entered the order.

AMPS
Acronym: auction market preferred stock. A Merrill Lynch proprietary term for certain preferred shares. This product was originated to compete with First Boston's STARS and Salomon Brothers' DARTS.

In effect, an issuer's preferred dividend is reset every 49 days to mirror prevailing money market conditions. Securities thus purchased are held more than the statutory 46-day holding period required for corporate holders to be eligible for the 70% "dividend received" exclusion under the IRS Code.

AMSTERDAM INTERPROFESSIONAL MARKET
See AIM.

AMSTERDAM STOCK EXCHANGE
The Amsterdam Stock Exchange is located in Holland (Netherlands) and, having been founded in 1602, is the oldest in the world. The exchange is international in scope and more than half its listed securities are of foreign-based companies. Trading is from 10:00 A.M. until 4:30 P.M., but Dutch issues may be traded for an additional six hours. Settlement terms are quite liberal and payment/delivery are to be made on the 10th business day following the trade.

AMT
See ALTERNATIVE MINIMUM TAX.

AN ACTUAL
Term used to identify the security underlying an option. For example, when discussing an option, the "actual" would be the security deliverable in satisfaction of the contract.

More common expression: "the underlying." Example: A call is an option to purchase the underlying at a stated price on or before a specified date.

ANC

Acronym: adjusted net capital. A term used by the Commodities Futures Trading Commission (CFTC) to set minimum financial requirements for futures commission merchants (FCM) registered with the CFTC. The general formula is: Specified current assets minus Adjusted liabilities, minus Capital charges. The adjusted liabilities include customer funds that must be segregated. ANC, by CFTC rule, must be at least 4% of such segregated funds.

AND INTEREST

Term used in conjunction with the trading of most outstanding bonds. It signifies that the buyer must pay (and the seller receive) the interest that has accrued from the last interest payment by the issuer up to, but not including, the settlement date for the contract.

Antonym: flat; that is, no accrued interest is payable by the buyer to the seller.

See also ACCRUED INTEREST, FLAT.

ANGEL

Slang for an investment grade debt security; that is, a debt security with one of the top four ratings. The term arises from the fact that such bonds are favored by institutional investors anxious to avoid criticism for their portfolio management.

Synonym: investment grade or bank grade.

Antonym: junk bond.

ANNUALIZED DISCOUNT

Term used of the dollar valuation of T-bills and contingent T-bill options.

The discount is stated as a percent and is based on a 360-day year. The dollar amount of the discount is based on the formula:

$$\frac{\text{Days to}}{\text{maturity}} \times \frac{\text{Price in}}{\substack{\text{basis} \\ \text{points}}} \times 0.277778 = \frac{\text{Face value}}{\substack{\text{in} \\ \text{dollars}}}$$

This formula is accurate for trades of $10 million or less. For larger trades, introduce another 7 into the constant repeating decimal of 0.2777778. This decimal represents 0.01 divided by 0.01 × 360 (in other words, the decimal factor for a basis point for 1 day).

ANNUAL REPORT

Popular term for the yearly report made by a company to its stockholders. Federal law requires all registered corporations to make such reports. They usually contain a balance sheet, an income statement, a list of changes in retained earnings, and how income of the corporation was used.

The report form filed annually with the SEC is called Form 10-K, which expands on items in the annual report. Shareholders may request Form 10-K from the corporate secretary for additional information.

ANNUITANT

Legal designation for a person who receives benefits from an annuity. Technically, the term is used of a person who has elected the type of payout to be made on the annuity.

The term also is used of a person who is currently purchasing accumulation units in an annuity plan or who has made a lump-sum purchase but has not yet elected a method of payout.

See also ANNUITY, ANNUITY UNIT, and ACCUMULATION UNITS.

ANNUITY

An investment contract sold by a life insurance company in which the annuitant receives regular payments for life, or for a fixed period, in exchange for the immediate or installment deposit of a specified number of dollars.

Technically, the premium paid by the annuitant purchases accumulation units. At the time when the annuitant elects a payout method, the annuitant gives up ownership of the accumulation units and, in exchange, receives the right to a guaranteed payout in accordance with the payout method elected.

ANNUITY UNIT

An accounting device used to convert accumulation units of an annuity into units on which the payments to an annuitant will be based. Used both of fixed and variable annuities. For example, over the years a contributor to a variable annuity has accumulated x accumulation units. Upon election of a payout method, the annuitant will receive y annuity units. This number is fixed. Because it is a variable annuity, however, the monthly payment will vary. The monthly payouts would not vary if the annuitant had been accumulating units of a fixed annuity.

ANNUNCIATOR BOARD

A mechanical paging device—prominently displayed on the walls of the New York and the American Stock Exchanges—that was formerly used to summon floor brokers, or other members, to a prearranged location for order executions or messages. Now, electronic paging devices are used.

ANSERM

Acronym for Association of Nagoya Stock Exchange Regular Members. ANSERM is a nonregulatory organization whose purpose is to promote mutual friendship, the exchange of ideas, and philanthropy. Its surveillance activities are strongly influenced by the JASD.

ANTICIPATED INVESTMENT RETURN

Term used in conjunction with the performance of annuity units of a variable annuity. When an owner of investment units of a variable annuity elects to annuitize and selects one of the annuity options (single life, one life and survivor, and the like) the insurance company assigns the annuitant a fixed number of annuity units. Because these annuity units will vary in performance, it is necessary to assign an arbitrary anticipated investment return (AIR). According to the annuity contract, the owner will receive monthly payment based on this AIR. The AIR, in turn, will be adjusted on a monthly, quarterly, or semiannual basis to conform to the actual experience of the separate account. It is in this sense that the annuity is said to vary.

ANTIPODEAN ISSUER

Term heard more often in Europe than in the United States, but, in all cases, it refers to an offering of securities by Australian and New Zealand issuers. Derived from the word antipodes, meaning on the opposite side, reference to Australia and New Zealand occurs because their geographic locations are on the opposite side of the rest of the world.

ANY-INTEREST-DATE CALL (AID CALL)

A feature of some municipal bonds whereby the issuer reserves the right to redeem the obligation on any date on which an interest payment is due. The redemption privilege may be at par, or at a premium, as outlined in the indenture.

AOAP

See FILL OR ANY PART.

AON

See ALL OR NONE

AOSERM

Acronym for Association of Osaka Stock Exchange Regular Members. Like ANSERM, AOSERM is a nonregulatory organization whose purpose is to promote mutual friendship, the exchange of ideas, and philanthropy. Its surveillance activities are strongly influenced by JASD.

APARS

See AUTOMATIC PRICING AND REPORTING SYSTEM.

APPRAISAL

See NOMINAL QUOTATION

APPRECIATION

1. Any increase in investor equity. For example, a client purchases a security for $25 per share and sells it at $32 per share.
2. Any increase over the "ratable cost" of an investment. For example, a zero-coupon bond has an adjusted cost of $450 and the bond is sold at $522.
3. In a broad sense, any increase in net worth resulting from an investment. In this sense, it is used as a synonym for total return. For example, "We anticipate that your total return on this investment, including reinvested cash flows, will be 15% per year over the next 10 years."

As a general rule, meanings 1 and 2 do not include dividends and interest; meaning 3 does.

APPROVED LIST

A list of investment vehicles considered acceptable for bank trust departments, financial institutions, and fiduciaries. The criteria for acceptability varies from jurisdiction to jurisdiction, but—in general—securities are either selected by statute or by a commissioner of securities for that state.

Also called the "legal list."

APPROVED PERSON

NYSE term: a person who is a director of a member corporation, or an owner of 5% or more of the voting stock thereof, but who is neither a member of the NYSE nor an allied member. An approved person must be qualified by the NYSE to serve in such a position.

See also MEMBER CORPORATION and ALLIED MEMBER.

APPROXIMATE MARKET

See NOMINAL QUOTATION.

APS

Acronym for auction preferred stock. APSs' were created by Goldman Sachs to compete with First Boston's STARS and Salomon Brothers' DARTS. These preferred issues have a dividend whose rate is reset each 49 days to mirror prevailing money market rates. In this way the holder has fulfilled the statutory 46-day holding period required for the 70% "dividend received" exclusion for corporate holders.

APT

Initials stand for Automated Pit Trading, an electronic trading system developed by the London International Financial Futures Exchange (LIFFE) for implementation after normal trading hours. It competes directly with Chicago's major commodities exchange's GLOBEX system.

ARBITRAGE

1. As verb: the act of buying and selling the same security in different marketplaces to profit from a disparity in market prices.
2. As verb: the act of buying one security coupled to a short sale of the same security to profit from a disparity of prices.
3. As noun: an offsetting security position that has a built-in profit.
4. As adjective or as past participle: to describe a security position that establishes a profit. For example, "His long position was arbitraged by a short sale."

See also ARBITRAGEUR.

ARBITRAGE BONDS

IRS term for bonds issued by a municipality if the proceeds of the sale are invested in other bonds paying a higher rate of interest than the municipality pays on its own bonds. If bonds are classified as arbitrage bonds, the IRS may revoke the tax exemption on the interest income the municipality pays on its bonds.

In practice, a municipality must clear with the IRS a bond issuance used for the prerefunding of their outstanding issues.

See also PREREFUNDING.

ARBITRAGEUR

A person who endeavors to profit from offsetting long and short security positions or from a disparity in market prices on different markets.

Although the term can be used of private individuals, the term generally is used of broker/dealers or their employees who conduct the arbitrage operations.

See also ARBITRAGE.

ARBITRATION

Industry-sponsored method to adjudicate controversies between members or between members and nonmembers. Arbitration provides a final, binding decision—provided the parties to the arbitration agree to abide by the decision before the arbitration proceedings begin. Each of the exchanges, the NASD, and the MSRB have provisions for the arbitration of industry disputes.

ARCDELTA RISK
The risk a futures portfolio incurs at specific price intervals, based on changes in trading ranges of commodities products. The risk can be measured and plotted.

ARCN
See ADJUSTABLE RATE CONVERTIBLE NOTE.

ARCO
Acronym: Atlantic Richfleld Company. ARCO also is used as the company's commercial logo.

ARIEL
A computerized trade matching program in the United Kingdom that enabled institutional holders to trade directly with one another, thereby bypassing the London Stock Exchange's system of fixed commissions, in use before October 27, 1986. The custom was similar to the Fourth Market in the United States. Its use has been virtually abandoned.

ARMS INDEX
Technical indicator named for Richard Arms, a journalist with *Barron's* in 1967.
Popularly known as TRIN.

ARM'S-LENGTH TRANSACTION
Any business arrangement negotiated by an unrelated or unaffiliated party to the transaction. Such a transaction avoids conflicts of interest and thus is not detrimental to the interest of a third party with whom either or both of the transactors is associated.

AR-OP
See ASSISTANT REPRESENTATIVE-ORDER PROCESSING.

ARP
See ADJUSTABLE RATE PREFERRED STOCK.

ARREARAGE
Term used of unpaid dividends on cumulative preferred shares. Although such unpaid dividends are not owed to the preferred shareholders—only bond interest is owed—the company promises that it will not pay any dividend to common shareholders until such arrearages are paid. For example, a company passes two $3 dividends on its cumulative preferred shares. The company will not pay any dividends to its common shareholders until it has paid the $6 arrearage.

ARRS
See AUTOMATED REGULATORY REPORTING SYSTEM.

ARTICLE 65
A section of Japanese securities law that prohibits a bank, trust company, or similar financial institutions from engaging in most aspects of securities business. Agency orders and principal transactions for its own investment account are permissible exceptions. It is similar in scope to the Glass-Steagall Act in the United States.

AS AGENT
A person who acts as a broker in a transaction and who assumes no financial risk. For example, "Today, we purchased 1,000 shares of XYZ at $55 as agent for your account."

The term often is used as a synonym for subagent. For example, Bill Smith works as a broker for Smythe & Sons. Smythe & Sons usually acts as a broker. Technically, Bill Smith is a subagent for his employer.

Synonym: as broker.

ASAM
Acronym for Automated Search & Match System. ASAM is a NYSE data base of persons affiliated with issuers of stocks traded on the exchange. The data base is culled from financial manuals, directorships, and so on. It is so arranged that the system can be searched for opportunists, sources of, or circulators of, "inside" market information if there is evidence of price influencing of listed securities.

ASCA (A.S.C.A.)
See ALL SUBSEQUENT COUPONS ATTACHED.

ASE
1. Acronym for American Stock Exchange. Sometimes referred to as the "Curb." Located in New York, the ASE is one of the largest exchanges in the United States. In recent years, the exchange has preferred to be initialed as the AMEX.
2. Acronym for Amsterdam Stock Exchange. The largest securities exchange in Holland. It is a leading European marketplace and it deals in many international issues. It also sponsors trading of the AMEX's Major Market Index (XMI).

ASE INDEX
Index of all common stocks listed on the American Stock Exchange.

Because it weights price changes to reflect the number of outstanding shares for individual stocks, the index is rather a measurement of the average value change than a measurement of average price change. For example, Company A has two shares outstanding at a price of $50. Company B has four shares outstanding at a price of $53. Total value: $312; average value $52. Today, A goes down 1 point; B goes up 1 point. Average price change is zero. Average value change is $+1/3$. New total value is $314 for six shares, or an average value of $52^{1}/3$. The ASE index will reflect this change in average value.

ASIAN CD
Certificate of deposit issued by a bank located in Asia. Most common locations: Tokyo, Hong Kong, or Singapore. Unless otherwise stated, it may be presumed that the CD is denominated in U.S. dollars.

CDs denominated in yen or in Singapore or Hong Kong dollars, while they enjoy relative safety of principal, are subject to currency exchange risks.

ASIAN DEVELOPMENT BANK
An international financial institution established to foster economic growth and social development in countries in Asia and in the perimeter of the Pacific Ocean. Headquartered in the Philippine Islands, the bank lends money to smaller or less-developed countries in that region of the world for projects designed to assist their economic growth.

Acronym: ADB.

ASKED PRICE
Commonly accepted industry term for the lowest price at which a dealer is willing to sell a security. Presumption: The asked price is for the accepted unit of trading, although on exchanges the number of shares available at the asked price normally is given. For example, a security is bid 29, asked 30.

Also shortened to "asked."

Synonym: offering price. For example, the bid is 29, the offer is 30.

ASPIRIN
Acronym for Australian Stock Price Riskless Indexed Notes. These government-guaranteed notes are backed by the Treasury of New South Wales. They guarantee repayment of the face value in four years. They pay no current interest; thus, they are zero-coupon. In exchange, the noteholder will receive—in addition to par value—the percentage increase by which the Australian Stock Index of All Ordinaries (common stock) rises above 1,372 points during that period. In effect, they are bonds with no downside risk, no regular return, but a percentage return that is coupled to the performance of the Australian stock market during their lifetime.

ASPIRIN COUNT THEORY

A lighthearted leading indicator of general market price movement. Concept: About a year after aspirin production rises in the United States, the market will fall, and vice versa if aspirin production decreases.

ASSESSABLE STOCK

An equity participation in a corporation; for example, common or preferred stock, which allows the issuer to require further cash infusions from the stockholders.

The concept has not been applicable for many years in the sale and transfer of publicly traded shares. Such shares are inscribed as follows:

Fully paid and nonassessable shares
of such-and-such corporation

The concept can be important in the interpretation of state securities laws, where the "gift" of assessable stock is actually considered a "sale," because of this further requirement for funds from the holder.

ASSESSED VALUATION

The value, often arbitrarily assigned, of property in a taxing municipality. The tax then is assigned in mills per dollar of assessed valuation. For example, a taxpayer's house and lot are assigned an assessed valuation of $10,000. If the ad valorem tax is 76 mills ($.076) per dollar of assessed valuation, the tax on the property will be $760. Concept of assessed valuation is important in analyzing municipal bonds whose debt service will be paid from property taxes.

See AD VALOREM; LIMITED TAX BOND.

ASSET

Any item of value owned by an individual or a corporation. Most common differentiations:
1. Current asset: an item of value that will be turned into cash within a year.
2. Fixed asset: an item of value that is used in the conduct of a business that, ordinarily, will not be converted into cash within a year.
3. Intangible asset: an item of value whose resale value is difficult to determine.

ASSET ALLOCATION

The distribution of cash, stocks, bonds, real estate, and other assets in an institution's portfolio. The percentage of each component is a function of the portfolio manager's assessment of market and interest-rate risk—and other factors—at the present time. The distribution may also reflect the institution's investment objectives and its present and future cash flow needs.

Nothing prevents the term from being used of the portfolio mix of an individual investor. For example, a security research service may recommend that portfolios be 10% cash, 45% bonds, and 45% stocks under present market conditions.

ASSET-BACKED SECURITY
Generic term for any security whose underlying collateral or cash flow is dependent on an item of value. Such items of value are often receivables of corporations; thus, we see names like CARS (for car loans), CARDS (for credit card loans), and so on.

As a general rule, while the concept is the same, the term *asset-backed security* is not used of securities backed by mortgages. Instead, such securities are popularly called "mortgage-backed securities" (MBSs) or "collateralized mortgage obligations" (CMOs).

ASSET FINANCING
General term: a loan made to the owner of an asset who, in turn, segregates the asset as collateral for the loan. For example, a corporation borrows against the collateral value of an asset, such as land, property, or plant.

Basic concept: rather than looking at a loan from the viewpoint of the lender, asset financing looks at a loan from a viewpoint of the borrower. For example, a corporation looks at its assets and asks: "How can I turn these assets into cash for the operation of my business?"

ASSET PLAY
Expression associated with the upward movement of an actively traded stock when no other fundamental reason is apparent. The concept: If there is no apparent reason for the upswing, technicians and salespersons suspect that a group of investors see undervalued assets on the corporation's balance sheet and are buying the stock in anticipation of an appreciation of these assets by other investors.

In effect, accounting aberrations of certain assets, tangible or intangible, are being carried below their actual worth. Thus, such a company may be worth more dead than alive—especially to a corporate raider.

ASSET STRIPPER
This is the English term for a corporate raider who assumes significant debt to acquire a target company. Once in control, the asset stripper sells off parts of the company to pay down or liquidate the liability. Many leveraged buyouts (LBOs), whether done by an outside corporate raider or by company management, are characterized by such "stripping."

US expression: corporate raider, or predator.

ASSIGN
1. General term: to sign, to sell, to transfer, or to give away.
2. Specific term: to impose an obligation on someone else. For example, the Options Clearing Corporation—upon notice of an option exercise by the owner of the option—assigns the obligation of complying with the terms of the option (e.g., a call, to deliver the security; a put, to purchase the security) on a member firm whose client wrote the option. Also used as a noun: assignment.

ASSIGNMENT & POWER OF SUBSTITUTION
Technical term for a form whereby a registered owner of a security transfers ownership. Generally, a registered security provides a form on its reverse side whereby the registered owner may assign ownership. Ownership also may be assigned on a separate piece of paper.

See also BOND POWER, STOCK POWER.

ASSIGNMENT NOTICE
Form whereby the Options Clearing Corporation notifies a member firm that an option has been exercised against one of its clients who wrote a security option. The member firm, in turn, must assign the exercise against one of its clients on either a random or a first-in, first-out (FIFO) basis.

Also called "assignment notice."

ASSISTANT REPRESENTATIVE-ORDER PROCESSING (AR-OP)
An NASD registration status applicable to a member firm employee who regularly accepts unsolicited customer orders. This employee, it is presumed, does nothing else that would require qualification as a general securities registered representative.

Qualification as an AR-OP is obtained by application and passage of an examination.

ASSOCIATED PERSON
General term: Any person associated with a broker/dealer as a proprietor, partner, officer, director, branch office manager, investment banker, or salesperson. Persons who perform ministerial or clerical functions are not associated persons.

ASSOCIATE MEMBER
American Stock Exchange term: a person who has purchased from the exchange the right to execute orders through a regular member of the exchange. Such members may trade and clear orders through the regular member but have no right of access to the floor of the exchange.

ASSOCIATE SPECIALIST
Exchange members who act as assistants to regular specialists. Associate specialists are, in effect, in training. They may execute orders as agents for regular specialists—but only under the supervision of the regular, or relief, specialist.

ASSOCIATION OF COMPENSATION FUND FOR CONSIGNED LIABILITIES IN COMMODITY FUTURES, INC.
See HOSHO-KIKIN SYSTEM.

THE ASSOCIATION OF FUTURES BROKERS AND DEALERS
See AFBD.

ASSOCIATION OF INTERNATIONAL BOND DEALERS
AIBD, domiciled in Switzerland, is composed of banks and broker/dealers engaged in primary and secondary markets for international debt securities. The members of AIBD act as underwriters and marketmakers and settle transactions in accord with the procedures set forth by the association. AIBD is similar in function and responsibility to the NASD in the United States, but it lacks governmental backing.

ASX
See AUSTRALIA STOCK EXCHANGE.

ATHENS STOCK EXCHANGE
A relatively small exchange—even for Greece. The market is open each weekday from 10 A.M. until noon, although after-hour trading is permitted until 2 P.M. Contract settlement is due for a fortnightly accounting on regular way transactions; thus, it copies the procedure of the ISE. It is a verbal marketplace, with no restriction on foreign membership.

ATP
Acronym for arbitrage trading program. Term used to describe investors who attempt to lock in market profits through the simultaneous purchase of stock index futures and the sale of the underlying stocks in that index or vice versa. Speed of execution is necessary to capture the profits available because of price variations.

Such arbitrage traders are often simply called "program traders."

AT RISK
Tax law term used as a criterion for a deduction against a tax liability.

General concept: To provide a deduction, the money invested in a business—either personal capital or borrowed money—must be at risk (i.e., able to increase or decrease in value). For example, a person invests in a business, and the general partner guarantees the return of all money invested. The investor's money is not at risk. Hence, no deduction will be allowed for depreciation. Tax advice is needed.

ATS
Acronym for adjustable tender security. ATS is a variable-rate municipal security developed and sold by Smith Barney Harris Upham & Company, a prominent broker/dealer and investment banker. The municipality resets its interest rate daily. There is a put option attached to the instrument that enables the holder to redeem the debt at face value. However, the put can only be exercised weekly or monthly; this gives the issuer some flexibility in its debt structuring and some protection against volatile yield curve aberrations.

See also AUTOMATIC TRANSFER SERVICE ACCOUNT.

ATSERM
Acronym for Association of Tokyo Stock Exchange (TSE) Regular Members. ATSERM is a nonregulatory organization in Japan comprised of all members of the exchange. Its purpose is the promotion of mutual friendship, the exchange of ideas, and philanthropy. Its surveillance responsibilities are strongly influenced by the JASD.

ATTEST
To swear or affirm as true. The term is used in legal documents when it is necessary to swear that the information contained therein is true.

AT THE CLOSE
Customer instruction on a market order that is to be executed on an exchange.

Basic concept: 30 seconds before the close, a bell signals the last half minute before the close. This at-the-close order should be executed during this time. The order is a customer instruction; no guarantee can be given that an execution will be obtained. The customer should understand the provisional nature of the order.

AT THE MONEY
Term used of a security option if the strike (execution) price and the market price are the same. For example, a put at 35 on ABC if the market price of ABC is 35.

The term abstracts from premiums paid or received and from the cost of executing the option contract. Thus, at the money should not be confused with the client's break-even point—either as holder or seller—on the option contract.

AT THE OPENING
Customer instruction on a limit order that is to be executed on the initial transaction in an exchange-traded security. If the instruction cannot be implemented, the order is to be cancelled.

Note: This instruction should not be placed on a market order. All market orders received before the initial transaction must be included in the initial transaction; this is exchange regulation.

ATTORNEY-AT-LAW
Any legally qualified person authorized to represent clients in court or in other proceedings requiring the services of a lawyer.

ATTORNEY GENERAL
Official title for the chief law enforcement officer of the U.S. government or of one of the United States. Frequently used abbreviation: AG.

ATTORNEY-IN-FACT
Any person, acting as agent, who has the written authority to represent someone in out-of-court proceedings. The person who acts as attorney-in-fact need not be a lawyer. For example, by signing a stock power, the registered holder authorizes the broker to act as attorney-in-fact to facilitate the transfer of the security to the new owner.

AUDIT TRAIL
This term identifies the attempt by the NASD and the major stock and options exchanges to track trade executions and to eliminate broker errors (DKs). To do this, each participating member must submit immediately such basic information as buy/sell, quantity, issue, price, contra party, time of execution, and firm capacity on-line to the NASD or exchange. In this way, errors are quickly identified.

AUNT AGATHA
See AUNT MILLIE.

AUNT MILLIE
This term is representative of the small shareholder; that is, the unsophisticated retail investor who relies on the professional broker/dealer as a financial physician and advisor. The expression is often used to emphasize suitability when making investment recommendations to less-knowledgeable customers; that is, those unable to distinguish risk from opportunity.

In the United Kingdom, known as Aunt Agatha; in Brussels as the Belgian Dentist.

AUSTRALIAN STOCK PRICE RISKLESS INDEXED NOTES
See ASPIRIN.

AUSTRALIA STOCK EXCHANGE (ASX)
The exchange is comprised of trading floors linked by a computerized trading system (SEATS). Official trading hours are 10:00 A.M. to 12:15 P.M. and from 2:00 P.M. until 3:15 P.M. Settlements are scheduled on a once-a-month basis, but shorter-term trade completions are not unusual.

The exchange's "All Ordinaries Index" provides investors with an accurate view of the performance of this market, because the index contains about 85% of all of the domestic issues traded on the marketplace.

AUTEX SYSTEM
A communications network using electronic screens to enable broker/dealers and other subscribers to show their trading interest in specific blocks of stock. If a mutual interest is found, the transaction is completed on a securities exchange or in the over-the-counter market.

AUTHORIZED SHARES
The maximum number of shares, either common or preferred, that a corporation may issue. The number of authorized shares is stated in the charter of the corporation. Corporations may issue fewer shares. Permission to issue more shares requires amendment of the corporate charter, based on the approval of the company's shareholders.

AUTO-EX
Acronym for Automatic Order Execution System. This American Stock Exchange system is used in conjunction with the exchange's AMOS system. AUTO-EX provides instant execution of the most active series in the exchange's Major Market Index options (XMI). AUTO-EX can immediately execute market and limit orders at the market in quantities of up to 10 contracts at a single price.

AUTOM
Acronym for Automated Option Market system, an on-line system developed by the Philadelphia Stock Exchange. AUTOM allows electronic delivery of options orders from member firms directly to the specific specialist in an option series. Execution information from the specialist is speeded back to the member firm as well as to the OPRA tape.

AUTOM is independent from PACE, the electronic system used by PHLX for stock orders.

39

AUTOMATED BOND SYSTEM
See ABS.

AUTOMATED CLEARINGHOUSE
A process provided by the Federal Reserve Banking System whereby funds are transferred electronically without the need to handle paper checks.

Popular abbreviation: ACH.

AUTOMATED CONFIRMATION TRANSACTION SYSTEM (ACT)
An NASD electronic system that enables members to submit, compare, and automatically clear their transactions through the National Securities Clearing Corporation (NSCC). Through a linkage of computer terminals in member firm offices, a marketmaker participating in a transaction can submit trade information immediately, have it automatically compared (with its terms "locked in" on T+1), and completed successfully at NSCC on the settlement date.

AUTOMATED CUSTOMER ACCOUNT TRANSFER SERVICE
Acronym: ACAT. A service of the National Securities Clearing Corporation (NSCC) that enables members to transfer customer accounts automatically via NSCC computerized facilities. Within five business days following the written instruction from the customer, and the validation thereof, the losing broker's account will be debited and the receiving broker's accounts will be credited with the customer's security and money positions.

As a general rule, option and investment company positions are outside this procedure.

AUTOMATED OPTIONS MARKET SYSTEM
See AUTOM.

AUTOMATED PIT TRADING
See APT.

AUTOMATED REGULATORY REPORTING SYSTEM (ARRS)
An NASD service that enables members to access the NASD immediately through a computer interface. ARRS can be used for ongoing reporting requirements of members as well as for petitions for extensions of time under Regulation T, or SEC Rule 15c3-3.

AUTOMATED SEARCH AND MATCH
See ASAM.

AUTOMATIC PRICING AND REPORTING SYSTEM

System used in conjunction with the Designated Order Turn-around (DOT) system on the NYSE for the pricing of odd-lot orders.

Concept: APARS accepts and stores orders from 1 to 99 shares until a round-lot transaction takes place in that stock. When the round-lot transaction occurs, the system prices those orders that are capable of execution and directs them back to the originating firms.

AUTOMATIC REINVESTMENT

Feature that permits an equity owner to receive dividend distributions in the form of new shares in lieu of a cash distribution. The feature is common to most mutual funds, which also permit the reinvestment of capital gains on fund portfolio transactions.

About 800 NYSE-listed corporations also have dividend reinvestment programs.

Since both programs are voluntary, the equity owner is liable to taxation in the year the distribution is made. However, under the Economic Recovery Tax Act, reinvestments of dividends from qualified utility shares in new shares of the same company were tax exempt: $750 on a single return, $1,500 on a joint return. This feature expired in tax year 1985.

AUTOMATIC TRANSFER SERVICE ACCOUNT

Banking term for those savings accounts from which funds can be transferred quickly and electronically to customers' checking accounts to cover checks. By using this system, the customers' savings accounts continue to earn interest until a check is written against savings balances.

Acronym: ATS.

AUTOMATIC WITHDRAWAL

Feature of many mutual funds that permits fundholder to receive a fixed-dollar amount each month or quarter. Check is sent to the holder, and dividends, capital gains, or share liquidation is used to pay for the withdrawals.

Also known as check-a-month plan.

AUTRANET

AUTRANET specializes in marketing "soft dollar" services in the European investment community; that is, it pays for computer, research, and systems services for institutional customers in exchange for commission business from that customer. The ratio of expense for commission revenues is negotiable between the customer and AUTRANET. The corporation is an affiliate of U.S. broker/dealer Donaldson Lufkin & Jenrette.

AVERAGE
1. As noun: a measurement of general price movement of a security or a group of securities. For example, the measurement of the Dow Jones Industrial Average.
2. As verb: to make purchases at various prices to achieve an advantageous price for an entire lot of securities. For example, "Let's buy over time to average the price."
3. As adjective: a qualifier for a noun implying normative performance. For example, a mutual fund's performance last year was average in terms of performance that was measured against the Standard & Poor's Index.

AVERAGE DOWN
Investment strategy often used by purchasers of securities.

Concept: Do not buy all at once; instead, buy multiple holdings at various prices as a security falls in market value. For example, a client wants to buy 10,000 shares of a stock. Instead of buying all at once, the client buys 2,000 shares; then, if the price falls, the client will purchase additional lots of 2,000 shares—up to 10,000—to attain an average price that is lower than the original purchase price.

Strategy can be profitable if stock is going through a sideways movement with up-and-down price variations.

AVERAGE LIFE
The number of years required for one half of a debt to be retired through a sinking fund, serial maturity, or amortizing payments. For example, the company issued 25-year bonds with a sinking fund that will begin in 5 years. The average life of the bond issue is 18 years and 7 months.

AVERAGE UP
Term describing the purchase of the same security at various times and prices above the lowest price paid. For example, an investor buys 100 shares at $22, $24, $26, and $28. The investor has averaged up 400 shares at an average price of $25.

Term also is used of sales at various times at prices above the lowest price received.

AVERAGING THE DOLLAR
Term inaccurately used of dollar cost averaging.

See also DOLLAR COST AVERAGING.

AWAY FROM ME
Term used by a marketmaker to identify a quotation, transaction, or market in an issue that did not originate with the marketmaker. For

example, in response to a customer inquiry, a trader may respond, "The bonds sold at par, away from me." Meaning: Someone else sold the bonds at par.

AWAY FROM THE BLUE
Jargon for an offering of municipal securities by a dealer who has not previously advertised it in the Blue List (book).

AWAY FROM THE MARKET
Term describing an order that cannot be executed because it contains a limit bid below, or a limit offer above, prevailing quotes for the security. For example, when the quote for a security is 25 to 25½, a limit order to buy at 24 is away from the market.

Unless the order stipulates immediate cancellation (e.g., fill or kill, or immediate or cancel), such orders are given to the specialist for later transaction if the limit can be met.

AWC
Acronym for Acceptance, Waiver, and Consent Agreement. A written plea entered in connection with a NASD disciplinary matter. In it, the accused, without admitting or denying the allegations, agrees to refrain from a cited questionable act and also agrees to accept a negotiated penalty.

AXE
Shortened form of "an axe to grind." Slang expression used by securities traders when they solicit business without disclosing to securities salespersons whether they are interested in buying or selling. In this way, the traders can get an indication of market interest before they commit themselves to one side of the market or the other.

B

B
Second letter of the English alphabet, used:
1. Lowercase in stock tables to designate that the annual dollar dividend was accompanied by the payment of a stock dividend in addition; for example, 2.45b.
2. Lowercase in older option tables to designate that an option series was not offered. Current usage: s.
3. Used uppercase as the fifth letter in certain NASDAQ symbols to designate that more than one class of common stock is outstanding; for example, EBNCB is for Equitable Bancorporation, Class B common stock.

4. Uppercase as the NYSE symbol for the Barnes Group, Inc., a manufacturer and distributor of precision mechanical springs.
5. An identifying symbol after the name of a company reporting financial information in the newspaper under a section for corporate sales and earnings reports. It reveals the locale where this company's common stock is primarily traded. In this case "B" means Boston Stock Exchange.

BA
See BANKER'S ACCEPTANCE.

BABY BELL(S)
Used individually and collectively as a nickname for the seven operating telephone companies divested by American Telephone & Telegraph under terms of a federal court decree. Each of these companies dominates a particular region of the United States. The baby bells are: Bell Atlantic, Ameritech, NYNEX, Pacific Telesis, BellSouth, U.S. West, and Southwestern Bell.

BABY BOND
A debt instrument with a face value of less than $1,000. Example: ATT has many $100 face value bonds outstanding.

Baby bonds were designed to appeal to the small, public investor in the early 1800s as the railroad industry used massive financing for their expansion efforts. "Baby" was created on the floor of the New York Stock Exchange to differentiate it from the regular ($1,000) obligations of those railroads traded there.

See CITIZEN BONDS and CONSOL.

BACKDATING
Mutual funds permitting a fundholder who did not originally sign a letter of intent to sign one with a prior date (up to 90 days) on it. This permits prior purchases, together with a present large purchase, to qualify for a reduced sales charge.

BACK DOOR SUBSCRIPTION
In connection with the NASD's interpretations for "hot issue" allocations, this term refers to a broker/dealer's sale to a conduit-type customer; that is, an institution's action for a buyer whose identity is not revealed to the firm. The NASD requires that the member obtain a representation from the institution that it is not circumventing the association's rules by acting as an agent for someone who is ineligible to subscribe to the issue. In effect, that the ineligible person is not coming in through the "back door."

BACK-END BONUS

An expression used to describe additional compensation to certain sales-persons in the securities industry. The term refers to an increased aggregate percentage commission payable to registered representatives (RRs). For example, a broker/dealer uses a tiered compensation payout grid. Each time an RR reaches a preset production breakpoint—let's say $250,000—all old production is aggregated with the new to award the salesperson the new percentage payout. In this way, first dollars are equal to last dollars in terms of commission payout.

BACK-END LOAD

1. Term used to describe early redemption penalties paid by holders of certain mutual funds registered under 12b-1 of the Investment Company Act. Holders of these funds who cash in at prevailing asset value during the first few years after purchase are subject to a penalty fee.

    Also called "deferred contingent sales charge."
2. A slang term for any hidden sales charge by a mutual fund that does not charge an up-front sales charge. The charge is hidden, in that the investor pays the charge indirectly; that is, through a higher operating charge against the assets of the fund.

    Note: In practice, the expenses of most no-load funds are comparable to the expenses of funds with a sales charge. Do not confuse the term *back-end load* with the distribution fee that some funds charge. Back end load is used exclusively of the charge levied if funds are withdrawn before a certain period following purchase.

    See also DISTRIBUTION PLAN or 12b-1 PLAN.

BACK-END RIGHTS

A term from corporate finance to designate management's gift to stockholders in a company that has become a takeover target. The privilege enables holders to exchange one right and one share for cash, preferred stock, and/or debt securities in that concern in the event an acquirer obtains a predetermined percentage of the outstanding stock and does not promptly consummate the takeover at a value at least equal to management's distributed package of cash and securities. Back-end rights serve to protect the financial interests of shareholders in an about-to-be-acquired company.

BACKING AWAY

Marketmaker fails to honor a firm bid for the minimum quantity. Action violates the Rules of Fair Practice of the National Association of Securities Dealers (NASD).

BACK MONTHS

Expression used in futures and option trading for the later months of trading. For example, if contracts are available for July, August, September, October, and January, October and January would be considered "back months."

BACK OFFICE

Those departments of a broker-dealer organization that are not directly engaged in sales or trading activity.

Back office functions are cashiering, accounting, various communications, and the record keeping of the clients' cash or margin accounts.

BACKSPREAD

A reversal of the popular ratio-spread technique. Most ratio spreaders buy one call and sell two calls with a higher strike price. A backspread also can involve the purchase of one call and the sale of two calls with a lower strike price.

BACK-TO-BACK LOANS

Swap arrangement whereby parties in different countries borrow money from each other in the other's currency. For example, a U.S.-domiciled company has Swiss francs, and a Swiss company has U.S. dollars, and they borrow from one another. These simple, direct arrangements avoid the expense of a third party and the resulting transaction fees.

If the borrowing entities are subsidiaries, the loans are also said to be parallel. Back-to-back loans imply that the lender/borrowers are independent companies.

BACK-UP

1. Verb: Describes the market action of debt securities when dollar prices rise and yields fall. Example: The bond market is backing up.
2. Verb: Describes the action whereby a bond portfolio manager sells one bond and purchases another of equal quality with a shorter maturity date.

Note: Do not confuse with the noun backup; that is, a person or system that will substitute for another.

BACKUP BID

See TAKE-OUT (3).

BACKUP LINE

Line of credit by commercial bank to issuer of commercial paper if placement of the paper is slow or is difficult to accomplish.

46

BACKWARDIZATION
English trade term that describes the situation in commodities markets when spot prices are higher than futures prices.

Synonym: inverted market.

BADEN
Tokyo Stock Exchange term for a telephone booth on its trading floor. The baden (pronounced baa–den) forms a communication link between the trading floor and the office of the member firm entering the order.

BAGGING A DEALER
Expression used to denote deception by a marketmaker or portfolio manager. "Bagging" indicates that a sale of stock is made to a block positioner at a price that is higher than the current market level. Concept: The issue is highly volatile and the dealer is not alert to the rapid change and thus buys the stock at an inflated price. The dealer is thus "bagged" as an investor, unless the dealer is willing to sell immediately at a loss.

BAGGING THE OFFERING
The practice of selling short an issue in registration, with the intent of covering the short with shares (or bonds) acquired from the new offering. The practice is based on the fact that the new offering may depress the price. In this way, the "bagger" can sell short above the offer price and cover with new shares at a profit.

The practice is now illegal under SEC Rule 10b-21.

BAG-TRADING
Colorful expression for the illegal act of prearranged trading on behalf of two customers in the futures marketplace. Using an intermediary (the "bag" man), the dealer buys one customer's contract at the low end of the trading range while, at about the same time, the dealer sells the same contract through the same intermediary at the high end of the range. The dealer (FCM) and the bag man then split the profit.

BAIKAI
See CROSS-TRADING.

BAILING OUT
Trading expression for the sale of a security quickly and without regard for the price. If the market turns and the trader is caught "long and wrong," the trader will often sell out—often at a severe loss. This is in line with the Street jingle: "He who lives to run away, lives to trade another day."

BAILOUT BONDS
Popular term for the long-term bonds of the Resolution Funding Corporation, an adjunct of the Resolution Trust Company (RTC), empowered under FIRREA (q.v.) to resolve the financial insolvencies of savings institutions.

Semiannual interest is U.S. guaranteed and free of state and local taxes. The first bonds were issued in 1989.

BAIT AND SWITCH
The unsavory, and at times unethical, practice of advertising an item at an advantageous price. When potential customers inquire about the item, they are pressured into buying higher-priced substitutes that are more advantageous to the salesperson.

BALANCED COMPANY
See BALANCED MUTUAL FUND.

BALANCED MUTUAL FUND
A management investment company that endeavors to minimize capital risk by investing in a portfolio with a varying percentage of bonds, preferred stocks, and common stocks.

BALANCE OF PAYMENTS (BOP)
Difference in dollars between total payments made for goods and services imported from, and receipts for goods and services exported to, foreign countries. Often a gross figure or computed on a country-by-country basis.

BALANCE OF TRADE
Dollar difference between a country's merchandise imports and its exports. Differs from balance of payments in that it does not include money paid for services or funds spent by citizens of one country traveling in the other.

BALANCE SHEET
Simplified financial statement showing the nature and amount of a company's assets, liabilities, and net worth (shareholders' or stockholders' equity) on a given date.

BALANCE SHEET EQUATION
Total assets = Total liabilities + Stockholders' equity (net worth). It is this equation, graphically represented in the balance sheet, that makes double-entry bookkeeping possible.

BALLOON INTEREST
Feature of serial bond issues in which earlier years' coupons are lower than coupon interest rates for later serial maturities.

BALLOON MATURITY
Feature of serial bond issues in which dollar amounts of earlier maturities are smaller than dollar amounts of later maturities.

BAN
See BOND ANTICIPATION NOTE.

B&B
English slang for "bed and breakfast" as applied to the securities market. This English technique—often also applied in a U.S. context—endeavors to lessen tax liability without sacrificing a security position.

The technique involves a sale as late as possible in the day and a repurchase as early as possible the next day. Because there is minimal market risk between the two days, the customer, in effect, maintains the same security position. On the other hand, the sale/purchase commissions and a one-day cost of carry on the security should offset one another. The customer, however, is flat overnight against adverse news and has offsetting tax considerations.

BANDWAGON ACCOUNT
Term used by a broker/dealer in referring to a customer who is not a trendsetter. In fact, that customer usually copies the investment activities of other persons. Thus, the expression is often used of a customer who "jumps on the bandwagon" after someone else has created a unique investment trend or securities position strategy.

BANIF
Short name for Banif de Inversiones Finanzaz, S.A., a wholly owned subsidiary of Banco Hispano-Americano, S.A., one of the largest banks in Spain.

BANIF serves as an investment manager for the largest pool of funds in that country, and it is also an advisor to the First Spanish Investment Trust, plc, a closed-end fund concentrated in issues traded on the Spanish stock market.

BANK
1. Any institution that accepts time and demand deposits and makes loans.
2. If such loans are to individuals and businesses, the term *commercial bank* is used.

3. If such loans are primarily made in the form of mortgages, the term *savings and loan* is used.
4. If the bank is primarily engaged in the raising of capital, both short- and long-term, for corporations, municipalities, or governments, the bank is called an "investment bank."
5. In the United Kingdom, banks involved in corporate investing or bills of trade are called "merchant banks."

BANK CHECK
A draft drawn by a bank upon itself. In the securities industry, a bank check is considered one of several forms of good trade settlement because payment is assured by the bank's obligation to honor the check. If requested by a third party, the bank normally will charge a fee for the issuance of a bank check.

Note: Do not confuse with a check drawn by a bank on its account with the Federal Reserve System. Such checks are a form of federal funds.

See also FEDERAL FUNDS.

BANKER'S ACCEPTANCE
Time draft that becomes a money market instrument when payment is guaranteed; that is, accepted by a bank. Used extensively in international trade.

Manufacturer accepts a discounted amount from the bank for the goods; importer pays face amount. The discount becomes in effect the interest to the purchaser of the accepted time draft because the purchaser will receive the full face value at maturity. Most BAs mature within 9 months, although shorter maturities are common.

Also called BAs.

BANK FOR COOPERATIVES (CO-OPS)
Supervised by Farm Credit Administration, a government-sponsored corporation, to make and service loans to agricultural cooperative associations.

BANK GUARANTEE LETTER
A letter from a commercial bank to a broker/dealer stating that a customer has funds on deposit and that these funds will be paid to the broker/dealer if certain activities occur in the customer's brokerage account.

A bank guarantee letter can serve as acceptable collateral for the writing of a short put in the customer's account.

BANK HOLDING COMPANY
A corporation engaged in many businesses through control of other corporations. However, the holding company's principal asset is ownership of a commercial bank. This form of business enterprise often is used to establish subsidiaries that are outside the restrictions of state banking laws.

BANK INSURANCE FUND (BIF)
An arm of the Federal Deposit Insurance Corporation (FDIC). It was created to insure depositor's savings accounts up to $100,000 at member banks. The enabling legislation for BIF is abbreviated FIRREA.

BANK INVESTMENT CONTRACT
See BIC.

BANK QUALITY
Refers to a debt security that has been assigned one of the top four credit ratings (i.e., S&P's AAA, AA, A, BBB).
Synonymous with bank grade.
See also LEGAL LIST.

BANKRUPTCY
The state of being insolvent; that is, liabilities exceed assets, with little hope of a reversal of this situation.

Under the laws of the United States, persons who are in the state of bankruptcy may petition to be declared bankrupt and to be protected from the immediate claims of their creditors. This same petition may be made by corporations and other business enterprises.

BARCLAYS SHARE PRICE INDEX
A popular capitalization-weighted index of 40 stocks traded in New Zealand. This special index reflects the market performance of the most important companies—although it is oriented toward natural resource companies domiciled in New Zealand. The index also serves as the basis of a futures contract traded there by means of a computerized order matching system.

BARE ASS
In the securities industry, this colorful term is used of the Boeing Company, the largest manufacturer of jet aircraft in the world. The term is derived from the company's stock symbol: BA.

BAREFOOT PILGRIM
A derogatory term for a public customer in the securities industry. It is supposed to identify a naive investor who has lost his or her shirt—and often his or her shoes—in the harsh world of securities trading.

BARGAIN
1. Verb: used as a synonym for negotiate. Example: They bargained back and forth.
2. Noun: in the United States, a security that is underpriced in terms of other securities of the same class or industry. Example: XYZ is a bargain at today's prices.
3. Noun: in England, a completed securities transaction. Example: They struck a bargain on the sale.
4. Adjective: used to describe an "as is" sale. Example: That was a bargain sale and may not be rescinded.

BARREL OF OIL (BOL)
A standard measure of crude oil volume, equal to 42 U.S. gallons of oil at 60 degrees Fahrenheit.

The term has extensive usage in economic reports; its price, for example, is a major component in the consumer price index (CPI). The term also is used in conjunction with certain tax-sheltered investments involved in oil exploration and development.

BARRON'S CONFIDENCE INDEX
Weekly index prepared by the publishers of *Barron's*. Index compares yields of higher-grade to lower-grade corporate bonds. As yields on lower-grade bonds fall, it shows that investors are more confident about the economy. Used for an insight into possible market sentiment about equity securities.

BARROW BOYS
A derisive term used in the English financial industry to distinguish securities traders from bankers. Allusion: traders are often working-class in both background and schooling and are from the lower social order. Bankers, on the other hand, traditionally stem from the aristocracy, have public school educations, and are from a higher stratum of society.

BASE
Acronym for Brokerage Accounting Systems Element. BASE is a computerized operations department that processes all transactions executed on the floor of the Boston Stock Exchange. When added to the exchange's BEACON system, it will immediately confirm executions, update specialist positions, and provide average inventory costs on a continuing basis.

BASE LENDING RATE
This is the percentage interest rate charged to a bank's best customers in the United Kingdom. It is similar to the prime rate in the United States. Just as the Federal Reserve influences the prime rate in the United States, so the Bank of England influences the United Kingdom base lending rate.

Also called "base rate."

BASE MARKET VALUE
Average value of traded securities at a certain time, used in construction of a market index. Movement is in terms of dollar change or percentage change from original base. For example, NYSE Index had an original base of 50.00 as of December 31, 1965.

BASE RATE
See BASE LENDING RATE.

BASH AND TRASH
Slang for the endeavor of analysts to deride the merits of another investment banker's takeover deal. "Bash" refers to the deriding of the junk bonds that will be issued, and "trash" refers to their deriding of the deal in general. For example, "There was a chorus of 'bash and trash' reports from Street analysts when AJAX proposed the takeover of COMET by the use of junk bonds."

BASIC
1. Noun, in capitals: a simple computer language used by the general public and other noncomputer specialists. Example: "My computer is programmed in BASIC."
2. Adjective: used as a synonym for elementary or essential. Example: Timely purchase is a basic investment strategy.
3. Acronym for Banking for Securities Industry Committee. Promotes standardization of securities operations and of certificate processing systems.

BASIS BOOK
Published by Financial Publishing Company of Boston, book contains coupon interest rates and time remaining to maturity. From these, one can compute yield to maturity given a dollar price, or a dollar price given yield to maturity.

BASIS POINT
By common agreement, .01% of yield on a fixed-income security. For example, if a bond's yield to maturity changed from 9.05% to 10.35%, there was a change of 130 basis points.

Also used with yield changes for securities sold at a discount from face value.

BASIS PRICE
1. Noun: arbitrary price set by floor official that will be used to execute certain odd-lot orders.
2. Noun: also used to designate a taxpayer's cost of acquisition for the computation of capital gains or losses.

BASIS SWAP
A transaction arrangement whereby contra parties exchange floating-rate obligations that are calculated on different indices. For example, Company A has a variable-rate liability based on the six-month T-bill rate. Company B has a variable-rate liability based on LIBOR. The companies may be inclined to swap liabilities if they feel that the other's rate index would save interest dollar expenses over the near term.

Also known as a "floating swap."

BASIS TRADING
Also called "yield trading." It is a term associated with wealthy or institutional-type investors who establish large underlying stock and index option futures positions. If index futures look cheap, relative to the underlying stocks, they buy the futures and sell the stocks short. When futures become overvalued, they do the opposite. The purpose of this very aggressive trading is to generate an overall rate of return on invested capital that is greater, and safer, than can be achieved in only one marketplace.

BASKET BOOK BROKER
See BBB.

BASKET TRADING
A practice used by some portfolio managers and investment partnerships with substantial investment capital. Rather than attempt to outperform the market, they try to match the performance of a particular market index or average. To do this, they assemble a portfolio—a basket of securities—that in composition and share volume will tend to track the index or average they want to follow.

Many variable annuities use such trading and often assemble a portfolio of mutual funds to achieve the desired effect.

Also called "market basket trading."

BB

An employee of the Chicago Board Option Exchange. He or she makes a memorandum of option orders that are away from the market and, thus, are not capable of execution at the present time.

See also BOARD BROKER.

BBB

1. NYSE designation for a basket book broker. A BBB is similar in function to an order book official (OBO) on the CBOE. In effect, a BBB is a "passive marketmaker," in that the BBB accepts limit orders for ESP (Exchange Stock Portfolio Equities) and executes them—always as agent!—when it is feasible to do so.
2. Standard & Poor's credit designation for a bond that is at the lower edge of investment grade. Such bonds are either severely influenced by changes in the economy or have minimal bond debt service coverage in the investment grade category.
3. NYSE ticker tape symbol for Baltimore Bancorp, a large bank holding company in Maryland.

BBI

An index that measures yield levels of municipal bonds.

See also BOND BUYERS INDEX.

BBL

Abbreviation for barrel of oil.

See BARREL OF OIL.

BB SYSTEM

Abbreviation for "broker's brokerage," a futures trading system in Japan that enables nonmembers of commodities exchanges to solicit and enter orders for exchange-listed contracts through members, with both organizations receiving compensation for their services.

BCC

1. Among self-regulatory organizations (SRO) the initials commonly used to denote Business Conduct Committee.
   See also BUSINESS CONDUCT COMMITTEE.
2. The NYSE stock symbol for the Boise Cascade Corporation, a large lumber and paper processor.

BD

Written Bd and used as an abbreviation for bond.

In newspaper transaction tables for U.S. government securities, the lowercase symbol b is used instead of Bd.

BD FORM
Document that broker/dealers must file with SEC. Contains information about principals, net capital compliance, and financial statements about firm. Must be constantly updated.

BEACON
Acronym for Boston Exchange Automated Communication Order routing Network. BEACON is an electronic system available for the entry and execution of market and marketable limit orders up to 1,299 shares. This system can also provide for execution at prices based on primary market openings, or the consolidated tapes, at the preference of the customer.

BEAR
See BEARISH.

BEAR BONDS
A Eurodebt issue with its redemption amount linked to the downward movement of a specific foreign stock index, such as the Nikkei Japanese stock index or the FAZ (Frankfurter Allgemeine Zeitung) German stock index.

Bear bonds are designed to appeal to Japanese and German investors in whose countries options and futures trading were considered illegal and are now considered unsuitable for domestic citizens. These issues offer holders a long-term put on the stock markets of these nations. Holders receive a premium over par value at maturity if the benchmark index declines below a predetermined figure.

See also BULL BONDS for opposite concept.

BEARDING
The practice of splitting a large order into smaller pieces for execution by a number of brokers. In this way, corporate raiders and large institutional investors can mask their strategies and discourage others who may want to piggyback their activities.

Bearding, of course, does not absolve the acquiror from complying with the provisions of SEC Rule 13D as it applies to the acquisition of 5% or more of the equity securities of a registered company.

BEARDS
Slang for the illegal practice of using "dummy" customer accounts as a repository for stocks purchased. In effect, the purchase is disguised and the identity of the beneficial owner is hidden. This practice, which is illegal, is used to avoid federal filing requirements or to avoid premature disclosure of merger or acquisition intentions.

BEARER SECURITY

Security is not registered in the name of the owner; instead, it is presumed to be the property of the holder, and transfer is completed by giving security to new owner.

Many older bonds were issued only in bearer format, although current trend is to issue bonds in registered format.

Many foreign equity securities are in bearer format; this gives rise to American Depository Receipts.

See also COUPON BOND and COUPON.

BEAR HUG

Slang term used in describing a takeover offer. Concept: The raiders' offer is sufficiently attractive to draw protests from shareholders if the board turns it down, but it really is not that attractive. Thus, the board of directors is caught in a "squeeze play"—they're damned if they do and damned if they don't accept the offer.

BEAR HUG LETTER

A written communication with an issuer threatening to buy control of that company unless certain specified measures are taken. It is a form of corporate blackmail done by a raider seeking a favorable reorganization or an offer of "greenmail." Bear hug letters have proven to be effective when management has a minimal ownership in the corporation.

BEARISH

Having the opinion that securities will fall in market value. Used of persons or of general market conditions. For example: "Mr. Smith is bearish," or "The market is bearish."

BEAR MARKET

Colorful, and metaphorical, term used to describe the fact that securities prices generally are declining. Term also may be used of an individual security. Example: Although the stock market is generally rising, there is a bear market for high-technology stocks.

See also BEARISH.

BEAR POSITION

Euphemistic term used in England to identify a short security position. One who has sold short and who does not own the underlying stock is positioned to profit from a drop in the price of the stock when the short position is covered. Term *bear* is from the 18th century London Exchange slang: to sell a bear (skin). Allusion: The skin was sold before the bear was caught, because the dealer considered that bear skin prices would fall. Today, in England, stock is often called a "bear skin."

BEAR RAID

Manipulation of the price of a security by short selling at prices lower than previous transaction prices. When the price was sufficiently low, the manipulator profited by repurchasing the security sold short at a lower price.

The practice is now illegal. Current SEC rules require that short sales of exchange-traded securities be made at a price that is higher than the last different price in the security. In effect, short sellers may not depress the price of a security by their short sale.

BEARS

Acronym for Bonds Enabling Annual Retirement Savings. BEARS are investment instruments designed to appeal to retirement plans and other financial institutions. BEARS holders receive the maturity value of bonds underlying calls not exercised by holders of CUBS, or by the aggregate exercise price itself if those calls are actually exercised.

See also CUBS.

BEAR SPREAD

An option strategy that involves the purchase and sale of options of the same class. Example: The purchase and sale of calls, or puts, on the same underlying.

Such a strategy is called "bearish" if the holder/writer will profit from a drop in the market. The term is used correctly only of vertical spreads.

In a *call* bear spread, the long leg has the higher strike price. In a put bear spread, the short leg has the higher strike price.

The strategy works because, as the market drops, the premium on the leg with the higher strike price will drop faster than the premium on the lower leg.

See OPTION SPREAD STRATEGY.

BEAR TRAP

Slang for a market situation where falling prices encourage short selling by speculators who believe that further declines are imminent. Soon after the short sales, the market reverses itself and prices start to rise rapidly. The bears are thus forced to cover the short positions at substantial losses. The speculators were literally trapped by the ensuing bull market rise in the underlying securities.

BED AND BREAKFAST TRANSACTION

English expression for the profitable sale of a security late in the day with a next-day repurchase, possibly at a lower price.

BEDBUG LETTER

Facetious expression for the deficiency letter sent by the SEC in response to the filing of a preliminary registration statement by a corporation about to distribute securities.

Concept: The SEC wants the "bugs" taken out of the registration statement before the securities are issued.

BELGIAN DENTIST

See AUNT MILLIE.

BELG-INDEX FUND

The Belg-Index is based on the performance of stocks listed and traded only on the Brussels Stock Exchange. In practice, there are 40 different Belgian companies in the index and these represent about 91% of the market's total valuation. This investment company (mutual fund) is sponsored and sold by Reyers Timmermans, a small Brussels stock brokerage company.

BELL

Trading on the exchanges begins and ends with a recognized signal, often a bell.

See also AT THE CLOSE.

BELLS AND WHISTLES

1. Used of special features attached to a security to attract investor attention. Example: The company put a lot of bells and whistles on that issue of preferred stock by adding subscription warrants.
2. Used pejoratively of sales presentations in which the salesperson emphasizes minor features of an investment and thus distracts the customer from features that may be disadvantageous for the purchaser.

BELLWETHER

One who assumes a position of leadership. Said of a security or industry that seems to lead a market movement or economic trend.

BELLY UP

Slang term to describe a company, or its securities, that threatens to go bankrupt and thus be worthless. Example: When faced with the low cost of foreign labor, many smokestack industries may go belly up.

Concept: A fish that has died in the water often floats in this position.

BELOW THE MARKET

A bid to purchase a security that is lower than the then highest bid price. For example, if the highest bid for a security is $23 per share, a bid at $21 is below the market.

Synonym: away from the market, although this expression also is used of offers above the market.

BENCHMARK
A standard for quantitative measurement. For example, the benchmark for the quarterly dividend rate on the variable-rate preferred stock was set at 75% of the two-year Treasury note auction rate during that period. Or, the London Interbank Offer Rate (LIBOR) is the benchmark for Eurodebt securities.

Note: Benchmark is a quantitative norm. To express a qualitative norm, use hallmark. For example, concern for the customer's needs and investment objectives is the hallmark of business ethics in the securities industry.

BENEFICIAL OWNER
The person entitled to all benefits of ownership even though a broker or bank holds the security. For example, a fundholder leaves shares of a mutual fund with the custodian bank, or a brokerage client leaves stock with his broker.

See also STREET NAME.

BENEFICIARY
Person who will receive the financial benefits of an asset, subject to certain conditions. Asset may be an insurance policy, an annuity, a trust, or other property.

BES
See BUSINESS EXPANSION SCHEME.

BESSIE
Nickname for Bethlehem Steel Corporation, derived from its stock symbol: BS.

BEST EFFORTS
Term used of an underwriting conducted on an agency basis. The distributor promises to do his or her best to sell the security but does not guarantee the sale by purchasing the security from the issuer. If the security is not sold, the underwriter receives no fee but he or she has no further financial obligation to the issuer.

See also BOUGHT DEAL.

BETA
An analysis of price volatility of a security in terms of Standard & Poor's Index. The S&P Index is given a value of 1. Securities with a beta

greater than 1 have in the past been more volatile than the S&P; those with a beta less than 1 have been less volatile. It is anticipated that this trend will continue, although the beta is subject to factual revision in terms of current comparisons of the security and the S&P Index.

BET THE JOCKEY NOT THE HORSE
Saying among horse racing fans that is echoed on Wall Street. The analogy suggests that traders should copy successful investors and insiders and not be concerned about individual companies. The philosophy is predicated on the opinion that such successful investors and insiders have superior timing patterns of purchases and sales because of their proximity to the situation.

BG
Meaning: bank guaranteed. This symbol often is used of debt securities if a commercial bank has guaranteed either the payment of principal or interest, or both, on a security.

Because the bank guarantee does not represent a deposit there is no insurance. Thus, the value of the bank guarantee for this security should be based on the credit rating of the bank.

BIC
Acronym for bank investment contract. A BIC is an interest in a portfolio that guarantees subscribers a specific yield over a predetermined period. BICs are guaranteed by a bank; in this way, they are similar to a GIC (guaranteed investment contract) issued by an insurance company.

BID
Price at which someone is willing here and now to purchase a security. Synonymous with bid price.

See also QUOTATION.

BID AND ASKED
The highest price (bid) at which someone is willing to purchase a security and the lowest price (offer) at which the same or another person is willing to sell a security here and now.

Synonyms: bid and offer; quote; quotation; market.

BID-IN-COMPETITION
An institutional investor solicits bids from several dealers for a block of bonds that it wants to sell. The bonds will be sold to the dealer with the highest bid.

BID PRICE

The highest price at which someone is currently willing to buy a particular security. On a registered stock exchange bid prices are stated orally in the trading crowd by members announcing price followed by the quantity desired. For example, the appropriate language for a bid price is "51⅝ for 1,000."

BID WANTED

Signifies that someone who is willing to sell securities wants someone else to give a price at which he or she is willing to buy. Bid need not be specific because seller is willing to negotiate the final price. Often used on published market quotation sheets.

Common abbreviation is BW.

BID WILL IMPROVE

Expression used by OTC traders in response to a request for a market from a seller. It signifies that the trader can pay more than the represented bid price, but first he or she wants a counterproposal from the prospective seller.

Acronym: BWI.

BIF

See BANK INSURANCE FUND.

BIG

See BOND INTERNATIONAL GOLD.

BIG BANG

A colorful term associated with the revision of operating rules of the International Stock Exchange of the United Kingdom and the Republic of Ireland on October 27, 1986. Under these rule changes, fixed commission charges became fully negotiable; members were allowed to function in a dual capacity (agent/principal); new and more comprehensive capital rules were adopted for member organizations; and some principals of member organizations could now be non-U.K. nationals.

BIG BOARD

The New York Stock Exchange.

BIG DRAGON

Term often used of Japan in its role as the most important financial power in the Asiatic sphere of influence. Following World War II, Japan quickly gained international prominence in the production and sale of automobiles, textiles, electronic and photographic equipment, and computer components. Ironically, Japan is now facing challenges from the "Little Dragons" of Asia, who are using the same strategies, particularly low-cost labor, that helped Japan to reach its prominence.

THE BIG FIVE
Term often applied to the five largest securities/commodities firms in Japan. Generally, they account for more than 50% of the total trading volume on each day. The five firms are: Nomura, Daiwa, Nikko, Yamaichi, and Kokusai.

THE BIGGER THE TOP, THE BIGGER THE DROP
Jingle used by technical analysts to presage a large drop in the price of a stock if there is a large top formation without significant corrections.

A top formation is represented by a horizontal price movement following a relatively long rise in the price of a stock. The longer the horizontal price movement (the top formation itself), the greater the probability of a subsequent and significant downward price movement if there is a penetration of the support level for the top movement.

BIGI
See BOND INVESTORS GUARANTY INSURANCE COMPANY.

BIG INDEX SWAP
A product initiated by Salomon Brothers to compete with Merrill Lynch's Dollar BILS. The product is a synthetic asset for institutional customers, whereby they can match or beat the return on the Salomon Brothers' Broad Investment Grade (BIG) bond index.

Under a Big Index Swap a customer is guaranteed a monthly return on a specified principal amount for a three- to five-year period. In return, the customer guarantees to pay Salomon monthly the LIBOR rate less 20 basis points. The difference is settled by checks based on the two rates. In effect, the swap is between two floating rates, which the customer can hedge by investing the principal in a LIBOR-based instrument during the calculation period.

BIG MAC
See MUNICIPAL ASSISTANCE CORPORATION FOR THE CITY OF NEW YORK.

BIG PRODUCER
Expression used of a registered representative who generates substantial revenues for a broker/dealer. Although the differentiation between little, medium, and large producer will differ from firm to firm, and during differing periods in the market cycle, it is generally admitted that

registered representatives in the $500,000 to $1,000,000 and up range in annual revenues are big producers.

BIG STEEL
Colloquial name for United States Steel Corporation, or for its shares.

BIG TELEPHONE
See MA BELL.

THE BIG THREE
1. In the United States, the three largest automakers, namely General Motors, Ford, and Chrysler.
2. In Switzerland, the three largest banking institutions, namely Credit Suisse, Swiss Bank Corporation, and Union Bank of Switzerland. The Big Three control about 70% of the new issue market in Switzerland.

BIG TICKET
1. Slang for any high-priced stock, particularly if the stock is felt to be overpriced.
2. Any large customer order for stocks or bonds that results in significant compensation for the salesperson who enters the order.

BIG UGLIES
Slang for issues currently out of favor with the investing public. This disfavor may be a perception on the part of the public, or it may be based on the fundamentals of the underlying industries or companies. As a result, the "big uglies" often sell at significant discounts to their underlying asset value.

BILLS
Short-term securities of the U.S. Treasury sold at a discount from their face value. Difference between purchase price and face value represents interest income if held to maturity.
  Other governments also use bills for short-term financing.
  Bill is synonymous with bills.
  See also TREASURY BILL, TREASURY-BILL AUCTION.

BILL STRIP
A Treasury-Bill auction in which the Treasury Department simultaneously offers bills of different maturities at one average price.

BINDER
A written memorandum of the terms and conditions of a contract that is meant to serve as a temporary agreement until a formal contract can be drawn and signed.

BITCH BOX
An unfortunate colloquialism for open, two-way, telephonic communication within a member firm.

See SQUAWK BOX.

BITS
Acronym for Bond Interest Term Security. This is a municipal security product developed and sold by Smith Barney Harris Upham, a prominent broker/dealer and investment banker. The product features a variable-rate interest coupon and a put feature so the holder can redeem the bond at par if the daily rate is not satisfactory to the holder.

BITSY
A word based on the phonemes of BTSI (Brokers Transaction Services, Incorporated). BTSI sells trade processing, surveillance, and reporting services to broker/dealers.

BLACK FCM
In Japan, black FCM unregistered futures commission merchant who seek domestic futures business and execute it on overseas commodities exchanges. Such FCMs operate on the fringe of illegality, and they are generally ostracized by local members of the securities and commodities exchanges.

BLACK FRIDAY
Expression used to designate any financial debacle. The origin of the term occurred in 1869 at the time of the gold panic and depression, but it was used in later years for any sharp market drop which, coincidentally, often occurred on Fridays.

In practice, the expression is used for any large market sell-off, no matter on which day of the week it happened.

BLACK KNIGHT
In corporate finance, a party who makes a tender offer or merger proposal that is hostile to present management of a company.

Antonym: white knight; that is, a tenderer who overcomes the unfriendly actions of a black knight.

BLACK MARKET BONDS
Trading in SEC-registered bonds by dealers outside the offering syndicate between the effective date and the date pricing restrictions are removed from members of the account. Often detrimental to distribution efforts of the syndicate.

BLACK MONDAY
Media-coined term used to designate the financial events of October 19, 1987. On that day, both price and volume record changes occurred as the Dow Jones Industrial Average plunged 508 points and NYSE volume skyrocketed to more than 600 million shares. Many used the term as a parallel to the Black Friday of the 1929 crash and felt that it presaged the start of another depression.

BLANK CHECK OFFERING
Expression used of an initial public offering (IPO) of the stock of a company that does not have an established business. In effect, subscribers give management discretion over the use and application of their money. In general, such offerings are successful only when speculation predominates the marketplace.

BLANK CHECK PREFERRED STOCK
Slang for the authorization given to company management to issue, at various rates and times, preferred shares without further specific approval of the common shareholders.

BLANKET BOND
A broker's insurance policy designed to protect the firm against fraudulent trading, check and securities forgery, and unexplained shortages of money and securities. Minimum coverages necessary in each of these categories range from $25,000 to $500,000, depending on that concern's SEC net capital requirement.

BLANKET CERTIFICATION FORM
NASD Form FR-1. Given by foreign brokers or dealers who purchase new-issue securities, which begin trading at an immediate premium, for their customers from NASD members. The form states that the foreign broker understands the NASD rules on hot issues and will abide by them.
See also HOT ISSUE.

BLANKET FIDELITY BOND
Insurance coverage required of brokers to protect firm against fraudulent trading, check and securities forgery, and security misplacement or

loss. Minimum coverage is required by industry rules and varies with firm's SEC net capital requirement.

Synonymous with blanket bond.

BLANKET RECOMMENDATION
Securities recommendations made to all customers regardless of their financial capability and investment objectives.

BLIND ADVERTISEMENT
Promotional material that reaches a mass audience through public media without identifying the name of its sponsor. Help wanted ads that describe a job to be filled but do not identify the hiring company would be included in this definition.

Blind ads are not unethical, but they could become illegal if they are used to disguise discriminatory hiring practices.

BLIND BROKERING
The use of an intermediary for an unnamed principal to bring borrower and lender together in a collateralized financing transaction. Often used in repurchase agreements (REPO) when an institution's money is loaned to an unidentified dealer against securities in that dealer's inventory.

BLIND POOL
Monies collected from many persons are managed for their profit. Periodic reports of profits are made to these contributors, but the contributors have no authority to manage the money nor to know how the money is employed.

In most states, blind pools are illegal except under the most stringent regulatory control.

BLIP
Term used to identify any deviation from what is considered normal or routine.
1. Used by analysts when a company announces quarterly earnings that were unexpected, but anticipates that the next quarter's earnings will be back to normal.
2. Used by chartists when a stock's price spikes up or down for no explainable reason. It is anticipated that the chart pattern will resume its normal movement in the near future.

BLITZKRIEG TENDER OFFER
From the German: lightning-like war. The term is used in mergers and acquisitions to describe a raider's attempt to take over a company in a quick military-like fashion. Using great speed and offering higher than

market prices, the raider asks shareholders to quickly sell their stock to facilitate control of the company.

BLOCK
A purchase or sale of a large number of shares or dollar value of bonds. Although the term is relative, 10,000 or more shares, or any quantity worth over $200,000, is generally considered a block. The use of a block for bond purchases and sales varies with the user and with normal market round-lot practices.

BLOCKED
Exchange floor terminology to advise block traders that their block cannot be crossed under existing market conditions at the trader's specified price. Generally, the condition exists because the spread is too narrow to permit a cross, or because another broker with time priority is willing to pay as much or offer as little as the trader in question. Example: Our cross at $57\frac{1}{2}$ is blocked by a broker with 1,000 to sell at that price.

BLOCK ORDER
As a general rule, an order to buy or sell 10,000 or more shares of the same security, or of any quantity if the dollar value is $200,000 or more.

BLOCK POSITIONER
A dealer who, to give liquidity to a seller, will take the opposite side of a trade. Block positioners must register with the SEC and, if members of the exchange, with the NYSE. Block positioners hope to profit by a rise in the value of the security, but they often offset a portion of their risk by arbitrage: the sale of calls or the purchase of puts.

Block positioners also sell securities to buyers of stocks or bonds. In many cases, they will sell short.

BLOOD LETTER
Quaint British term for a European underwriter's letter to a law firm asking for a legal opinion about an issue's exemption from the U.S. Securities Act of 1933. If the underwriter is willing to state that the offering will be sold exclusively to non-U.S. investors, and that care will be exercised to ensure that the security will not "leak back" into the United States, the law firm will generally state that the security qualifies as a private placement under Section 4(2) of the '33 Act.

BLOTTER
A record of daily activity transacted at a broker/dealer. The SEC requires that the broker/dealer keep separate records to reflect purchases

and sales, money received and disbursed, securities accepted and delivered, and the location of all securities under that firm's control.

The term *blotter* had its origins in the days before automation when these records were handmade pen-and-ink entries.

BLOWOUT

1. Term used to describe the immediate sellout of a new issue of securities. You will often see the term used as a verb form; for example, the issue was blown out the window.
2. Slang expression to describe the dissipation of a customer's assets through frequent trading or poor investments. The combination of frequent trading—with concomitant commissions—and poor investments will quickly reduce the client's assets.
Synonym: churning or twisting.
See also GOING AWAY and HOT ISSUE.

BLUE CHIP

A widely known company that is a leader in its industry and has a proven record of profits and a long history of dividend payment.

In poker playing and in casino play, the blue chip is usually the one with the highest value.

BLUE-COLLAR WORKER

Expression used to designate nonmanagement, nonadministrative personnel in industry. Because such workers often wear heavy-duty clothing—usually blue—they were dubbed with this name.

BLUE LIGHT

NYSE trading floor term for an official request to registered competitive marketmakers (RCMMs) to help with a block trade. The Blue Light is an electronic message alert asking RCMMs to assist the specialist in taking the contra side of a block trade. In this way, the RCMM(s) and the specialist give liquidity to the marketplace on block trades.

BLUE LIST

A list published each business day by Standard & Poor's that contains the par value, issuer, coupon rate, yield to maturity, and the dealers who make markets in municipal bonds. The Blue List also contains some corporate bond offerings and prerefunded municipal bonds offered by the same dealers.

Also called "Blue Book."

BLUE MONDAY
Term originated by the media to describe the phenomenon that—more often than not—the DJIA goes down on Mondays. The unexplainable statistics may arise from the fact that unfavorable news often occurs over the weekend.

BLUE ROOM
An ancillary trading room that is part of the New York Stock Exchange floor complex. Distinguished by its color, hence the name.

BLUE SHEET INFORMATION
Securities and Exchange Commission (SEC) enquiries of selected broker/dealers requiring identification of trade participants, pertinent details of their transactions, and possible affiliation with the issuer. The request is so called because of the color of the paper containing the SEC's solicitation of information. This information must be sent directly to the SEC by electronic means.

BLUE-SKYING
General term used for the qualification of securities for sale in any of the United States under their securities laws. Also used for the registration of broker/dealers or their agent.

The expression *blue sky* means lacking in substance (e.g., right out of the blue—having no worth). These state laws provide that new securities issuers qualify by providing information about the issue and the issuer so buyers may judge the issue's value.

Generally, issues senior to securities already blue-skied (or a further issuance of securities already listed on a national exchange) are exempt from blue-sky procedures. Legal advice is needed.

See also UNIFORM SECURITIES AGENT STATE LAW EXAMINATION.

BLUE-SKY REGISTRATION
1. The qualification of a broker/dealer to do securities business in one of the 50 states.
2. The qualification of an agent of a broker/dealer to solicit buy and sell orders for securities from the residents of one of the 50 states. Many states require the Series 63 USASLE Exam (Uniform Security Agent State Law Examination) as a qualification.
3. The qualification of a nonexempt security by the issuer for sale within one of the 50 states. This qualification may be by notification, coordination, or qualification. As a general rule, Treasuries, agencies, municipals, and securities registered on a national exchange do not need separate blue-sky qualification.

BNL

1. NYSE ticker tape symbol for Beneficial Corporation, which is devoted to consumer loan activities.
2. Initials for the Banco Nationale del Lavoro, Italy's largest commercial bank.

BOARD BROKER

An employee of the Chicago Board Option Exchange who makes a memorandum of option orders that are away from the market and thus not capable of execution at the present time. The board broker may execute orders on an agency basis, and, if this is done, the board broker notifies the member who entered the order.

See also ORDER BOOK OFFICIAL.

BOARD OF ARBITRATION

The arbitrators who are chosen to decide a controversy in the securities industry. Three or five members from the board hear individual cases requiring arbitration.

See also ARBITRATION and CODE OF ARBITRATION.

BOARD OF DIRECTORS

The group of persons, elected by vote of the stockholders, who make important management decisions and who elect the officers of a corporation. Members of the board of directors are control persons under the securities laws of the United States, and the securities they own are restricted.

Frequently abbreviated BD.

Often used interchangeably with board of governors for governing body of exchanges and associations of broker/dealers.

BOARD OFFICIAL

Those employees on the floor of the International Stock Exchange of the United Kingdom and the Republic of Ireland who accept and record public orders for options in a special book and who, at the first practical opportunity, execute such orders. Their function is similar to that of the order book official (OBO) on the CBOE.

BOARD OF GOVERNORS

1. Chief elective body of the National Association of Securities Dealers.
2. Board of Governors of the Federal Reserve System.

BOARD ROOM

1. The place where corporate directors periodically meet to set policy, declare dividends, and make executive management decisions.

2. In the parlance of the Street, the place in which brokers' desks are located and where they can meet with, or phone, customers to transact business. The board room often contains a ticker tape and other information sources for the use of the broker and customers.

BO DEREK
Slang for the U.S. Treasury bonds 10s of May 2010. Term derives from the title of a popular movie (*10*) and the name of its star whose beauty and figure ranked at the top of a 1 to 10 scale.

BO DEREK STORY
Term for a company that is perceived to be of the highest quality; that is, similar to the movie *10* in which Bo Derek was starred and was depicted to be the most perfect (a "10") woman in terms of physical qualities.

BODY RAIN
The term has received two relatively tasteless meanings:
1. A time of profuse perspiration as displaced executives look for jobs because of layoffs, takeovers, and mergers.
2. The period following the crash of 1929 when many speculators were financially ruined and committed suicide by leaping from the windows of tall buildings.

BOERSENZEITUNG INDEX
A popular index of performance of the German stock market. The index is composed of 30 blue-chip issues, all equally weighted. The index uses September 1959 as its base and it is updated every 30 minutes.

BOGEY
Trader's terminology for a particular target, whether it be a price or yield objective. For example, "That customer has a bogey of $8^{1}/_{2}\%$ for the sale of commercial paper in his portfolio." Term probably arises from military slang: a bogey; that is, an unidentified flying object on a radar screen.

BOILERPLATE
1. Used of pro forma information that is provided to conform to certain laws, but that—in general—has little positive content. For example, the red herring caveat on a preliminary prospectus.
2. A pejorative term for any form of professional cant or other insincere printed statement whose value is relatively meaningless. The term is not used of false statements.

BOILER ROOM
Place where brokers, often illicitly, conduct high pressure—hence the name—telephone sales campaigns for highly speculative securities.

BOLSA
The Spanish word for a purse. By long-term attribution, this term is applied to a stock exchange and thus parallels the French (bourse) and Italian (borsa) usage for an exchange.

There are four stock exchanges in Spain, with the exchange in Madrid being the largest and having the most trading activity.

BOM
See BRANCH OFFICE MANAGER

BOMBAY STOCK EXCHANGE (BSE)
The largest stock exchange in India. Although the BSE is open for business for only a short time during the day, it does have an index of 30 stocks that serve as a barometer of economic activity in India.

BONA FIDE ARBITRAGE
An arbitrage in good faith; that is, offsetting buy and sell transactions that have a built-in profit.

BOND
1. Any debt security, such as an IOU or a corporation promissory note.
2. A debt security with a maturity of more than 7 to 10 years. Used in distinction to note, a debt security with a shorter time to maturity. Often an issuer will describe a debt security as a bond that other issuers would call a note.
3. Money or property deposited as a pledge of good faith.
4. One's word given as a pledge of future performance. Example: "My word is my bond."

BOND ANTICIPATION NOTE (BAN)
Short-term municipal note used as interim financing. Principal and interest on the BAN will be repaid from the proceeds of a forthcoming bond issue.

BOND BROKER
1. Brokers who transact bond orders on the floor of the exchanges.
2. Brokers in the municipal bond market who do agency transactions for institutional clients.

BOND BUYERS INDEX (BBI)

An index that measures yield levels of municipal bonds. The index contains two measurements of yield. The 20-bond index contains bonds that have an average rating of A+; the 11-bond index contains bonds that have a rating of AA. Each index is of newly issued municipal bonds selling at par. Both the trend of yields and the spread between the two indices gives dealers, underwriters, and institutional buyers an insight into interest-rate trends and their accompanying market risk. The index also contains the aftertax yield of 20-year government bonds as a measure of comparative yield.

BOND DADDIES

Also referred to as "Memphis Bond Daddies," these organizations were high-pressure telephone sales boiler rooms that specialized in the sale of municipal, government, and agency securities. Operating in Memphis, Little Rock, and Palm Beach, these boiler room operations gained their reputation from high-pressure selling, large markups, and account churning.

BOND INTEREST TERM SECURITY

See BITS.

BOND INTERNATIONAL GOLD (BIG)

An investment vehicle for gold trading founded by Alan Bond, a wealthy Australian entrepreneur. Under the umbrella of Mr. Bond's international gold interests, this corporation invited public subscription for its shares which—in turn—were collateralized by gold bullion, the main assets of his concern. In effect, an investment in this company was a play on the value of gold bullion in world markets.

BOND INVESTORS GUARANTY INSURANCE COMPANY (BIGI)

An insuror of the timely payment of interest and the repayment of principal to holders of selected municipal securities. BIGI is equally owned by American International Group, Bankers Trust, Xerox Credit, and Salomon Inc.

This group not only competes with MBIA and AMBAC, it also insures municipal unit investment trusts, municipal bond funds, and substantial municipal portfolios. Premiums are set as a percentage of the par value of the securities insured.

BOND POWER

A separate form for an owner's assignment and power of substitution which, when signed, transfers ownership of a registered bond to a new owner.

BOND RATIO

A measurement of a corporation's leverage. The ratio is found by dividing the total of a corporation's bonds with more than one year to maturity by the total of those bonds plus the stockholders' equity. For example, if the total of bonds is $10 million, and the stockholders' equity is $30 million, the bond ratio is:

$$\frac{\$10 \text{ million (bonds)}}{\$40 \text{ million (bonds + equity)}}$$

Except for utilities, where higher bond ratios are usual, bond ratios in excess of 33% are considered highly leveraged.

See also LEVERAGE.

BOND WASHING

Term used of an unethical, if not illegal, procedure associated with bond trading in England.

Background: Some English bonds trade ex-interest, rather than on an accrued interest basis. To avoid taxes, these bonds are sold before ex-date to nontaxable holders. After ex-date, the bonds are repurchased at a price that represents the original price plus the interest amount. In this way, the "interest" becomes a capital consideration, rather than a currently taxable event.

BONUS ISSUE

See CAPITALIZATION ISSUE.

BON VOYAGE BONUS

This is the original designation for what has subsequently become known as "greenmail"; that is, the payment of a premium for shares held by a prospective predator to avoid a proxy contest for control of a company. Such an agreement is always accompanied by another agreement whereby the predator promises not to acquire additional shares for an extended period.

BOOK

1. The record of either indications of interest for a proposed underwriting or the record of the syndicate activity of the members of an underwriting account. For example, ABC Brokerage is managing the book.
2. See also SPECIALIST'S BOOK.

BOOK ENTRY (SYSTEM)

A recordkeeping process for securities whereby the names of registered holders—for either stocks or bonds—is maintained in a computerized or other recordkeeping procedure. The central concept is this: no certificate is available. Book entry systems are used for listed options, U.S. Treasuries, and agency securities.

BOOKRUNNER
English term for the lead (managing) underwriter of the syndicate involved in the distribution of securities. The bookrunner keeps a record of each member's allocation, the "pot" for institutional investors, and so forth. As in the United States, the bookrunner receives an additional fee for its services.

BOOK VALUE
Take total assets minus intangibles, subtract all liabilities and the par value of preferred stock. Divide by the number of outstanding common shares. Quotient is the book value.

Although book value can be a deceptive measurement, it is used by many to make a gross selection of common shares that may be underpriced. Book value should not be an ultimate criterion for security selection.

Also called the "net tangible value" or the "liquidating value per common share."

BOOT
1. In capital letters, an acronym for branch office operations training. BOOT is a formal system of instruction used by brokerage firms with decentralized branch offices. BOOT is designed to teach new employees the fundamentals of order entry, recordkeeping, and cashiering procedures.

    Generally, the BOOT program is more detailed and suited to customer relations and problems than to training headquarters operations personnel.
2. This term is also used to identify start-up procedures needed to activate computerized programs and to load those programs into the system.

BOOTSTRAP ACQUISITION
Term used in conjunction with a friendly corporate takeover. First, when threatened with a takeover, the target company exchanges some of its assets for outstanding shares held by the dissident shareholders. Then, the target company sells the rest of the firm to a friendly acquirer. In this way, the friendly acquirer obtains 100% of the target company for less than it would have paid. In effect, the target company has helped to finance part of its own takeover.

BOP

See BALANCE OF PAYMENTS.

BORROWING POWER

In general, the amount of money that may be borrowed against equity securities pledged as collateral.

Under Regulations T, U, G, and X of the Federal Reserve, broker/dealers and banks may lend up to 50% of the purchase amount on such securities, provided they are listed on an exchange or traded on the NASDAQ National Market System. Other equity securities and listed options have no borrowing power.

Separate rules apply to other securities. In general, the borrowing power on corporate bonds, municipals, and governments is set by the exchanges, the NASD, or the MSRB.

BOSTON STOCK EXCHANGE (BSE)

The BSE is an important regional stock exchange located in Boston, Massachusetts. The BSE has a trading linkage to both the NYSE and the Montreal Stock Exchange.

BOT

BOT is often used to abbreviate bought.

See also BALANCE OF TRADE.

BOTTOM

Term used by traders and chartists to refer to a price level through which an issue, or the market in general, is not expected to fall without encountering substantial buying pressure by investors.

If used historically, the term often is used in conjunction with qualifying terms, such as *double bottom, triple bottom,* and so on.

BOTTOM FISHER

Slang for a prospective buyer who is looking to buy a security at its lowest price.

Bottom fishers appear after an extended decline, or during bankruptcy proceedings, and attempt to buy at distressed prices.

BOTTOMING OUT

A market technician's term used to signify that the decline in a stock (or the market in general) is apparently coming to an end. Needless to say, such a cessation of a drop in prices does not necessarily mean that the price will rise. If demand equals supply, there could be an extended accumulation of the stock. Only when the accumulation is completed, or underlying fundamentals change and demand increases, will the stock begin to rise. Indeed, instead of stabilizing (i.e., reversing its trend), it may consolidate—which means, return to its former pattern of falling lower.

BOTTOM LINE
1. The net profit, after interest and taxes, of a corporation or other business enterprise.
2. The result of any endeavor. Example: "If we do it right, the bottom line will be a quality product."

BOUGHT DEAL
Synonym for a firm commitment underwriting in which the syndicate (the group of underwriters) guarantees performance by buying the securities from the issuer.

The expression implies financial risk for the syndicate. Underwritings that do not imply financial risk are called "best efforts."

BOUNCE
1. Whenever delivery of a security by the seller, or the seller's agent, is refused by the purchaser—for whatever reason—it is said to be "bounced."
2. Whenever a security's price falls precipitously downward and then soon recovers its old price level, the security is said to have "bounced."
Synonym: downward spike.

BOUNCED STOCK
Slang for a rejected delivery from one dealer to another.

The official term is *reclamation.* A reclamation may result from a bad delivery; that is, a certificate in wrong form or denomination, a certificate without a proper assignment, a certificate that is stolen, or a certificate that is forged or counterfeit.

THE BOX
Industry term for the physical location of securities in safekeeping. Because of federal and industry rules on safekeeping and segregation of customer securities, there are many boxes. Some boxes are eligible for stock loans or for repledging to a bank to finance customer margin accounts.

Also called "stock box" and referred to as "in the box."
See also HYPOTHECATION and REHYPOTHECATION.

BOX FORMATION
See TRIANGLE FORMATION.

BOX SPREAD

An option position that has four components. There is a long call–short put position with identical expiration dates and exercise prices; this establishes the bullish side of the position. Then, there is a long put–short call position with its own exercise prices and expiration dates. In effect, the investor has set all four corners of the possible market activities.

From the bettor term, *to box,* whereby the bettor selects four opposing positions—and bets on each—on the presumption that the reward will exceed all of the bets made.

BP

See BASIS POINT.

BRACKET

The ranking of individual investment bankers in an underwriting. The term refers to the financial responsibility of the firm, in terms of takedown, in the distribution; thus, the higher the bracket, the greater the financial responsibility.

Typical bracket terminology, from highest to lowest, is: manager (co-manager), special, major, mezzanine, submajor, first regional, second regional.

Occasionally, the term is used to show a special business relationship with the manager of the underwriting or the issuer.

BRANCH OFFICE MANAGER (BOM)

A person in charge of one or more of a member firm's branch offices. Such persons must pass a special exchange examination. Exchange rules also require that persons who actually supervise the sales activities of three or more registered representatives must pass the Sales Supervisory examination (Series 8).

BREADTH OF THE MARKET

A comparison of the number of issues traded with the number of issues listed for trading. For example, if 2,000 issues are listed and 1,600 are traded on a given day, the breadth of the market is 80%. Market trends are considered to be corroborated only if there is a reasonable breadth of the market.

BREADTH OF THE MARKET INDEX

A measurement of the number of issues advancing versus the number of issues declining on a given day or as a moving average.

Many measurements are used: advances divided by declines, as a percentage; advances minus declines, as a net positive or negative number.

The measurement, consistently followed, is an insight into investor sentiment and is used extensively by market analysts.

Also called "Advance Decline Index."

BREAK
1. Bookkeeping imbalance either within a brokerage firm or between two brokers.
2. Sudden, significant price decline of a security.
3. Sudden good fortune.

BREAK EVEN
A transaction in which the income received equals the expenditures made.

BREAK-EVEN POINT
Dollar value at which a transaction will neither gain nor lose. Generally computed on gross prices without commissions, although accuracy requires that the adjusted cost of acquisition be compared to net proceeds of sale.

See also BREAK-EVEN POINT ON OPTIONS.

BREAK-EVEN POINT ON OPTIONS
1. Long call break-even is strike (or exercise) price plus premium.
2. Long put break-even is strike price minus premium.
3. Short uncovered call break-even is strike price plus premium.
4. Short covered call break-even is purchase price minus premium.
5. Short put break-even, if covered by short stock, is price at which underlying stock was shorted plus premium.
6. Short uncovered put break-even is strike price minus premium.

BREAKFAST OPTION
Slang expression to describe the fact that some Standard & Poor's Index options were referenced to the opening, rather than the closing, of the market on the third Friday of the expiration month. This was done by the SEC to mute the extreme market volatility on "triple witching days." Breakfast referred to the fact that the major marketplaces began trading at 8:30 A.M. Central Time.

BREAKING THE SYNDICATE
Termination of the agreement among underwriters (a syndicate) for a specific offering of securities. Members are then free to dispose of unsold securities and are no longer bound by restrictive price agreements.

BREAKOUT
Price of a security emerging from a previous trading pattern. The new price "breaks out" above the high (or below the low) trading pattern lines that enclose all other prices for that security in the preceding period. Breakouts are used by technical analysts to predict substantial upside or downside movement.

See also TRADING PATTERN.

BREAKPOINT
Dollar level of purchases, either lump sum or by accumulation, which qualifies a mutual fund holder for reduced percentage sales charge.

See also LETTER OF INTENT (1) and RIGHT OF ACCUMULATION.

BREAKPOINT SALES
Unethical practice. Soliciting mutual fund purchases in dollar amounts that are slightly below eligibility for reduced sales charge. Sales within $1,000 of a breakpoint may be considered breakpoint sales.

BREAKUP VALUE
1. English term: net asset value per share. American synonym: book value.
2. The value of the component parts of a corporation if they were to exist as independent entities. Example: The breakup value of American Telephone & Telegraph is $78 billion.

BRIDGE FINANCING
Short-term corporate borrowings used as an interim step before the issuance of securities. Commercial banks are the usual providers of this form of financing prior to the completion of an underwriting, although some brokerage firms also provide such loans.

Also called "bridge loans."

BRIDGE LOAN
Short-term financing provided while borrower seeks longer-term loan.

BRITISH FUNDS
The common terms for English government bonds. In exchange dealings, these bonds are subdivided into "shorts" (up to 5 years), "intermediates" (from 5 to 15 years), and "longs" (more than 15 years.)

British funds are also called "gilts" or "government stock."

BROAD TAPE

Common name for a subscription news service that provides timely financial information. So called because tape provides detailed information, as opposed to narrow tapes of stock exchange transactions.

Often used for Dow Jones tape, although expression may include Reuters, Munifacts, Associated Press, or United Press International.

BROKEN AMOUNT

English terminology for what we would call an "odd lot." For stocks, this is a trade for less than 50 shares (on 50-share traders) or 100 shares (on 100-share traders); for bonds, any debt security with a par value of less than 100 pounds.

Also called a "broken number."

BROKEN CONVERTIBLE

A convertible bond or preferred that is selling at a yield competitive with yields on nonconvertible securities of the same class. This occurs if the market has no prospects for a rise in the value of the common stock; thus, the market is unwilling to pay extra for the conversion feature. When this occurs, the price of the convertible will tend to fall to a level to provide a yield that is competitive with nonconvertible fixed-income securities and the convertible is said to be "broken."

BROKEN NUMBER

See BROKEN AMOUNT.

BROKER

Person or firm acting as intermediary between buyer and seller.
See also AGENT.

BROKERAGE ACCOUNTING SYSTEMS ELEMENT

See BASE.

BROKER ASSOCIATION

As defined by the CFTC a broker association is two or more members of an exchange who share:
1. Responsibility for executing customer orders.
2. Access to unfilled customer orders.
3. Profits or losses associated with their brokerage or trading activities.

BROKER LOAN

Short-term secured loan made by broker from commercial bank to finance customer security positions.

The expression also is used of loans made by a bank to specialists or to broker/dealers to carry proprietary accounts.

See also CALL LOAN and REHYPOTHECATION.

BROKER'S BROKERAGE
See BB SYSTEM.

BROKER'S COLLATERAL LOAN
See BROKER LOAN.

BROKERS TRANSACTION SERVICES, INCORPORATED
See BITSY.

BROKING
English securities industry term for acting as an agent and charging a client a commission for services performed. The American equivalent is called "brokering."

Webster considers the word to come from the Spanish *alboroque,* meaning, "to give a drink to the other party upon completion of a trade."

BROUGHT OVER THE WALL
Term used to describe the finance department's confidential use of research persons to enhance a particular investment banking deal. Technically, the research person is now privy to "inside information" and thus may no longer provide opinions about the underlying company.

Allusion: The use of the research person's expertise by corporate finance has breached the "Chinese Wall" that should separate investment banking from sales and trading within a member organization.

BRUSSELS STOCK EXCHANGE
One of the four stock exchanges located in Belgium, the Brussels Stock Exchange is the largest and the most active. The exchange is open for trading from 12:30 P.M. until 2:30 P.M.—although there is no limitation on trading after that time. Trades are done on a cash and forward basis, with cash trades settling on the next business day and forwards settling on a fortnightly basis.

BSE
1. Boston Stock Exchange (q.v.).
2. Bombay Stock Exchange (q.v.).
3. Brussels Stock Exchange (q.v.).

BTSI
See BITSY.

BUBA
Derivative from the German word for a grandmother or a guardian angel. Buba has become the quaint term used by Germans for the Bundesbank, the regulator of national banks in Germany. The Bundesbank controls banks, all financial activities, and—in practice—the value of the principal unit of currency, the deutsche mark.

BUCK
1. Jargon: a U.S. dollar or multiple thereof.
2. U.S. government securities trading term for an even dollar quote, either for the bid or the asked. For example, a U.S. Treasury bond has been trading in the 97–98 range. The quote could be: 28 to a buck. Meaning: bid $97^{28}/_{32}$, asked 98.

BUCKET SHOP
An establishment whose brokers accept customer orders but who do not immediately execute them. Later, the order is executed at a price that is advantageous to the broker but is confirmed to the customer at the earlier prevailing price. Practice is illegal under the Securities Exchange Act of 1934 and is forbidden by industry regulations.

BUCKSHOT BUYING
Term used of programmed transactions in low-capitalized over-the-counter stocks. In an "enhanced" index, an institution may buy enough of a low-capitalization company to remove the float from market. This, in turn, will cause the price to rise and thus show good results for the program. The big risk is that the holdings may not be able to be sold, because of lack of demand or an illiquid market.

BUDGET
1. The anticipated cost of a project or enterprise. For example, we have a budget of $4 million for the rollout of the new computers.
2. The difference between revenue and expenses for a specific time period, usually one year, for a corporation or government. For example, XYZ Corporation expects a budget deficit in the first quarter.
3. The act of allocating assets for the initiation or completion of a project. For example, "We have budgeted $10 million for the project."

BUG

1. Noun: slang—an unanticipated problem in the programming of a computer that does not show up until processing begins.
2. Verb: slang—to pester or annoy others to do an action that they have previously refused to do. Example: "He is a successful salesperson because he bugs his clients until they buy."

BUKKO

Japanese word for manager. In Japan, where a person's training can entail most of one's working life, it is not unusual for someone to rotate through all departments of a firm before appointment as manager. This may take years and provide a broad spectrum of knowledge about every aspect of the firm. This practice has serious drawbacks in the financial industry, where individuals quickly become specialists in complex products and intricate trading techniques.

BULGE BRACKET

Slang for the major participants in an underwriting syndicate, so called because they subscribe to and sell the largest portion of the offering. The firms in the "bulge bracket" are typically listed at the top of the tombstone advertisement.

An underwriter with slightly smaller subscriptions is said to be in the "mezzanine bracket."

BULK SEGREGATION

Customer-owned securities held in street name but kept separate from firm-owned securities. Securities are not individually registered in name of the customer nor otherwise identified as belonging to specific individuals.

BULL

See BULLISH.

BULL BONDS

A Eurodebt issue with the redemption amount linked to the upward movement of a specific foreign stock index, such as the Nikkei or the FAZ (Frankfurter Allgemeine Zeitung) stock index.

Bull bonds are designed to appeal to Japanese and German investors in whose countries options and futures trading was deemed illegal. It is now just "unsuitable" for domestic customers. In effect, bull bonds are a long-term call on the stock market and holders receive a premium over par value at maturity if the benchmark index rises over a predetermined figure that was established at the time of issuance.

See also BEAR BONDS for the opposing concept.

BULLDOG SECURITIES

Debt securities of foreign issuers that trade in England and whose face values and interest payments are denominated in pounds sterling. Typically, these securities are investment grade with longer-term maturities.

U.S. analog: Yankee bonds.

BULLET

Financial term for a debt financing with a single maturation date (as opposed to serial bonds). If the issue is noncallable and nonrefundable it is said to be a "hard bullet." If the issue provides for a sinking fund for premature retirement it is said to be a "soft bullet." Asset-backed securities also include a designation of hard or soft bullet but that description refers to the existence (or not) of a bank guarantee of principal repayment. The expression *term financing* is also used.

BULLETIN BOARD SERVICE

See OTC BULLETIN BOARD DISPLAY SERVICE.

BULLETS

In its plural form, the term refers to a lump-sum payment into an insurance company's GIC for a qualified pension plan. These single payments earn interest at a guaranteed rate for the 1–5 year term of the contract.

BULLISH

Used of persons or of the market. State of believing that price will rise or will continue to rise. For example: "We feel that the market will turn bullish within the next two months," which means "we" think there is an advancing market.

BULL MARKET

A market for stocks, bonds, or commodities that is generally marked by rising prices.

The origin of the metaphor is unknown, but the concept is clear: A period marked by general enthusiasm, often thoughtless and overly speculative, for the value of financial assets.

BULL PEN

Nickname applied to the area in a typical member firm where the registered representatives (RRs) work and meet their clients. The area may have cubicles for the individual RRs, or it may be quite open. Generally, the larger producers have individual offices.

The term is also used of a similar area in the investment banking function where interns and newly hired financial personnel work.

BULL POSITION

English term used to signify a long position in a security. Thus, the person is able to physically deliver the security if sold and thereby profit from a rise in the security's price.

BULL SPREAD

An option strategy that involves the purchase and sale of options of the same class. Example: The purchase and sale of calls, or puts, on the same underlying.

Such a strategy is called "bullish" if the holder/writer will profit from a rise in the market. The term is used correctly only of vertical spreads.

In a *call* bull spread, the long leg has a lower strike price. In a *put* bull spread, the higher strike price.

The strategy works because, as the market rises, the premium on the leg with the lower strike price will rise faster than the premium with the higher strike price.

See OPTION SPREAD STRATEGY.

BUMP-UP CD

An innovative product of the Crossland Savings Bank. It is a certificate of deposit with a fixed rate of interest for the length of the deposit. However, if interest rates rise during the period of the deposit, the holder has a one-time right of requesting that the new rate apply to the remainder of the term. A drop in interest rates, on the other hand, does not lower the original rate.

BUNCHING

1. Combining round-lot orders for convenience in executing them on the floor.
2. Combining odd-lot orders, with permission of customers, to save an odd-lot differential (if any).

BUNNY

Colloquial name for Playboy Enterprises, Inc., a well-known magazine publisher, hotelier, and operator of entertainment clubs. The name comes from the company's popular commercial logo.

BUNNY BONDS

Slang for a rather unusual bond, in that the holder may hop back and forth upon any interest-rate payment date to a larger investment (at par) or to cash, at the option of the investor.

BURNED OUT TAX SHELTER

Slang for an investment vehicle that no longer produces tax-deductible write-offs for subscribers, but which—in turn—now begins to return declarable income.

More formal expression: The tax shelter has reached its crossover point and the participants now receive fully taxable income.

BUSINESS CONDUCT COMMITTEE (BCC)

A group of industry professionals appointed by each of the self-regulatory organizations (SROs) to continuously monitor the members' compliance with that organization's rules and regulations. Generally, this organization has the authority to censure, fine, suspend, or even expel a member who violates the rules and regulations. Such decisions may be appealed to the SEC.

Also called "District Business Conduct Committee" within the NASD.

BUSINESS CYCLE

1. Term used of time from top of one rise in gross national product through one fall in GNP back to original base line. In past, business cycles have tended to average about 2½ years.
2. Time it takes a manufacturing company to turn raw materials into sold finished products.

BUSINESS DAY

Day on which the principal securities marketplaces are open for trading.

See also REGULAR-WAY TRANSACTION.

BUSINESS EXPANSION SCHEME (BES)

A plan adopted by the British government to attract venture capital to start-up and buyout companies. It offers individuals tax relief for a number of years following such investments.

BUSINESS MIX TEST

A term used in SEC Rule 11a 1-1(T) that relates to the ability of stock exchange members and member organizations to trade as principal on an exchange. Under the rule, a member is qualified to act as principal if, during the preceding year, more than 50% of gross revenues were derived from such activities as underwriting, acting as broker for customers' securities transactions, or distributing securities issued by other persons.

BUSTED CONVERTIBLE
A convertible bond or preferred stock that is selling at or near the price at which it would sell were it not convertible. For example, at a time when general interest rates are 10%, a convertible bond with a 6% coupon is selling at 62; that is, to have a current yield at approximately 10%. In effect, the marketplace has given up—at least for the present—on the convertibility of the bond and prices it as though it were not convertible.

Synonym: broken convertible. Such bonds are said to trade at their "investment value" as a bond. There is no special premium for convertibility.

BUST-UP PROXY PROPOSAL
Term for the request made to shareholders to approve the sale or liquidation of a company. Usually, this request is made by dissident shareholders who seek to oust present management or who wish to gain control of the company or its parts.

BUST-UP TAKEOVER
A corporate finance technique often used in mergers and acquisitions. A corporation is bought out by the use of borrowed money, either bridge loans or junk bonds. Subsequently, the debt is paid down by the sale of portions of the acquired corporation.

BUTTERFLY SPREAD
Option strategy. Client sells two calls, then buys two calls, one with strike (exercise) price higher and one with a strike price lower than short calls. Client is partially hedged in either direction and hopes to profit from call premium received and restricted movement of underlying stock.

BUY
As a noun, a synonym for bargain. For example, "It's a buy." Also used as an adjective. For example, "It's a buy situation."

BUY AT BEST
This is the trade instruction underlying a market order to buy. In practice, this substitute instruction is used in over-the-counter trading if the purchaser wants a large block of securities and wants the broker/dealer to act as an agent. There is no requirement that all of the purchases be made at the same price.

BUY-BACK

Term used in conjunction with the repurchase by an issuer of its own securities. Such securities will then either be retired or placed "in the treasury."

The buy-back of bonds is often in conjunction with a sinking fund or a refinancing.

The buy-back of equities, to avoid any allegation of manipulation, is usually done in accord with SEC Rule 10b-18, or the tender offer regulations 14D or 14E.

BUY-DOWN LOAN

Term for a mortgage loan in which the builder subsidizes a portion of the buyer's interest payments for the first three years or more. To make monthly mortgage payments more appealing to the buyer, the builder, for example, agrees to pay the difference between a lower rate of interest, let's say 9%, and the then prevailing mortgage interest rate, let's say 13%. This is a mortgage interest savings of 4% for the first three years.

BUYERS' MARKET

Condition in which the anticipated supply so exceeds demand that buyers can dictate prices and terms of sale. For example, the world surplus of oil has produced a buyers' market.

Antonym: sellers' market.

BUYER'S OPTION

Securities contract between two broker/dealers in which the seller attempts to settle before the date agreed upon at the time of the contract. In this case, the buyer has the option of agreeing to settle before the agreed upon date or of refusing to do so without prejudicing its rights in this transaction.

BUY-IN

Follows a failure by seller to deliver securities. Broker must buy in to obtain the securities which the contra party did not deliver in accord with industry rules. Term used of broker-to-broker transactions. Industry rules set times for buy in procedures.

See also CONTRA BROKER.

BUYING CLIMAX

A sudden upward movement in the market value of a security characterized by a gap in the prices between one trading session and the following. Used in technical analysis, and often considered an indication that a security has been overbought and price will fall.

BUYING POWER

Used for general margin accounts. The dollar value of securities that may be purchased in terms of the special memorandum account entry without generating a margin call. If marginable equity securities are purchased, buying power is two times the SMA entry under Federal Reserve rules in effect in 1990. For example, client has SMA entry of $1,000. Client may buy marginable securities worth $2,000 without generating a margin call. If a security is not eligible for margin purchase, the special memorandum account entry may be used on a dollar-for-dollar basis.

BUYING SIGNAL

A point in a sales presentation to a potential buyer where the buyer shows interest in the product. For example, a salesperson is presenting the benefits of a particular convertible security and the client asks: "How many shares of stock will I receive if I convert?"

Generally, an efficient salesperson will, if the product is otherwise suitable to the client, ask for the order if the client gives a buying signal.

BUYING THE SPREAD

Expression used both in the options and futures marketplaces to identify the simultaneous sale of a near-term contract and the purchase of a long-term contract. Because the strike price is the same, the long-term contract will cost more. Thus, the transactor of this spread position pays the difference between the sale and purchase prices.

BUY-IN PROCEDURE

The buyer's remedy if the selling broker/dealer fails to deliver the purchased security. Two business days after giving written notice of intent to the delinquent seller, the buyer may purchase the promised amount of that security in the market and hold the delinquent seller responsible for any loss that may be incurred.

Also called "close-out."

See also SELL-OUT PROCEDURE.

BUY MINUS

Instruction from buyer to purchase only on dips in market price, or at last previous price if that is lower than previous different price.

See also MINUS TICK, DOWNTICK, and ZERO-MINUS TICK.

BUY SIGNAL

A term used by chartists. It means that their technical measurements of previous price movements indicate the appropriateness of a purchase at the present time.

Generally, buy signals occur when the price of a security does not break through a support level, or when the price of a security penetrates a preestablished moving average. Market volume is also an important consideration.

BUY STOP ORDER
Customer instruction on a buy order to broker, or specialist, on the floor of an exchange. If the market price touches this price, or if there is a transaction above this price, the broker is to execute a market order at the best available price. For example: BUY 500 LMN 52 STOP. The customer is giving the following instruction: if there is a transaction at 52 or above, immediately buy 500 LMN at the best available price. The transaction at 52 or above is said to elect, activate, or trigger the stop and thus turn it into a market order to buy.

BUY THE BOOK
Instruction from trader or institutional account to buy all shares available from specialist's book at current offer price. Trades also will be made with other members in the crowd who are willing to sell at that price.

BUZZ WORD
Jargon: a word or expression that is considered state of the art and is used by experts to identify a problem or its solution. As this word or expression flows into current usage by nonexperts, it is called a "buzz word."

Buzz words are often misunderstood by their users. Many buzz words are neologisms. Example: Telephone sales can often be time-consuming.

A rapid method of screening potential clients by telephone is called "telemarketing." This buzz word now becomes the expression to solve all sales problems.

BW
See BID WANTED.

BWI
See BID WILL IMPROVE.

BY-PASS TRUST
A testamentary trust that permits a surviving spouse to receive income from the assets in trust during his or her lifetime. After the survivor's death, the property passes to the grantor's other heirs, as designated in the by-pass trust agreement.

C

C

The third letter of the English alphabet, used:
1. As a Roman numeral designation for 100. Often used in parlance for a $100 bill; thus, a "C note."
2. As the fifth letter in the stock symbol of certain NASDAQ/NMS stocks as an identifier that the particular stock no longer meets the NASD's qualifications for trading on NASDAQ. For example, WSTXC stands for Westronix, Inc., an issuer with total assets of less than $750,000 or fewer than 300 shareholders. It is subject to delisting at the next NASDAQ meeting.
3. Uppercase by the NYSE as the symbol for Chrysler Corporation, a major automotive manufacturer.

CA

Abbreviation often used in bond tables and in offering sheets for callable.

CABINET BID/OFFER

On option exchanges, a procedure used to make accommodation transactions in relatively worthless option contract positions. It is a nonauction procedure enabling investors to close out option positions, either long or short, for 1¢ per share.

CABINET BONDS

NYSE term for listed corporate bonds that are infrequently traded. So called, because current bids and offers, if any, are filed in cabinets by price and time of entry. The infrequent trades are completed when a buyer or seller uses the cabinet entries to find the other side of the trade. Modern methods employ the Exchange's Automated Bond Service.

CABINET CROWD

Term for members of the New York Stock Exchange who trade in inactive bonds (those that are seldom traded). The term derives from the practice of filing all orders for such bonds on cards in metal racks called cabinets. Orders are removed only if canceled or if a contra party is willing to accept the stated bid or offer.

See also ACTIVE BOND CROWD and AUTOMATED BOND SERVICE.

CABINET SECURITY

Exchange-traded securities that do not have an active market, principally stocks that trade in 10-share units and many inactively traded bonds. Name arises from practice of placing orders, according to buy-sell and limit prices, on small cards in assigned places in metal cabinets on the floor of the exchange. Orders remain in cabinets until broker who entered them removes them from cabinet, or contra broker accepts bid or offer.

CABS
Acronym for Capital Appreciation Bonds. This is a service mark of Salomon Brothers Inc for zero-coupon municipals.

CAC INDEX
An index of the 241 common stocks listed on the Paris Bourse. The index is based on the opening price of these stocks. The index is not updated throughout the day; instead, a new index price is computed on the opening of each subsequent business day.

CAC 40 INDEX
An index of the 40 most popular issues traded on the Paris Bourse. Unlike the CAC Index, the CAC 40 Index is updated throughout the market day and is the basis for index futures and index options contracts. The 40 stocks comprise about 50% of the total FF (French franc; also Fr.F.) capitalization of the Paris Bourse.

CAES
Acronym for Computer Assisted Execution System.

CAES is an NASD-sponsored communication system that links stock exchange broker/dealers to OTC marketmakers. CAES permits these broker/dealers to automatically direct order flow for exchange-listed securities to the OTC market for execution, if this is a better market.

THE CAGE
The cashiering function of a member firm or of one of its branch offices.

CALENDAR
Industry term for list of upcoming securities offerings. Usually preceded by type of security. For example, municipal calendar, corporate bond calendar.

CALENDAR SPREAD
Option spread endeavoring to profit from the purchase of an option in a farther month and from the sale of an option of the same class in a nearer month. Example: buy October 50 call, sell closer July 50 call; or buy October 45 put, sell closer July 45 put.

Called "horizontal spread" if strike (exercise) prices are the same. Called "diagonal spread" if strike prices are different.

Calendar spreads are bullish if investor will profit from upward movement of underlying stock; bearish if investor will profit from downward movement of stock.

CALL

1. Verb: the action whereby a company elects to redeem a security prior to its maturity date.
2. Noun: an option to buy a stated number of shares of a security at a stated price on or before a specified date.

CALLABLE

Security which, at option of the issuer, may be redeemed prior to maturity for bonds or be repurchased by issuer if security is preferred stock. Early call often requires issuer to repurchase security at a premium above par value.

See also CALL PREMIUM, CALLABLE BOND, and CALL FEATURE.

CALLABLE BOND

Bond that may be called by issuer on or after a specified date.

CALLABLE PREFERRED

Term identifying a preferred issue that may, at the option of the issuer, be retired at a preestablished redemption value. The prospectus of the issue will outline the call price and the conditions under which the issue, or a portion thereof, may be retired by the issuer. Most preferred issues are callable.

CALLABLE SWAP

An exchange of interest-rate obligations (fixed for floating rate, or vice versa) in which the counterparty has an option to cancel the swap arrangement after a prescribed time. The subscriber pays a significant premium for the option to cancel.

CALLED AWAY

1. A security that is called by the issuer from a client's account.
2. A security that a client must deliver because a short call is exercised against a client's account.

CALL FEATURE

Bonds accompanied by call date and redemption price. For example, ABC 9% bonds have a call feature on February 1, 1995, at 105.

CALL LOAN
Loan made by broker, upon deposit of appropriate collateral, to finance margin activities of customers. Loan is callable at any time by either party.

Also called "broker loan," or "broker's collateral loan."

See also BROKER LOAN; REHYPOTHECATION.

CALL LOAN RATE
The rate of interest charged by banks when brokers deposit margined securities as collateral for loans used to finance client margin accounts. The margin interest, in turn, will be based on the call loan rate.

The process of depositing margined securities is called "rehypothecation."

Also termed *call money rate.*

Synonym: broker's (collateral) loan rate.

CALL OPTION
Privilege given to holder of option to purchase a specified number of shares, or dollar face value of bonds, at a specified price on or before expiration date of option. Option comes into being when buyer, or holder, and writer, or seller, agree upon a premium for the privilege.

See also CALL; PREMIUM; EXPIRATION; STRIKE PRICE.

CALL PREMIUM
1. Dollars, or points, paid by issuer if preferred stock or bonds are redeemed at option of issuer prior to maturity.
2. Dollars per share paid by buyer of an option for privilege of buying a call for a specified number of shares at a specified price on or before expiration date.

The premium paid for selling a put for a specified number of shares at a specified price by a certain date is known as a "put premium."

See also INTRINSIC VALUE and TIME VALUE PREMIUM.

CALL PRICE
Money a corporation must pay to redeem its senior securities. For bonds, the call price usually is a percentage of par value. For preferred stock, the call price is the dollar price per share.

CALL PROTECTION
Time between original issue date of security and earliest date when issuer may exercise right to redeem security prior to original maturity date.

Also called "cushion."

CALVET
Composite word used for the California Department of Veterans Affairs. CALVET was created under California state law to look after important public affairs. CALVET has legal status to issue municipal revenue bonds.

CAMPS
Acronym for Cumulative Auction Market Preferred Stock. CAMPS were created by Oppenheimer & Co. to compete with First Boston's STARS and Salomon Brothers' DARTS. CAMPS are basically preferred shares whose dividend is reset every 49 days to mirror prevailing money conditions. Holders are entitled to the "dividend received" exclusion if they are corporations and hold the shares more than 46 days.

CANADIAN DOLLAR
The primary unit of currency in Canada. Frequent abbreviations: Can$ or $C.

CANADIAN INSTITUTE OF CHARTERED ACCOUNTANTS (CICA)
A nationwide body in which public accountants in good standing in Canada are granted membership. Although CICA makes accounting practice announcements affecting corporate audit practices, professional ethics are regulated under provincial control. To be a member of CICA, a public accountant must have a college degree and practical working experience, and must pass a series of local examinations.

CANADIAN INTEREST COST
See TRUE INTEREST COST.

CANADIAN/U.S. PRINCIPAL SECURITIES
See CUPS.

CANCEL
Instruction to void a prior order to buy or sell, or price, or amount. May or may not be accompanied by new instruction.

CAN CROWD
Slang expression for bond brokers who trade cabinet securities.
    See also CABINET SECURITY.

CANDLE CHART
See ROSOKU-ASHI.

C&D ORDER
Abbreviation for a "cease and desist" order.

C&D orders often are sought by the SEC and CFTC to halt an ongoing practice by someone acting against the federal securities or commodities trading laws. This is required because the SEC and the CFTC do not have civil or criminal jurisdiction.

C&D REIT
See CONSTRUCTION & DEVELOPMENT REIT.

CAP
The "cap" is the highest interest rate the issuer is willing to pay on a bond issue, or the highest price at which the underwriters are willing to attempt to make an offering of stock.

CAPITAL APPRECIATION AND PROTECTION INSURANCE
See CAPTN.

CAPITAL APPRECIATION BONDS
See CABS.

CAPITAL ASSET
For IRS purposes, all equity and debt issues of value.

Money market securities are not considered capital assets. Exception: A sale of Treasury bills before maturity can generate a capital gain or loss if sold above or below the ratable value in terms of purchase price and maturity value. Tax advice is needed.

CAPITAL BUILDER ACCOUNT (CBA)
A Merrill Lynch Servicemark for its margin account with a debit card and check writing privileges. CBA accounts are geared to the young professional who is just beginning to accumulate capital. Security purchases may be made in CBA accounts. CBAs are similar to the highly successful CMA (Cash Management Account) of Merrill Lynch but require only $5,000 in cash or securities to be opened, rather than $20,000 as required in CMA accounts.

CAPITAL GAIN
Securities transaction in which the proceeds of the sale exceed the adjusted cost of acquisition. May arise from prior purchase and subsequent sale, or prior sale and subsequent purchase (short sale), or sale of a gifted

security above the basis price, or sale of a security received from a bequest at a price above fair market value established by an administrator or executor.

See also CAPITAL LOSS; LONG TERM; SHORT TERM.

CAPITAL GEARING

An English term for what in the United States is called the "capitalization ratio" of a corporation. Thus, capital gearing measures the percentage of bonds, preferred stock, and common stocks in the capital of a corporation, thereby measuring the company's ability to finance and carry debt or equity in its day-to-day operations.

CAPITALINK

An electronic system in its pilot stage that enables direct issuance of securities to institutional investors. Following announcement by a prospective issuer, subscribers to the system enter their individual bids for the security. If accepted, either partially or fully, the placement (pursuant to SEC Rule 415) bypasses the need and expense of a broker/dealer underwriter. Obviously, only prestigious issuers who are up to date with their information filings at the SEC can succeed with these offerings.

CAPITAL INTERNATIONAL INDICES

A series of measurements of worldwide stock performances owned and maintained by the Morgan Stanley Group, Inc.

The indexes cover 2,000 equities domiciled in 21 countries outside the United States. As such, the indexes reflect stock market performance on a global scale. The indexes have great appeal to international investors who are endeavoring to gauge their own portfolio performance.

CAPITALISATION ISSUE

See SCRIP (2).

CAPITALISM

An economic system in which private ownership dominates and determines the production and distribution of goods and services for financial profit.

Capitalism can coexist with socialism; that is, a partial ownership of certain industries or public services.

Antonym: Communism; that is, an economic system in which all, or practically all, means of production are owned by the state.

CAPITALIZATION

General term for sources of a company's funds that are evidenced by either longer-term bonds or stock. Current liabilities (in which bonds that will mature in one year or less are numbered) are excluded from capitalization. In addition to the par value of outstanding preferred and common stock, paid-in surplus and retained earnings are included in capitalization.

See also CAPITALIZATION RATIO.

CAPITALIZATION ISSUE

In England, a free distribution of stock to common shareholders in proportion to their existing holdings in the company. Also called "scrip" or "bonus issue."

In the United States, such distributions are known as stock dividends, split-ups, or spin-offs.

See also SCRIPT.

CAPITALIZATION RATIO

Measurement of longer-term sources of funds used by a corporation in terms of funded debt (bonds), preferred stock, and common stock.

Normally stated as a percentage. For example, company has longer-term debt of $10, preferred stock of $5, and common stock of $35 (including surplus). Total capital is $50. Bond ratio is 20%, preferred stock ratio 10%, common stock ratio 70%.

See also DEBT-TO-EQUITY RATIO; LEVERAGE.

CAPITAL LOSS

Securities transaction in which the proceeds of a sale are less than adjusted cost of acquisition.

CAPITAL MARKETS

General term used for both primary and secondary markets that deal in securities with maturities of more than one year.

For example, stocks and long-term bonds are traded in the capital markets. Or, LMN Corporation, because of financial difficulties, has had difficulty in entering the capital markets.

It is also a general term for the institutional market in the securities industry; that is, the stock and bond market transactions made by fiduciaries. The term tends to include broker/dealer proprietary trading, transactions by mutual funds, pension and profit-sharing plans, bank trusts, corporate investors, and many eleemosynary institutions.

Antonym: money markets; that is, markets for securities that will mature in one year or less. Longer-term securities with variable rates and put features are considered to be part of the money market.

CAPITAL SHARES

1. It is the English term for common stock; that is, the basic unit of equity ownership in a corporation. Some American corporations use the term also; for example, the capital shares of American Telephone & Telegraph.
2. A class of shares issued by dual-purpose investment companies, as opposed to income shares. Capital shares entitle the owner to any appreciation in value plus all gains on transactions in any shares of the company. Capital shares may also go down in value due to market activity or because they are liquidated to provide the minimum prearranged income for the income shares. In effect, the income shares are similar to cumulative preferred shares.

CAPITAL STOCK

Term often used of all sources of equity capital for a corporation. Common usage: synonym for common stock. For example, American Telephone & Telegraph issues capital stock but everyone will call them common shares.

Also called "capital shares."

See also COMMON STOCK.

CAPITAL STRUCTURE

1. The component parts of a corporation's permanent or relatively permanent sources of funds. In practice, the practical breakdown is made between funded debt (bonds with maturities of more than one year), preferred stock, and common stock. In the computation of the relative value of common stock, par value, paid-in surplus, and retained earnings are used.

   Synonym: capitalization.
2. The total capital of a company from all sources, including current liabilities.

CAPITAL SURPLUS

Dollar amount by which price paid by original purchaser exceeds par value of securities. For example, issuer sells stock at $15 that has a par value of $5. The $5 is entered in common stock account on balance sheet, and $10 is entered in capital surplus account. Same principle used if company sells stock reacquired and held in the treasury above par value.

Also called "paid-in capital."

CAP ORDERS

Acronym for convert and participate, the term is applied to large buy or sell orders left with an exchange specialist that authorize the specialist to use conditional market judgment in their execution.

In effect, CAP orders are "percentage orders" left with exchange specialists. Such orders are not reflected in prevailing quotations; they do, however, become market or limit orders after a specified percentage of volume occurs in a designated security.

Also called "hook" or "on the hook" orders.

CAPPING
Term used to describe the manipulative practice whereby a person who has previously sold call options sells the underlying stock to depress its value and thus prevent, or discourage, the exercise of the calls against the account.

The practice is illegal.

CAPS
See CONVERTIBLE ADJUSTABLE PREFERRED STOCK.

CAPTIVE INSURANCE COMPANY
Term identifying an affiliate of a company that insures plant and equipment of the parent company. In effect, the establishment of a captive insurance subsidiary is a form of self-insurance that may result in significant savings.

Many captive insurance subsidiaries are set up outside the United States (offshore) for tax and regulatory purposes. Often, such subsidiaries also insure other companies.

CAPTN
Acronym for capital appreciation and protection insurance. A form of variable life policy that enables the owner to switch investment premiums between several investment choices. These choices may include a number of mutual funds or zero-coupon bonds. Yields and realized profits remain tax sheltered as long as they remain undistributed.

Variously known as universal life, directed life, and multipurpose life policies.

CARDS
A servicemark of Salomon Brothers standing for certificates for amortizing revolving debts (CARDs). In effect, the holder of credit card receivables (i.e., the financing bank) uses the receivables as collateral for short-term debt instruments. In this way, the bank lessens its need for reserves to protect assets that are now "off its books."

CARIBBEAN VACATION

A euphemism in the financial industry for an SEC-imposed short suspension from the securities business. The term arises from the 30–60 day suspensions that the SEC frequently imposes on individuals for violations of securities laws. The allusion is that such suspended persons—since they are not permitted to work nor to be on the premises of their employers—spend the "down time" on an island in the Caribbean.

CARP

See CONTROLLED ADJUSTABLE RATE PREFERRED STOCK.

CARROT EQUITY

An English euphemism for a capital contribution to a corporation that permits an even larger purchase of equity if the corporation reaches certain financial targets. In effect, it is an investment with an option to buy more (the carrot) of the company.

CARRY

See COST OF CARRY.

CARRYOVER

Provision of tax law of United States that permits individual taxpayer, who sustains net capital loss in excess of annual deduction of $3,000 against income, to carry over the remainder into the subsequent tax years until it is offset against either capital gains or income.

CARS

See CERTIFICATE FOR AUTOMOBILE RECEIVABLES.

CARTEL

Italian: *cartello*, a letter of defiance.

A group of countries or businesses, usually international, that band together to control prices or distribution of a commodity, thus assuring a great profit in most cases.

Practical synonym: a monopoly.

CASH & NEW

A speculative practice on the International Stock Exchange of the United Kingdom and the Republic of Ireland whereby a customer can roll a position from one account period (ordinarily two weeks in length) into the next one. The rollover is effected by selling for cash on the last day of the period and reestablishing the position on the following Monday. The practice, by exchange rules, may not be repeated for more than seven account periods.

See also ACCOUNT DAY.

CASH BASIS

1. Accounting method that credits money only as it is received.
2. Optional method allowed to holders of Series EE savings bonds. Holder may elect to pay tax on increased redemption value only when it is received at redemption. For example, client buys Series EE bond at 50% of face value and bond will mature in eight years. Client may elect to pay tax on 6.25% of face value each year or pay tax on 50% of the face value when bond matures.

CASHBOX COMPANY

Term applied to an issuer who raises cash for the purpose of making non-specific investments in the stock market. In effect, investors put their money in a blind pool and have no effective control over the company's business or investments. Shareholders, since they have no product or service to rely upon, are placing their trust in management's capabilities as investors.

CASH CALL

An English euphemism for a rights offering. Thus, in the English marketplace, if an issuer wants to increase its equity capital, it offers subscriptions to new stock. Present stockholders, therefore, are required to contribute more cash—hence the name—to maintain their present proportionate ownership in the company.

CASH COMMODITY

A completed commodity contract that requires immediate settlement and delivery. A cash commodity is used in contrast to a futures contract. A futures contract is a completed contract that requires settlement and delivery sometime in the future. As time passes, a futures contract becomes a cash (or spot) commodity.

Synonym: "spot commodity."

CASH COW

1. Slang for any company that has a substantial operating surplus without any immediate need for reinvestment of the surplus in the business. Thus, the company often pays a large dividend to its stockholders.
2. Slang for a municipal bond that pays a large amount of tax-free interest to its bondholders.

CASH FLOW

Accepted measurement is earnings after interest and taxes, and preferred dividend if applicable, to which the annual depreciation charge for fixed assets is added.

The cash flow measurement is indicative of the earning power of a company, but can be deceptive. Many recent articles in scholarly journals dispute accepted measurement standards.

Cash flow is calculated as follows: company has annual aftertax earnings of $50 million. Company also had depreciation charge of $5 million and preferred stock dividend of $2 million. Cash flow is:

$50,000,000	
−2,000,000	For preferred dividend
$48,000,000	For common stockholders
+5,000,000	Depreciation
$53,000,000	Cash flow

CASH FORWARD MARKET

See TBA MARKET.

CASHIERING DEPARTMENT

Function within a broker/dealer organization that is responsible for the physical handling of securities and maintenance of inter-broker records.

This department also handles receive and deliver functions, transfer responsibilities, dividend and interest records, the vault and its safekeeping function, proxy statements and proxy reports, reorganization, and all other responsibilities that center on broker-customer and broker-broker financial relationships.

CASH IMMEDIATE MARKET

Term is analogous to regular way settlement in the corporate bond market, but the term is restricted to trades in pass-through securities. In the case of conventional pass-throughs, settlement must be no later than seven business days following the trade date.

A cash immediate market for GNMA pass-throughs permits the trade to be settled any time in the current month, but no substitution of comparable GNMA issues is permitted; only the issue that is the subject of the contract is deliverable.

CASH INDEX PARTICIPATION

See CIP.

CASH MANAGEMENT ACCOUNT (CMA)

Proprietary servicemark of Merrill Lynch & Company for its central brokerage accounts that permit securities trading, provide a checking account, and a debit/credit VISA card.

Generally, CMA accounts are margin accounts, but cash accounts also are permitted for custodians, trusts, estates, and corporations.

CASH MANAGEMENT BILL

A short-term U.S. Treasury bill occasionally offered by the Treasury Department to restore depleted cash balances or to meet current debt obligations.

CASH-ON-CASH

A method of computing return (yield) on an investment whereby the return is simplified in the following formula:

$$\frac{\text{Annual return in dollars}}{\text{Total dollar amount invested}}$$

The formula avoids the pitfalls of both current yield and yield to maturity (call, if applicable), but it oversimplifies the problem of "opportunity value" derived from the resale value of the asset. Used principally of limited partnerships where the resale value is difficult to compute but basis is easy to compute.

CASH ON DELIVERY (COD)

Used typically on buy orders entered by institutional investors, many of whom are prohibited from delivering cash unless an asset is received in its place. Example: "If I give you $1 million, you must give me something worth $1 million."

Also called "delivery versus cash" (DVC).

CASH-OUT TIME

Term used in conjunction with CIPs, EIPs, and VIPs. It is a specific date each quarter when the holder of that particular index participation option can receive its closing index value upon exercise of the accompanying privilege.

CIPs, EIPs, and VIPs are currently the subject of an injunction requested by the major commodities exchanges because of their similarity to futures contracts.

CASH RATIO

Measurement of a corporation's liquidity. Compares cash and marketable securities to current liabilities. Indicator of company's ability to meet immediate claims of creditors.

See also ACID-TEST RATIO, CURRENT RATIO, and CURRENT ASSETS.

CASH SALE
A securities transaction in which delivery of the certificates, and payment, is scheduled for completion on the same day as the trade itself.

CASH SETTLEMENT
1. In the United States, the description of a transaction that requires delivery and settlement on the trade date.
2. In the United Kingdom, the description of a transaction that requires delivery and settlement on the first business day following the trade date. Typically, British government bonds, options, new issues, and rights subscriptions settle for cash on the next business day.

CASH TRANSACTION
Securities transaction, usually negotiated, that settles on the same day as the trade. Cash transactions are frequent in Treasury bill market but uncommon in other markets where regular way transactions prevail.
Also called "cash sale."

CASUAL PASS
Term for an innocent and informal contact by a raider of a target corporation's management. If management is not frightened into submission, the raider can back away without further announcement or adverse publicity.
Also called a "teddy-bear pat."

CATASTROPHE CALL
The term is used in conjunction with most municipal revenue bonds. In effect, the provision in the bond indenture requires redemption (issuer call) if natural events (a catastrophe) take place and impede the flow of revenues that should be realized from the project financed by the revenue bonds. Because the project is generally insured by commercial carriers, the issuer's issuance coverage will be sufficient to implement the redemption requirement.

For example, the collapse of a bridge from a hurricane would be a catastrophe. In law, this is called a *force majeure;* that is, an unanticipated event that can excuse performance on a contract.

CATNIPS
See SERIAL CATS and CATS.

CATS

1. Acronym for Certificate of Accrual on Treasury Securities. A form of security that is proprietary to Salomon Brothers. CATS represent ownership in a payment of future interest or principal on selected U.S. Treasury securities. In effect, CATS are zero-coupon bonds with underlying governments as the investment. The bonds themselves (both principal and interest coupons) are held in trust by a commercial bank.
2. Acronym for Computer-Assisted Trading System. An electronic trading system of the Toronto Stock Exchange. Under this program, certain stocks can be traded without first going to the auction floor.

CAVEAT EMPTOR

Latin: let the buyer beware.

Term frequently used in the securities industry to warn anyone who eagerly purchases any security without an appropriate consideration of risk or without adequate diligence about the issuer.

CAVEAT VENDITOR

Latin: let the seller beware.

In effect, a warning by regulators of the securities industry. It is directed toward broker/dealers and their agents: Obey federal, state, and industry rules and regulations, or face criminal, civil, or economic sanctions.

CB

Initials for convertible bond; that is, a debt security exchangeable for a fixed number of common shares. In practice, convertibles are considered as equity securities for regulatory purposes.

CB is used primarily in the Japanese marketplace; the U.S. marketplace generally uses the initials CV.

CBA

See CAPITAL BUILDER ACCOUNT.

CBI

See CERTIFICATE OF BENEFICIAL INTEREST.

CBMM

Acronym for competitive basket marketmaker. A CBMM is a NYSE member registered to make bids and offers in ESP (exchange stock portfolios), a market basket of stocks worth about $5 million each. Since the CBMM makes bids and offers for his personal trading account, he gives liquidity to this special security product developed for institutional investors.

CBO

Acronym for Collateralized Bond Obligation. The CBO, in effect, is a debt security collateralized by a pool of "junk" bonds. These bond pools are more diversified, pay higher rates of interest if none of the bonds are in default, and have less collective risk (and thus a higher rating) than the individual bonds in the portfolio because the risk of selection is lowered.

CBOs are patterned after CMOs.

CBOE

Acronym for Chicago Board Options Exchange. Nation's first and largest organized marketplace for the exchange trading of specific put and call options.

C-BONDS

Used for long-term obligations of corporate issuers. The usage is analogous with the expression "T-bonds" to signify long-term Treasury issues.

CBS STOCK TREND INDEX

A market index comprised of the values for most stocks traded on the Amsterdam Stock Exchange. It is calculated seven times daily during exchange trading hours. The information is supplied by the Dutch Central Bureau of Statistics—hence the initials CBS. The index excludes investment funds, property funds, and holding companies because their underlying securities are already part of the index.

CBT

See CHICAGO BOARD OF TRADE.

CCA

Initials for: current cost accounts, an English accounting term used to provide a realistic valuation of a firm's balance sheet.

By recognizing the distorting effect that inflation can have on a balance sheet, this valuation approach assigns current market costs to specified balance sheet assets. It thereby avoids the use of actual costs, which in practice may be considerably lower, and which could be misleading in evaluating the company.

CD

See CERTIFICATE OF DEPOSIT.

CDSL

See CONTINGENT DEFERRED SALES LOAD.

CEASE AND DESIST ORDER
See C&D ORDER.

CEDE
This is the nominee partnership entity of the Depository Trust Company (DTC), the quasi-cashiering department of the securities industry. The partnership name is used as the registration form for stocks and bonds left in DTC's custody. This greatly simplifies the transfer of securities following a trade.

CEDEL
An institution headquartered in Luxembourg that serves banks and broker/dealers as a clearing corporation for Eurobond transactions.

CEILING
This expression is used to designate the highest price, or highest interest rate, that is acceptable to the purchaser (or issuer) of a security. It always refers to a maximum number needed to arrange a transaction between a buyer and seller. For example, "The issuer has placed a ceiling of 9% on the issue."

The term *ceiling* is used interchangeably with *cap*.

CEMETERY SPREAD
A tongue-in-cheek expression used by option traders when spread premiums move in the wrong direction. Normally a spread trader who puts on a spread at a debit expects premiums to so widen that the spread can be taken off at a profit. The opposite is true if a spread is put on at a credit. When the premiums go in the wrong direction, the spread trader is getting "killed"—financially, of course—and this gives rise to the expression "cemetery" spread.

CENTRAL BANK
Bank organized for benefit of government of a country. Issues currency and administers monetary policy. U.S. counterpart is the Federal Reserve System.

CENTRALE DE LIVRAISON DE VALEURS MOBILERES S. A. LUXEMBOURG
The full title for the second largest clearing organization in Europe for foreign-issued securities (see CEDEL).

CENTRAL REGISTRATION DEPOSITORY (CRD)
The CRD, sponsored by the NASD, is a computerized system for the maintenance of records for all registered personnel. The system also en-

compasses many state blue-sky registrations. Centralization permits easy recordkeeping and especially the annual renewals required by many of the states.

CENTRAL SCHOOL DISTRICT
See CSD.

CENTRAMART
The silent broadcast system used to tie Philadelphia Stock Exchange executions into the national trade reporting system; that is, the consolidated tape.

The system has been in operation since 1988 and is currently manually operated, although it should soon be linked to the ITS trade system employed by all domestic stock exchanges.

Popularly called the "ticker" by exchange members.

CEO
Acronym for chief executive officer. The corporate officer, reporting only to the board of directors, whose responsibility it is to carry out policies established by the board. How much of the day-to-day responsibilities the CEO exercises depends on how much has been delegated to other management officials.

CERTIFICATE
Evidence of security ownership. In most cases, the evidence is a piece of paper, properly inscribed, that states the name of the issuer and the conditions under which the issue was made. Generally, the certificate is fully transferable. In recent years, there has been an increasing trend to book-entry security ownership; that is, the evidence of ownership is kept on the books of the issuer and transfer is made by offsetting journal entries. For example, security options, and many issues of Treasury bills, notes, bonds, and agency securities. Also:
1. Any document representing equity or debt of the issuer.
2. A debt instrument with an original maturity of one year or less. Exception: Some certificates of deposit have longer maturities.

CERTIFICATE FOR AUTOMOBILE RECEIVABLES
CARs, as they are popularly called, are two- to three-year debt securities collateralized by pools of bank and finance company car loans. Because CARs give higher than comparable Treasury security interest rates, they are attractive to institutional investors.

CERTIFICATE OF ACCRUAL ON TREASURY SECURITIES
See CATS (1).

CERTIFICATE OF BENEFICIAL INTEREST

A CBI is evidence of an undivided ownership interest in a business created under a legal trust. As such, a CBI differs little from common stock and is often called "a share of beneficial interest." However, unlike common stockholders, owners of CBIs do not elect successors to the trustees. The trustees elect their own successors.

CERTIFICATE OF DEPOSIT (CD)

Debt instrument issued by commercial bank. Promises to pay principal and fixed rate of interest at maturity, normally one year or less. Amounts of $100,000 or more with 30 or more days to maturity are exempt from interest ceiling imposed by Regulation Q of Federal Reserve and are negotiable and actively traded in money market.

CERTIFICATE OF INCORPORATION

See CHARTER.

CERTIFICATE OF INDEBTEDNESS

A short-term, fixed-coupon debt security formerly issued by the U.S. Treasury with maturities of 90 days to one year. CIs have been replaced by 180-day and one-year Treasury bills.

CERTIFICATE OF LAND APPRECIATION NOTES

See COLA (2).

CERTIFICATE OF (TIME) DEPOSIT

A debt security issued by a commercial bank in exchange for funds that are to be left on deposit for a period of 30 days to one year, although longer-period CDs are available. Generally, the interest rate is fixed and is paid at maturity, or at more frequent intervals.

Holders of nonnegotiable CDs generally have to pay a penalty for premature redemption. Negotiable CDs are issued in bearer form and are readily marketable at prevailing money market rates.

CERTIFICATE ON GOVERNMENT RECEIPTS

See COUGARs.

CERTIFICATES FOR AMORTIZING REVOLVING DEBTS

See CARDs.

CERTIFIED CHECK

A personal check drawn on a commercial bank that the bank guarantees to honor upon presentation. The bank, upon certification, sets aside sufficient funds from the writer's account to redeem the certified check.

Note: Do not confuse with bank check, a check drawn by the bank on itself, or with Federal Funds check, a check drawn by the bank on its account with the Federal Reserve. Certified checks are clearinghouse funds.

CERTIFIED FINANCIAL MANAGER
A Merrill Lynch designation for financial consultants (RRs) who have completed an in-house course. This course is a series of continuing education programs and includes instruction in financial planning, risk management, insurance, wills and estates, fixed-income securities, communication. The course was designed to compete with the courses of the College for Financial Planning. Successful completion of the assigned courses gives the RR the right to be called a "certified financial manager" and to use the initials CFM on business cards.

CERTIFIED FINANCIAL PLANNER
A certificate awarded to persons who have successfully completed a course prepared by the College for Financial Planning located in Englewood, Colorado. The courses are administered both in residence or via correspondence, and completion is tested by examination. The course includes financial concepts, terminology, strategies, and, in effect, is a form of continuing education for RRs employed by member firms.

Persons who successfully complete the six portions of the program are permitted to designate themselves as a certified financial planner (CFP) on their business cards and other correspondence.

CEW
See CURRENCY EXCHANGE WARRANT.

CFM
See CERTIFIED FINANCIAL MANAGER.

CFO
See CHIEF FINANCIAL OFFICER.

CFP
See CERTIFIED FINANCIAL PLANNER.

CFTC
See COMMODITIES FUTURES TRADING COMMISSION.

CGT
An English abbreviation for capital gains tax; that is, a special rate for this type of income as opposed to ordinary earned income.

The expression is not used in the United States.

CHA-CHA
Colloquial name used to identify both the company and the common stock of Champion International, Inc., a prominent manufacturer of building materials. Name is derived from the symbol for the stock: CHA.

CHANGE OF MODE PAYMENT
See CMOP.

CHAPDELAINE AUTOMATIC TRADING SYSTEM (CHATS)
An automated order entry and execution system for government securities developed by Chapdelaine and Co., a government and municipal securities dealer in New York City. Although its availability was initially restricted to primary dealers, the system also permits nonprimary dealers and institutional investors to use it. A transaction fee is levied upon users of this computerized system.

CHAPTER 10
A reference to a section of the federal bankruptcy statutes whereby an insolvent entity may petition the court for protection from its creditors and for the appointment of an independent manager (trustee in bankruptcy) to reorganize the company. If granted, the company continues its operations free from immediate obligations to its creditors while it undergoes restructuring and recapitalization.

Often written "Chapter X."

CHAPTER 11
A reference to a section of the federal bankruptcy statutes whereby an insolvent entity may petition the court for protection from its creditors while present management attempts to reorganize the company. If granted, the corporation will be freed from immediate obligations and management will try to restructure the company, debt payments, and the like.

Also written "Chapter XI."

CHARM
A computer information processing system used by the International Stock Exchange of the United Kingdom and the Republic of Ireland to compare daily transactions (also called "bargains") made between members. CHARM is similar to the NYSE's SIAC system for trade comparisons, and it works in tandem with the Talisman system to complete settlements.

CHARTER
Common term for certificate of incorporation, a state-validated document giving legal status to a corporation.

Also called "certificate of incorporation."

CHARTIST
Market technician who makes buy-sell decisions based on plotted price movements of a security.

See also POINT AND FIGURE CHART.

CHASING THE MARKET
An expression used of a customer who originally entered a limit, rather than a market, order and who then watches the market move away from the limit: if a buyer, the price moves up; if a seller, the price moves down. Finally, the customer has to enter a market order to complete the transaction. However, the execution price is at a level different from that originally intended by the customer. In effect, the customer has chased the market.

CHASTITY BONDS
These are nonconvertible corporate debt securities with built-in protection for the holder in the event of a corporate takeover attempt. In the event of a takeover, a tender offer, or a LBO, the holders of these bonds are authorized to turn in the bonds for redemption at par value. In effect, the bondholders are protected from the probable decline in bond rating that will occur if the company substantially increases its debt-to-equity ratio.

CHATS
See CHAPDELAINE AUTOMATIC TRADING SYSTEM.

CHATTEL MORTGAGE
A loan agreement that places a lien on such personal property as furniture, automobiles, jewelry, or other personal possessions that are pledged as collateral for the repayment of the loan.

CHEAP
Term often used to indicate that the price of a particular security is relatively low when compared to previous prices for the same security, or when compared to the securities of other companies in the same industry.

Cheap tends to be a judgment of present price in terms of present value. Underpriced tends to be used of present price in terms of future value.

Common antonym: fully priced.

CHEAP STOCK
Corporate shares distributed while the concern is still in a developmental or promotional stage, or issued to promoters for a consideration well below the proposed public offering.

CHECKING THE MARKET
Canvassing marketmakers to determine best bid or offer for a security. May be done by telephone, telex, or other electronic media.

CHECK KITING
Issuing a check without sufficient funds in the account, in the hope of depositing a second check into the account before the first check is presented for payment.

CHERRY PICKING
Slang expression for choosing the best of something while ignoring what is less attractive.

The SEC uses the term regarding Rule 14b-1 and the intent of issuers to be fair and reasonable in soliciting names of beneficial owners. If issuers solicit names, they should do so from all broker/dealers and banks; in this way, the issuers would not show discrimination by forcing only large brokerage firms to search their records for the names of beneficial owners.

CHICAGO BOARD OF TRADE
Nation's largest exchange for trading of futures contracts. Well known for grains and metals futures, CBT also trade futures in fixed-income securities and currencies. Parent organization of Chicago Board Options Exchange (CBOE).

CHICAGO BOARD OPTIONS EXCHANGE
See CBOE.

CHICAGO MERCANTILE EXCHANGE (CME)
Second largest commodities exchange. Specializes in futures in poultry, eggs, live cattle, and other agricultural commodities. Parent of International Monetary Market, specializing in currency futures.

Also referred to as the MERC.

CHICKEN CONVERTS
Humorous term coined by traders to identify the Holly Farms 6% subordinated convertible debentures due February 15, 2017. "Chicken" refers to the principal business activity of the issuer. Each $1,000 bond is convertible into 16.84 shares of common stock of Holly Farms.

CHIEF EXECUTIVE OFFICER
See CEO.

CHIEF FINANCIAL OFFICER (CFO)
In a corporation, the individual who has the responsibility to oversee the management of the company's money, investments, and tax liabilities. Included also is the responsibility of overseeing, planning, and supervising the corporate budget.

CHIEF OPERATING OFFICER (COO)
In a corporation, the individual responsible for the day-to-day management of the company. If the chairman is the chief executive officer, the president normally will be the chief operating officer.

CHINESE ARBITRAGE
See REVERSE HEDGE.

CHINESE MARKET
Term used by traders to signify that they are willing to buy above the lowest offer, or sell below the highest bid, but only in significant quantities.

CHINESE PAPER
The name given to new securities that are used in lieu of cash to acquire a company. The value of these securities is often questionable, because the newly merged company ends up with diluted equity or overburdening debt. Whether or not a pun was intended, "Chinese paper" in the current environment is also known as "junk bonds."

CHINESE WALL
A slang expression to designate the communication barrier that should exist between the finance/research areas of a member firm and the trading/sales areas. The term signifies that the finance area possesses "inside information" that must not be communicated to others until such time as the fact becomes public.

The barrier is moral, rather than physical, but it usually involves the use of code names and other subterfuges to prevent premature leaking of material information.

CHIPS
Acronym for Clearing House Interbank Payment System. CHIPS is an electronic, international check-transfer system that can move dollar balances between participating U.S. and foreign financial institutions anywhere in the world.

CHUMMING

A slang expression for the creation of artificial transactions on one exchange to equalize the price with transactions made on another exchange. When options were traded on multiple exchanges, this was sometimes done to make sure that prices were the same on both exchanges.

The analogy is to the practice of commercial fishermen who use chum (chopped up fish or refuse from fish canning factories) to attract fish to the fishing boat.

Chumming violates SEC rules.

CHUNNEL

A popularized English term that combines "channel" and "tunnel" to identify the Euro-Tunnel plc. This enterprise is engaged in the development and construction of a tunnel from England to France below the English Channel. The tunnel will permit direct train and auto traffic from England to the Continent.

CHURNING

Excessive trading in an account, with connotation that buy-sell activities are against financial interests of customer. Unethical activity and often actionable at law by offended party. Courts judge degree of control over the account, broker profits versus customer profits, and turnover of original capital to decide if churning has occurred.

CI

See CERTIFICATE OF INDEBTEDNESS.

CIB

See COMPOUND INTEREST BONDS.

CIC

Acronym for Canadian Interest Cost.
See TRUE INTEREST COST.

CICA

See CANADIAN INSTITUTE OF CHARTERED ACCOUNTANTS.

CICI

Acronym for Computer-to-Computer Interface. CICI is an NASD term for an automated communication relationship between marketmakers or between marketmakers and selected customers. In effect, CICI enables marketmakers to receive and execute orders electronically in OTC securities.

CIF
See CORPORATE INCOME FUND.

CINCINNATI STOCK EXCHANGE (CSE)
The nation's first fully automated stock exchange. Transactions are arranged by members via the computer facilities of Control Data Corporation without benefit of a physical trading floor in a central location. It is now owned by the CBOE.

CINS
See CUSIP INTERNATIONAL NUMBERING SYSTEM.

CIP
Acronym for Cash Index Participation. CIP was developed by the Philadelphia Stock Exchange. CIP was designed to enable the average investor to participate pricewise in the whole market by purchasing this one security. CIP is similar to a mutual fund in that its value is based on a structured portfolio similar in concept to the DJIA or the S&P Index. It is similar to a mutual fund, also, in that dividends from the underlying securities in the portfolio are passed through to the CIP holder. Unlike mutual funds, CIP does not assess a management fee. It is now the subject of a court-issued injunction because of its similarity to a futures instrument.

A CIRCLE
Industry term for indications of interest taken while security is in registration. Registered representative makes list of potential clients for new issue and circles those who are interested.

CIRCUIT BREAKERS
A generic term used by industry leaders and regulators of some proposed solutions to the price volatility that may be caused by various kinds of programmed trading, particularly index arbitrage. Circuit breakers would apply when certain market conditions occur. Among the solutions proposed as circuit breakers are: trading halts, higher margin requirements, denial of the use of automated trading systems, or price movement limits on index futures contracts. It is envisioned that one or more of these controls should cushion the impact of market volatility and thus quiet small investor concerns.

CIRCUS
Acronym for combined interest rate and currency swap. CIRCUS involves an exchange between two parties of fixed- and floating-rate obligations in different currencies. In effect, the swap is made because the two parties

have diametrically opposed opinions of currency and interest-rate trends. For example, if a person swaps fixed-interest obligations in one currency for floating obligations in another currency, that person is engaging in a CIRCUS transaction, and he or she believes that short-term rates will rise on the "floater" and that the fixed-income currency will depreciate versus the currency of the floater. Obviously, the other party to the swap would not agree to the swap unless he or she held an opposing point of view.

CIS
Acronym for Computer Information Services. CIS sells trade processing, surveillance, and reporting services to broker/dealers and commodity futures merchants.

CITATION
Citation is an affiliate of Merrill Lynch & Co. and is responsible for its "soft dollar" business. In effect, the affiliate solicits commission business in exchange for "soft dollars"; that is, in the form of research subscriptions, computer services, or portfolio analysis.

CITIZEN BONDS
Originated by Prudential-Bache Securities, these are municipal bonds that can be purchased in denominations of $1,000 or less to provide greater public participation. A single jumbo-sized certificate is issued, held by the Depository Trust Company, and ownership, transfer, and secondary market transactions are made in the Prudential-Bache computerized operations system.

THE CITY
That region in the eastern portion of London wherein is concentrated England's principal financial services organizations. It is the counterpart of New York's Wall Street.

A CLAIM
A legal right to a future distribution.
1. In conjunction with a distribution by an issuer, if the entitled new owner fails to reregister before the company closes its books, the new owner can acquire the distribution only by making a claim against the old owner.
2. The same is true if the new owner fails to reregister and wishes to receive a proxy. To do so, the new owner must make a claim against the old owner.
3. The same is true if the new owner fails to reregister and thus fails to get a cash dividend, interest, or return of principal.

Generally, such a failure to reregister in time is caused by the old owner's late delivery of the certificate. In such a case, the new owner's broker will not accept delivery unless it is accompanied by a "due bill" or "due bill check" for the distribution. This establishes the claim against the old owner.

CLARA BOW
Clara Bow was the "It" girl of the 1920s. IT was also the NYSE ticker symbol of International Telephone and Telegraph Co.

Although the symbol for the company is currently ITT, there is some recurring popularity for the concept because of current media commercials sponsored by International Telephone and Telegraph.

CLASS
1. Used of securities with similar features. For example, bonds are a class of security.
2. Used of options with similar features. For example, all calls of an underlying security are one class, all puts are another class. Definition is important because option position and exercise limits generally are determined by class.

CLASS ACTION
Legal term for a grievance filed on behalf of a group of shareholders or other injured parties. In effect, because all of the persons in the group have an identical complaint, they will be represented in court by a single action under a single attorney (or group of attorneys). This approach also appeals to legal counsel because the awards are generally quite large and represent larger fees for counsel.

CLASS OF OPTION
This term identifies all put options on the same underlying security as a class. All call options on the same underlying security constitute a second class.

CLASS 1 RAILROAD
Industry category used to distinguish those railroads in the United States that have annual revenues of more than $10 million. Practically, these are the only railroads that can borrow money through debt securities without either a commercial bank assurance or a parent company guaranty.

CLAWBACK PROVISION
Slang for a provision that usually occurs in the underwriting agreement of public property that is being "privatized"; that is, sold to the public.

Because such sales often generate a large international demand for the resulting securities, the "clawback" provision permits the selling government to so restrict overseas subscriptions that domestic demand is satisfied first. For example, when British Airways plc and British Gas plc were sold, the British government scaled back American and Canadian orders in favor of domestic U.K. buyers.

CLAYTON ANTITRUST ACT
Passed in 1919, this federal law is designed to prevent business monopolies, unfair competition, or restraint of trade in any domestic industry.

CLC/PLC
Acronym for Construction Loan Certificate/Project Loan Certificate. CLC/PLC is a GNMA debt security comprised of two distinct parts: a two-year construction loan that is used to construct the project, and a 40-year project loan that refunds the construction loan and provides longer-term financing for the project. In effect, the lender can bail out after two years, or exchange it for the 40-year project loan. The latter obligation is constructed like a standard GNMA pass-through with all of the government guarantees associated with these securities.

CLEAN
Term used by block positioners if they are able to match buy-and-sell orders from customers without the need to take the security into inventory. Example: "We did a clean trade for 50,000 ABC." In other words, they had a seller of 50,000 and found a buyer without taking inventory risk.

"Clean on the tape" is often used if the transaction appears on an exchange tape.

The term *natural* is often used as a synonym for clean. Example: "We did a natural for 50,000 ABC."

CLEAN ON THE PRINT
Expression used by block positioners of exchange-listed stocks. The expression is an announcement to the firm's sales force that it brought buyers and sellers together in sufficient quantity so the block trade may be executed on the floor without a need for the firm to act as principal to facilitate the trade.

CLEAN PERIOD
Slang term in Japan for the period before a corporate issuer announces a forthcoming offering of equity securities. During the "clean period" the issuer may negotiate with various underwriters, and underwriters may

act for themselves and for customers, but they must be very careful not to destabilize the marketplace for similar securities of the same issuer.

CLEAR
1. Comparison and verification of details of a securities trade as preparation for final settlement.
2. Performance of clearing function for another brokerage firm. For example, ABC clears for XYZ.

CLEARING AGENCY
An intermediary between contra brokers who validate the terms of their transactions and arrange for payments and deliveries. The function of a clearing agency is to reduce the number of physical settlements and to assign allocation responsibilities among trade participants. .

CLEARING AGREEMENT
1. A contract between broker/dealers in which one agrees to execute, compare, confirm, and settle the other's securities transactions on a fee basis.
2. A contract between banks whereby one agrees to honor, accept, and process the other's checks through the Federal Reserve Banking System.

CLEARING HOUSE FUNDS
Monies represented by a personal or a corporate check that must go through local or regional bank clearing function before an account credit is given to payee. Used in distinction to federal funds, which are immediately usable by payee. Most securities transactions outside of money market are payable in clearing house funds.
See also FEDERAL FUNDS.

CLEARING HOUSE INTERBANK PAYMENT SYSTEM
See CHIPS.

CLEARING MEMBER ACCOUNTING AND CONTROL SYSTEM
See C/MACS.

CLEARING MEMBER TRADE AGREEMENT
See CMTA.

CLIENT SERVICE REPRESENTATIVE (CSR)
CSR is an alternate title for registered representative or account executive. The inference is that the CSR is a salaried employee, while the RR works on a salary plus adjustment or directly on a commission basis.

The term *CSR* originated with discount brokerage firms, although some full-service brokerage firms use CSRs to screen walk-ins, to handle one-time transactions, or to execute orders for house accounts.

CLIFFORD TRUST
Temporary inter vivos trust (between living persons). Assets are pledged for 10 or more years. Income from assets is paid to a specified party. At end of trust, assets revert to grantor. IRS considers income a gift to recipient, so legal advice is needed.

See also INTER VIVOS TRUST.

CLOSE
1. Final transaction in listed security on a business day.
2. Next-to-last column in financial report of stock and bond transactions. Final transaction price given.
3. Last 30 seconds of market trading. Time is marked by continuous ringing of bell on NYSE and ASE.
4. As verb: transfer of money and securities following an underwriting. For example, "They close the deal on Tuesday."

CLOSE A POSITION
To remove the risk inherent in an investment by making an offsetting transaction that gives the client no further risk or options. For example, a client owns 500 shares of ABC. The client is at risk if ABC declines in value. The client sells 500 ABC and delivers the shares to the new owner. The client has closed the position and has no further risk. Offsetting transactions that exclude risk but leave other optional decisions open (e.g., a short against the box) are not considered as closing a position.

CLOSED-END MANAGEMENT COMPANY
Management investment company that issues a fixed number of shares. Generally, shares are not redeemable at option of shareholder. Redemption, therefore, takes place through secondary market transactions. Most closed-end management company shares are listed for trading on exchanges.

CLOSED-END MORTGAGE
Provision of indenture of mortgage bond that prohibits issuing corporation from repledging same collateral without permission of first mortgage holders who have the prior claim on pledged assets in the event of default.

CLOSELY HELD
Term refers to a company whose common stock is predominantly held by a few owners, but there are sufficient shares held by others to form a base for secondary market trading. If this latter case is not true, the company is said to be privately held.

See also FLOAT (1).

CLOSE OUT
This is the generic term for the procedure taken by either party to a transaction if the contra broker defaults. Thus, if the contra broker fails to deliver, the purchasing broker will "buy in" to complete the contract. A "sell out" occurs if the contra broker fails to pay. Buy-ins and sell-outs are the financial responsibility of the contra brokers and will be charged to them. They, in turn, will debit their customer for the fail.

CLOSING A MARKET
This is jargon used when the traders narrow the difference between bid and offer prices (the spread). They do this by raising the bid, or lowering the offer (asked) price, or by a combination of both.

CLOSING PURCHASE
Writer of an option makes a purchase of same series, thereby giving the writer a net zero position. For example, writer of five XYZ April 45 calls subsequently buys five XYZ April 45 calls.

CLOSING QUOTATION
Marketmaker's or specialist's final bid and offer at time trading ceases on a particular trading day.

CLOSING SALE
Term used of exchange-traded options if a transaction reduces or eliminates a long position in an option series. Example: A client purchases 5 XYZ JAN 65 puts. A subsequent sale of 5 XYZ JAN 65 puts would constitute a closing sale and would eliminate the position.

CLUB FINANCING
Term used in Eurobond underwritings. The term is used to designate an underwriting by a group of similarly sized banks each of whom subscribes to an equal amount of the issue.

C/MACS
Acronym for Clearing Member Accounting and Control System. C/MACS is a computer driven communication linkage between some member firms and the Options Clearing Corporation. Through it, members can:

1. Retrieve daily options activities and position reports.
2. Exercise valid long positions.
3. Give OCC instructions for same-day security and cash collateral movements.

CME
See CHICAGO MERCANTILE EXCHANGE.

CMO
See COLLATERALIZED MORTGAGE OBLIGATION.

CMOP
Initials represent Change of Mode Payment, a service offered by the Depository Trust Co. (DTC) to enable participants to change the frequency by which they receive dividends from selected unit investment trusts and variable preferred stocks. Payments on those issues can be requested on a monthly, quarterly, semiannual, or annual basis, or be changed periodically at the preference of the investor. Changes are arranged between DTC and the transfer agent in a computer-to-computer interface.

CMS
See COMMON MESSAGE SWITCH.

CMTA
Acronym for Clearing Member Trade Agreement. The agreement is a standard Options Clearing Corporation form that permits exchange members to execute, clear, and settle contracts through a clearing member. This procedure facilitates recordkeeping of the opening and closing of options contracts and the collection of execution brokerage expenses.

CMV
Frequently used abbreviation for current market value in ledger displays of margin accounts.

CNS
A prevalent method of clearing and settling securities transactions. See also CONTINUOUS NET SETTLEMENT.

COATS
Acronym for Canadian Over-the-Counter Automated Trading System. COATS is an electronic quotation and trade reporting system for Canadian issues not listed on any Canadian stock exchange. It is similar to

the NASDAQ system in the United States. At present, COATS is still a pilot project in the province of Ontario.

COATTAIL INVESTING
This term refers to the practice of buying and selling the same securities as do well-known persons or institutions as soon as their activities are publicized. In effect, such participants are using the research of prominent market investors. Because of the built-in time lag this practice is fraught with great risk.

Also called "piggyback investing."

COB
Initials, and commonly used, for "Commission des Operations de Bourse." COB is the French version of the SEC in the United States. Thus, it is a regulatory agency responsible for the proper functioning of financial markets in France.

COBOL
An approximate acronym for Common Business Oriented Language. This is a popular business-oriented computer language developed especially for typical commercial activities.

COCKING A SNOOK AT THE MARKET
This is a quaint English expression used to describe a marketmaker's bid and offer at the same price. This practice is frowned upon in the United Kingdom because it forces the order flow to the marketmaker who has bid and offered at the same price, and it interferes with any competitor's ability to profit on a transaction because there is no spread and, hence, no margin of profit.

From the English expression "to cock a snook"; that is, to thumb one's nose. The origin of the expression is unknown.

COCKROACH FACTOR
Term coined by federal and securities industry regulators to describe the actions of some registered representatives when their brokerage firm becomes subject to public scrutiny. In an allusion to the durable and infamous insect, these salespeople scurry to a new firm when exposed to the light of discovery of their improprieties.

COCONUTS
A light-hearted nickname given to Coastal Caribbean Oil Co. by traders on the Boston and Philadelphia stock exchanges. The nickname is derived from a play on its ticker symbol: CCO.

COCOONING
Used by securities analysts to describe certain practices of the food processing industry whereby food is prepared for microwaving in family kitchens. In effect, it is the industry's application of "fast foods" techniques for home food preparation.

COD
See CASH ON DELIVERY.

CODE OF ARBITRATION
National Association of Securities Dealers' rules for submission and arbitration of controversies involving money or securities transactions between members or members and customers.

See also ARBITRATION and BOARD OF ARBITRATION.

CODE OF PROCEDURE
National Association of Securities Dealers' rules for the adjudication of trade practice complaints, alleged to be in violation of the Rules of Fair Practice.

CODM
Acronym for call option deutsche marks. This is a conventional currency contract arranged as a European option to enable the holder to buy a predetermined amount of German currency at a fixed price stated in U.S. dollars.

As a European option, the option may be exercised only on a specific date in the future; thus, it differs from an American option that can be exercised any time between purchase and expiration date.

COD TRANSACTION
Frequently used designation on institutional client buy orders. Broker buys for client's account and will deliver to client's agent. Upon delivery, agent will pay for cost of purchase.

Also called "DVP" (deliver versus payment) and "DAC" (deliver against cost).

COF
See COST OF FUNDS.

COIL FORMATION
See TRIANGLE FORMATION.

COINCIDENT INDICATOR
A measurement of economic or financial activity that tends to move in the same direction and at the same time as the gross national product (GNP).

COLA
1. Acronym for cost of living adjustment. For example, in 1990 there was a 4% COLA added to Social Security payments.
2. Acronym for Certificate of Land Appreciation note. This is a debt security created by Merrill Lynch to raise capital for AMFAC/JMB Hawaii, Inc. Among other features, this note, which matures in 2008, entitles its holder to 4% in annual cumulative interest plus an additional 6% in additional payments dependent upon the issuer's cash flow surplus.

COLD CALLING
A popular term in the United States for an unsolicited personal visit or any oral communication with a customer or a potential customer. This, together with referrals, is probably the chief source of new customer accounts.

In England, under the Financial Services Act of 1986, this practice was made a criminal offense except in accordance with certain limited rules and procedures.

Cold calling is also prohibited in some Canadian provinces.

COLLAR
In connection with a new issue of securities, this term signifies the lowest interest rate that bond purchasers may accept, or the lowest price an issuer may accept as a guarantee from the underwriters of stock.

Antonym: see CAP.

COLLATERAL
An asset pledged by a borrower to a lender. If there is a default, the collateral may be taken or sold by the lender to repay the loan.

COLLATERALIZE
To put up an asset as a pledge that a loan will be repaid. For example, to collateralize a margin loan by the deposit of stock with the broker.

COLLATERALIZED BOND OBLIGATION
See CBO.

COLLATERALIZED MORTGAGE OBLIGATION (CMO)
A CMO is a debt security collateralized by a portfolio of other securities-for example, a portfolio of GNMA modified pass-throughs. In effect, they have the same credit rating as the collateral.

CMOs are normally issued in denominations of $1,000, pay semiannual interest, and semiannual partial repayments of principal.

COLLATERAL TRUST BOND
Corporate debt security which pledges a portfolio of securities, usually held in trust by a bank, as protection for the purchasers of the bond. Securities may be those of subsidiaries or of other corporations and may be either debt or equity securities.

Also called "collateral trust certificate."

COLLECTION RATIO
An important measurement of the efficient use of corporate assets.

The ratio, in effect, measures how quickly a corporation turns a dollar of "accounts receivable" into cash on the corporate balance sheet. For example, if Corporation A turns an accounts receivable dollar into cash in 35 days, it is more efficient than Corporation B that takes 60 days to do the same thing.

Ratios vary by industry. In practice, a year-to-year comparison is the best insight of the efficiency of a particular company.

COLLEGE CONSTRUCTION LOAN INSURANCE CORPORATION
See CONNIE LEE.

COLOR
Jargon: background information. Used in the financial services industry to describe market conditions, investor preferences, price levels for yield spreads between benchmark issues, or between alternative investments.

COLTS
Acronym for Continuously Offered Longer-Term Securities. COLTS are offered by the International Bank for Reconstruction and Development (World Bank) to fund its general operations. As the title implies, COLTS are an open-ended distribution of 3- to 30-year bonds with some zeros. Rates may be fixed or variable as determined by bank management at the time of each offering. Four agent broker/dealers, all internationally prominent, act as underwriters and distributors.

COMBINATION ORDER
Long call and long put, or short call and short put, on same underlying security having different expiration months or different strike prices. For example, buy XYZ April 50 call, buy XYZ July 45 put. Order ticket will give the net debit, on long combination, or the net credit, on short combination, that is acceptable to customer. Order will be executed only if conditions can be met.

COME BACK
1. Verb: used as two words—the act of returning to an original state. Example: The market is temporarily depressed and will come back to its old high.
   Note: In England, the expression implies a return to a lower state. Example: The market will come back.
2. Noun: used as one word—the result of the act of returning. Example: "That was quite a comeback." Implication is that the return is a repetition of a former success.

COMEX
Acronym for Commodity Exchange Incorporated in New York City. Formed by merger of four prior exchanges. Comex trades futures in metals, petroleum, coffee, sugar, and financial instruments.

COMFORT LETTER
Letter of indemnification often given by an issuer or seller of a security to its investment banker as underwriter or sales agent. In a comfort letter, the offeror agrees to reimburse the investment banker for realized litigation losses and expenses resulting from material omissions or misrepresentations in a registration statement, merger proposal, or tender offer.

COMING IN
A term used both by equity and bond traders when describing a market situation that is turning from positive to negative. For example, the expression "the market is coming in" means that sellers are materializing and will depress prices from their current levels.

COMING TO ME (CTM)
Qualifying language used by over-the-counter traders when they represent a quote that is not their own. For example, the price is $19\frac{1}{2}$–20, coming to me.

The price expresses another dealer's firm market, but it does not represent the market at which the trader is willing to buy or sell.

COMISSAO DE VALORE MOBILIARIOS
See CVM.

COMMERCIAL BANK
A national or state chartered institution that accepts savings, time, or demand deposits. These deposits, in turn, are used to finance short- and intermediate-term loans to individuals, businesses, and governments.

COMMERCIAL PAPER
Unsecured promissory notes of corporations, issued to provide short-term financing, sold at a discount and redeemed at face value. Exempt from registration if maturity is 270 days or less. Highly competitive with other money market instruments.

COMMERZBANK INDEX
This index is the oldest measurement of stock market performance in Germany. It is named after Commerzbank, one of Germany's largest banks.

The index is computed once each day at noon. It is capitalization weighted and represents the accumulated value of 60 widely traded German stocks.

COMMINGLING
Using customer securities in same loan agreement with member firm securities. Prohibited by federal law and by industry regulations.

See also SEGREGATION.

COMMISSION
Fee charged by a broker for buying or selling securities or property for the account of a customer.

COMMISSION HOUSE BROKER
See FLOOR BROKER.

COMMITMENT FEE
1. Money paid as an incentive to investors by an issuer of securities to be distributed some time in the future. The issuer has no current need for the money but is willing to pay a fee for the certainty that the funds will be available when needed.
2. Points paid by a prospective borrower to a bank to guarantee the availability of funds in the future. Often used with mortgages on residential property. As such, points represent a form of interest and are tax deductible.

COMMITTEE FOR AN INCOMPETENT

Term used for a court-appointed person or institution directed to handle the legal, personal, or financial affairs of someone judged to be physically or mentally unable to handle his or her own affairs.

The term generally is shortened to committee. Example: The court appointed a committee to handle her affairs while she is recovering from a stroke.

Security transactions effected by a committee constitute a "legal" transfer and require supporting documentation.

COMMITTEE ON UNIFORM SECURITIES IDENTIFICATION PROCEDURES

Its numbering system—9 characters, 7 numbers, and 2 letters—permits a standardized computer identification of debt securities issued in the United States after 1970. For example, the CUSIP number 43755 42AF applies only to the XYZ 5 ½% bonds that will mature in 1994. CUSIP identifiers for stocks have 9 numbers.

Also called "CUSIP number."

COMMODITIES FUTURES TRADING COMMISSION

Federal regulator of commodities exchanges and futures trading, located in the District of Columbia.

COMMODITY EXCHANGE INCORPORATED

See COMEX.

COMMODITY POOL OPERATOR

Acronym is CPO. Any person or enterprise that solicits funds to pool them for trades in commodities futures contracts on behalf of the owners of the funds. Such pool operators must register with the National Futures Association (NFA) and comply with the provisions of the Commodities Exchange Act.

COMMODITY SWAP

An exchange of variable payment liabilities between two parties made on the proviso that the basis on which payments are made will not be a financial instrument benchmark but will be considered a spot price transaction. Thus, the prices will not be part of a futures index.

Commodity swaps may also involve the exchange of different physical commodities in specific amounts on a future date.

COMMODITY TRADING ADVISOR

Acronym is CTA. A person who provides others, for a fee, with advice on futures contract tactics or strategies. CTAs must register with the National Futures Association (NFA) and comply with the provisions of the Commodities Exchange Act.

COMMON LAW
1. Legal precedents derived from court decisions over a period of years, rather than from specific legislative decrees.
2. Used to distinguish such precedents from statute law.
3. Used to distinguish general legal statutes from specific laws. Example: The law of agency derives from common law, rather than from securities law.

COMMON MARKET
See EUROPEAN ECONOMIC COMMUNITY.

COMMON MESSAGE SWITCH
Acronym is CMS. CMS is an electronic switching device that links member firms with the floors of the New York and American Stock Exchanges. Order instructions are routed electronically; that is, switched to the appropriate floors for execution. Executed orders are returned to the initiating member firm by the same system.

COMMON STOCK
Class of ownership, or equity, security with residual claims on assets of corporation after claims of bondholders, other creditors, and preferred stockholders are settled. Charter of corporation defines the rights of common stockholders. Generally, common stockholders control management and company policy through voting rights.

COMMON STOCK EQUIVALENTS
Name given to securities that may, with or without the addition of money, be exchanged for common stock. Convertibles, rights, warrants, and long calls are typical common stock equivalents, but only under certain conditions.

COMMON STOCK RATIO
That percentage of a corporation's relatively permanent capital that comes from common stock, paid-in surplus, and retained earnings. Bond ratio, preferred stock ratio, and common stock ratio total 100%.

COMMUNISM
1. As a political system, the centralized control of social and economic forces by a strong and totalitarian political faction that is self-perpetuating.
2. As an economic theory, a transition phase between capitalism and

socialism. It is characterized by governmental control of production facilities and the distribution of goods and services. Ultimately, production facilities should be transferred to the workers who produce the goods and services.

COMMUNITY PROPERTY
Legal concept: Assets acquired during a marriage are deemed to be acquired half and half by each party to the marriage. As a result, in those states that have community property laws, the consent of both parties is required to effect transfer or other disposition of such assets.

COMP
Slang term used by traders asked to bid for (or offer) debt instruments to a portfolio manager. The term signifies "in competition" and means that two or more dealers are requested to state a price (or yield) at which a transaction will take place with a customer. The expression could be: "We are asked for a comp bid on the Mohawk 7s of '99."

Using more than one dealer to arrive at a price or yield assures the customer of a fair price level.

COMPANION CMO
An offshoot of a conventional collateralized mortgage obligation (CMO) marketed almost exclusively to retail customers. In exchange for about $1/4$ point more in interest, these bonds serve as a buffer for the conventional CMOs sold as part of the same issue. In effect, if interest rates fall, these bonds will be called first; if rates rise, they will be prepaid last by underlying mortgage holders.

Because they are always disadvantaged vis-à-vis the institutional classes (tranches) of the same issue, companion CMOs are more volatile.

COMPARISON
Notice exchanged between brokers who are parties to a trade to verify and confirm details of the trade prior to settlement.

Also called "comparison sheet."

See also DK.

COMPENSATING BALANCE
A banking term used by commercial banks when they make unsecured loans. In exchange for a lower rate of interest on a loan (or even a line of credit), the borrower agrees to leave a specific minimum sum of money in a demand deposit account, bearing nominal or no interest, to "compensate" the bank for its willingness to lend money at a lower rate. Whether a compensating balance is worthwhile financially depends on the amount required and the preferential loan rate.

COMPETITIVE BASKET MARKETMAKER
See CBMM.

COMPETITIVE BID
Price and terms offered to an issuer by an underwriter. Issuer will award securities to the underwriting syndicate that provides the highest bid or most advantageous terms, in accord with prearranged conditions for the award. Many municipal, utility, and railroad securities offerings are competitive.

COMPETITIVE OPTIONS TRADER
Acronym is COT. A COT is a NYSE-registered options trader. The COT provides liquidity to the marketplace by augmenting the dealer activities of the specialist. Comparable to the marketmaker function on most other option exchanges, the COT will bid and offer, or buy and sell, for personal accounts to accommodate public orders in all option series dealt in on the NYSE.

COMPETITIVE TRADER
A member of an exchange who trades in stocks on the floor for an account in which he has an interest.
Also known as a registered trader or floor trader.

COMPLIANCE
1. The act of being in conformity with the laws, rules, and regulations of the securities industry.
2. The concept of self-policing, whereby SROs set rules and regulations to protect customers and to observe federal securities laws.
3. That department of a member firm that advises management of procedures aimed at obedience with federal, state, and local laws, and with industry standards. Such a department also enforces internal regulations of the firm.
4. As an adjective to qualify certain words, such as compliance manual, compliance standards, compliance officer, and the like.

COMPLIANCE REGISTERED OPTIONS PRINCIPAL (CROP)
Person registered as options principal who is responsible for a firm's compliance with options rules and regulations. Must make periodic reports and suggestions to senior management following periodic audits of option transactions and their supervision. Generally, a CROP may not have any sales functions.

COMPO
Contraction for: in competition. An invitation to a dealer by a customer that the dealer, in competition with other dealers, submit a competitive bid/offer for a block of securities. The dealer with the best bid/offer then completes the trade in an over-the-counter transaction.

COMPOUND INTEREST
Also called "interest on interest," it is a borrowing charge calculated on the principal amount of a loan *plus* the unpaid interest from preceding interest periods. For example, the interest on margin debit balances is compounded monthly.

Future value tables will show the amount owed, or owned, at varying compound rates of interest. To program a pocket calculator, key: CE; 1 + rate of interest as a decimal; x. Each time the = is keyed, it will compound the interest for the designated number of interest periods. Multiply by the principal amount in dollars to get the future value.

COMPOUND INTEREST BONDS (CIB)
Used of municipal bonds issued at a significant discount from face value that pay no periodic interest. At maturity, the bond is redeemed at par. The difference between the original purchase price and par value represents interest income.

See also ZERO-COUPON BOND.

COMPREHENSIVE CRIME CONTROL ACT OF 1984
This act revised some federal statutes regarding criminal practices in securities-related transactions. Among other prohibited practices, this law prohibits the counterfeiting of municipal and corporate securities, or the forging thereof. The law also extended the scope of federal bank bribery statutes to include other types of financial institutions.

COMPUTER-ASSISTED EXECUTION SYSTEM
See CAES.

COMPUTER-ASSISTED ORDER ROUTING AND EXECUTION
See CORES.

THE COMPUTER FRAUD & ABUSE ACT OF 1986
A federal law which, in general, makes it a crime for a broker/dealer to perpetrate a fraud in a securities transaction while using the facilities of a computer. The law becomes operable if more than $1,000 worth of damages is involved.

COMPUTER INFORMATION SERVICES
See CIS.

CONC
This is a commonly used contraction of the word "concession", a price discount often granted by one dealer to another as a professional courtesy for helping to distribute an offering of securities.

CONCESSION
1. Corporate underwritings: dollar remuneration per share or per bond given to members of selling group who successfully market the securities.
2. Municipal underwritings: dollar discount from public offering price. Given to members of the Municipal Securities Rulemaking Board (MSRB) who are not members of the account if they purchase bonds for their own or the accounts of customers.

CONDITIONAL CALL OPTIONS
SEC-registered contracts issued by corporations with high-coupon debt outstanding. These contracts provide purchasers with the right to receive a non-call-for-life bond with the exact terms as the outstanding bond if the outstanding bond is called. The issuer receives tax benefits, both currently and in the future, while the bondholder is assured of high income for the life of the instrument. In effect, these conditional call options are warrants providing call protection insurance to the holders of otherwise callable securities.

CONDITIONAL SALES AGREEMENT
See CSA (1).

CONDOR SPREAD
Slang used by professional traders in index options to designate certain vertical spreads. It is a condor if it is a vertical bull and bear (four positions, therefore). Condor spreads may be put or call positions.

Condor spreads do not have any strike prices in common. The two long legs are in the middle, with the short legs bounding them to imitate the wide wingspan of the condor. The spread, therefore, covers a wide range of index volatility. Example: With the OEX at 197.57, a condor spread would be long the OEX 195 and 200, and short the OEX 190 and 205. All expirations would be the same month. The four positions could be puts or calls.

CONDUIT THEORY

Nickname for IRS treatment of income received by qualified investment organizations, principally regulated investment companies. Interest and dividends received, as well as net capital gains, are passed along to investors for their personal tax liability without subjecting the investment company to federal and local taxation. Hence, term *conduit* or *pipeline*.

See also PIPELINE THEORY.

CONDUIT-TYPE CUSTOMER

Term used to describe an institutional client doing business with a broker/dealer who does not disclose the principals for whom it is transacting business. Typical conduit-type customers include banks and trust companies.

Conduit-type customers are required to represent to the broker/dealer that they know their customers and that federal securities laws and industry regulations are not being violated.

Frequently used synonym: omnibus account on an undisclosed basis.

CONFERENCE OF SECURITIES ASSOCIATIONS

See CSA (2).

CONFIDENCE INDEX

See BARRON'S CONFIDENCE INDEX.

CONFIRM

See CONFIRMATION.

CONFIRMATION

Commonly called a "confirm." The confirmation is a notice to a customer that payment is due on a purchase, or that net proceeds are available on a sale of securities.

Federal securities law requires that a confirmation be sent promptly following each purchase and sale. Notices for dividend reinvestment programs, however, may be sent on a periodic basis.

CONFLICT OF INTEREST

Term used to describe a financial situation where a person prejudicially places personal affairs before those of constituents that the person is supposed to serve or represent. The term is not limited to financial profit; it also may include social or political conflicts.

One example of a conflict of interest would be for a registered representative to purchase a security for a personal account just before recommending it to customers.

CONGLOMERATE
Description of a corporation that controls a number of other concerns in unrelated business fields. The term is descriptive only. In practice, many companies diversify business activities to moderate the effects of economic cycles without being called conglomerates.

CONGRATULATORY ORDERS
Term used to designate the myriad of orders, both buy and sell, presented to a new member of the Tokyo Stock Exchange. The principal contributor is usually the "godfather" of the new member. This token of congratulation is intended to help the new member start off business in the right direction.

CONNIE LEE
A nickname for the College Construction Loan Insurance Corporation. Connie Lee is a direct guarantor or insuror of debt issues sold by universities and colleges that have insufficient creditworthiness to market them directly. Authorized by federal legislation, Sallie Mae (Student Loan Marketing Association) is an equity participant in Connie Lee which, in turn, helps rehabilitate and modernize educational facilities without direct access to domestic bond markets.

CONSENT TO SERVICE
Legal document authorizing someone to act as attorney to accept orders of any lawful process or proceeding brought against person who signs the document. Filing of consent to service is required with each application for registration as broker/dealer or agent under Uniform Security Agent rules.
See also BLUE-SKYING.

CONSERVATOR
A court-appointed fiduciary whose responsibility it is to manage the assets of someone legally deemed to be incompetent.
In practice, the distinction between a conservator and a committee is semantic. Usually a committee is appointed if a person is physically or mentally incompetent. A conservator may be appointed for a person who is a compulsive gambler or a spendthrift.
See COMMITTEE FOR AN INCOMPETENT.

CONSIDERATION
A consideration is something that makes an informal promise legally binding; usually, it is something of value given in return for the promise.
Although the term is used both in the United States and in the United

Kingdom, in the latter it is used more frequently in conjunction with the transfer of securities for value received. For example, the transfer of ABC securities from father to son was completed for a nominal consideration.

CONSOB
A government-appointed regulatory authority in Italy with jurisdiction over that country's stock market practices. The largest stock exchange within its jurisdiction is the Milan Stock Exchange.

CONSOL
An infrequently used term for a bond with a face value of less than $1,000.
See BABY BOND.

CONSOLIDATE
Term frequently used by market technicians to designate that a previous trend (either up or down) has, after a pause, again started.

CONSOLIDATED BALANCE SHEET
A financial document showing the combined assets, liabilities, and net worth of a parent organization. The combined balance sheet does not break out the components that come from subsidiary corporations.

Most American parent corporations use consolidated balance sheets, although the annual report may represent the input, or profitability, of the subsidiaries.

CONSOLIDATED MORTGAGE BOND
Term bond with a single coupon rate of interest issued to obtain funds to refund previously issued mortgage bonds at different interest rates and maturities.

CONSOLIDATED QUOTATION SYSTEM
Acronym is CQS. A system that collects from all market centers the current bid and asked prices, with sizes, of listed stocks. These bids and sizes are then disseminated to subscribers. For example, the Quotron Financial Data Base is a CQS. Line 20 of Quotron represents current bids and offers not only from the NYSE but also from the other exchanges or the Third Market if these are better than the NYSE quotes.

CONSOLIDATED TAPE
Process whereby all transactions in listed stocks, whether made on principal exchange, other exchanges, or in OTC market, are reported on the tape of the principal exchange. At present there are two networks: Net-

work A for NYSE issues, Network B for ASE and regional exchange issues. Process is sponsored by Consolidated Tape Association, made up by exchanges and the National Association of Securities Dealers (NASD).

CONSOLIDATED TAPE ASSOCIATION
Acronym is CTA. A group of exchange and over-the-counter representatives who administer a joint industry plan for timely reporting of listed securities transactions, whether executed on an exchange or in the over-the-counter market.

CONSOLIDATED TAPE (SYSTEM) (CTS)
Acronym is CTS. An electronic system that receives and disseminates volume and last sale prices for listed stocks from all markets in which they are traded.

There are two networks: A, for trades of NYSE-listed stocks; B, for ASE-listed and regional-exchange-listed stocks. The tape display does not give the location of the trade, although it formerly did so.

CONSTANT DOLLAR PLAN
Method of formula investing. Client determines number of dollars in stocks and number in bonds in a fully invested portfolio. At stated periodic intervals, buy-sell action in either portfolio will bring accounts back to prestated dollar level.

Called "constant ratio plan" if percentages, rather than dollar amounts, are used.

CONSTANT RATIO PLAN
A program of formula investing. The investor establishes a ratio of fixed income to equity securities to be maintained in a portfolio, and fixed time schedule for portfolio adjustment. Example: An investor sets a 60–40 bond to equity ratio with a semiannual period of adjustment. Every six months, the investor will sell either bonds or stocks and reinvest the proceeds to return to the original preestablished ratio. The procedure presumes that bond and stock prices move in opposite directions.

CONSTRUCTION & DEVELOPMENT REIT
A mortgage real estate investment trust that lends short-term funds to builders and developers of commercial and residential properties.

Abbreviation: C&D REIT.

CONSUMER CREDIT PROTECTION ACT OF 1968
This federal law requires that lenders provide borrowers with current (and future) terms and conditions associated with interest charges and expenses. It is also called the "Truth-in-Lending Act."

SEC Rule 10b-16 requires that such a truth-in-lending statement be sent to customers who open margin accounts. Periodic updates are also required if rates or conditions are changed.

CONSUMER MARKETS
Industry term used to designate the retail part of the securities industry, as opposed to the institutional (or capital markets) part of the industry. Many member firms divide their sales efforts and operations into a "consumer markets" and a "capital markets" side.

CONSUMER PRICE INDEX (CPI)
The CPI is compiled monthly by a government agency of the United States. The CPI, which is based on the comparative prices of a market basket of consumer items—including food, clothes, shelter, transportation, and entertainment—gives users an insight into the relative cost of these items on a month-to-month basis. Thus, CPI also shows inflationary or deflationary trends.

The CPI is also important because it is used as the basis for the assignment of Social Security cost-of-living adjustments (COLAs)

CONTANGO
1. In the English securities markets, an arrangement whereby a trader can carry over a long or short securities position from one account trading period to another without payment or delivery. See ACCOUNT DAY.
2. In American commodities markets, term is used if futures contracts trade at higher prices than spot prices. The difference is usually the carrying charges involved in a future delivery of the commodity.

CONTANGO DAY
See CONTANGO (1).

CONTEMPT OF COURT
An action, or the omission of an action, that interferes with the orderly administration of justice. Persons declared in contempt of court may be fined or imprisoned.

Generally, contempt of court is a misdemeanor. Do not confuse with obstruction of justice—such as perjury, falsification of evidence, suborning a juror, and the like—which is usually a felony.

CONTINGENT DEFERRED SALES LOAD (CDSL)
CDSL is a term used in the mutual fund industry to designate a sales charge (load) that is charged not when the customer buys the fund but, on a contingent basis, when the fund is redeemed.

Funds that charge a CDSL are regulated under SEC Rule 12b-1 of the Investment Company Act. The deferred sales charge is generally applied on a sliding scale; for example, 5% if redemption is in the 1st year, 4% if redemption is in the 2nd, and so on.

Most funds that have contingent deferred sales load—also called a "back-end load" or "exit fee"—also apply a distribution fee on an annual basis to compensate the fund for advertising costs and to compensate registered representatives (RRs).

CONTINGENT IMMUNIZATION

Term used to describe a bond portfolio management strategy. In the beginning, the bond portfolio is so managed and traded to maximize gains and return in excess of that achievable by passive management.

A minimum acceptable yield is set (called the "base yield"). If the return drops to the minimum yield, the portfolio is immunized in the usual manner (using the duration of the bonds) to lock in the minimum yield thereafter.

CONTINGENT ORDER

Order for the purchase or sale of a security and the sale or purchase of another if the swap can be made at a stipulated price difference.

See also SWAP.

CONTINGENT VALUE RIGHTS (CVR)

An inducement used in takeover agreements to entice holders to surrender their shares. CVR is a supplemental provision entitling the holders to receive additional, future compensation if the company meets a predetermined financial or stock price goal.

CONTINUATION

Term used on the International Stock Exchange of the United Kingdom and the Republic of Ireland to describe the fact that large institutional investors who bought and sold the same securities on a continuous basis could aggregate their trades and thus be eligible for reduced commissions. In effect, the normal 1/2% rate could be reduced to 1/8%.

Continuation was based on the fact of fixed commissions and certain rebates. Following the "big bang" on October 27, 1986, all commissions on the ISE are negotiable; thus, the term is no longer in common usage.

CONTINUING COMMISSIONS

In the past, contractual mutual funds were popular with some investors. It was the practice to pay continuing commissions on such plans to retired registered representatives (RRs) or their widows or beneficiaries if this was stipulated in the contracts between the RRs and member firm.

Although NYSE and NASD rules differ slightly on this matter, such continuing commissions are not permitted on new business or new customers introduced to the firm.

CONTINUOUSLY OFFERED LONGER-TERM SECURITIES
See COLTS.

CONTINUOUS NET SETTLEMENT (CNS)
Prevalent method of clearing and settling securities transactions. National Securities Clearing Corporation interposes itself between brokers, thereby establishing a securities balance account. Broker's balance account is adjusted upward or downward each day, depending on whether the firm was a net buyer or seller on that day. Money balances are adjusted similarly, and shares or funds can be withdrawn according to net balance.

Opposite: window settlement whereby seller delivers securities to buyer and receives payment.

CONTRA BROKER
Broker on the other side of the transaction. Thus, buying broker has selling broker as contra broker.

Also spelled as one word.

CONTRACT NOTE
In England, the equivalent of the confirmation notice sent by American broker/dealers following a purchase or sale.

See CONFIRMATION.

CONTRACT REPO
See TERM REPO.

CONTRACT SHEET
Prepared daily by Securities Industry Automation Corporation (SIAC) from information given by brokers and contra brokers. Brokers compare their transaction records to prepare for settlement. Items not in agreement with records are DKd, slang for don't know, or marked QT, questioned trade. Discrepancies are usually resolved quickly so settlement may be made on proper day.

CONTRACTUAL PLAN

Method of periodic accumulation of mutual fund shares through the use of a plan company or a participating unit investment trust. Client agrees to purchase a fixed dollar amount of the fund by periodic investments over a 10-year or 15-year period. In return, client receives certain plan features and often receives decreasing term life insurance as part of program of financial planning.

Also called "prepaid plans."

See also FRONT-END LOAD, LOAD SPREAD OPTION, PLAN COMPLETION INSURANCE, and PLAN COMPANY.

CONTRA PARTY

The party to the other side of a trade. Example: To a seller, the contra party is the buyer.

In practice, contra broker is the more commonly used expression.

CONTRARIAN

In the financial industry, a contrarian is someone who—as a general rule—takes an opinion that is in opposition to that taken by the majority.

Examples of a contrarian approach to the market are myriad. For example, investors who buy depressed stocks for a turnaround are contrarians. Investors who sell into a rising market (to preserve profits) and buy into a falling market (to buy undervalued securities) are contrarians.

As a general rule, contrarians are intermediate- to longer-term investors who buck current trends for longer-term rewards.

CONTROLLED ADJUSTABLE RATE PREFERRED STOCK

Acronym is CARP. A preferred stock whose dividend is periodically adjusted to reflect current Treasury security rates plus a premium.

"Controlled" adds this concept: The issuer promises to maintain a base of assets to ensure that the company will be able to pay the adjusted rate dividend.

CONTROLLER

Term that designates the work area of a broker/dealer responsible for preparing, maintaining, and auditing the firm and customer financial reports, and the records and statements of accounts, as prescribed by federal law and SEC rules.

Often spelled: comptroller.

CONTROLLERS DEPARTMENT

A work area in a broker/dealer organization that is responsible for preparing and maintaining the firm and the customer financial reports, plus records and statements as prescribed by law or SEC rules.

Also called the "controller."

CONTROL PERSON

Generic term for someone who can influence corporate decisions. Control can arise from voting power, because person owns 10% or more of corporation's voting shares, or because person is director or elected officer of corporation.

Also called "affiliated person" in certain contexts.

See also CONTROL STOCK.

CONTROL STOCK

Voting shares owned by a control person. Shares may have been acquired by private purchase, purchased in the public marketplace, or by bequest or gift. Concept usually applies to the aggregate shares held by family members.

See also CONTROL PERSON.

CONVENIENCE SHELF

An abbreviated registration statement for a public offering of securities. A convenience shelf can become effective under SEC Rule 415 without pricing information and the names of nonmanaging underwriters; however, the size of the offering cannot be increased.

Often called "phantom shelf."

Note: Do not confuse with the traditional shelf registration, which requires more information and also permits greater versatility to the registrant.

See also SHELF REGISTRATION STATEMENT.

CONVENTIONAL OPTION

Put or call contract negotiated outside a listed option marketplace. Because of a limited secondary market, very few conventional options are negotiated.

CONVENTIONAL PASS-THROUGH

A security, issued by a savings bank, a savings and loan, or a commercial bank, that represents an interest in a pool of mortgages. There is no government guarantee of interest and principal payments, although such conventional pass-throughs often are insured commercially.

Antonym: modified pass-through, which is U.S. government guaranteed.

CONVERSION

1. Feature permitting owners of certain bonds and preferred stock to exchange these securities for a fixed number of common shares.

2. Feature of many mutual funds whereby owners of one fund may exchange shares for shares of other funds under same management without additional sales charges.
3. Illegal use of assets held in trust for another for one's personal advantage.
See also CONVERSION RATIO and FAMILY OF FUNDS.

CONVERSION BOND
See CONVERTIBLE GILTS.

CONVERSION PARITY
Mathematical statement of equality between value of underlying common stock and theoretical value of convertible security. For example, if a bond is convertible into 40 shares of common stock and stock has market value of $22 per share, conversion parity is $880; that is, 40 times $22.
See also CONVERSION PREMIUM and CONVERSION RATIO.

CONVERSION PREMIUM
Dollars in excess of market price of a convertible security over conversion parity. May also be stated as a percent. For example, convertible bond is selling at $990. Conversion parity is $880. Premium is $110, $990 minus $880. Or, premium is 12.5%, $110 divided by $880.

Percent of conversion premium provides critical insight into risk of ownership of convertibles. Low premium centers risk on changes in market value of underlying common stock; high premium centers risk on convertible as a fixed-income security.

CONVERSION PRICE
Fixed-dollar value often used by corporation to state conversion ratio of convertible securities. For example, a bond is convertible into common shares at $40 per share. Thus, conversion ratio is par value, $1,000, divided by $40, or 25 shares.

Conversion price is theoretical and presumes convertible selling at par. Conversion feature goes with security, and convertible may be exchanged for common stock at option of holder.

As a general rule, if company splits stock or pays a stock dividend, the conversion price will change because convertible will be exchangeable for a larger number of shares.

CONVERSION RATIO
Statement of the relationship between a convertible bond and the number of common shares into which it is convertible. Example: A bond with

a face value of $1,000 is convertible into 40 shares of common stock. As a ratio:

$$\frac{\$1,000 \ (1 \ \text{bond})}{40 \ (\text{shares})} = X \ (\text{Conversion Price})$$

This shows that the theoretical conversion price of the common stock is $25.

See CONVERSION PARITY to find the practical application of conversion ratio to the actual market prices of the convertible bond and the underlying common stock.

CONVERT AND PARTICIPATE ORDERS
See CAP ORDERS.

CONVERTIBLE
Class of corporation securities that is convertible into a fixed number of shares of other securities of same corporation. Convertibles usually are debentures or preferred shares that may be exchanged for a fixed number of common shares.

CONVERTIBLE ADJUSTABLE PREFERRED STOCK
Acronym is CAPS. A class of preferred stock that (1) has an adjustable dividend rate that is periodically pegged to Treasury security rates and (2) permits the holder to exchange the CAPS for common stock equal in market value to the par value of the preferred.

CAPS usually permit the issuer, if CAPS are tendered, to redeem for cash, rather than cause an undue dilution of the common stock of the company.

CONVERTIBLE GILTS
English Treasury obligations (gilts) with an option attached, whereby the holder may exchange the present holding for a longer-maturity issue under certain circumstances. This conversion privilege is the equivalent of a European option in that it is exercisable only on a certain date.

The longer-maturity bond is called a "conversion bond" and may or may not be in existence at the time the holder exercises the option.

CONVERTIBLE UNIT INVESTMENT TRUST
See CUIT.

CONVEXITY
A term used in conjunction with duration to measure interest-rate risk on intermediate- and longer-term bonds with coupon interest. The terms do not apply to zero-coupon bonds.

Duration is defined as the midpoint (in time) of the present values of the cash flows from a bond. This is a measure of interest-rate risk.

If interest-rate changes cause the midpoint to shorten (the duration is shortened), the bond is said to have "positive" convexity. If interest-rate changes cause the duration to lengthen, the bond is said to have a "negative" convexity. Callable bonds often have negative convexity, and for this reason increase the interest-rate risk if they are selling at a premium.

COO
See CHIEF OPERATING OFFICER.

COOKED BOOKS
Slang: The financial records of a company have been falsified to persuade investors to purchase or to achieve unrealistic profits. Generally, the expression implies an intent to deceive.

Note: Do not confuse with legitimate accounting practices that temporarily provide a more profitable picture of the company.

Such accounting practices always are included in the footnotes to the financial statements.

COOLING-OFF PERIOD
Commonly used expression for statutory 20-day period that 1933 Act interposes between filing of preliminary registration and effective date of public sale. SEC may shorten or lengthen period. Time is used by SEC to review registration and by issuer and underwriter to examine issue and registration statement more closely.

Also called "cooling period."

CO-OPS
See BANKS FOR CO-OPERATIVES.

COORDINATION
A form of eligibility requirement for the public offering of securities under the blue-sky laws of many states. If registration is required in a state, and coordination is the method prescribed, an offering may be made to citizens domiciled within that state concurrent with the effectiveness of the issuer's SEC-filed registration statement.

COPs
Acronym for municipal certificates of participation. The word is popularly used in the plural as COPs. COPs are similar to corporate collateral trust bonds; that is, a municipality enters into a lease-purchase arrangement for such things as computers or telephone systems, with the

equipment used as collateral for the financing. The equipment is usually paid off in 7–11 years from operating budgets of the municipality and thus does not become part of the bonded debt of the municipality.

COPENHAGEN STOCK MARKET
One of four stock markets in Scandinavia, this Danish exchange is better known for bond, rather than stock, trading. For trading purposes, the Copenhagen Stock Market is open on weekdays from 9:30 A.M. until 3:30 P.M. and all trading is done electronically. Contract settlement is due on the third working day after the trade date (except Friday trades, which settle the following Tuesday).

COPPER A TIP
English marketplace expression that means to do the opposite of what touts advise. In effect, it is the same as the United States concept of contrarian investing strategies. Thus, when English investors were given "golden information" by advisors of dubious stature, they turn the gold into a baser metal. From the verb *to copper;* that is, to cover with copper.

CORBEILLE
The French term for a trading pit, *corbeille* signified the old location of securities trading on the Paris Bourse. Pit trading on the bourse survived for more than 160 years, but it has now been supplanted by electronic methods. In the old pits, bids and offers were shouted aloud in a way that is similar to trading on the U.S. commodities marketplaces.

CORE CAPITAL
The term is used in conjunction with the financial requirements of thrift institutions. Core capital is the bank's common stock, surplus accounts, perpetual preferred stock, and minority interests in consolidated subsidiaries. In effect, core capital is real and reliable money derived from stockholder equity. Under proposals from the Federal Home Loan Bank Board, core capital must equal at least 2% of total assets.

CORES
Acronym for Computer-Assisted Order Routing and Execution System. CORES are used for the routing and handling of orders on the Tokyo Stock Exchange. The concept is similar to that of the DOT system on the NYSE, in that orders for designated stocks can be entered, recorded, and executed by pairing the order with comparable contra orders at that trading post.

A CORNER
See CORNERING THE MARKET.

CORNERING THE MARKET

A person, or group of persons working in concert, acquires such a large position in a security that persons who have made short sales of the security cannot cover without paying sharply inflated prices.

CORPORATE EQUIVALENT YIELD

Yield on a corporate bond selling at par that must be achieved to equal the yield on a government security selling at a discount. Cash flow on discounted government security reflects tax on interest income and maximum corporate tax on capital gains.

Used by government bond dealers in their offering sheets to show possible advantage, or disadvantage, of an investment in government bonds at the offered price.

CORPORATE FINANCING COMMITTEE

Standing committee that assists the Board of Governors of the National Association of Securities Dealers. It examines documents filed with the SEC by underwriters to determine the fairness of the markup.

CORPORATE INCOME FUND

A fixed-unit investment trust. Portfolio usually contains fixed-income securities. Most CIFs feature monthly payment of net investment income. Portfolio is supervised but not managed.

CORPORATION

An assocation, usually of many persons, chartered by a state to conduct business within that state. Federal government also charters corporations.

Corporation is a legal person and thus is independent of life of underlying persons and provides owners with limited personal liability for debts of the corporation.

Difference between corporation and partnership is often very close. Legal advice is required for appropriate tax treatment of income.

CORPUS

Latin: body.
1. The assets underlying a trust agreement.
2. Of a debt security, the principal amount, as opposed to the coupons representing future interest payments.

CORRESPONDENT

A broker/dealer, bank, or other financial services organization that provides services to other organizations in markets to which the other organization does not have access.

Securities firms may have correspondents in foreign countries or on exchanges of which they are not a member. Usually correspondents are linked by private wire.

COST AVERAGING
See DOLLAR COST AVERAGING.

COST OF CARRY
Out-of-pocket expense paid by investor during period that a security position is maintained. For example, client with long margin position has a cost of carry in margin interest; client with short margin position has cost of carry in dividends paid to the lender of the borrowed securities. Although cost of carry does not include the possible investment value of funds tied up in accrued interest or equity tied up in a short account, these must be considered in computing true return on an investment.

Also called "carry."

COST OF FUNDS (COF)
1. In the brokerage industry, COF is used to designate a broker/dealer's expense in borrowing money to finance inventory positions.
2. In the banking industry, it is the expense of obtaining deposits; that is, the interest that must be paid to finance loans to borrowers.
3. In mortgage banking (under the California Plan), it is a three-month blended rate of interest payable by the district savings and loan associations in that Federal Home Loan Bank (Freddie Mac) area.

COST OF GOODS SOLD
Accounting entry that represents the costs of material, labor, and other production costs of goods sold during an accounting period.

General practice is to make a separate entry on corporation income statements of depreciation of plant and equipment, and sales and administrative expenses. In this way, the cost of goods sold can be compared more exactly from one accounting period to another.

COST PURCHASE ACCOUNTING
An accounting system that permits a corporation that owns less than 20% of another corporation's stock to include in its own income only the cash dividends received from this investment.

Antonym: equity purchase accounting.

COT
See COMPETITIVE OPTIONS TRADER.

COUGARS
Acronym for Certificate on Government Receipts. Trade name for the former A.G. Becker Paribas's instruments evidencing interests in principal or coupon payments to be made in the future on specific issues of U.S. Treasury bonds. Modeled on the Merrill Lynch TIGRs and Salomon Brothers CATS.

COUNTRY FUND
A broad name for an investment company whose portfolio holdings are limited to common stock concerns domiciled in one specific country. For examples, in 1989 and 1990 there were many closed-end investment companies making initial public offerings: The Spain Fund, The Germany Fund, The Italy Fund, The Korea Fund, and so forth.

COUNTRY OF ORIGIN
Term used in the foreign currency option market to designate the sovereign government that issues the particular currency underlying an option.

COUPON
1. Interest rate, expressed as a percentage of par or face value, that issuer promises to pay over lifetime of debt security. Coupon rate is annual. Normal practice is to pay half the amount semiannually.
2. Small, detachable certificate that is removed from main certificate and presented for payment of bond interest.
     See also BEARER SECURITY.

COUPON BOND
Bond with small detachable certificates to be presented as evidence of interest payments due that is not otherwise registered in name of owner.

   Industry rules presume that municipal bond transactions are for coupon bonds unless otherwise agreed before completion of trade; or unless "registered" is the only available form.

COUPON PASS
Term used of the daily activities of the Fed's FOMC (Federal Open Market Committee) as it endeavors to fine-tune money and credit in the U.S. economy. Under this concept, the "desk" (FOMC's trading arm) canvasses dealer banks and nonbank dealers to determine their long/short inventory in Treasuries. Based on this information, the FOMC will arrange to buy-sell certain specific issues (coupons) to either inject or withdraw bank reserves and thus alter available credit.

COUPON ROLLOVER DATE

The quarterly or semiannual date on which a new interest rate will be established for payments on a floating-rate security. Depending on the issuer, the new rate will be pegged at a specific percentage above LIBOR for Eurofloaters, or above the U.S. Treasury bill rate for domestic floaters.

COUPONS-UNDER-BOOK-ENTRY-SAFEKEEPING

See CUBES.

COVENANT

Those portions of indenture or bond resolution in which issuer promises to do, or not to do, certain activities. Covenants are for benefit of bondholders and may, with permission of bondholders, be voided or changed.
Also called "restrictive covenant."

COVER

1. Term used in investment banking to describe the difference, either in net interest cost or dollars, between the winning and the second-place bid. For example, "The cover was only 0.15% in net interest costs on the Ajax deal."
2. Verb designating a closing transaction on an option, future, or short-sale contract. For example, "I covered my short position at a profit of $3 per share." Also used of short against box when client instructs broker to deliver box securities against short position.
3. Of corporations: the ability to pay fixed charges on debt securities by earned income. Important in ratings of bonds.

COVER BID

This is the second-highest bid in a competitive distribution. The spread between the winning bid and the cover bid gives an insight into the validity of judgments of value made for the underlying security.

COVERED BEAR

U.K. term for someone who sells short versus a long position, and who intends not to cover the short with delivery of the long position but with the purchase of stock at a price lower than the short sale price. The strategy, if completed in the same account period, permits settlement by a single check for the profit or loss.

COVERED OPTION

If option writer has another security position that protects the broker against financial risk, the short option is said to be covered. For example, owner of 300 shares that are held by broker sells 3 call options against long stock position. Cover may not fully protect broker; in which

155

case, broker will mark to the market. Short covered option itself, however, requires no margin.

See also NAKED OPTION and UNCOVERED OPTION.

COVERED STRANGLE

An equity option position in which the writer of a straddle (short call and short put) is also long the underlying stock. Thus, in exchange for two premiums, the writer accepts the risk of being called or put.

The term is also used of a short combination, with the call strike price above the current market price of the underlying, and the put strike price below the current market price of the underlying. While such a strangle has less risk than a straddle write, it also generates less premiums because both options are out-of-the-money.

CP

Common abbreviation for commercial paper. CP is short-term discounted debt instruments issued by corporations (and some municipalities) to meet current cash requirements. Corporate CP is exempt from registration under the '33 Act if it initially has 270 days or less to maturity.

CPI

See CONSUMER PRICE INDEX.

CPO

See COMMODITY POOL OPERATOR.

CQS

See CONSOLIDATED QUOTATION SYSTEM.

CRAM-DOWN DEAL

Slang expression used by investment bankers if a merger is so arranged that shareholders have no option but to accept the compensation offered. For example, in a merger or LBO, if stockholders are offered only "junk bonds"—with no choice of cash or stock—it would be an example of a "cram-down" deal.

CRASH

Street term for a sharp and sudden plunge in securities prices, usually the prices of common stocks. As a general rule, a crash is accompanied by large trading volume. The October 19, 1987, event in which the DJIA dropped by 508 points (on a base of 2,700) and trading volume jumped to over 600 million shares versus an average volume of 200 million, is generally conceded to have been a crash.

The term *spike* is used of similar sudden plunges in the price and rise in the trading volume of individual securities. Spike, on the other hand, is also used of upward price movements.

CRAZY MARY
Nickname for the common shares of Community Psychiatric Centers, a large corporate owner of mental hospitals. The nickname is derived from its NYSE ticker symbol: CMY.

CRD
See CENTRAL REGISTRATION DEPOSITORY.

CREDIT AGREEMENT
Document prepared by a broker/dealer and presented to every customer who uses credit to purchase, carry, or trade securities with that firm. A copy of this agreement—which details the terms, conditions, and arrangements by which credit will be provided, the margin to be deposited or maintained, and when and how interest is charged—must be given to each credit customer of the firm. SEC Rule 10b-16 obligates the broker/dealer to give this document to the customer.

CREDIT BALANCE
1. In cash accounts: monies on deposit with broker or uninvested proceeds of sales. May be withdrawn at will.
2. In margin accounts: proceeds of short sales. If margin account is mixed (i.e., account contains both long and short positions), broker usually nets credit and debit balances.
3. Free credit balances may be withdrawn at will. Additional credit balances required by Reg-T on short sales are not free credit balances.
   See also SECURITIES INVESTORS PROTECTION CORPORATION (for treatment of credit balances).

CREDIT DEPARTMENT
1. General term for the margin department of a broker/dealer.
   See also MARGIN DEPARTMENT.
2. Specific term for the work area of a broker/dealer or a commodity broker who investigates the creditworthiness and the line of credit to be extended to customers.

CREDIT ENHANCEMENT

A term used by credit analysts to identify letters of credit or surety bonds or other forms of insurance that back debt instruments. Usually such backing raises the rating of the bond to AAA.

Such credit enhancement is used both by issuers whose credit rating is low and by issuers who have high credit ratings but who wish to enhance it for investor appeal and thus be in a position to issue debt at lower coupon interest rates.

Although credit enhancement is paid for by the issuer, it is ultimately paid for by the buyer in the form of lowered rates of return.

CREDITOR

A person, whether real or legal, to whom a debt is owed. Example: In a margin account, the broker/dealer becomes a creditor.

CREDIT SHELTER TRUST

A trust that provides for the maximum use of the $192,800 tax credit (in effect, exempting $600,000 from estate taxation) upon the death of a U.S. person who is also a spouse. By placing $600,000 in the trust, these assets become aftertax dollars. They can then be used for the benefit of the surviving spouse and other beneficiaries. The remainder of the estate passes tax free to the surviving spouse to be subject to estate tax upon his or her death. Thus, two $192,800 estate tax credits will be obtained.

It is not unusual to place insurance in such a trust and thus take it out of the estate of the decedent.

Professional tax advice and legal counsel are needed.

CREDIT SPREAD

A long and short position in options of the same class (puts, or calls). It is called a "credit spread" if the net premiums (plus the premium received minus the premium paid) results in a credit in the client's account.

Also called a "money spread."

Credit spreads become profitable if the premium differential so narrows that the client can close the position at a lower cost than the proceeds of the spread.

CREDIT UNION

A state or federally chartered savings institution that is owned, managed, and operated as a cooperative association by its members for their own financial benefit. Eligible member depositors and borrowers are linked by a common interest, be it occupational, fraternal, educational, or residential. The primary purpose of a credit union is to lend money to its member depositors at relatively low rates of interest.

CREDIT WATCH
The term used by Moody's and Standard & Poor's or other credit-rating services to designate the fact that an issuer's debt securities may be subject to a ratings review (usually a lowering).

Such credit watches are announced by the rating services following some economic event, such as a class action suit, a proposed issuance of junk bonds, a merger, and the like that could lower the creditworthiness of the issuer.

CREEPING TENDER OFFER
Term used by the SEC to describe the private or open market purchase of a significant percentage of an issuer's stock by one or more persons acting in concert. The purpose is to gain control without the benefit of a prior public notification by means of a proxy statement.

CRIIMI MAE
Popular term for CRI Insured Mortgage Association, an exchange-listed company (CMM) operating as a real estate subsidiary of CRI, Inc. As a REIT, Criimi Mae manages real estate limited partnerships specializing in federally insured mortgages on multifamily housing.

CRI INSURED MORTGAGE ASSOCIATION, INC.
See CRIIMI MAE.

CROP
See COMPLIANCE REGISTERED OPTIONS PRINCIPAL.

TO CROSS
Broker acts as agent for both a buyer and a seller in a completed transaction. Example: A floor broker with both a buy and sell order for the same amount of shares, after following proper floor procedures, completes both transactions by having her customers buy and sell to each other.

CROSS-CURRENCY INTEREST-RATE SWAP
See CIRCUS.

CROSSED MARKET
If any broker's bid is higher than the lowest offer of another broker, or vice versa, the market is said to be crossed. This occasionally happens. The rules of the National Association of Securities Dealers (NASD) for NASD Automated Quotations (NASDAQ) forbid dealers to cross the market intentionally.

CROSS-HEDGE

An attempt to limit or prevent monetary loss in an established security or commodity futures position by buying or selling another security or futures contract in a different instrument which has similar market reactions. Example: A client has a long position in GNMA pass-throughs. A cross-hedge could be effected by the sale of U.S. Treasury note futures. A client who has written a call on 90-day CDs could cross-hedge by purchasing 13-week U.S. Treasury bill put options.

CROSSOVER POINT

Term used of limited partnerships to describe a point in time when the income received exceeds the cost of maintenance, operations, production, and so forth. In effect, the time when the enterprise is no longer a tax shelter but generates taxable income.

CROSS-TRADING

In the United States, cross-trading designates the internalization of commodities orders; that is, executing customer orders against in-house proprietary orders without exposing them to other bids and offers in open outcry in the commodity pits. The practice is illegal.

In Japan, the practice is legal and is known by the name "baikai." Baikai order crossing is permitted for customer orders after the market is closed but only if the futures merchant traded the same number of contracts at the same price during the market day.

CROWD

Exchange term for those members who come to the post to seek an execution and who, because no execution is currently available, remain there. They, together-with the specialist, form a crowd.

See also TRADING POST.

CROWN JEWEL DEFENSE

A management strategy to thwart a hostile takeover. The strategy centers on an agreement to sell to a third party the company's most valuable asset, or assets—hence the term—to make the company less attractive to the raider.

Such a defense will bring stockholder suits if the asset is sold for less than its fair market value.

CROWN LOAN

The term is taken from the name of Henry Crown, a Chicago industrialist who pioneered the concept. A crown loan is a loan from a high-bracketed family member to a lower-bracketed family member. When the lower-bracketed borrower invests the money, it is taxed at his or her lower rate.

A 1984 Supreme Court decision validated the concept, but only if the loan is made at prevailing interest rates.

The practice has little applicability following TRA 86 because the investment income of the borrower (after the first $1,000 of income) is taxed at the parent's tax bracket.

CRT
Initials for cathode ray tube. Although in recent years other video display devices have been used to project prices and news, the initials CRT are still in use. A form of CRT is in use to administer the principal examination to officers of broker/dealer organizations.

CRUMMEY TRUST
A legal instrument, named for its originator, which enables its beneficiary to accept valuable assets on a continuing basis from any person and to provide that donor with an annual exclusion from federal gift taxes. Characteristically, this trust is drawn for the benefit of a minor and it has the power to receive additional donations by parents and relatives over the ensuing years. Each contributor is entitled to the yearly maximum $10,000 gift exclusion.

CRWNS
Acronym (pronounced "crowns") for currency related warrants to acquire certain U.S. Treasury note securities. These warrants, with one- and two-year expiration dates, permit purchase of U.S. Treasury 11⅝s of '94 at designated fixed prices. The exercise price, while stated in U.S. dollars, is denominated in deutsche marks at the exchange rate of 3.152 per dollar.

CS
A frequently used abbreviation for common stock.

CSA
1. Acronym for Conditional Sales Agreement. Often used in the private placement of equipment trust certificates. The issuer pledges a minimal amount of equity; however, title to the equipment does not pass to the issuer until the entire debt is repaid.
2. Acronym for Conference of Securities Associations. CSA is the Japanese counterpart of the Securities Industry Association (SIA) in the United States. Neither organization has governmental status but is used primarily for financial discussions and mutual member interest—although the government may listen to their suggestions.

CSA is composed of:
The Securities Dealers Association of Japan.
The Bond Underwriters Association.
The Investment Trust Association.
The Tokyo Stock Exchange.
The Association of Tokyo Stock Exchange Regular Members.

CSD

Abbreviation for "central school district," a quasi-government entity created by a municipality to provide educational services to its residents on the grade and high school levels. As such, the CSD is authorized to issue bonds for construction and renovation of educational facilities, and such bonds are serviced by *ad valorem* real estate taxes (plus tuition charges in some cases) levied on residential and commercial real estate in the district.

As a general rule, CSD bonds form "overlapping debt" for the municipality that created the school district, and, in the event that revenues are insufficient, the municipality will be obliged to make up for the shortfall.

CSD bonds are always so designated on the bond certificate.

CSE

See CINCINNATI STOCK EXCHANGE.

CSFB

An identifier for Credit Suisse First Boston Corporation. CSFB is a partnership to foster the commercial banking and investment banking interest of its two founders, Credit Suisse and First Boston Corporation. Although this Europartnership is independent of either founder, it is influenced significantly by the economic and political maneuvers of its parents.

CSFB is a major player and a significant primary and secondary market participant in European securities markets.

CSI LEVY

CSI (Council for the Securities Industry) is a sort of watchdog and ombudsman for the public interest in the financial community of the United Kingdom. To support its activities, there was a levy of 60p (about $1) on customer transactions of 5,000 pounds or more. Often this levy was absorbed by the brokerage firm.

Although the levy is still charged, the role of the CSI was greatly curtailed with the passage of the 1986 Financial Services Act in Britain.

CSR

See CLIENT SERVICE REPRESENTATIVE.

CT

Abbreviation for certificate; that is, a debt instrument with an original maturity of up to one year.

CT also is used interchangeably with CTE, the more common abbreviation for certificate. Here certificate means the engraved paper used to evidence equity or debt participation in the issuer.

CTA

See CONSOLIDATED TAPE ASSOCIATION and COMMODITY TRADING ADVISOR.

CTF

See CT.

CTM

See COMING TO ME.

CTS

See CONSOLIDATED TAPE (SYSTEM).

CUBES

Acronym for Coupons-Under-Book-Entry-Safekeeping. CUBES was a U.S. Treasury program in effect from January 5 through April 30, 1987, whereby holders of physical coupons stripped from selected government bonds were able to include them for book-entry ownership at a Federal Reserve Bank. Through CUBES, over 400,000 physical coupons were made automatically payable at maturity by the Fed's electronic system. CUBES are not included in nor interchangeable with the Federal Reserve's STRIPS program.

CUBS

Acronym for Calls Underwritten by Swanbrook. CUBS are annual options on zero-coupon Treasury securities that result in a guarantee of annual interest rate to holders exercising them at expiration. Swanbrook Limited Partnership is a Nevada-based investment firm and is the issuer of these call options. Swanbrook uses the custodial and processing facilities of Security Pacific National Bank of Los Angeles (SEPACO). The calls are fully covered by the underlying instrument.

See also BEARS.

CUFF QUOTE

Slang: an educated guess about the bid and asked prices for an issue. A cuff quote is given without actually checking the current market with marketmakers.

CUIT

Acronym for Convertible Unit Investment Trust. This was an E. F. Hutton product created to provide a steady income stream and potential capital growth through investment in a diversified portfolio of convertible bonds and convertible preferred stocks.

CULPEPER SWITCH

The computerized message switching center located in Culpeper, Virginia, to transfer federal funds and U.S. Treasury securities between member banks of the Federal Reserve System.

CUM

1. Abbreviation for cumulative preferred stock. The abbreviation is used in Moody's and in Standard & Poor's stock guides. Generally, however, the abbreviation is omitted in newspaper listings because almost all issues of preferred stock are cumulative.
2. Latin: with. Used to designate that a transaction will be accompanied by a distribution. For example, cum rights, or cum dividend (q.v.).

CUM DIVIDEND

Cum is Latin for "with." Securities are sold with a dividend if the current buyer is entitled to the next dividend to be paid. Normally, securities are sold with a dividend if the trade is made on or prior to the fifth business day before the company's preestablished record date. Transactions for cash (i.e., same-day settlement) and for mutual funds are exceptions to the general rule.

CUM RIGHTS

In Latin, cum means "with." Normally, buyers will receive rights accompanying the purchase of securities if the trade is made on or prior to the date on the prospectus accompanying a rights distribution.

CUMULATIVE PREFERRED

A feature of certain preferred shares, established by the issuing corporation, assuring the holder that, if any preferred dividends are passed by the corporation, such passed dividends plus any current dividend will be paid to the preferred stockholder before any dividend is paid to common stockholders. Almost all currently issued preferred shares are cumulative.

CUMULATIVE VOTING

Privilege occasionally given to common shareholders by the corporation's charter. The privilege permits shareholders to allocate their votes in any manner they please. Thus, a holder of 100 shares—if five persons are to be elected to the board—may assign his 500 votes (100 shares times five vacancies) to a candidate of his choice. Through cumulative voting, minority shareholders can, if they act in concert, make sure that at least one or more persons on the board will represent their interests.

CUPS

Acronym for Canadian/U.S. Principal Securities. This Bankers Trust product was designed for retail speculators in the currency markets. CUPS are a debt security of a Canadian issuer. The holder has the right to receive payment in either Canadian or U.S. funds but need not decide which currency to request until just before the maturity date.

CURB

Nickname for American Stock Exchange. Prior to 1921, the ASE was known as the New York Curb Exchange because it worked outdoors on Broad Street—literally on the curb. Oldtimers still refer to the ASE as the Curb.

CURB TRADING

1. Securities industry expression for transactions that take place on the American Stock Exchange. The ASE or AMEX—as it has been known since its move to Trinity Place in New York in 1921—was originally known as the New York Curb Exchange.
2. The practice on some commodities exchanges—often considered improper—of liquidating positions by exchange members after the closing bell signaling the end of trading for the day.

CURRENCY EXCHANGE WARRANT (CEW)

CEWs are a Bear Stearns product designed to appeal to currency speculators who believe that the Japanese yen will lose value in terms of the American dollar during the five-year life of this warrant. The warrant is purchasable in conjunction with a debt security and has a separate premium, which is used to offset the cost of borrowing. If the dollar rises versus the yen in a significant way, holders of the warrant can exercise it anytime during the five-year period.

CURRENCY IN CIRCULATION

A popular misnomer for money in circulation. Currency is only coins and paper money. Money is a broader term and includes demand deposits, which are balances in checking accounts.

CURRENT ASSET
Item of value owned by a corporation that either is cash or can become cash within one year. Most common current asset entries on a corporation's balance sheet: cash, marketable securities, accounts receivable, and inventory.

CURRENT COUPON
See GINNIE MAE PASS-THROUGH; CURRENT PRODUCTION RATE.

CURRENT COUPON BOND
Any bond, whether corporate, municipal, or government, whose coupon rate of interest is close to its yield to maturity. For example, if a bond's current coupon is 15% and its yield to maturity is 15.4%, it is said to be a current coupon bond. So called because the bond's cash flow is competitive with other bonds of the same class and it is less sensitive, short-term, to interest-rate changes.

CURRENT LIABILITY
Term used in balance sheet bookkeeping and financial statement analysis: the sum of all debts, currently owed, that will become due within one year.

CURRENT MARKET VALUE
Norm used in margin account ledgers for the resale value of securities long in the account. Used as a basis for marks to the market. Closing price for listed securities is used to determine current market value; bid price is used for OTC securities.

Also called "long market value" if client owns security, or short market value if client owes security.

CURRENT MATURITY
Used to designate the remaining lifetime of an already outstanding bond. For example, a bond with an initial 20-year maturity has a current maturity of 15 years at the end of its first 5 years.

CURRENT PRODUCTION RATE
Maximum coupon rate of interest that may be placed on currently generated GNMA Modified Pass-Throughs. On these securities the current production rate is 1/2% below the rate at which the mortgage is issued to the home owner. For example, if the current FHA-VA mortgage rate is 16 1/2%, the current production rate is 16. The sponsoring bank uses the 1/2% to cover the clerical cost of processing the mortgage; the 16% passes through to the GNMA pass-through holder.

CURRENT RATIO

Common measurement of a corporation's liquidity. Ratio is computed by dividing current assets by current liabilities. For example, a corporation with current assets of $2.5 million and current liabilities of $1 million has a current ratio of 2.5 to 1. Generally accepted norm is 2 to 1, although utilities are an exception and permit a lower ratio.

CURRENT SINKER

Slang: a bond with a sinking fund obligation that is presently operative. A corporation is currently obligated to retire a portion of an outstanding bond issue either by a call or by an open market purchase.

If a bond is selling at a discount, the fact that it is a current sinker will tend to enhance its market value because the issuer will tend to buy through an open market purchase, rather than call a portion of the issue at the call price.

CURRENT YIELD

Percentage measured by taking annual dividend interest from an investment and dividing by current replacement cost. Closing price is used on OTC securities.

Most important measurement for security holder who intends to spend the cash flow because it permits her to compare yield with other possible investments of the same amount of money.

Normally, total dividend for previous year is used. If anticipated dividend is used in computation, it is called "estimated" or "anticipated" current yield.

Also called "current return."

CURRENT YIELD BASIS

One of two formerly acceptable methods used to determine the return on capital of a mutual fund. The method adjusts the current price by the previous distribution of capital gains and compares this number with the net distribution of dividend and interest income during the previous year.

Formula:

$$\frac{\text{Net dividend / Interest income}}{\text{Current offer price} + \begin{array}{c}\text{Capital gain paid} \\ \text{in last 12 months}\end{array}}$$

Antonym: historical yield basis.

CURTESY

See CURTSY.

CURTSY
Slang: the legal interest a man has in the real property held in the estate of a deceased wife.

Alternate spelling: curtesy.

CUR YLD
Abbreviation: current yield. Used in newspaper tables of bond transactions on the NYSE and ASE to show the simple interest an investor will receive if the bond is purchased at current prices.

Formula:

$$\frac{\text{Annual interest payment}}{\text{Current market price}}$$

Note: Newspaper bond tables often give to maturity yields for government, agency, and municipal bonds. Thus, CUR YLD is only used if current yield is being computed.

CUSHION
If associated with time, the years between issue date and the earliest callable date of a security. For example, this bond will mature in 20 years, but it has a 5-year cushion. Translation: the bond is callable, but there are 5 years between its issue date and its earliest callable date.

CUSHION BOND
A bond, currently callable, whose market price—in terms of competition with other bonds of similar coupon and rating—is artificially suppressed because of its call price. For example, a bond, callable at 105, that should sell at 120; it is selling at 107, however, because the marketplace fears it will be called. Its price is said to be cushioned.

Although cushioning works against the bondholder as interest rates decline, it works for the bondholder if interest rates rise. In other words, the bond will, in many cases, tend to remain stable during a period of interest-rate changes because the call price and the market price are close.

CUSHION THEORY
Because short sales must be made on upticks, they do not depress the market for a security. Short positions, therefore, have only one future effect: a rise in prices as short sellers buy to cover. A total large short position—while bearish short-term—is bullish long-term. Market analysts look to total short positions that exceed average daily volume by 1½ to 2 times as quite bullish. This is called the "cushion theory."

Because many current short sellers are borrowing to deliver against exercised short calls, most market analysts restrict short sale analysis to that made by members for proprietary accounts.

See also SHORT INTEREST THEORY.

CUSIP
See COMMITTEE ON UNIFORM SECURITIES IDENTIFICATION PROCEDURES.

CUSIP INTERNATIONAL NUMBERING SYSTEM (CINS)
A foreign security identification being developed at the request of the SEC to expedite foreign clearances and settlements. CINS is like CUSIP (Committee on Uniform Security Identification Program) in that it is a 9 alphanumeric symbol that is compatible with U.S. broker/dealer operations. When fully adopted, CINS will unify settlement procedures no matter where executions are effected.

CUSTOMER
1. Any person for whom, or with whom, a broker/dealer executes a transaction, or for whom it holds funds or securities in an account created for that purpose. As a general rule, principals of the broker/ dealer, even if they have brokerage accounts with the broker/dealer, are not considered customers.
2. Any person who may become a customer of a broker/dealer. Many of the rules and regulations of the industry are written to cover the ethical conduct that must govern relationships not only with present customers but also future customers.

CUSTOMER'S AGREEMENT
See MARGIN AGREEMENT; HYPOTHECATION AGREEMENT.

CUSTOMER'S LOAN CONSENT
A written agreement that brokers ask their margin customers to sign. It permits the broker to borrow margined securities, to the amount of the debit balance, for use in delivery against short sales made by other customers and for use by the broker to cover certain fails.

CUSTOMER'S MAN
A term used in prior times to describe a man or woman who served as a registered representative (RR).

See also REGISTERED REPRESENTATIVE.

CUSTOMER STATEMENT
See STATEMENT OF ACCOUNT.

CUTTING A MELON

Slang: any distribution of profits by means of cash or stock dividends. The term is not restricted to distributions to equity owners; it also includes bonuses paid to employees.

CV

Abbreviation for convertible. Used in newspaper stock and bond tables, and in stock and bond guides, to designate any security that may, at the option of the owner, be exchanged for a fixed number of common shares, usually of the same issuer.

CVM

Acronym for Comissao de Valores Mobiliarios. CVM is the Brazilian name for a governmental agency similar in function to the SEC. CVM's powers, however, are more extensive than those of the SEC.

CVR

See CONTINGENT VALUE RIGHTS.

CYLINDERS

A term used in foreign exchange markets for certain currency futures options. A cylinder combines a long put and a short call based on estimations of the currency's future performance. The premium from the call substantially lowers the cost of the put alone.

Cylinders, also known as "tunnels" or "fences," can set a floor and a ceiling (a collar) around foreign currency exposure. Needless to say, the long put and short call are "on the same side of the market," and the strike prices must be carefully chosen to protect from the upside risk caused by the short call.

D

D

Fourth letter of the English alphabet, used:
1. Lowercase in stock transaction tables to designate a new low for the previous 52 weeks. Thus, d 21⅞ designates a new low. The next day the 52-week high/low figures will be changed to reflect this; the previous low figure will be replaced by 21⅞.
2. Temporarily, as the fifth letter in a NASDAQ/NMS security traded over the counter to designate that a reverse split has recently occurred. Thus, for a while, LMNO may be symboled as LMNOD.
3. Alone in uppercase, D is the NYSE tape symbol for Dominion Resources of Virginia, a major utility.

DAILY ADJUSTABLE TAX-EXEMPT SECURITIES

Acronym: DATES. A type of municipal industrial development revenue bond designed by Salomon Brothers Inc. Key feature: The interest, which is calculated daily and distributed monthly, is based on an index of 30-day tax-exempt commercial paper published by the Munifacts Wire System. Added feature: DATES can be tendered to the issuer at any time at face value plus accrued interest to the day of redemption.

DAILY BOND BUYER

Trade publication of the municipal bond industry, although it contains news of value to all fixed-income investors. Published daily, Monday through Friday.

See also BOND BUYERS INDEX and THIRTY-DAY VISIBLE SUPPLY.

DAISY CHAIN

Slang, for a pattern of fictitious trading activity by a group of persons buying and selling. The unsuspicious person drawn into the chain bails out the persons who created the manipulation. He, in turn, has no one to whom to sell because the activity was manipulative.

DAMAGES

The monetary compensation awarded to someone who was injured by the negligent action of another. As a general rule, court-awarded damages, unless they are punitive, are not taxable income to the recipient.

D&B

See DUN & BRADSTREET.

DARTS

Acronym for Dutch Auction Rate Transferable Securities. An adjustable rate preferred stock originally issued by Goldome Florida Funding Corporation. This preferred stock is nonconvertible. Its dividend rate is reset every 49 days by competitive bids (Dutch auction). Each party submits a rate at or above which the holder is willing to "buy"; that is, continue to hold the stock. The maximum rate is 125% of the 60-day AA commercial paper yield.

DATED DATE

The date from which accrued interest is calculated on bonds and other debt instruments that are newly offered. For example, if the dated date is May 1 and settlement is May 25, the buyer will pay 24 days of accrued interest to the issuer. This money will be regained when the first interest payment is paid.

DATE OF DECLARATION
The day on which a dividend distribution is announced by the board of directors of a corporation.

DATE OF PAYMENT
The date set by the board of directors of a corporation for the distribution of a cash, stock, or other distribution.

More frequently used: payment date.

See also PAYMENT DATE.

DATE OF RECORD
The date set by the board of directors of a corporation for its securities transfer agent(s) and registrar to close their books to further changes in ownership registration. Those identified as owners at the close of business on the date of record will be the recipients of the distribution declared by the board of directors.

DATES
See DAILY ADJUSTABLE TAX-EXEMPT SECURITIES.

DAWN RAID
See PREMIUM RAID.

DAY LOAN
A one-day loan made by a broker/dealer to finance the purchase of securities. The securities thus purchased are used as collateral for the loan while more permanent financing is being arranged.

DAY ORDER
An order to buy or sell securities that expires at the end of the trading day unless it is either executed or canceled. All orders are presumed to be day orders unless otherwise designated by the person who enters them.

DAY-TO-DAY REPO
This is an open-ended repurchase agreement that has a one-day effective life. The agreement is cancelable on 24-hour notice; but if not canceled, the REPO is automatically renewed at an interest rate adjusted to current market conditions.

DAY TRADE
A commitment and a decommitment made on the same day: a purchase followed by a long sale, or a short sale followed by a short cover. Special margin maintenance requirements apply.

DBA

1. Acronym for Dealer Bank Association. In this sense, DBA is an organization that represents commercial banks that engage in municipal securities trading. As such, these dealer banks are members of and ascribe to the rules of the Municipal Securities Rulemaking Board (MSRB).
2. Abbreviation for "doing business as. . . ." This expression is abbreviated d/b/a or D/B/A. For example, AJAX Partners, d/b/a Phoenix Associates. The term is also used of private individuals who use another name for their business enterprises.

DBCC

See DISTRICT BUSINESS CONDUCT COMMITTEE.

DBL

Initials stood for Drexel Burnham Lambert, Inc. Often used on corporate and municipal calendars to represent this major underwriter when it was an ongoing concern. It filed for bankruptcy protection in 1990.

DB-25

Short name for the Deutsche Bank 25, a model portfolio of 25 German blue-chip stocks. This portfolio is designed to track the stock market's performance in that country. This indexed portfolio provides institutions with more liquidity than if they attempted to deal in the underlying issues themselves.

DD

See DELAYED DELIVERY.

DDB

See DOUBLE-DECLINING BALANCE METHOD.

DDN

See DOCUMENTED DISCOUNT NOTES.

DE

1. Used on order tickets by RRs to designate that the RR used discretion (DE = discretion exercised) in entering that order for the customer's accounts. Such discretion may be used only if the customer has given prior written authorization and the member firm has accepted the discretionary authorization.
2. The consolidated tape symbol for Deere & Company, a large manufacturer and distributor of farm equipment whose shares are listed on the NYSE.

DEA
See DESIGNATED EXAMINING AUTHORITY.

DEAD CAT BOUNCE
Colorful slang heard each year in December on the Street. It is a reference to the partial recovery of issues that were depressed by tax selling. If the stocks were substantially oversold, this rally may continue even into the following January, causing a January rally.

DEADHEAD
Slang term unfortunately used by securities traders to identify, from its stock ticker symbol DH, the securities of Dayton Hudson Corporation.

DEALER
An individual or firm who, as a matter of regular business, purchases or sells securities for a proprietary account and risk.
 Also called a "principal."

DEALER BANK
1. A commercial bank that makes a continuous market in government and agency securities.
2. A separately identifiable department of a bank that is registered as a municipal securities dealer with the Municipal Securities Rulemaking Board (MSRB).

DEALER FINANCING
An economic arrangement between a marketmaker and a financial institution whereby a collateralized loan is made by the financial institution to the marketmaker to carry its inventory of stocks and bonds. Through such loans, a securities dealer can provide sizable liquid market positions with a minimum amount of its own capital.

DEALER LOAN
A collateralized loan by a bank to a marketmaker in corporate, municipal, or government securities to finance its trading position. Dealer loans are arranged on a day-to-day basis, and the interest rate is negotiated according to competitive conditions.

DEALER MARKET
A securities market in which virtually all transactions are effected between principals acting for their trading or investment accounts. Thus, few agency transactions are effected. Both the municipal securities and the U.S. government securities markets are predominately dealer markets.

DEALER PAPER
Commercial paper sold by its issuer to a broker/dealer who, in turn, sells it to institutional investors for a small markup. The presumption on dealer paper is that the dealer will maintain a secondary market for the commercial paper.

DEALER'S CONCESSION
See SELLING CONCESSION.

DEALER'S TURN
Jargon for the profit a broker/dealer, acting as a marketmaker, realizes if he or she buys at the bid and sells at the offer price for a security. Generally, a dealer's turn is available only if there is a relatively stable market prevailing for a security.

DEAL FLOW
Corporate finance department term used to designate the rate at which new investment banking proposals come to the attention of other investment banking associates; in effect, how fast does a deal flow through the investment banking area. Paradoxically, riskier deals tend to flow faster than conservative deals.

DEALING FOR NEW TIME
Term from the English securities market designating a purchase or sale of securities for the next account trading period. This activity is permitted during the last two days of the present account period.
   See also ACCOUNT DAY.

DEALING WITHIN THE ACCOUNT
In English securities markets, a purchase and a sale, or a short sale and an agreement to repurchase, executed within the same two-week account period. Because these trades offset one another settlement can be made by a single check for the differences.

DEAL STOCK
Street term for an equity issue that is rumored to be the potential target of a merger, takeover, reorganization, or an LBO. Such issues are "in play" and lure speculators and risk arbitrageurs prior to the formal announcement. Needless to say, if there is no deal, the speculators can lose large amounts of money. If there is a formal announcement, the price rise may be minimal because speculators and arbitrageurs have already pushed up the price with their purchases.

DEAR MONEY
Term used by traders and economists to describe the fact that interest rates are high because money and credit are scarce. In this context, "dear" means excessive or very expensive.

DEATH-BACKED BONDS
These bonds are also known as "policyholder loan bonds." The expression is associated with a private placement originated by Prudential-Bache Securities and Morgan Stanley. The bonds are collateralized by loans to life insurance policyholders and are so named because the loans will be repaid from the insurance policy if the borrower dies.

DEATH PLAY
Macabre expression for this situation: The CEO or principal stockholder of a corporation is dying and it is predicted that the company will be broken up and sold off. The speculation is that the parts of the company are worth much more than the whole, and the death of the strong-willed previous owner will subject the company to dismemberment and a rally.

DEATH VALLEY CURVE
An English corporate finance term. The concept: A newly reorganized company—often following a leveraged buyout—is losing so much of its equity capital so fast that it simply cannot borrow sufficient further funds to maintain its existence.

DEB
Abbreviation for: debenture.

DEBENTURE
1. In the United States, a longer-term debt security that is unsecured by any collateral and thus is junior to other debt securities of the same issuer. Only the good faith of the issuer backs the issue. If issued for 10 or less years, it is not unusual to have such securities called "notes."
2. In the United Kingdom, it is the highest, not the lowest, ranking debt issue of a corporation. In the United Kingdom, debentures are typically secured by a mortgage on the issuer's property.

DEBIT BALANCE
Money owed by a margin account customer to a broker for funds advanced for the purchase of securities.

DEBIT SPREAD

A long and short position in options of the same class (puts, or calls). It is called a "debit spread" if the net premiums (plus the premium received minus the premium paid) results in a debit in the client's account.

Debit spreads become profitable if the premium differential so widens that the client can close out the position with greater proceeds than the original cost of the position.

DEBT CEILING

The maximum dollar debt limit a government, agency, or municipality may incur legally without specific further authorization of a higher debt limit by Congress or other legislative body.

Also called "debt limit."

DEBT-EQUITY SWAP

Concept: An issuer, using the distribution facilities of a broker/dealer, exchanges a newly registered issue of stock for outstanding bonds of the same issuer. As a general rule, a debt-equity swap will improve the corporation's balance sheet by lowering the amount of long-term debt and will often increase earnings after interest and taxes.

DEBT INSTRUMENT

General name for any certificate that evidences a loan between a borrower and a lender.

Commonly used equivalent terms, although there are differences in the payment of interest on the debt, are *bill, note, bond, certificate of indebtedness, certificate of deposit, banker's acceptance, commercial paper, receiver's certificate.*

DEBT LIMIT

See DEBT CEILING.

DEBTOR

A person, either real or legal, who owes money, or other assets, to another. For example, persons who purchase debt securities or who sell short in a margin account are debtors.

DEBT SECURITY

General term for any security that represents money loaned and that must be repaid to the lender at a future date.

More specific terms are *bill, note, bond, debenture, commercial paper, certificate of deposit, banker's acceptance.*

DEBT SERVICE
1. The annual interest payment on a debt that is not self-amortizing.
2. The annual interest and principal payment on a debt that is self-amortizing.
   The second meaning is more common.
   See also LEVEL DEBT SERVICE.

DEBT SERVICE COVERAGE
1. In general, the income flow of a corporation or municipality in terms of the net annual payment of interest and principal. For example, Center City has $25 million in revenues to cover a debt service of only $3 million per year.
2. Specifically, the ratio of available income to annual debt service. Thus, in the example given above, the ratio of revenue to debt is $8\frac{1}{3}$ times. As a general rule, municipalities should have a minimum debt service coverage of 4 to 1.

DEBT SWAP
A cross-currency swap in which each party actually exchanges the entire underlying debt obligation. There is an immediate exchange of currency so as to provide the contra party with sufficient funds to satisfy the principal responsibility. Each party then assumes the other's obligation to make interest and principal payments on the debt over its lifetime.

DEBT-TO-EQUITY RATIO
Measurement of leverage in a corporation's financial structure. Formula varies. Less common: total long-term debt divided by stockholders' equity. More common: long-term debt plus par value of preferred stock divided by common stockholders' equity. Use of term, therefore, must be carefully reviewed to make sure which set of figures is being used. Second measurement is more properly a measurement of securities with fixed charges (bonds and preferred) against securities without fixed charges (common).

DECEDENT
Legal name for a person who is deceased. Because death causes the property of the decedent to pass to his or her estate, industry rules require that, upon notification of the death of a customer, the member firm must cancel all open securities orders and take no further action in the account without the advice of counsel or the legal representative of the decedent's estate.

DECK

1. The collection of unexecuted orders in the possession of a member. The term is used both in the equity and the futures markets.
2. Nickname derived from the stock symbol DEC for Digital Equipment Corporation, a leader in the electronic computer industry.

DECLARATION DATE

See DATE OF DECLARATION.

DECLARATORY JUDGMENT

Judicial pronouncement that expresses the opinion of the court about a matter of law without ordering anything to be done about it.

DEEP BID (OFFER)

Trader's jargon for a bid or offer of significant size that is somewhat away from the prevailing market. It is used as an advisory to salespersons that a large order may be executed if and when market prices reach that level.

DEEP DISCOUNT

See DEEP DISCOUNT BOND.

DEEP DISCOUNT BOND

Term used of a bond originally issued at or near par that is currently selling below 80% of its par value. For example, the Fischbach Corp. 8½ of '05 are currently selling at 61. $610 per bond. This represents a deep discount from the original par value of $1,000.

Term is not used for bonds sold at an original issue discount.

DEEP IN THE MONEY

Used of options. A call, for example, has a strike (exercise) price 5 or more points below the current market price of the underlying security, or a put has a strike price 5 or more points above the market price of the underlying security. Term, however, is relative to strike and market prices.

See also DEEP OUT OF THE MONEY.

DEEP OUT OF THE MONEY

Used of options. A call, for example, has a strike (exercise) price more than 5 points above market price of underlying security, or a put has a strike price more than 5 points below market price of underlying security. Term is relative and depends on strike and market price of securities.

DEEP POCKET

Colloquial term for a person of wealth. In context, the term is used of securities liability litigation where the defendants are usually those most likely to be able to afford payment of a sizable judgment. For example, in our litigious society, lawyers for the plaintiff will sue the deepest pocket.

DEEP SIX

Nautical term for a sunken ship in six fathoms of water; thus, one that will never sail again.

Often used as a verb: to deep six (i.e., to reject something as valueless). For example, we should deep six that idea; or the market deep sixed the news.

DEFALCATION

Legal term: the misappropriation of funds or other assets by a fiduciary or other person in a position of trust. Depending on the amount involved, defalcation may be a misdemeanor or a felony, and may subject the perpetrator to civil and criminal penalties.

Reasonable synonym: embezzlement.

Also used of the funds misappropriated.

DEFAULT

Used of debts if the debtor fails to meet an interest payment or to repay the principal. The debt agreement, however, may define default in other ways.

DEFEASANCE

Used in finance, either municipal or corporate, of the action whereby a present debt is effectively removed from the balance sheet by pre-refunding.

Concept: An issuer has an outstanding debt. Additional money is borrowed and escrowed to maturity in U.S. government securities with a maturity that is the same as the previous issue (or its call date). Because funds are in hand for the previous debt's retirement, the debt, and any restrictive covenants attached thereto, are effectively removed from the issuer. Only the requirement of the new debt remains.

DEFEASED BOND/EQUITY SWAP

Procedure used by many corporate guarantors of industrial development bonds (IDBs) to pre-refund the bonds. Under this procedure the guarantor arranges to swap its common stock for a similar dollar amount of U.S. Treasury securities. The bonds are escrowed to maturity, or to earliest call to pre-refund the issue of IDB. The dealer who arranged the swap then sells the common stock and thereby recovers its costs for the U.S. Treasury securities.

DEFERRED AMERICAN OPTION
A put or a call option with this restrictive qualifier: it is not exercisable for a designated period following its creation. Following this period, the option may be exercised anytime up to and including its expiration date.

DEFERRED CHARGES
Expenses incurred by a corporation to improve or promote the long-term prospects of the business. These expenses are summarized on the corporation's financial statements and are charged off against earnings over a time period. If prepaid, such charges become an asset until they are charged off. For example, prepaid insurance that overlaps a fiscal year. If unpaid, they become a liability. For example, the discount at which an issue of bonds was sold by the issuer.

DEFERRED DIVIDEND SHARES
The expression refers to certain equity issues of Australian companies. They are called "deferred" because they have junior ranking to ordinary common stock and will have their dividends postponed until a specified time in the future. When they are dividend paying, such shares will have equal status with other outstanding common shares.

DEFERRED PAYMENT ANNUITY
Annuity contract whereby annuitant makes a lump-sum or installment deposit of premiums. Annuity payoff does not start until a later date at the election of the annuitant.

DEFERRED PAYMENT NOTES (DPN)
A Eurodollar security combining some features of a debt security with some features of a securities option. The debt security is fixed rate, but requires only a 25% initial payment, with final payment due several months later. If, during the period, interest rates rise dramatically, thus dollar value falls, the purchaser can refuse further payment, thus limiting loss to the initial 25% payment. If interest rates fall, the purchaser will complete payments and will have a leveraged play on interest rates during the period between initial and final payment.

DEFERRED PROFIT-SHARING PLAN
Acronym: DPSP. Permits corporations registered with Revenue Canada to sponsor employee retirement plans. Under such plans, the employer can contribute the greater of 20% of wages or $3,500, thereby reducing taxable income for the year.

DEFERRED SHARES

In the United Kingdom, deferred shares are a type of equity share that has greater voting rights or greater residual claims, or both, to extra dividends. In this latter regard they are similar to participating preferred shares in the United States.

In some instances, deferred shares have dividends deferred for a number of years; but when dividends are started, they have a cumulative arrearage that must be paid before dividends are paid to ordinary shareholders.

DEFICIENCY LETTER

Written statement from SEC to issuer during the registration process. Suggests revisions or addition of other information to the preliminary registration statement. Although a deficiency letter does not necessarily delay the registration, an effective date will not be assigned until the deficiency is corrected.

DEFICIT REDUCTION ACT OF 1984

Popularly called: "DEFRA," or "DRA." This 1984 tax act:
1. Reduced long-term holding period from more than 12 months to more than 6 months. (There is now no capital holding period.)
2. Changed from 16 days to 46 days the minimum holding period for corporate investors to be eligible for an 85% dividend exclusion. (It is now a 70% exclusion.)
3. Requires holders of newly issued market discount bonds to treat some of the discount annually as ordinary interest income.

Tax advice is needed.

DEFINED BENEFIT PLAN

Under ERISA rules, a participant receives a guaranteed pension at retirement. Thus, contributions to each participant's plan will vary according to age and actuarial assumptions. The amount of the pension is specified and varies with salary. Typically, the pension is 60% of average wages over a predetermined time period.

See also DEFINED CONTRIBUTION PLAN.

DEFINED CONTRIBUTION PLAN

Under ERISA rules, specified annual payments, usually based on a percentage of salary, are made to the retirement account of participants. The retirement benefits, therefore, will vary according to the investment experience of contributions made to the plan.

Also called "dollar purchase plan."

See also DEFINED BENEFIT PLAN.

DEFINITIVE SECURITY

A permanent stock or bond certificate issued to replace a temporary certificate. Occasionally issuers will give temporary certificates at the time of a new issue or stock split/dividend.

See also GLOBAL CERTIFICATE.

DEFLATION

An economic period generally marked by a period of lowered consumer prices and, thus, marking an increase in the purchasing power of money.

More commonly used: disinflation.

Antonym: inflation.

DEFRA

See DEFICIT REDUCTION ACT OF 1984.

DELAYED DELIVERY (DD)

Settlement of a securities contract after regular way delivery. For example, if regular way settlement is next business day, a contract to settle on the second business day would be a form of delayed delivery.

DELIVER ORDER

See DO.

DELIVER VERSUS PAYMENT (DVP)

When delivery is made to the customer's bank, the bank will pay in cash, or by check, for the customer's account. It is a frequently used transaction settlement procedure by institutional accounts.

Also known as deliver against payment; delivery against cash; or, from the other side of the trade, receive against payment.

DELIVERY DATE

See SETTLEMENT DATE.

DELTA

Greek letter D. Delta, by inference to the proportional change between two quantities in differential calculus, is used of options to state the change in the option premium for each 1 point change in the price of the underlying stock. For example, a delta of .75 means that the premium tends to increase by 3/4 point for each point that the underlying stock goes up. For options in the money, delta will always approach 1 as the option nears expiration. Same concept is true of puts as stock goes down.

Also called the "hedge ratio."

See also HEDGE RATIO.

DELY
Abbreviation: delivery.

DEMAND DEPOSIT
Banking term for customer assets that may be drawn against by check or draft. In its simpliest terms, deposits in bank customer checking accounts. The deposit may arise from cash or other deposits in the customer's account or by credit if the bank extends a loan to the customer.

DEMAND LINE OF CREDIT
Arrangement made with a commercial bank whereby a customer may borrow, up to a preset maximum dollar amount, on a daily basis (i.e., upon demand).

DEMAND LOAN
A loan with no fixed maturity date which is payable upon demand—that is, immediately—by the party granting the loan. In practice, the terms *demand loan* and *call loan* are synonyms.

DEMERGER
Pronounced: dee–merger. An English finance term used:
1. To designate a spin-off by a company of a subsidiary to its shareholders. The spun-off company can then act independently.
2. To designate the sale by a parent company of its ownership in a subsidiary to the management of the subsidiary. The new company can then act independently (and often as a competitor) of the original parent.

DENKS
A tongue-in-cheek acronym for: dual-employed, no kids. A type of family unit in which both members are employed but do not have the responsibility of child rearing; thus, they are able to enjoy more luxuries or to invest more. Similar to DINKS (q.v.) but the latter may infer that one of the parties holds down two jobs (double income) and the other none.
    See also DEWKS.

DENOMINATION
Number of shares or principal amount of bonds inscribed on the face of a security.
    See also GOOD DELIVERY.

DEPLETION
Accounting term for a theoretical pool of funds set aside from a corporation's annual earnings for the replacement of a natural asset that is be-

ing used up. For example, oil from a well, ore from a lode. Because it is usually impossible to replace the asset, the depletion is usually given in the form of a credit against taxes due by the corporation.

DEPOSITORY
An entity that receives and holds securities for subscribers.

The most popular depository is the Depository Trust Co. (DTC). It is a major factor in DVP/RVP (Deliver versus Payment/Receive versus Payment) transactions for banks and brokerage firms because it "immobilizes" certificates and arranges for book-entry transfers between participating members.

DEPOSITORY INSTITUTIONS DEREGULATION ACT OF 1980 (DIDA)
DIDA is a federal law that provides for the orderly phaseout of the restrictions on interest and dividend rates paid on accounts maintained for customers by banks and other thrift institutions. A special committee (DIDC) has been authorized to develop new government-insured interest-bearing deposits to compete with money market mutual funds.

DEPOSITORY INSTITUTIONS DEREGULATION COMMITTEE (DIDC)
DIDC is an ad hoc group authorized by federal law to develop government-insured interest-bearing deposit accounts at banks and other thrift institutions that can compete with money market mutual funds.

DEPOSITORY PREFERRED STOCK
Term used for an issue of high par value preferred stock that is deposited with a bank. The bank, in turn, issues many more shares of a lower par value preferred stock that is entitled to a proportionate interest in the deposited security. This technique could be used to circumvent share limitations imposed on the corporation by corporate bylaws.

DEPOSITORY TRUST COMPANY (DTC)
A central securities certificate depository, and member of the Federal Reserve System, through which members may arrange deliveries of securities between each other through computerized debit and credit entries without physical delivery of the certificates.

The DTC is industry owned, with the NYSE as the majority owner.

DEPRECIATION
Theoretical sum of money that represents the loss of value of a tangible asset over time because of use or of obsolescence. The sum is deducted from purchase price of a fixed asset to give its residual value for balance sheet accounting. A similar sum is deducted from the corporation's income for that year.

See also CASH FLOW; STRAIGHT-LINE DEPRECIATION; DOUBLE-DECLINING-BALANCE METHOD; SUM-OF-THE-YEARS'-DIGITS METHOD.

DEPRESSION
Term used to describe the long-lasting period of curtailed business and economic activities in the United States from 1929 through the 1930s. For example, during the Depression many banks and businesses failed. Usually called the "Great Depression."

The term also is used of any continued period marked by deteriorating securities and commodities prices coupled to a period of depressed personal savings and decreased industrial production.

DEPTH
1. Ability of the market to absorb either a large buy or a large sell order without a significant price change in a security.
2. Degree of general investor interest in the market. For example, the depth of the market index compares the number of issues traded with the number of issues listed. The greater the number of issues traded, the greater the market depth.

DERIVATIVE PRODUCT(S)
Popular term of the 80s and 90s to designate tradeable equity, debt, or futures instruments stemming from specific underlying securities or commodities. Such products may or may not be the responsibility of the issuer.

Popular derivatives are options (equity, debt, currency, and index) that are not the responsibility of the issuer. Other derivatives are asset-backed securities, including mortgage-backed, CMOs (collateralized mortgage obligations), "baskets of securities," TIGRs, CATS, COUGARs, all of which are ultimately the responsibility of the issuer.

DESIGNATED CONCESSION
Order given to a syndicate. The order, for a number of shares or bonds, designates the nonmembers of the account who are to receive the concession for the sale of the securities. For example, an order for 1,000 bonds designates that the concession for 400 is to go to A, 300 to B, and 300 to C.

DESIGNATED EXAMINING AUTHORITY
Acronym: DEA. A self-regulatory body with responsibility for oversight of a particular broker/dealer. Because most broker/dealers have memberships on several exchanges and in the NASD and MSRB, it often is confusing if several authorities exercise surveillance. Under DEA, one

of the regulators assumes the job for the others, thus, duplication of effort, confusion, and contradictions are avoided.

DESIGNATED NET
Order given to a municipal security syndicate by a nonmember of the MSRB, for example, by an insurance company to a municipal underwriting syndicate. The order, executed at the public offering price, directs that the concession be credited to the accounts of at least three members of the syndicate designated by the insurance company.

Frequently used by institutional municipal investors to reward account members who have presented sales ideas or other valuable research information.

DESIGNATED ORDER
Also referred to as a directed order, this is an institution's purchase request for a newly registered security placed with the manager of the underwriting group. In entering the order, the institution indentifies which syndicate and selling group members it wants credited for specific quantities of the issue purchased. The customer thus receives and settles on a single, large quantity confirmation instead of many smaller ones.

See also DESIGNATED NET and DESIGNATED CONCESSION.

DESIGNATED ORDER TURNAROUND (DOT)
Electronic switching service provided to NYSE members whereby market orders for 1 to 2,099 shares are routed directly to the specialist. The specialist represents such orders in the crowd. If no contra broker is found, the order is executed against the book (i.e., buy orders against the best offer on the book; sell orders against the best bid). The specialist does not charge the member firm for the service if an immediate transaction is made.

On the NYSE, DOT transactions account for more than 50% of all trades—although a much smaller percentage of total volume.

DESIGNATED PRIMARY MARKETMAKER
See DPM.

DESIGNATED SECURITY
As defined in SEC Rule 15c2-6, a designated security is a non-NASDAQ equity issue, traded over the counter, whose tangible assets are $2 million or less.

DEUTSCHE TERMINBOERSE GMBH
See DTB.

DEVALUATION
Official lowering of value of one country's currency in terms of the exchange rate for another country's currency. For example, if the United States was to state that starting tomorrow $1 will be exchanged for 1,000 Italian lire instead of today's rate of $1 for 1,100 lire, this act would devalue the dollar. Reason: holders of lire could buy more U.S. goods tomorrow than they could today. Devaluation normally is the result of an unfavorable balance of trade. Currency spent abroad returns to the home country in the form of purchases of that country's goods. The norm may be a specified amount of gold, silver, or a basket of currencies.

If the issuing government unilaterally lowers such currency values, it usually is an endeavor to spur its own exports and to stem imports of another country's goods and services.

DEWAP
Acronym for Department of Water and Power, of the City of Los Angeles, California. Used also of the municipal revenue securities issued by that municipal entity.

DEWKS
Tongue-in-cheek acronym: dual-employed, with kids. This is the largest and fastest growing segment of the U.S. population as more and more persons endeavor to put together parenting and business careers. With both the husband and wife working in business, despite the financial drain of children, they have a substantially higher income and standard of living than would be otherwise possible.

DIAGONAL SPREAD
Option strategy based on a long and short position in the same class of option. For example, long a call and short a call, where the strike prices are different and the expiration months are different.

The diagonal spread strategy is bullish or bearish depending on the difference between the strike prices and the price of the underlying security, relative to the strike prices and their expiration months.

DIALING AND SMILING
A euphemism for a salesperson's cold calls to build a roster of customers for business. To attract and motivate unseen strangers, salespersons must not only phone (dialing) but must also exude a personal warmth and concern (smiling) if they are to be successful.

DIAMOND FORMATION
See TRIANGLE FORMATION.

DIDA

See DEPOSITORY INSTITUTIONS DEREGULATION ACT OF 1980.

DIDC

See DEPOSITORY INSTITUTIONS DEREGULATION COMMITTEE.

DIE

Acronym for Designated Investment Exchange. DIE is a U.K. term introduced under the Financial Services Act. Under the act, a DIE is any stock exchange located outside the United Kingdom that provides trade visibility and fairness of pricing for its listed issues. If this is determined, the exchange will be "designated" by the Securities Investment Board (SIB) as an acceptable marketplace for U.K. investors.

DIFF

The Euro-Rate Differential (hence the initials) is a futures contract introduced in 1989 on the Chicago Mercantile Exchange (CME). The purpose of the contract is to lock in an interest-rate spread (differential) between the U.S. dollar and either the British pound, the West German deutsche mark, or the Japanese yen. Although the contract is designed primarily for institutions dealing in international markets, it can also be used by currency speculators.

DIFFERENCE CHECK

A single settlement check for the differences between total costs and net proceeds of trades to be satisfied on the same day. Under the Fed's Regulation T this is permitted for same-day substitutions. On the other hand, if the purchases and sales were made on different dates in a corporate security, each trade must be settled individually.

DIFFERENTIAL

Compensation to a dealer for the completion of an odd-lot transaction for a customer. Term is specific to odd-lot transactions on exchanges where the differential—commonly ⅛ point, although there are exceptions—is added to purchases and subtracted from sales.

Term also is used generally of any trading situation where the dealer widens his quote because the customer is buying or selling a relatively small amount of the security. For example, a government security dealer widens his quote from 95.16 bid—95.20 offered to 95.10 bid—95.24 offered because a customer only wishes to buy $10,000 face amount of the bonds.

DIGITAL INTERFACE SERVICES

See DIS.

DIGITS DELETED

Exchange tape designation when tape has been delayed. Normally, all digits and variations are displayed. With digits deleted only the variations are displayed.

For example, normal transactions might read:

$$45\text{-}^7/_8........46\text{-}^1/_8........46\text{-}^1/_4$$

With digits deleted, tape would display:

$$5\text{-}^7/_8........6\text{-}^1/_8........6\text{-}^1/_4$$

The viewer is expected to supply the missing digits.

DIME

When used in connection with the yield on a debt security, this slang expression designates 10 basis points, or .10%. Example: "I will buy if you will raise it a dime."

DINGO

Acronym for discounted investment in negotiated government obligations. This is the Australian version of government-issued securities stripped of interest coupons. The securities, which are sold at deep discounts, are similar in concept to TIGRs, CATS, and Treasury STRIPS.

DINKS

Acronym for double-income, no kids. This term is often used by analysts when referring to young married professionals with no children who became financially secure and who were investors in the U.S. economy during the 80s. Previously, the term for such professionals was *Yuppies* (Young Urban Professionals), although that term had no intimation of marriage as does Dinks.

DIP

A small temporary drop in the price of a security, usually a few points but certainly not more than 10% of the current price. In general, dips are a form of profit taking following a rise in the price of a stock, and astute investors use such dips as an opportunity to buy more shares.

DIP LOAN

Acronym for "debtor-in-possession" loan; that is, a loan, usually by a commercial bank, to a bankrupt organization. The purpose of this financing is to enable an insolvent corporation to continue its day-to-day operations while it is in the jurisdiction of a federal bankruptcy court.

DIRECTED ORDER
See DESIGNATED ORDER.

DIRECTIONS UNIT INVESTMENT TRUST
See DUIT.

DIRECTOR
Person elected to serve on the board of a corporation or trust. In the latter case, the more common expression is "trustee."

Powers of a board of directors is given in corporation's charter.

In recent years, *affiliated persons* has become the general term for directors, elected corporate officers, and holders of 10% or more of outstanding shares of a corporation.

DIRECT PAPER
Term used of commercial paper that is sold by a corporation to investors without the use of a broker/dealer or a bank as an intermediary.

DIRECT PARTICIPATION PROGRAM (DPP)
General term used by National Association of Securities Dealers (NASD) for partnership agreements that provide a flow-through of tax consequences to the participants. Subchapter S corporations, which provide tax consequences similar to partnerships, are usually included in this concept.

REITs, pension, and profit-sharing plans, individual retirement accounts, annuities, and investment companies are usually excluded from the definition of direct-participation programs.

DIRECT PLACEMENT
Used of an issuer's sale of a new security to one or more institutional clients without the assistance of a broker/dealer.

Occasionally used of private placement where broker/dealer acts as an agent. This later usage is more commonly called a "private placement."

DIRT BAG
A term used of a person considered to be a sneak and a crook. Although the term is not restricted to investments, it has been introduced as evidence by the government in the prosecution of various violations of securities laws. In effect, a "dirt bag" is someone who is not to be trusted.

Also called a "sleaze bag."

DIRTY STOCK

Securities industry slang for a stock certificate not in proper deliverable form between NASD/NYSE members. It may mean that the certificate is mutilated, counterfeit, or in nontransferable form; for example, in the name of a decedent, alien corporation, or it is "legended" (not registered with the SEC).

DIS

Acronym for Digital Interface Services. DIS is an NASD pilot program that enables subscribers to convert transmitted market information into information that can be displayed on the user's own terminals. Thus, the NASD date in digital form can be sent to a firm's dedicated computer and then routed to the actual marketmaker for that broker/dealer.

DISC

Acronym for domestic international sales corporation. The term is used of an offshore entity created by a U.S. corporation to provide tax advantages for foreign exporters of U.S. merchandise to foreign countries. DISCs enable U.S. companies to compete effectively with subsidized foreign competitors. The IRS permits certain tax exemptions under complex, closely controlled rules.

DISCIPLINARY REPORTING PAGE
See DRP.

DISCLOSURE REPORTING PAGE
See DRP.

DISCO BROKER

Contraction for: discount broker (q.v.); that is, an SEC-registered broker/dealer that charges substantially lower commissions than full-service brokers. As a general rule, discount brokers do not provide securities research options and often curtail the other ancillary services that are associated with securities brokerage services.

DISCOUNT

1. Noun: the dollar (or point) difference between the price of a security and its redemption value. Example: A bond with a face value of $1,000 is selling at a $50 discount if its current market value is $950.
2. Adjective: used to describe a security selling at a discount or offered for sale at a discount. Example: Treasury bills are discount securities.
3. Verb: the act of factoring the long-term effects of news into one's estimate of the present value of a security. Example: The stock has gone

down in value because the market is discounting the news of a threatened labor strike.

Also used as a past participle. Example: The news is discounted.

DISCOUNT BOND

A bond, originally sold at or near par, which is currently selling below its par value.

Also called a "discounted bond."

See also DEEP DISCOUNT BOND.

DISCOUNT BROKER

Exchange members who will provide execution-only services for clients and, as a result, charge lower, or discounted, commissions.

The principal difference between discount brokers and full-service brokers is that the latter will give investment advice and portfolio suggestions. Discount brokers enter orders for clients who wish to buy or sell. They also provide margin accounts and, occasionally, custodial service. They do not provide advice or other research services.

Discount brokers cater to a clientele of customers who make their own investment decisions and who do not expect the broker to supply investment opinions.

Also called "discount houses."

DISCOUNTED INVESTMENT IN NEGOTIATED GOVERNMENT OBLIGATIONS

See DINGOs.

DISCOUNTER

The term applied to a broker/dealer that offers all customers a substantial reduction in commission, compared to that charged by full-service member firms. Important names in this category are Charles Schwab & Co. and Quick & Reilly Corp.

DISCOUNT HOUSE

See DISCOUNT BROKER.

DISCOUNT RATE

Interest rate charged by the Federal Reserve when member banks borrow from the Fed against eligible securities as collateral. The discount rate, which the Fed changes from time to time to implement its monetary policies, becomes the floor beneath which the member banks will not loan money. For example, if the discount rate is 12%, a bank would lose money if it reloaned the funds at 12% or below.

See also DISCOUNT WINDOW.

DISCOUNT SECURITIES

Debt instruments issued without a fixed interest rate that are offered and traded until maturity at a value below the face amount of the security. Common examples: U.S. Treasury bills and commercial paper. At maturity, the difference between the purchase cost and maturity value represents interest income. If longer-term, such securities are called "original issue discounts."

Note: Do not confuse with securities issued at or near face value that are currently selling at a market discount.

DISCOUNT WINDOW

Term for the loan facility provided by the Federal Reserve Bank whereby member banks can borrow against the collateral value of eligible securities.

See also DISCOUNT RATE.

DISCOUNT YIELD

Measurement of return that computes interest on face value of security, rather than on dollar amount invested. Used in figuring yield on U.S. Treasury bills. The formula is:

$$\text{Yield} = \frac{\text{Discount}}{\text{Face amount}} \times \frac{360 \text{ days}}{\text{Days until maturity}}$$

Example: If a client buys a $10,000 Treasury bill for $9,500 when 180 days remain to maturity, the discount yield is calculated as follows:

$$\text{Yield} = \frac{500}{10000} \times \frac{360}{180}$$

$$\text{Yield} = 0.05 \times 2$$

$$\text{Yield} = 10\%$$

Also called "discount basis."

See also EQUIVALENT BOND YIELD (to compare with regular method of computing current yield).

DISCRETIONARY ACCOUNT

Brokerage account that permits a designated employee of the member firm to make investment decisions on behalf of a client. The investment decisions include buying and selling and the selection of the securities. Authorization for such accounts must be given in writing by the customer and must be accepted by an officer of the member firm.

Member firm customers may verbally give discretion about time and price for specified trades. This limited discretion does not require written authorization.

DISCRETIONARY ORDER
An order to buy or sell that an employee of a member firm entered because she has limited power of attorney over a client's account.

Industry rules require that such orders be marked discretionary, be entered in accord with the customer's investment objectives, and be approved promptly by a designated person in the member firm.

DISINTERMEDIATION
Term describing the action of an investor who has left funds on deposit with a portfolio intermediary (e.g., a bank, savings and loan, or insurance company) removes those funds and makes a direct investment in other securities. Example: A bank depositor who receives $5\frac{1}{4}\%$ on a passbook deposit withdraws funds to purchase Treasury securities paying 11%.

Disintermediation occurs when rates on direct security investments are substantially higher than the rates paid by portfolio intermediaries.

DIS-PREMIUM
A euphemism for the disappearance (i.e., "decline") of the offering price soon after a junk bond issue is marketed by its underwriter(s). With public and institutional aversion to the junk bond market in the early 1990s it became apparent that public and private placements of such issues (even if they could be sold quickly) dropped to discount prices.

DISPROPORTIONATE IN QUANTITY
Term used by the NASD in its interpretation of the allocation of a "hot issue" by a broker/dealer. The term applies to sales of more than 100 shares, or $5,000 face value of bonds, to persons in these occupational categories:
1. The managing underwriter's finder for this offering, its accountants, attorneys, financial consultants, and members of their immediate families.
2. Senior officers, securities department employees of commercial banks, savings banks, insurance companies, and investment companies, or other persons who influence the investment decisions of these institutions.

DIST
On exchange ticker tapes, DIST designates an exchange distribution.
See also EXCHANGE DISTRIBUTION.

DISTRESS POSITION
Term used by traders and marketmakers to identify proprietary positions that are being held at a loss. Thus, if a long position was initially purchased at higher than prevailing prices or if a short position was established at lower than current prices. If these positions were closed out it would obviously cause the firm financial distress.

DISTRESS SALE
The sale of a security under adverse market conditions, such as a margin call or to meet net capital requirements. Such distress sales usually lead to large losses. A popular axiom on Wall Street is: "Sell 'em when you want to, not when you have to."

DISTRIBUTION
General term used to designate the sale of a large block of stock. The distribution may be primary, as in an underwriting, or secondary, as in an exchange distribution.

DISTRIBUTION AREA
Term describing a relatively narrow price range for a security over a relatively long time. For example, a stock trades between 36 and 38 for a six-week period. Called a "distribution area" because the implication is that sellers are disappointed but buyers are willing to purchase the security at those prices. In practice, it is difficult to tell whether the primary cause for the sideways price movement comes from sellers, who are distributing, or from buyers, who through their limit orders are accumulating.

DISTRIBUTION PLAN
A plan whereby a mutual fund charges certain distribution costs, both advertising and RR fees, against the assets of a fund.
See the 12b-1 Fund for a fuller explanation.

DISTRIBUTION STOCK
Stock sold publicly by persons affiliated with the issuer pursuant to an effective shelf registration.

DISTRIBUTOR
Term for the underwriter of mutual fund shares.
Also called "wholesaler."
See also UNDERWRITER.

DISTRICT BUSINESS CONDUCT COMMITTEE (DBCC)
Committee appointed by the members within 1 of the 11 districts of the National Association of Securities Dealers (NASD). The DBCC is em-

powered to hear trade practice complaints against a member or a person associated with a member under the Code of Procedure.

See also BUSINESS CONDUCT COMMITTEE and CODE OF PROCEDURE.

DISTRICT UNIFORM PRACTICE COMMITTEE
See UNIFORM PRACTICE COMMITTEE.

DIVERSIFICATION
Process whereby an investor, to reduce the risk of selection, spreads investment dollars over many securities or uses a single investment with a portfolio invested in many securities.

DIVERSIFIED
Term used of management investment companies—both closed and open-ended—if at least 75% of its assets are represented by four forms: cash, government securities, securities of other investment companies, and other securities. Purpose: so no more than 5% of the management company's total assets are invested in the securities of any one issuer and they hold no more than 10% of the voting securities of any issuing corporation.

DIVERSIFIED COMMON STOCK COMPANY
A management investment company that has substantially all of its assets invested in a portfolio of common stocks of companies engaged in a wide variety of industries.

Often called "a diversified common stock fund."

DIVERSIFIED MANAGEMENT COMPANY
An investment company that has at least 75% of its assets represented by: (1) cash and cash items; (2) government securities; (3) securities of other investment companies; and (4) other securities, limited to securities of one issuer having a value not greater than 5% of the management company's total assets and no more than 10% of the voting securities of the issuing corporation.

DIVIDED ACCOUNT
A corporate underwriting agreement in which syndicate members sign a contract with the issuer as a group but limit their individual liability to the specific quantity of shares or bonds that they individually underwrite.

See also EASTERN ACCOUNT and WESTERN ACCOUNT.

DIVIDEND

1. A distribution of cash from net profits or of securities made at the discretion of the board of directors to the equity shareholders of a corporation. Cash dividends are taxable to the recipient. Generally, stock dividends are not taxable at the time of receipt.
2. A distribution of cash from net income made by a regulated investment company. Under Subchapter M of the IRS Code, the tax treatment of such distributions is dependent on the original source: long- or short-term capital gains, interest income, or security dividends.

DIVIDEND CAPTURE

General name for a variety of techniques whereby purchasers of stocks acquire dividend distributions with a minimum amount of market risk. These strategies include: dividend rollovers, auction rate preferred shares, sales of covered calls, and stock portfolios hedged by bond or stock index futures or options.

DIVIDEND DEPARTMENT

Work area in a broker/dealer organization that accepts, allocates, pays, and claims dividend and interest distributions associated with securities that are in the firm's custody or within the firm's responsibility.

DIVIDEND EXCLUSION

Amount of dividends not subject to federal taxation.

For domestic corporations, current law excludes 70% of the dividends received from an equity issue of another domestic corporation. Not every domestic issuer qualifies, so tax advice is required. There is no exclusion for individuals receiving dividends.

DIVIDEND/INTEREST DISBURSING AGENT

An institution, usually a commercial bank, that distributes dividend or interest checks to the holders of specific securities upon instruction from that issuer's directors or trustees.

The disbursing agent uses the official record of the registrar to identify the appropriate recipients.

DIVIDEND PAYOUT RATIO

A method of comparing payout ratio of companies within the same industry or companies in general. Comparison is relative and, of itself, has no further investment decision value. Companies with high dividend payout ratios usually are not considered growth companies.

The formula is:

$$\frac{\text{Annual common stock dividend}}{\text{Earnings available for common stock}}$$

DIVIDEND RECORD
A widely used publication of the Standard & Poor's Corporation that contains statistical information about dividends and dividend payment announcements of publicly held security issuers.

DIVIDEND ROLLOVER
A tax-advantaged dividend capture technique used by some U.S. corporations. Concept: Purchase a high-yield utility stock or preferred stock, or both, and sell it more than 46 days later after an ex-dividend date. The dividend received is 70% tax free. Under normal and stable interest-rate trends, the market price of the stock should be close to the price at which the stock was purchased.

DIVIDEND STRIPPING
This term describes the other side of a dividend rollover; that is, in response to a customer's request to buy a forthcoming dividend, the broker/dealer sells it short to the customer just before the ex-dividend date and, soon after, buys it back from the customer (remember, it is less the dividend) to cover the short position. Settlement is so arranged that it is after the record date. The net effect is for the broker/dealer to pay the dividend out of its own pocket to the lender of the stock. This strips the dividend from an otherwise riskless transaction.

DJ
See DOW JONES & COMPANY, INC.

DJIA
See DOW JONES INDUSTRIAL AVERAGE.

DK
See DON'T KNOW.

DM
Initials for: deutsche mark. DM is the primary unit of currency in Germany.

The initials also are used to designate the currency options in deutsche marks that are traded on the Philadelphia Stock Exchange.

DNC

An order instruction that means "do not cross." This instruction may be made on stock exchange floor tickets in conjunction with index program executions. Because the same stocks are represented in several stock indexes, and because it may be necessary to sell one basket while buying another basket, orders are marked DNC to avoid a "wash sale" consideration.

DNE

Order ticket initials standing for: discretion not exercised. This situation arises when the customer has given discretion to an employee of the member firm but, in this particular case, the customer initiated the trade, not the registered representative.

DNI

See DO NOT INCREASE.

DNR

See DO NOT REDUCE.

DO

Acronym for deliver order. A DTC mechanism for book entry settlements by broker/dealer participants. It is an automated service, sponsored by DTC to expedite settlements between members. Buyers are credited and sellers are debited with the security position on settlement date. It helps eliminate late or erroneous deliveries.

DOCUMENTARY STAMP TAX

A state or local tax imposed on the transfer of real property. In Florida, the tax also is effective on the transfer of debt and equity securities within that state. It is paid by the seller.

In England, the tax is payable by the buyer of ordinary (common) shares to reregister certificates.

DOCUMENTED DISCOUNT NOTES

Acronym: DDN. Commercial paper pledged by member banks as qualified collateral at a Federal Reserve District Bank. To qualify as acceptable collateral, the DDN must be accompanied by a letter of credit written by a commercial bank, or guaranteed by a private insurance company not related to the commercial paper issuer.

DOEA

Acronym for Designated Options Examining Authority. A self-regulatory organization responsible for inspecting member firm compliance with the rules of the various option exchanges. Under the SEC's present plan, only the ASE, CBOE, NASD, and NYSE can be DOEAs.

DOG AND PONY SHOW
Colloquial term for an informational seminar used to introduce a new product or service. Such seminars are often given by broker/dealers to stimulate the interest of its own registered representatives. Frequently, the seminars center on particular companies, and participants, who may include potential customers, have an opportunity to discuss company policies and products with corporate officials. Generally such seminars are given in many different locations.

Dog and pony show is an allusion to old-time vaudeville acts that traveled from place to place.

DOING BUSINESS AS
See DBA.

DOL
Acronym for Department of Labor. The DOL is the cabinet-level agency that has jurisdiction over pension and profit-sharing plans subject to ERISA laws. The DOL establishes the rules and reporting requirements for such plans. It also regulates the relationship of such plans with bankers, brokers, and investment advisors.

DOLLAR AVERAGING
Incorrect contraction of the expression "dollar cost averaging." As such, securities regulators consider its use objectionable.

See DOLLAR COST AVERAGING for the correct usage.

DOLLAR BEARS
Term used for traders and speculators who believe that the value of the U.S. dollar will decline in the forseeable future. Although there is often a large amount of volatility in the major world currencies, these speculators consider the U.S. dollar a prime subject for decline because of the constant U.S. trade deficit.

DOLLAR BILS
Acronym for Bond Index-Linked Security. Dollar BILS are a Merrill Lynch product that are a 10-year zero-coupon debt instrument. BILS are priced initially according to the current performance of the Merrill Lynch Index of 506 high-grade corporate bonds with maturities of 15 years or more. Dollar BILS are designed for small institutions because at maturity they return the full principal price plus the future value of 25 basis points (4.24%). The bonds are backed by the credit of Merrill Lynch.

DOLLAR BONDS
1. Long-term municipal revenue bonds usually quoted in dollars (i.e., in points), rather than in yield to maturity.
2. Bonds of foreign issuers sold in the United States and denominated in U.S. dollars.
3. Bonds, denominated in U.S. dollars, that are issued, bought, and sold in foreign countries.
   Also called "Eurobonds," although such bonds are traded in Mexico and Japan.

DOLLAR COST AVERAGING
Method of formula investing based on the periodic investment of equal dollar amounts in the same security. The result in every case will be an average cost per unit that is less than the average of the prices paid. Method, however, does not guarantee a profit. There will be a profit only if sale price exceeds average cost per unit.

Dollar cost averaging can be used for the purchase of management investment company shares (mutual funds) and in the sharebuilder plans offered by many broker/dealers.

DOLLAR PRICE
Term used of the quote for a bond that is expressed as a percentage of that instrument's face value. Example: A bond quoted at 98½ means that the dollar price will be 98½% of the bond's face value; that is, $985 if the bond has a face value of $1,000.

Term is used to distinguish from basis price; that is, a bond quote given in terms of yield to maturity. For example, the bond is priced at 10.72%.

DOLLAR ROLL
A form of questionable financing in the Ginnie Mae securities market. A dollar roll involves the purchase of a TBA (terms to be announced) Ginnie Mae and a concurrent sale of that security for settlement in a later month. Because the purchase and sale will be paired off on the same dealer's books, no money is necessarily deposited and the commitment represents an uncollateralized forward settlement trade. Depending on the investor's perception of interest-rate trends, the sale will be made first and then the TBA contract will be made for a settlement in a future month.

DOMESTIC INTERNATIONAL SALES CORPORATION
See DISC.

DOMICILE

In law, one's principal home and permanent residence. The law is complex, and legal advice is needed.

The term is important for income and estate tax considerations. In general, to probate an estate and to transfer securities for a decedent, it is necessary to have an affidavit of domicile and a tax waiver from the state in which the decedent was domiciled.

DO NOT INCREASE

Abbreviation: DNI. An instruction that is placed on good-till-cancelled buy limit and sell stop orders on the NYSE and ASE. In the event of a stock split or stock dividend, the customer does not want the quantity of his or her order increased on the ex-date of the distribution.

To illustrate, there is to be a stock dividend of 10%. Normally the stock price would be multiplied by $^{10}/_{11}$ and the order quantity would be increased by $^{11}/_{10}$. The customer who enters a DNI order does not want these calculations to apply; he or she wants the original order to stand. The customer will do his or her own reentering of the order.

DO NOT REDUCE

Instruction that may be added to good-till-cancelled (GTC) limit buy orders and sell stop orders—also to sell stop limit orders—telling specialist that on ex-dividend day the customer does not want the order reduced by the amount of a cash dividend.

DNR instruction does not affect the handling of stock dividends. Special rules apply.

DON'T FIGHT THE TAPE

An expression of analysts and traders to caution against using personal prejudices or feelings in making investment decisions. In fact, it does not make any difference what the fundamentals are if the market is going the other way; right now it is more profitable to join the crowd, rather than go counter to it.

DON'T KNOW

Industry term for a questioned trade (one where there is some discrepancy in the transaction records) on the comparison sheet for daily trades between broker/dealers.

See also QT.

DONUT TRADE

Term used of a somewhat tainted U.S. government securities transaction. Specifically, it is a term reverse repurchase agreement with a hole in the middle. Thus, a customer of a broker/dealer finances a government securities position for 30 days (typically) but, at month end, takes back the collateral and returns the money. The following day (or soon after) the original financing is reestablished at the old valuation. In effect, the hole in the donut enhances the ratings of both firms because ratings are usually based on month-end financial statements.

DOOMSDAY VALUE
A popular tax term in England when referring to an investor's cost basis for calculating capital gains and losses. When the capital gains tax (CGT) was imposed in England on April 6, 1965, investors were permitted to use that date's closing prices as the basis for future liability—this gave them a one-time "step-up" in value. Because this was a one-time event, the name "Doomsday" caught on. This is an obvious reference to the *Doomsday Book* (correctly, *Domesday Book*) completed in AD 1086 on the direction of William the Conqueror. This book was based on a survey of all lands in Britain and listed the legal owner and the value as determined at that time.

DORMANT ACCOUNT
A customer securities account in which there has been no securities or money activity for an extended time.

It is not uncommon for the brokerage firm to determine that such an account is dormant and to cease doing business with the customer.

If the customer cannot be found, there may be a presumption of death of the customer, or abandonment of the assets. In such cases state "escheat" (pronounced "ess-cheat") laws take over the ownership of the assets.

DOT
See DESIGNATED ORDER TURNAROUND.

DOUBLE-BARRELED
Use of municipal revenue bonds if the payment of interest and the repayment of principal is further guaranteed by another municipality that will make the payments from general taxes. For example, a housing authority issues revenue bonds. The bonds are double-barreled if a city or state pledges to pay interest and principal if rents from the housing project are insufficient. Do not confuse with overlapping debt (i.e., a bond with two issuers).

DOUBLE BOTTOM
Description of a stock's price movement if it reaches, on two different occasions, the same low price. For example, on two occasions in the past year or so, a stock dropped to 36. Technical analysts see the double-

bottom price as a support level. Hence, a subsequent drop below this price is a sign of a continued decline in price.

Term also can be expanded, such as *triple bottom,* and so on.

See also DOUBLE TOP.

DOUBLE-DECLINING-BALANCE METHOD
Depreciation method that accelerates depreciation in earlier years and lowers it in subsequent years. Starts with percentage of straight-line depreciation, doubles it, and applies same percentage in subsequent years. For example, if straight-line depreciation is 10%, DDB is 20%. Both methods meet at scrap value, although DDB will usually get to scrap value earlier, thus it has a tax advantage in earlier years.

DOUBLE DIPPING
1. Any conflict of interest.
2. Slang: the practice whereby a corporation finances construction through an issue of industrial revenue bonds by the municipality in which the property will be located. The corporation double dips in that it raises capital at lowered rates and uses accelerated depreciation to recover costs. Pending legislation would eliminate one of the "dips" by requiring straight-line depreciation.

DOUBLE EXEMPTION BOND
Colloquial expression for a bond whose interest payments are not subject to federal and state taxation. This privilege is generally limited to municipal bonds if the holder is domiciled in the same state as the issuer of the bond.

DOUBLE OPTION
An English term for what in the United States is known as a *straddle;* that is, a long put and long call (or a short put and short call) at the same strike price and with the same expiration date. Everyone is agreed up to this point.

If the strike prices differ, terminology may be confusing. Conventional (OTC) options with differing strike prices are often called "spreads"; standardized (listed) option terminology, if there are differing strike prices (or differing expiration dates), tends to center on the word "combination."

DOUBLE TAXATION
Feature of the tax law in the United States whereby the income of dividend payers is taxed before the distribution of dividends. The dividends, in turn, are again taxed at the recipient's level. Example: The earnings

of a corporation are taxed. The corporation then pays dividends that are taxable to the individuals receiving them.

Exception: dividend recipients to whom the "conduit" theory applies. Example: Certain trusts and regulated investment companies, who pass through the dividend untaxed. The final recipient pays the taxes.

DOUBLE TOP

Description of a stock's price movement if it reaches, on two different occasions, the same high price. For example, on two occasions in the past year or so, a stock rose to 42. Technical analysts see the double-top price as a resistance level. Hence, a subsequent rise above this price is a sign of a continued rise in price.

Term can also be expanded, such as *triple top,* and so on.

See also DOUBLE BOTTOM.

TO DOUBLE-UP

A strategy that reaffirms the original reason for investing—either a purchase or short sale—by doubling the risk of the original investment. For example, if a client buys 1,000 shares of LMN at $50 and, when the stock drops to $45, the client buys another 1,000 shares, he or she is doubling up. Note that the client is reaffirming confidence in the security. Note also that the client needs a 10% rise in the stock from $45 to $50 to break even. Following the double-up, the client needs only a 5% stock price rise from $45 to the doubled-up average price of $47.50 to break even.

Doubling up is a sophisticated strategy and generally should be used only by wealthy investors who can afford to accept the doubled risk.

DOUBLE WITCHING DAY

The Japanese version of the U.S. "triple witching" day. In Japan, both futures on the Nikkei Index and the TOPIX Index expire at the conclusion of the third trading day before the 10th day of March, June, September, and December. The Nikkei Index trades on the Osaka Exchange and the TOPIX Index trades on the Tokyo Exchange. These are weighted indexes and many of the stocks are different in the two indexes—as a result, many arbitrage situations exist.

DOWER

Term used for the legal interest a woman has in the estate of her deceased husband.

DOW JONES & COMPANY, INC.

Publisher of research and advisory services to the securities industry. DJ is the publisher of *Barron's* and *The Wall Street Journal* and is the proprietor of the Dow Jones Averages, which is the most popular of the measurements used to track the general movements of stock market prices.

DOW JONES AVERAGE
Measurement of market price movement based on 65 stocks: 30 industrials, 20 transportation, and 15 utility issues. Relatively few persons follow the composite average; instead, they follow the industrial average, DJIA, and the relative movement of the other two averages.

DOW JONES INDUSTRIAL AVERAGE
A measurement of general market price movement for 30 widely held NYSE-listed stocks. Called an "average" because no adjustment is made for the number of shares outstanding in the component stocks. Average is found by adding the prices of the 30 stocks and dividing by an adjusted denominator. Over the years, because of stock splits, stock dividends, and substitutions of stocks, the denominator has been changed from 30 to .505. The 30 component stocks and the current denominator can be found in *The Wall Street Journal* in the footnotes to the chart of the average.

DOWN-AND-OUT OPTION
Term used of a block of at least 10 call options with the same exercise price and expiration date carrying this provision: If the underlying stock declines by a predetermined, agreed-upon amount in the marketplace prior to the expiration date, the exercise privilege is immediately canceled and the option becomes worthless.

Listed options are not subject to the down-and-out provision.

DOWN DELTA
See DELTA.

DOWNSIZING
A euphemism for the reorganization of a company that results in a lowering of the number of employees and its payroll. Downsizing often occurs after a period of rapid expansion, when it is realized—either because of return on capital or a recession—that the company would be better managed if it would stick to its most profitable areas of business.

DOWNTICK
Sale of a listed security at a price that is lower than the price of the previous regular-way transaction. For example, the last regular-way transaction was at 29. If the next regular way transaction is at 28⅞ or below, it is said to be a "downtick."

See also REGULAR WAY-TRANSACTION; MINUS TICK; ZERO-MINUS TICK.

DOWNTREND LINE
See TRENDLINE.

DOWN UNDER BONDS
Eurobonds denominated in Australian or New Zealand dollars. Such bonds are offered originally in European markets. Because they are not registered in the United States, they may not be acquired by U.S. investors until they are "seasoned"; that is, are actively traded for a time and are thus no longer subject to U.S. legal restrictions.

DOWPAC
Acronym for Dow Jones Put and Call Option. An over-the-counter option contract developed by Oakley, Sutton Investment Corporation, an investment adviser. The contract permits the holder to buy, or sell in the case of a put, a package of eight stocks, in different predetermined quantities, most of which are issues used to calculate the Dow Jones Industrial Average.

DOW THEORY
Interpretation of primary market trend. The Dow Theory holds that there is no primary market trend (i.e., a trend that will last—either upward or downward—for a year or more) unless there is substantial correlation between the movements of the industrial, transportation, and utility averages.

DPM
Acronym for designated primary marketmaker. DPM is a title used by the CBOE to identify the firm (or individual) primarily responsible for maintaining fair and orderly markets in selected nonequity options. This is under the exchange's Modified Trading System (MTS). In effect, the DPM has a function similar to that of the specialists on the major stock exchanges.

Trading in equity options features competitive marketmakers on the CBOE.

DPN
See DEFERRED PAYMENT NOTES.

DPP
See DIRECT PARTICIPATION PROGRAM.

DPSP
See DEFERRED PROFIT-SHARING PLAN.

DR

1. Commonly used designation, Dr, of a debit in a client's account with a brokerage firm. For example, a client's statement reads $2,500 Dr, which signifies that the client owes the brokerage firm $2,500.

   From the Latin *debetur,* abbreviated Dr. meaning it is owed.

2. When used in this fashion, particularly on corporate or municipal calendars, these initials identify Dillon, Read & Co., Inc., a major underwriter of securities in the financial community.

DRA

See DEFICIT REDUCTION ACT OF 1984.

DRAFT

A negotiable instrument that will, if endorsed, transfer money from the account of the payer to the account of the payee. Significant difference from a check: a check is a debit on the books of the issuer as soon as it is issued; a draft is not a debit until it is presented for payment.

DRAFT DELIVERY

A settlement procedure whereby securities are delivered to a buyer with an unsigned check attached as a condition of acceptance.

The buyer must sign the check already drawn for the contract amount payable to the seller. Only when this check is signed and presented to the deliverer is the trade considered as "settled."

DRAW BACK

The expression signifies that an underwriter's retention in a specific syndicate offering has been reduced by the manager. In other words, the underwriter has fewer shares or bonds to offer to its own customers from its underwriting commitment, because the manager has drawn back shares or bonds into the "pot" for sale to institutional accounts.

DRAWDOWN SCHEDULE

An estimated list of payments to be made to a contractor in the course of the completion of a construction project. The schedule of such payments is usually set forth in the contract of a municipal or a REIT loan.

DRESSING UP A PORTFOLIO

A term used to describe the policy of portfolio managers whose endeavors are subject to periodic scrutiny; for example, a quarterly or semiannual report to investors or pension fund holders.

To make sure that all looks well, the manager makes sure that at the time for the cut-off for the report to fund holders, only "in vogue" stocks are in the portfolio. This is done by selling off high-risk stocks just before the end of the reporting period and substituting more palatable stocks. Except for the transaction costs, such "dressing up" does little for the performance of the portfolio.

Also see WINDOW DRESSING.

DREW'S ODD-LOT THEORY

A hypothesis, on a theory of Garfield Drew, that one may predict a general market trend opposed to the trend of odd-lot transactions. Thus, if odd-lotters are buying, sell; if selling, buy. The theory has no present value.

See also ODD-LOT THEORY.

DRIP

Acronym for dividend reinvestment plan. Program whereby some corporations offer current shareholders the option of using dividends to purchase more shares in the corporation. Often such shares purchased through dividend reinvestment are purchased at a discount, typically 5%, from current market value.

More than 800 companies whose shares are listed on the NYSE offer such plans. Because the shareholder has the option of taking the dividend in cash or reinvesting, the dollar value of the reinvestment is taxable in the year of purchase.

DRIP-FEED TECHNIQUE

An English term that is also called "evergreen funding." The concept is simple: Installment payments are used to capitalize the start-up of a newly reorganized company. Thus, as needed, new capital is added to the company in a way that is analogous to the feeding of a plant by the gradual dripping of moisture and plant nutrients.

DROP-DEAD DAY

Used in financial circles to describe the last possible day on which an important event can take place. For example, the debt limit will expire tomorrow and Congress has done nothing to raise the limit: tomorrow is "drop-dead day."

DROP-LOCK

Colloquial term for a feature that often accompanies the issuance of floating-rate note. Using this feature, the holder may convert the floating-rate note into a fixed-rate note if prevailing interest rates drop to a specified level during the life of the instrument.

See also FLOATING-RATE NOTE.

DROP-LOCK SECURITY
A floating-rate security with interest payments pegged to changes in a popular interbank loan rate as they occur. LIBOR is commonly used. However, if the rate used as the peg falls to a predetermined level, the drop-lock security automatically changes to a fixed-rate security until its maturity date.

DRP
Acronym for Disciplinary Reporting Page. This is an attachment to the standard Form U-4 employee application for registration with the NASD, NYSE, and other exchanges. This attachment solicits details in a standardized format about the disciplinary history of an applicant. By thus standardizing the information in a brief format, it is possible to temporarily transfer registration until further information is received.

DRT
Abbreviation: disregard tape. This designation is used on orders sent to exchanges if the buyer/seller wants to authorize the floor broker to use personal judgment to determine the time or price, or both, of the execution.

More popular usage: NH; that is, order not held.

DTB
Acronym for Deutsche Terminboerse Gmbh. This is the official name of the German Options and Financial Futures Exchange. The DTB is designed to function in competition with similar exchanges throughout the world; it must also be in conformity with other German exchanges.

Cash deposits and settlements are linked to the Hessische Landes-Zentral Bank, which acts as the DTB's agent. Securities are deposited with the Frankfurter Kassenverein, which is similar to the DTC in the United States. Only major German banks are shareholders in DTB; no foreign institutions are eligible.

DTC
See DEPOSITORY TRUST COMPANY.

DUAL BANKING SYSTEM
General term for the U.S. form of commercial banking. Under the Federal Reserve Banking Act of 1913, a commercial bank may elect to register and to be regulated by either the Federal Reserve or by an individual state banking commission. Both subject their members to continuous scrutiny and high operating standards.

Of about 14,000 commercial banks in this country, 40% are members of the Federal Reserve banking system and they control about 75% of all deposits in the United States.

DUAL CAPACITY
This term is used equally in the United States and the United Kingdom following the "big bang" in 1986.

The term refers to the fact that a securities firm may act either as a broker (agent) or dealer (principal) in executing different transactions in the same security, or even for the same customer in the execution of different transactions. It is prohibited to act as both broker and dealer on the same transaction.

DUAL CURRENCY CONVERTIBLE
This is a debt instrument of an overseas subsidiary domiciled in England. It is convertible into stock of the parent company but at a ratio of currency exchange determined at the time of issuance. For example, if the U.K. subsidiary of a U.S. company issued a dual currency convertible, it could be issued and traded in pounds sterling, but it could also be convertible into 50 shares of the U.S. parent's common stock traded in U.S. dollars. All things being equal, the convertible's value would be a function of the ratio of pounds to dollars.

DUAL CURRENCY YEN BONDS
Japanese-issued securities, offered in the European marketplace, in which the periodic interest is payable in yen. The principal amount, however, is repayable in some other currency at a specified rate of exchange.

DUAL LISTING
A misnomer for a security that is listed on one exchange and is also traded on a second or third exchange. Generally, an issuer does not file a listing application with more than one exchange. If a second exchange trades the security, it usually means that the SEC has permitted the second exchange to conduct unlisted trading on its premises.

The term is not used of a security listed for exchange trading that also is traded over the counter. In this case, the over-the-counter trading is referred to as "the third market."

DUAL-PURPOSE COMPANY
A form of closed-end management investment company that initially distributes two classes of securities in equal amounts in a single offering. Generally, one class will be designated capital shares, and the other will be designated income shares. Each class will have its own privi-

leges. By issuing equal amounts of each class of shares, an investor of $1 in one type may reap the results of $2 worth of investment because all income goes to one class of security and all capital growth to the other class.

DUAL SERIES ZERO-COUPON DEBENTURE
Two distinct securities offered by the same issuer at the same time in an endeavor to appeal to different segments of the market. Typically, one security is a short-term (1 to 5 years) zero-coupon note; the second is a long-term (20 to 30 years) fixed-coupon bond. The issuer, by offering both bonds at the same time, hopes to achieve a net interest cost that will be less than the cost of issuing each security separately.

DUAL TRADING
1. The simultaneous trading of a stock or a bond on two stock exchanges or marketplaces. In this regard, it is a form of arbitrage.
2. The ability of a commodity exchange member to transact both for a client's account and for a personal account in the same commodity on the same day. This potential conflict of interest is permitted in the commodities exchanges, but it is forbidden on the NYSE without specific consent from the customer.

DUBLIN STOCK EXCHANGE
This stock exchange is officially part of the International Stock Exchange of the United Kingdom and the Republic of Ireland (the old London Stock Exchange).

This affiliate employs a call market each business day at 9:30 A.M. and again at 2:15 P.M., although after-hour activity is allowed until 5:30 P.M. Settlement, as in England, is scheduled at the end of each two-week account period.

DUE BILL
Document attached by selling broker to delivered securities that gives title to the buyer's broker for a specified number of shares or dollars.

A due bill is attached if seller sold securities with a dividend, interest, or other distribution but delivery occurred too late to make buyer the holder of record. The due bill, in effect, rectifies this failure to deliver on time to make the buyer the holder of record. For example, buyer purchases 100 XYZ with a dividend. Record date is May 15; delivery is made by the seller's broker on May 16. Buyer's broker will accept securities only if a due bill for the dividend is attached.

Also called "due bill check" (q.v.).

DUE BILL CHECK
A due bill for a cash dividend on stock or an interest payment on registered bonds. The due bill check is postdated and can be deposited on the payment date designated by the issuer of the underlying securities. For example, a stock was purchased with the dividend. However, the certificate cannot be delivered to the buyer in time to make the buyer the holder of record. The buyer will not accept the certificate unless a due bill check for the amount of the dividend to which the buyer is entitled has been attached to the certificate.

DUE DILIGENCE MEETING
A meeting held to discuss and review the detailed information included in the registration statement and to begin negotiation for the formal underwriting agreement. SEC rules require that such a meeting between officers of the issuing corporation and prospective members of the underwriting syndicate be held between the filing of the preliminary registration statement and the effective date of the offering.

DUE-DUE BILLS
Tongue-in-cheek name for short-term floating rate instruments collateralized by poor-quality automobile receivables. Due-due is a sound-alike name for "doo-doo"—a vulgar description of the low quality of the pledged collateral. Banks and finance companies are often the securitizers of such poor obligations.

DUE-ON-SALE CLAUSE
Clause often contained in a mortgage instrument whereby the full balance due the lender must be paid at the time there is a sale of the underlying real estate. This clause precludes the assumption of the existing mortgage, which often has very favorable terms, by the new purchaser of the property.

DUFF AND PHELPS
A Chicago-based research organization that rates debt securities of many utility, bank, finance company, and industrial issuers.

DUIT
Acronym for Directions Unit Investment Trust. DUITs were invented by the former firm of E. F. Hutton to achieve capital appreciation through investment in a diversified portfolio of securities. This "in-house" investment company was comprised of a fixed portfolio of 30 undervalued stocks selected by Hutton's computer research capabilities.

DUMP

1. To sell a security at a sacrifice price. Example: "Let's dump it."
2. In computer terminology, to erase a database, or to transfer a portion of data from one base to another to detect program errors.
3. The nickname used for Dome Petroleum, a large Canadian producer of crude oil, derived from its American Stock Exchange ticker symbol: DMP.

DUMPING

1. The removal of stored information from the database of an automated computer system. Dumping is normally done when the system's capacity is reached.
2. Slang for a practice prohibited by the CBOE. Dumping is the sudden entry of a large number of market and immediately executable limit orders for options on the order book official (OBO). This practice can excessively burden or impede trading in a particular option series. In practice, it may even lead to a trading halt.

DUN & BRADSTREET (D&B)

A corporation, headquartered in New York City, that specializes in credit reporting and collection. Its subscription services are widely used by broker/dealers and other commercial enterprises to obtain credit information about current and prospective customers-

DU-OP SECURITY

Contraction of: dual option. A warrant that contains two options: the holder may subscribe either to an issue of common stock or an issue of preferred stock. In this way, the holder may profit if the common stock rises in value, or may elect to choose preferred stock for income.

DURABLE POWER OF ATTORNEY

An authorization to act on behalf of another, including the purchase and sale of securities, in which the designee's power will survive the disability or incompetence of the grantor. As usual, this power of attorney terminates upon the death of the grantor.

DURATION

An important term in bond portfolio management. Although there are many definitions, two are more prevalent:

1. The point in time at which the paper loss of principal equals the increased return from the reinvestment of cash flow from coupons if interest rates rise.

2. The midpoint of the present value of all cash flows to be received from a bond held to maturity, provided all cash flows are reinvested (Macaulay's definition, 1938).

Both definitions are an approach to bond portfolio management and a method of moderating interest-rate risk. Duration changes as a bond approaches maturity and as interest rates change. The speed of such changes is called the "convexity" of a bond.

DUTCH AUCTION

General concept: Bidders do not bid up for a purchase; instead, seller offers down until a satisfactory price is reached.

In practice, an offering that is accepted at a price sufficient to sell all of the items for sale. For example, if 30,000 items are offered, and bidders bid 30 for 10,000 and 29 for 15,000 and 28 for 5,000, the issue will be sold at 28 because the total bids are for 30,000 and that satisfies the needs of the seller.

If the property offered is in multiple units, the price is lowered until buyers for all of the property are found. The weekly auction of Treasury bills is a classic Dutch auction.

DUTCH AUCTION RATE TRANSFERABLE SECURITIES

See DARTS.

DVP

See DELIVER VERSUS PAYMENT.

DVP TRANSACTION

Initials for deliver versus payment. A purchase of securities on behalf of a customer who promises full payment at the time the certificates are delivered to an agent bank or broker/dealer.

Synonym: COD (cash on delivery) transaction.

In practice, such transactions are permitted only in institutional-type accounts.

DWARFS

Slang for Federal National Mortgage Association (Fannie Mae) securities with 15-year original maturities and presumed 7-year average lives, as opposed to regular, conventional pools with 30-year original maturities and presumed 12-year average lives.

Both regular and dwarf pools are assembled in minimum pools of $1 million.

DWR
When used on corporate or municipal calendars, these initials stand for Dean Witter Reynolds, a subsidiary of Sears, Roebuck and Company, and a major underwriter of securities.

DYNAMIC HEDGING
Euphemistic term used of index arbitrage activity by some institutional portfolio managers. Typically, it involves large and rapid portfolio switches from stocks to index options or index futures contracts and vice versa. In early 1990 it encompassed a strategy using "portfolio puts" by introducing a third-party broker/dealer to cushion some (or all) of its market risk.

DYNAMITER
Industry slang for high-pressure salespersons.

The term is pejorative and is used of salespersons employed by "penny stock" firms that convince customers to part with their money in get-rich-quick schemes.

E

E
Fifth letter of the English alphabet, used:
1. Lowercase next to the dividend in stock transaction tables to designate that some method of computation is used, other than the product of the last quarterly dividend multiplied by 4. Often means that a capital gain accompanies the dividend; for example, the distributions of closed-end funds.
2. As the fifth letter in a NASDAQ/NMS symbol to designate that the company is late in filing its required documents with the SEC. As such, the company may be subject to federal penalties and delisting from NASDAQ.
3. Uppercase on the NYSE tape, this letter stands for Transco Energy Company, a major supplier and transporter of natural gas systems in the eastern part of the United States.

EAC
See EQUITY APPRECIATION CERTIFICATES.

EAFE
Acronym for Europe, Australia, and Far East stock index. EAFE is a portfolio of 900 different stocks selected by Morgan Stanley as the basis of futures contracts and listed option contracts overlying them. These

900 stocks represent more than 60% of the aggregate market value of the stocks traded on exchanges in 16 different countries.

EAGLE
NYSE title for its computer command system for on-line retrieval of information stored in its FOCUS, LEGAL, and REGIS subsystems. Access to this information is highly restricted and is tightly controlled by the exchange.

E&OE
Initials for: errors and omissions excepted. This legend often appears on customer statements and is intended to absolve the broker/dealer of liability if an accidental mistake is made in preparing the statement.

EARLY BARGAIN (EB)
English marketplace term for transactions executed after 3:30 P.M., London time. Such trades are submitted for comparison on the morning following trade date, just as though they had occurred the following day.

Although EB trades carry the same settlement date (by account period) as trades completed earlier on the same day, they will be DKd if they are submitted on the same day as the transaction.

EARLY BIRD RECEIPTS (EBR)
Similar in concept to CATS and TIGRs, this name is given to stripped U.S. government securities issued by Lazard Freres & Co.

See CATS and TIGRs.

EARLY EXERCISE
Term used if an option holder chooses to buy (call) or sell (put) before the expiration date of the contract.

From the viewpoint of the writer of the option, early exercise results in an early assignment.

EARNED SURPLUS
See RETAINED EARNINGS.

EARNINGS BEFORE TAXES (EBT)
Commonly used expression for earnings of a corporation after payment of bond interest but before payment of federal and other taxes.

EARNINGS PER SHARE (EPS)
Net income of a corporation after taxes and required payments to preferred shareholders.

Called "primary earnings per share" if corporation also has convertible securities or other common stock equivalents outstanding. Fully diluted EPS also will reflect effect of conversion or exercise of stock options. For example, a company has primary earnings of $4.00 per share and fully diluted earnings of $3.50. This means, right now all common shareholders have an EPS of $4.00; but if all the convertible securities on the stock were exercised, the earnings would be $3.50.

EARNINGS REPORT
Popular name for the income statement of a corporation; that is, a statement showing the corporation's revenues and expenses over a given period. Generally, earnings reports are issued quarterly and annually.

EARN-OUT
Mergers and acquisitions terminology for future supplementary payments that must be made for the acquisition of a business. These payments are not part of the original purchase price; instead, they are extra payments to be made if future earnings of the acquired business exceed a specified minimum dollar threshold.

EARN-OUT RIGHT
Term used to describe the entitlement given to the seller of a business to additional compensation based on the level of future earnings of the company. Thus, the seller receives an immediate payment for control of the business, but more remuneration may be forthcoming if the company meets specified revenue or net income goals.

EASIER
Term used by industry professionals to designate that bid prices (or transaction prices) are falling in value. For example, the market is easier.
   Also used as a participle. Example: Bond prices are easing.

EASTERN ACCOUNT
Commonly used underwriting account for municipal securities. Basic concept: Syndicate as a group assumes financial responsibility for success of the venture. Thus, gains or losses for participants in the account are not dependent on what they sell, but on their participation in the account. Example: In a divided account, member A has a 10% participation. Member A sells 15% of the bonds, but the entire syndicate only sells 80% of the bonds it bought. Member A would be responsible for 10% of the remaining bonds despite overselling its percent participation.
   Also called "divided account."
   See also WESTERN ACCOUNT.

EASYGROWTH TREASURY RECEIPTS

Acronym: ETR. Stripped U.S. Treasury bonds made into zero-coupon debt securities by Dean Witter Reynolds, Inc. There is a single payment of cash at the maturity of the certificate. ETRs are similar in concept and function to TIGRs, CATS, and COUGARs.

EASY MONEY

Slang term for an economic situation in which interest rates are low and the money supply is plentiful. The most popular criterion for easy money is the Federal Funds Rate: the interest rate banks pay one another for the loan of overnight funds. The Federal Reserve Board, through the powers granted to it, is probably the greatest influence on whether money is easy or not.

EASY QUALIFIER LOANS

See EQUAL LOANS.

EATING SOMEONE'S LUNCH

Slang expression used to indicate the aggressiveness of a competitor. The analogy: The aggressive company is taking food from another person's mouth by aggressive pricing and promotion. Some years ago, for example, Kodak was accused of "eating Polaroid's lunch" as it began to sell instant film. Court judgment in favor of Polaroid appears to have borne this out.

EATING STOCK

1. Used of a block positioner or marketmaker who is obliged to buy stock in a falling market.
2. Used of an investment banker who has purchased a security from an issuer for resale but who is unable to sell it at the present time.

Both terms imply the inability to sell the stock immediately at a profit, as would generally be the case of a dealer or underwriter.

EB

See EARLY BARGAIN.

EBT

See EARNINGS BEFORE TAXES.

EC

See EUROPEAN ECONOMIC COMMUNITY.

ECONOMIC LIFE
The time period within which the cost of a fixed asset can be depreciated against current earnings. Theoretically, the economic life represents the time frame within which that asset will yield useful service to the business. Land has an infinite economic life; hence, it may not be depreciated. The economic life of most other assets is fixed by the tax code and ACRS (Accelerated Cost Recovery System).

ECONOMIC RECOVERY TAX ACT OF 1981
See ERTA.

ECP
Commonly used initials for Euro-commercial paper.

Euro-commercial paper is used by companies outside the United States to borrow short-term funds for ordinary operations, short-term inventory needs, and the like. Euro-commercial paper is similar to commercial paper in the United States but does not have the usual regulatory restraints.

ECU
See EUROPEAN CURRENCY UNIT.

EDGAR
Acronym for Electronic Data Gathering, Analysis, and Retrieval. EDGAR is a computer program sponsored by the SEC. The program permits registered issuers to file electronically, rather than by hard copy, the required reports to the SEC. As a result, public subscribers to these reports can have instant access to this updated information by means of a computer interface.

EDGE
1. Slang: an advantage. Example: Federal securities law forbids the use of inside information because it would give the edge to one person over another.
2. Used as a short form for the Edge Act, or securities issued thereunder.

EDGE ACT
Federal law, passed in 1919, permitting commercial banks to conduct international business across state lines. As a general rule, domestic banks may only conduct business in the state where they are chartered.

Often, you will hear securities related to such interstate banking activities called "Edge Act securities."

EDR
See EUROPEAN DEPOSITORY RECEIPT.

EEC
See EUROPEAN ECONOMIC COMMUNITY.

EFFECTIVE DATE
Date when a registered offering may begin to be made. Usually it is the 20th day following the filing of a registration statement with the SEC, unless the SEC has issued a deficiency letter requiring the issuer to make certain adjustments in the registration statement.

SEC, either on its own initiative or upon request by the issuer, may set an earlier effective date.

EFFECTIVE LIFE
1. The time remaining on an unexecuted open order entered by a customer. For example, at many member firms good-till-cancelled orders have an effective life of 31 days.
2. The expected life of a self-amortizing security based on the experience of other securities of the same class. For example, although GNMA pass-through securities are based on 30-year self-amortizing mortgages, the expected life may be much shorter.

EFFECTIVE SALE
Common expression for the price of the round-lot transaction on an exchange that determines the execution of an odd-lot order. For example, if a client enters a market order to buy 50 shares of a listed security, and the next round-lot transaction is at 33, that sale will be effective. The odd-lot buyer will pay 33 plus a differential (if any) of $1/8$ point payable on odd-lot transactions.

EFP PROGRAM
See EXCHANGE FOR PHYSICAL PROGRAM.

EIP
Acronym for Equity Index Participatnts. EIPs are the American Stock Exchange's counterpart to the PHLX's Cash Index Participations (CIPs). The EIP, on the other hand, is an option based upon the performance of the Major Market Index (MMI) or the Institutional Index (II) traded on the AMEX. Like the CIP, holders do receive a proportionate share of the dividends paid to holders of the underlying stocks. There is no specific expiration date on EIPs. It is the subject of a court-issued injunction because of its similarity to a futures contract.

EITHER/OR ORDER

An exchange order that combines a limit with a stop order for the same security. Execution of one instruction requires cancellation of the other; that is, either the limit or stop order because each is on an opposite side of the market.

See also ALTERNATIVE ORDER.

EITHER WAY MARKET

A market situation in which there is an identical bid and offer (asked) price for a security. Term also is used if there are identical interest rates on bank deposits.

Common synonym: locked market.

EL BIG BANG ESPANOL

A lighthearted term for some recent reforms in the Spanish stock markets. The reforms have embraced two concepts: an SEC-like body in Spain to monitor and supervise a revised code of market trading rules, and a computer linkage of the regional exchanges in Barcelona, Bilbao, and Valencia with the principal exchange in Madrid.

ELBOW

Designation of a sharp change in the slope of a yield curve. Example: If there were a steady rise in yields for maturities from 1 to 7 years, then a pronounced flattening of the slope from 7 out to 30 years, the change at 7 years would be called "an elbow."

ELECTING SALE

1. Round-lot transaction that causes either a round-lot or an odd-lot stop order or a stop-limit order to become a market or limit order. For example, a customer has entered a sell stop order at 55; a transaction occurs at 54$\frac{7}{8}$; the stop order to sell at 55 is elected and is now a market order to sell.

   See also ODD LOT and ROUND LOT.
2. Transaction at a price that a member, usually a specialist, has guaranteed to another customer. For example, a specialist has stopped an order at 55. A transaction at 55 elects the stop, and the specialist must execute at the guaranteed price.

ELECTION STOCK

Also known as "political" stock, the term is used in Japan to describe an equity that is about to be manipulated upward and thus should be appealing to persons running for political office. The concept is this: A candidate can buy the stock now and in a few months sell it at a good profit to pay off campaign expenses.

ELECTRONIC ACCESS MEMBER
A person who has purchased from the NYSE the right to use the trading floor facilities to buy and sell securities through the electronic communications and execution capabilities of a regular member organization.

ELECTRONIC DATA GATHERING ANALYSIS, AND RETRIEVAL
See EDGAR.

ELEEMOSYNARY INSTITUTION
Greek: *eleemosyne*, meaning mercy or alms. A legal or recognized charity that may be religious, social, or political. Such organizations are philanthropic and nonprofit and, as such, are tax-exempt. Great care must be exercised if brokerage accounts are opened for such institutions to make sure that all recommendations are suitable and that the institution is properly empowered to have securities accounts.

ELEPHANTS
A somewhat derogatory term for large institutional investors. The term signifies that, because of their huge assets, these customers are capable of moving markets with their buy-sell programs. The concept is that these elephantine organizations have no qualms about trampling small retail investors in their eagerness to buy or sell portfolio securities.

ELEVATOR BONDS
A slang term that is used in the underwriting market for Eurobonds. If an issue is priced too high for an easy and immediate sale, the underwriters have no other choice than to hold the bonds in inventory. To describe this event, they say: "Send them down in the elevator"; that is, from the trading floor down to the bank vault.

ELIGIBLE SECURITY
Widely used term, which may refer to:
1. Securities traded by Federal Open Market Committee.
2. Securities that a Federal Reserve bank will accept for loans at the discount window.
3. Securities that have loan value under Regulation T, whether in the general, special bond, or special subscription accounts.
4. Securities that a carrying broker may deposit at the Options Clearing Corporation as collateral for short option positions.
5. Securities that exchange members may trade in the OTC market although they are listed on the exchange.

ELLIOTT WAVE THEORY
A popular technical analysis of trends in the Dow Jones Industrial Averages, formulated in 1938 by the late Ralph Elliott.

Using a system that counts and measures price changes in the DJIA, an Elliott analyst predicts future trends in the average. From this, one then can deduce the next likely broad market movement for most stocks.

EMANCIPATION
Legal term for the passage of a person from a status of servitude to freedom. Commonly used applications:
1. A person, not yet of legal age, who is permitted to enter into binding contracts. For example, the court permits a minor to sell a piece of property.
2. A person, although a minor, who is permitted to act as an adult because of special economic reasons. For example, mother and father die in an accident; they have three children ages 17, 11, 9. The 17-year-old is permitted by the court to act as guardian for the 11- and 9-year-old children. The 17-year-old child has been emancipated by the court.

EMBARGO
A government-imposed restriction on the export of goods from its country to another country. This action may have political, military, or economic motivation. From the Spanish *embargar,* to prohibit.

EMBEZZLEMENT
Misappropriation of a customer's or firm's assets, often in the form of checks or securities certificates. Persons associated with the securities industry who embezzle, even if full restitution is made, generally are barred from future employment in the industry. By industry rule, brokerage firms must carry a blanket fidelity bond to protect it from such unlawful actions by employees.

EMERGING MARKETS FREE INDEX
See EMF.

EMF
Acronym for Emerging Markets Free index. EMF was innovated by Morgan Stanley Capital International (MSCI) to monitor stock market price movements in Mexico, Malaysia, Chile, Jordan, Thailand, the Philippines, and Argentina. These countries were chosen because they offer immediate and direct access to foreign investors.

EMINENT DOMAIN
The sovereign right of government to appropriate the assets of a private party for the general welfare of the public. Just and equitable compensation must be paid for the property taken. Eminent domain usually is associated with real estate transactions, and it could affect paydowns on GNMA, FHLC, and conventional mortgage loans in some circumstances.

EMPLOYEE RETIREMENT INCOME SECURITY ACT OF 1974
See ERISA.

EMPLOYEE STOCK OWNERSHIP PLAN
See ESOP.

EMPLOYEE STOCK OWNERSHIP TRUST
See ESOT and ESOP.

EMPTY HEAD AND PURE HEART TEST
A tongue-in-cheek description of SEC Rule 14e-3, sub-paragraph (b). The rule prohibits any person, other than the bidder in a tender offer, from trading in that security while in possession of material, nonpublic information about the deal. Sub-paragraph (b) provides an exemption for financial institutions—but only if:
1. The trader did not know the information, and
2. The financial institution had created, surveilled, and enforced reasonable policies and procedures to avoid violations of the rule; for example, prepared a restricted list.

EMS
These initials stand for European Monetary System, a compatible exchangeable currency proposal for implementation in Common Market transactions. EMS permits the use of a member country's own currency in satisfaction of mercantile transactions. Of course, it also assumes each country will continuously stabilize the value of its currency through adherence to the European Exchange Rate Mechanism (ERM).

ENDORSE
1. To guarantee. Examples: to endorse a conventional over-the-counter option; to endorse a certificate as signed by the registered owner.
2. To sign a certificate, as registered owner, so title may be transferred. Examples: to endorse a check; to endorse a stock or bond.

ENDORSEMENT FEE

Money paid by put and call brokers and dealers to an NYSE member organization for its guarantee of client performance in connection with the writing of a conventional OTC option. Generally, the fee is about $6.25 per contract, although higher fees may be negotiated.

ENGLISH AUCTION

Marketing method occasionally used by issuers for public offerings of their securities. Each of the bidding broker/dealers independently submits a bid for a specific quantity of the issue at a price it deems reasonable for investment or profitable resale.

The issuer sells the securities to as many of the best bidders, at their prices and quantities, as are needed to distribute the entire offering. Example: In a 300,000-share offering, if an issuer received five 100,000 share bids at 39, $39^{1}/_{8}$, $39^{1}/_{4}$, $39^{3}/_{8}$, and $39^{1}/_{2}$, it would sell 100,000 to each of the top three bidders. The bidders, in turn, would establish their own reoffer prices.

ENTREPRENEUR

French: a person who undertakes. In practice, a person who undertakes a business enterprise.

The connotation of the word is that the enterprise entails a considerable amount of ingenuity and risk. Hence, the adjective, entrepreneurial, meaning inventive and risky.

EOE DUTCH STOCK INDEX OPTION

The European Options Exchange in Amsterdam offers a European-style index option based on the performance of 20 Dutch companies whose stock is traded on the Amsterdam Exchange. Although other options on the EOE can be traded American-style, this option can be exercised only on its day of expiration.

EOM

Abbreviation for: end of month. Brokerage compensation for security salespersons is based on the settlement date, not the trade date. Thus, for those salespersons who are compensated solely on commission production, it is important that their sales efforts be geared to the settlement of transactions.

EOM LOANS

Acronym for early ownership mortgages. EOM loans are marked by these provisions: During the first 6 years the payments are sufficient to pay off the mortgage in 30 years. After the 6-year period, the payments increase, although the rate stays the same; as a result the loan is paid off in less than 30 years. Thus, there is early ownership.

EQUALIZING SALE
Term formerly used of a short sale executed on a national securities exchange at a minus tick or zero-minus tick. This is still allowable under SEC rules if that price constituted a plus or zero-plus tick had the sale been made on the principal exchange where the issue was traded. The current SEC reference price for short-sale transactions is the last published sale on the consolidated tape.

EQUAL LOANS
EQUAL is an acronym for: easy qualifier loans. The concept was originated by the Federal Home Loan Mortgage Corp. (Freddie Mac) to help more home buyers to obtain fixed-rate mortgages. As an alternative to graduated payment mortgages (GPM) or adjustable-rate mortgages (ARM), EQUAL requires that all payments in the early years be for an equal amount, but at a rate that is about 1/4% higher than typical home loans at the time of origination.

EQUIPMENT TRUST CERTIFICATE
See ETC.

EQUITY
1. Security representing residual ownership in a corporation. If there is no preference in payment of dividends, it is called "common stock"; if preference is shown among owners, it is called "preferred stock."
2. Liquidating value of a client's margin account. For example, if client owns securities worth $30,000 and the client's debit is $12,000, the equity in the account is $18,000.

EQUITY APPRECIATION CERTIFICATES (EAC)
One of three forms of securities created when common shares are tendered in response to a management proposal for reorganization. The concept was developed by Shearson Lehman Hutton and functions like an Americus trust. Thus, in exchange for their shares, common stockholders receive a 30-year bond, a preferred share, and an EAC. The EAC entitles its holder to any stock appreciation above the par value of the bond component. In effect, they are no longer voting owners, but they have some of the rights of ownership.

EQUITY INDEX PARTICIPANTS
See EIP.

EQUITY KICKER

Slang for an offering of debt securities that is convertible or that is accompanied by a warrant to subscribe to common stock in the company. The company usually can sell the bonds at a lower interest rate and the purchaser has the opportunity to share in the future financial success of the company.

See also EQUITY.

EQUITY NOTES

Also called "a security purchase contract." Equity notes are debt instruments that will automatically become shares of common stock of the same issuer after a set time period. This financing technique originated in 1982 and was popular for a time with some large commercial banks.

EQUITY PURCHASE ACCOUNTING

Accounting practice that permits a company holding 20% or more of another company's stock to include in its own net income a percentage of the other company's income equal to its percentage share in the other company. For example, if Company A held 25% of Company B, and Company B reported annual earnings of $2 million, Company A could include $500,000 in its net reported income.

EQUITY REIT

A real estate investment trust (REIT) that uses stockholder equity to buy and lease commercial and residential property. Generally considered a conservative security.

EQUITY SECURITY

A certificate that designates a proportional ownership in a corporation: principally common and preferred stock.

Rights, warrants, convertibles, and long call options are considered the equivalents of equity securities in many situations. For example, in determining whether a sale at a loss is a wash sale for taxation purposes.

EQUITY-TYPE SECURITY

Securities that are neither common nor preferred stock but that are capable of conversion, subscription, or exercise for either of these securities. Equity-type securities would include convertible bonds, rights, warrants, and long calls.

Also called "common-stock equivalents," and the term is important because the purchase of such equity-type securities during the "tainted" period of a sale of the underlying security at a loss will constitute a wash sale.

EQUIVALENT BOND YIELD

Used to compare the discount yield on money market securities to the coupon yield on government bonds. Example: A Treasury bill with a 90-day maturity is sold at a discount yield of 12%. The purchase price is $97,000, the discount is $3,000. The equivalent bond yield is:

$$\frac{\$3,000}{\$97,000} \times \frac{365}{90} = 12.54\%$$

The number 365 is used because interest on government bonds is computed on a 365-day year, rather than the 360-day year used for T-bills.

EQUIVALENT TAXABLE YIELD

Comparison of the nontaxable yield on a municipal bond to the taxable yield on a corporate bond at a client's tax bracket. For example, a client in the 40% tax bracket is offered a municipal bond with a yield of 12%. The corporate bond yield after tax that equals the nontaxable yield on the municipal is calculated thus:

$$\frac{\text{Municipal yield}}{1 - \text{Tax bracket}} = \frac{12}{1 - .40} = \frac{12}{.60} = 20\%$$

ERD

Acronym for Escrow Receipt Depository program. This is a book-entry system administered by the Options Clearing Corporation to facilitate the handling of escrow receipts issued by custodian banks. Through the use of a multientry rollover form, custodian banks can readily deposit, withdraw, and reallocate escrow receipts collateralizing options on different series of the same class. The program sharply reduces the movement of securities and the issuance and reissuance of escrow receipts.

ERISA

Acronym for Employee Retirement Income Security Act, passed in 1974, that gives governmental jurisdiction over the establishment, operation, and funding of most nongovernmental pension and benefit plans.

ERISA FIDUCIARY

A person who provides a pension or other employee benefit plan covered by the Employee Retirement Income Security Act with investment advice, or who has discretionary authority over the management of the assets of the plan. Such fiduciaries have an obligation to act solely in the interest of the plan, and to work for the exclusive purpose of providing it with benefits and prudent administration.

ERM

Acronym for exchange rate mechanism. ERM is the term for an agreement among participating member countries to intervene in the financial marketplace, whenever necessary, to hold the value of their own currency within a narrow trading range of about $2^{1}/_{2}\%$.

ERR

Symbol used in the futures marketplaces to designate quotations deemed to be erratic. Such a designation may be used if bid and asked prices fluctuate wildly, or result in "locked" or "crossed markets."

ERRORS AND OMISSIONS EXCEPTED

See E&OE.

ERTA

Acronym for Economic Recovery Tax Act of 1981. ERTA was a broad-based law designed to encourage savings and investments. It did this by introducing "All Saver" certificates, lowering capital gains taxes, raising the threshold for gift and estate taxes, and by granting retirement savings incentives—particularly the IRA account. The law contains many other features.

ESAE

See EXCHANGE SUPERVISORY ANALYST EXAM.

ESCHEAT

A state law regarding the disposal of abandoned property (e.g., bank balances, unpaid insurance policies). These properties are governed by escheat (pronounced ess–cheet) laws. Normally, such assets revert to the state, but rightful owners subsequently can claim the property.

See also ABANDONMENT.

ESCROW

Assets placed with an independent third party to insure that all parties to a contract fulfill its terms. For example, a client purchases a contractual mutual fund at a sales charge of $500. The sales charge is wholly or partially refundable under certain circumstances. The $500 will be placed in escrow until the client either fulfills the conditions of the contract or rescinds it.

Also called "escrow account."

ESCROW RECEIPT

A paper often used by writers of call option contracts who have underlying securities on deposit with an exchange-approved bank. The bank issues an escrow receipt to broker, thereby guaranteeing delivery of shares to broker if call is exercised against writer.

ESCROW RECEIPT DEPOSITORY PROGRAM
See ERD.

ESOP
Acronym for employee stock ownership plan. Also called "employee stock ownership trust" (ESOT).

Plan whereby employees of a corporation can buy out all or part of the corporation for which they work. Tax advice is needed.

ESOT
An identifier for "employee stock ownership trust." Used synonymously with "employee stock ownership plan."

See also ESOP.

ESP
See EXCHANGE STOCK PORTFOLIO.

ETC
Commonly used abbreviation for: equipment trust certificates; that is, serial debt obligations secured by a lien on movable equipment, such as diesel locomotives, railroad cars, buses, and the like.

ETR
See EASYGROWTH TREASURY RECEIPTS.

EURO BONDS
Bonds issued by European or American corporations. Bonds have interest and principal payments in dollars. As a general rule, such bonds are not registered with the SEC and cannot immediately be sold in the United States.

EURO CD
Short-term time deposits issued by European banks. The deposits are made in Eurodollars, and interest and principal repayment are in Eurodollars.

See also LIBOR.

EUROCLEAR
A Brussels-based organization that serves member banks and dealers with clearing facilities for transactions in Eurobonds and Yankee bonds.

EURO-CURRENCY
Bank deposits in a country other than the one in which those monies are denominated. Example: U.S. dollar deposits in a London bank are Eurodollars; French franc deposits in an Italian bank are Eurofrancs, and so on.

EURODOLLAR
Common term for dollars held by banks in European countries. Such dollars, originally received by European merchants for goods sold to American companies, will be used to pay for intercountry trades or for petroleum purchases; in this case, they become petrodollars. If such dollars are used to pay for trade with the United States, they become regular dollars on deposit with banks in the United States. Many European debt securities are issued with payment promised in Eurodollars.
See also EURO BONDS.

EURODOLLAR SECURITY
A stock or bond of a United States or foreign issuer that is denominated in dollars, and the dollars are deposited in one or more European banks. Such securities may not be initially offered to U.S. persons because they are not SEC-registered in accord with U.S. securities laws.

EUROLINE
A line of monetary credit made available to a customer by a bank located outside the United States. Euroline credit terms are stated in the specific currency of a European country.

EUROMARCHÉ
In anticipation of the dropping of trade barriers in the Common Market in 1992, this is an English proposal to trade a "common European list" of major stocks on the ISE. It reflects discussions with major Continental stock exchanges to provide market exposure to interested investors via the ISE's SEAQ system of trading.

EUROMONEY/FIRST BOSTON STOCK INDEX
An ongoing statistical survey of price performance of about 1,300 stocks in 17 world markets. The index is sponsored and compiled by First Boston Company and published each month in *Euromoney* magazine.

EUROPEAN COMMUNITY
See EUROPEAN ECONOMIC COMMUNITY.

EUROPEAN CURRENCY UNIT
Also used: ECU. ECUs are a weighted package of currencies of the member nations of the European Economic Community; that is, the Common Market. The weighting is periodically adjusted to reflect the trade balances of the countries. By using ECUs to settle trades between nations, the member nations partially diversify the risk of volatile currencies.

EUROPEAN DEPOSITORY RECEIPT
Commonly abbreviated: EDR. A negotiable instrument issued by a European bank to represent ownership of a specific number of shares in a non-European corporation. The bank holds the underlying shares. The receipts are traded, and the bank's records are changed to reflect these transactions.

EUROPEAN ECONOMIC COMMUNITY
Also known as EEC, EC, the European Community, and the Common Market. EEC is an economic alliance comprised of most countries in Western (non-Soviet) Europe. It functions like a multigovernment cartel by removing trade barriers between members and imposing import duties on nonmembers who import into the community. EEC was founded in 1957 and in 1992 will take on special importance as more trade barriers are lowered between the members.

EUROPEAN MONETARY SYSTEM
See EMS.

EUROPEAN OPTION
A put or call privilege that has this restriction: It can be exercised by its holder only on the expiration date or during the five-day period prior to that date.

Such options may be for stocks or bonds.

EUROPEAN-STYLE EXERCISE
A contract qualifier for most listed options traded in Europe and some listed options traded in the United States (e.g., the S&P 500 Index Option). The holder of a European-style option can exercise the option only on the last day (or perhaps also the day before) it expires.

EUROPEAN TERMS
Expression used in currency transactions. It states the number of units of a foreign currency required to purchase one U.S. dollar. Example: If Swiss francs were offered at 2.0181, European terms, it would mean that a Swiss franc is worth $.4955; that is, $1 divided by 2.0181.

EUROPEAN WHOLESALE MARKET
See EWM.

EUROPE, AUSTRALIA, & FAR EAST STOCK INDEX
See EAFE.

EURO-RATE DIFFERENTIAL
See DIFF.

EVALUATION
Term commonly used of the endeavor to estimate the worth of an investment portfolio. Listed stocks are valued at closing prices; OTC stocks, at the bid price. The value of infrequently traded bonds is based on third-party estimations. The same is true of fixed assets that have no established marketplace.

EVALUATOR
Independent third party who assigns a resale value to an asset for which a limited market exists.
    See also EVALUATOR'S FEE.

EVALUATOR'S FEE
Fee charged by an evaluator. Many portfolios must be evaluated periodically, either by law or to establish redemption price. Example: A unit investment trust contains letter bonds for which no ready market exists; the units, however, are redeemable. The evaluator establishes an estimate of the resale value of the bonds and charges a fee for this service.

EVEN-BASIS SWAP
A sale of one fixed-income security and the purchase of another effected without any change in the yield on the investor's portfolio. Such a swap may change average maturities, or face value, but it does not change yield.

EVEN KEEL
Nautical term used to describe the fact that the Federal Reserve's monetary policy will remain unchanged. Example: Despite the recent refunding of $20 billion in notes by the U.S. Treasury, it seems that the Fed will maintain an even keel.

EVENT RISK
A term coined by industry analysts to refer to unpredictable corporate actions that could have a dramatic impact on the value of a company's stocks or bonds. Generally, the "events" are such that management has

considerable control over them, and they would include restructurings, asset write-downs, spin-offs, and leveraged buyouts.

EVERGREEN FUNDING
A picturesque English finance term used in association with the recapitalization of new or newly reorganized companies. The concept refers to a steady stream of capital into these companies by means of installment payments, rather than by lump-sum payments.

EVERGREEN PROSPECTUS
Term used when an offering of securities registered with the SEC will be made on a continuous basis. Classic evergreen prospectus: those used to offer open-end investment company shares.

An evergreen prospectus, while remaining substantially the same, will be periodically updated to reflect changing company conditions.

EWM
Acronym for European Wholesale Market. EWM is a proposal to list the most popular European companies on all major stock exchanges in Europe. If successful, investors will gain greater liquidity for their holdings and will be able to buy and sell those shares in multiple currencies in their appropriate countries.

EXCEPTION REPORT
A computerized document prepared for compliance and audit personnel. This report extracts information from the daily activities of the broker/dealer that exceed pre-established parameters. For example, an exception report based on a universe of 10,000 daily transactions shows that only 100 exceeded $50,000 in value, or exceeded 5,000 shares in volume, or represented more than 5% of a client's assets. In making such "exceptions," the report points compliance and audit personnel in the direction of transaction that prima facie could represent compliance problems or audit problems.

EXCESS MARGIN
Dollar value of client's equity above initial Regulation-T margin (Reg-T excess) or maintenance requirement (maintenance excess). For example, a client has securities worth $50,000 in a margin account with a debit balance of $20,000. Client has equity of $30,000; this is $5,000 greater than the current $25,000 Reg-T initial margin and $17,500 greater than maintenance requirement of $12,500.

See also SPECIAL MEMORANDUM ACCOUNT.

EXCESS MARGIN ACCOUNT SECURITIES

As defined in SEC rules, excess margin account securities are those above and beyond the value of what is necessary to finance the debit balance in a client's margin account.

In practice, securities worth more than 140% of the client's debit balance must be segregated; thus, they are identifiable and will not be jeopardized if the broker/dealer becomes insolvent.

EXCESS RESERVES

Banking term that signifies that the total reserves of a bank on deposit with the Federal Reserve plus the cash on hand exceeds the statutory reserve requirement based on the bank's deposits. For example, if a bank has a statutory requirement of $1,000,000, its reserves with the Fed are $800,000, and it has cash in its vault of $250,000 (a total of $1,050,000), the bank has an excess reserve of $50,000. Excess reserves may be withdrawn, lent to other banks, or lent to customers.

See also FEDERAL FUNDS.

EXCHANGEABLE DEBENTURE

Similar to convertible securities, except that the holder can exchange the debenture for shares of a company in which the issuer has an equity interest. For example, CIGNA Corporation, an insurance company, has an 8% exchangeable debenture due in 2007. Holders may exchange it for 23.36 shares of Paine Webber Group common stock.

EXCHANGE ACQUISITION

This is a non-publicized customer bid for a block of stock to be purchased exclusively from one or two NYSE member organizations and/or their clientele. The bid is circulated internally at those firms, seeking contra sellers for this proposed transaction. When sufficient sell orders are accumulated, all orders are sent to the floor of the Exchange where they are crossed with the block purchaser's at a price within the spread of the prevailing quotation. The seller's incentive to participate is the buyer's assumption of all transaction expenses, including commissions and stock transfer taxes.

EXCHANGE CONTROLS

This term is used of governmental regulations relating to the buying and selling of foreign currencies.

EXCHANGE DISTRIBUTION

Nonpublicized sale of a large block of stock through an exchange. Offer is made through one or two member firms. When sufficient buy orders are accumulated, trade is made on the floor within existing market.

Completed transaction is then announced on exchange tape. Seller pays all transaction costs.

Tape symbol: DIST.

EXCHANGE FOR PHYSICAL PROGRAM
Common acronym: EFP. A trading technique that involves futures on an index and the component stocks. The stock index is used as a benchmark. Sophisticated computer programs show aberrations in the spread between the futures and the stocks. The trader will try to profit by arbitraging; that is, by buying the index future and selling the stocks short, or vice versa. As the spreads return to their historical norms, the positions are closed out at a profit.

EXCHANGE RATE
This is a price, or value factor, at which the currency of one country can be exchanged for that of another. For example, the exchange rate of U.S. dollars for French francs is 5.0674; this value factor means that a person with one U.S. dollar can purchase 5.0674 French francs.

In the past, the exchange rate often has been artificially pegged by the countries involved. At the present, most exchange rates are determined by market forces.

EXCHANGE STOCK PORTFOLIO (ESP)
ESP is a NYSE-listed product designed to reflect market movements in the S&P 500 Index. ESP is a basket of securities in one ownership package. The package is composed of 462 NYSE issues and 38 other stocks. ESP is primarily designed for institutional investors who can buy a "market basket" and also avoid some of the volatility associated with programmed trading activity.

EXCHANGE SUPERVISORY ANALYST EXAM (ESAE)
A qualification test that must be passed by member-firm employees responsible for the approval of research reports that will be distributed to the public. It is a two-part exam that tests the knowledge of financial statement analysis; the second part of the exam tests the candidate's knowledge of NYSE and ASE research standards of suitability.

EXCHANGE-TRADED OPTION
Technical term for what is popularly called a "listed option."

See also LISTED OPTION.

EXCHANGE-TYPE COMPANY
In the past, persons could exchange their personal holdings of securities for shares of diversified mutual funds without a capital gain tax liabil-

ity. The management companies that permitted such exchanges were commonly called "swap funds."

Such exchanges are no longer permitted by the IRS.

EX CLEARING HOUSE
Expression used to identify a transaction that is completed between the contra brokers without the use of a clearing facility.

Such transactions are infrequent. Ex clearing house transactions usually arise when the buyer requires guaranteed physical delivery of the security.

EX-DIVIDEND
Security contract that does not entitle buyer to the next dividend on the security. Trade is ex-dividend because settlement date is after the record date that determines the holders who will receive the dividend.

See also EX-DIVIDEND DATE.

EX-DIVIDEND DATE
Date on or after which buyer will not receive the next dividend on a security. On regular-way transactions, ex-dividend date is the fourth business day before the record date.

See also REGULAR-WAY TRANSACTION.

EXECUTION
Popular term for a transaction between a buyer and a seller.

Also called a "trade."

EXECUTIVE SHARES
A U.K. term used to describe shares purchased on the installment plan over a 1–3 year period. In such a financing, issuers may permit buyers to pay for their shares in predetermined installments on specific dates. The buyer turns in the previously received certificate plus a check for the next installment and receives the next certificate. When the final payment is received, the buyer receives an "executive share" certificate. This last certificate is equal to all other outstanding shares and is fully listed on the exchange.

EXECUTOR
A person, qualified in a probate court, who is named in a valid legal instrument known as a will to fulfill the last wishes of a decedent, satisfy the claims of tax collectors and creditors and, in general, act in a prudent fiduciary capacity to settle that estate by distributing its remaining assets to legitimate beneficiaries.

EXECUTRIX
A female named to act in a valid will. The term *executor,* without any designation of the sex of the person, is now commonly used.

EXEMPT ACCOUNT
A NYSE interpretation of its margin rules on the purchase of U.S. government securities and certain mortgage-backed securities. Under this interpretation, individuals with net tangible assets of at least $16 million, and broker/dealers subject to regulation by the United States, to any of its agencies, or to state and municipal regulation, are exempt from the minimum margin requirements.

EXEMPT SECURITIES
1. Securities exempted from the registration requirements of the Securities Act of 1933. Example: Government and municipal securities.
2. Securities exempted from certain provisions of the Securities Exchange Act of 1934 in terms of margin, registration of dealers who make a market in them, and certain reporting requirements. Example: A class of equity securities of a corporation that now has less than 300 holders is exempted from quarterly and annual reporting. Also called "exempted securities."

TO EXERCISE
This is a word with several applications in the securities industry.
1. In connection with a securities option, this is the act of buying or selling shares of underlying stock from or to someone, pursuant to a privilege granted to that person at some earlier time.
2. In connection with a conversion privilege written into the indenture of a bond or terms of a preferred stock agreement, this is the holder's act of exchanging a convertible security for a specified number of shares of underlying common stock.
3. In connection with an issuer's right to retire a bond or preferred stock via a call feature, this is the company's act of requiring holders to tender their bond/stock in exchange for a cash payment.

EXERCISE AN OPTION
See TO EXERCISE.

EXERCISE LIMIT
Maximum number of contracts of the same class of option that may be exercised within five consecutive business days. The maximum exercise limit for some equity-type options is 8,000 contracts.

EXERCISE NOTICE
Advisory form submitted to Options Clearing Corporation by broker stating that it demands fulfillment of terms of a long option contract. OCC will then assign performance to a broker representing a writer of contract.

Incorrectly used of client; it is a broker who enters Exercise Notice upon request of client.

EXERCISE PRICE
Dollar value per share at which holder of long option may elect to exercise.

See also STRIKING PRICE.

EXHAUST LEVEL
Jargon for the price level at which a customer's margin account must be liquidated. In general, it is the firm's or the exchange's minimum equity level at which either more margin must be deposited or the account will be terminated. This will be done by selling off long positions or covering short positions.

EXIMBANK
Popular name for the Export-Import Bank of the United States, which was established in 1934 as an independent federal agency. It facilitates exports and imports by borrowing from the U.S. Treasury to finance them. It provides direct credits to foreign borrowers, export insurance for U.S. businesses, and export credit guarantees.

See also EXPORT-IMPORT BANK OF THE UNITED STATES.

EXIT FEE
A term associated with certain mutual funds. In effect, it is a penalty levied on the early redemption of fund shares. Generally, early redemption means in the first few years after purchase. The penalty may be in cents per share, or it may be a percentage of the redemption value.

See DEFERRED CONTINGENT SALES LOAD.

EXIT STRATEGY
Corporate finance term for a financing technique recommended to issuers of second quality securities. The strategy entails an immediate "bridge" financing provided by a merchant banker (investment banker) coupled with a commitment to issue long-term junk bonds in about six months. The proceeds from the bonds will be used to repay the banker for the bridge loan.

EXIT TRANSACTION
Term created by the PORTAL System (Private Offerings, Resale and Trading through Automated Linkages) to identify the sale of an unregistered security by a broker/dealer member of the system to a non-PORTAL participant. When a PORTAL security (subject to SEC Rule 144A) leaves the system—that is, is sold to an overseas buyer—a full report of the transaction is filed with the NASD by the member participant. The information is then given to the SEC.

EX-LEGAL
Term from municipal trading: a security that does not have attached the legal opinion of bond counsel. Trades can be made but buyer must be informed that delivery will be ex-legal. Most currently issued municipal bonds have the legal opinion printed directly on the bond certificate.

EXPENSE RATIO
Ratio, usually expressed in cents per $100 of investment, that compares mutual fund expenses for management fee and other overhead expenses to average net asset value of outstanding shares. Normally given in annual report of fund. For example, an expense ratio of 43 cents means that an investor pays 43 cents per year per $100 of investment in the fund for the services of the fund. Expenses are withheld by fund from current income and are not an out-of-pocket cost to investor.

See also OPERATING RATIO.

EXPIRATION
An option or privilege ceases to have value. Examples: An equity-type option expires on the Saturday after the third Friday of a particular month; a security is convertible until April 15, 1994; and so on.

EXPIRATION CYCLE
Cycle of three-month intervals for which option contracts ordinarily will be traded. There are three quarterly cycles beginning with January (JAJO), February (FMAN), and March (MJSD). Usually three or more of the four months in each cycle are traded at same time. When the current month expires (e.g., January), the last month in the cycle will begin to trade on the next business day. Thus, the October contract will be added to the currently traded April and July contracts.

In practice, stock options now trade: current month, following month, and next month in that cycle.

EXPIRATION DATE
Saturday after the third Friday of the contract month for equity-type options. Option expires worthless at 10:59 P.M., Chicago time, unless it is previously exercised by the holder.

EXPIRATION MONTH
See EXPIRATION CYCLE; EXPIRATION DATE.

EX—PIT TRANSACTION
A futures transaction executed off the trading floor of the commodity exchange where such business is usually transacted. The place on the trading floor where such transactions usually take place is called the "pit." Ex-pit transactions are extremely rare and, for the most part, are illegal.

EXPORT-IMPORT BANK OF THE UNITED STATES
Common acronym: EXIMBANK. The bank, which is an independent agency of the United States, aids in the financing of exports and imports between the United States and foreign countries.

The debt obligations of EXIMBANK are guaranteed by the full faith and credit of the United States.

See also EXIMBANK.

EXPOSURE
1. The dollar amount of financial risk involved in an investment.
2. The maximum dollar amount of credit that a broker/dealer will extend to a customer between trade and settlement date. By extension, if ultimate settlement is not to be completed until a future date (e.g., short option contracts and commodity futures) the total dollar amount of risk that a broker/dealer will undertake on behalf of a customer.

EXPRESS LANE
A NYSE programming device that is incorporated into its Super DOT order entry and execution system. This device is intended to operate only when predetermined market conditions prevail; that is, when a key indicator (the DJIA) moves up or down a specified number of points from the previous day's close. When this occurs, program-type trades are prohibited from using the Super DOT system; instead, only retail customer market orders of 2,000 shares or less will be given priority—hence the term *express lane*—to be executed before other trades.

EX-RIGHTS
Status of the underlying security on the day after the rights and their accompanying prospectus are distributed to present security holders. On or after that date, the security and the rights trade separately and the buyer of the security from a previous holder will not get the rights.

EXTENDABLE DEBT SECURITY

A debt obligation that gives the holder the option at maturity of redeeming at face value or continuing to hold the security for a predetermined time. If the holder chooses to retain ownership, the interest rate will be adjusted according to a preset formula. Generally, the formula is based on a spread over Treasury issues of comparable maturity.

EXTENDING

Term that describes the purchase of debt securities with maturities longer than those usually bought for portfolio purposes. The purchase of longer-than-usual maturities is an indication of portfolio manager confidence in the future and is usually done to pick up higher yields than those available for shorter-term instruments.

EXTENSION SWAP

A purchase of one debt security and the sale of another, with the result that the client's time to maturity is lengthened.

Common synonym: maturity swap.

EXTRAORDINARY

Used with income or charges on corporation income statements. In every case, term signifies a one-time event, for example, the write-off of a loss, or the sale of property.

EXTRAORDINARY INCOME/CHARGES

A one-time expense entry on the income statement of a company. Called "extraordinary" with the implication that there will be no similar entry in the future.

See also NONRECURRING CHARGE.

EYE BEEM

Jargon used by traders and exchange members for the common stock of International Business Machines (IBM).

Also used: Big Blue. This is based on the characteristic color of the company's logo.

F

F

Sixth letter of the English alphabet, used:
1. Uppercase to mean foreign in corporate sales and earnings reports.
2. To signify "fast" in commodities markets; that is, rapid price fluctua-

tion and large volume. A fast market may excuse a broker who misses the market.

3. To designate "flat"; that is, a bond that trades without accrued interest. Generally, such trading marks bonds that are in default.

4. As the fifth symbol in the ticker (tape) symbol of a NASDAQ/NMS stock of Canadian origin. Challenger Intl., for example, is CSTIF.

5. Uppercase to signify the common stock of Ford, a major automotive manufacturer.

F

F is the official logo of the French franc and is often so depicted on the country's currency and postage stamps. This depiction is used to have the symbol compete with the logo for the Japanese yen (¥) or the British pound (£).

FACE AMOUNT CERTIFICATE

Debt instrument that obliges issuer to pay a stated amount, the face value, on a fixed date more than 24 months after issuance. May be purchased lump sum or by installments. Rate of interest is fixed, although additional interest may be paid if issuer's income from investment warrants it.

See also FACE AMOUNT CERTIFICATE COMPANY.

FACE AMOUNT CERTIFICATE COMPANY

A type of investment company that issues debt instruments obligating the payment of a stated sum of money (face amount) on a date in the future in return for deposits made by an investor. May be lump sum or period payments. Minimum maturity: 24 months. Generally, the investor will receive a fixed rate of interest, but the company will often pay additional interest if its investment income warrants it.

FACE VALUE

Value of a bond stated on the bond certificate. It is also the redemption value at maturity, although, if issuer calls bond before maturity, there may be a premium added to face value as redemption price.

Also called "par value." This usage of par value is limited to bonds. See also PAR VALUE.

FACILITATION ACCOUNT

A Federal Reserve term adopted by the New York Stock Exchange to identify a broker/dealer whose transactions are executed by another broker/dealer. If the original firm initiates proprietary transactions through a second broker/dealer, the executing firm must treat that firm as it would any customer and obtain appropriate margin (or a cash deposit) in a timely fashion.

FACILITATION ORDER
Option exchange term. It signifies an order for the proprietary account of a broker/dealer. Called a "facilitation order" because it is to be executed in whole or in part as part of a cross with that firm's public customer. Example: A customer wants to sell 100,000 shares. The broker/dealer has a "natural" for 25,000 shares; that is, buy orders from customers. The broker/dealer may enter a facilitation order for the remaining 75,000 shares. The order ticket must be marked as such: "facilitation order."

FACTOR
1. Technical name for an extender of credit that is used to purchase, carry, or trade corporate securities. Thus, brokers and banks are factors in their role of carrying margin account transactions for clients.
2. A firm that buys receivables from other organizations at a discount from the face value of the receivables.
3. That proportion of the unpaid principal amount of a mortgage when related to the original principal (face value) amount. For example, Ginnie Mae Pool #25792 was originally issued with a mortgage amount of $3,257,980. Its factor is now 0.57543; that is, $1,874,739.40 remains unpaid. Holders of pass-throughs receive a monthly statement of the factor of their investment that remains to be paid.

FACTORING
1. The sale of accounts receivable owned by a company to another company. The sale is made at a discount to provide cash flow to the seller and a source of profit to the buyer.
2. In the securities industry, factoring refers to the financing of security positions. Example: A dealer borrows against securities in inventory, or a customer borrows against portfolio securities in a margin account.

FADED
Term used to designate that previously given prices have either been withdrawn or have been revised downward. Example: The market for ABC has faded.

FADING
Term used on stock exchanges when a marketmaker takes the other side of the trade on public customer orders. Rather than see the business

transferred to another exchange, some brokers on regional exchanges will act as the contra side of customer orders and offset the position elsewhere.

The word is taken from an expression in dice: to fade is to bet against the thrower. For example, "I'll fade you."

FAIL CONTRACT
Any securities contract that has not been honored or completed.

See also FAILED TO RECEIVE and FAILED TO DELIVER.

FAILED TO DELIVER
Past-due contract between brokers where the seller has not presented the security to the buyer for payment.

Normally used as a noun; also used as a verb: "The broker failed to deliver."

FAILED TO RECEIVE
Past-due contract between brokers where the buyer has not made payment because seller's broker has not yet made delivery.

Normally used as a noun; also used as a verb: "The broker failed to receive."

FAIL POSITION
Industry term describing a broker/dealer's inability to deliver securities to the buyer's broker because his customer did not deliver the securities sold. Or, looked at from a buying broker's viewpoint, the inability of a selling broker to deliver securities purchased.

In practice, a broker/dealer will have a net fail position. It will be a fail-to-receive position if other brokers did not deliver securities to satisfy his clients; it will be a fail-to-deliver position if he was not able to satisfy the delivery needs of brokers to whom his clients sold.

FAIR MARKET VALUE
Price at which a buyer and seller are willing to exchange an asset. Generally synonymous with current market value determined by the competitive forces of supply and demand operating in a free and open marketplace. Endeavors to rig the price to favor the buyer or seller are manipulative and violate federal laws.

NASD also defines it in terms of swaps against syndicate offerings: the price that a dealer normally would pay for the security in the ordinary course of business if there were no swap involved.

FAIRNESS OPINION

A comment by an expert in mergers, acquisitions, or leveraged buyouts that the tender price is reasonable and in the best interest of the shareholders. It is often provided (for a fee) by an independent investment banker to the potential acquirer to forestall litigation about the terms of the deal.

FALLEN ANGEL

English term for a debt security of high quality that has been downgraded by a rating agency into what is now referred to as a "junk" bond. The deterioration of the issuer's business prospects and its ability to pay its bond debt service is the usual cause for such a decline.

FAMILY OF FUNDS

Mutual funds, each with a different investment objective, that are managed by the same investment manager. Generally, funds in the same family are exchangeable on a dollar-for-dollar basis, although usually there is a fee for administrative expenses, and there may be an additional sales charge if a client switches from a fund with a lower sales charge to a fund with a higher sales charge.

IRS considers the exchange a sale followed by a purchase, thus there may be a tax consequence on the shares swapped.

FANCY

Slang for FNCI (q.v.), an acronym for the Financial News Composite Index.

FANNIE MAE

Nickname for the Federal National Mortgage Association. Also used of the debt securities of the FNMA; for example, "I bought some Fannie Maes."

See also FEDERAL NATIONAL MORTGAGE ASSOCIATION.

FAQS

Acronym for Firm Access Query System. A computerized service provided by the NASD to its members. Through FAQS, members may access the NASD database of pending securities registrations, and may schedule qualification examinations and review the results thereof.

FARMER MAC

Nickname for the Federal Agricultural Mortgage Corporation, a government agency sponsored by the Federal Farm Credit System. Farmer Mac securitizes farm real estate loans by pooling the loans and selling them as a security. Because its interest and principal are ultimately guaranteed by the U.S. Treasury, Farmer Mac joins Fannie Mae, Ginnie Mae, and Freddie Mac in secondary market transactions in mortgage-backed securities.

FARMER'S HOME ADMINISTRATION
Acronym: FHDA. FHDA, an agency of the Department of Agriculture, grants loans for farms, homes, and community facilities in rural areas of the United States.

FAR MONTH
A term used both in the options and futures business to designate the trading month farthest in the future. For options this may be as many as five months, for futures a year or more.

Antonym: near month or spot month.

FARTHER OUT, FARTHER IN
Use of maturity dates (or expiration dates) on options. The concept: One's obligations or opportunities are extended or retracted.

See also DIAGONAL SPREAD.

FASB
See FINANCIAL ACCOUNTING STANDARDS BOARD.

FASCISM
General term for a socioeconomic system in which the government dominates production and distribution of goods and services by the control of private industry.

Term is pejorative. It infers that such domination is primarily intended to promote national esteem rather than the good of the populace.

Often called "the right," as distinguished from the left, another term for Communism.

FAST
Acronym for Fast Automatic Stock Transfer. FAST is a service provided by the Depository Trust Co. (DTC) through the maintenance of jumbo-sized certificates with principal transfer agents in major financial centers. Through FAST, DTC members can authorize withdrawals of stock in appropriate denominations, cause it to be re-registered into customer name, and deliver it to the beneficial owner within 24 hours following the instruction to do so.

FAST AUTOMATIC STOCK TRANSFER
See FAST.

FASTBACS

Acronym for First Automotive Short-Term Bonds & Certificates. FAST-BACS were a Drexel Burnham Lambert product modeled after Salomon Brothers' CARS. In effect, these securities were asset-backed securities collateralized by receivables on auto loans held by commercial banks.

FAST MARKET

Term designating a rapid volume of activity in a class of listed option. Floor officials initiate special exchange procedures to manage order flow efficiently. New orders may be delayed, and if a fast market cannot be controlled, it may be necessary to use a rotation to establish an orderly market.

FAT CAT

A slang expression used to designate:
1. Any very wealthy person.
2. A person who receives preferential treatment, either financially or politically.
3. An investor who has profited beyond expectation in a deal.
4. A person who is so successful that he or she has become lazy.

FAT LADY

Jocular expression for the First Atlanta Corporation, a large bank holding company, based on a play on its NASDAQ symbol, FATL.

FAVORITE FIFTY

Term describes the 50 largest equity holdings of major institutional investors. Often used in the past to describe major institutional holdings that resisted downside moves in bear markets.

Also called "first-tier investments."

FAZ INDEX

FAZ is an abbreviation for the Frankfurter Allgemeine Zeitung. The FAZ Index is based on the price movements of 100 high-quality stocks traded in the German marketplace.

Some Eurobonds have their redemption value linked to this index.

FBO

Initials representing "for the benefit of . . .," an expression used in identifying a legal trust account at a broker/dealer. In the interest of conserving space in the title of the account the letters FBO are used after the name of the trustee and before the name of the trust's beneficiary. For example, it might read "John Smith, trustee FBO Margaret Jones, under trust dated (UTD) June 4, 1989." (The specific date is cited because Margaret Jones might be the beneficiary under several trusts in which John Smith is the trustee.)

F/C
1. First call date; that is, the earliest date at which the issuer of a debt security or preferred stock may call the security for premature redemption.
2. First coupon date; that is, the first interest payment that the issuer will make to holders of a bond. The term is not used unless the first interest payment will be less than, or more than, the regular six months between interest payments.

FCM
See FUTURES COMMISSION MERCHANT.

FCOP
See FOREIGN CURRENCY OPTIONS PARTICIPANT.

FCP
Acronym for Fonds Communs de Placement. FCPs are a form of mutual fund recognized in France. There are no restrictions on their investments, and portfolio managers may be quite aggressive in both long and short-term markets. FCPs are organized as joint ownerships within unit trusts.

FDIC
See FEDERAL DEPOSIT INSURANCE CORPORATION.

FED
See FEDERAL RESERVE BOARD and FEDERAL RESERVE SYSTEM.

FEDERAL AGRICULTURAL MORTGAGE CORPORATION
See FARMER MAC.

FEDERAL CREDIT AGENCIES
General term for U.S. government-sponsored agencies that supply financial aid to specific institutions, classes of individuals, or economic segments of society. Example: There are federal credit agencies that supply credit to farmers, farm cooperatives, students, exporters, small businesses, and savings and loan associations.

FEDERAL DEPOSIT INSURANCE CORPORATION (FDIC)

Membership corporation sponsored by the federal government to insure repayment of savings and time deposits if a member bank becomes insolvent. Current coverage is $100,000 per separate account at each insured bank.

FEDERAL FARM CREDIT BANKS

Formerly, the Federal Land Banks, the Federal Intermediate Credit Banks, and the Banks for Cooperatives issued their own securities. The Federal Farm Credit Banks was organized to consolidate and reduce financing costs for these banks.

Since 1980, the securities issued have been called the Federal Farm Credit Banks Consolidated System-wide Bonds.

FEDERAL FINANCING BANK

Acronym: FFB. A government bank, supervised by the Treasury Department, established to consolidate and reduce financing costs of those federal agencies whose obligations are guaranteed by the federal government. Examples of such agencies: Export-Import Bank, the U.S. Postal Service, and the Tennessee Valley Authority.

FEDERAL FUNDS

Excess reserves of member banks of the Federal Reserve system. These excess funds can be loaned to other member banks, usually on an overnight basis, at the federal funds rate.

Term also used of any immediately usable funds that can be used to pay for government securities transactions. In this sense, the term includes cleared credit balances in client accounts, in special memorandum accounts (SMAs) in margin accounts, checks drawn by a member bank of the Fed on its account with the Fed, and—with the increased popularity of money market funds—transfers from these funds to the client's cash or margin account.

FEDERAL FUNDS RATE

Negotiated interest rate charged by a bank that loans excess reserves to a bank that needs to increase its reserves.

Probably the most sensitive indicator of monetary conditions because it is an overnight rate and, unlike the prime and discount rates, is a market rather than a posted rate.

FEDERAL HOME LOAN BANK

The FHLB serves savings banks, savings and loan associations, and cooperative banks in much the same way the Federal Reserve serves commercial member banks. The FHLB regulates these banks and lends money against acceptable collateral.

FEDERAL HOME LOAN MORTGAGE CORPORATION

Abbreviation: FHLMC. Nickname: Freddie Mac. Government-sponsored corporation owned by FHLMC. Purpose is to purchase qualifying conventional residential mortgages from FHLMC members, which it then packages under its own name and assurances and resells to the public.

FEDERAL HOUSING ADMINISTRATION

FHA, operating under the Department of Housing and Urban Development (HUD), insures mortgage loans, principally on residential housing.

FEDERAL INTERMEDIATE CREDIT BANKS (FICB)

Government-sponsored corporation that makes loans to banks and other credit institutions engaged in agricultural financing projects.

See also FEDERAL FARM CREDIT BANKS.

FEDERAL LAND BANKS

Supervised by Farm Credit Administration, the FLB are owned by farmers through land bank associations. FLB makes agricultural purpose loans to farmers and ranchers secured by first mortgages on real estate.

See also FEDERAL FARM CREDIT BANKS.

FEDERAL NATIONAL MORTGAGE ASSOCIATION

Nickname: Fannie Mae. Government-sponsored, publicly owned corporation was created to give liquidity in the secondary market for FHA-insured and for some conventional mortgages. Mortgages are purchased from approved holders using the proceeds from the sale of FNMA debentures and notes.

FEDERAL OPEN MARKET COMMITTEE

Committee of Federal Reserve governors and of presidents of six Federal Reserve Banks. Purpose: to make short-term monetary decisions to achieve long-term objective of Fed as regulator of money and credit supply.

Chief tool is the sale of government securities to decrease money supply, or purchase of government securities to expand money supply.

FEDERAL RESERVE BOARD

A statutory board of seven members, appointed by the President and with the advice and consent of the Senate for terms of 14 years, to regulate banking and credit activities in line with the goals of the Federal Reserve Act of 1913.

Principal tools: setting reserve requirements, open market activities, establishing the discount rate, controlling credit in the margin purchase of securities.

Commonly abbreviated Fed or FRB.

See also FEDERAL RESERVE SYSTEM.

FEDERAL RESERVE SYSTEM

Commonly means the Federal Reserve Bank, the 12 district banks, and the member banks of the Federal Reserve. Basically, a membership corporation, sponsored by the Federal Reserve Act of 1913.

The FRS has two functions: to act as a central bank and fiscal agent of the United States and to regulate credit in the American economy.

Also abbreviated FRB or Fed.

See also FEDERAL OPEN MARKET COMMITTEE.

FEDERAL RESERVE WIRE SYSTEM

See FED WIRE.

FEDERATION INTERNATIONALE DES BOURSES DE VALEURS

See FIBV.

A FED PASS

A Federal Open Market Committee (FOMC) term for an action that will increase reserves, and thereby credit, in the banking system. The FOMC constantly monitors the money supply and the inventory of the primary dealers. To make a Fed Pass, the FOMC could buy securities or arrange certain reverse repurchase agreements that will increase the money supply and thereby fine-tune the economy.

FED WIRE

Abbreviation for Federal Reserve Wire Network. The FED Wire is a communication facility operated by the Federal Reserve Banking System to transfer funds and book-entry securities between subscribers to the wire.

Member banks and U.S. government security dealers are primary subscribers to the wire. These are called "primary dealers."

FEEMAIL
Disparaging slang for the legal fees charged by attorneys to settle stockholder suits that attempt to bar management from ransoming shares held by prospective corporate raiders.

For further information about the repurchase of shares from corporate raiders, see also GREENMAIL.

FELONY
In law, a more serious crime than a misdemeanor. Root of word is Scottish and means a wicked person. Generally, a felony is punished by jail sentences of more than one year. The law defines which crimes are considered felonies.

In the securities industry, certain violations of securities law are defined as felonies. Adjudication of guilt in such cases is reserved to the federal courts and is not part of the administrative decisions of the SEC.

FENCES
See CYLINDERS.

FENCE SITTER
Slang: a retail customer or portfolio manager who is unable to come to a decision about the merits of an investment opportunity.

ff
Also: FrF. Initials used to designate the French franc, the primary currency unit in France.

FFB
See FEDERAL FINANCING BANK.

FGIC
Acronym for Financial Guaranty Insurance Company. FGIC is a consortium of financial institutions and brokerage firms that insures municipal securities and municipal unit investment trusts against default.

The fee is paid by the issuer, or the UIT, and the insurance covers both interest and principal payments on the bonds covered. FGIC is similar in function to AMBAC and MBIA.

FHA
See FEDERAL HOUSING ADMINISTRATION.

FHDA
See FARMER'S HOME ADMINISTRATION.

FHLB
See FEDERAL HOME LOAN BANK.

FHLMC
See FEDERAL HOME LOAN MORTGAGE CORPORATION.

FIBV
Known in the United States as the International Federation of Stock Exchanges, its official title is Federation Internationale des Bourses de Valeurs. This is an organization of 33 stock exchanges in 28 countries and its purpose is to promote closer collaboration and to contribute to the development of securities markets.

FICB
See FEDERAL INTERMEDIATE CREDIT BANKS.

FICO
Acronym for The Financing Corporation. FICO was created by the U.S. Treasury Department and the Federal Home Loan Bank Board to finance and recapitalize FSLIC (Federal Savings and Loan Insurance Corporation).

Because FSLIC is insolvent, FICO was authorized by Congress to interpose itself between the 12 Federal Home Loan Banks and the capital markets. Although FICO is not guaranteed by the U.S. government, it carries the moral obligation of the U.S. government.

FICO STRIPS
Obligations of the Financing Corporation for which interest and principal payments are marketed separately in a manner similar to Treasury STRIPS.

See also FICO.

FICTITIOUS CREDIT
A credit in a client's account that represents the proceeds of a short sale and the margin required by Regulation T. It is called "fictitious" because the client may not withdraw the credit since both the proceeds and the margin protect the broker and the lender of the borrowed securities.

Opposite: a free credit balance (i.e., funds on deposit with a broker that may be withdrawn whenever the client chooses).

FICTITIOUS ORDER
Buy or sell instructions given to a broker by a person, or persons, attempting to manipulate the price of a security. Such orders are called "fictitious" because, as a general rule, these persons do not intend to

honor their commitment; instead, they seek only to create the illusion of activity in the security and thus influence its market price.

See also FICTITIOUS CREDIT.

FIDDLING WITH THE BOOKS
An English expression used to describe fraudulent corporate record-keeping, which lures investors with fictitious earnings or assets.

Also called "creative accounting" or (in the United States) "cooking the books."

FIDELITY BOND
Insurance policy that protects broker/dealers from loss caused by mis-placement of funds or securities, check forgery, fraudulent trading practices, or securities forgery. Policy covers such activities by employees, officers, or partners. Exchange and NASD rules set the amount of insurance that is required.

Also called "fidelity bond insurance" or "blanket fidelity bond."

FIDUCIARY
Person entrusted with the control of assets for the benefit of others. Most states have laws governing the conduct of fiduciaries.

Fiduciaries are generally court-appointed: executors of wills, administrators of estates, receivers-in-bankruptcy, and committees for incompetents. Trustees also are considered fiduciaries. The document of appointment usually limits the power of fiduciaries and sets guidelines for their activities.

Custodians under Uniform Gifts to Minors Acts are fiduciaries in the sense that they may not alienate assets for their own benefit. They are not, however, directly governed by a written court-approved document governing the conduct of such accounts.

FIELD GOAL
Industry slang for U.S. Fidelity & Guaranty Corporation. Its trading symbol, FG, is the same as that employed in football for a field goal.

FIFO
See FIRST IN, FIRST OUT.

FIGS
Acronym for Future Income Growth Securities. A Paine Webber municipal product patterned after the GAINS originated by Goldman Sachs.

Concept: The bond is issued at a discount; then, after a number of years, it pays a fixed rate of interest based on a par value of $1,000. Example: The bond sells at $500; in eight years it becomes a $1,000 face value bond paying 9% annual interest until its maturity.

FILL
Commonly used industry term for the execution of an order to buy or sell a security.

Execution of less than the amount designated in the order is called a "partial fill."

FILL OR KILL (FOK)
A limit order to buy or sell that the client instructs, as follows: "If this order cannot be executed immediately at its limit price, cancel the entire order." FOK orders, although they may be buy or sell orders, are usually buy orders.

FOK orders, in most cases, are for a significant quantity of the security—one that would otherwise cause a significant price change if a market order to buy-sell were entered.

If the order is not executed, the client will want to reassess his or her strategy.

FILOS
Acronym for Fixed Interest Limit Order Service. FILOS is an International Stock Exchange of the United Kingdom and the Republic of Ireland computer service to complement its SEAQ Fixed Interest Market Maker Service. FILOS is designed to permit subscribers to display orders and contingent prices for second-line fixed-income securities and thereby attract interested contra parties.

FIMBRA
Acronym for Financial Intermediaries Managers & Brokers Regulatory Association. FIMBRA is the result of the merger of NASDIM and LUTIRO. These two trade associations were merged to give a single jurisdiction over smaller OTC firms, life assurance brokers, and unit trusts in Great Britain. FIMBRA is registered with the SIB under England's Financial Services Bill.

FINAL DIVIDEND
English financial term: the final cash dividend paid to shareholders in a particular year. English custom requires a final dividend to be approved by the stockholders. A final dividend is descriptive only and does not imply that other dividends were paid in the same year.

FINANCE ISSUE

Japanese identification for an upcoming public offering of an equity security (stock, convertibles, bonds with warrants attached). Under Minister of Finance (MOF) regulations, each phase of the underwriting from preliminary discussions to public sale and actual payment date requires specific market "postures" by underwriters and nonunderwriters to prevent price manipulation.

FINANCE PAPER

Commercial paper issued by companies engaged primarily in extending credit to customers of their firms. Well-known issuers of finance paper include General Motors Acceptance Corporation, Ford Motor Credit Corporation, Household Finance Corporation, and CIT Financial Corporation.

The term also is used of registered debt offerings of such corporations with maturities greater than 270 days.

FINANCIAL ACCOUNTING STANDARDS BOARD (FASB)

An independent body of certified public accountants that studies bookkeeping practices and publishes opinions about these practices. Generally, corporations abide by these standards in the preparation of financial reports.

FINANCIAL AND OPERATIONAL UNIFORMED SINGLE REPORT

See FOCUS REPORT.

FINANCIAL FUTURE

Futures contract for interest-sensitive securities: T-bills, T-notes, T-bonds, CDs, and GNMA pass-throughs.

Trading is governed by the Commodities Futures Trading Commission (CFTC) and requires special registration.

Trend of financial futures trading is often an indicator of interest rates, but interpretation of trend requires sophisticated assessment of the basis, which is the difference between cash and futures price.

FINANCIAL GUARANTY INSURANCE COMPANY

See FGIC.

FINANCIAL INSTITUTION NUMBER

See FINS.

FINANCIAL INSTITUTIONS REFORM, RECOVERY, AND ENFORCEMENT ACT OF 1989

See FIRREA.

FINANCIAL INTERMEDIARIES MANAGERS & BROKERS REGULATORY ASSOCIATION
See FIMBRA.

FINANCIAL PLANNER
1. An individual or an organization that helps others to plan for educational needs, retirement planning, or estate planning.
2. A registered representative (RR) who specializes in retirement planning.
3. A person licensed by a state or registered with the SEC as an investment advisor.
4. A person who has graduated from the College of Financial Planning in Denver, Colorado.
5. A person chartered by the American College (Bryn Mawr, Pennsylvania) as a chartered financial planner (ChFP).
6. A member of the International Association of Financial Planners (IAFP).

Numbers 2 and 3 have regulatory standing; 4, 5, and 6, although non-accredited academic institutions, have professional standing.

FINANCIAL PRINCIPAL
A National Association of Securities Dealers' examination for a person qualified to prepare and approve member firm's financial statements and computation of net capital requirements.

FINANCIAL SECURITY ASSURANCE, INC.
FSA is similar in purpose to municipal insurance companies in that they insure, for a fee, the principal and interest for subscribing corporate issuers. The debt must be backed by mortgages or other select receivables to qualify for this insurance.

The fee for such insurance is paid by the issuer; but because issues that qualify have AAA rating, the fee for insurance can be quickly repaid by the lowered cost of borrowing.

THE FINANCING CORPORATION
See FICO.

FINDER'S FEE
Remuneration to a person who refers business to another. For example, "The finder's fee for the referral of Company A to Company B in their merger was $500,000."

FINOP
Acronym for financial and operations principal.

Under MSRB and NASD rules, persons responsible for the maintenance of financial records or the approval of financial reports must qualify as a FINOP through a qualification examination.

Each member must have at least one such designated principal. See also MUNICIPAL SECURITIES RULEMAKING BOARD and NATIONAL ASSOCIATION OF SECURITIES DEALERS.

FINS
Acronym for Financial Institution Number. An identifying number assigned to a banking participant in the Depository Trust Company's (DTC) Institutional Delivery (ID) System. Through FINS, a broker/dealer executing a customer order either "cash on delivery" (COD) or "receive versus payment" (RVP) can do so electronically. After details of the transaction are confirmed by the broker/dealer, the system will:
1. Automatically transfer the security to the agent's bank on settlement date by means of DTC's book entry system.
2. Automatically debit the purchaser's account and credit the seller's account with the trade proceeds on the records of DTC.

FIP
Acronym for Fixed Income Security Options Permit. FIP is a license that may be purchased from the ASE. It permits licensees to trade in interest-rate options for their own account on the floor of the American Stock Exchange.

FIREWALL
A colorful metaphor to describe the legal barrier that must be erected by a bank holding company if it owns or controls a broker/dealer. If the Glass-Steagall Act is repealed, it will also apply to broker/dealers doing a banking business. In essence, a barrier must be established to prevent banking and brokerage activities from spreading into the other area. For example, the bank could not lend to its securities affiliate or finance underwriting activities. The broker/dealer affiliate must register with the SEC and be subject to its regulations.

FIRM ACCESS QUERY SYSTEM
See FAQS.

FIRM COMMITMENT
The underwriter, either through negotiation or competition, agrees to buy the securities to be issued. The underwriter, therefore, owns the se-

curities. If the securities are sold at the public offering price, the underwriter usually makes a profit. If the securities are not sold at the public offering price, the underwriter may have a diminished profit or a loss. In no case can the underwriter make a profit from a sale above the public offering price (unless the securities are exempt) because federal law requires that a bona fide public offering be made.

Also called "firm commitment underwriting."

See also FREERIDING; WITHHOLDING; BOUGHT DEAL.

FIRM MARKET
See FIRM QUOTE.

FIRM ORDER
1. A buy or sell order on behalf of a broker/dealer's proprietary account.
2. A buy or sell order given to a broker/dealer. Normally, set terms and conditions are established for a fixed time. The order can be executed within that time without further confirmation from the customer.

FIRM QUOTE
Also: firm market. A quotation made by a dealer who is prepared to buy or sell immediately at least the minimum quantity associated with trades in that security.

Generally, the minimum quantities are 100 shares of stock. In the block markets for stocks, the minimum quantities are higher. Secondary market Treasury quotes generally are firm for $100,000 face amount. In the secondary markets for corporate and municipal bonds, unless such quotes are given AON (all or none) the minimums are for 5 and 25 bonds, respectively.

Ethics of the industry require that any quote not firm be identified as either a nominal or a subject quote.

FIRREA
Acronym for Financial Institutions Reform, Recover, and Enforcement Act of 1989. This legislation was initiated to resolve the crisis of failing thrift (savings and loan) institutions in the United States.

FIRST AUTOMOTIVE SHORT-TERM BONDS & CERTIFICATES
See FASTBACS.

FIRST BOSTON GLOBAL INDEX
See EUROMONEY/FIRST BOSTON GLOBAL STOCK INDEX.

FIRST CALL DATE
See F/C.

FIRST COUPON DATE
Used only of newly issued bonds if the first interest payment will be less than, or more than, six months from the issue date. Example: The LMN lls of '05, dated 5-1-95, F/C 1-1-96.

After an irregular first coupon, all subsequent coupon payments are made on a semiannual basis until maturity.

See also F/C.

FIRST DEALINGS
English stock exchange term for the earliest time that transactions are allowed for settlement at the end of the next account period (usually a fortnight). First dealings can be as early as 9 A.M. Greenwich time two business days before the start of that account period; but normally it is on Monday morning at the beginning of that period.

FIRST IN, FIRST OUT
Accounting method of assigning cost to inventory used to produce salable goods.

Opposite: last in, first out—LIFO.

Accounting method is choice of corporation, and IRS approval is required to change more than once.

Important note: on sale of securities, IRS presumes FIFO unless owner designates that some other method of valuation was used.

FIRST MONEY
Picturesque term used in the operations area of broker/dealers. It represents the quantity times the contract price; for example, 100 shares at $50 represents "first money" of $5,000, and it does not include commissions and other charges that will be added to (on purchases) or subtracted from (on sales) that amount.

FIRSTS
Acronym for Floating Interest Rate Short Tranche Securities. The term is associated with a Shearson Lehman collateralized mortgage obligation (CMO) security. In effect, one tranche (class) of the debt is short term (the FIRSTS) and has a floating interest rate pegged to LIBOR (London Interbank Offered Rate). The long-term portion of the issue carries a traditional fixed-interest rate.

FIRST SINKING FUND DATE
Also: FSF. The earliest date at which the issuer of a debt security obligates itself to begin sinking fund payments. The bond indenture designates the methods that may be used, either by the issuer or the bond

trustee, for the early retirement of the bonds. Such methods include calling the security for redemption or making open market purchases.

FIRST-YEAR REPUBLICAN JINX THEORY
A lighthearted market indicator: The market will go down in the first year of incumbency of any Republican president, even of a second term. The theory is waggish and has not been proved in practice.

FISCAL AGENT
Manager of securities sales for the U.S. government or one of its agencies. Responsible for obtaining capital by distributing its debt instruments. For example, the Federal Reserve is the fiscal agent of the U.S. government.

FISCAL POLICY
Economic term used to designate actions by either the president or Congress that affect spending practices by the government. Fiscal policy is used to differentiate such practices from monetary policy; that is, actions by the Federal Reserve Board that affect the money supply in the United States.

FISCAL YEAR
Any consecutive 12-month period of financial accountability for a corporation or other governmental agency. Often abbreviated FY with a date. For example, FY May 31. The firm's fiscal year goes from June 1 to May 31 of the following year.

TO FISH
Slang: an endeavor by a dealer to find out the buyer or seller when another broker/dealer wants to trade a significant quantity of a security. Generally, such information is confidential.

However, federal law requires self-disclosure in certain situations; and the rules of the NASD, if the contra party is acting as agent, require the revelation of the other side of the trade if this is demanded. This rule is to prevent certain conflicts of interest, hot-issue problems, insider trading, and the like.

A FIT
As a noun: signifies ability of an investor to purchase securities that meet the portfolio needs of the investor in terms of credit rating, price, yield, and so on. For example, "We've got a fit with the AJAX 14s priced to yield 15.50."

FITCH
Shortened term for Fitch Investors Services. Fitch provides corporate bond ratings that give investors an insight into the degree of credit risk entailed in investing in the bond of the corporation.

See also FITCH SHEETS.

FITCH SHEETS
A chronological record of successive trade prices for listed securities maintained by Fitch Investors Services. For example, "I found the price in the Fitch Sheets."

FIVE & TEN
Industry jargon used to identify the F.W. Woolworth Company, a major retailer and a stock included in the Dow Jones Industrial Average.

THE FIVE HUNDRED
See FORTUNE 500.

$500 RULE
Under Regulation T, a broker/dealer need not invoke buy-in, sell-out procedures against an account if the cash deficiency is less than $500. For example, a client buys securities worth $10,000 plus $287.50 commissions. Client's check is for $10,000, but the client is out of town and cannot be reached. The broker need not liquidate a portion of the account to recoup the $287.50 commission that was not included in the check.

FIVE PERCENT GUIDELINE
One of NASD Rules of Fair Practice that is used to define fair and reasonable in the determination of markups, markdowns, and commissions. It is an ethical, rather than a mathematical, criterion and permits exceptions based upon other relevant factors that pertain to the transaction.

Also called "five percent rule."

See also PROCEEDS SALE and RISKLESS TRANSACTION.

FIXED/ADJUSTABLE CUMULATIVE PREFERRED STOCK
An innovative issue of preferred stock created by Bankers Trust New York with a variety of characteristics. For the first five years, it carries a fixed dividend. Subsequently, the rate is adjusted quarterly, pegged 25 basis points above the higher of the three-month T-bill, 10-year T-note, or 30-year T-bond. During this period there is a 15% cap and an 8% collar. And, after the first five years, holders are entitled to an additional

dividend if the common stock's cumulative dividend in the previous quarter is in excess of 93 cents per share.

FIXED ANNUITY
Investment contract sold by an insurance company for an immediate or installment payment of premiums. When annuitized, the insurance company guarantees periodic fixed payments to the annuitant, either for life or for alternate periods—according to the election made by the annuitant. By guaranteeing payments, the insurance company assumes both the mortality and the investment risks of the annuitant.

FIXED ASSETS
Accounting term for assets of a corporation that are not readily salable and which represent the depreciated value of property, equipment, and other tangible assets.

FIXED-CHARGE COVERAGE
Comparison of corporation's income before interest and taxes with annual interest payments on funded debt. For example, income before interest and taxes is $10 million and bond interest is $2 million per year. The fixed-charge coverage is 5.

Fixed-charge coverage is a measurement of the safety of a bond and enters into rating by bond-rating services. It is, however, a relative number because a large coverage may indicate that a company is under-leveraged and has not fully used its borrowing potential.

Also called "times fixed charges."

FIXED-DOLLAR SECURITY
A nonnegotiable debt instrument that can be redeemed at the holder's option for a dollar value set forth in a schedule of fixed prices. Example: Series EE Savings Bonds are fixed-dollar securities. The redemption value is set monthly and varies with the prevailing established interest rate and the time that it has been held by the owner.

FIXED-INCOME SECURITY OPTIONS PERMIT
See FIP.

FIXED LIABILITY
Balance sheet terminology for corporate debt obligations that will mature in more than one year. The time to maturity is the governing factor; thus, bonds, notes, and debentures will be included.

Also called "funded debt."

On the balance sheet of municipalities, fixed liabilities are called "bonded debt."

FIXED-PAYMENT MORTGAGE
See FPM.

FIXED-PRICE OFFERING
SEC-registered underwritten offerings are usually fixed-price offerings. In effect, the underwriters purchase the issue from the issuer at a fixed price and then sell the registered offering to the public at a price that is stated in the prospectus.

Only when the offering is completed, or the contract among the underwriters is terminated, may the participants in the syndicate and selling group sell the security at a price different from their preset and advertised price.

FIXED-RATE AUCTION PREFERRED STOCK
See FRAPS.

FIXED-RATE LOAN
A loan with a preset rate of interest. Of itself, the term does not state whether payments will be self-amortizing; that is, include interest and a partial repayment of principal, or interest only.

Term is used to distinguish from floating-rate loan; that is, a loan whose rate of interest will be periodically adjusted to prevailing rates.

FIXED-TERM REVERSE MORTGAGE
The concept is similar to an IRMA. In effect, a homeowner is permitted monthly borrowings against the equity in a home but only for a limited time. For example, the borrowings are permitted only for a period of, let's say, 12 years. At the end of that period, the loan plus accrued interest must be repaid.

FIXED TRUST
Term used of those unit investment trusts that have a fixed portfolio of securities. To be distinguished from participating trusts, the normal organizational form of a plan company that sells units in a contractual mutual fund.

Fixed trusts usually invest in a type of security. For example, in corporate bonds, government bonds, and municipal bonds to provide steady income to unit holders.

FLAG FORMATION
Term from technical analysis to designate a pattern of stock price movements that, in general, resembles a triangle with the apex to the viewer's right.

Usually indicates an indecisive subsequent move in the stock's price. Often used by technical analysts to buy an option straddle so a profit may be obtained from either an upward or downward move in the price of the security.

Also called a "pennant," "triangle," or "coil."

FLASH PRICES

If the volume on an exchange is so great that current displays show transactions occurring more than five minutes ago, it is customary to interrupt the tape display to flash a current price for a widely traded security. For example:

ABC   XYZ   FLASH LMN
52   31   24

The LMN price represents an interruption and is a current price.

FLAT

1. A bond that trades without accrued interest. This may arise because the bond is in default; an income bond before semiannual interest is declared; or any bond that trades so settlement date is coupon payment date.
2. With reference to yield curve measurements, any class of bonds whose intermediate and long-term returns are similar. If short-, intermediate-, and long-term rates are similar, the expression "flat yield curve" is used.
3. In financial analysis, a quarter in which earnings are neither above nor below the earnings of the previous quarter. For example, "Earnings for ABC have been flat during the past three quarters."
4. It identifies a marketmaker's or trader's position when it has neither a long nor a short position in a particular security (i.e., the marketmaker has a net zero position).
5. It is used to describe an underwriter's position when it has completely sold its commitment to customers.

FLAT MARKET

A market that is typified by a horizontal price movement because of little or no market activity in the security.

Do not confuse with stabilization, consolidation, or distribution. Each of these terms often is associated with active trading during a sideways price movement having an indecisive future movement. A flat market implies a sideways movement because there is little or no activity in the security.

FLAT SCALE
Municipal bond expression: there is little difference between short-term and long-term yields over the maturity range of a new serial maturity issue.

FLAT YIELD
English term: the annual interest paid divided by the current market price. Thus, it is the equivalent of current yield as this is measured in the United States.

As with current yield, the measurement does not take into account possible gain or loss that will arise if the instrument is held to maturity.

FLB
See FEDERAL LAND BANKS.

FLEX-DARTS
The service mark of a Salomon Brothers product meaning Flexible Dutch Auction Rate Transferable Securities. This corporate equity issue is designed to reduce the number of Dutch auctions during the year yet permit a new dividend rate to be set for the next 49 days. The "flexibility" feature of this instrument permits the issuer to extend its dividend rate for up to one year but, in reality, the dividend auction is held quarterly.

FLEX REPO
Abbreviation of: flexible repurchase agreement. A flex repo is a long-term master contract between a borrower and a lender with securities pledged as collateral. At some time in the future, the borrower must repurchase the collateral. In the meantime, the principal amount may be expanded or contracted, and the interest rate will be adjusted to market conditions.

FLIGHT TO QUALITY
Term used to describe the changes in portfolio management policies during adverse economic conditions. Although the general use of the term refers to the sale of lower-rated bonds and the purchase of higher-rated bonds, it also refers to the sale of speculative stocks and the purchase of investment-grade (blue-chip) stocks.

Barron's Confidence Index, by measuring yield spreads of higher versus lower rated bonds, is an endeavor to anticipate stock market movements based on the increase or decrease of investor confidence shown by the flight to quality, or the opposite.

FLIP-FLOP BONDS
Colorful term for a World Bank perpetual bond that can be exchanged for a three-month note, back into the bond, or put back to the issuer at par value. In effect, the investor can change back and forth or redeem depending on the level of interest rates.

FLIP-OVER PROVISION
A provision introduced into the charter of a target company on the occasion of an unfriendly takeover attempt. Under this provision, preferred shares are granted the privilege of conversion into the common stock of that company, or into common shares of an acquiring company that is forcing the merger. Such a conversion makes takeover much less attractive, because it increases the number of shares that will have to be acquired, or dilutes the percentage of ownership.

Possible analogy: certain turtles and crustaceans will die if they are turned on their backs; to survive they must flip over.

See also POISON PILL.

FLIPPED TRADES
An expression originating with the Midwest Securities Trust Co. (MSTC), an authorized clearing agency registered with the SEC. Flipped trades are transactions compared by MSTC members through its facilities but ultimately destined for settlement at another clearing agency; for example, the DTC. The second clearing agency has its clearance and settlement facilities electronically linked with MSTC.

FLIPPER
Jargon with two meanings in the securities industry:
1. A customer who buys a new issue and immediately sells it in the aftermarket. Although this is not condoned, it is done by trading clients who buy a "hot issue" and immediately take the aftermarket profit.
2. Nickname for the FPL Group (formerly Florida Power & Light) based on its NYSE tape symbol, FPL.

FLOAT
1. The number of shares in the hands of the public; thus, it gives insight into the number of shares available for trading. Example: "ABC has a small float."
2. Float also is the time lag in the check-clearing process. Float may be advantageous to the checkwriter, or disadvantageous to the check depositor, depending on the number of days it takes for a check written to appear as a debit, or a check deposited to appear as a credit.

FLOATER
Slang expression for floating-rate notes (i.e., of debt securities whose semiannual rate of interest is indexed to a money market interest rate).

FLOATING AN ISSUE
Industry jargon for the issuance and public distribution of a new issue of securities. For example, "LMN is floating an issue of convertible debentures."

FLOATING DEBT
Term primarily used in municipal security analysis for debts that will mature within five years.

Also called "bonded debt."

FLOATING INTEREST RATE SHORT TRANCHE SECURITIES
See FIRSTS.

FLOATING-RATE NOTE
A note, usually with a 5- to 7-year maturity, whose stated rate of semiannual interest is indexed to some pre-established money market rate. The money market rate may be an average of T-bill rates or some other sensitive market rate.

Because rate is variable, the holders of FRNs have substantially reduced interest-rate risk.

FLOATING SUPPLY
Term most commonly used of the dollar value of municipal bonds offered in the Blue List. For example, the floating supply is about $2.5 billion.

Also used of individual securities to designate quantity of an issue in the hands of persons willing to sell at current levels. Example: "We estimate that the floating supply is no more than 50,000 shares."

FLOATING SWAP
See BASIS SWAP.

FLOOR
1. Often used interchangeably with the term *collar* to refer to the lowest price or lowest interest rate acceptable to the issuer/purchaser of a security. Thus, it is an absolute minimum number required to arrange a transaction.
2. Also used in a relative sense to designate the relationship between two rates. Thus, the Fed raised the discount rate last week, thereby raising the floor at which banks will lend money.

3. Used to designate the trading area of an exchange, a commodity market, or the over-the-counter trading area within the premises of a broker/dealer. For example, "You will find Jim on the bond trading floor upstairs."
See also UPSTAIRS MARKET.

FLOOR BROKER
Popular name for commission house broker. Term designates a member of an exchange who, as an employee of a member firm, executes buy and sell orders received from the customers of the member firm.

FLOOR GIVE UP
See GIVE UP.

FLOOR OFFICIAL
Exchange term for a member or an employee of the exchange who is authorized to settle disputes in the auction procedure. Thus, if a dispute arises about priority or precedence in the settling of an auction, or if there is a question about the existence of a fair and orderly market, the normal procedure is to call upon a floor official for an on-the-spot judgment. In practice, the judgment of the floor official is accepted.

FLOOR TICKET
Industry terminology for the written summary of customer instructions contained on the original order ticket. The format and content of floor tickets are prescribed by the exchanges where they are received.

A floor ticket may not be given verbally from one member to another; instead, the physical piece of paper must be so transferred that responsibility is established and the duplication of order executions is prevented.

Industry rules specify the kind of information that must be contained on floor tickets.

FLOOR TRADER
Member of an exchange who is registered as a competitive trader. Such members trade for their own accounts and are governed by rules that approximate the rules that govern specialists.

FLOTATION
English term for an offering of securities; for example, to float a loan, or to float some shares. In the US the tendency is to use a word such as recapitalization to designate a public offering or private placement of stocks or bonds.

FLOWER BONDS

Certain designated issues of U.S. Treasury bonds that are acceptable at par in the payment of estate taxes if the bonds were owned by the decedent at the time of death. The last of currently outstanding flower bonds will mature in 1998.

Also called "estate tax anticipation bonds."

FLOW OF FUNDS

Used in conjunction with bond resolution of municipal revenue issues. Flow of funds statement usually establishes this priority: (1) operation and maintenance, (2) bond debt service, (3) expansion of the facility, (4) a sinking fund for the retirement of debt before the original maturity. Bond resolution will give precise flow of funds application; it differs from issue to issue.

Also called "flow of funds statement."

FMAN

Acronym for February, May, August, and November. Designation of the months for the quarterly expiration of option series assigned to some classes of listed options. Current practice is to offer a maximum of three expiration months at one time.

FNCI

Acronym for Financial News Composite Index. Slang: fancy. A price-weighted stock index of 30 equities developed by the Financial News Network. Fourteen of the 30 stocks are from the Dow Jones Industrial Average and FNCI is designed to closely track the movements of the Dow. The Pacific Stock Exchange trades European-style options based upon this index.

FNMA

See FEDERAL NATIONAL MORTGAGE ASSOCIATION and FANNIE MAE.

FOB

1. On corporate and municipal calendars, FOB is used to designate the First Boston Corporation, a major broker/dealer and investment banking firm.
2. In commerce, FOB means "free on board." In effect, it means that the seller of merchandise will ship to a buyer's single destination point at a price that includes both the merchandise and the cost of transportation. The buyer, in turn, is required to transport the merchandise from the ship to the warehouse or shop.

FOCUS REPORT
Acronym for Financial and Operational Combined Uniform Single report. Broker/dealers must make such reports to SROs (self-regulatory organizations) on a monthly and quarterly basis. Reports detail capital, earnings, trade flow, and other pertinent information.

FOK
See FILL OR KILL.

FOMC
See FEDERAL OPEN MARKET COMMITTEE.

FONDS COMMUNS DE PLACEMENT
See FCP.

FOOTSIE
Slang for: FT-SE. This is the Financial Times-Stock Exchange Index. This index of the 100 largest publicly owned stocks traded on the London Stock Exchange is as popular in England as the Dow Jones or the Standard & Poor's are in the United States.

THE FORBES 500
Directory of the 500 largest publicly owned corporations, compiled by *Forbes* magazine. Directory compares and ranks each of these companies by sales, assets, profits, and market value of shares.

FORCED CONVERSION
Term used to describe this situation: A convertible security is selling above its call price because of the market value of the underlying common shares. Issuer calls the convertible security at the call price. Owner of the convertible is forced to convert to common shares, to sell the convertible, or to accept a loss of potential value by accepting the call price.

FORCE MAJEURE
Legal term: a disruptive event that may excuse one or both parties to a contract from completion of the contract.

Such disruptive events may include acts of God; for example, earthquakes, floods, and the like, or catastrophic social events, such as war, revolution, nationalization of property, and so on. Often such events are included in the terms of the contract; at other times, they may be defined in the law.

FORECAST

1. The act of predicting, either short or long term, the course of financial events, such as the stock or bond market, trends in the economy, interest rates, or the fortunes of individual companies. Generally, the term *analyst* is used of persons who forecast based on measurable present and past events.
2. The written or spoken statement that evidences the act of forecasting.

FORECLOSURE

The legal procedure brought by the holder of a mortgage (creditor) or the representative of a deed of trust (trustee) for the purpose of claiming deeded property in satisfaction of a defaulted debt. Example: When XYZ Company failed to make its interest payments, the trustee moved to foreclose under the provisions of the deed of trust (indenture).

FOREIGN BOND

See YANKEE BOND.

FOREIGN CURRENCY OPTION

Acronym: FCO. Put or call options for packages of individual foreign currencies traded on the Philadelphia Stock Exchange.

FOREIGN CURRENCY OPTIONS PARTICIPANT

Acronym: FCOP. A licensee of the Philadelphia Stock Exchange who, in exchange for a one-time fee, is authorized to conduct a principal or customer business in selected foreign currency options on the floor of the exchange.

FOREIGN EXCHANGE RATE

See EXCHANGE RATE.

FOREX FILTER

A service mark of Salomon Brothers for a foreign currency contract intended to eliminate foreign exchange risk associated with investments in the U.S. stock market. It is a currency agreement, with Salomon Brothers as the contra party, in which a foreign investor insures against gains or losses in a U.S. stock portfolio that arise solely from differences between the exchange rate and the spot rate at the maturity of the FILTER contract.

Because it is designed to offset such currency differences, the FILTER contract is a variable hedge agreement for the foreign investor.

FORM 3

Document filed with the Securities and Exchange Commission by officers, directors, and holders of 10% or more of equity securities of a company registered with the SEC. Document states beneficial ownership of stock or other security that may be converted into equity security: rights, warrants, options, or convertibles. The form is available from the SEC.

FORM 4

Document filed with the Securities and Exchange Commission by officers, directors, and holders of 10% or more of equity securities of a company registered with the SEC to reflect net changes in security ownership. Document must be filed within 10 days after the end of month in which the changes occur. The form can be obtained from the SEC.

FORM 8K

Public report that must be filed with the Securities and Exchange Commission by a reporting corporation. Report must be filed in the month following any material event that affects the company's financial situation. Criterion: Would this event materially affect the buying or selling of the corporation's securities? The format of the report is established by the SEC.

FORM 10K

Report that must be filed annually with the Securities and Exchange Commission by reporting corporations. This includes all listed corporations and corporations with 500 or more shareholders and with assets of $1 million or more. The SEC outlines information that must be included in the report. Summary of 10K report must be included in the annual report that is to be sent to registered shareholders.

FORM 10Q

Report that must be filed quarterly with the Securities and Exchange Commission by reporting corporations. Summary of the report must be sent to stockholders.

Investment companies do not file quarterly reports; instead, they send semiannual reports to shareholders.

FORM 13D

A form that must be filed with the SEC and which is named after the SEC's Rule 13D. Under Rule 13D, anyone who acquires 5% or more of a registered company's outstanding stock must file a report with the SEC within 10 days of attaining that threshold amount.

FORM 13G

A form that must be filed with the SEC and which is named after the SEC's Rule 13G. Under Rule 13G, broker/dealers, insurance companies, banks, or investment companies must file notice with the SEC if they acquire 5% or more of the equity of a registered company in the ordinary course of their business. This form must be filed within 45 days after the end of the calendar year if the above-named position is still in inventory at that time.

FORM RE-3

A NYSE advisory document used by member firms to report rule infractions and other misdeeds by an employee of the firm. The Enforcement Department of the NYSE then decides whether to proceed with further action against the offender.

FORM S-1

A comprehensive form for the registration of securities with the SEC prior to a public sale. The form includes detailed information about the issuer, the security, and the method whereby the offering will be made.

FORM S-2

A form of securities registration that is less detailed than Form S-1. Public companies with a three-year history of reporting to the SEC under the provisions of the Securities and Exchange Act of 1934 may use Form S-2. This shortened form permits the detailed information required in Form S-1 to be included by reference to the company's latest annual and quarterly reports. Purchasers of the securities will receive these reports together with the shortened prospectus.

FORM S-3

An abbreviated SEC securities registration form that can be used by corporate officials and control persons to sell personally owned stock at various times and at prevailing market prices.

Form S-3 also can be used by highly capitalized and widely held corporations with good credit ratings to make offerings over a two-year period.

Also called "shelf registration."

FORM T

An NASD form on which members report equity transactions that are executed outside normal market hours. Certain transactions are exempted from this reporting requirement, but—in general—most equity transactions completed outside trading hours must be reported.

FORMULA INVESTING

Investment strategies based either on time or on profit and loss experience. All are based on pre-established rules that minimize emotional prejudices.

Principal applications: dollar cost averaging, a method of risk reduction based on the periodic investment of equal dollar amounts; constant dollar plan, a method of so allocating profits in a bond/stock portfolio that the profits in one portfolio are reinvested in the other so there will be—according to a prestated time frame—a basic balance between equity and fixed-income investments.

FOR THE BENEFIT OF . . .

See FBO.

FOR THE PLAN OF . . .

See FPO.

FORTRAN

Acronym for Formula Translation System. The most complex of the computer languages. The other popular computer languages are BASIC and COBOL.

THE FORTUNE 500

Directory of the 500 largest U.S. industrial corporations, compiled by *Fortune* magazine. The directory compares sales, net income, and stockholders' equity. Frequently the second 500 are given in a subsequent issue of *Fortune*. The same criteria are used. Financial and utility corporations are not included in the directory.

FOR VALUATION ONLY

Term (and abbreviation FVO) used on the periodic pricings of securities prepared at the request of a customer. Such pricings are not for trading purposes; instead, they are to give an estimate of current or historical prices for the use of the customer. Such FVO valuations may be for estate purposes, to determine the fair market value of a gift, for the equitable distribution of property, and so on.

FORWARD

See FORWARD CONTRACT.

FORWARD BARGAIN

Typical settlement terms for share transactions executed on the International Stock Exchange of the United Kingdom and the Republic of Ireland (ISE). Regardless of trade date, ISE requires the closing of the account period every second Friday, with full payment due on all outstanding positions on the following Monday. (Instead of the usual fortnight, some account periods are scheduled to run for three weeks because of holidays on settlement date.)

FORWARD CONTRACT
Completed transaction in a commodity, security, or financial instrument at a negotiated rate with a future settlement date. For example, a forward contract for 100,000 ounces of silver at $6.54 per ounce with a delivery date on March 15.

Because the forward contract is completed, it may be used as a cover for a sale of a futures contract.

Forward contracts are available for most commodities, precious metals, and government securities and agencies.

FORWARD PRICING
Term used to describe SEC regulation of bid-offer prices for mutual funds. Under forward pricing, all incoming orders to buy and sell become effective on the next net asset valuation of fund shares.

Sell orders are executed on the net asset valuation (minus any redemption charge). In practice, funds do not charge for redemptions.

Buy orders are executed at the public offering price. No-load funds have the same buy and redemption prices.

FORWARD PURCHASE UNDERWRITING
An underwriting technique whereby a corporation can raise capital by issuing stock at a price that is higher than prevailing levels if the company is willing to defer receipt of the proceeds until a later date.

FORWARD RATE
The dollar price at which payment versus delivery will be made on a specific future date for a commodity, currency, or certain types of debt instruments. It is a completed contract and not a futures or an option.

FOR YOUR INFORMATION (FYI)
Often used as a prefix to a quote. It means that marketmaker is unwilling to trade at that price but is supplying the quote as a courtesy. Price can be used for valuation, but is not a firm quote.

FVO, for valuation only, is often used as a substitute for FYI.

FOUR-CORNER ARBITRAGE
Term used to identify the near-simultaneous purchase of an international stock and sale of its corresponding shares of ADR in the United States, based on price differences in the two markets. (The opposite transaction procedure would also qualify.) It is "four corner-ed" in that, in addition to real price differences in the two markets, both issues values are also influenced by currency fluctuations in their respective countries.

THE FOUR PILLARS
Canadian term for the four major participants in its institutional markets: principal banks, trust companies, life insurance companies, and broker/dealers in securities. Because of the "little bang" on July 1, 1987, and the corresponding increase of foreign competition, it is expected that the lines of demarcation between the "four pillars" will gradually be eliminated.

FOURTH MARKET
Term commonly used for a computerized subscription service. Subscriber s can enter orders, either to buy or to sell. Computer then searches for the other side of the trade. Service is used by institutional investors, who trade directly with each other and do not use a brokerage firm.

See also INSTINET.

FPM
Acronym for fixed-payment mortgage—as opposed to a graduated payment mortgage (GPM). In this type of mortgage, the monthly dollar payments remain the same over the life of the mortgage; with GPMs, monthly payments may be lower in earlier years and higher in later years.

FPO
Initials representing "for the plan of . . .", a term used in the account title for a retirement plan at a broker/dealer. The letters FPO follow the name of the plan administrator and precede the name of the plan's owner. For example, although the designation for an IRA (individual retirement account) or a Keogh (a self-employed person's retirement account) also appears, the title may look like "XYZ Bank IRA, administrator FPO Harry G. Brown."

FRACTIONAL DISCRETION ORDER
Order to buy or sell that gives the executing broker discretion, within a prestated limit, for the execution of the order. For example: "Buy 2,000 ABC 45, discretion one-half point" (i.e., maximum price 45$\frac{1}{2}$).

FRAGMENTATION
SEC-coined term to describe the fact that order flow for a particular security is dispersed among many market centers. As a result, it is impossible to determine which is the principal market for the security.

FRANKED INVESTMENT INCOME
A term used of investment trusts (mutual funds) in England. The term refers to investment income received by the trust from companies that have already paid corporate taxes on such distributions. Under U.K. law, such dividends when distributed are not again subject to corporate taxation.

FRANKFURT RUNNING INDEX
This index is a minute-by-minute measurement of the performance of 30 blue-chip stocks traded on the Frankfurt Stock Exchange. Using share prices as of December 31, 1987, as a benchmark, this index measures the same stocks as those found in the Boersenzeitung Index but measures them continuously, rather than only once a day.

Formerly known as the KISS Index.

FRANKFURT STOCK EXCHANGE
The Frankfurt Stock Exchange is the largest of the exchanges in Germany and it accounts for approximately 70% of all stock and bond trades in that country. Although the floor is open officially only from 11:30 A.M. until 1:30 P.M., the floor's trading technologies have promoted this bourse's popularity. In addition, there is an active and permitted OTC activity after trading hours to handle the interests in German companies traded in London and New York. Contract settlements are set for the second business day after trade date.

FRAPS
Acronym for Fixed-Rate Auction Preferred Stock. A Salomon Brothers product, FRAPS are a preferred stock whose dividend rate is subject to change every 49 days by means of an auction among prospective buyers. The shares are maintained in book entry format and are redeemable at a premium during the early years following issuance.

FRAUD
Fraud is a legal term for a purposeful deception that results in financial loss to another. Generally, fraud results from misrepresentation, concealment, or omission of material facts, or from the employment of artificial devices or contrivances intended to deceive. Fraud is prohibited by federal and state law and is subject to prosecution, fine, or imprisonment under securities laws.

FRB
See FEDERAL RESERVE BOARD.

FREDDIE MAC
See FEDERAL HOME LOAN MORTGAGE CORPORATION.

FREE BOX
Industry slang for a bank vault or other secure location used to store fully paid customer securities.

Many broker/dealers use the Depository Trust Company (DTC) as a free box for their customer-owned securities.

FREE CREDIT BALANCE
Cash held by a broker in a customer's account that may be withdrawn by the customer at any time.

Free credit balance should not be confused with the credit that results from a short sale. This latter credit is held in escrow to secure the loan of securities made to the client when the short sale was made.

Entries in the special miscellaneous accounts (SMAs) of margin customers are not considered free credit balances.

FREE CROWD
Term often used of the active crowd for bond trading on the New York Stock Exchange.

See also ACTIVE BOND CROWD and CAN CROWD.

FREED UP
Term signifying that members of an underwriting syndicate are no longer bound to sell the security at the price agreed upon in the agreement among underwriters. For example, "The manager was unable to stabilize the offering, so the account was freed up."

Also called "free to trade."

FREE ON BOARD
See FOB (2).

FREE-RIDER BANKS
A British expression for small banks that originally made loans to less developed countries (LDCs) at a rate of interest that *no longer reflects* the adjusted interest rate evidenced in the new loan agreements with these countries. In effect, these banks are "free-riding" the new loan agreement.

FREERIDING

1. NASD rule violation that results if a member of an underwriting account withholds a portion of a public offering and resells it at a profit.
2. Used of customers who buy, then sell at a profit, without depositing money to show ability and intent to pay. Regulation T requires that such customer accounts be frozen for 90 days. Freeriding is prohibited in margin accounts.

See also FROZEN ACCOUNT.

FREE RIGHT OF EXCHANGE

Term used if a security holder may change the security from bearer to registered format, or vice versa, without charge.

See also REGISTERED SECURITY.

FREE STOCK

1. Stock fully paid for and free of any encumbrances; for example, a margin loan that may be sold by the customer or delivered out in registered format.
2. Stock that is held by an issuer following a private placement but that will be delivered out free of any restrictive legend. In this case, the stock is free and may be sold without further restriction.

FREE TO TRADE

See FREED UP.

FREIT

Acronym: (pronounced: free it) finite life real estate investment trust. An investment trust whose underlying assets are restricted to real property, such as raw land, commercial real estate, residential housing, developmental or mortgage financing, or any combination thereof. It differs from a typical REIT in that these assets must be liquidated at a predetermined time in the future. The proceeds are then distributed to the unit holders who, individually, bear the tax consequences.

FRICTIONAL COST

Term often associated with portfolios that replicate a specific index in terms of issues, dollar value, number of shares, and so on. By definition, the frictional costs (commissions, portfolio management fees, and the like) will cause the assembled portfolio to underperform the benchmark index unless certain adjustments are made to overcome the frictional cost.

FRIED EGGS

Part of the insider trading jargon of Wall Street, "fried eggs" is used to identify the fraction five-eighths. For example (in a shout across the floor), "It's selling at 55 and fried eggs (55⅝)." It is both quaint and a way of clarifying the quote.

FRIVOLITY THEORY
A lighthearted market indicator with a lead-in time of about one year. Using figures published annually in *The World Almanac*, the dollars spent on household operations are compared with the dollars spent on restaurant meals and drinking. If the latter frivolous expenditures go above 36%, or below 33%, people are too frivolous, or not frivolous enough, and the market is expected to decline.

FRN
See FLOATING RATE NOTE.

FRONT-ENDING AN ORDER
Term describing block orders where a broker/dealer agrees to buy a portion of a block with the provision that he will execute the remainder of the order as agent. For example, "We front-ended the order for 100,000 shares by taking 25,000."

FRONT-END LOAD
Contractual purchase plan used by many mutual funds. In exchange for some privileges, customer agrees that a large portion of first year's contributions will be used to offset total sales charges over the life of the contract.
   See also LOAD SPREAD OPTION.

FRONT OFFICE
Brokerage term used to identify sales and trading personnel. As a general rule, the term is used to include revenue producers in a member firm, including sales management; and the term is used in opposition to "back office"—that is, operations and other support personnel.

FRONT-RUNNING
Industry slang for someone who, with prior knowledge of an impending block transaction in a security, buys or sells options in that security.

FROZEN ACCOUNT
Regulation T requires cash account customers to pay promptly and not make a habit of selling securities before they are paid for. Customers who violate this rule have their account frozen for 90 days. During this period, such customers must pay in full for purchases before the buy order is entered, and sell orders will not be entered unless the broker has the certificates in hand.
   See also FREERIDING (2).

FROZEN ASSET
An item of value which, by law or other restriction, may not be liquidated or otherwise disposed of during a fixed time period.

FSA
See FINANCIAL SECURITY ASSURANCE, INC.

FSF
See FIRST SINKING FUND DATE.

FT—ACTUARIES WORLD INDEX
This is a statistical monitor of the price performance of 2,400 securities
traded in 23 countries throughout the world. As such, the index represents over 70 percent of those countries' market values. This index appears daily in the *Financial Times* (of London), and is a joint production
of FT, Goldman Sachs, Wood Mackenzie, and two U.K. actuarial organizations.

FTD
Past-due contract between brokers where the seller has not presented
the security to the buyer for payment.
    See also FAILED TO DELIVER.

FTR
A past-due contract between brokers where the buyer has not made payment because seller's broker has not yet made delivery.
    See also FAILED TO RECEIVE.

FT-SE
See FOOTSIE.

THE FULL
See HANDLE.

FULL DISCLOSURE
General principle of ethical sales: the seller must fairly represent the
item being sold. In U.S. securities law, this principle is incorporated in
the Securities Act of 1933 that regulates the public sale of corporate securities. The concept of disclosure also is applied in the Securities Exchange Act of 1934 to secondary markets for most corporate securities.

FULL FAITH AND CREDIT
Expression signifying that an issuer's reputation and taxing power are
pledged in the payment of interest and the repayment of principal for a

specified debt security. U.S. government securities and general obligation bonds of states and municipalities are backed by the full faith and credit of the issuer.

FULL TRADING AUTHORIZATION
Industry term for the document whereby the owner of an account gives full power of attorney to an employee of a broker/dealer to make buy-sell transactions for the client.

See also TRADING AUTHORIZATION.

FULLY DILUTED EARNINGS PER SHARE
Computation of corporate earnings applicable to each share of common stock that would be outstanding if all convertible and exchangeable securities were tendered for common shares at the beginning of the accounting period.

If such conversion had not been made, and earnings were divided among the previously outstanding shares, the term *primary earning per share* is used.

FULLY DISTRIBUTED
Term used when a public offering of securities is successfully sold to institutional and retail customers. A public offering is not fully distributed if large portions of the offering are sold to traders and other dealers.

FULLY MODIFIED PASS-THROUGH SECURITIES
Pass-through securities are debt issues with fractional claims upon a specific multimortgage portfolio. The issuer, for a fee, distributes funds received, either principal or interest, to the holder.

Such a security is said to be "modified" or "fully modified" (both expressions mean the same thing) if the distributions are to be made whether or not they are received. Thus, the distributions are guaranteed. In practice, this guarantee is made by the Government National Mortgage Association.

FULLY PAID AND NON-ASSESSABLE
This terminology appears on virtually all stock certificates issued in the United States. In practice, it means that, in the event of bankruptcy and dissolution of the company, the owner of the certificate can lose no more than the amount paid to acquire the security.

Earlier in United States history and before the passage of certain protective state laws, if a corporation sold securities below their par value, the subscriber could—if the company became bankrupt—be forced to pay the difference between the subscription price and the par value.

FULLY TAX-EXEMPT SECURITY

A municipal obligation whose interest payments to holders is not subject to federal, state, or local taxation. Generally, this exemption applies to holders who are domiciled in the same state as the issuer of the security. Some states, however, distinguish between individual and corporate holders in the application of this exemption.

Often called "triple tax exempt."

FUNDAMENTAL ANALYSIS

Quantitative approach to forecasting based on a corporation's balance sheet and income statement. The strengths and weaknesses, as shown by arithmetic formulas and by other measurement of economic and industry trends, can indicate future price movements in the security.

See also TECHNICAL ANALYSIS.

FUNDED DEBT

Balance sheet terminology for those corporate liabilities with maturities of more than five years.

On corporation balance sheets, funded debt is usually identified as long-term liabilities.

The exact meaning of the term can only be determined from the context. Thus, fixed liabilities (bonds with a maturity of more than one year) and funded debt are often used interchangeably.

See also FIXED LIABILITY.

FUNDS

1. Any accumulation of usable money.
2. Popular name for both mutual funds and unit investment trusts.
3. In England, the debt securities issued by the government of the United Kingdom. Commonly: the funds.

FUNDS RATE

Negotiated interest rate charged by a bank that lends excess reserves to a bank that needs to increase its reserves or to a government securities dealer who needs it to settle transactions. The funds are usually loaned overnight, at the "federal" rate.

See also FEDERAL FUNDS RATE and FEDERAL FUNDS.

FUNGIBLE

Any bearer instrument that is freely transferable and equal in all respects to any other instrument of the same class of the same issuer. Perfect example: a dollar bill that you lend is paid back by another dollar bill.

As a general rule, common stock of the same issuer is fungible. Other securities, with different maturities, call dates, or par value, are not fungible.

FUNNEL SINKING FUND
Term used of the sinking fund provision for a number of an issuer's outstanding debts. Under the funnel provision, the issuer may combine sinking fund payments from several issues. In this way, the monies can be used to retire the most expensive of the issues. Example: A corporation has two bonds outstanding, one with a 12% coupon, the other with a 14½% coupon. Under a funnel sinking fund, the monies that would be set aside to retire both issues can be combined to retire the 14½% bonds.

FUTURE INCOME GROWTH SECURITIES
See FIGS.

FUTURES COMMISSION MERCHANT
Acronym: FCM. Any business entity that solicits or accepts orders for the purchase or sale of commodities futures contracts or exchange-traded commodity options.

Such organizations must register with the Commodities Futures Trading Commission (CFTC) and are regulated by the National Futures Association (NFA).

FUTURES CONTRACT
Completed, but transferable, agreement to make or take delivery of the object of the contract at a specified time at a specified price. The most common futures contracts center on commodities and financial instruments.

A futures contract should not be confused with an option contract. An option contract is not completed and leaves with the buyer of the option the choice of requiring or not requiring the completion of the contract.

FUTURES MARKET
General name for marketplaces where contracts for the future delivery of commodities and certain financial instruments are traded according to pre-established conditions.

The principal futures marketplaces are: Chicago Board of Trade, Chicago Mercantile Exchange, COMEX (New York), Kansas City Board of Trade, and New York Futures Exchange. There also are futures markets in London and Canada. Spot (cash) markets for commodities exist throughout the world.

FUTURE VALUE OF A DOLLAR

The amount of money a dollar will become during a specified time period at a specified rate of compound interest. The formula is:

$$(1+R)^n$$

where: 1 is the original dollar,
R is the compound rate of return,
n is the number of time periods.

Thus, $1 invested at 8% for 10 years compounded semiannually would be computed by:

$$(1+0.04)^{20}$$

Note: Because of semiannual compounding, the rate was divided by 2 and the number of periods increased to 20. The answer is:

$$2.1911$$

FUTURE VALUE OF AN ANNUITY

The number of dollars that will be achieved if a person invests a fixed number of dollars, at a fixed rate of compound interest, for a fixed number of years. The formula is:

$$\frac{(1+R)^n-1)}{R}$$

where: R is the rate of return,
n is the number of compounding periods.

Thus, a client who puts $2,000 per year into an IRA for the next 25 years at 11% compounded return will have:

$$228,826.52$$

The formula presumes that the annual contribution into the annuity is made at the *beginning* of each year.

FVO

See FOR VALUATION ONLY.

FX

Abbreviation for foreign exchange; that is, the rate at which foreign currencies may be exchanged for U.S. currency and vice versa.

FY

Any consecutive 12-month period of financial accountability for a corporation or other governmental agency.
See also FISCAL YEAR.

FYI

The commonly used annotation to notes or copies of correspondence; meaning: for your information.

G

G

This is the seventh letter of the alphabet, used:

1. Lowercase in stock transaction tables to denote that the dividend is paid in Canadian funds, although the prices are in U.S. dollars.
2. Uppercase in the NASDAQ/NMS symbol as the fifth letter if an OTC bond is convertible; for example, FCBNG is the symbol for Fluorocarbon Co. convertible 8% debentures due January 15, 2011.
3. Uppercase alone to represent Greyhound Financial Corporation, a large conglomerate involved in business systems, food services, and equipment leasing.

GAAS

Acronym for Generally Accepted Auditing Standards. GAAS is a system of audit quality controls set forth and overseen by the Financial Accounting Standards Board (FASB). The SEC has also adopted these standards and permits their use in the filing of the mandatory financial statements with the commission.

GAIJIN

Japanese word for foreigner. Although all non-Japanese people can be so labeled, the term is used particularly of those non-Japanese broker/dealers who are established in Japan and thus compete directly with the "Big Four" Japanese brokers: Nomura, Daiwa, Nikko, and Yamaichi. The gaijins are usually the most prestigious of the brokerage firms in the United Kingdom or the United States.

GAIMUIN

Japanese term for a salesperson of a registered broker/dealer who is authorized (qualified) to do sales and sales promotion work *outside* of the employer's physical offices. Such persons must register with the Minister of Finance (MOF). This is normally done through the Japanese Association of Securities Dealers (JASD). Qualification is contingent upon passage of a special examination or equivalent supervisory experience.

GAIMU KOUI

Japanese term for the actual sales and sales promotion activity done outside the offices of a registered broker/dealer in that country.

See GAIMUIN for further details about the registration and qualification of the personnel who do such activities.

GAINS
Acronym for Growth and Income Securities. This is a type of tax-exempt issue created by Goldman Sachs. Concept: The security is issued originally at a deep discount and pays no interest for a fixed number of years. At this time, it becomes a regular bond with a fixed par value and pays a predetermined semiannual interest. Example: The bond is issued at $500. In nine years, it becomes a $1,000 face value bond paying 8% interest.

GAN
See GRANT ANTICIPATION NOTE.

GAP
Term used of a stock's price trend if the range for one trading session does not overlap a portion of the subsequent trading session. For example, range on Monday 40 low to 40½ high; range on Tuesday 41 low to 41½ high. There was a gap in the trading pattern.

A gap often is a sign of a reversal because the market is overbought or oversold.

See PRICE GAP.

GAP OPENING
Street term used to identify an opening transaction that is significantly higher/lower than the previous market day's closing price. Generally, if there is to be a gap opening, the specialist will give indication notice on the tape to attract contra brokers. Although there is no legal definition of a gap, a good rule of thumb is 1 point for stocks selling below $20, 2 points for stocks selling between $20 and $100, and 5 points for stocks selling above $100.

GARAGE
Nickname for the annex floor to the north of the main trading floor of the New York Stock Exchange.

GARDEN LEAVE
A U.K. term for a meritorious employment practice in England as well as in the United States. It provides that, if an employee resigns to compete with that firm (either personally or on behalf of someone else), its employee must immediately retire from that business for up to 90 days. This practice is designed to prevent that person from stealing customers, business, or trade secrets from the former employer. It is as-

sumed that, in the interim period, the former employer (i.e., broker/dealer) will attempt to retain the customer base and prospective business relationships. In the meantime, it is assumed that firm will continue to pay benefits to the "beached" former employee.

GAS 100
Acronym for Global Analysis Systems 100 International Equity Index. It is a two-tiered index, which uses all 100 international issues in its computation and a second tier that uses only the 58 non-Japanese components in its measurement. Merrill Lynch is the sponsor of GAS 100.

GATORS
Acronym for Government and Agency Term Obligation Receipts. GATORS were originated by Moseley, Hallgarten, Estabrook, and Weeden to compete with CATS and TIGRs and are substantially the same as these and similar zero-coupon treasuries.

GCO
Acronym for GNMA Collateralized Obligation.
   See COLLATERALIZED MORTGAGE OBLIGATION.

GD
1. NYSE symbol for General Dynamics, a large U.S. defense contractor and a major participant in the aerospace industry.
2. An order qualifier on purchase or sale instructions on the London options marketplace. GD signifies "good for the day only" and means that the order—if not executed—expires at the end of the trading day.

GEARING
Slang for the percentage of debt in terms of total capital in an investment. For example, if the total capital of an investment is 10 million, debt of 4 million would indicate a 40 percent gearing and a 60 percent shareholder equity.

GEISCO
Acronym for General Electric Information Services Co., a communications linkage between ISCC and CEDEL to share international transaction and settlement information involving PORTAL (SEC Rule 144A) securities. Current data communications linkage involves ISCC software called "Global" Compass but this is deemed too cumbersome for PORTAL activities.

GEM

Acronym for growing equity mortgage. A home real estate mortgage whose initial payments of principal and interest are based on 25 years. However, the annual payments are increased 4% each year. Because the increase will be applied totally to the reduction of the principal amount, equity is increased and the mortgage will be amortized in 15 years.

GEMM

Acronym for gilt edged marketmaker. GEMM is used of any of the recognized dealers in U.K. government securities. These firms are members of the International Stock Exchange of the United Kingdom and the Republic of Ireland and make continuous two-sided markets in gilts. They are the principal means whereby the Bank of England fine-tunes the U.K. money supply.

GENERAL ACCOUNT

Federal Reserve term for a client's margin account. All equity transactions in which a broker maintains a creditor relationship with the customer must be made in the general account. Some transactions, however, may be made in special margin accounts (e.g., subscriptions, bonds, convertibles, and arbitrages).

See also EQUITY.

GENERAL ELECTRIC INFORMATION SERVICES CO.

See GEISCO.

GENERAL MOTORS BELLWETHER

Popular market theory. It holds that General Motors common stock signals general market direction for the four-month period following a new high, or low, of GM stock. If GM does not, within that time frame, set another new high or low, the market will reverse direction.

GENERAL OBLIGATION BOND

A municipal security whose interest and principal payments are backed by the full faith, credit, and taxing power of the issuer. Usually included in this category are limited tax bonds to be repaid from real estate taxes and special assessment bonds to be repaid by user fees.

Popularly abbreviated GO.

GENERAL SERVICES ADMINISTRATION

Acronym: GSA. Government agency created to construct, purchase, and manage government properties. GSA also is empowered to sell such facilities. The stockpiling of strategic materials and their distribution also is part of the mandate of GSA.

GSA may issue participation certificates. These debts are guaranteed by the United States; thus, interest is exempt from state and local taxation, although it is subject to federal taxes.

GENERIC SECURITY

An expression used to designate a newly issued publicly owned security that as yet has no track record; that is, any history of how the security will react to different market scenarios.

The term is often used of new real estate backed issues because it is not known how fast the mortgagees will "pay down" the principal amount of their loans; thus, it is not known how long will be the average life of the investment nor the yield to maturity on the original investment.

GENSAKI RATE

Rate associated with repurchase agreements for Japanese bonds traded in yen. The rate is comparable to the yen CD market, but there are adaptations made for Japanese and international investors.

Gensaki agreements may not be offered publicly in the United States.

GES

Acronym for Guaranteed Execution System. GES is a nonautomated small order execution system on the Boston Stock Exchange, analogous in purpose to DOT (NYSE), SOES (NASDAQ), PACE, and the like.

GES handles orders for 1,299 shares or less, based upon prevailing prices in the Consolidated Quotation System (CQS).

GETTING HEAVY

A term used in conjunction with a decline in prevailing prices for a security, or for the market in general. Generally, the term is used to designate that sellers are trading in volume and thereby depressing prices. For example, "ABC is down 2 points and trading is getting heavy."

G-5

A political term used to designate the "Group of Five"; that is, the finance ministers of the United States, Britain, Japan, Germany, and France. The original purpose of the group's meeting in 1985 was to lower the value of the US dollar in terms of other world currencies.

Also used as G-7 if the finance ministers of Italy and Canada are included.

In nonpolitical contexts, G-7, G-8, and G-10 are used to designate significant groups of management-type persons.

GG

Abbreviation: government guaranteed. GG often is used in the footnotes of statistical tables or other listings of debt securities to designate issues that are guaranteed either by the U.S. government or the foreign government in which the securities were issued.

GHOSTING

Term used of a form of collusive manipulation of stock prices by two or more securities firms.

It is called "ghosting" because one firm dictates price levels and the other firm follows its lead. The investing public, on the other hand, is led to believe that the price level is determined by the opinions of several "independent" marketmakers.

GHOST SHORTING

This colloquial term describes a marketmaker's improper act of selling a security not owned and not even bothering to borrow it in order to make delivery to the purchaser.

Also called "naked shorting."

See also GHOST STOCK.

GHOST STOCK

Slang for stock sold short by a firm or customer and neither borrowed nor delivered to the purchaser. It is also called a "naked short," and the initiating seller hopes that the price declines before the buyer initiates buy-in procedures.

GIC

See GUARANTEED INVESTMENT CONTRACT.

GIFT TAX

A federal tax levied on the donor of a gift in excess of $10,000 to any one individual in one year. The limit is $20,000 if the donor is married and the spouse concurs in the gift.

The tax is graduated according to the amount in excess of $10,000; however, the tax is integrated with the estate tax of the individual.

Legal advice is needed. There is no federal tax on gifts between spouses, but many states have such taxes or legislate a different threshold.

GILT

English slang: an obligation of the United Kingdom. American slang: blue-chip investment.

GILT-EDGED

Technically, the edges of a book that has been gilted; that is, covered with gold leaf. By implication, anything of the highest quality or value. Example: You would have to look long and hard to find securities that are more gilt-edged than these.

Term applied to the security of a corporation that has proved, over time, its ability to pay continuous dividends or interest. It refers more often to high-quality bonds than to stocks.

GILT-EDGED MARKETMAKER

See GEMM.

GINNIE MAE

See GOVERNMENT NATIONAL MORTGAGE ASSOCIATION.

GINNIE MAE PASS-THROUGH

A security that represents a proportional interest in a pool of mortgages. The security is called a "pass-through" because homeowners send monthly mortgage payments to a bank, which passes through the security holder's share of the payment after deducting a service charge.

Timely payment of interest and principal is guaranteed by the Government National Mortgage Association (GNMA or Ginnie Mae). Original principal amount is stated on the security certificate, but remaining unpaid principal is reduced monthly.

Technical name for these securities is GNMA Modified Pass-Through, because the coupon rate or production rate on the certificates is modified by the deduction of 1/2% from the loan rate of the mortgage pool. This deduction pays for the sponsoring bank's services. The principal is passed through without deduction.

See also HALF-LIFE.

GINNIE MAE II (GNMA II)

A form of Ginnie Mae pass-through serviced by Chemical Bank. Concept: The pass-through is based on a number of mortgage pools with differing interest rates and maturities. It is hoped that Ginnie Mae II, by including pools from various areas of the United States and with varying interest rates, will tend to standardize the paydown of these pass-through securities. Unwanted paydown of Ginnie Maes is one of the negative features of these securities.

GINZY

Commonly: the ginzy. Used as a noun. Example: "I arranged the ginzy."

This slang expression designates a transaction in a futures contract at a price that is unfavorable to the executing broker. The hope: the broker will do more business with the customer at prices that are beneficial.

This practice, which we would call a "loss leader" in other marketing efforts, violates the Commodity Exchange Act.

GIT
See GUARANTEED INSURANCE TRUST.

GIVE ME A LOOK AT
Industry slang used by traders, particularly on exchanges, when they want a current quotation and size for the market in a particular security. Example: "Give me a look at Bare Ass?" Translation: "I would like the quote and size for Boeing Corporation." Fortunately, there is no listed corporation called Moon Industries.

GIVE UP
Term used when an exchange member, acting as an agent for another member, designates that party as the person with whom the contra broker has traded. For example, Member A trades with Member B and "gives up the name of" Member C as the person with whom Broker B has traded.

The term also is used if a customer of one firm, while traveling, enters an order to buy or sell with another firm, with the instruction that his or her regular broker handle the clearing details of the transaction.

GLAMOUR STOCK
Popular term for an equity security that is highly recommended for growth and that is currently favored by portfolio managers seeking aggressive growth.

Concept: Glamour is what is in vogue.

GLASS-STEAGALL ACT
Federal law that prohibits commercial banks from owning broker/dealer affiliates. Bank holding companies, however, may own such affiliates. Law forbids commercial banks from owning, underwriting, or trading corporate securities for proprietary accounts. Law also forbids banks from underwriting most municipal revenue bonds.

GLOBAL ANALYSIS SYSTEMS 100 INTERNATIONAL EQUITY INDEX
See GAS 100.

GLOBAL CERTIFICATE

In foreign debt security offerings, it is customary to represent the total debt by one certificate; hence, the term *global*.

After 90 days, the global certificate is broken up into definitive pieces, each represented by individual certificates that are distributed to the subscribers according to their individual purchases.

GLOBAL FUND

An investment company or managed pool of investments whose portfolio is comprised of securities; denominated both in U.S. dollars as well as those in other currencies. In this regard, a global fund is distinguished from an international fund (q.v.) that contains only foreign securities.

GLOW WORM

Street slang for the stock of Corning Glass, derived from its symbol: GLW.

More common: Glass Works. This is derived from the official name: Corning Glass Works Corporation.

GNMA

Government-owned corporation, nicknamed Ginnie Mae, that facilitates financing in the primary mortgage market by (1) purchasing mortgages from private lenders to encourage construction and (2) guaranteeing the timely payment of principal and interest on certain pools of mortgages.

See also GOVERNMENT NATIONAL MORTGAGE ASSOCIATION.

GNMA MORTGAGE-BACKED SECURITIES DEALERS ASSOCIATION

An industry-sponsored group of dealers devoted to furthering member interests. The group is dedicated to education, trading, and operations. It also advises, through lobbying, anyone interested in these securities.

GNMA PRODUCTION RATE

See PRODUCTION RATE.

GNMA STANDBY

A put option on GNMA securities.

This negotiated option to sell at a fixed price hedges the originator of the pool of mortgages during the period between the assembly of the pool and its sale to a dealer from dramatic rises in the production rate; that is, the rate at which GNMA will guarantee the mortgages.

The premium (fee) is usually ¼% of the face value, although it may be higher. Unlike other put options, the buyer of the standby must give the writer 30 days' notice before exercise.

GNMA II
See GINNIE MAE II.

GNOMES
1. Jargon made popular by the television program "Wall $treet Week" for the 10 widely followed technical analysts whose composite opinion is used by the program to indicate the short-term direction of the market. For example, "This week our gnomes are 3 up, 3 neutral, 4 down, for a net of minus 1." From the Greek *gnome* (gnomay), an opinion; then introduced into Germanic folklore to signify a shriveled person who delivers this opinion: the gnomes of Zurich.
2. Slang for Freddie Mac mortgage pools with 15-year, rather than 30-year, maturities, and also a shortened average life.

GNP
See GROSS NATIONAL PRODUCT.

GO AROUND
When the Federal Open Market Committee canvasses primary bank and nonbank dealers for their bids and offers, the process is called a "go around."

GO BOND
See GENERAL OBLIGATION BOND.

GODFATHER
On the Tokyo Stock Exchange, a member who sponsors and assists a new member in preparing for admission and eventual prosperity on that exchange. It is not unusual for a new member of the Tokyo Stock Exchange to ask one of the "Big Four" (Nomura, Daiwa, Nikko, or Yamaichi) to act as "godfather."

GOFFEX
Originally the acronymic name of the German Options and Financial Futures Exchange modeled after the similarly named Swiss entity SOFFEX. As the organization proceeded to incorporate, it changed its name to DTB (Deutsche Terminboerse Gmbh.)

GO-GO FUND
Popular name for investment companies that specialize in highly speculative ventures.

GOING AWAY
Also: going away order.

The term is from municipal bond underwriting. Concept: The buyer is going to hold the bonds to maturity; thus, there will be no immediate effect on the remainder of this underwriting nor on the secondary market for the bonds. Example: A sale to other dealers may quickly provide competition in the secondary market, whereas a sale going away gives an ultimate noncompetitive buyer. For this reason, the syndicate manager will give priority to the confirmation of orders that are "going away."

GOING PRIVATE
Corporations whose common shares are owned by 500 or more persons are said to be public. They continue to be public as long as 300 or more persons own such stock.

To go private means to repurchase shares in such a way that there are less than 300 owners. Corporations with less than 300 owners of any class of equity security are nonreporting corporations under the 1934 Act, and are said to be "private."

See GO PRIVATE.

GOING PUBLIC
Initial public offering of the common shares of an issuer. Concept: Previously, either the company had sold no shares, or such shares as existed were traded privately between the company and its owners.

See GOING PRIVATE and GO PUBLIC.

GOLDEN BOOT
Term used to designate the layoffs of older employees with minimal incentives and financial benefits. Such layoffs may be disguised as "voluntary" but are often coerced under the veiled threat of termination without any financial benefits. As such, these layoffs may violate EEOC guidelines against discrimination because of age and the like.

GOLDEN CROSS
In Japan, a market technician's powerful indicator of a forthcoming rise in prices. This bullish sign occurs when the 80-day moving average of stock prices crosses from below the 200-day moving average of stocks on the Tokyo Stock Exchange.

GOLDEN HANDSHAKE
Euphemistic term to describe an incentive plan geared to entice employees into early retirement. Such a plan may include salary continuation programs, continued health and insurance benefits, a lump-sum pension payment, and so on. Such plans are aimed at creating openings for younger employees or to lower (ultimately) payroll or benefit costs, or both.

GOLDEN HELLO
Slang in the English securities marketplace to signify a large start-up bonus paid to new employees to induce them to join a particular securities organization.

GOLDEN PARACHUTE
One uses a parachute in the event of an air disaster to descend to the ground safely. Analogy: A company anticipates a takeover or other financial adversity that may "ground" present executives. Thus, the executives vote themselves termination or other retirement benefits that will—no matter what the fortunes of the company—provide them a safe passage to financial security.

GOLDEN SHARE
In the United Kingdom, a situation where the seller retains voting privileges to elect the issuer's board of directors. This occurred in the privatization of Britoil, plc, where the British government sold its interest in that company but the buyers were not in a position to elect the board of directors.

GOLD FIX
In London, the twice-daily setting of the price per ounce of bullion gold. This price becomes the worldwide standard for the price of gold and of gold bullion futures. The fixing is picturesque: three dealers sit at a table and, as the price is changed (up or down), they are at liberty to hold the flag in front of them up until the price reaches a level that they feel will satisfy their orders, both received and anticipated. When all three flags are lowered, the price is fixed.

GONE FOR A BURTON
Quaint local English slang for a sharp market decline. The term originated when an RAF pilot in World War II was shot down and killed. In explanation, it was said that "he had gone for an ale in Burton-on-Trent." That was quickly shortened and used to signify financial destruction in a falling market.

GOODBYE KISS

Tongue-in-cheek expression for the payoff of an unwanted suitor by a company threatened by a takeover. The pirate's stock is purchased at higher than market prices; hence, the expression "goodbye kiss."

Similar in concept to "greenmail."

GOOD DELIVERY

Industry term for a certificate that meets certain standards and thus is negotiable among brokers. These standards apply to proper denomination, endorsement, signature guarantee, and other qualifications. If a certificate is in good deliverable form and is presented by the selling broker, it must be accepted by the buying broker.

GOOD FAITH DEPOSIT

1. Deposit required by member firms when a customer, unknown to the firm, enters an order to buy or sell. Usually a good faith deposit is 25%.
2. Deposit, usually 1 to 5% of the principal amount of the issue, made by competing municipal underwriters with the issuer. Losing syndicates have the deposit returned. The winning syndicate leaves the deposit with the issuer and it becomes part of the final settlement for the issue.

GOOD MONEY

Street slang: federal funds; that is, money that may be used immediately without passing through the clearing process.

In practice, good money is represented by: cash, cleared credit balances in a member firm client's account, a check drawn by a member bank of the Federal Reserve on its Federal Reserve account, and funds transferred by the Fed Wire.

Checks that must pass through clearing, and the proceeds of securities sales that do not settle on the same day, are not good money.

GOOD NAME BROKER

Industry term for a contra broker suggested by SIAC (Securities Industry Automated Clearing) if there is a "break" on the contract sheet.

Concept: A break is a mismatch between the buying and selling broker. Thus, both brokers will DK; that is, don't know the transaction. SIAC will volunteer the name of another mismatch. In this way, a few calls between mismatched brokers will quickly establish the correct matches and settlement/delivery can be established.

GOOD TILL CANCELLED ORDER (GTC)
An order to buy or sell, usually at a limit or stop price, that remains in effect until cancelled by the customer. Although the order and its terms remain in effect indefinitely, industry practice is to require periodic verification from the customer that the order should remain in force.

GOOFBALL
Colorful industry slang for the shares of Wilson Pharmaceutical Corporation, a manufacturer of ethical drugs among which are included some psychoactive and mind-altering drugs. The expression builds on popular slang for tranquilizers.

GOOSE JOB
This vulgar expression refers to the influence of a trader who, in the face of a limited supply of a stock, increases the demand for a stock.

In practice, industry rules prohibit an industry professional from purchasing stocks in such a way that prices are forced up. Thus, industry professionals may buy at present prices or below; but as buyers they may not push up prices for a security.

GORIKA
An electronic order and trade routing system under development by the Tokyo Stock Exchange. It is similar to the NYSE "order book" and it will disclose market depth at all prices for interested prospective broker participants.

See SAITORI.

GORILLA
Street slang for the shares of General Instrument Corporation derived from its NYSE symbol: GRL.

GOVERNMENT AND AGENCY TERM OBLIGATION RECEIPTS
See GATORS.

GOVERNMENT BROKER
1. In the United States, the term identifies a securities firm that acts as an intermediary between two government securities dealers who prefer to trade anonymously. In this regard, the term is similar to the term *broker's broker* in the municipal securities markets.
2. In the United Kingdom, the term applies to a firm called Mullens & Company. Mullens acts for the Bank of England on behalf of the English government. At the direction of the Bank of England this firm buys and sells gilts through various marketmakers.

GOVERNMENT NATIONAL MORTGAGE ASSOCIATION (GNMA)
Government-owned corporation, operating within the Department of Housing and Urban Development (HUD); facilitates financing in the primary mortgage market by:
1. Purchasing mortgages from private lenders to encourage construction.
2. Guaranteeing the timely payment of principal and interest on certain pools of mortgages.

Nickname is Ginnie Mae. The name often is used of the securities of the GNMA.

GOVERNMENTS
General term for the negotiable and marketable securities issued by the U.S. Treasury.

The term does not include nonnegotiable securities of the U.S. government, currency, or securities of government agencies.

THE GOVERNMENT SECURITIES ACT OF 1986
Federal law that regulates broker/dealers in U.S. government securities and agency securities. Banks and securities firms that transact in those securities must register with the SEC *and* with their own regulators (e.g., securities firms with the NASD; banks with their regulators). Exempt are organizations that:
1. Handle U.S. savings bonds exclusively.
2. Execute less than 500 trades a year.
3. Act only as fiduciaries.
4. Engage only in REPO (Reverse REPO) transactions.
5. Are registered with the Commodities Futures Trading Commission (CFTC) and whose government trades are incidental to such business in futures.
6. Are a branch or agency of a foreign bank whose customers are non-U.S. citizens.

GOVERNMENT SECURITIES BROKERS ASSOCIATION
A trade group of government securities brokers organized to lobby in Washington to present the industry's ideas and viewpoints to Congress. These firms act as intermediaries for government dealers trading anonymously and formed their organization in 1986 to promote mutual economic interests.

GOVERNMENT SECURITIES CLEARING CORPORATION
Initials: GSCC. This is an offshoot of the National Securities Clearing Corporation (NSCC), which was founded originally to settle OTC trans-

actions. GSCC was founded in 1986 to compare and make net settlements in government securities for participating dealers.

GOVERNMENT TRUST CERTIFICATES
See GTC.

GPM
Acronym for graduated payment mortgage. A real estate mortgage loan with a fixed interest rate. Monthly payments, however, rise during the first 10 years, then level off. The end result, since the additional payments reduce principal, is to reduce the effective life of the mortgage.

Also see GEM for a similar concept for the life of the mortgage to decrease the principal balance over a shorter time.

GRADUATED CALL WRITING
A program of selling call options against an underlying stock position at increasing strike prices and increasing premiums as the stock price rises. If the strategy is successful, the result is the sale of the entire stock position at the call prices at an average price (including premiums and dividends) that is higher than the original prices of the options. Also known as "incremental return writing strategy."

Should the options not be exercised, the premium income will cushion downside stock fluctuations. In effect, a client with 1,500 shares sells 5 calls at 50, then 5 calls at 55, then 5 calls at 60. If called, the client will garner the increased strike prices, the increased profit on the underlying, and the increased premiums. If not called, the premiums will cushion downside risk.

GRADUATED PAYMENT MORTGAGE
See GPM.

GRANDFATHER CLAUSE
A provision generally written into new rules that permits persons previously engaged in certain specific functions and procedures to continue to qualify without undergoing new tests or other qualification procedures.

Also called "grandfathering."

GRANDFATHERING
Industry jargon for the recognition of continued professional work over a defined time period in such a way that the incumbent of a job does not have to pass a new qualification examination. Example: There will be a

new industry examination for financial advisors, but persons who have served as registered representatives for the previous five years will be grandfathered.

GRANNY BOND
English term: a government-sponsored savings bond which may be purchased only by those in retirement or who are receiving governmental income payments. The interest is indexed to the British consumer price index, but the floor is a 4% minimum.

GRANT ANTICIPATION NOTE
GANs are municipal securities issued in expectation of federal government monies to be received for a specific project. The notes are a form of bridge financing to begin work on a highway, water facility, and the like. The federal government statutes will spell out the ways in which the monies are to be used.

GRANTOR RETAINED INCOME TRUST
See GRIT.

GRANTOR TRUST
Legal term for the conduit used to entitle ownership interests in a pass-through security. In effect, the grantor trust provides equity units of participation in an instrument holding title to an issue of debt securities collateralized by mortgages, credit card receivables, automobile loans, or other asset-backed instruments.

GRATUTY FUND
Special fund that provides death benefits for the next of kin of deceased members of the exchanges. Fund is made up of contributions from the members. NYSE fund payment varies from $20,000 to $100,000 depending on the tenure of the decedent. The ASE fund payment is $75,000.

GRAVESTONE SALES
A derogatory term used in Japan to describe high-pressure securities sales tactics much like the concept of "boiler room" sales in the United States. The term is derived from an unsavory practice in Japan of selling family gravestones in a culture that is dedicated to ancestor honor, with an overtone that the sellers either fail to deliver on their promises or what they deliver is lacking in real value.

GRAVEYARD MARKET

Colorful term used to describe a bear market in which many investors have substantial paper losses and thus are not able to sell without realizing the losses of substantial amounts of capital. The other side of the coin is this: Those who did not suffer paper losses and who, instead, have either substantial cash or large gains, feel that it is too early to jump back into the market. They feel that the market has not yet bottomed.

GRAY KNIGHT

Colorful term used in mergers and acquisitions for a second bidder for a takeover target.

The second bidder is not a "White Knight" because it is not coming to the rescue of the target. Nor is it a total enemy of the target, a "Black Knight." That only leaves one color, a mixture of white and black: gray!

GRAY MARKET

1. The purchase of open-end mutual fund shares by a broker/dealer at a price above the net asset value for resale to its customers. This practice is unethical if the broker/dealer has signed a sales agreement with the underwriter of the fund.
2. In England, "if and when issued" secondary market sales made during the period when a security is in the hands of its underwriters and before the actual distribution. English law, unlike that of the United States, does not forbid such sales.

GREED INDEX

This 10-factor index, each of which is graded 1 to 10, gives an insight into the personal habits of portfolio managers. With a high of 100, scores below 30 are bullish; scores above 60 are bearish. A form of contrarian analysis; that is, managers, on balance, tend to buy at the top and sell at the bottom. Thus, low ratings are good and high ratings are bad.

Here is a list of the 10 factors:
1. Buy new money management vehicles.
2. Expected rate of return on equities.
3. Prefer stocks to bonds.
4. Are fully invested; that is, cash is low.
5. Invest for aggressive growth.
6. Acceptance of new ideas.
7. Ratios of positive commentary.
8. Institutional activity.
9. New-issue interest.
10. Money manager personal investments.

GREENFIELD VENTURE

Quaint British term for a venture capital deal by a group without a previous track record. Thus, neither the new company nor the capital suppliers has a record for the other to gauge prospective success because both are "start-up" operations.

A GREENIE

Picturesque term used on the floor of the New York Stock Exchange for a memorandum on green paper given by the specialist to indicate the opening price of a stock. If such a memorandum is given to a broker whose stock was used to determine the opening price, the broker must compare the price with that of the contra broker for the execution price to be valid.

GREENMAIL

Slang: used in conjunction with takeover bids, tender offers, or unfriendly proxy fights. The concept is similar to blackmail.

Greenmail involves the purchase of a significant block of stock for one of two purposes: either to sell the block to a corporate raider, or to tender it to the company for a premium price. Because the sale of the block to a raider would threaten the continuity of management, management feels impelled to buy the shares at a premium, rather than have the shares sold to an unfriendly corporate raider.

GREEN SHOE

Provision in an underwriting agreement that permits the syndicate to purchase additional shares at the same price as the original offering. In this way, the underwriting group can cover shares sold short without financial risk.

Also called "the green shoe clause."

GRESHAM'S LAW

This postulate was made in the 16th century by Sir Thomas Gresham, an English economist. The law states that, if a country has two forms of currency, hoarding will take the currency with the higher intrinsic value out of circulation. Example: When the United States in 1964 began to circulate copper-clad coins, it quickly caused the hoarding of the silver coins then in circulation.

GRIT

Acronym for grantor retained income trust. GRIT is an estate-tax saving device that is predicated on the grantor's survival of the trust termination date. GRIT is an irrevocable trust with at least a 15-year life. It allows the grantor to transfer assets but retain the income of the trust for the life of the trust. Upon termination, the remainderman (who owns the property) now also gets the income. The grantor now pays a gift tax based on the original value of the gifted property. The gift tax could be at a rate that is fully covered by the unified gift and estate tax credit permitted by law. Upon the grantor's death, such a gift is added back to the estate of the grantor at the value as of the day of the gift, not its current value. Therein lies the principal estate tax saving.

GRIZZLY
Verbal acronym for a Growth Retirement Investment Zero-Coupon Treasury Certificate. GRIZZLYs were originated by Swanbrook Limited Partnership. Issued by Security Pacific National Bank of Los Angeles as custodian for Swanbrook's underlying government securities that collateralize the issue. The GRIZZLY represents ownership of a specific amount of a bond underlying Swanbrook's CUBS and BEARS (q.v.).

GROSS LEASE
A short-term commercial loan in which the landlord pays all expenses incidental to ownership. The tenant is responsible only for the lease payments and for maintenance and operating expenses.

Antonym: net lease, in which the landlord pays only taxes and all other operating, maintenance, and insurance expenses—plus the payment of a net sum—are the obligation of the tenant.

GROSS MARGINING
Term used on the Chicago Mercantile Exchange (CME) regarding the carrying of positions in futures contracts. Under gross margining, the "Merc" requires each member to deposit margin daily not for its net position but for all of its open positions. For example, if a member has 100 open long positions and 50 open short positions in the same commodity, it must deposit margin on all 150 open positions, not on the net position of 50 contracts.

GROSS NATIONAL PRODUCT
Dollar value of the final goods and services produced in the U.S. economy. The GNP is considered the principal coincident indicator of the state of the American economy. Looked at from the point of view of users, the GNP is equal to the national income.

On a quarterly basis the Bureau of Economic Analysis (Department of Commerce) compiles and reports two GNPs: the normal, which is the total for the quarter, and the real GNP, the total after the effects of inflation are removed.

GROSS SELECTION
Depends on the context. Most common usage: a preliminary selection before the final selection is made.

GROSS SPREAD
Dollar difference between the public offering price of a new issue of securities and the proceeds to the issuer. The gross spread is further subdivided into the manager's fee, the dealer's (or underwriter's) discount, and the selling concession.

GROSS UNDERWRITING SPREAD
The dollar difference between the public offering price of a new issue of securities and the proceeds to the issuer.
    See also UNDERWRITING SPREAD.

GROSS YIELD
The yield to maturity on a bond purchased at a discount. Because the cash flow does not take into consideration the tax consequences of the tax on interest income or the tax on capital gains, it is gross before taxes.
    Because of taxes, many bond offering sheets also will include the effective yield for corporations in the highest tax bracket so the buyer may measure the actual return on invested dollars.

GROUP LESS CONCESSION ORDER
See DESIGNATED CONCESSION.

GROUP NET ORDER
Buy order given to manager of a municipal securities syndicate. Purchaser, who is a nonmember, agrees to pay the public offering price and to leave the entire spread in the account for the benefit of the syndicate. Group net orders are priority orders and are confirmed before typical retail orders.
    See also MEMBER TAKEDOWN.

GROUP OF FIVE
See G-5.

GROUP ROTATION

Technical and market analysis term that centers on the fact that the stocks of a particular industry go in and out of fashion. Thus, when Industry A goes into fashion, portfolio managers jump in to make it too "pricey," and then they jump to Industry B because it is now underpriced. The term does not infer that there is conscious manipulation of the prices of one industry over the other; rather, it is an inference that there is an element of "follow the leader" in portfolio management as there is in any industry.

GROUP SALES

Term refers to the sale of SEC-registered offerings by the manager of the syndicate to institutional investors. The shares come from the "pot" established by the syndicate. Credit for the sale is proportional to the takedown of the individual members of the syndicate.

GROUP UNIVERSAL LIFE POLICY

See GULP.

GROWING EQUITY MORTGAGE

See GEM.

GROWTH AND INCOME SECURITIES

See GAINS.

GROWTH STOCK

Equity security of a company that is expected to increase in market value at a relatively rapid rate. Growth usually is a function of rapidly increasing earnings, although special situations may cause a stock to be considered a growth stock.

Growth stocks usually are marked by a relatively high price-earnings ratio and a low dividend payout ratio.

GS

When used on corporate and municipal bond calendars, these initials stand for Goldman Sachs & Company, a major underwriter of securities.

GSA

See GENERAL SERVICES ADMINISTRATION.

GSBD

Acronym for Government Securities Brokers and Dealers. A form of SEC registration for government securities dealers after July 25, 1987. Under federal law, those firms not registered as general securities brokers under the 1934 Act with the SEC must register as GSBDs if they wish to act as brokers or dealers in government securities. This requirement applies also to dealer banks (or separate trading units within banking institutions) with this exception: the registration of banks must be with their own regulators, rather than with the SEC.

GSCC

See GOVERNMENT SECURITIES CLEARING CORPORATION.

GSOP

Acronym for Government Security Option Permit. GSOPs are three-year privileges offered by the CBOE that enable holders to deal as marketmakers in these specialty instruments. These permits do not require that the permit holder be a member, nor do they carry a right to purchase a membership in the exchange.

GTC

Initials that are used to signify:
1. On an order to buy or sell, that the order is valid until it is cancelled by the customer. Industry or member firm practice is to require periodic revalidation of such orders; for example, at the end of 31 days, or every six months.
2. Government Trust Certificates. These are U.S. government guaranteed (90%) refinancings of loans to foreign countries enabling them to buy American military equipment. GTCs were created in 1988, and such loans enabled these countries to pay less interest for their loans originally negotiated in the early 1980s. GTCs have no provisions for prepayments, calls, or sinking funds.

GTD

See GUARANTEED BOND.

GUAN

An infrequently used abbreviation for a stock or bond that is guaranteed.

GUARANTEED ACCOUNT

An account of one customer that is guaranteed by another customer. The guarantee involves the payment of margin debits, or performance on option contracts. Such accounts require that the guarantor provide full and specific assurances in writing.

GUARANTEED BOND
Concept: A *guaranteed stock* is a preferred stock whose dividend payments are guaranteed by someone other than the issuer. A *guaranteed bond* is a bond whose interest and principal payments are guaranteed by someone other than the issuer. Example: The bonds of ARCO Pipeline, a subsidiary of Atlantic Richfield Corporation, are guaranteed by the parent corporation.

See also GUAN.

GUARANTEED EXECUTION SYSTEM
See GES.

GUARANTEED INSURANCE TRUST
Acronym: GIT. A hybrid product that combines some features of a UIT with some features of a guaranteed income contract issued by an insurance company. GITs are designed to appeal to small and medium-sized nontaxable retirement funds. In practice, a broker/dealer will pool several GITs to form a unit trust with the GITs as the principal assets. Then, participation units having face values as low as $1,000 are offered to interested buyers.

Generally, the broker/dealer will maintain a secondary market, although most units are bought and held.

GUARANTEED INVESTMENT CONTRACT
GICs are investment contracts sold by insurance companies to pension and profit-sharing plans, usually for a period of 3 to 10 years. The pension or profit-sharing plan makes a large capital investment; in return, the insurance company guarantees a specific rate of return on the invested capital. The insurance company assumes all market, interest-rate, and credit risks on the securities that are held in trust to collateralize the obligation. The pension or profit-sharing plan assumes all inflationary risk.

GUARANTEED SPREAD
A proposal by a broker/dealer to a customer in conjunction with a swap. Concept: In return for the customer's commitment to buy a new security at a price that will be determined, the broker/dealer agrees to buy from the customer those securities held by the customer at a predetermined spread between the two prices.

The guarantee is illegal if corporate securities are involved. It may be fraudulent if exempt securities are involved and the guarantee creates a contract value that is fictitious.

GUARANTEE LETTER
Letter issued by a commercial bank on behalf of a customer who has written a put option. The letter, which specifies both the dollars and the put contract involved, promises to pay a specified sum when, and if, an assignment notice is presented.

GUERILLA GROUP
A municipal underwriting term. Concept: The underwriting group is composed of only a few members, who thereby assume large capital risks.

In practice, municipal accounts attempt to minimize the individual risks of the participants by including a large number of underwriters in the account.

GULP
Acronym for group universal life policy. GULP is a form of employee benefit plan made available by many financial services firms. GULP centers on a form of term life insurance but adds savings features and residual value not found in most whole life policies. As a group policy, GULP features economies not found in personal universal life policies. GULP policies are "interest-rate sensitive" and returns may vary. Often GULP policies are offered not only to the employee but also to other immediate family members.

GUN JUMPING
Industry slang for:
1. The illegal act of soliciting buy orders before an SEC registration is effective.
2. Buying a security based on information that is not yet public.

GUNNING
A slang term for market manipulation. In this case, the manipulation occurs when a person or a group of persons purchases a security at increasing prices. The goal is to lure greedy investors, who will end up holding securities with inflated values.

Manipulation is outlawed by the Securities and Exchange Act of 1934 and by state securities laws.

GUNSLINGER
A 1960s term for an aggressive portfolio manager who purchased highly speculative stocks, or who used leverage to increase returns. Subsequent bear markets and economic downturns helped to remove most of these speculators.

GYP-EM
A jocular term used to describe graduated mortgage payments. See GPM for a description of such mortgages.

H

HAIRCUT
Industry term for the valuation of securities used to compute the broker/dealer's net capital. The haircut varies with the class of security, its market risk, and time to maturity. The haircut may vary from 0% to 30% (which is common for equity securities) to 100% for fail positions that have little chance of being settled in the member firm's favor.

HALF-LIFE
Term used of GNMA pass-throughs. It is the time after issuance when it is estimated that one half of the principal amount on a pool of mortgages shall have been repaid. Based on FHA experience of prepayment and default, GNMA pass-throughs are presumed to have a half-life of 12 years. In practice, the half-life of a specific pool may be longer or shorter than 12 years.

HAMMERED
An English term for a stock exchange member who became insolvent.

The term originated when the London Stock Exchange hammered a bell during trading hours and announced to the other members that this or that member firm was now insolvent.

HAMMERING THE MARKET
Picturesque metaphor used by traders to reflect the downward pressure on the market caused by heavy selling. In effect, speculators and investors have become pessimistic and their selling, either constant or in waves, is causing the market to drop rapidly.

Used both actively and passively; for example, "The programmed trading is hammering the market . . ." or, "The market is being hammered by aggressive selling."

HANDLE

Also called "the handle," or "the full."

Concept: Only the 8ths, 16ths, or 32nds of the bid and asked prices are quoted. The presumption is that industry professionals know the "handle," or the percentage amount that is involved.

Example: A quote of a government at 16-20 omits the handle. The full quote could be—to those acquainted with the current market for the security—$98^{16}/_{32}$ bid and $98^{20}/_{32}$ offered.

HANDS-OFF INVESTOR

Expression used to describe a capital contributor to a corporation who is willing to accept a passive role in its day-to-day operations.

HANDS-ON INVESTOR

An investor who makes a major capital contribution to a business enterprise and who expects to play an active role in its day-to-day management. "Active" may mean in an advisory role, or through a seat on the board of directors, or as a manager or officer.

HANGNAIL

A cute nickname for Houston Natural Gas Corporation. Hangnail is based on the NYSE ticker symbol: HNG.

HANG SENG INDEX

An index that measures the price change movements of 33 stocks traded on the Hong Kong Stock Exchange.

It is similar in concept to the Dow Jones Average of Industrial Stocks. However, the Hang Seng Index represents about 70% of the market value of all stocks traded on the Hong Kong Exchange. The Dow Jones Average represents only 25%, approximately, of the stocks traded on the NYSE.

HAPPINESS LETTER

A letter signed by an officer or branch manager to a customer—either new or continuing—to ensure that the relationship between the customer and the broker/firm is satisfactory.

Such "happiness letters," as they are picturesquely called, are usually required by the broker/dealer's legal department whenever a customer account:

1. Is introduced to the firm or transferred thereto,
2. or is subjected to unusual activity,

3. or changes investment objectives,
4. or buys something of questionable suitability.

The purpose of the letter is to forestall customer complaints or future litigation.

HARD BULLET ASSET-BACKED SECURITIES

A debt obligation collateralized by credit card receivables, but with a "maturity guarantee" by a bank issuer in case principal collections are insufficient to meet principal requirements at maturity.

HARD DOLLARS

Actual dollars paid for the research or other services provided by a firm to a client. The expression is used in contrast to soft dollars. For example, a computer analysis of a client's portfolio may cost $3,000 hard dollars; or $10,000 soft dollars, if the client directs portfolio transactions through the firm that provided the computer service.

Antonym: "soft dollars." This term is used when payment is made in kind; for example, commissions in exchange for research services or other statistical services, or if payment is made by a third party.

HART-SCOTT-RODINO ACT

A short-name title for Section 7A of the Clayton Antitrust Act.

In practice, this section requires a prior screening by the Federal Trade Commission and the Justice Department of possible federal antitrust violations.

Specifically, a 15 to 30 day waiting period is mandated for this screening if a prospective purchaser would hold $15 million or more of the acquired company's assets and 15% or more of that company's voting stock.

HEAD AND SHOULDERS

Bar chart pattern of a stock's price movement marked by a shoulder line, neck line, and head line conforming, in general, to a person's upper torso. As the price movement approaches the shoulder line on the right, technicians consider the trend as bearish—a head and shoulders top. The reverse pattern is upside down, with the head at bottom. Such a pattern is considered bullish—and called a "head and shoulders bottom."

HEAF

Acronym for Higher Education Assistance Foundation. HEAF is a private guarantor of student educational loans and, as such, is a significant participant in the U.S. government's student loan program. HEAF specializes in guaranteeing loans to finance technical school training, junior colleges, and two-year degree programs.

In general, HEAF, if a student defaults, insures the loan repayment and is, in turn, partially reimbursed by the government. If not, it will honor the loan out of its reserve fund.

HEALTH INDUSTRY BOND INSURANCE COMPANY

Abbreviation: HIBI. A bond insurance program backed by Crum and Forster and American Health Capital Management to assure payment of interest and principal to holders of debt securities in qualifying health care institutions. HIBI does not limit its insurance to nontaxable debt. Generally, HIBI-insured issues carry AAA ratings.

HEAVEN AND HELL BONDS

Slang for a unique product of Mitsui & Co. (USA).

Heaven and hell bonds are parts of a Eurobond issue linked to the performance of a specific U.S. Treasury issue. The holder of a "heaven" bond receives par plus a premium if the U.S. Treasury bond *outperforms* the Eurobond issue. The holder of a "hell" bond receives par plus a premium if the U.S. Treasury bond *underperforms* the Eurobond issue. Interest on both bonds is nominal: 3–4% annually; their value is in the premium paid under differing circumstances.

These bonds are similar in concept to bull and bear bonds (q.v.) but differ in their benchmark index and type of underlying security.

HEAVY

Industry term that designates a preponderance of offers in the market for a particular security. A heavy market for a security, or the market in general, implies a probable decline in the security, or market. Example: The unfavorable balance of trade report issued last week has tended to make a heavy market.

HEDGE

Used both as a verb and a noun to indicate reduced risk.

A hedge involves an offsetting securities position that limits loss. A hedge that eliminates the possibility of future gain or loss is a perfect hedge.

Example of a perfect hedge: A client holds appreciated stock and sells short against the box.

Example of an imperfect hedge: Buy a stock and sell a call. Client is hedged against loss by the amount of the premium received.

See also BOX.

HEDGE CLAUSE
Statement that appears in a research report, market letter, or other security valuation in which the writer disclaims responsibility for the accuracy of information that the writer took from what are considered to be reliable information sources. The intent is to remove liability for the accuracy of the information, although the writer is not absolved from negligence in the use of the information.

HEDGED TENDER
SEC Rule 10b-4 prohibits the tender of borrowed stock. However, if long stock has been tendered and the tenderer anticipates that not all of the tendered stock will be accepted, the tenderer may want to sell some of the stock short. In this way, the tenderer will hedge against a possible decline of the stock following the partial acceptance. Such a short sale is called "a hedged tender."

HEDGE FUND
Slang term for a limited partnership that speculates in securities. Limited partners have limited risk, but their rewards are shared by the general partners.

Term also is used of funds that use hedging techniques. For example, calls, puts, margin, and shorting to increase return.

HEDGE RATIO
A ratio of the number of option contracts needed to hedge a position in the underlying equity based on the beta of the underlying.

For example, a client is long 100,000 shares of LMN, which has a beta of 1.15. To hedge this position, the client could buy 1150 long puts, or sell 1150 covered calls. Reasoning: the underlying will tend to perform as though it had a dollar value equal to 115,000 shares of stock; thus, it should be hedged as such. Remember: the word *hedge* means to take an offsetting position; that is, on the opposite side of the market from the underlying. Long puts and short calls are on the other side of the market from the long position because they partially protect on the downside.

See also DELTA.

HEDGE WRAPPER
An expression used to designate this strategy: a customer who is long the underlying stock buys a put and sells a call. No matter which way the underlying moves, the customer stands to benefit—although losses

are possible. If the underlying does not move, the customer benefits from the difference between the income in (from the call) and premium paid (on the put). If the stock moves up, the customer will be called at a profit; if the stock moves down, the customer is hedged (hence, the name) by the put. The strategy is also used with index options but requires that the customer have a diversified portfolio of stocks similar to the overlying index.

HELSINKI STOCK EXCHANGE
Located in the capital of Finland, this exchange is one of the smallest in Europe because foreign ownership of Finnish companies is severely restricted. Trading hours are from 9:30 A.M. until noon, but afternoon trading is permitted for another two hours. Settlement takes place on the fifth banking day after trade date.

HELSINKI STOCK EXCHANGE AUTOMATIC TRADING & INFORMATION SYSTEM
Popularly known by its acronym HETI, this is a computerized program to support securities trading on the Helsinki Stock Exchange. The system coordinates both exchange trading and trading done in the offices of Finnish brokerage firms.

HEMLINE THEORY
Stock market theory that the trend in the hemline of women's dresses is accompanied by a corresponding trend in the prices for stocks. For example, if hemlines are trending down, stock prices are trending down; if up, stock prices are trending up. Obviously, there is an upper limit on this theory.

The concept anticipates that the hemlines will serve as a leading indicator by about six months.

HETI
See HELSINKI STOCK EXCHANGE AUTOMATIC TRADING & INFORMATION SYSTEM.

HIBI
See HEALTH INDUSTRY BOND INSURANCE COMPANY.

HIBOR
Acronym for Hong Kong Interbank Offered Rate. HIBOR, an obvious analog of LIBOR, is similar to the prime rate in the United States and

forms a pricing standard for interest costs in the Far East. HIBOR is an "inside market" for interest rates made available only to prestigious banking and financial institution members in southeast Asia.

HIGHBALLING
Fraudulent swap technique. A client's holdings are purchased by the dealer above current market value so he does not have a loss. However, the client swaps for a new holding above its market value. The dealer accepts the "loss" on the purchase so he can build in a present gain on the sale.

HIGH FLYER
An expression that is aptly used of stocks with extreme price volatility. "High flyers" are stocks "in vogue" that are marked by extremely high price-earnings ratios and characterized by rapid price movements in reaction to business news about the company. In the latter part of the 1980s, computer issues and high-technology companies tended to be in the category of high flyers.

HIGH-GRADE BOND
A bond with a rating of AAA or AA.

HIGH-INCOME TRUST SECURITIES
See HITS.

HIGHJACKING
This is a literal translation of the Japanese word *nottori*.

The word is used in Japan to identify a takeover situation. It (highjacking) is also used in the United States of merger and acquisition activities.

HIGHLY CONFIDENT LETTER
A letter, pioneered by Drexel Burnham Lambert in conjunction with certain issues of "junk bonds," stating that they were highly confident (but without official commitment) and that they would be able to successfully market an offering of a particular type of security. Such a letter often arose in connection with a tender offer, or a leveraged buyout, where significant amounts of money would be needed from an issue to have the funds to purchase control of a company.

HIGHLY LEVERAGED TRANSACTION
See HLT.

HIGH STEPPER

Conventional industry term for a growth stock that combines high technology, high price volatility, and an "in vogue" status with investors and portfolio managers. Thus, the stock had all the ingredients to attract large cash flows in a competitive high-volume marketplace.

HIGH-YIELD BONDS

Industry term for "junk bonds"; that is, bonds with ratings of BB (Moody's Ba) or lower. Bonds with no rating are often placed in the same category.

Such bonds often have yields of 400 plus basis points above Treasuries of comparable maturities because of the default risk inherent in the bond. Unfortunately, both terms are deficient: high yield because it is euphemistic; junk bond because it is pejorative. In fact, only about 600 companies in the United States (out of 5,000 publicly traded) merit an investment grade rating; thus, "junk bonds" are the only access some companies have to the credit markets.

HISTORICAL YIELD

Originally, the yield on a mutual fund that took the annual dividend and divided it by the average public offering price. With the abrogation of the SEC's Statement of Policy in 1980, funds have been free to compute yield by any reasonable method. Most funds now take annual yield and divide it by a reasonable average. Money market funds typically use yield to average life.

A HIT

As a noun the term is used to designate:
1. A large monetary loss—either realized or on paper. Thus, an investor who had a rapid 10% loss would be said to have had a "hit."
2. A large monetary gain—either realized or on paper. Here the analogy is with the term used in baseball, *to make a hit.*
3. Slang—a capital penalty against a balance sheet asset that is judged ineligible for consideration under the SEC rule for the computation of net capital by a broker. Example: "We computed our net capital, but we had to take a hit on the value of stock exchange memberships."

As a verb the term is used to designate:
1. The borrowing of money; for example, "The company hit its stockholders for another large bond issue."
2. The appearance of news or rumors; for example, "It didn't take that rumor long to hit the Street."

HITS

Acronym for High-Income Trust Securities. This is a unit investment trust that was sponsored by Drexel Burnham Lambert. The trust featured high-yield, lower-quality bonds—popularly known as junk bonds—and thereby diversified the risk that may come from an individual investment in any of the bonds.

HIT THE BID

Expression used when a seller is willing to accept the bid made by a buyer. For example, if the quote is 18 to a quarter, a seller who hits the bid sells at 18.

HLT

1. Acronym for highly leveraged transaction—a euphemism for a bank loan to a company with a disproportionate amount of debt. What constitutes disproportionate will often vary by industry and traditional debt structures. Thus, in the United States, debt to equity ratios tend to be smaller for industrial and service companies than for utilities and banks. And, in Japan, debt to equity ratios tend to be much larger than in the United States.
2. NYSE ticker symbol for Hilton Hotels Corporation, one of the world's largest hotel chains.

HOEKMAN

Title of those members of the Amsterdam Stock Exchange (ASE) who have a function similar to that of the specialists on U.S. exchanges. The hoekman indicates quotes, takes and matches orders from other members, and also buys and sells as principal. It is also the hoekman's duty to report prices of actual transactions for the exchange's records and computer screens. As with U.S. specialists, they have assigned stocks and are expected to maintain "fair and orderly" markets.

HOLDER IN DUE COURSE

Legal term: a person who, in good faith, purchases an asset before the determination it was defective, stolen, or that its title was tainted.

Generally, the holder in due course is considered immune from claim or criminal prosecution. As a result, claims are made against the original purchaser for failure to apply due diligence to ascertain ownership if the item is stolen, or against the original seller if the item is defective.

HOLDER OF RECORD

Official title of the person whose name is on the books of a corporation at the close of business on an assigned day as the registered owner of an asset. Dividends, in the case of stock—and interest, in the case of bonds—will be paid to holders of record on the assigned day.

Holder of record is an identifiable event. Member firms, through the use of due bills, justify inequities that result because securities transaction were not completed in time to make buyers the holders of record in line with contract provisions.

HOLDING COMPANY
Under federal law, this is any corporation, partnership, trust, association, or organized group of persons that owns or controls 10% or more of the outstanding voting securities of a public utility company.

Term also is used of any company organized to own and manage other companies.

HOLDING PERIOD
The time that an investor owns a capital asset. On purchases followed by a sale, the IRS computes a long-term holding as follows: take the date following the purchase date; long-term holding begins on that calendar date one year later. For example, a purchase is made on February 28 in a non-leap year. The next day is March 1. One year later, the holding is long-term. There is a different computation of holding period on gifts and bequests. Tax advice is needed.

HOME
In usage: a home. Slang for a seller looking for a buyer in a difficult market. The buyer is referred to as a home. Example: "We're looking for a home for 100,000 shares."

The term is used when no evident buyer is available, or if buyers are making an unrealistic bid, or if the quantity bid falls far short of the amount of the security available for sale.

HOME RUN
This analogy from baseball is used to designate anyone who combines two concepts: a large profit in a short time. For example, "His purchase and resale of AJAX Corporation for a $40 million profit was a home run in anyone's league."

HOMES
In England, the designator of National Home Loans: the originator of a debt instrument representing the pooled mortgages of British homeowners. Similar in concept to Ginnie Mae pass-throughs in the United States, HOMES are backed by private insurors—although they have tacit approval of the Bank of England and the Inland Revenue Service.

HONG KONG STOCK EXCHANGE

This exchange marketplace is second only to Tokyo in terms of volume and trading activity in Asia. Trading is held each business day from 10:00 A.M. until 12:30 P.M. and from 2:30 P.M. until 3:30 P.M. No after-hour trading is permitted. Settlement the regular way is the next business day.

Its Hang Seng Index of market performance is followed worldwide.

HOOK ORDERS

See CAP ORDERS.

HORIZONTAL COMBINATION

A merger of two companies that produce substantially the same products. Thus, the merger produces economies of scale by eliminating duplicative management and support personnel. Example: A merger of two large steel companies.

Note: Do not confuse with horizontal spread as used in option terminology. A *horizontal spread* is the purchase and sale of options of the same class with the same strike price, but with different expiration months. Example: "Sell an April 50 call and buy a July call on the same security."

HORIZONTAL PRICE MOVEMENT

A term describing a succession of transaction prices in a security that are relatively the same. For example, a security that has a price range of between $8 and $10 per share over 1 or 2 months has a horizontal price movement.

Many persons use sideways price movement to describe the same series of prices. Key concept: The price does not vary substantially over time. As such, a horizontal price movement is indecisive and does not indicate a trend in the price of the security.

HORIZONTAL SPREAD

Technically, a horizontal spread is the purchase and sale of an equal number of contracts of options of the same class with the same striking price, but with different expiration months. For example:

> Buy 5 ABC April 60 calls
> Sell 5 ABC Jan   60 calls

Also called a "calendar spread."

HOSHO-KIKIN SYSTEM

This system augments the guaranty of the Japanese commodity exchange community by settling client equity liabilities in the event that a commodity futures merchant becomes insolvent. It was established in 1975 as a nonprofit foundation and is recognized by several ministries with industry jurisdictions.

Also known as: Association of Compensation Fund for Consigned Liabilities in Commodity Futures, Inc.

HOT ISSUE

NASD term for an SEC-registered public offering with an over-the-counter bid that is higher than the fixed public offering price on the day the security is first offered for sale. For example, a syndicate offers an issue at $31 per share. At the end of the trading day, the OTC bid is $32 per share. This is a hot issue and special rules apply to the syndicate's distribution of the security.

See also FREERIDING and WITHHOLDING.

HOT PANTS

A nickname for the common shares of Helmerich & Payne Corporation, a contract driller of oil and gas wells. The nickname is derived from the NYSE ticker symbol: HP.

HOT STOCK

1. Securities that are stolen.
2. Securities that rise rapidly in price on the sale date.
   See also HOT ISSUE.

THE HOUSE

1. A large broker/dealer organization with many offices and employees interconnected by internal wire systems; for example, Shearson Lehman Hutton is a large house.
2. A bank or broker/dealer dominated by a well-known person; for example, the House of Morgan.
3. Designation of a securities or commodities clearing agency set up to compare, confirm, and settle transactions; for example, "The house says that we owe 1,000 shares of ABC."
4. Collective name for the contra bettor in a gambling casino; for example, "The vigorish favors the house."

HOUSE ACCOUNT

A customer account held by a broker/dealer that is active but not assigned to a specific salesperson. Such house accounts often arise from a traditional relationship between the firm and the customer; for example, a pension and profit-sharing account that has always been at a particular firm. House accounts continue to generate commission business, but the allocation of production credits is generally lower than the ordinary allocation; for example, 10% rather than 25%, or it is used by the branch manager in return for favors.

HOUSE CALL
Wall Street euphemism for a margin maintenance call; that is, a request for additional funds in a margin account to meet either the firm's or the industry's maintenance requirements.

Antonym: T-call; that is, a request for funds to meet an initial margin requirement on a purchase or short sale as required by Regulation T of the Federal Reserve Board.

HOUSE MAINTENANCE REQUIREMENTS
The lowest dollar levels to which the equity in a customer's margin account may decline before more equity must be supplied, or collateral will be liquidated. The requirement is set by the broker/dealer and is somewhat higher than the levels mandated by the self-regulatory organizations in their minimum maintenance requirements.

See also MAINTENANCE REQUIREMENT.

HOUSE RULES
A broker/dealer's internal policies and procedures pertaining primarily to the opening and handling of customers' accounts and customers' activities in those accounts. House rules are often more strict than industry rules.

HOUSING AND URBAN DEVELOPMENT (HUD)
Department of the federal government that fosters, through loan guarantees and other measures of public policy, lower-income and middle-income housing in the United States.

HOUSING STARTS
One of the 12 leading indicators of movement in the U.S. economy. A change in the number of housing starts can severely affect a number of industries: banking, construction, forest and wood products, and other industries that supply materials for housing.

HUD
See HOUSING AND URBAN DEVELOPMENT.

HUMPTY DUMPTY BOUNCE
Taken from the nursery rhyme, this is a lighthearted allusion to corporate management's ability to write-down (write-off) large losses and expenses in one accounting period—thereby virtually assuring the next quarter's earnings will look very positive. For example, an automotive

company closed a plant and stopped research on a particular vehicle and took a $500 million loss this quarter.

Such write-offs are not illegal and make a lot of financial sense, but they do make it difficult to compare corporate quarterly figures.

HUMPTY DUMPTY FUND
In late 1983, the details of the AT&T breakup were known: The holder of 10 AT&T shares would receive 10 shares of the new AT&T and 1 share of each of the 7 "spun-off" operating companies. As a result, any holder of the old AT&T that did not hold a multiple of 10 would become partially disinvested because cash would be given in lieu of fractional shares of the operating companies.

A unit investment trust was formed. Any holder of AT&T stock could deposit any number of shares. The depositor would receive a fractional interest in the fund. As a result, the fund did what the nursery rhyme could not do: It "put Humpty Dumpty together again."

HUNG BRIDGE LOAN
Industry jargon for a temporary loan by an investment banker that could not be converted into long-term financing because of prevailing market conditions. Typically, the merchant banking arm of a broker/dealer makes a short-term loan to a client, anticipating repayment when the client issues a longer-term security. If market conditions interfere with the success of that offering the broker/dealer is hung for its reimbursement.

HUNKERING DOWN
Street jargon used by traders to signify an ongoing endeavor to lower one's risk in a position. For example, a trader, to accommodate a customer, took a large position in a stock; now he or she is trying to gradually sell off the position to lower risk exposure.

From "hunkers"; that is, one's haunches. To hunker is to squat on one's heels—and by analogy, to protect oneself by lowering one's profile.

HYBRID ANNUITY
An insurance company investment contract that combines features of both a fixed and a variable annuity in varying percentages, as elected by its subscribers.

HYBRID INVESTMENT
A trading vehicle whose investment value depends on more than one type of convention or supply/demand coalescence. For example, a futures or option contract whose value is related to supply/demand vectors and forces in its marketplace but whose ultimate value is dependent

upon an equity, debt, or index fluctuation in another marketplace. Thus, a divergence in market prices may create arbitrage situations (profit) or increase risk exposure.

HYPOTHECATION
Term refers to the pledging of securities or other assets as collateral for a loan while still keeping ownership. For example, if a client buys securities on margin, the securities are held by the broker (i.e., they are hypothecated, as a pledge that the client will repay the loan).

HYPOTHECATION AGREEMENT
Written agreement between customer and broker/dealer that details the rules under which the account is opened and carried. Principal parts of the agreement: securities purchased on margin are held by the broker/dealer; these securities may be repledged by the broker/dealer to finance the account; the broker/dealer may sell the pledged securities, if needed, to protect its financial interest in the account.

Also called "customer agreement" or "margin agreement."

I

IA
See INVESTMENT ADVISOR.

IADB
See INTER-AMERICAN DEVELOPMENT BANK.

IB
1. Commodity trading abbreviation for: introducing broker. An introducing broker is a futures commission merchant who is a member of the National Futures Association who gives up customer execution and clearance to another member.
2. A sometimes-used abbreviation for the World Bank. The technical abbreviation is IBRD: International Bank for Reconstruction and Development.

IBIS
Acronym for International Banking and Investment Services. IBIS is a computerized currency trade system located in Valley Forge, Pennsylvania.

The service prepares confirmations, arranges settlement, gives up-to-date currency positions, and gives credit exposure to its customers throughout the world.

IB RATE

See INTERBANK RATE.

IBRD

See WORLD BANK.

I BUY

Commonly used expression in the over-the-counter markets by traders who are buying for their own accounts. The expression acknowledges transactions, avoids human error, and emphasizes the dealer role of the trader.

The expression is particularly important for recordkeeping by the trader. Example: If the customer of a member is selling, the trader for the same firm is buying. Thus, accurate terminology is required to maintain inventory positions.

ICC

See INTERSTATE COMMERCE COMMISSION.

IC/VC

See INVESTMENT COMPANY AND VARIABLE CONTRACT PRODUCTS.

ID

See INSTITUTIONAL DELIVERY SYSTEM.

IDB

See INDUSTRIAL DEVELOPMENT BOND and INTER-DEALER BROKER.

IDBI

See INDUSTRIAL DEVELOPMENT BOND INSURANCE COMPANY.

IDD

Acronym for Index Disclosure Document. IDD is a special explanation of the features that surround Index Participations (IP). This document supplements "Characteristics & Risks of Standardized Options." This is the document that must be presented to a prospective options customer prior to approval by a registered options principal and the transaction of index option trades in the account.

IDIOT

Tongue-in-cheek acronym: institutional detection of inside-information offices and techniques. The term, which represents a hypothetical governmental office, was coined by counsel representing investment banking firms and is an attempt to spoof regulatory criticism of the financial industry in light of trading scandals. Congressional calls for more compliance and greater surveillance to detect improper use of nonpublic information prompted this suggestion for a formalized governmental group to oversee the investment banking activities of broker/dealers.

IDR

See INTERNATIONAL DEPOSITORY RECEIPT.

IET

See INTEREST EQUALIZATION TAX.

IF COME ORDER

Customer order to purchase a specific bond issue from a broker/dealer if that firm can find and buy these securities from a current holder of that security.

IFX OPTIONS

Fungible foreign currency options tradable on either the Philadelphia or the International Stock Exchange of the United Kingdom and the Republic of Ireland that are cleared by the Options Clearing Corporation (OCC). This intercontinental linkage of exchanges and contracts was pioneered in early 1986, and these instruments are often referred to as "international options."

IIEDS

See INDIVIDUAL INVESTOR EXPRESS DELIVERY SERVICE.

ILLIQUID

Used of a security that does not enjoy an active secondary market; thus, the holder may find it difficult to sell the security and thereby go back to cash.

IMA

See INTERNATIONAL MARKET AGREEMENT.

IMBALANCE OF ORDERS

This term is used to describe a premarket opening situation on an exchange. There is an overabundance of either buy or sell orders for a security and the amount is such that it overwhelms the specialist's ability to establish a balance between supply and demand. In this circumstance, the specialist will announce on the tape that contra orders are needed to set a fair opening price. The tape announcement could appear:

LMN   OPENING DELAYED INFLUX OF BUY ORDERS

This will tell interested sellers that they may be able to sell at a substantially higher price on the market opening.

IML
Acronym for Institut Monetaire Luxembourgeois. A government agency established to supervise banks in that country. It is also responsible for oversight of CEDEL, the settlement depository for international securities transactions which is also domiciled in Luxembourg.

IMM
See INTERNATIONAL MONETARY MARKET.

IMMEDIATE FAMILY
Under the National Association of Securities Dealers' rules on Freeriding and Withholding, certain sales are prohibited to brokerage employees and their immediate family. This latter term includes parents, mother- or father-in-law, brothers or sisters, and brothers- or sisters-in-law, children, and any relative to whose support the prohibited employee contributes.

IMMEDIATE-OR-CANCEL ORDER
See IOC.

IMMEDIATE PAYMENT ANNUITY
A single payment annuity contract with the election of annuity payments to begin immediately. The payments, usually monthly, are for the life of the subscriber, or for a specified number of years, according to the election made.

IMMEDIATE REPORTING ON QUOTE
See IRQ.

IMMUNIZATION
Term used in bond portfolio management when interest-rate risk has effectively been removed from the portfolio. The strategy takes place when the portfolio manager so adjusts the duration of portfolio bonds that it conforms to the time when the manager will need the funds in the account. In this way, any principal loss caused by a rise in interest rates

will be offset by increased return from the reinvestment of the cash flow (coupon interest) at higher than anticipated rates. Immunization is not easy to attain because bond duration can vary with the maturity time of bonds, their coupon rate of interest, and prevailing competitive interest rates.

IMRO
Acronym for Investment Management Regulatory Organisation. This is an SRO in the United Kingdom under the Financial Services Bill. IMRO has supervisory authority over investment managers, advisors, trustees of collective investment plans, and pension fund administrators who join the industry trade group.

INACTIVE BOND CROWD
New York Stock Exchange term for those listed bonds that trade infrequently. Limit orders to buy or sell such bonds are stored in steel cabinets to the side of the bond trading floor. Brokers with orders to buy or sell such bonds can seek a contra broker's order in the cabinet, with the trade completed in the bond trading area.

INACTIVE STOCK/BOND
A particular security that trades infrequently or trades in relatively low quantities.
Caution: The term is relative both to trading and to volume available. Example: Many 10-share traders on the New York Stock Exchange— usually preferred shares—trade in large blocks in the OTC market. Thus, they are inactive in one marketplace and active in another.

INADVERTENT RESTRICTED STOCK
Expression used when an insider buys stocks of a publicly traded company and uses stock of the insider's company to pay for the stock. If the seller accepts this form of payment—in effect a swap in kind—the stock thus acquired continues to be restricted. Such stock may be sold only after it has been held at least two years.

IN AND OUT COVERAGE
An International Stock Exchange of the United Kingdom and the Republic of Ireland term for the insurance coverage required for its members. In effect, this coverage is a fidelity bond protecting customers of members against improper activities by officers and employees of the members. Minimum coverage of any member is 100,000 pounds sterling.

IN-AND-OUT TRADER

A day trader, who generally keeps no overnight position in a security or commodity and who endeavors to profit from intra-day price fluctuations.

IN-AND-OUT TRANSACTION

Slang for a purchase and sale of a security completed within a brief time, often on the same day. The technique is used by traders, specialists, and marketmakers able to trade with low transaction costs and minimum capital risk. Some full-service brokers and most discount brokers provide speculators with lower commission charges on the in-and-out transactions completed the same day.

INCENTIVE STOCK OPTION (ISO)

Economic Recovery Tax Act (ERTA) of 1981 provides this form of executive compensation. Under ISO of ERTA, executive pays no tax when option is exercised.

INCOME BEFORE TAXES

See EARNINGS BEFORE TAXES.

INCOME BOND

Bond that promises to pay interest only if earned or to the extent it is earned. Income bonds are normally exchanged for outstanding bonds of a bankrupt company that is being reorganized.

Also called "adjustment bond."

INCOME COMPANY

An investment company whose principal objective is to provide investors with current income higher than that usually obtainable from other securities. Thus, a diversified portfolio of utility common stocks assembled by a mutual fund normally would be designated as an income company (fund).

INCOME INVESTMENT COMPANY

Popular classification of a management investment company whose primary investment objective is to provide maximum income to fundholders.

INCOME SHARES

A class of securities issued by dual-purpose investment companies, the other class of shares being capital shares. All income from both classes of shares accrues to the income shareholders; all capital gains accrue to the capital shareholders.

Because there is a minimum income guarantee, the income shares become the equivalent of cumulative preferred shares.

INCOME STATEMENT
Commonly used term for the numeric description of the income, expenses, interest and taxes paid, and the net profit of a company during a specific accounting period. Except for mutual funds that issue semiannual income statements, publicly traded corporations issue both quarterly and annual statements of income.

Also called "profit and loss statement."

IN COMPO
Contraction for: in competition.

Most frequent use: an invitation to a buyer or seller to submit a bid or offer that will compete with bids or offers from others.

IN CONCERT
Two or more persons, together or through an agent, try to achieve an investment goal. There are restrictions against such efforts.

See also ACTING IN CONCERT.

THE INCREDIBLE JANUARY EFFECT
Title of a book written by Robert Haugen and Josef Lakonishok in which they expound this theory: investor returns in January of any year are greater than the combined returns of the other 11 months of that year. The authors contend that this is not a U.S. phenomenon but is worldwide—even in countries without a capital gains tax.

INCREMENTAL RETURN WRITING STRATEGY
See GRADUATED CALL WRITING.

INDEMNIFICATION
In a contractual relationship, indemnification is the assurance by one party that it will make whole the other party under certain circumstances. In the securities industry, the term is used primarily of underwriting agreements in which the issuer guarantees to indemnify the members of the syndicate if suit is brought that questions the legality of the offering.

See also LETTER OF INDEMNIFICATION.

INDENTURE

The written deed of trust between an issuer and its bondholders. The indenture details the terms, conditions, and repayment provisions for the debt. Under the Trust Indenture Act, the indenture must also provide for the appointment of a trustee to oversee the agreement.

INDEX

A broad-based measurement of general market trend. The measurement is called an "index" because security prices are weighted to reflect the number of shares outstanding and the index, as a result, gives an insight into value change rather than only price change. Principal examples: the NYSE and ASE indices, the Standard & Poor's Index, and the NASDAQ OTC Index.

INDEX ARBITRAGE

General term used to describe a trading tactic whereby "baskets of stocks" and stock futures contracts are bought or sold, or both, according to their deviation from a recognized stock index. Generally stocks are bought and futures are sold—or vice versa—so one position hedges the other. The tactic is called an "arbitrage" because there is a locked-in profit that can be made.

INDEXATION

The act of forming an equity portfolio in such a way that it will track a pre-established index used as a benchmark. The act of indexing need not mirror the components of the index—just its performance.

In general, indexation is often called "passive portfolio management," as opposed to active portfolio management whereby the portfolio manager endeavors to outperform a pre-established index.

Portfolio charges, management fees, and other overhead costs will often make it impossible to mirror the results of the index.

Also see FRICTIONAL COST.

INDEX CALL

A feature written into the indenture of a bond issue. Under an index call, the issuer may call—that is, retire the bond issue at a price keyed to prevailing government bond rates, rather than at a fixed-dollar price.

The index call is rarely used.

INDEXED BOND

A debt security whose principal amount at maturity (no matter whether it be zero-coupon, fixed-coupon, or variable-coupon) is linked at the time of maturity to value of a specific commodity. This commodity could be gold, silver, crude oil, and so on.

For example, Goldman Sachs underwrote a bond for Standard Oil (Ohio) that is pegged at maturity to the value of West Texas Intermediate crude oil.

INDEX FRONTRUNNING

Frontrunning can be a form of price manipulation. It occurs if someone with prior knowledge of what another is going to do acts before that person in order to profit. Thus, if a broker/dealer knows that a client is about to enter an order for an index option and aggressively buys the underlying stocks or buys the option first so the client pays more, the broker/dealer would be frontrunning.

This term is also used of index futures and the underlying basket of stocks (depending on the valuation of the stocks in terms of the index futures) and their subsequent purchase or sale based on a knowledge of client intentions. It is *not* frontrunning to anticipate the activities of others through proper market analysis.

INDEX FUND

A fund with a portfolio of securities that includes many of the same securities composing a popular index and in the same quantity as the index. Thus, over time, the fund should mirror the performance of the index.

INDEX PARTICIPATION (IP)

A generic term for a broad-based option encompassing a basket of common stocks. Most index participations are based on stocks found in the S&P 500 or the Dow averages.

For example, the Philadelphia Stock Exchange calls its version Cash Index Participation (CIP); the American Stock Exchange calls its version Equity Index Participations (EIP); the CBOE calls its version Value of Index Participations (VIP); and the NYSE calls its version Exchange Stock Participations (ESP). This latter index participation is comprised of 462 Big Board issues and 38 non-Big Board issues. They are all subject to a court-issued injunction because of their similarity to futures contracts.

INDEX PROGRAM

A method of portfolio management, both in terms of securities chosen and number of shares, so the market performance of the assembled shares will "track" the performance of a chosen index: Dow Jones, Standard & Poor's, Value Line, and the like. The concept: The client is "buying" the index without the investment of the dollars required to duplicate the index.

Index options are based on this principle. An index program actually assembles shares to provide similar performance.

INDICATED MARKET

Numbers quoted for price ideas only. The marketmaker or specialist has no actual bids or offers at the stated prices and seeks prospective orders at those levels.

See also SUBJECT MARKET.

INDICATED ORDER

Technically, this is not an order. Rather, it is an indication of interest in a purchase or sale. It permits that broker to seek a contra order, but validation from the client is needed before a binding order can be executed.

INDICATION

A price range within which a security may trade. Indications are often given if normal trading cannot begin, or if it was halted because of an imbalance of orders on one side of the market.

INDICATION OF INTEREST

Indication by a client that he may be interested in the purchase of a security currently in registration with the SEC. This is not a firm commitment by either the client or the underwriter, and such indications must be reconfirmed by the client when the registration is effective.

INDIVIDUAL IDENTIFICATION

As a general rule, brokers must segregate fully paid and excess-margined securities.

Bulk segregation is the most commonly used method of segregation; that is, all street-name securities that fall into either of these categories are held in a special vault and individual certificates are not identified.

Some brokers choose individual identification of the securities in their vaults. This can be done by registering the securities in the client's name or by using identification marks. Example: A penciled inscription of the client account number on the certificate.

INDIVIDUAL INVESTOR EXPRESS DELIVERY SERVICE

Also known as IIEDS, this is the official title for the NYSE's Rule 80A. This rule is also known as the "side car" rule.

In effect, the rule says that, if the S&P Index or the Dow Jones Industrial Average rises or declines by a predetermined amount on the same day, institutional program orders entered via the DOT system will be rerouted for five minutes to give ordinary customers execution priority.

INDIVIDUAL PROPRIETORSHIP

Term used to describe a one-man business, or what we would call "a mom-and-pop business."

Such business enterprises are easy to establish—often requiring no more than the public statement that there is a business—but such businesses lack permanence, often find raising capital difficult, and are frequently subject to interruption because of sickness.

Individual proprietors represent business expenses on a separate tax form; otherwise the taxation of an individual proprietorship is the same as that of a person earning personal service income.

INDIVIDUAL RETIREMENT ACCOUNT (IRA)
Personal retirement program for employed persons. Under present law, an employed person with a specified limited amount of earnings may deposit up to $2,000 of earned income annually depending upon that person's earnings. The deposit is (1) a deduction from income and (2) tax sheltered until withdrawn at age 59½ or later. Withdrawal must begin no later than the calendar year in which person becomes 70½. Deposits must be made under a qualified plan, and the deposit is not tax deductible if the employed person is otherwise covered by an employer's plan.

See also IRA ROLLOVER.

INDIVIDUAL RETIREMENT ROLLOVER ACCOUNT
See IRRA.

INDIVIDUAL REVERSE MORTGAGE ACCOUNT
See IRMA.

INDIVIDUAL SEGREGATION
Method used by some brokers to identify fully paid client securities left with the broker. The segregation may be effected by registering the security in the client's name, or by attaching an identification with the client's name to certificates registered in the name of the broker.

INDUSTRIAL DEVELOPMENT BOND (IDB)
Municipal revenue bond whose debt service is paid from net lease payments made by an industrial corporation to the municipality. For the interest income to be exempt from federal taxation for the bondholder, the corporation must use the facilities to improve civic services or for pollution control activities.

Also called "industrial revenue bond."

INDUSTRIAL DEVELOPMENT BOND INSURANCE COMPANY
Abbreviation: IDBI. A bond insurance program sponsored by Corroon and Black, with policies written by Continental Insurance Company.

IDBI assures payment of both interest and principal for qualifying industrial and commercial development projects. Once so insured by IDBI, the bonds have the highest rating.

INDUSTRIAL REVENUE BOND
See INDUSTRIAL DEVELOPMENT BOND.

INDUSTRY GROUP
General term for different companies within the same business area. Example: A group of international oil companies would include Exxon, Royal Dutch, Texaco, Mobil, and Shell.

Although the individual business fortunes will vary among the competitors, general economic trends will tend to be favorable or unfavorable for the group. Hence, the term *group rotation;* that is, market activity will tend to center now on one industry group, now on another. Many market analysts base their recommendations on group rotation.

INFLATION
An economic condition characterized by persistent increases in the amount of money in circulation and continuously rising prices for goods and services. As a result, the purchasing power of individual dollars deteriorates as their value is cheapened.

IN FOR A BID (OR OFFER)
Equity block trading term used to describe an institutional client's request for a bid/offer from a broker/dealer's proprietary account for a significant amount of stock. Once negotiated, the request results in a binding capital commitment, subject to that firm's ability to transact at that price on the floor of an exchange.

INFRASTRUCTURE
Generic term for the fundamental facilities provided by a municipality for its citizens. Included are roads, communications, sewers, schools—in other words, facilities provided by the capital, rather than the operating budget, of the municipality. In times of budgetary crises, it is often easier for politicians to neglect the infrastructure, rather than tighten the belt in operating expenses. This often leads to neglect of the infrastructure.

The term is often used in an Official Statement of a municipal bond issue to discuss a municipality's growth, the use of funds from the issue, or in anticipation of later problems and the need for more funds to repair the infrastructure.

IN HAND

Term used by salespersons and traders for orders given to them for execution during a limited time, such as a morning, a day, an hour, and so on.

Used in contradistinction to "indicated" or "in-touch" orders. These orders are not official instructions to buy or sell; "in hand" orders are.

INITIAL MARGIN

Term from Regulation T of the Federal Reserve to designate the percentage that must be supplied by a customer who places himself at risk in a margin account. At the present time, the initial margin is 50% of the purchase price or 50% of the proceeds of a short sale. Regulations G and U apply similar standards if a person purchases securities with money borrowed from a bank (U) or from another lender (G) to purchase, carry, or trade in a nonexempted security.

INITIAL MARGIN REQUIREMENT

The minimum amount of equity a customer must deposit when initiating transactions in a margin account. The requirement, by class of security, is set forth in Regulations T, G, and U of the Federal Reserve Board.

INITIAL PUBLIC OFFERING

IPO is used to describe an issuer's first public offering of a security of any class, although the term tends to be limited to common stock. The term is also used to designate an offering of previously authorized but unissued securities.

INJUNCTION

Court order directed at a person or group of persons to prohibit a specific activity or to require the performance of a specific action in conformity with federal securities laws. The SEC often will petition for an injunction against parties who are the subject of an inquiry, thereby preventing a continuation of a questionable practice until the case is concluded.

IN-LINE BUYER-SELLER

A buyer-seller of a significant quantity of a security who is willing to deal at prevailing price levels. The designation means that the buyer-seller is seeking a contra offer/bid that will provide the size satisfactory to meet its requirement.

IN-PLAY

Term used by arbitrageurs and finance associates to describe a company that is a prime target for a takeover, either hostile or friendly.

Thus, to make a takeover attempt attractive to current shareholders, an offer is made substantially above the current market. This will draw others in to buy the "cheap" shares, or to make a counterproposal at a higher price. In this way, the company is "in-play."

INS
Acronym for Institutional Net Settlement. INS is an extension of the Talisman service on the International Stock Exchange of the United Kingdom and the Republic of Ireland for institutional investors. INS is similar in function to DTC in the United States: it permits institutional investors to settle trades at the end of the account period by a single difference check, despite the fact they may have made many trades through many brokers during that period.

INSEAD
Acronym for Institut Europeen d'Administration des Affaires. INSEAD is a leading business school located outside Paris and is renowned for its on-campus business executive programs.

INSIDE INFORMATION
Legal and industry term for material information that (1) would influence the purchase or sale of a company's security and (2) has not been publicized in a widely used medium. For example, a company suffered a dramatic loss and this fact has not yet been announced publicly.

INSIDE MARKET
Inside market quotes are the bid or asked prices at which one dealer will buy from or sell to another. In contrast, retail market quotes are the prices at which customers may buy or sell to the dealer.

Also called "wholesale" or "inter-dealer" market.

INSIDER
Slang for a person who (1) controls a corporation, (2) owns 10% or more of a company's stock, or (3) has inside information. The term is used most often of the directors and the elected officers of a corporation.

See also INSIDE INFORMATION.

INSIDER TRADING
This expression implies the use of material nonpublic information to make a securities transaction (either a buy or a sell) thereby working to the detriment of the contra party who does not have this information. Such use of inside information can be construed as a violation of the Securities and Exchange Act of 1934. To violate the law, the user of inside information need not be an affiliate of the company or a member of his or her family. Tippees and others who have received and used the inside information in a clandestine manner have also been judged to have violated the law.

THE INSIDER TRADING SANCTIONS ACT OF 1984
An amendment to the Securities and Exchange Act of 1934. Under this amendment, the SEC may seek civil or criminal penalties, or both, against:
1. Anyone who purchases or sells securities while in possession of material nonpublic information.
2. Anyone who communicates material nonpublic information to someone who buys or sells securities.
3. Anyone who aids and abets someone in the purchase or sale of securities while possessing material nonpublic information.

Fines may be levied up to three times the amount of the illegal profit gained (or losses avoided). The law is also applicable to derivative products.

INSOLVENCY
1. A debtor who is unable to meet obligations as they come due and payable in the normal course of business.
2. Any corporation or individual who has liabilities exceeding assets at any given time.

Insolvency generally leads to a court petition resulting in bankruptcy proceedings under federal law.

INSTALLMENT SALE
1. A securities transaction in which the contract price is set, but the proceeds are paid, over time, in installments. As a general rule, gains or losses on such transactions are considered to be prorated for tax purposes.
2. A sale in which the seller agrees to defer receipt of the proceeds until a later date and, perhaps, in more than one payment. Under IRS rules, the seller is accountable for the federal tax on the transaction upon receipt of the proceeds, and in the same proportion of profit or loss, as the payments are received. Generally used to defer the payment of taxes.

INSTANTANEOUS INDEX
This is a gauge of price movements of 50 issues traded on the Paris Bourse. From 10 A.M. until 5 P.M., this index reflects price movements on a real time basis; hence, its name. It was originally conceived as an improvement on the CAC Index, but in practice the CAC 40 remains more popular than the innovation.

INSTINET
Computerized trade execution service, Institutional Networks Corporation, registered with the SEC as a stock exchange. Exchange permits

subscribers to search the system for the opposite side of a trade, without the cost of brokerage fees. Used by many mutual funds and other institutional investors. Trades are reported on the composite tape if the security is listed.

See also FOURTH MARKET.

INSTITUT EUROPEEN D'ADMINISTRATION DES AFFAIRES
See INSEAD.

INSTITUT MONETAIRE LUXEMBOURGEOIS
See IML.

INSTITUTIONAL CD
Generic name for any certificate of deposit in denominations in excess of $100,000—the upper limit of federal deposit guarantees. Sophisticated institutional buyers of such instruments are usually more sensitive to the credit rating of the issuing institution than are typical public banking customers.

INSTITUTIONAL DELIVERY SYSTEM
Acronym: ID. A trade notification and settlement system developed and maintained by the Depository Trust Company (DTC). ID facilitates payment and delivery between broker/dealers for securities transactions made by their institutional-type customers. Basically a book-entry system, ID facilitates transfers between the institutions' custodian banks and the broker/dealer.

INSTITUTIONAL HOLDINGS CMOs
See PLANNED AMORTIZATION CLASS.

INSTITUTIONAL INVESTOR
Although individual brokerage firms may use different dollar parameters for this classification, the most typical designations include:
1. A bank, savings and loan, insurance company, or registered investment company with assets of $100 million or more.
2. A registered investment advisor with more than $100 million under management.
3. A person, either natural or legal, with total assets of at least $100 million.

The definition, therefore, is sufficiently broad to include individuals, partnerships, corporations, or trusts with substantial investible funds. If a brokerage firm handles both retail and institutional business, there is usually a different sales and support service for institutional clients.

INSTITUTIONAL NET SETTLEMENT
See INS.

INSUBSTANTIAL QUANTITY
The NASD places certain restrictions on broker/dealers in their allocations of "hot issues." Exception: the allocation of an insubstantial quantity to certain purchasers.

In its interpretation of this rule, the NASD has said that an allocation
of 2,000 or fewer shares, or $25,000 face value of bonds, is an insubstan-
tial quantity.

This interpretation applies to the entire group given below:
1. The managing underwriter's finder for this offering, its accountants,
   attorneys, financial consultants, or members of such persons' immediate family.
2. Senior officers, securities department employees, or persons influencing securities activities in the following:
   a. A domestic commercial bank or trust company.
   b. A domestic savings bank or savings and loan association.
   c. An insurance company.
   d. A registered investment company.

Total sales to persons in these groups in excess of the parameters
given would violate the rules on "hot issues."

INTANGIBLE ASSET
1. Items of value owned by a corporation whose true worth is difficult
   and, at times, impossible to determine. Examples: patents, copy-
   rights, and trade or service marks.
2. Goodwill also is an intangible asset. In a merger/acquisition, the dollar difference between the purchase price of the acquired company
   and its net tangible asset value is called "goodwill." IRS rules permit
   goodwill to be listed as an intangible asset and to be amortized, on a
   consolidated balance sheet, over a 40-year period.

INTEGRATED MARKETMAKING
Also known as "side-by-side" trading. The term identifies an NASD
member who makes continuous bids and offers in an equity security and
makes bids and offers in over-the-counter options on the underlying securities. Although the practice is not illegal, it could open the door to
manipulative price abuse.

INTEGRATED SECURITIES COMPANY
A designation used by the Japanese Minister of Finance to identify
those securities firms licensed to engage in all four categories of securities business, which are:

1. Dealing; that is, to act as a principal in the trading of securities,
2. Brokerage; that is, to act as an agent in the execution of customer transactions,
3. Underwriting; that is, to engage in financings and refinancing through public offerings,
4. Selling; that is, to make retail offerings of publicly traded securities.

INTER ALIA
Latin: among other things.

The term often appears in complaints filed against broker/dealers or its representatives, or both. The term highlights several specific charges, but includes by inference other charges. Example: "We charge ABC, inter alia, with unauthorized trading and churning." The idea: These are but two of the unethical practices with which the broker/dealer is charged.

INTER-AMERICAN DEVELOPMENT BANK
Acronym: IADB. A bank organized to promote and advance the economic and social development of member countries located in Latin America. The bank is owned by the governments of various countries in the Western Hemisphere.

INTERBANK MARKET
General name for spot and forward currency transactions. International banks and multinational corporations are the principal participants in this market.

Foreign currency options listed and traded on the Philadelphia Stock Exchange are based on the interbank market.

INTERBANK RATE (IB RATE)
The percentage of interest at which commercial banks are willing to buy and sell excess reserves among themselves. The term is similar to federal funds; however, federal funds may be bought and sold both by banks and nonbanks.

INTER-DEALER BROKER (IDB)
A British term used to designate intermediaries who effect transactions between primary dealers in English government securities. They are similar in functions to "brokers' brokers" in the United States in that they are used to maintain anonymity between transactors and receive a fee for their services.

INTEREST
1. Money paid for the use of money. In general, debt instruments and other loans have a predetermined rate of interest that is to be paid for

the use of borrowed money. The rate may be fixed, variable, or zero depending on the indenture. Debts whose interest is not paid in a timely fashion are said to be in default.
2. Used to describe an equity participation in a partnership; for example, a partnership interest.
3. Used synonymously for an intent to buy (or sell); for example, the registered representative canvassed his or her clients for indications of interest in a new public offering.
4. Used to describe a benefit that may accrue from some action or activity; for example, "Jim could not become engaged in the sale because of a conflict of interest."

INTEREST EQUALIZATION TAX (IET)
A special excise tax on the purchase by U.S. citizens of foreign securities from foreign owners. The law was designed to curb the outflow of capital from the United States. The law was repealed in 1974.

INTEREST ON INTEREST
A frequently used synonym for compound interest. Compound interest is not based on the original principal; instead, during each period of compounding, the rate is applied to the accumulated principal and accrued interest. Thus, the interest will increase over time because the base (principal plus accrued interest) is constantly increasing.
Antonym: simple interest.

INTEREST-RATE OPTION
Acronym: IRO. A put or call in which the underlying is specific bills, notes, or bonds issued by the U.S. Treasury, or certificates of deposit with a specified face value. Because the premiums on these nonequity options are especially sensitive to interest-rate trends, they are called "interest-rate options."

INTERIM DIVIDEND
English term: the periodic cash distributions made to shareholders. Example: The company made three interim dividends of 50p and a final dividend of 75p.
See also FINAL DIVIDEND.

INTERMARKET
1. Of stocks: trades of the same security made on different exchanges.
2. Of bonds: the sale of one type of bond and the purchase of another type of bond. Example: A sale of Treasuries and a purchase of corporate bonds would be an intermarket trade.

3. In corporate finance: the sale of one asset and the acquisition of another. Example: IBM sold Satellite Business Systems and bought an 18% stake in MCI Communications.

See also INTERMARKET TRADING SYSTEM and CONSOLIDATED TAPE.

INTERMARKET FRONTRUNNING
The term refers to transactions in index futures that are initiated when one hears of an impending index program execution in the stock market; in effect, the index future action is taken in anticipation of the effect that will be caused by the stock transactions.

Such activities may be in violation of NYSE rules, which are validated by the SEC. It is anticipated that the CFTC will also make the action unethical.

INTERMARKET SURVEILLANCE INFORMATION SYSTEM
See ISIS.

INTERMARKET TRADING SYSTEM (ITS)
Electronic system that links the floors of the American, Boston, Midwest, Pacific, Philadelphia, and New York stock exchanges. The system provides a comparison of bids and offers on the exchanges. A buyer or seller, therefore, can choose the best market. The actual transaction is completed outside the system by telephone or telex.

See also CONSOLIDATED TAPE.

INTERMEDIARY
A person or organization helping an investor to make, or to implement, investment decisions (i.e., persons who permit the investor to buy into a portfolio of securities). For example, an insurance company, a bank, or a mutual fund are called "portfolio intermediaries." Persons who assist an investor with the execution of orders to buy or sell, or who provide investment advice, are called "marketing intermediaries."

INTERMEDIATE TERM
A relative expression for a period somewhere between a short and a long time.
1. When used of fundamental security analysis: intermediate is between 6 months and 1 year. For example, "We expect the stock to rise in the intermediate term."
2. When used of debt securities: intermediate term signifies that 2 to 10 years remain to maturity.

INTERMEDIATION

The placement of investment dollars with a portfolio intermediary; the intermediary, in turn, invests the dollars in securities, mortgages, or other investments. The investor accepts the investment judgment of the intermediary.

The opposite term is *disintermediation*. In this situation, the investor withdraws dollars left with the portfolio intermediary to make direct security investments.

INTERMOUNTAIN POWER AGENCY

Acronym: IPA. A legal entity and political subdivision of the state of Utah, organized in 1977, to own, acquire, construct, and operate electric power facilities within the state. IPA finances its activities through the issuance of municipal revenue bonds.

INTERNALIZATION

SEC term for a practice of broker/dealers making over-the-counter markets for listed securities. Specifically, internalization means executing customer orders as principal without exposing to the customer the possibility of a better execution that may be available in different market centers.

INTERNAL RATE OF RETURN

Acronym: IRR. A finance term from real estate investing. It endeavors to recognize the fact that, in real estate investing, shifting values caused by interest and depreciation make the computation of return difficult. Generally, IRR is computed by dividing actual dollars invested by net rents and the residual value of the property minus interest paid on the mortgage during its lifetime. In effect, therefore, IRR is an endeavor to compute the time value of money in the investment.

INTERNATIONAL BANK FOR RECONSTRUCTION AND DEVELOPMENT

Acronym: IBRD.
　　See WORLD BANK.

INTERNATIONAL BANKING AND INVESTMENT SERVICES

See IBIS.

INTERNATIONAL DEPOSITORY RECEIPT

Acronym: IDR. A negotiable equity instrument issued by a commercial bank to represent a specific number of shares in a corporation that is not domiciled in that bank's native country. The bank holds the underlying shares. Transfer of the depository receipt is effected by the bank on its own records. Similar to the ADR, EDR, and JDR in concept, although the IDR is more flexible because it can accommodate domestic trading in all international securities.

INTERNATIONAL FEDERATION OF STOCK EXCHANGES
See FIBV.

INTERNATIONAL FUND
An investment company or managed pool of investments whose portfolio is comprised of securities denominated in currencies other than U.S. dollars.

INTERNATIONAL MARKET AGREEMENT (IMA)
A contract between the Options Clearing Corporation (OCC), the American Stock Exchange (AMEX), and the European Options Exchange (EOE). Under IMA the terms are set forth under which the EOE will trade the AMEX's Major Market Index (XMI) and such trades will be cleared by the OCC. In this way, XMI became the first international option traded by a link between an American and a foreign securities exchange.

INTERNATIONAL MARKET INDEX
Originated by the American Stock Exchange, this product gauges the market performance of 50 stocks representing 10 foreign nations traded in the United States. In effect, the index is an option with cash settlement traded on the AMEX. It is also called the "ADR Index Option," in that it enables investors to subscribe to foreign issues with their currency fluctuations without the inconvenience of foreign currency conversions.

INTERNATIONAL MONETARY MARKET (IMM)
A division of the Chicago Mercantile Exchange that provides a marketplace for futures contracts in foreign currencies, silver coins, and U.S. Treasury bills and notes.

INTERNATIONAL OPTIONS
See IFX OPTIONS.

INTERNATIONAL SECURITIES CLEARING CORPORATION
See ISCC.

THE INTERNATIONAL SECURITIES REGULATORY ORGANISATION
See ISRO.

INTERNATIONAL STOCK EXCHANGE OF THE UNITED KINGDOM AND THE REPUBLIC OF IRELAND
This is the successor organization to the London Stock Exchange. The formal name (popularly abbreviated ISE) was officially adopted following the merger of the LSE with ISRO. The reorganization involved two separate functional responsibilities: as a Registered Investment Exchange (RIE) and as a Self-Regulatory Organisation (SRO).

INTERNATIONAL TIER TRADING
See INTIER.

INTERPOLATION
Mathematical procedure for the approximation of either price or yield when the actual bond's maturity falls between listed maturity dates. For example, if the bond yield table gives the price for 11 years and 11 years and six months, and your bond is 11 years and three months, take a price that is halfway between the two prices. The same principle applies to yield differences.

INTERPOSITIONING
A potentially unethical practice whereby a broker employs a second broker to complete a transaction between a customer and a marketmaker. The customer, therefore, pays for two agency transactions. The customer pays more or receives less than he would have if the original broker had dealt directly with the marketmaker.

INTERSTATE COMMERCE COMMISSION
Acronym: ICC. A federal agency that has jurisdiction over common carriers doing business across state boundaries. Offerings of equipment trust certificates fall under its jurisdiction. Other debt securities and equity issues of these same issuers are under the jurisdiction of the SEC.

INTER VIVOS TRUST
Trust, either temporary or permanent, established by one living person for the benefit of another. Term is used in contrast to a testamentary trust; that is, a trust that will be operative only when the person who established the trust dies.

INTESTATE
Legal term for a person who dies without leaving a valid will to direct the disposition of assets in the estate.

IN THE BOX
See THE BOX.

IN THE MONEY
Expression used of any option series if the strike (exercise) price and market price are such that the option holder could exercise at a profit, independent of the premium and other transaction costs. For example, if a call is held at a strike price of 30 and the stock is at 32, the call is in the money.

See also INTRINSIC VALUE.

IN THE TANK
Slang: a security or an entire securities market that is quickly losing value. For example, "ABC is going in the tank."

IN THE YELLOW
A United Kingdom term to designate the best bid and offer for a security traded on the SEAQ system (q.v.)

In the SEAQ system, these prices are culled from the other prices offered and displayed against a yellow background to gain the viewer's attention.

INTIER
Abbreviation for: International Tier Trading, a NYSE prototype of a trading system designed to facilitate international trading on the exchange.

INTIER is a computerized screen that links marketmakers in international issues and makes it possible for members to deal directly with them from the floor of the NYSE.

IN TOUCH WITH
Industry jargon used by salespersons to signify that they know a customer who has an interest in buying or selling a particular security but who has not entered a specific order to do so. The expression is used to try to locate a contra party who will complete the transaction.

INTRINSIC VALUE
Arithmetic statement of the dollar difference between the strike (exercise) price of an option and the market price of the stock, if the option can be exercised at a profit. For example, the strike price of a put is 40 and the stock is at 37. The intrinsic value is 3. If an option is at or out of the money, it has no intrinsic value.

INVENTORY

1. The dollar value of raw materials, goods in progress, or completed goods that a corporation owns.
2. The net security position, either long or short, that a dealer or specialist has in a security.

INVENTORY TURNOVER

A measurement of a corporation's efficient use of assets in terms of turnover of saleable goods.

The best formula: cost of goods sold divided by average inventory for the year. Year-end inventory can also be used. For example, a corporation's cost of goods sold is $12 million and its average inventory is $2 million. Its inventory turnover is 6 (times a year).

INVERTED MARKET

See BACKWARDIZATION.

INVERTED SCALE

The scale is the schedule of offering prices for bonds with serial maturities.

The scale is said to be inverted if the net yields for shorter maturities are greater than the yields on longer maturity bonds.

INVERTED YIELD CURVE

Term describing the graph of yields on similar debt securities if short-term yields are higher than long-term yields. For example, "The yield curve on AA utility issues is inverted."

See also YIELD CURVE and NEGATIVE YIELD CURVE.

INVESTMENT ADVISER (IA)

A person who, for a fee, gives counsel to others regarding the purchase, sale, or holding of securities and other financial investments. Such persons are subject to the Investment Advisers Act of 1940 and must register with the SEC.

There are many exceptions to registration (e.g., general circulation newspapers, broker/dealers, persons who give advice to a limited number of persons); as a result, the category of IA is more important under state law. Legal advice should be sought by anyone who intends to sell investment advice for a fee.

INVESTMENT ADVISERS ACT OF 1940

Act that requires those who sell investment advice for a fee to register with the SEC. In general, the act applies to those who sell advice to 15 or more persons on an interstate basis. There are numerous exceptions; the most important are banks, brokers, and general-circulation newspapers. State laws often differ widely from federal law for investment advisers. Legal advice is needed if one intends to sell investment advice for a fee.

INVESTMENT ANNUITY
See WRAPAROUND ANNUITY.

INVESTMENT ASSETS
Technical term used by the regulators of the suitability of securities option activity in a client account. Investment assets include cash, stocks, bonds, and other assets and investments used to produce income or capital appreciation.

Concept: The regulators will not sanction the use of more than 15 to 20% of such investment assets in the purchase of put and call options. Reason: Long puts and calls are "wasting assets," with an expiration date at which they become worthless.

INVESTMENT BANKER
General term for a broker/dealer who assists corporations with the distribution of securities or with other money management or public relations services.

Investment bankers do not take time and demand deposits and, as a general rule, do not make short-term loans to corporations, as do commercial banks. In many other respects, however, commercial and investment banks compete for government and municipal securities business.

Also called an "underwriter."

INVESTMENT COMPANY
A corporation engaged primarily in the business of investing and trading in securities. The definition includes face-amount certificate companies, unit investment trusts, and management companies.

The definition excludes holding companies, banks, broker/dealers, and insurance companies.

INVESTMENT COMPANY ACT OF 1940
Public legislation that regulates the issuance of investment company securities. The law is administered by the SEC. The act sets standards for the organization, operation, and pricing of investment company securities, their public sale and reporting requirements, and, in many cases, for the allocation of portfolio investments.

INVESTMENT COMPANY AND VARIABLE CONTRACT PRODUCTS

Acronym: IC/VC. NASD term for a form of limited registration, either as principal or representative, that qualifies an individual to sell (representative) or manage the sale of (principal) investment company shares or variable annuity contracts.

Qualification is by an examination. Persons so qualified are limited to the sale of such products.

Antonym: General Securities Representative Examination, which qualifies for the sale of all securities products.

INVESTMENT GRADE

Term used of the top four ratings made by a national bond-rating service. Such ratings give an insight into the credit risk (i.e., of the risk of bankruptcy) of the issuer of a bond or other debt instrument.

Popular designations: Standard & Poor's, or Fitch, both of which use AAA, AA, A, BBB. Moody's uses Aaa, AA, A, Baa. Moody's also uses MIG-1, 2, 3, 4 for investment-grade municipal notes.

Bonds rated BB (Moody's: Ba) or below are considered speculative and are popularly called "junk bonds."

See also JUNK BOND and PRUDENT MAN RULE.

INVESTMENT HISTORY

Term applicable to the NASD rule on Freeriding and Withholding if a sale of a hot issue is made to decision makers of institutional-type accounts. As a general rule, sales of hot issues may be made if the amount is small and is in line with the history of investment in the account. Usually, this history embraces a reasonable time (e.g., 3 years) and a reasonable number (e.g., 10) of securities transactions. The rule does not list specific measurements.

INVESTMENT LETTER

The written agreement between a seller and a buyer in a private placement of securities.

In the investment letter, the buyer states that he or she is acquiring the security as an investment and does not intend to reoffer the securities publicly.

Because the sale is accompanied by an investment letter, the securities purchased are often referred to as "letter stock" or "letter bond."

See also LETTER STOCK.

INVESTMENT MANAGEMENT REGULATORY ORGANISATION

See IMRO.

INVESTMENT QUALITY
See BANK QUALITY.

INVESTMENT SKELETON
Industry slang. It refers to speculative securities that are worthless or were purchased contrary to one's general investment objectives, or which failed to meet expectations.

The concept is a pun: "Everyone has an (investment) skeleton in their closet."

INVESTMENT TAX CREDIT (ITC)
A 10% tax credit permitted to the purchaser of certain tangible assets in the year that the purchase is made. The typical credit is 10% of the cost. The purpose of the law is to encourage the purchase of certain assets that enhance employment or public service. Tax advice is needed because the tax credit varies and can be recaptured as taxable income if a premature sale of the asset is made. Most ITCs were repeated by TRA 86.

INVESTOR
An *investor* is a general term for anyone who puts money to use in the hope of producing income, interest, or an increase in value.

In practice, the term may be distinguished from a *saver;* that is, a person who uses money to produce current income without any risk of capital loss. The term is also used in distinction to a speculator; that is, a person who uses money in the pursuit of short-term investment profits.

Unless otherwise stated, it is to be presumed that an investor is not concerned with short-term price fluctuations but has a time horizon of one year or more for the investment.

INVISIBLE CALENDAR
A general term used to describe prospective distributions of securities. The concept includes both issues that have been announced (the visible calendar) and those shelf registrations and other issues that are dependent on changes in the interest rate (the invisible calendar). Municipal securities, in particular, do not need to be registered with the SEC, and their issuance is often dependent on interest-rate changes and the resulting "window of economic opportunity" that presents itself. Such offerings are made quickly and with little prior notification to the financial community.

INVOLUNTARY UNDERWRITER
See STATUTORY UNDERWRITER.

IOA
Acronym for International Operations Association, a division of the U.S.-based Securities Industry Association (SIA). IOA has a membership of approximately 700 broker/dealers, banks, and institutional investors, and its goal is to help standardize the settlement terms for foreign securities transactions in the United States.

IOC
Acronym for immediate-or-cancel (order). An order that restricts the time of execution but does not restrict the size. Example: Buy 2,500 LMN 52 IOC. The customer instruction says: I want to buy 2,500 shares at a limit price of 52 right now. Buy all 2,500 if you can. If you cannot, buy 2,400, or 2,300, and so on. Whatever portion of the order cannot be filled should be canceled.

Antonyms: FOK (fill or kill)—buy/sell all of the order right now, or cancel the entire order. Also, AON (all or none)—buy/sell whenever you can, but I will accept only a complete trade at my price.

IO/PO
Acronym for Interest Only/Principal Only. IO/PO is a term associated with certain mortgage-backed securities (either MBSs or CMOs) in which interest payments and principal payments are traded separately and independently of one another; in effect, the interest payments are "stripped" from the principal repayment. Such IO/POs have all of the interest-rate risk features characteristic of zero-coupon bonds.

IP
1. See INDEX PARTICIPATION.
2. NYSE stock ticker symbol for International Paper, a large manufacturer of paper and paper products found in the Dow Jones Industrial Average.

IPA
See INTERMOUNTAIN POWER AGENCY.

IPO
See INITIAL PUBLIC OFFERING.

IRA
See INDIVIDUAL RETIREMENT ACCOUNT.

IRA ROLLOVER

Provision of the tax law that permits a person who terminates employment and who receives a lump-sum distribution of pension benefits to reinvest in an individual retirement account (IRA) within a period of 60 days. Funds thus rolled over continue to be tax sheltered until withdrawn.

IRB

Acronym for industrial revenue bond. An IRB is a debt security issued by a municipality. The proceeds are used to build a commercial facility. The net lease payments received from the renting company will be used to amortize the bond debt service. Because of the contract between the issuer and the renter, the rating on such bonds will tend to reflect the creditworthiness of the renter.

Pollution control bonds are the most common form of IRB.

There is a statutory limit on the dollar amount of IRBs that may be issued for nonpublic use.

IRISH DIVIDEND

A derogatory expression for a reverse split; that is, a stock split that results in fewer shares outstanding.

See SCOTTISH DIVIDEND.

IRMA

Acronym for individual reverse mortgage account. IRMAs, originated in England, permit elderly homeowners to borrow up to $1,000 per month against their equity in their home, as long as the borrowers are alive and live in the home. The loan comes due when the owners decide to sell the house or when they die. In this way, elderly persons who are otherwise poor may use part of their equity as collateral while they live. Generally, when the owners die the beneficiaries have the option of paying off the loan or selling the house (with the IRMA debited against the proceeds) as the estate is settled.

IRMAs are true reverse mortgages; thus, interest accrues against the outstanding loan. Just as monthly mortgage payments cause a mortgage to be paid down, so IRMA monthly payments cause the outstanding loan to go up.

IRO

See INTEREST-RATE OPTION.

IRQ

Acronym for Immediate Reporting on Quote. IRQ is an electronic linkage of some member firm order departments to selected specialist marketmaking books on the floor of the NYSE.

Firms and specialists that subscribe to this service can direct orders up to 1,000 shares directly into the system for execution. Buy orders are executed against the offer, and sell orders are executed against the bid— just as they would if sent through the DOT system. The report is simply faster.

In eighth-of-a-point markets, IRQ provides the same price that would be provided were the order sent through a floor broker or the DOT system.

IRR
See INTERNAL RATE OF RETURN.

IRRA
Acronym for individual retirement rollover account. Under prevailing IRS rules an individual under 70½ years of age may transfer money from a qualified retirement account, *without penalty*, providing those monies are deposited in an IRRA account within 60 days after withdrawal.

IRREDEEMABLES
In the United Kingdom, these are debt securities with no dated date nor maturity date. In general, such securities are redeemable at the issuer's request or option, or upon special events, such as a takeover.

Such securities are rare in the United States and when extant are called "perpetuals."

IRS
Acronym for Internal Revenue Service. The IRS is a federal agency that is responsible for the collection of individual and corporate taxes and for the surveillance and enforcement of U.S. tax laws.

The IRS may not assess criminal penalties. It may, under the guidance of the tax laws, assess civil penalties.

ISCC
Abbreviation for International Securities Clearing Corporation, a wholly owned subsidiary of the National Securities Clearing Corporation (NSCC) in the United States. It was formed in late 1985 to support international clearances in foreign and foreign-issued securities. It is registered with the SEC under Section 17 A of the 1934 Securities and Exchange Act and is one of two international clearing associations utilized by the NASD in the PORTAL system for unregistered issues placed or resold, or both, in the United States.

ISE

See INTERNATIONAL STOCK EXCHANGE OF THE UNITED KINGDOM AND THE REPUBLIC OF IRELAND.

ISE/NIKKEI 50

An index of 50 Japanese common stocks based on their prices.

The ISE/NIKKEI 50 is picked up each day in Tokyo by Nihon Keizai Shimbum (NIKKEI), which follows these stocks as they are traded on the Tokyo Stock Exchange. When the Tokyo Stock Exchange closes, the index value is picked up by the ISE (International Stock Exchange of the United Kingdom and the Republic of Ireland), where trading in these same stocks continues through SEAQ International.

In effect, ISE/NIKKEI is a global index monitored for more than 12 hours on each market day.

ISIS

Acronym for Intermarket Surveillance Information System. ISIS is a data base of trading information maintained by the surveillance departments of the various stock exchanges in the United States. In effect, each exchange can match trade information—including contra parties—and thereby analyze such information for possible trading violations by market participants.

ISLAND REVERSAL

Term used by technical analysts.

Concept: There is a reversal from down to up or up to down. However, between the two trends there are a number of trades marked on both sides by a gap both on the up and the down side.

Example: Stock moves regularly from 35 to 50. Stock gaps to 51 and trades over a time period to 52. Then, following a gap to $50\frac{1}{2}$, the stock trades down to 40. The trades from 51 down to $50\frac{1}{2}$ form an island, and the technicians call it "an island reversal."

ISO

Acronym for incentive stock option. A form of permitted executive compensation. If the executive exercises the option, no tax is due at the time of exercise.

ISRO

Acronym for International Securities Regulatory Organisation. ISRO is a professional trade association of U.K. brokers and dealers who participate in nondomestic debt and equity and options transactions. ISRO has been approved as an SRO under England's Financial Services Bill of 1986.

ISSUE
1. The act of distributing securities to investors.
2. Any class of securities. For example, the Treasury bonds that will mature in 2002, the ABC common shares, the XYZ $4^{1}/_{4}\%$ preferred stock.

ISSUED AND OUTSTANDING
Term used for the number of a corporation's authorized shares that are held by investors, including corporate officers.

The term does not include unissued shares and those Treasury shares repurchased by the company.

ISSUE PRICE
This is the initial price at which underwriters make an offering of securities. In corporate offerings the issue price is fixed until the syndicate is terminated, although participating broker/dealers may receive selling concessions and dealer discounts for actual services rendered.

Also called PUBLIC OFFERING PRICE.

ISSUER
A corporation, trust, or association legally empowered to distribute its own securities.

Definition also includes governments, governmental agencies, municipalities, and political subdivisions thereof if these latter are empowered to distribute their own securities.

ISTANBUL STOCK EXCHANGE
This bourse is intended to deepen Turkey's capital markets. Trading is from 9:30 A.M. until 12:30 P.M. each business day, with after-hour activity permitted. Settlement is scheduled for the third business day following the trade date.

This market was reopened in 1985. It is relatively inactive because it is dominated by banking interests.

ITAAWASE TRADING
This is a proposed method of trading commodity future contracts in Japan. It is similar to the auction markets in the United States in that it publicizes contract prices and quantities. Then, when contra offers are received, they are transacted and the trade completed. In effect, the Itaawase trading method provides a continuous market.

See also ITAYOSE TRADING.

ITAYOSE TRADING

Vocalization: "Tan-itsu-yakujo." In this method of trading—which is used both on the commodities exchange in Japan and in the afternoon (1–3 P.M.) session of the Japanese exchanges—orders to buy and sell are accumulated until a single price can be set that will satisfy both supply and demand. This results in a single trade price for that issue or contract on that day.

ITC

This is a tax credit permitted to the purchaser of certain tangible assets in the year when the purchase is made. The typical credit is 10% of the cost.

See also INVESTMENT TAX CREDIT.

ITS

The electronic system that links the floors of the American, Boston, Midwest, Pacific, Philadelphia, and New York stock exchanges.

See also INTERMARKET TRADING SYSTEM and CONSOLIDATED TAPE.

J

J

The tenth letter of the alphabet, used:
1. Uppercase as the NYSE symbol for Jackpot Enterprises, a large manufacturer of slot machines.
2. As the fifth letter in the symbol of certain NASDAQ/NMS equity securities to designate that the stock is issued by a quasi-governmental entity. For example, SLMAJ is the publicly owned common stock of Student Loan Marketing Association, an agency founded to fund, promote, and guarantee loans for college educations.

JACUZZI LOAN

Tongue-in-cheek term for an uncollateralized loan that is both weak and easily subject to default. The analogy: The lender's money could easily flow "down the drain" just as the water in a Jacuzzi.

JAGR (pronounced "Jaguar")

Acronym for Junk and Government Receipts. Developed by Merrill Lynch, JAGR is a new product to counter public aversion to junk bonds. Because most junk debt used for acquisition in the 1980s was issued as PIK (payment-in-kind) they did not pay cash in the early years after issuance. This blended instrument combined short-term government securities with long-term junk bonds, thus creating a synthetic interest rate. The government issues paid cash interest until they matured; at which time, the junk bond was expected to pick up and pay cash interest thereafter.

JAGUAR
See JAGR.

JAJO
Abbreviation for January, April, July, October. JAJO stands for the successive expiration months of successively offered option contracts. Normal practice is to have three of the four months offered in series at any single time.

Alternatives: FMAN and MJSD. Listed options are normally offered in one or the other series so option expiration dates are spread throughout the year.

JAMES BOND
Slang: U.S. Treasury bonds that mature in 2007. Allusion is to the fictional hero who uses the pseudonym "Agent 007."

THE JANUARY EFFECT
See THE INCREDIBLE JANUARY EFFECT.

JAPANESE DEPOSITORY RECEIPT
See JDR.

JAPANESE DIVIDEND ROLLOVER
Also called a "dividend capture." In effect, the technique is based on one of the vagaries of Japanese tax law, which permits dividend payouts but not capital gains payouts under certain circumstances.

Under the rollover (capture), a Japanese insurance company buys a high-yielding American stock before ex-dividend date (thus, it gets a dividend) and sells the stock almost immediately for seller's option delivery after the record date. The negotiated price of the sale is such that there is a capital loss approximately equal to the dividend gained. The dividend is converted to yen and distributed to the policyholders of the insurance company.

See also DIVIDEND CAPTURE.

THE JAPAN INDEX
This is an AMEX option product. The underlying for the option is the closing price of 200 stocks traded on the Tokyo Exchange. Calculated in yen and translated into dollars, the index then becomes the basis for the

strike price and premium. This contract is traded on the floor of the AMEX.

JAPAN SECURITIES CLEARING CORPORATION (JSCC)
JSCC is the Japanese counterpart of SIAC and DTC in New York. Membership in JSCC is limited to members of the Tokyo Stock Exchange.

JSCC serves as a clearing and settlement facility for all securities (including bonds, warrants, foreign issues, and the like) traded on the Tokyo Exchange.

JASD
Acronym for Securities Dealers Association of Japan. Although that is its technical name, the association is almost universally referred to as JASD. It is similar in function to the NASD. Although membership is optional, the JASD was authorized in the Japanese Securities and Exchange Act of 1973 and all trade practices in Japan are regulated by the JASD.

JASDEC
Short name for the Japanese Securities Depository Center. JASDEC is an adjunct of the Tokyo Stock Exchange and was founded in 1984. Its purpose is to compare and settle members' transactions. It is similar in function and scope to the DTC in the United States.

JDR
Abbreviation for Japanese Depository Receipt. Similar to an ADR, these registered receipts represent ownership of a specific number of shares in a non-Japanese corporation. Upon sale, the receipts are transferred by the depository to the new owner only on its own records. The underlying securities remain on deposit.

JEEP
Slang based on the first two phonemes of GPM, an acronym for graduated payment mortgage. Under a graduated payment mortgage, payments in the early years are lower than in the intermediate and later years.

GPMs are also known as "GYP-EMs."

JELLY ROLL SPREAD
Colorful terminology occasionally used by professional traders in index options. The jelly roll spread combines long and short positions in the same index option, but with different classes (i.e., put and call) and for different expiration months. A typical jelly roll OEX spread might combine the following:

LONG OEX NOV 190 Call
SHORT OEX DEC 190 Call
LONG OEX NOV 190 Put
SHORT OEX DEC 190 Put

In equity options parlance, this would be a "put and a call time (horizontal) spread."

JENNY TEL
Wall Street abbreviation and identifier for General Telephone & Electronics Corporation.

JEWISH DENTIST DEFENSE
An antitakeover defense developed by Joseph Flom, a partner in the law firm of Skadden Arps Slate Meagher and Flom.

When Sterndent, a dental supply company, was threatened by a takeover by Magus, a Kuwaiti concern, Flom had customers and suppliers complain that they did not want to be owned by an Arab firm. Magus then reconsidered its proposal and backed away from its intended takeover—hence the name.

JGB
Acronym for Japanese government bonds. These yen-denominated debt securities are issued by the Imperial Japanese Government to finance its budgetary programs. JGBs are similar in stature in Japan as U.S. government bonds are in the United States.

JITTERS
See MARKET JITTERS.

JOBBER
English securities term for a marketmaker on the ISE. The term is analogous to that of the specialists on U.S. exchanges, with this exception: The jobber acts only as a principal. His contra parties are brokers for the public and other jobbers.

JOBBER'S TURN
English securities term for the spread—that is, the difference between the bid and asked prices—of the quote given by a jobber. Example: In a quote of 170 p bid and 190 p offered, the jobber's turn is 20 p.

JOHANNESBURG STOCK EXCHANGE
The JSE is open for trading from 9:30 A.M. until 1:00 P.M., and again from 2:00 to 4:00 P.M. After-hour trading in gold shares is permitted for over-

seas orders. Regular way settlement is on the seventh business day following the trade date.

The JSE is noted for illiquidity because of USA (Union of South Africa) rules governing the flight of capital from the country. In practice, the greatest number of stocks traded represent gold mining shares. Many USA gold mining shares are available in ADRs and are actively traded OTC in this country.

JOINT ACCOUNT

1. A brokerage account that involves two or more clients.
   See also JOINT TENANTS WITH RIGHTS OF SURVIVORSHIP and TENANTS IN COMMON.
2. An investment banking account, or syndicate.
   See also EASTERN ACCOUNT and WESTERN ACCOUNT.

JOINT ACCOUNT AGREEMENT

Form that must be signed by all parties to a joint account. Although the details of such joint accounts may differ, one thing is common: any party to the account may make purchase or sale transactions. This protects the broker. Assets, whether held in the account or transferred out, are in joint name and are for the benefit of all account owners.

JOINTLY AND SEVERALLY

Expression used in Eastern accounts for municipal underwritings. Such accounts are undivided and the entire account is responsible for the entire offering. Thus, an account member with 3% of the participation who sold 3% of the offering would still be responsible proportionately for any unsold bonds in the offering.

See also SEVERALLY BUT NOT JOINTLY (for divided accounts) and EASTERN ACCOUNT.

JOINT TENANTS BY THE ENTIRETIES

Abbreviation: Ten. by Ent. A form of joint ownership recognized and legally used in only a few states. Such tenancy is restricted to husband and wife. It is similar to joint tenant with right of survivorship, but there are nuances in terms of disposition, assessment, and the like that require legal advice.

JOINT TENANTS IN COMMON

Frequently used abbreviations: TIC, or Ten. in Com. In this form of joint ownership, two or more persons maintain a collective securities/commodities account with a broker/dealer, each having a fractional financial interest in the assets in the account. At death, the decedent's estate shares in the percentage of value attributable to that party's participation in the account.

JOINT TENANTS WITH RIGHTS OF SURVIVORSHIP (JTWROS or WROS)
Two or more persons who maintain a collective account with a broker, but there is no specific fractional financial interest. Upon the death of one party, his ownership passes immediately to the other party. There is no probate, but there could be estate taxes if the decedent's portion, except in the case of a spouse, exceeds estate tax exemptions.

JOINT VENTURE TENDER
Term used to describe two or more companies that pool capital to take over another company. If successful, the victors either will jointly own the venture or divide up the assets of the acquired company. Example: In 1983, Martin Marietta and United Technology unsuccessfully tried a joint venture tender for Bendix Corporation.

JSCC
See JAPAN SECURITIES CLEARING CORPORATION.

JTWROS
See JOINT TENANTS WITH RIGHTS OF SURVIVORSHIP.

JUBILEE
See YEAR OF THE JUBILEE.

JUMBO CERTIFICATE
1. The form of security custodial service whereby the DTC holds in the nominee name of CEDE large deposits of securities made by members of the Depository Trust. These certificates may be of varying sizes. Nothing prevents, for example, securities owned by the customers of Merrill Lynch from being comingled with those owned by customers of Salomon Brothers. Having thus formed a jumbo certificate, DTC on its own books lists the amount attributable to the individual member firms.
2. The certificate that is evidence of time deposits in denominations of $100,000 or more. Such certificates generally have a coupon rate of interest, a fixed maturity, and are readily negotiable.

JUNIOR SECURITY
From the Latin, *juvenis,* meaning younger.
1. Used absolutely of common stock, the security that has the last claim on corporate assets in the case of dissolution of the company.
2. Used relatively of any security that is subordinate to another in its claim on corporate assets. Thus, debentures are junior to secured bonds, preferred stock is junior to any debt security, and so on.

JUNK AND GOVERNMENT RECEIPTS
See JAGR.

JUNK BOND
Industry expression for bonds with a credit rating of BB or lower. Such bonds have speculative overtones.

JURISDICTION
The right of a regulatory body to hear a case, and the corresponding power to render a judgment. For example, "This case involved a claim of fraud and thus the NASD decided that it did not have jurisdiction; instead, it recommended that the clients seek their remedies at law."

K

K
Eleventh letter of the alphabet, used:
1. Lower or uppercase to signify 1,000. From the Greek, *kilion,* a thousand. Used with an Arabic number, it multiplies that number by 1,000; for example, 24K = 24,000.
2. Uppercase in computer language to designate a kilobyte.
3. As the fifth letter in a NASDAQ/NMS symbol to designate a nonvoting common stock; for example, PHELK designates Petroleum Helicopters' nonvoting common.
4. Alone uppercase as the stock symbol for Kellogg, Inc., a major manufacturer of breakfast products in the Unites States and the United Kingdom.

K is not used in the securities industry. Instead, the Latin M (1,000) is used, as in 20M and 1OM. This abbreviation is used to give buy/sell instructions for bonds to designate the face value of the bonds.

KABUTO-CHO
Name for the financial district of Tokyo and used in practice as Wall Street is used in the United States to signify the place where financial dealings are conducted.

KAFFIRS
Wall Street slang for South African mining shares as a general class of securities. The word stems from the tribe of native black workers who work in the mines and make them function profitably.

The word was originally used only of the Xhosa tribe in South Africa but eventually came to be used of all black workers. From the Arabic *kafir* (pronounced kay–fear), meaning an infidel or nonbeliever.

KAISHIME GROUPS
Japanese name for groups of stock manipulators who "corner" a specific issue for the purpose of extracting "greenmail" from the management of these companies. In effect, they monopolize the stock and then sell it back to management at a significant profit.

KANGAROOS
Slang term used in a general way to describe Australian common stocks ("ordinaries"). The obvious reference is to the marsupial most closely connected with that continent.

KANSAS CITY BOARD OF TRADE (KCBT)
A commodities exchange located in Kansas City, Missouri. Its brokers specialize in agricultural commodities and futures contract trading.

KB BELGIAN INDEX FUND
A mutual fund sponsored by the Kreditbank (KB) of Belgium. The fund is indexed to the market performance of the Brussels Stock Exchange and contains stocks of 22 companies that constitute 75 percent of that market's total capitalization.

KCBT
See KANSAS CITY BOARD OF TRADE.

KEEP IN MIND
Acronym: KIM. A customer or salesperson memorandum to a marketmaker that gives the price or size, or both, at which they would be buyers or sellers of a particular security. It is a nonbinding indication of interest.

KEEPWELL AGREEMENT
Also: keep well. A contract between a parent company and a third party in which the parent company agrees to cause a subsidiary to maintain certain minimum financial ratios or net worth. This arrangement arises to protect the integrity of a prospective financial deal between the subsidiary and the third party.

KEOGH PLAN
Self-employed persons are permitted to make tax-deductible contributions to a retirement plan. The plan may be a defined contribution, a defined benefit, or a profit-sharing plan; this is determined by the owner of the plan and is incorporated into the plan documents.

Defined benefit and profit-sharing plans need legal advice.

Defined contribution plans permit the self-employed person to contribute 20% of gross self-employed income (or $30,000, whichever is less) into a tax-sheltered plan. As with IRA plans, withdrawals before age 59½ are subject to a 10% penalty. Withdrawals based on actuarial expectations must begin the year the owner becomes 70½.

Tax advice is needed by those who are the beneficiaries of another person's Keogh plan.

See also VOCON.

KEOP
Acronym for Key Indicator Operational Report. A weekly report mandated by the NYSE from member organizations who carry or clear customer accounts. Purpose: to enable the NYSE to quickly identify any member firms that are experiencing operational difficulties in the processing of their business, which difficulties, in turn, could jeopardize the quantity or quality of the firm's net capital.

KEY INDICATOR OPERATIONAL REPORT
See KEOP.

KEYNESIAN ECONOMIST
This financial philosophy is named for its founder, John Maynard Keynes (rhymes with "canes"), a British economist who flourished in the 1930s and 1940s. This school of economic thought advocates governmental control of the economy in times of recession by spending and tax adjustments. In effect, Keynesian economic thought makes the government the "employer of last resort" in poor economic times. This school of economy greatly influenced the New Deal and the "pump priming" that marked the early days of the presidency of Franklin Delano Roosevelt.

KEYNESIAN THEORY
Also simply: Keynesian. An economic theory, named after the late John Maynard Keynes, a prominent British economist. This theory is based on the belief that liberal government spending programs are needed to stimulate and maintain continuing economic growth in a country's gross national product. This theory, in times of depression and recession with elevated unemployment rates, would make the government the employer of last resort to revive the economy.

KEY REVERSAL
An expression used by technicians to describe the chart pattern of a stock that *rehit* a record high or low in the stock. A key reversal does not forecast a changing trend; instead, it usually means that there is simply a pause before the stock penetrates the old level high or low.

KICKBACK

1. An illegal rebating scheme.
2. Any systematic program to rebate or reduce commissions charged by a broker to a customer.

In general, a kickback made to influence a decision is considered unethical or illegal. If given because of the volume of business, it may not be unethical.

KICKER

A special feature or added benefit of a security. Term is generally used as a noun. For example, "This bond has a floating rate, and—as a kicker—you can put it to the issuer at par in five years."

KIDDIE TAX

Jocular term used in conjunction with a feature of the Tax Reform Act of 1986. Under this feature, investment income received by a minor under 14 years of age is taxed as follows:

$1 to $500	untaxed
$501 to $1,000	15% tax
$1,001 or more	taxed at the parents' bracket

The "kiddie tax" does not apply to earned income nor to gift taxes that are paid by the donor.

After the age of 14, the minor (and subsequent major) would pay taxes at his or her bracket on taxable income, although the bracket may be applied somewhat differently if the minor is a deduction on the parents' return.

KILL

Slang: cancel. Examples: kill the bid, kill the offer, fill or kill.

KILLER BEES

Jargon for a law firm, proxy solicitor, public relations firm, and a bank to provide credit. These are held on retainer by a corporation as a continuing defense against a hostile takeover through tender offers or a proxy contest. This team of specialists is in the hive and, as "killer bees," are ready to protect the company from all unfriendly outsiders.

KIM

See KEEP IN MIND.

KIND ARBITRAGE
The near-simultaneous profitable purchase and sale of substantially identical securities in the same marketplace, based on price differences which prevail in their separate trading values.

KISS INDEX
Acronym for Kurs–Information–Service–System.
> This long-name title for the index was abandoned some years ago.
> See also FRANKFURT RUNNING INDEX.

KITING
The unwise and flighty practice of sustaining credit or of raising money by causing prices to soar.
> See also CHECK KITING.

KIWIS
Slang for a five-year floating rate note marketed by the Student Loan Marketing Association (Sallie Mae) in the United States. The interest rate is denominated and payable in New Zealand dollars. The variable rate is set at $1\,3/4$ percentage points less than the New Zealand bill rate. This rate was chosen because, at the time of issuance, the rate was higher than comparable rates available on U.S. securities.

KLSE
See KUALA LUMPUR STOCK EXCHANGE.

KNIFE
Word derived from the phonemes of NYFE.
> See also NEW YORK FUTURES EXCHANGE.

KNOCKOUT
Colorful name used for the shares of Coca-Cola Company, Incorporated. The term is derived from the company's NYSE ticker symbol: KO.

KNOW YOUR CUSTOMER
Industry obligation, imposed by New York Stock Exchange's Rule 405 but equally implied by other industry rules, that requires a brokerage firm and its registered representatives to know the important facts about the customers with whom they do business. The rule requires due diligence because what may be unimportant for one customer may be very important for another.

KONDRATIEFF CYCLE

Named after Nikolai Kondratieff, a Soviet economist. In his view, Western capitalist economies are subject to major cycles of 50 to 60 years in duration. Since Kondratieff claims to have predicted the 1929/30 depression and market collapse, it would seem that we are to expect another financial downturn soon.

KOP

The initials designate the three largest rival banks to the Union Bank of Finland. These banks are the Kansallis, the Osake, and the Panki. KOP helped organize the Optionsmaklare, the major equity options exchange in Finland.

KP

When used on corporate and municipal bond calendars, these initials identify Kidder, Peabody & Company, a major underwriter of securities.

KRUGERRAND

Legal tender in the Republic of South Africa, the Krugerrand has a value of RSA 25 rand. The coin contains one troy ounce of "feingeld" (puregold) and thus its value fluctuates as the value of gold bullion fluctuates. In recent years, as a protest against South African apartheid policy, many U.S. dealers will no longer buy (but will sell) this South African coin.

KUALA LUMPUR STOCK EXCHANGE (KLSE)

This exchange was originally affiliated with the Singapore Stock Exchange but is now independent and is the largest securities exchange in Malaysia. The exchange uses an "open outcry" system. There are two trading sessions daily, Monday through Friday. Settlements are scheduled on a weekly basis.

L

L

Twelfth letter of the alphabet, used:
1. Uppercase in typewritten manuscript (often with a serif, such as £) to designate pound sterling.
2. Uppercase in typewritten manuscript to designate Italian lira (more common, Lit).
3. As the fifth letter in NASDAQ/NMS symbols to represent nonvoting stock of a government-founded company; for example, SLMAL represents nonvoting stock of the Student Loan Marketing Association.

4. Uppercase as the ticker symbol of Loblaw Companies, Ltd., a major food wholesaler in Canada.
5. Uppercase to represent 50 in Roman numerals, although this is not used to designate securities quantities.

LAFFER CURVE
The graphic expression of an economic theory founded by Professor Arthur Laffer, a government advisor and economist, which holds that there will be a growth in economic output if tax rates—particularly on businesses—are cut. This theory was the foundation of President Reagan's dramatic tax cuts of 1981 and following, and the beginning of "supply side" economics. Unfortunately, neither the President nor Congress was willing to undertake the other side of the theory: the dramatic cut of governmental spending.

LAISSEZ-FAIRE CAPITALISM
French: let (it) act. A theory of capitalism which holds that the economy works best when market forces (i.e., supply and demand) are permitted to operate without intervention. Thus, the theory would have the government eschew all intervention in the economic order, or keep such intervention at a minimum. In practice, laissez-faire capitalism has not worked and has resulted in revolution wherever it has been absolutely implemented. Some governmental control of business forces is always required.

LANDOWNER ROYALTY
This is a share of the gross production of an oil or gas well—usually ¹/₈ percent—paid to the owner of the land from which the oil or gas is removed. The landowner royalty is paid without any financial contribution to the development of the well on the part of the owner.

LAPPING
A fraudulent scheme, also known as a Ponzi scheme, which takes money stolen from current participants in the scheme to repay persons who were victimized earlier. Theoretically, such a scheme will continue indefinitely until no new persons can be bunkoed into the ever-widening circle of victims.

LAPSED OPTION
An option that has expired unexercised and therefore is worthless.

LARGE ORDER EXECUTION
See LOX.

LAST DEALINGS

A British expression frequently used on the International Stock Exchange of the United Kingdom and the Republic of Ireland to designate trades that occur on the last day of the account period. The account period is usually a fortnight in length and all trades made during that period must be settled at the end of the period.

LAST IN, FIRST OUT (LIFO)

Method of inventory valuation. Under LIFO, the last items received into inventory are considered to be the first items sold. In an inflationary period, this would cause the cost of goods sold to be higher than the cost of goods sold if first in, first out (FIFO) valuation were used.

By increasing the cost of goods sold, LIFO valuation will decrease working capital, profits, and taxes.

LAST SALE

Industry usage for the most recent transaction in a specific security. The term is used of stock exchange transactions. The last sale is important for the application of the uptick rule for short sales, and often limits buying and selling transactions of specialists and floor traders.

Common usage reserves the term *closing sale* for the last trade of the day.

LATE TAPE

Term used if the exchange tape is significantly behind schedule in the reporting of completed transactions. As a rule of thumb, if the tape is two or more minutes late, initial digits of the transaction price will be deleted. For example, a transaction at $45^{1}/_{2}$, when the tape is late, would appear $5^{1}/_{2}$.

A LAUGH

Quaint term used by order clerks and stock exchange floor members to signify a fractional price of $^{1}/_{2}$. For example, a price of $22^{1}/_{2}$ could be expressed as "twenty-two and a laugh."

Although the expression was originally intended to be used jocularly, the expression quickly caught on and is now used extensively.

LAUNDER

To "clean up" money obtained illegally through the drug trade or from organized crime. Generally, the laundering is done by so funneling the money through other legitimate businesses that the "paper trail" is very difficult to follow.

The U.S. Treasury requires that all transactions of $10,000 or more in cash be identified on a prescribed form. Nevertheless, it is difficult to trace such laundering.

LAUNDER MONEY

To transfer money through several financial institutions to conceal its illegal source.

See SEC RULE 17a-8, which is designed to prevent the laundering of money through an account with a broker/dealer.

THE LAUNDRY BUSINESS

Tongue-in-cheek expression for "wash selling," a market manipulation practice outlawed in the Securities and Exchange Act of 1934. In this context, wash selling describes the practice of creating artificial transactions—usually by buying and selling for your own account in quantity—so unsuspecting investors are brought to believe that an accumulation is taking place prior to a takeover bid. This may push up the price of the security and at that time the wash seller will unload previous holdings at a profit.

LAUTRO

Acronym for Life Assurance and Unit Trust Regulatory Organisation. LAUTRO is a trade association in the United Kingdom that regulates life insurance companies unit trust managers and their trustees. In Britain, a unit trust is similar in form and function to a mutual fund in the United States.

LAY OFF

Used in conjunction with a standby underwriting if the manager of the syndicate allocates unused rights to the syndicate members.

LAY UP

Slang term derived from the sport of basketball to designate an easy execution of an order to buy or sell a security. Example: In today's market, 10,000 shares should be a lay up.

LBO

This is the purchase of a controlling interest in a company through the use of borrowed money.

See also LEVERAGED BUYOUT.

LBO STUBS

These are the publicly owned equity securities of a company after a leveraged buyout (LBO) has been completed and the issuer is now a "private" concern. It is difficult to determine the true value of such minority interests in the absence of a public market for the remaining securities (the "stubs").

LDC

See LESS DEVELOPED COUNTRIES.

LEAD MARKETMAKER (LMM)

This is a category of marketmaker on the Chicago Board Options Exchange (CBOE) who is authorized to assist the order book official (OBO) in expediting the opening rotation in the OEX (S&P 100 Index) option.

The lead marketmaker is appointed on a month-to-month basis by the CBOE's Market Performance Committee and is obliged to quote firm two-sided quotes and to facilitate customer order imbalances in all OEX index option series that are being traded within a given area of strike prices.

Once the opening rotation is completed, other marketmakers join in the competition for trades.

LEAD REGULATOR

1. In the United States, because of the wide diversity of business done by broker/dealers and the large number of regulators (SROs), it often happens that one regulator investigates and then reports to other SROs. For example, it is not uncommon for the NYSE to investigate an action and then report to other SROs. In this role, the NYSE is the "lead regulator."
2. In the United Kingdom, under the Financial Services Act, each bank, broker/dealer, investment trust, or insurance company has a "lead regulator" appointed to investigate its activities in terms of capital adequacy and good business conduct. Every endeavor is made to avoid a duplication of regulatory oversight by other organizations that may have jurisdiction.

LEAKY LETTER OF CREDIT

Conventional letters of credit (LOC) are often issued by banks in conjunction with the issuance of a security either as collateral or as a guarantee of performance. If the issuing bank is itself a credit problem or has had its credit rating recently downgraded, the LOC is said to be "leaky."

LEASE

A legal contract whereby an owner grants use of its assets for a fixed (time) period for a fixed fee (rent) to a lessor. Such leases may include any asset that is usable. In recent years, there has been an increased use of leases to permit exchange memberships to be used by others for an annual fee. The most common use of leases is in the rental of real estate, and this may include not only the use but also mining rights for oil, natural gas, or other minerals.

LEASE REVENUE BOND

A variety of a "shadow" bond in which a municipality obtains financing for a public project outside of its budget (credit) limitations. As a result, the municipality does not secure that instrument. Instead, tolls, rental payments, user assessments, and the like are the only protections for the bondholders. No governmental body interposes itself between issuer and bondholder.

LEASE UP
The act of filling a commercial building with rent-paying tenants for periods specified in a contract known as a lease agreement. Broker/dealers often own or occupy such buildings and the lease agreement is often critical to that firm's profitability.

LEFT-HAND FINANCING
Colloquial term used to describe borrowing collateralized by assets which, in double-entry bookkeeping, are listed on the left-hand side of a corporate balance sheet. Concept: Asset-rich companies, by using these assets, can obtain capital at lower than usual costs.

LEG
Describes one or the other side of a transaction that partially offsets an existing position without closing out the position. For example, a client buys a call at 50. To turn this into a call spread, the client could add a leg by selling a call at 60.

You will also see the term to *take off a leg* if one side of a spread is closed, leaving the other side as either long or short.

LEGAL
Also: legal item, or legal transfer. Commonly used as a noun. Example: It's a legal.
1. Term is capitalized but is not an acronym. It refers to a centralized computer data bank of NYSE customer complaints, enforcement information, and the findings of exchange examiners in their audit of the records and activities of a member firm.
2. Term is used of a certificate registered in the name of a corporation, trust, or deceased person. The transfer agent will not effect transfer unless the certificate is accompanied by supporting documentation. As a result, buying brokers are not required to accept legals; instead, the selling broker must first have the security transferred to street name. It is then delivered to the buying broker.

LEGAL AGE
Age at which, under the law of the state of residence, a minor reaches majority. This is an important concept for persons with multiple residences or who are under the Uniform Gift to Minors Act.

LEGAL INVESTMENT
A security that is considered to be eligible for selection by a fiduciary for the portfolio which the fiduciary manages. As a general rule, securities within the top four ratings of a national rating service are considered to be legal investments.

LEGAL LIST
Various states restrict the investments of fiduciaries to specific securities on a list prepared by the state. As a general rule, the securities are specified high-quality debt and equity securities.

See also PRUDENT MAN RULE.

LEGAL OPINION
A statement of counsel given to an issuer of municipal securities that specifies that (1) interest income is exempt from federal taxation, (2) enabling legislation permits the issue, and (3) no restrictive covenant on prior issues is violated by this issue. Although the legal opinion is subject to future adjudication, no syndicate will accept an issue for sale without a legal opinion.

LEGALS
See LEGAL TRANSFER.

LEGAL TRANSFER
Industry term for a security that is so registered that documents, other than a stock/bond power, are required to effect its transfer from a seller to a buyer. Buying brokers will not accept securities requiring legal transfer; it is the selling broker's obligation to complete the legalities so the certificate is transferrable.

Securities registered under the Uniform Gift to Minors Act are not considered legal transfers, but securities registered to a corporation or to a deceased person are.

LEG BREAKER
See SHERIFF.

LEGGING
Jargon for an ultimate two-sided position of which only one side has currently been established. For example, "I'm legging a spread but I only have the long call in place."

The expression may be used of any risk arbitrage (it is presumed that a bona fide arbitrage has both legs in place), an option spread, or a straddle or combination. However, since such two-sided positions are basically "hedged" there is great risk if the legging is delayed.

Antonym: to "take off a leg"; this is the reverse of legging.

TO LEG INTO A HEDGE
A hedge is any offsetting security position.

To leg into a hedge, as this term is used by securities traders, describes the intention to create an offsetting position in a security by executing one side now and waiting until some later time to execute the other side of the trade. They hope that the subsequent position can be effected at a better price than the one now prevailing.

See also LEG.

LEHMAN INVESTMENT OPPORTUNITY NOTES
See LION.

LEMON
Quaint expression used to designate any investment or product that gives poor performance or results. The expression can be used of things, whether tangible or intangible; for example, "That is certainly one lemon of an automobile," or "My investment in ABC stock turned into a lemon."

LENDER OF LAST RESORT
Member banks of the Federal Reserve may borrow against eligible securities; the monies thus borrowed may be loaned or used to fulfill reserve requirements. In this way, the Fed is "the lender of last resort." The ability of members to borrow is not without restrictions, however, and for this reason the discount window and the moral suasion of the Fed come together in this concept of lending.

See also DISCOUNT WINDOW.

LENDING AT A PREMIUM
If a short seller must pay the lender of the borrowed securities, the security is lending at a premium. For example, the lender requires a premium of $1 per day per 100 shares for the loan of the securities. The premium is over and above the requirement that the loaned securities be (1) marked to the market and (2) reimbursed for any dividends/interest payable.

LENDING AT A RATE
When a person sells short there is a credit in that account. If the short seller demands payment for the money that is held in escrow to protect the lender of the securities, the securities sold short are said to be "lending at a rate."

LENDING FLAT

Term used of the borrowing of securities collateralized by cash if no fee is paid by the borrower nor interest paid by the lender. Term refers to short sales.

Antonym: lending at a rate; that is, interest paid by the lender who has the use of the cash collateral. Lending at a premium; that is, a fee paid by the borrower for the use of the certificate.

LE PETIT BANG

A facetious term used of the French government's attempt to deregulate that country's financial industry. Using methods similar to the British deregulation of 1986, the French government permitted foreign banks and brokerage firms to purchase equity interests in French financial institutions and thus become members of the Paris Bourse.

LESOP

Acronym for leveraged employee stock ownership plan. LESOP is a program by which employee pension and profit-sharing plans can easily convert or exchange assets for shares in the underlying issuer-employer. This places a large block of ownership in friendly hands and thereby discourages corporate predators.

The leverage arises when the company lends money to the pension plan, or issues convertibles to it with payment made on the installment basis. If convertibles are used, the company purchases a block of common stock in the marketplace and puts them in reserve against a subsequent conversion. Generally, conversion takes place only if a prospective raider comes on the scene to threaten the existing management.

LESS A . . .

Term used to designate a concession granted to a member who helps in the distribution of a security. Examples: "Less a buck"; that is, the selling dealer will be permitted to buy a security at $1 under the public offering price, thereby making a profit when it is resold at the public offering price; "less a quarter," which means the concession, on a bond sale, would be a quarter point (i.e., $2.50).

LESS DEVELOPED COUNTRIES

Acronym: LDC. LDC is a "buzz word" in the financial industry for countries considered economically primitive; that is, with low per capita income, a great deal of inflation, and extensive negative balance of payments and borrowings. LDCs as a group are often referred to as belonging to the Third World.

LESSEE

The person who enters into a contractual agreement to rent an asset from someone for a fixed time in return for the periodic payment of a fixed sum of money. The terms of the contract will determine whether the lessee or the lessor is responsible for maintenance and insurance.

Synonym: renter, although in context the word may be deceptive.
Antonym: lessor.

LESSEE MEMBER

A real person who has leased the use of a membership (a seat) on an exchange from a member for a fixed time for a fixed fee. For example, when exchange memberships were selling at $250,000, a person leased a membership for $40,000 per year. The lessor member was getting 16% on invested capital; the lessee was leveraging a $40,000 investment, with a chance for a return on the other $210,000, to get the total return on the $210,000 and the income from the use of the seat.

LESSOR

The person who enters into a contractual agreement to rent to someone an asset for a fixed time in return for the periodic payment of a fixed sum of money. In addition to the payments received by the lessor, current tax laws permit the lessor to depreciate the value of residential and commercial property and, in the case of newly purchased qualifying equipment, to be eligible for investment tax credits.

Antonym: lessee.

LETTER BOND

A bond sold privately with ability for transfer or resale subject to terms of an investment letter.

LETTER OF CREDIT

Popular acronym: LOC. A LOC is a document issued by a commercial bank that enables the subscriber to draw monies as needed at the issuing bank. The subscriber pays an annual percentage fee to the issuing bank even if the credit is not used.

LOCs have extensive world usage in commerce, in international business, and are also used extensively by broker/dealers to establish credit with clearing associations. For example, a broker/dealer could provide a letter of credit to the OCC to take care of the varying margin obligations of its positions with the OCC.

LETTER OF FREE CREDIT

A written statement from one broker/dealer to another on behalf of a purchasing customer. The letter of free credit attests to the availability of funds to fully pay for securities that are to be delivered versus payment. Regulation T mandates this procedure if the purchasing customer regularly instructs that payments are to be made COD (cash on delivery) or POD (payment on delivery). Such letters are used only with institutional accounts.

LETTER OF INDEMNIFICATION
An agreement stating that one party to a business contract will compensate one or more other parties for losses incurred as a result of the venture. This agreement is fairly common in corporate finance activities involving mergers, acquisitions, and private placements. In public offerings, such agreements generally are limited to prospective litigation costs or penalties.

LETTER OF INTENT
1. A written promise by a mutual fund shareholder to invest, during a 13-month period, a specified sum of money to qualify for a reduced percentage sales charge.
2. A preliminary contract between two parties negotiating a merger or an acquisition.

LETTER SECURITY
The name given to an unregistered security that is purchased privately from the issuer. The term arises because the issuer, in the private sale, asked the purchaser to state in a letter that the purchase was made as an investment and not for purposes of immediate resale.
See also INVESTMENT LETTER.

LETTERS OF ADMINISTRATION
A court-issued certificate that empowers a court-appointed administrator to settle the estate of a decedent who left no will.
Securities in such an estate cannot be sold or reregistered unless this court certificate, dated within the past six months, is submitted to the transfer agent for inspection and acceptance.
See also INTESTATE.

LETTERS TESTAMENTARY
A court-issued certificate that empowers the executor of an estate to settle the decedent's affairs as quickly as possible under the terms of the recognized will.
Securities in this estate cannot be sold or reregistered unless this court certificate, dated within the past six months, is submitted to the transfer agent for inspection and acceptance.

LETTER STOCK (LETTER BOND)

Popular term used to designate stocks/bonds that have been purchased privately from an issuer and thus have not undergone the process of SEC registration. As such, both letter stock and letter bonds may be difficult to transfer because the transfer agent knows their restricted status.

Also known as "stock (bond) with an inscription" or "stock with a restriction" because the certificate may be inscribed to designate the fact that they were purchased privately.

The term *letter stock* is so denominated because the issuer will ordinarily require of the private purchaser a letter designating the fact that the securities were purchased as an investment and not for resale.

See also INVESTMENT LETTER.

LEVEL

1. Noun: often used synonymously for the price or yield at which a security may be bought or sold, or at which a customer may be interested in a purchase or sale. Example: "I'd be interested in those bonds at the 8.50 level."
2. Verb: price or yield area where activity in a security will tend to remain for a time period. Price or yield may be higher or lower than present prices. Example: "We expect the market to level at 1350 until the last quarter of the year."

LEVEL DEBT SERVICE

Requirement of a municipality's charter that the annual debt service (i.e., the combined total of interest and principal payments) be approximately equal each year. The purpose is to provide for effective budgeting of the tax revenues of the municipality.

LEVEL I SERVICE OF NASDAQ

Subscription service that provides, on an electronic screen, the highest bid and lowest offer of NASDAQ-traded securities. The market maker is not identified.

This service is used by brokerage firms to give up-to-date information to account executives and clients.

See also NASDAQ.

LEVEL II SERVICE OF NASDAQ

Subscription service that provides, on an electronic screen, the market-makers and their bids and offers for NASDAQ-traded securities.

This service, available to institutional investors and to the traders of NASD members, is used to give competitive information on NASDAQ-traded securities.

See also NASDAQ.

LEVEL III SERVICE OF NASDAQ

Subscription service that provides, on an electronic screen, the market-makers and their bids and offers for NASDAQ-traded securities.

It also permits subscribers, who are registered marketmakers, to compete by entering their own bids and offers for the securities in which they are reg istered. In effect, therefore, Level III is an electronic marketplace.

See also NASDAQ.

LEVEL PLAYING FIELD

Expression used to denote equality among competitors in a specific marketplace or under particular market conditions. For example, in a given market environment, all participants should be subject to the same trading rules, the same tax requirements, the same capital requirements, and the same disciplinary risks.

It would violate the concept of a "level playing field" were one nation to have restrictive import quotas while another did not, or for one nation to permit collusion in the fixing of prices while the other does not, or—particularly—to permit "dumping"; that is, sales below cost to gain market share at a disadvantage to the other nation.

LEVERAGE

In finance, the term *leverage* is applied to:
1. The control of a large amount of money by a small amount of money. For example, a warrant or a long call controls a large amount of money with a small amount.
2. The use of borrowed money at a fixed rate of interest to achieve a greater rate of return. For example, a client buys on margin or a company borrows money.

See also TRADING ON THE EQUITY and BOND RATIO.

LEVERAGED

A business or financial enterprise that uses borrowed money at a fixed rate of interest in an endeavor to achieve a greater rate of return on the total invested capital. For example, "An investor leveraged his equity by buying the security in a margin account."

LEVERAGED BUYOUT (LBO)

Acronym: LBO. Jargon for the purchase of a controlling interest in a corporation through the use of borrowed money. The concept includes the idea that the resulting consolidated balance sheet will contain debts that are to be paid off from assets currently on the balance sheet of the acquired company, or from cash flows generated by that company. Insurance companies, commercial banks, or venture capital organizations are often the sources of such borrowed funds.

LEVERAGED COMPANY

A business enterprise whose total capital comprises both equity and debt. Industrial corporations with more than one third of their capital in the form of long-term debt are said to be highly leveraged.

Leverage is an endeavor to increase the return on equity by accepting an increased risk of bankruptcy; that is, an inability to meet the interest and principal payments on the debt.

LEVERAGED INVESTMENT COMPANY

1. An open-end investment company whose charter permits bank loans as part of the invested capital of the fund.
2. A dual-purpose fund with both income and capital shares. Because all dividends go to the income shares, and all capital gains to the capital shares, the investors in both classes of shares, in effect, leverage each other.

See also LEVERAGE.

LEVERAGED LEASE

A lease contract for equipment that is substantially financed by a nonrecourse loan. The lessee has the use of the equipment without the outlay of capital. The lessor retains the residual value of the depreciated asset when the contract expires and the immediate advantage of the investment tax credit and depreciation writeoffs.

See also DEPRECIATION; INVESTMENT TAX CREDIT; and NONRECOURSE LOAN.

LEVERAGED LEASE TRANSACTION

An equipment lease contract in which the cost of the equipment is substantially financed by a nonrecourse loan. The lessee gains use of the equipment for its business uses without a substantial outlay of capital. The lessor, who remains the owner, obtains depreciation benefits and the investment tax credit, and retains the residual value of the asset when the contract expires.

LEVERAGED RECAP

Abbreviation for: leveraged recapitalization plan. In effect, this is a corporate finance strategy to discourage corporate raiders. Under the plan, a company substitutes as much debt as possible for equity by borrowing and then distributing as much as possible of the company's assets to the shareholders in the form of cash. As a result, the company is now highly leveraged and is no longer as attractive as it originally was to the raider.

LEVERAGE TRANSACTION MERCHANT (LTM)

This is a futures commission merchant (FCM), registered with the CFTC, who is permitted by exemption to deal in selected over-the-counter futures instruments. As a general rule, such off exchange futures trading is prohibited. However, those FCMs who were already in the business before June 1, 1978, can be grand-fathered from current rule compliance with the authorization of the CFTC.

LF

Initials used on corporate and municipal bond calendars to designate Lazard Freres & Company, a major underwriter of securities.

LIABILITY

In finance, any claim for money against the assets of a company. Thus, all debts—whether short-term or long-term—are liabilities. However, securities, whether common or preferred, have no claim on the assets of a company.

LIBERTARIANISM

Although the term is used primarily of those who propose freedom of conduct in any circumstance, or who propose that freedom of will is superior to any other restraint, the term is also used as an ultimate form of "laissez-faire" capitalism in which all citizens should be permitted to control their own business and social destinies.

LIBID

Acronym for London Inter-Bank Bid Rate. The bid in a quotation representing the rate of interest at which U.S. dollar deposits retraded within the English banking community.

The offer side of this quotation is called LIBOR (offered rate).

LIBOR

Acronym for London Inter-Bank Offered Rate. It is the rate at which deposits of U.S. dollars are traded in London. LIBOR is often used as the base for the determination of the changes in the interest rate on Eurodollar notes that have a floating rate.

LIEN

A claim against property made to a creditor. For example, a margin account customer gives the broker a lien against assets in the account, or a bond gives the bondholder a lien against the company's plant.

LIFE AND UNIT TRUST INTERMEDIARIES REGULATORY ORGANISATION
See LUTIRO.

LIFE ASSURANCE AND UNIT TRUST REGULATORY ORGANISATION
See LAUTRO.

LIFEBOAT FUND
Term used to describe the $20 million financing set up in 1985 to rescue some members of the Kuala Lumpur Stock Exchange who sustained large forward contract losses due to a crisis involving Pan-Electric Corporation. The financing was dropped in 1987 when the involved members were able to unwind their positions.

LIFEBOAT ISSUE
Term used in the United Kingdom for an issue of stock or bonds whose proceeds will be used to save a company that is otherwise sinking into bankruptcy.

In the United States, we use other terms. If bonds, we may call such debt "junk bonds." If stock, it may be referred to as a "bridge financing."

LIFFE
Pronounced: life.

See LONDON INTERNATIONAL FINANCIAL FUTURES EX-CHANGE.

LIFO
See LAST IN, FIRST OUT.

A LIFT
Term used to designate an upward movement in the price of a security because of buying pressure.

In the United States, the term is neutral and descriptive; for example, heavy buying by mutual funds gave a lift to the market.

In the United Kingdom, the term often suggests a form of manipulation in that the buyers are aggressive and are doing so without regard to the fundamentals of the company; for example, speculators are giving a lift to XYZ Company.

LIFTING A LEG
Expression used when an investor with a hedged investment removes one or the other part of the hedge. For example, a client with a long call and a short call (i.e., a call spread) makes a closing sale of the long call.

This leaves the client with a short call outstanding. The client has lifted a leg.

See also LEG.

LIFTING A SHORT
Term used by traders in commodities futures. Lifting a short describes the closing of a short position; that is, the obligation to deliver, by purchasing futures contracts for the same commodity in the same delivery month. On the records of the clearing house, the customer has a zero net position.

LIGHT BID/OFFER
Expression used by equity traders to indicate that their bid or offer is not equal to or better than the best prevailing bid or offer. The expression indicates institutional interest if and when the market moves up or down from present levels. Example: "I'm not buying, but I've got a couple of light bids if prices fall."

LILCO
Acronym and short name identifier for: Long Island Lighting Company, a large public utility whose shares are listed on the NYSE. LILCO also is used as the company's commercial logo.

LIMITED
1. In the United States, the term is used in conjunction with a partnership interest in an enterprise where the limited owners have no voting privileges and liabilities are limited to the money contributed to the enterprise.
2. In the United Kingdom, an official suffix (abbreviated Ltd.) of a corporation. The concept: Owners are limited in their obligations to the debt of the company. In recent years, the suffix plc (public liability company) has become common.
3. The name of a large retail ready-to-wear chain store with the NYSE symbol LTD. Official name: The Limited.

LIMITED ACCESS TO BOOKS AND RECORDS
Generally, the right of a shareholder to inspect certain records of a corporation.

Specifically, of companies registered with the SEC, the requirement that shareholders be given an annual report, regular quarterly announcements, plus—as required—interim reports of significant activities as and if they occur. In most cases, shareholders receive such interim reports through newspaper press releases.

LIMITED DISCRETION
Written authorization given by a client to a registered representative. The authorization permits the representative to close existing option positions and, within the last days prior to expiration, to exercise option positions without prior consultation or approval from the client.

LIMITED EXERCISE OPTION
Term coined by the CBOE to describe an option contract which may not be exercised prior to the fifth business day before the expiration of the contract. In this way, a limited exercise option is similar to European options for debt and equity securities.

At the time of writing, there are no limited exercise options traded.

LIMITED PARTNER
A member of a partnership who has no vote in the management of the partnership. Limited partners are also called "silent partners." Their potential loss is limited to their capital contribution, and usually they receive a fixed dollar return that is payable in full before the general partner shares in any profits.

LIMITED TAX BOND
A form of general obligation municipal bond used by cities and other local municipalities. The bond and its interest are paid from real estate taxed at a specified rate on the assessed valuation of property.

See also AD VALOREM and MILL.

LIMITED TRADING AUTHORIZATION
Brokerage account in which the client permits an account executive, through a written agreement with the brokerage firm, to make discretionary buy and sell transactions in the client's account. The authorization is limited in the sense that the account executive may sell and reinvest the proceeds of the sale but may not remove assets from the account.

Also called "discretionary account."

LIMIT ORDER
A type of buy or sell order used by some customers in the secondary market for securities. The customer establishes a limit price (i.e., a maximum buying price or a minimum selling price). Brokers will endeavor to get a better price for the customer if this is possible, but the broker may not violate the limit price set by the client.

LIMIT ORDER INFORMATION SYSTEM (LOIS)
An electronic communication system that reveals the specialists' books on participating stock exchanges. The system reveals the locale, quanti-

ties, and prices. The system provides competition and protects against disadvantageous executions if a better execution is available elsewhere.

LIMIT ORDER SYSTEM (LMT)
The Limit Order System is an integral part of the Designated Order Turnaround (DOT) system on the NYSE. Under the Limit Order System (LMT), limit orders in quantities up to 2,099 shares are stored and automatically executed if a contra order is available. Upon execution, the system generates a report back to the firm that entered the order.

LIMIT PRICE
A price qualifier set by the customer on his or her order to buy or sell. If it is a buy limit order, the customer requires that the purchase be made at or below the limit price. If it is a sell limit order, the customer requires that the sale be made at or above the limit price.

LINE OF CREDIT
Arrangement that enables a prospective borrower to obtain a maximum sum of money during a predetermined time period. For example, "The ABC Bank gave its client a $1 million line of credit for 6 months."
See also SPECIAL MISCELLANEOUS ACCOUNT.

LINE-OF-CREDIT REVERSE MORTGAGE
A real estate loan that uses the borrower's home as collateral. They are unlike IRMAs, however, in that there is generally no monthly payout; instead, under the line-of-credit reverse mortgage, money may be borrowed as needed for larger expenses. Under such a reverse mortgage, principal and interest are generally deferred until the death of the client or the sale of the residence.

LINKED TRANSACTIONS
See ADJUSTED TRADING.

LION
Acronym for Lehman Investment Opportunity Notes. This was a trademarked product marketed by Lehman Brothers Kuhn Loeb, Inc., now a subsidiary of American Express, known as Lehman Brothers.
LIONs are similar to TIGRs and CATS in that they represent ownership interest in future principal and interest payments of selected U.S. government securities.

LIQUID ASSETS
Cash and marketable securities are generally considered liquid assets. The expression is commonly used in the analysis of corporate financial

statements, but is also used of brokerage clients to determine the suitability of certain relatively illiquid investments for their portfolios. For example, " This investment is not suitable unless the client has $50,000 in other liquid assets."

LIQUIDATION
1. The process whereby securities or other assets are sold to produce cash.
2. The term also is used in the securities industry to describe an involuntary sale of securities in a client's account. For example, "When the client failed to meet the call, the broker met the call with a liquidation."

LIQUIDITY
1. The quality of an asset that permits it to be converted quickly into cash without a significant loss of value.
2. On an issue-by-issue basis, liquidity refers to the ability of the marketplace to absorb a reasonable amount of buying and selling without excessive price volatility.
See also MARKETABILITY.

LIQUIDITY DIVERSIFICATION
Technique used by portfolio managers whereby bond portfolios are diversified by maturities. This reduces interest-rate risk because the cash flow from frequently maturing securities can be reinvested at advantageous rates.

LIQUIDITY RATIO
An infrequently used ratio that compares cash and marketable securities owned by a company to its current liabilities. It is the most strict of the measurements of corporate liquidity.
See also ACID-TEST RATIO; CURRENT RATIO; QUICK ASSET RATIO.

LIQUID YIELD OPTION NOTES
See LYON.

LISBON STOCK EXCHANGE
One of the smallest and least active of European exchanges, this exchange is located in Lisbon, the capital of Portugal. Trading is from 9:30 A.M. until 1:00 P.M., Tuesdays through Fridays, with after-hour trading permitted. Settlement is scheduled for the third business day following the trade date.

LISTED OPTION

A class of put or call option that has been admitted to trading on a registered exchange. The decision to trade the class of option is made by the exchange.

The term *listed option* is popularly used; technically, it is an *exchange-traded option.*

LISTED STOCK

The stock of an issuer who has applied for and received the privilege of having the stock traded on a registered stock exchange. As a general rule, the exchange will delist the stock if it fails to maintain the continuing qualifications for listing.

LITIGATION

A lawsuit or legal proceeding involving at least two disputants. In general, the term *litigation* is limited to civil suits.

Because controversies between broker and customer generally involve entitlements to money or securities, the industry provides arbitration facilities to reduce the number of judicial cases that must be opened.

LITTLE BANG

Expression used to describe the legislation in the province of Ontario (Canada) whereby foreign securities dealers were permitted, starting on July 1, 1987, to register in Ontario and to begin to compete for business there. The term is modeled after the so-called "big bang," which originated in England in October 1986, and which deregulated securities brokers there.

LITTLE DRAGONS

Term used of four Asian nations (Singapore, Hong Kong, South Korea, and Taiwan) who, because of low labor costs, competitive production, and aggressive sales, are a threat to the "big dragon," Japan, on the western rim of the Pacific.

LIVE FREE MORTGAGE

Term used to identify a home loan made to lure buyers by offering a no-payment provision for the first few months in return for an obligation to refinance later at higher than market rates. Thus, the no-payment loan carries a very short life and, when used as collateral in a GNMA or FHLMC security, causes that pool of mortgages to prepay more rapidly than anticipated.

LIVING DEAD

An oxymoron used in two ways:

1. To describe a company on the brink of insolvency; that is, one that is barely operating on a day-to-day basis.
2. To describe a stock price that is not moving as expected. In effect, it is used by RRs as an alibi for a stock they recommended but that is moving sideways, or somewhat down, but not up.

LIVING TRUST

See INTER VIVOS TRUST.

LMM

See LEAD MARKETMAKER.

LMT

1. Abbreviation used on security orders to buy or sell that also set a maximum price (buy limit) or a minimum price (sell limit) at which a customer will accept an execution.
2. See LIMIT ORDER SYSTEM.

LOAD

Industry term for either the percentage sales charge (load) or the open-end investment company shares (load fund) if there is a sales charge when such shares are purchased.

See also NO LOAD.

LOAD SPREAD OPTION

Misnomer for annual sales charge allocation on some contractual mutual funds. It is not an option of the customer. Under this method, the total sales charge may not exceed 9% of the contract. However, during a contract's first four years, up to 20% of any year's contributions to the fund may be credited against the sales charge, if total charges in the first four years are not over 64% of one year's contributions by the planholder.

See also CONTRACTUAL PLAN.

LOAFS

A British tongue-in-cheek expression standing for "large open area floor spaces." In effect, the term is pejorative for the large spaces used by securities salesmen and traders in a typical brokerage office.

In the United States, with no pejorative meaning, the term used is *boardroom.*

LOAN CONSENT

The specific approval given by a customer to a broker/dealer whereby the broker/dealer may lend securities to itself or to customers to complete short sales. The loan consent is usually part of the margin agreement form but a separate customer signature is required.

Also called the "stock loan agreement" or the "loan consent agreement."

LOAN STOCKS

In the United Kingdom, where corporate equity is called "shares" and debt is often called "stock," this term is the equivalent of what we in the United States call "debentures." (See DEBENTURES for the British meaning of that term.)

In effect, loan stock is an asset secured only by the general credit of a corporation. In the event of a corporate liquidation, holders of loan stock will be paid off only after all secured creditors are paid, although loan stock owners take precedence over equity claimants.

LOAN VALUE

The maximum percentage credit, based on the current market value of an eligible security, that a broker may extend to a margin account customer if the customer (1) makes a commitment through an initial purchase or (2) deposits fully paid securities into a margin account. Regulation T of the Federal Reserve Board sets the loan value on listed equity and convertible securities and on some NASDAQ-traded securities. The exchanges or the brokers establish the loan value on other types of securities.

LOB

Partial acronym for an unsecured *lease obligation bond;* this is a modern term for a debenture whose proceeds are used to build and lease an operating plant for a public utility. If the lessee defaults on payments, the bondholders become general creditors (debenture holders) of that utility. They do not have a specific claim on the asset built with the proceeds of the loan.

LOBBY NOTE

Term associated with some borrowings by thrift institutions. It is incorrect to represent they are insured by federal regulators because these instruments are not covered by law. They are subordinated liabilities of those banks, not savings accounts. They often carry interest-rate payments significantly higher than these banks pay on their CDs.

LOBSTER TRAP

A defense mechanism used by a company that has convertible securities outstanding to prevent an unfriendly takeover. The mechanism prohibits conversion into common shares by any holder of the convertible if the holder owns, or would own, 10% or more of the voting shares.

This colorful analogy is derived from the design of real lobster traps: they catch and hold large lobsters, but they permit small lobsters to escape.

LOC

See LETTER OF CREDIT.

A LOCAL

Term associated with a futures exchange member who trades primarily for his or her own account and risk. The term has longstanding usage on the Chicago Board of Trade (CBT) and the Chicago Mercantile Exchange (MERC). A local, in effect, designates initiation of an "on-floor" transaction for the member, as opposed to initiation of "off-floor" transactions sent to the trading pits for execution from a member firm's offices.

LOCH

Acronym for London Option Clearing House. LOCH compares and settles option transactions made by members (or their customers) in the United Kingdom. It is similar in function to the OCC in that it grants and guarantees option contracts and collects margin to assure their validity.

LOCKED IN

Industry slang for an investor who is unwilling or unable to sell because a sale will actualize a paper gain or loss.

LOCKED IN TRADE

Term used of a transaction in a marketplace's automated system. The term is used both of exchange and NASDAQ trades in that both contra parties are automatically "captured," compared, and submitted for settlement. In such a system, the number of fails and mistaken trades approaches zero because there can be no comparison without both parties to the trade in the system.

LOCKED MARKET

A temporary situation in a highly competitive market signifying that the bid and offer prices are the same. Once the offsetting buys and sells are completed, the market will unlock.

LOCKUP

1. On the occasion of the preparation of a final competitive bid for an underwriting, the representatives of the syndicate are sequestered until the competitive bids are opened at the office of the issuer. In this way, the participants, except for the manager's agent, have no way of compromising the secrecy of the sealed bid.
2. A secret sales agreement between principal stockholders and someone intent on the acquisition of a company. This secret agreement often precedes the purchaser's tender offer to other public stockholders for the balance of that company's stock.

See also LOCKED IN and LOCKED MARKET.

LOIS

See LIMIT ORDER INFORMATION SYSTEM.

LOLLIPOP

Street slang for a sucker; that is, a customer who is willing to buy anything offered if it comes with a persuasive story. Needless to say, such persons are frequently duped and lose large amounts of investment funds.

LOLLIPOP TACTIC

A colorful slang expression used to describe a company's endeavor to thwart a hostile takeover. In this tactic, certain current shareholders are given the right to tender shares at a premium price—but only if an undesirable bidder acquires a predetermined number of the outstanding shares. Thus, the deal tastes good to everyone except the hostile suitor.

LOMBARD RATE

The German banking system's equivalent of the Federal Reserve's discount rate in the United States. It is the rate of interest the central bank of Germany charges other commercial banks when they borrow money collateralized by German government securities.

LONDONCLEAR

Written LondonClear, this is an automated clearing facility for CDs traded in the secondary market in London. LondonClear does not charge for the clearing service but does charge a custodial fee. LondonClear is affiliated with EuroClear, a service offered primarily for Euro-issues traded outside the United States.

LONDON FOX

Short name for the London Futures and Options Exchange. London Fox was established to complement activity on the London International Financial Futures Exchange (LIFFE) and specializes in the automated trading of coffee, cocoa, and raw sugar futures. Orders are entered directly into the computer and matched with contra orders; there is no trading pit nor open outcry.

LONDON INTERNATIONAL FINANCIAL FUTURES EXCHANGE
Acronym: LIFFE. A newly organized futures exchange in England that permits speculators, hedgers, and arbitrageurs to trade selected financial instruments. All of the instruments are sensitive to interest-rate change. Contracts currently are available for Eurodollars, pound sterling CDs, and long-term U.K. government issues.

LONDON STOCK EXCHANGE
See INTERNATIONAL STOCK EXCHANGE OF THE UNITED KINGDOM AND THE REPUBLIC OF IRELAND.

LONG AND WRONG
Traders slang to indicate ownership of a security that has declined in value. For debt instruments it means the trader guessed wrong on interest-rate direction; and, consequently, when rates increased, the value of fixed-rate obligations dropped. For equity holdings, the value dropped in response to supply and demand factors putting pressure on prices.

LONG BOND
1. An investor's position in a debt security: the security is owned and title can be transferred by sale or gift.
2. A debt security with a maturity date that is more than 10 years away. In this latter sense, the expression is generally used in the plural. For example, "The portfolio is almost entirely in long bonds."

LONG COUPON
1. A new issue of bonds or notes on which the first coupon payment will be greater than the usual six-month coupon period. For example, a bond dated April 1 with the first coupon to be paid on December 1. Normally, subsequent coupons will be at six-month intervals.
2. Interest-bearing bonds with maturities in excess of 10 years.

LONG HEDGE
Strategy used to lock in a future yield on fixed-income securities if a drop in interest rates is anticipated. Two strategies: (1) Buy a futures contract on the security. *Risk:* The investor can lose more than the good faith deposit on the purchase if interest rates rise dramatically. (2) Buy a call option on the security. *Risk:* The purchase of the call automatically

makes the investor's breakeven point the execution price plus the premium paid. Thus, the call may not be profitable unless a drop in interest rates is dramatic.

LONG LEG
This term identifies the position owned by a client who holds an offsetting position in a security. For example, a client puts on a call spread in a class of option. The long call is the long leg.

See also LEG.

LONG POSITION
Financial term signifying ownership, the right to transfer ownership, and financial risk if the asset (e.g., bond, stock, option, or other security or commodity) declines in value.

Term is also used of securities owned by a client that are in the possession of client's agent. For example, "The client's securities are long with his broker."

Long can also mean that a broker/dealer owns more stocks or bonds than she has contracted to deliver (e.g., a broker/dealer has a net long position in ABC).

LONG TERM
1. Noun: As defined by the Internal Revenue Service, a holding period for securities in excess of 12 months.
2. Adjective: Refers to bonds whose maturity is greater than 1 year.

LONG-TERM DEBT
1. A debt instrument with more than 10 years to maturity.
2. In financial statement analysis, long-term debt is variously used. It always means more than 1 year to maturity in balance sheet bookkeeping, but analysts may change their usage of long term to cover bonds of 5 or 7 years, or longer terms.

LONG-TERM GAIN
A profit on a capital transaction that is eligible for preferential tax treatment. On a purchase followed by a sale, a long-term gain can result if the asset was held more than 12 months.

Special rules apply if the asset was received through a gift or bequest.

LONG-TERM LOSS
A loss sustained on the sale of a capital asset that was held more than 12 months.

LOOK-BACK OPTION

A put or call privilege in commodities. It enables the holder to buy or sell, as the case may be, at the most advantageous price available during the life of the option. Example: The holder of a 60-day silver call could purchase silver at the lowest price available in the cash market during the 60-day period, even if silver is currently selling at a higher price. Such look-back options usually have premiums that double those that would be paid for a fixed-price option. Look-back options were originated by Mocatta Metals Corporation, a major participant in the precious metals market.

THE LOOK THROUGH RULE

Popular name for SEC Rule 11al-2, which restricts proprietary trading by members and member organizations. In effect, if an associated person of a member firm enters an order, the accepting broker must consider it; that is, "look through" the order, as though it had come from the member firm itself and part of the orders under restriction according to the rule.

LOR PRODUCT

Designation for Leland, O'Brien, Rubinstein, Inc., the creators of Portfolio Insurance and—most recently—SuperShares. Portfolio Insurance and SuperShares are investment techniques designed to appeal to portfolio managers and to enable them to participate in market trends. In practice, Portfolio Insurance causes great market volatility, while SuperShares do not.

See also PORTFOLIO INSURANCE and SUPERSHARES.

LOSS LEADER

Universally applied term that designates merchandise offered at a known loss to entice a buyer into a store in the hope that, while there, the buyer will also purchase other items on which there is a profit.

The use of "loss leaders" is not common in the financial community; but such "lures" are used in terms of "free checking" in exchange for relatively large constant bank deposits, or for lowered securities commissions in exchange for subscriptions to other products and services.

LOUSY LOUIE

Colloquial name used to identify Louisiana Land & Exploration Company, a concern engaged in oil, gas, and mining ventures. The name is derived from its NYSE ticker symbol: LLX.

LOX

Acronym for large order execution. A Chicago Mercantile Exchange proposed rule that would permit the off-floor assembly of purchase and sale orders in offsetting quantities. Thus, it would be possible to "cross" such orders on the floor. The cross would be by public outcry, thus brokers with orders could participate in the transaction. Basically, the procedure will be initiated to forestall manipulation and to permit institutional block-size crosses of hedging positions.

LS

Abbreviation for: last sale.
   See LAST SALE.

LTD

See LIMITED.

LTM

See LEVERAGE TRANSACTION MERCHANT.

LUFTHANSA SYNDICATION

Tongue-in-cheek term for investment bankers, acting as a team, who flew into Frankfurt, Germany, to launch a deutsche mark debt offering and immediately flew back to Britain. The concept: Their efforts in Germany were temporary, but their base of operations (and profits) were elsewhere.

LULLING LETTER

Street term for a brokerage firm's letter to a customer on the occasion of a recent investment that lost money. The letter from the firm's management tells the customer not to worry; the next product to come along will probably act better.

   The purpose is to placate the customer, to give the customer confidence, and—indirectly—to persuade the customer not to initiate litigation.

LUMP SUM

1. A form of mutual fund investing whereby the initial investment is the only investment (except for dividend reinvestments) made into the fund.
   Antonym: periodic investments, or dollar cost averaging.
2. The payment of a single premium to fund a life insurance policy or a fixed or variable annuity in perpetuity. Subsequent growth is based on the internal return of the policy or annuity.
3. A single payment made from a qualified pension and profit-sharing plan to a retiree or upon separation from the company or termination

of the plan. If the recipient is not yet 70½ years old, such lump-sum distributions may be invested in a rollover IRA to continue the tax shelter.

LUTIRO

Acronym for Life and Unit Trust Intermediaries Regulatory Organisation. LUTIRO is a trade organization in the United Kingdom that regulates insurance and unit trust (mutual fund) intermediaries in connection with their day-to-day activities in these products. LUTIRO competes with LAUTRO (q.v.) for the same constituency, although their oversight differs somewhat.

LYON

Acronym for Liquid Yield Option Note(s). A Merrill Lynch product that combines the capital needs of its investment banking client with the investment needs of its retail customers. LYONs are callable zero-coupon securities with a put option that becomes operative in the third year after issuance. The call price reflects a fixed rate of interest; thus, the call price increases over time. The same is true of the put feature.

In some cases, the debt security is convertible into common stock, but at an increasing conversion ratio to reflect the accrued interest on the zero-coupon bonds.

M

M
Thirteenth letter of the alphabet, used:
1. Following a number, M stands for 1,000 times the number; for example, 10M=10,000.
2. On the pink sheets, published daily by the National Quotation Bureau, M before the name of a stock signifies that the security is eligible for margin purchases.
3. In parentheses, (M) is often used to designate that a security is traded on the Midwest Stock Exchange.
4. Followed by a number, M stands for the nation's money supply as variously measured by the Federal Reserve. For example, M1, M1A, M2, and so on.
5. As a doubled uppercase, MM, to stand for one million. More commonly abbreviated MYN.
6. As a triple uppercase, MMM, to stand for Minnesota Mining, a large manufacturer of adhesives, building products, and so on. MMM is one of the 30 stocks that comprises the Dow Jones Industrial Average.

M1

Also: M-1. Used as an identifier of the basic component of the money supply: currency in circulation plus bank demand deposits. Because this definition lacks some precision, M-1a and M-1b (defined below) were invented in 1980.

In practice, economists regroup M-1a and M-1b back into M-1 as the kind of money supply that most immediately affects the U.S. economy.

M1a

Also: M-1a. A current gauge of the money supply that combines currency and demand deposits but excludes U.S. government, domestic, and foreign bank proprietary deposits, checks in the Federal Reserve's float, and currency held in bank vaults. Thus, it is a more stringent definition of money and demand deposits.

M1b

Also: M-1b. A broader gauge of the money supply than M-1a. It adds to M-1a the dollar amounts in checking-like deposits, such as NOW and Super-NOW accounts, at savings banks and other thrift institutions.

M2

Also: M-2. A broader definition of the money supply in that it includes all monies in M-1a and M-1b and adds overnight repurchase agreements, money market mutual fund shares, savings and small time deposits at commercial banks and thrift institutions.

M3

Also: M-3. A continued expansion of the definition of the money supply. M3 is M2 plus large time deposits ($100,000 and over) and term repurchase agreements at commercial banks and thrift institutions.

M4

Also: M-4. The last measurement of the money supply, M4 is M3 plus other liquid assets, such as U.S. savings bonds, commercial paper, and bankers' acceptances.

As a general rule, newspaper reports of the money supply do not include M4, although it is given in the Federal Reserve's reports, because it is not part of the target area expansion set by the Federal Reserve.

MA BELL

Used by investors and traders alike to designate American Telephone & Telegraph, the world's largest communication network.

The term is endearing and designates the long-term image of the company in its advertising of maternalism and concern for others in the use of the telephone to "reach out and touch someone."

MAC
See MUNICIPAL ASSISTANCE CORPORATION FOR THE CITY OF NEW YORK.

MACARONI DEFENSE
A jocular term for a corporate defense strategy designed to thwart a hostile takeover. It calls for a threatened company to issue bonds that expand to a mandatory higher redemption value when a takeover is proposed by a raider. The expanding redemption value—much like the expansion of cooking macaroni—should discourage an unfriendly merger proposal.

MACROECONOMIST
Academic term for someone who studies, measures, and predicts the flows of funds, goods, and services on a world or national scale. In this sense, a macroeconomist endeavors to measure the economic events that influence financial, political, and social decisions and to quantify growth, recession, surplus, and trends in the big economic picture.

Antonym: microeconomics (also called "fundamental analysis"), which endeavors to measure financial trends in individual corporations.

MACRS
Acronym for Modified Accelerated Cost Recovery System. MACRS (which followed ACRS) was initiated by the Economic Recovery Tax Act of 1981 (ERTA) and modified by the Tax Reform Act of 1986 (TRA).

These acts divide assets into two categories: real and personal. Real assets must use straight-line depreciation. Personal assets are divided into classes (3-, 5-, 7-, 10-, 15-, and 20-year property) and may use accelerated depreciation.

Form 4562 is used for the filing of income tax reports on the depreciation of such properties. Tax advice is needed.

MAD BOMBERS
So-called nickname given to foreign firms in Japan engaged in program trading there. The term originated in February 1990 when firms engaged in index arbitrage between the futures and stock markets in Japan sold baskets of stocks on the Tokyo Stock Exchange, precipitating substantial declines in the Nikkei stock average.

MAD DOG

Nickname for the common shares of McDonnell Douglas Corporation, a large defense industry contractor. The nickname is derived from its NYSE ticker symbol: MD.

MAE WEST SPREAD

Named after the popular life preserver used by pilots, the Mae West spread can return profits during periods of market stagnation. The spread combines a short straddle and a long strangle.

The strategy involves a credit in the account that results from a short, at the money, straddle. There is a small debit from the long strangle. The end result is, in most cases, a profit on the expiration of the positions.

See also STRANGLE.

MAGIC-T THEORY

This is a market timing technique and philosophy originated by a technical analyst named Terry Laundry.

Simplistically, this theory holds that the market moves up and down for the same time period—only the amount of the upward or downward movement differs. Moreover, the theory holds that there are two highs and lows for each issue each day. Thus, the way to profit is to buy when the volume for the low declines and to sell when the volume for the high declines.

MAINTENANCE CALL

A notice to a margin account customer sent by the carrying broker. The notice states that the client's equity is insufficient to meet industry or brokerage rules. The call is for a specific amount of money and must be met promptly by a deposit of funds or securities. If the call is not met, the broker will liquidate sufficient securities in the account to remove the maintenance deficiency.

Also called "maintenance margin call."

MAINTENANCE REQUIREMENT

1. As an absolute dollar amount, industry rules require that a client's equity be $2,000 or more in a margin account with a debit balance.
2. As a relative dollar amount, industry rules require that a client's equity be a stated percentage of long or short market values. Most brokerage firms require that the client's equity be 30% on listed stocks, convertibles, and corporate bonds held in margin accounts. There are special maintenance requirements on other securities.

MAJOR-BRACKET UNDERWRITER

An investment banking organization that consistently subscribes to the largest portion of security distributions and whose name, therefore, appears near the top of tombstone advertisements and on the front page of the prospectus.

Associated terms for underwriters who are not major-bracket underwriters: *mezzanine, second tier, third tier.*

MAJORITY CONTROL

Ownership by a person, or a group of persons working in concert, of 50% or more of the voting stocks of a corporation constitutes majority control.

In practice, effective control often can be exercised by persons with less than 50% of the voting stock.

MAJOR LEAGUE BUYER/SELLER

A picturesque term used to describe a buyer or seller of large amounts of publicly traded stock. For example, a person who normally buys blocks in the 6–7 digit quantity is a major league buyer. The same concept applies to large sellers.

MAKE A MARKET

A broker/dealer who habitually maintains competitive quotations for one or more specific issues, and who stands ready to buy and sell at those stated prices.

Noun: marketmaker.

MAKE-UPS

English slang for a "third-party" settlement. "Make-ups" are frequently used in the tradings of gilts in the United Kingdom if the trade occurs in the same account period. For example, a dealer buys gilts from another dealer and, within the same settlement period, sells them to a third dealer. The buying dealer requests that the gilts be delivered to the third dealer who, in turn, either remits or collects the cost differential from the original buyer.

MALONEY ACT

Section 15.A of the Securities Exchange Act of 1934. The amendment, sponsored by the late Senator Maloney, permits the registration of self-policing associations of securities dealers.

The National Association of Securities Dealers (NASD) is registered with the SEC under this provision of the 1934 Act.

Also called the "Maloney Amendment."

MANAGEMENT BUY-IN
See MBI.

MANAGEMENT BUY-OUT
See MBO.

MANAGEMENT COMPANY
An investment company that provides day-to-day management of a portfolio of securities and that permits the investment manager to sell the portfolio securities and reinvest the proceeds in other securities.

Management companies may be either closed or open-end. This latter form, popularly called a "mutual fund," is by far the most popular form of investment company.

MANAGEMENT GROUP
Official title for the organization that serves as investment advisor of an investment company. The management group may, in addition to its advisory service, provide the investment company with legal, clerical, public relations, and portfolio execution services.

Often, the management group may advise many funds with differing investment objectives. In this case, such funds may be in the "same family of funds" and may be exchangeable for one another without an additional sales charge.

MANAGING UNDERWRITER
The investment banker who represents one or more similar organizations in its dealings with an issuer of securities. As managing underwriter, this investment banker works with the issuer, organizes the syndicate, arranges for a selling group, maintains the syndicate books, and stabilizes the security's price during the distribution. In return for these services, the managing underwriter receives an extra financial benefit from the gross profit of the other underwriters.

M&A
Acronym for mergers and acquisitions. A special unit within a broker/dealer's corporate finance department. This special unit attempts to find business enterprises suited for purchase by, or amalgamation with, its investment banking clients. M&A also advises companies that are the subject of a takeover attempt.

MANILA STOCK EXCHANGE
The largest of the stock exchanges in the Philippines. Activity is relatively inactive which, in turn, is a manifestation of the political unrest there.

The exchange is open on weekdays from 9:30 A.M. until 12:10 P.M. Settlement is scheduled for cash within five business days.

MANIPULATION
The act of depressing or raising securities prices artificially so that prices do not represent true value. This is done by creating an appearance of active buying or selling, either alone or in concert with others. Manipulation violates federal securities laws and is subject to criminal and civil penalties.

MANNY HANNY
An endearing term for the Manufacturers Hanover Trust Company, a large commercial bank headquartered in New York and a member of the Federal Reserve Banking System.

MANUAL EXEMPTION
This is a privilege that enables broker/dealers to offer unlisted securities to persons domiciled in a state without the obligation of an annual re-registration of those securities. This exemption is permitted because registration is expensive, the paperwork is extensive, and there is no evidence that such constant registration will prevent "penny stock" scams in any event.

This is not an exemption from original registration; just from the onus of re-registration.

MAPLELEAF SERIES
Nickname for a product created and offered exclusively to non-U.S. customers of Merrill Lynch Capital Markets, Inc. It is a Euro-Canadian warrant to purchase a specific amount of a specific issue of Canadian government bonds. Example: Series I permits the holder to buy the Government of Canada $10\frac{1}{4}$% bonds due in 2004 at a price of Can$ $87\frac{1}{2}$.

MAPS
Acronym for market auction preferred stock. A variable-rate preferred issue whose dividend rate is reset every 49 days by a Dutch auction. Holders who are dissatisfied with the new rate can redeem their shares at face value.

MAPS are immediately callable by the issuer if the dividend rate ever exceeds the CD equivalent rate of 60-day AA-rated commercial paper.

See also DUTCH AUCTION.

MARGIN

1. The client's equity in a securities account that has an outstanding loan of money (a long margin account) or a loan of securities (a short margin account).
2. The client's good-faith deposit when the client buys or sells a futures contract. In this sense, margin ensures performance at the prescribed future time.

Substantial additional margin can be required on a daily basis if the futures contract goes against the purchaser or seller.

MARGIN ACCOUNT

A brokerage account in which a client may maintain a creditor/debtor relationship with the broker. The client may owe money loaned for the purchase of securities, or securities loaned for sales made short. Regulation T of the Federal Reserve System regulates the conduct of margin accounts, although industry rules may further limit the maintenance of credit in such accounts.

MARGIN AGREEMENT

A document signed by a margin account customer that details the conduct of accounts in which the broker loans money or stock to a customer.

Commonly called the "customer agreement" or the "hypothecation agreement."

See also HYPOTHECATION AGREEMENT.

MARGIN CALL

A broker's notice to a customer following a purchase or a short sale for funds sufficient to satisfy the initial margin requirements of Regulation T. The dollar amount of the margin call will be the requirement on the activity, as specified by Regulation T, minus any available funds in the account.

Technically, a margin call may result from an activity in either a margin or a cash account.

MARGIN DEPARTMENT

Common name for the group within a broker/dealer's operations area that monitors client accounts so there is a record of client holdings, short sales, debits and credits, and the compliance of such accounts with Reg-T, exchange, and member-firm requirements for the extension or maintenance of credit.

Also called the "credit department" or the "cash-margin department."

MARGIN OF PROFIT
In financial statement analysis, margin of profit answers this question: How much of the income received from a sales dollar remains after the cost of goods sold (and administrative expenses, if these are not originally included) are subtracted from income from sales? For example, if sales income is $100 and cost of goods sold is $80, the margin of profit is $20, or 20% of sales.

See also OPERATING RATIO.

MARGIN REQUIREMENT
Percentage of the purchase price or of the proceeds of a short sale that a client must account for if he puts himself—and thus his broker—at risk by a commitment. Although Regulation T determines this percentage requirement if a client purchases or sells short listed securities, industry rules often specify higher margin requirements.

MARGIN SECURITY
Although the technical definition is more extensive, a margin security is one that may be purchased or sold short in a margin account and that permits the client to maintain a debtor/creditor relationship with his or her broker.

MARGIN STOCK
As used in Federal Reserve regulations, this term applies to those issues for which the Federal Reserve allows banks, broker/dealers, and other registered lenders to extend a specified percentage of credit to purchase, carry, or trade in them.

MARGIN/SUBSTITUTION
See SUBSTITUTION.

MARITAL DEDUCTION
Also: unlimited marital deduction. Under present tax laws, a decedent may leave to a spouse all, or any part, of an estate without the payment of estate taxes.

This unlimited marital deduction does not avoid estate taxes, it simply postpones them until the death of the surviving spouse. As a result, proper estate planning for estates in excess of $600,000 requires legal advice.

MARKDOWN
1. The difference between a dealer's bid and asked price. It is the dealer's spread looked at from the viewpoint of a seller.

2. A sudden drop in a dealer's quote to reflect a drop in market values. Investors generally call this a "sale price."
3. A reevaluation of the syndicate price by a municipal bond account if the market is unreceptive.

MARKETABILITY
Although marketability is synonymous with liquidity on the sell side, on the buy side the term implies that buyers can purchase reasonable amounts of a security without severely raising its market price. Thus, a security has good marketability if it can be easily resold or readily purchased in an active secondary market.

MARKETABLE LIMIT ORDER
An instruction to buy or sell that has a maximum (buy) or minimum (sell) price established by the customer. However, because of present market conditions, the customer's limit prices better the current market; hence, the order can be executed immediately. This concept is of particular importance in the opening or reopening of the market.

MARKET AUCTION PREFERRED STOCK
See MAPS.

MARKET AVERAGE
An indicator of general stock price movements based on the sum of the market values for a selected sample of stocks, divided either by the number of stocks or by a divisor adjusted for stock splits or other changes in capitalization. The Dow Jones Industrial, Transportation, and Utility averages are classic examples of market averages.

MARKET BASKET
See BASKET TRADING.

MARKET BREAK
1. Any major decline in an index of selected common stocks. For example, "Bad inflationary figures and persistent high interest rates caused a severe market break today."
2. In the parlance of the SEC, the term is almost exclusively used of the October 19, 1987, 508-point drop in the Dow Jones Industrial Average—the largest one-day drop to date in the history of the NYSE.

MARKET DISRUPTION
A euphemism used by the SEC to describe stock market events of October 13, 1989. When UAL pilots were unable to assemble financing for a proposed buyout, the DJIA dropped 191 points. It was, at that time, the second worst one-day decline in NYSE history. Because the DJIA quickly made up for the decline, the phenomenon is called a "disruption," rather than a "break."

MARKET EYE
A new financial information service sponsored by the International Stock Exchange of London that is designed to augment the SEAQ service but at a lower cost. Market Eye is transmitted by BBC and is received through a special desk top system. Market Eye provides current market information plus statistical data on U.K. equities, gilts, and international issues traded in London.

MARKET-IF-TOUCHED ORDER
Acronym: MIT. An instruction permitted only on some exchanges. Buy MIT orders are entered below the market and are to be executed at the market if the issue trades at or below the established price. Sell MIT orders are to be executed at the market if the issue trades at or above the established price. Thus, in terms of market dynamics, MIT orders are exactly the opposite of buy and sell stop orders.

MIT orders are used extensively in commodity futures trading.

MARKET INDEX
Market averages and indices are general measurements of market movement.

Averages emphasize price movement.

Indices, because they include weighting of prices in terms of outstanding shares, emphasize changes in value for outstanding shares.

In practice, the marketplace assesses all of the factors, and, as a result, there is substantial similarity between price and value trends.

MARKET INDEX OPTION ESCROW RECEIPT
See MIOER.

MARKETING OF INVESTMENTS BOARD
See MIB.

MARKET JITTERS
A term used by analysts to describe a period of selling that is the result of investor reaction to economic news. This news may be bad, or not as good as expected. During this period, market prices will tend to trend

downward. Typically, as investors become fearful—hence the term *jitters*—they will tend to sell until the news becomes better. The term does not endeavor to judge the news itself, but rather the resulting state of general fear that affects market participants.

MARKET LETTER

A form of sales literature issued by a broker/dealer for distribution to customers. It centers on economic, political, or supply/demand factors that may affect securities prices. For example, "If money is in short supply and investors are bearish, do not expect your security to go up." Market letter must be approved by a designated person within the issuing firm, must be retained in the records of the firm, and must conform to the general norms for all sales literature.

MARKETMAKER

A dealer who is habitually willing to buy or sell a round lot of a security at his stated bid or offer.

MARKET MULTIPLE

The multiple is another name for the *price-earnings ratio*. The comparison of the multiple for an individual security with the multiple for a group of stocks;—for example, the S&P Index—is called the "market multiple." The market multiple will give an indication whether a stock is overpriced or underpriced. As a general rule, such market multiples are better indicators if the comparison is made between one company and other companies in the same industry. Example: A company selling at a multiple of 9 while other companies in the same industry are selling at 12 may be an indication that the first company is undervalued.

MARKET-ON-CLOSE ORDER

Acronym: MOC. An instruction given to a stock exchange floor broker to buy or sell at the best available price during the 30-second period that designates the close of trading. The customer has no assurance that the order will be executed or, if executed, that the price will be the final trading price of the day.

MARKET ORDER

If one starts with the concept that the market for a security is the highest bid and the lowest offer, a market order is an order to buy or sell a specific number of shares at the best available price once the order is received in the marketplace.

See also GOOD TILL CANCELLED ORDER, LIMIT ORDER; STOP ORDER.

MARKET ORDER SYSTEM OF TRADING
See MOST.

MARKET OUT CLAUSE
A feature found in most underwriting agreements. Under this market out feature, the investment banker (underwriter) can terminate its firm commitment to the issuer before the formal closing of the contract if certain material events occur that impair the investment quality of the securities about to be offered.

MARKET OVERSIGHT SURVEILLANCE SYSTEM
Acronym: MOSS. A computerized market monitoring system, operated by the SEC, which incorporates the monitoring systems of the self-regulatory organizations into a single database. Purpose: to facilitate analysis of unusual market activity in a security or group of securities that could indicate manipulation, insider leaks, and the like.

MARKET PERFORMANCE COMMITTEE
Acronym: MPC. This is a NYSE group of members and allied members who continuously monitor the marketmaking activities of specialists. The group evaluates each specialist unit in terms of trading, price differentials, and liquidity of the market for each stock. MPC has authority to allocate newly listed stocks (or reallocate already listed issues) among the specialist units as they consider this or that unit capable of doing a better job in the public interest.

MARKET PRICE
For exchange-traded securities, the last reported sale price.

In the over-the-counter market, a consensus of marketmaker quotations can be used.

If a rarely traded security is involved, expecially for the evaluation of an estate on the day of death, the opinion of analysts and traders in the same or similar securities is often used.

MARKET RAID
See PREMIUM RAID.

MARKETS AND TRADING COMMISSION (MTC)
A proposed U.S. government agency designed to replace both the Securities and Exchange Commission (SEC) and the Commodities Futures Trading Commission (CFTC). If enacted into law this new agency would have jurisdiction over both securities and commodities contract market-

places in the United States. Headed by a 5-person commission, appointed by the President (with consent of the Senate), they would dictate policy and oversee implementation in all marketplaces, both physical and capital-oriented.

MARKET SWEEP

A mergers and acquisitions term used in this context: When a tender offer is terminated, the buyer usually has a relatively large portion of the company. At this time, it makes a second offer to institutions at a price that is slightly above the tender price. This moves the institutions to give up their shares and, before the market can react to the end of the tender, the buyer has effective control of the company.

MARKET TONE

A market is said to have good market tone if dealers and marketmakers are willing to trade actively on narrow spreads between bid and asked prices.

MARKET VALUE

See CURRENT MARKET VALUE.

MARKING

A manipulative action by a trader or investor involving the execution of an option contract at the close that does not represent the fair value of the contract and that results in a net improved equity position in the client's account.

A MARKING NAME

U.K. term for a certificate registered in the name of a bank, broker/dealer, or a nominee other than the beneficial owner.

In the United States, the similar form of registration is called "nominee name" or "Street name" registration.

The term is not used of "book-entry" registration.

MARK TO THE MARKET

A request by a party to an unsettled contract who has become unsecured because of a change in the market value of the underlying instrument.

The most common marks are:

1. A request for more margin if a stock sold short goes up in value.
2. A request for more margin if a short call that is uncovered, or a short put that is uncovered, goes against the writer.
3. A when-issued security declines in value before settlement date.

MARKUP

1. The dollar difference between the bid and asked price for a security. Also called the "spread." In this sense, markup is the dealer's potential profit if he can consistently buy and resell at his quoted prices.
2. *Markup* is a term used if there is a sudden rise in prices and a dealer or an underwriter of municipal securities increases the asked price to reflect this increased demand for the security.

MARRIAGE PENALTY

The term is used of a quirk in the U.S. tax code whereby married persons who file jointly actually pay more in taxes than they would if they were unmarried and were to file as individuals.

There is no marriage penalty on gift and estate taxes, only on income taxes in certain circumstances.

MARRIED PUT

Expression used if a client buys a security and, on the same day, buys a put and elects to hedge the stock with the put. If this election is made, the put premium, if the put expires, is not a capital loss; instead, the premium paid for the married put is added to the purchase price of the underlying stock to get the client's basis for the stock. Tax advice is needed for the method needed to marry the stock and the long put.

MARUYU

Term used to describe the Japanese system to encourage savings. Under this system, 80% of the interest paid on deposits is exempt from taxation.

The system began over 100 years ago and centered on accounts with the Japanese Post Office Savings Bank. This central account, in terms of deposits, is about three times as large as the next largest commercial bank in the world. Deposits in other savings banks are also subject to the tax exemption.

MARXISM

A form of economic theory that advocates the collective; that is, public ownership of the means of production. It is similar to Communism, although Communism embraces both the concept of public ownership of the means of production and adds the public planning of production changes and a centralized government (praesidium) to oversee these changes.

The events of late 1989 in Eastern Europe have shown that Marxism is no longer viable in these countries. Whether or not the centralization of political and planning power will also change remains to be seen.

MAS
Acronym for Monetary Authority of Singapore. MAS is a governmental agency that is responsible for the supervision and regulation of the financial industry in Singapore. Originally centered on the regulation of banking, MAS in 1986 also took over the regulation of the securities industry.

MASTER LIMITED PARTNERSHIP
See MLP.

MASTER OF BUSINESS ADMINISTRATION
Common abbreviation: MBA. An intermediate academic recognition between that of BBA (bachelor of business administration) and DBA (doctor of business administration). Generally, MBA candidates must choose between an emphasis in finance, management, or marketing.

In the mid-70s through the 80s, either an MBA or a JD degree was considered a prerequisite to a finance position with most broker/dealers.

In many schools, candidates may also choose to work on a MPA (master of public administration) if they wish to follow a finance career in city or state government.

MAT
Abbreviation often used for "maturity"; that is, the date the principal amount of a debt security must be repaid to creditors.

Also: Mat and M/D or MD.

MATCHED AND LOST
Report sent back from an exchange floor if a client's market order is not executed at the price reported on the tape. Although exchange regulations give priority to the first bidder at a price, the same rules give precedence to other bidders with large orders once the first bidder is filled. It is possible, therefore, for a buyer or seller who misses the first transaction, because of time priority, to miss subsequent transactions at that price because of order size.

MATCHED BOOK
Broker/dealer term that describes an equal borrowing and loan situation. The broker/dealer can make a profit if the borrowings are made at one rate of interest and the loans at a higher rate. Repurchase agreements (repos) and reverse repurchase agreements are used to achieve a matched book and thus finance the dealer's security inventory.

MATCHED ORDERS
Purchases and sales of the same security by the same beneficial owner at the same time and price. The purpose is to give the impression of extensive trading in the security. Matched orders, which are usually made through different brokers, are violations of the Securities Exchange Act of 1934.

MATCHED SALE-PURCHASE TRANSACTIONS
Used by the Federal Open Market Committee to fine-tune member bank reserves and their ability to extend credit. The procedure involves the sale of government securities and a contingent provision to repurchase the securities at the same price in the future. The Federal Reserve pays interest for the money thus acquired at competitive rates.

TO MATCH FUND
Used as a verb: the act of borrowing money with a repayment date that is the same as the date on which the same amount of money will be due to you from a different borrower. Example: "$100,000 is due to me on April 23. If I borrow $100,000 that also must be repaid on April 23, I can be said to match fund."

Banks, through the sale of CDs, and broker/dealers, through repurchase agreements, match fund extensively. It is quite profitable if the interest rates favor the person who is match-funding.

MATIF
Acronym for Marche a Terme d'Instruments Financieres. MATIF is a futures exchange in Paris where contracts for 7–10 year French government bonds with a nominal 10% coupon are traded. Trades are made in French francs. In the late 1980s, as part of deregulation, foreign investors were permitted to trade these contracts for hedging, speculation, or arbitrage.

MATIF is a competitor in the area of government securities futures with LIFFE (London International Financial Futures Exchange).

MATRIX TRADING
Traditionally there are yield spread differences between fixed-income securities of the same class with different ratings, or between fixed-income securities of different classes. When these spreads diverge from traditional ranges, astute traders can profit by buying and selling the right securities if the ranges subsequently return to traditional patterns.

Matrix trading is a form of bond swapping.

MATURE LIQUID CONTRACT

As defined by the Chicago Merchantile Exchange (CME), this is a futures instrument that has traded at least 10,000 contracts per day for six consecutive months. In these instruments dual trading by members is prohibited! That is, on the same day, members cannot act as principal (for themselves) and as agent (for customers) in those futures contracts. A similar ban on S&P 500 Index futures has been in effect since 1987.

MATURITY DATE

The specified day on which the issuer of a debt security is obligated to repay the principal amount, or face value, of a security. It is rare for an equity security to have a maturity date, although dual-purpose mutual funds assign a maturity date for income shares.

Also called "maturity."

MAX

Acronym for Midwest Stock Exchange Automated Execution System. This is an electronic linkage between the Midwest exchange and the Intermarket Trading System (ITS).

MAX permits the MSE to accept and automatically execute up to 1,099 shares of any dually listed issue at a price that equals the best price represented in the ITS system.

MAXIMUM SLIPPAGE

A term used of a corporation that is having great difficulty in preserving its capital. The term, therefore, is an extension of the expression *slippage*—which may occur to any corporation.

Despite the inclusion of the expression *maximum,* maximum slippage does not yet mean that no one will lend it further capital; in effect, the company is not moribund.

MAY DAY

1. Internationally used distress call.
2. Used in the United States to describe May 1, 1975, the day the SEC required that all securities commissions become unregulated and subject to negotiation.

In practice, such negotiation is used extensively in institutional trading and with very large retail accounts. Most retail trades are subject to a prestated "statement of charges" that apply equally to almost all retail trades.

May Day—or its equivalent—has slowly spread to almost all countries with active securities trading.

MBA

1. Initials used to designate the academic achievement of master of business administration (q.v.).
2. Acronym for merchant banking acquisition (q.v.).

MBCS

Acronym for Municipal Bond Comparison System. MBCS is sponsored by the NASD through the National Securities Clearing Corporation (NSCC).

MBCS will accept daily municipal trade data from Municipal Securities Rulemaking Board (MSRB) members and will clear these transactions by (1) gaining contra party acceptance of the trade terms and (2) facilitating settlement by book entry debits and credits where this is possible.

MBEARS

A trademarked acronym originated by Morgan Stanley & Co. for Municipal Bond Exempt Accrual Receipts. MbearS are similar to Salomon Brothers' M-CATS in that they represent investment interest in municipal securities stripped of their interest payments. MbearS are collateralized by pre-refunded municipals. The stripped interest coupons are then offered in registered format. Buyers get tax-free interest on an annual basis.

MBI

Acronym for management buy-in. MBI is the English equivalent of a venture capital investment.

Under an MBI, a group representing capital contributors purchases stock (or even control) in a relatively new enterprise and expresses confidence in present management by retaining it to run the business. The purchase may be of newly issued stock (or even a repurchase from dissatisfied stockholders).

As a general rule, venture capital contributors buy a combination of a marketable idea *and* management; thus, it is uncommon to replace management in these circumstances.

MBIA

See also MUNICIPAL BOND INSURANCE ASSOCIATION.

MBO

Acronym for management buyout. The term describes the purchase of a company from existing stockholders by current management. The buyout, if it involves extensive borrowing, is also called a "leveraged buyout" (LBO). LBO is more popularly used in the United States, with MBO used more frequently in Europe.

Do not confuse with the infusion of new capital from a venture capital firm; this is called a "buy-in," not a buyout.

MBS

Acronym for mortgage-backed security. The concept of an MBS centers on the pooling of mortgages and their resale in the form of a single security to new owners. Generally, the mortgage originator retains an agency relationship to the pool and processes the mortgage payments but has no principal risk. Principal risk is assumed by the purchaser of the pass-through securities. In many cases, principal repayment and the prompt payment of interest may be guaranteed by a third party.

See also GINNIE MAE MODIFIED PASS-THROUGH.

MBS differ from CMO (collateralized mortgage obligations) in that the mortgage originator in a CMO retains ownership but uses them as collateral for additional debt securities.

MBSCC

Acronym for Mortgage Bond Securities Clearing Corporation. This is an industry-sponsored entity that facilitates ownership transfer between participants in the various mortgage-backed securities and pass-throughs. MBSCC is patterned after the Depository Trust Company (DTC), in that it permits trade comparisons and the transfer of monies and securities by book entry debits and credits.

M-CATS

Salomon Brothers acronym for: Municipal Certificates of Accrual on Tax-Exempted Securities. M-CATS represented an investment interest in the tax-exempt coupons stripped from pre-refunded municipal bonds. M-CATS were sold in two kinds: coupon M-CATS that provided tax-exempt income; and principal M-CATS that provided capital gains on the discounted principal amounts.

MCC

See MORTGAGE CREDIT CERTIFICATES.

McFADDEN ACT

Federal law, passed in 1927, that gave to the states the authority to regulate commercial banks within their borders. The effect of this law was to restrict—and, in some cases, to prohibit—branch banking within those states.

MCS
See Muni-Comparison System.

MDS
Acronym for Market Data System. MDS is a communications device that automatically captures and continuously displays in summary form the trade and volume statistics generated by activities on the NYSE's trading floors.

MEATBALL
Colorful nickname used by traders and salespersons to identify the common stock of Wilson & Co., a meatpacker and a distributor of meat specialties. The nickname is derived from the slang term used to describe one of its products.

MEDIUM-TERM BOND
The expression is practical rather than legal. Bonds, or notes, with maturities from 2 to 10 years in the future are usually called "medium-term" or "intermediate-term bonds."

If a medium- or intermediate-term bond is called a "note," it usually implies that the security is not callable by the issuer.

MELLO-ROOS FINANCING
Mello and Roos were two California politicians. They sponsored 1982 legislation to foster the development of real estate based on the promise of tax revenues. Although the original bill was intended to foster rural development, nothing in the bill prevents its use to foster urban development, also.

MEMBER CORPORATION
A term used to signify that a broker/dealer organization has purchased a seat on a stock exchange in the name of a corporate entity.

MEMBER TAKEDOWN
Term means that a syndicate member will buy bonds from the account at the takedown or member's discount price and sell them to the customer at the public offering price.

The term is used of retail sales of primary municipal offerings. Member takedown sales have the lowest priority when subject orders are directed to the syndicate manager. An underwriting spread on municipal offerings is divided into the manager's fee and the takedown, which includes additional takedown and the concession.

Often written with a hyphen between member and takedown.
See also DESIGNATED NET; GROUP NET ORDER; TAKE DOWN.

MEMORANDUM OF UNDERSTANDING (MOU)
The term is used to designate an agreement between the SEC and the securities regulators of a foreign country regarding mutual regulatory interests.

At present, only two such MOUs are in effect:
1. With the United Kingdom's SIB that enables U.S. broker/dealers to work in the United Kingdom without regard to that country's unique net capital rules.
2. With Brazil's CVM pledging cooperation in cases involving insider trading, regulatory disclosure, financial qualifications, and some cases of manipulation and securities fraud.

MEMPHIS BOND DADDIES
See BOND DADDIES.

MERC
Popular jargon identifier of the Chicago Mercantile Exchange.

MERCATO RISTRETTO
This is the Italian name for the Unlisted Securities Market (USM), and a common identifier of small companies whose shares are traded (alongside the larger companies traded) on the Rome, Milan, Turin, Genoa, Florence, and Naples stock exchanges. Thus, these shares are not technically *unlisted;* but they have requirements that are substantially below those for full listing, are more speculative, and have greater financial risk.

From the Italian: restricted market.

MERCHANT BANK
A British term for the rough equivalent of commercial bank in the United States: A bank that takes demand and time deposits. There is, however, a difference: Merchant banks in England may underwrite new issues of corporate securities. The underwriting of corporate securities is not permitted under the banking laws of the United States.

MERCHANT BANKING ACQUISITION (MBA)
A corporate finance term originated by the First Boston Corporation.

The term embraces a "bridge loan" by an investment bank to a client that enables that client to acquire another company. Later, the loan will be repaid with interest when the client corporation does a long-term financing.

The MBA can be highly profitable for the merchant bank; it achieves an advisory fee, interest on the bridge loan, and usually a profit on the underwriting of the permanent financing.

MERGER
Popular name for the union of two corporations. Merger generally implies a friendly union and states nothing about the name of the resulting company. Acquisition also is used of the union of two corporations. Acquisitions may be friendly or unfriendly and generally result in the loss of corporate identity for the acquired company.

MERGERS AND ACQUISITIONS UNIT
See M&A.

MESSAGE SWITCHING
Also called "message switching unit." An automated communication procedure that links sales, operations, and trading locales by means of a computer. The MSU of the NYSE routes orders, stores information, and relays execution prices to subscribing member firms.

MEXICAN STOCK EXCHANGE
The name by which this exchange is known throughout the Latin-American world is Bolsa Mexicana de Valores.

Because 10 of its top stocks constitute over half of its market value and are closely tied to the petroleum industry, this exchange is the most volatile of all stock exchanges, although the Austrian Stock Exchange with its 102% change in 1989 runs a close second.

The exchange is open daily from 10:30 A.M. until 1:30 P.M. with no after-hour market activity. Settlement is on the second business day after trade date and is subject to price modifications based on changes in the Mexican peso.

MEZZANINE BRACKET
Popular name for those underwriters who, while not the major underwriters of an issue, generally subscribe for the next largest portion of the issue.

MEZZANINE FINANCING
Term used in conjunction with leveraged buyouts. As opposed to pure debt financing, the term refers to financing a takeover by preferred stock or convertible subordinated debentures. In this way, the resulting company's equity capital is expanded, rather than its debt, and it satisfies important creditors that the new owners will have a larger financial commitment to the merged corporations.

M FORMATION
See DOUBLE TOP/BOTTOM.

MIB
Acronym for Marketing of Investments Board. The MIB is a quasi-governmental body established by means of the Financial Services Act of (1986) to oversee and regulate prepackaged investments, such as life insurance and unit trusts (mutual funds), in the United Kingdom.

To provide for economies and for efficiency, the MIB was merged into the SIB to function collectively with the Securities and Investments Board (SIB).

MIBOC
Acronym for Marketing of Investments Board Organising Committee. In the United Kingdom, this was the forerunner of the MIB which—in turn—was merged into the SIB (q.v.).

MICROECONOMIST
Academic term for a person who studies, measures, and predicts the fortunes of individual companies. In this sense, the term is used synonymously with *fundamental analyst.*

The term is also used of the study, measurement, and prediction of the financial activities of households (both collectively and as an average). Thus, this study has great impact on marketing projections, changes in market share, spending habits, inventory needs, and so on, of manufacturers and providers of services.

See also MACROECONOMIST.

MIDGETS
Slang for mortgage pools of GNMA securities with a 15- rather than the usual 30-year maturity. The presumed prepayment period is 8 years on midget pools; it is 12 years on 30-year pools. Only the original maturity period differs; midget pools, like the regular GNMA pools, have a minimum principal amount of $1 million in underlying mortgages.

MIDWEST STOCK EXCHANGE
A registered national exchange, located in Chicago. In addition to providing trading facilities for the securities listed there, the MSE also provides a marketplace for many securities traded on the NYSE.

MIDWEST STOCK EXCHANGE AUTOMATED EXECUTION SYSTEM
See MAX.

MIG

Acronym for Moody's Investment Grade. MIG ratings are given by Moody's to relatively short-term municipal debt issues. The four ratings that are given are:

MIG 1 — Best quality.
MIG 2 — High quality.
MIG 3 — Favorable quality.
MIG 4 — Adequate quality.

As with all debt ratings, the ratings are the opinion of the rating service and are subject to review.

MILAN STOCK EXCHANGE

Although it is the largest of Italy's stock exchanges, it has serious problems. Because no law forbids it, insider trading is rampant and much of this occurs outside of regular trading hours (10 A.M. until 2 P.M.). In addition, contract settlements are notoriously slow—often taking six or more weeks to complete. Paper flow control is the heart of the problem and no solution is currently in sight.

See also MONTE TITOLI.

TO MILK

To exploit. An analogy drawn from the term meaning to extract the nutritional fluid from an udder or breast.

Used in the securities industry in several senses:

1. To extract all of the "good things" from an account or a customer; for example, to milk an account dry.
2. To achieve all of the profit from an investment situation; for example, "He really milked that investment and when he sold there was nothing left for the buyer."
3. To drain all of the information from a source; for example, "They milked that information for all it was worth."

MILL

One 1,000th part of a dollar ($.001), or 1/10th of a cent. Municipalities usually state property taxes in mills and multiples thereof based on the assessed valuation of the taxable property. For example, if the assessed valuation of property is $1 million and the tax is 8 mills per dollar of valuation, the total tax would be: $1,000,000 times . 008, or $8,000.

Sometimes spelled mil.

MINI MANIPULATION

Manipulative transactions in an option stock so its price movements are sufficient to cause a premium change in an option position previously established. Mini manipulation is difficult to detect, but it can be easily seen that a small movement in the underlying stock would be multiplied many times if the manipulator has a large position in an underlying option.

MINI-MAX
A Salomon Brothers procedure that enables investors to benefit from foreign currency fluctuations without exposure to significant risk. This is a currency-linked money market strategy that permits subscribers to choose a minimum return on investment and still have upside potential in the upper end of a specified range. In effect, the investor can choose either the minimum (mini) or the maximum (max) return while Salomon Brothers provides the other side of the range. The strategy combines (1) a foreign currency spot trade, (2) a repurchase agreement of a short-term nondollar instrument in that currency, and (3) a "range forward" currency contract versus the U.S. dollar.

MINI-MAX OFFERING
A variation of a best efforts—all or none—underwriting. In a mini-max, there is a minimum number of shares required for the offering to be effective, but a maximum number of shares that may be sold in the offering. As in a "best efforts" underwriting, the underwriter has an agency relationship with the issuer.

MINIMUM LENDING RATE
Acronym: MLR. The interest rate charged to banks in Great Britain when they borrow from the Bank of England. It is comparable to the discount rate charged by the Federal Reserve to its member banks.

MINIMUM MAINTENANCE REQUIREMENTS
The minimum equity, or margin, required either by exchange or National Association of Securities Dealers (NASD) rules, or by brokerage firm requirements.
1. There is a $2,000 maintenance in all accounts with a debit balance or a short position.
2. The exchanges and the NASD require a 25% maintenance on long margin accounts, and, as a general rule, 30% on short margin accounts.
3. Many member firms have special maintenance requirements on debt securities, option accounts, or on securities selling below a specified dollar value per share.

MINIMUM PRICE CHANGES OMITTED
An announcement that appears on the consolidated NYSE and ASE tapes if reports of trades are more than 10 minutes late. Following this

announcement, only trades that fluctuate by more than $1/8$ point from the preceding report on that security are printed on the tape.

When the lag time is substantially reduced, normal reporting continues.

MINIMUM VARIATION
As a general rule, securities trading is in points, with a minimum price variation. In securities that trade in terms of points alone, the minimum variation is $1/8$ of a point, although government notes and bonds normally trade in minimum variations of $1/32$. If securities normally trade on a yield basis, the minimum variation is 1 basis point (i.e., a variation of .01% of yield). Of course, any security may trade at the last transaction price. In this case, there is no variation.

A MINOR
Someone who has not reached the age of majority in his or her state or residence. Brokerage accounts for minors are undesirable because losses can be recouped when the minor reaches majority. Court-appointed guardians and custodians under Uniform Gift to Minors Accounts can make legally binding investment decisions on behalf of a minor, and such accounts are permitted.

MINORITY INTEREST
1. Any group of corporate owners that, collectively, own less than 50% of the voting shares of a corporation.
2. A corporation that owns, usually as an investment, less than 50% of another corporation.
3. A person, either real or legal, who lends long-term funds to another corporation is also said to have a minority interest.

MINT
See MUNICIPAL INSURED NATIONAL TRUST.

–
See MINUS.

MINUS
Used as a word or as a symbol $(-)$.
1. Sales to underwriters or other dealers are often made minus a concession or reallowance.
2. A sale in the marketplace that is lower than the previous price is called a "minus tick" (q.v.).

3. If the closing sale in a security is lower than the previous day's close, the stock table will list the change (e.g., as $-\frac{1}{4}$).
4. The discount at which a closed-end fund is selling below the net asset value of the fund.

MINUS TICK
Industry jargon for any transaction price that is lower than the previous transaction price. For example, if the previous sale was 20 and the next sale is 19$\frac{7}{8}$, the sale at 19$\frac{7}{8}$ is said to be on a minus tick.
See also ZERO-MINUS TICK.

MIOER
An SEC acronym for Market Index Option Escrow Receipt. This is a written representation (escrow receipt) by a qualified bank stating that the writer of an index option has on deposit cash, cash equivalents, and marginable equity securities (or any combination thereof) *equal* to the margin required for the uncovered sale of that index option.

MIP
1. Acronym for monthly investment plan. A generic term for the periodic investment of small sums in the shares of a given company. MIP customers could purchase full and fractional shares. The term is not used of periodic purchases of mutual funds; instead, dollar cost averaging is used.
2. Acronym for mortgage insurance premium. An annual fee paid to the FHA or to a private insurance company to protect grantors of mortgages against loss due to defaults by borrowers or from losses due to natural hazards to the underlying property.

MIRROR SUBSIDIARY
Mergers and acquisitions term. The term describes the action of an acquiring firm when it places unwanted assets of its target into the shell of a subsidiary corporation at its prevailing book value. The shell subsidiary is then sold and the proceeds used to reduce the debt incurred by the acquisition.

In effect, the acquiring company and the acquired are looked at in a mirror. Those that duplicate activities of the acquirer are packaged and sold.

MISCELLANEOUS LIABILITIES
Entry on corporate financial statements to designate liabilities whose payment date is not yet determined. Adverse legal judgments under appeal, deferred taxes under adjudication, and other similar indeterminate liabilities would be included under this heading.

MISDEMEANOR

Under federal securities law, an action that is considered to be a minor violation of the law. Generally, misdemeanors will result in a fine, rather than imprisonment.

Antonym: felony.

MISERY INDEX

A graphic representation of consumer discomfort as interpreted by an economist at Prudential-Bache Securities.

It graphs two components together: the unemployment rate (using federal statistics) and consumer expectations of inflation (using University of Michigan statistics). If these two measurements trend downward (i.e., misery is diminished), it is expected that optimism will increase—and so will stock prices.

MISSING THE MARKET

Term describing the fact that an agent failed to execute a transaction at a price that was available, and that the subsequent transaction was disadvantageous to the customer. In this case, the agent must make up the amount lost by the client. The term implies negligence on the part of the agent but not fraud. Thus, the action is nonfeasance, but not malfeasance.

MIT

See MARKET IF TOUCHED ORDER; MUNICIPAL INVESTMENT TRUST.

MITI

Used in Japan to stand for the Ministry of International Trade and Industry.

MITI shares regulatory oversight and jurisdiction of the commodity futures industry in Japan with the Minister of Finance (MOF).

At present, MITI is starting to exercise control of the developing currency futures business in Japan. That business is not yet recognized, but it is rapidly gaining in popularity as giant Japanese trading houses and U.S. FCMs begin to participate in that market.

MIXED ACCOUNT

A client's margin account containing both long and short security positions.

MJSD

Initials for: March, June, September, and December, which are the expiration months for certain stock and debt options traded on option exchanges. As a general rule, no more than three of the expiration months are traded at any one time.

Index options also offer three expiration months for trading, but the months are successive rather than in three-month intervals.

MKT

Abbreviation for the word *market*. Its most prevalent use is on customer order instructions to buy or sell at the best available price at the time the order reaches the trading area.

ML

Abbreviation used on corporate and municipal bond calendars to identify Merrill Lynch & Company, a major underwriter of securities.

MLP

Acronym for master limited partnership. An MLP is a legal entity that provides subscribers (owners) with the income flow-through of an ordinary limited partnership plus the marketability feature that accompanies listed stock on an exchange.

The Tax Reform Act of 1986 caused all new MLPs to be taxed as corporations and thus substantially reduced their appeal as a tax shelter.

Unlike regular C-Corporations, MLPs have a limited life span and will, at a point in time, be liquidated.

MLR

See MINIMUM LENDING RATE.

MM

1. Abbreviation frequently used to designate a dealer who acts as a marketmaker.
2. When following a whole number, the initials stand for 1 million. Example: 1MM means 1 million, 2MM means 2 million.

   As a general rule, MYN is a more frequently used designation than MM.

MMA

Industry abbreviation for: money market account.
See MONEY MARKET ACCOUNT.

MMC

See MONEY MARKET CERTIFICATE.

MMID

Acronym for marketmaker identifier. This is a four-letter identifying code assigned by the NASD to broker/dealers who enter quotations into the NASDAQ trading system. Examples: The code for Merrill Lynch & Co. is MOTC (Merrill Over the Counter), and the code for Salomon Brothers Inc is SALB.

MMM
1. The ticker symbol for Minnesota Mining and Manufacturing Corp., a conglomerate listed on the New York Stock Exchange. Among the multitude of its products is Scotch Tape.
2. An advanced degree accorded by Northwestern's Kellogg Business School. It stands for a master's degree in management and manufacturing.

MMMF
Acronym for money market mutual fund. Popular name for open-end investment shares that invest in short-term money market securities in an endeavor to provide investors with (1) relatively risk-free investments that (2) give a daily payment of competitive short-term interest rates.

MMP
See MONEY MARKET PREFERRED.

MO
1. Frequently used symbol in newspaper summary earnings reports. When used following the name of the company, it signifies that the principal marketplace for the shares of the security is the Montreal Stock Exchange.
2. It is the ticker symbol for Philip Morris Inc. on the NYSE.

MOBILE HOME CERTIFICATE
A variety of Ginnie Mae (GNMA) security that represents mortgages on mobile homes. Although these securities generally have shorter maturities than other Ginnie Mae securities, they have the same guarantees for the repayment of principal and for the timely payment of interest.

MOB SPREAD
This is also known as the "munis-over-bonds spread."

In effect, the MOB spread is based on the decimal quotient found when the typical yield on munis of a certain rating and maturity is divided by the yield of Treasuries of similar maturity. At the time of writing, for example, the MOB spread is 0.875; thus, for each $1 of return on a 20-year Treasury, an investor in 20-year AA-rated munis will receive 87.5 cents.

Because the safety of a muni will never reach that of a Treasury, the spread becomes an important factor in investment decisions, tax considerations, and in the purchase or sale (or spreading) of financial futures contracts.

MOC
See MARKET-ON-CLOSE ORDER.

MODIFIED ACCELERATED COST RECOVERY SYSTEM
See MACRS.

MODIFIED PASS-THROUGH
The term is generally associated with the Ginnie Mae Modified Pass-Through.

In this context, *modified* means guaranteed; that is, a packager of mortgages originally backed by the Veterans Administration or the Federal Housing Authority takes the mortgage pool to the Government National Mortgage Association (GNMA). It, in turn, guarantees performance on the mortgages in regard to the prompt payment of interest and the repayment of principal. It does this by guaranteeing that the original backers (VA or FHA) will repurchase the mortgages if there is a default.

Once "modified" by GNMA, the pool and its participations are readily salable by government securities dealers to their customers. Because this guarantee is not a *direct* obligation of the United States, interest is subject to federal, state, and local taxation.

MODIFIED TRADING SYSTEM
See MTS.

MOFTAN
Japanese slang for the individual at a domestic bank, securities firm, or insurance company who has personal responsibility for dealings with the Japanese Minister of Finance (the MOF part of *moftan*).

The person so designated as *moftan* is expected to keep current with changing events at this governmental agency *and* to be able to influence favorable consideration for his employer. Because of the almost omnipotent power of the MOF, this position is very important.

MONETARIST
A follower of the financial belief that governmental control of the economy should be limited to the control of the supply of money. In effect, a monetarist believes that an annual expansion of—let's say—2.5% in the money supply is desirable. Minor variations are permissible but major incursions either by the Fed or by Congress will adversely affect the economy. Example: In a recession, a monetarist would moderate the re-

cession by controlling the money supply; a Keynesian economist would increase governmental spending. Supply-side economics is a variation of monetarist economics.

Nobel Laureate Milton Friedman is the name most commonly associated with the monetarist theory of economics.

Also called "monetarist economist."

MONETARY AGGREGATES
Formal name for the money supply. It is measured in various ways, generally by decreasing liquidity.

See M1, M2, M3, and M4.

MONETARY AUTHORITY OF SINGAPORE
See MAS.

MONETARY POLICY
1. General term that describes the actions of the Federal Reserve as it controls the supply of money and credit in the U.S. economy.
2. Term, usually qualified by an adjective, to describe the direction of the Fed's policies. For example, the Fed's monetary policy is expansive.

THE MONEY LAUNDERING CONTROL ACT OF 1986
A federal law that criminalizes the knowing participation in certain illegal activities in the transfer of money. The purpose of the law is to deny anyone the right to conceal ownership of unlawfully derived funds or to avoid federal or state reporting requirements.

MONEY MARKET
1. An abstraction for the dealers and their communication network who trade short-term, relatively riskless, securities.
2. The securities traded in the money market. The principal securities are: U.S. Treasury bills, banker's acceptances, commercial paper, and negotiable certificates of deposit.

Repurchase agreements and reverse repurchase agreements, although they are not securities, are also considered part of the money market.

MONEY MARKET ACCOUNT
Acronym: MMA. A special bank savings account that provides an interest rate higher than the usual $5\frac{1}{4}\%$ given to time savings accounts. Generally, a minimum account balance is required, such as $2,500 or more. The interest rates on MMAs are generally competitive with that earned by money market mutual funds.

MONEY MARKET CENTER BANK
Any large bank located in a major city that plays an active role in the issuance and trading of short-term financial instruments. These instruments include bankers' acceptances, commercial paper, and certificates of deposit.

MONEY MARKET CERTIFICATE
Acronym: MMC. A savings instrument offered by many thrift institutions. Generally, an MMC has a $10,000 minimum face value and a maturity of 26 weeks although other face values and maturities are available. The percentage of interest is guaranteed and is tied to the prevailing six-month Treasury bill rate at the time of issuance. There is a cash penalty, both in principal and interest, for the premature redemption of an MMC.

MONEY MARKET FUND (MMF)
Popular name for open-end investment shares that invest in short-term money market securities in an endeavor to provide investors with (1) relatively risk-free investments that (2) give a daily payment of competitive short-term interest rates.

MONEY MARKET PREFERRED
Acronym: MMP. A class of equity security whose dividend is payable every 49 days. At that time, the rate is recalculated to reflect current market rates for the next dividend period. Holders who are dissatisfied with the calculated rate may sell their shares in a special auction. If there are insufficient buyers to take care of dissatisfied sellers, the rate is recalculated at 110% of the commercial paper rate then obtainable for AA-rated companies.

MONEY MULTIPLIER SECURITY
Also called "Zerials." Initiated by Salomon Brothers, these securities are zero-coupon offerings of the same issuer, but with a choice of different maturities. Because the longer-term obligations are sold at a lower price than shorter-term obligations, but all are redeemed at par at maturity, the investor can double, triple, or quadruple his or her money by choosing the appropriate maturity date.

MONEY RATE OF RETURN
Annual yield expressed as a percentage of invested asset value. The calculation involves dividing annual dollars received by the value of assets employed to receive it.

MONEY SPREAD

Common term for a vertical option spread. For example, a client buys a call at 40 and sells a call at 50, with both calls expiring in the same month. This client is moderating the risk of a long call at the lower price by using the premium on the short call to defray part of the cost of the long call. The opposite would be true if the client bought a call at 50 and sold a call at 40.

MONEY SUPPLY

General term for the currency and demand deposits which are readily available for use in the economy of the United States.

The basic distinctions, established by the Federal Reserve, are M1, M2, and M3. The distinctions are based on the frequency of the use of "money" in the economy. M1 is by far the most important and is closely followed by economists.

Here are the key subdivisions of M1:

M1a: currency in the hands of the public and checking accounts, including monies on deposit with money market funds.

M1b: savings accounts.

M2 and M3 include time deposits with banks, Eurodollar deposits in the United States, short-term commercial paper and bankers acceptances, and Series EE Savings Bonds.

MONKEY WARD

Colloquial name used of the shares of Montgomery Ward Corporation before it was acquired by Mobil Oil Company. This colorful name undoubtedly will be revived if Mobil Oil, as it has announced, spins off Montgomery Ward as an independent corporation.

MONORY SICAVs

The term is named after the proponent of a 1979 French law affecting some mutual funds. Under this law, many French mutual funds must have at least 30% of their assets invested in French-issued bonds and 60% in French-issued stocks. This leaves little for foreign investing.

As a result of this dedication to French industry, such mutual funds are a popular investment vehicle for French insurance companies.

MONTE TITOLI

Name given to the Italian system for securities settlement.

The expression, which arises from the Milan Stock Exchange, is an antiquated manual system of trade comparisons and physical deliveries. Although the exchange does have access to both EuroClear and CEDEL settlement systems, any trade processed through Monte Titoli may take months to complete.

MONTHLY INVESTMENT PLAN
See MIP (1).

MOOCH
1. Noun: any person who invests before he or she investigates because of a desire to profit. For example, "His book is full of mooches looking for a fast buck in penny stocks."
2. Verb, transitive or intransitive: to borrow or beg small amounts without the intention of repaying; to steal. For example, "As a broker, she is always mooching from her customers."

MOODY'S
Popular name for Moody's Investors Service, a registered investment adviser. Moody's is best known for its company reports, which appear periodically in bound form for: Governments and Municipals, Industrial, and Utility Corporations.

Its bond ratings also are extensively used to qualify the credit ratings of corporate and municipal issuers and to determine whether the security is investment (bank) grade. The principal investment grade ratings are: Aaa, Aa, A, and Baa.

See also MIG.

MOODY'S INVESTMENT GRADE
See MIG.

MOODY'S RATING
A rating quality assigned by Moody's Investors Service to a specific debt instrument issued by a corporation. Moody's Investors Service is one of four research oriented institutions that rate (qualify) corporate bonds.

MOON BONDS
Bonds that are "far out"; that is, have maturities that are 20 or more years in the future.

MOPS
See MULTIPLE OPTION PUT SECURITIES.

MORAL OBLIGATION BOND
Term popularly given by the securities industry to those municipal bonds authorized by one session of a state's legislature in such a way that subsequent sessions are not legally bound to follow the directives first given. Buyers, therefore, have an implied moral obligation of future legislatures to pay interest and principal, but there is no legal obligation to do so.

MORAL SUASION
Term popularly used of the Federal Reserve's ability to persuade compliance with its general monetary policy outside of its statutory ability to do so. For example, a call from the Fed chairman to a member bank asking it to participate in the sale of securities, or to lower its bid in the T-bill auction, would exemplify moral suasion.

MORGAN STANLEY CAPITAL INTERNATIONAL WORLD INDEX (MSCI)
A Morgan Stanley owned product that tracks price performance of selected equities throughout world markets. MSCI was acquired in 1986 from Capital International S.A. (Geneva). MSCI was started in 1968 and it contains about 1,400 companies in 19 countries. It represents about 60% of the total capitalization of the stock exchanges on which these issues are traded.

MORGAN STANLEY WORLD INDEX
See MORGAN STANLEY CAPITAL INTERNATIONAL WORLD INDEX.

MORRE
Acronym for Montreal Exchange Registered Representative Order Routing and Execution System. This mouthful is an electronic system that connects the MSE and the Boston Stock Exchanges. The system enables traders and investors to execute orders in selected issues in U.S. dollars on the Boston Exchange if that price is more favorable than the price available on the MSE. MORRE will accept market orders for execution at the best bid or offer price in amounts from 100 to 1,299 shares.

MORTALITY RISK
The financial risk assumed by life insurance companies when they write a policy for a fixed premium and a fixed face value on a given individual with his or her actuarial life expectancy. A similar mortality risk is involved when an insuror writes a fixed annuity and guarantees payments for the life of the annuitant, or the annuitant and a survivor. The writer of a variable annuity policy also assumes mortality risk if the annuitant elects to receive payments for life. In the latter case, however, the mortality risk is somewhat lessened because of the variable payouts.

MORTGAGE-BACKED SECURITY
See MBS.

MORTGAGE BANKER

General name for the middleman between the originator of a mortgage (e.g., a bank or credit union) and the investor who assumes the mortgage risk by purchasing the mortgage. This gives liquidity to the original lender and passes the mortgage risk, with its reward, to the investor.

MORTGAGE BOND

A longer-term debt security that promises to pay interest and to repay principal, and that pledges real property, either land or plant or both, as collateral for the loan. Mortgage bonds are always designated as such, and the indenture will specify whether the mortgage is 1st or 2d and will state the restrictions on the further issuance of bonds.

MORTGAGE BOND SECURITIES CLEARING CORPORATION

See MBSCC.

MORTGAGE BROKER

An agent who, for a commission, arranges real estate loans for purchasers of property.

Unlike mortgage bankers, mortgage brokers do not service the loan after the financing is completed.

THE MORTGAGE CORPORATION

A U.S. government-sponsored corporation that was created in 1970 to purchase qualifying conventional residential mortgages from members of the corporation—FHLMC, or Freddy Mac—which it then packages under its own name and assurances and resells to the public.

See also FEDERAL HOME LOAN MORTGAGE CORPORATION.

MORTGAGE CREDIT CERTIFICATES

Acronym: MCC. Sanctioned by the Deficit Reduction Act of 1984, these are annual credits that can be issued by state and local governments. The MCC then are applied against that mortgage subscriber's federal tax liabilities. In effect, MCCs enable the local governments to subsidize mortgage payments at federal government expense. In this way, public housing projects are encouraged.

MORTGAGE ENFORCEMENT

Term associated with the pooling of mortgages having similar terms and interest rates for submission to a government agency for approval and guarantee. Once approved and guaranteed, such mortgages are said to be "enforced."

MORTGAGE INSURANCE PREMIUM
See MIP (2).

MORTGAGE POOL
Term used to designate a group of mortgages on the same class of property, the same interest rate, and substantially identical maturity dates. For example, a mortgage pool might contain mortgages with a total face value of $2,100,503.56 at a rate of 16% that will mature in 29 years and 6 months.

MORTGAGE POOL ORIGINATOR
Descriptive title for any mortgage banker, either commercial or thrift, that assembles real estate loans on similar classes of property, then issues a new security representing a fractional interest in that multi-mortgage portfolio, and distributes monthly to certificate holders the monthly interest and principal payments of the mortgagees. A fee is charged for this latter service.

The securities are said to be "mortgage-backed"; the monthly distribution is called "a pass-through"; and if the pool is guaranteed the securities are said to be "modified." Hence: Ginnie Mae Modified Pass-Throughs.

MORTGAGE REIT
Term designating a real estate investment trust (REIT) that uses the capital provided by the trustholders as a leveraged investment. The trust, in turn, borrows money from a commercial bank and relends it. The trust hopes to profit from the spread between the interest paid to the bank and the interest paid by the borrower. Mortgage REITs can be highly profitable in times of stable interest rates but are highly speculative if interest rates rise.

MORTGAGING-OUT
Somewhat derogatory term for the following activity. A group of people (or one wealthy person) purchases a company that carries a large amount of debt in relation to equity. The group then builds up its revenues and cash flow (primarily through acquisitions) and borrows an even larger amount of money based upon the newly enlarged company. The proceeds of the second financing are used to pay off the original invested capital, leaving the company saddled with enormous debt, which it may or may not be able to support with future operations.

MOSS
See MARKET OVERSIGHT SURVEILLANCE SYSTEM.

MOST

Acronym for Market Order System of Trading. This is an electronic linkage between the Toronto Stock Exchange and the American Stock Exchange. MOST, which works in tandem with PER, the ASE's order system, permits an order flow for dually listed stocks so the order can be executed automatically on the market that gives the best price.

MOTORS

Common trading nickname for the common shares of General Motors Corporation, the largest manufacturer of automobiles in the United States.

The nickname is not used of the Class E or Class H shares of General Motors.

MOU

See MEMORANDUM OF UNDERSTANDING.

MPC

See MARKET PERFORMANCE COMMITTEE.

MS

Abbreviation used on municipal and corporate bond calendars for Morgan Stanley & Company, a principal underwriter of securities. It is also the NYSE ticker symbol for the broker/dealer's holding company.

MSCI

See MORGAN STANLEY CAPITAL INTERNATIONAL WORLD INDEX.

MSE

1. Midwest Stock Exchange, Inc., located in Chicago. MSE trades many local issues as well as many of the securities listed on the NYSE and ASE.
2. Montreal Stock Exchange. MSE trades shares of many Canadian companies and options on these shares. MSE is subject to the regulatory jurisdiction of the Quebec Securities Commission.

MSRB

See MUNICIPAL SECURITIES RULEMAKING BOARD.

MTC

1. Initials stand for Markets and Trading Commission (q.v.), a proposed government agency with jurisdiction over securities and commodities marketplaces.
   See also MARKETS AND TRADING COMMISSION.

2. New York Stock Exchange ticker symbol for Monsanto Co. Inc., a large U.S. chemical and fabric company.

MTN

Initials used to designate: medium-term notes. Such MTNs are used to complement an issuer's commercial paper to finance short- to intermediate-term operations. By adding MTNs to its financial debt securities, an issuer can offer debt at anytime, anywhere, and in any currency with maturities ranging from five months to 10–15 years.

Such MTNs are not underwritten; instead, the corporation posts its intended rate, and investment bankers then compete for the right to publicly distribute the paper.

MTS

Acronym for Modified Trading System. MTS is used by the Chicago Board Options Exchange (CBOE) for selected nonequity options.

For most of its options, the CBOE uses order book officials (OBOs) as agents to record and execute options, and it uses marketmakers (MMs) who act as principals to provide continuous markets and the necessary liquidity.

For certain nonequity options, the CBOE uses a system of designated primary marketmakers (q.v.) to provide a combination of the same functions.

MUD

Acronym for municipal utility district. MUDs are political subdivisions set up by municipalities to provide certain utility-related services: water, sewers, electric power, fire protection, and so on. As such, MUDs may issue tax-exempted municipal bonds. Bond debt service is provided by a special property tax on the residents of the district.

MULLET

Mullets are thoughtless fish who, apparently, will follow any bait. Thus, this term is used by salespersons for naive, thoughtless investors who will buy anything that is popular with the crowd.

Needless to say, such investors are easy prey for unscrupulous salespersons who are anxious to create unnecessary activity in an account.

MULTICURRENCY CLAUSE

A paragraph found in a typical Eurocurrency loan that permits the borrower to repay in another currency when the loan comes due and if a new loan is to be created immediately.

The borrower may be able to profit if repayment can be made by using a depreciated currency.

MULTI-PART ORDER

A Philadelphia Stock Exchange/Board of Trade creation that permits the simultaneous entry of an order to buy or sell, or both, a stated number of foreign currency option contracts, *and* a stated number of foreign currency futures contracts. Execution of one part based upon a predetermined spread between prices of these contracts is contingent upon execution of the other part of the transaction. Thus, the spreader or hedger avoids a "one leg" execution; in effect, the entire position is put on at once if the conditions are met.

MULTIPLE OPTION PUT SECURITY

Acronym: MOPS. Term coined by the former brokerage firm of E.F. Hutton to identify municipal bonds with 30-year maturities, but with 2-, 3-, and 5-year put options attached to the certificates. As a result, it is a long-term security that has an effective price floor because of the put options. In effect, the original bond will trade near par as though it were a short- to intermediate-term bond.

MULTIPLIER

Term applied to the reciprocal of the Fed's reserve requirement on deposits. For example, at a 20% reserve requirement ($^1/_5$), the reciprocal is 5/1. Thus, a deposit of $100,000 in a bank requires a reserve of $20,000; the remaining $80,000 could be a base for loans of $400,000. Theoretically, $100,000 in cash could expand into $500,000 in loans. In practice, banks are more conservative, but the multiplier does apply to a limited extent.

Also called "multiplier effect" (q.v.).

MULTIPLIER EFFECT

Term used to describe the expansion of credit in the U.S. banking system. The multiplier effect arises from the reserve requirement imposed on member banks by the Federal Reserve. Theoretically, the expansion of credit is the reciprocal of the reserve requirement. Example: A 20% reserve requirement will multiply credit five times if money is deposited in a commercial bank. In practice, many banks have excess reserves; thus, the full multiplier effect is not achieved.

MULTIYEAR RESCHEDULING AGREEMENT
See MYRA.

MUNI

Popular contraction for any municipal security. In terms of the issuer, securities issued by any state, political subdivision thereof, or agency thereof. In terms of taxation, any security whose interest payments are exempt from federal income tax liability.

Plural: munis.

MUNICIPAL ARBITRAGE
This form of arbitrage entailed the issuance of tax-exempted debt at a fixed rate of interest with the proceeds of the offering invested in U.S. government securities at a higher rate of interest. In practice, the two issues would have similar maturities. Because of the difference in rates, and the fact that the municipality did not pay federal taxes, there was a profit for the municipality.

The TRA of 1986 sharply curtailed this practice.

MUNICIPAL ASSISTANCE CORPORATION FOR THE CITY OF NEW YORK
Also known as: MAC or Big MAC. MAC is a state governmental agency, organized as a public benefit corporation, to provide financing assistance and fiscal oversight for New York City. It was organized in 1975 by the New York State legislature and is empowered to incur debt, refund and redeem New York City obligations, and, in general, to oversee the financial affairs of New York City.

MUNICIPAL BOND
A debt security that is issued by a state, city, or other political subdivision chartered by the state. All municipal bonds have these elements in common: (1) there is enabling legislation to permit their issuance and (2) the interest income is exempt from federal taxes.

MUNICIPAL BOND COMPARISON SYSTEM
See MBCS.

MUNICIPAL BOND EXEMPT ACCRUAL RECEIPTS
See MBEARS.

MUNICIPAL BOND INSURANCE ASSOCIATION (MBIA)
An insuror, jointly owned by a consortium of insurance companies, that insures the timely payment of interest and the repayment of principal by municipal bond issuers. The insurance fee is paid by the issuer. Bonds so insured have the highest rating (AAA) and thus the issuer can sell the bonds at lower interest rates. In practice, the lower interest rate fully offsets the premium paid to the insuror.

MUNICIPAL CERTIFICATES OF PARTICIPATION
See COPs.

MUNICIPAL CERTIFICATES OF ACCRUAL ON TAX-EXEMPTED SECURITIES
See M-CATS.

MUNICIPAL INSURED NATIONAL TRUST
Acronym: MINT. A service mark of former broker/dealer Moseley, Hallgarten, Estabrook, and Weeden for a tax-free bond fund. MHEW acted as the trust's sponsor.

MINT was a municipal investment trust that features monthly net investment income payments derived from a diversified portfolio of municipal securities.

MUNICIPAL INVESTMENT TRUST (MIT)
A municipal investment trust, or MIT, is a form of unit investment trust that provides a diversified investment in a portfolio of municipal securities. Purpose: to give the holder monthly income exempt from federal taxation.

MUNICIPAL NOTE
In general, notes are shorter-term municipal debt obligations. Almost always, debts of 2 years or less are described as notes. The term note also is used of debt obligations with 2 or more years to maturity. In practice, therefore, a note is a security that the issuer describes as a note. Normally, notes are noncallable.

MUNICIPAL OPTION
In the parlance of municipal securities trading, this is an offering of bonds to another dealer at a fixed price for a limited period. Within that time frame, the offering firm must honor the original terms if the dealer decides to exercise the privileges of purchase.

Note: Do not confuse with municipal bonds with a put option privilege. This privilege accompanies ownership and is granted by the issuer.

MUNICIPAL SECURITIES RULEMAKING BOARD
Registered with the SEC under the 1975 amendments of the '34 Act, the MSRB proposes rules and provides arbitration facilities to broker/dealers and bank dealers in municipal securities. Members of the MSRB continue to report to their original self-regulatory organization, as established under federal law, but they agree to conform to the rules established by the MSRB and approved by the SEC.

MUNICIPAL SECURITY
See MUNICIPAL BOND.

MUNI-COMPARISON SYSTEM (MCS)

Written as MuniComparison, MCS is a division within Depository Trust Co. (DTC). MCS provides for a broad range of automated validation and settlement procedures between members in a broad range of municipal transactions. This section of Public Securities Depository Trust Co. (PSDTC) provides for book-entry settlements between participating members; the ability to compare and settle "when issued" bonds; and extended settlements, if requested, for regular way and when issued trades.

MUNIFACTS

A subscription service provided by *The Daily Bond Buyer* that disseminates information about municipal securities. Munifacts is similar in format to Dow Jones and Reuters in their respective fields of news.

MUNI MAC

Unofficial name for a government-sponsored agency authorized by Congress and modeled after the Federal Home Loan Mortgage Corporation (Freddie Mac).

The purpose of Muni Mac is to purchase and repackage municipal securities, with each "pool" having securities with similar terms. The pools are then securitized and the resulting debt is sold to investment bankers for resale to the public. The proceeds of the sale repays the original purchase price to Muni Mac.

Guarantees, if any, are made by the underlying municipal issuers and not by the federal government. Interest payments retain their tax-exempt nature.

MUNIS-OVER-BONDS SPREAD

See MOB SPREAD.

MUSICAL CHAIRS BONDS

A tongue-in-cheek expression for "Zombie Bonds" (q.v.).

MUTATIS MUTANDIS

Latin for a necessary change in terminology caused by differing circumstances but without any alteration in essential points. In form, it is an ablative absolute and thus may stand apart grammatically. For example, a municipal Official Statement is—mutatis mutandis—the equivalent of the final prospectus on a registered offering.

The expression literally means "necessary changes having been made" and is often used in foreign translations or comparisons of substantially similar instruments.

446

MUTILATED SECURITY

Any certificate for a security that has: (1) the name of the issuer or the issue obscured; (2) a portion of the security missing, perforated, or so cut that the security cannot be properly identified, or transferred, or that will prevent the purchaser from exercising the rights of an owner. It is the obligation of seller to rectify a mutilation by asking the transfer agent to guarantee all rights of ownership to a buyer.

MUTUAL FUND

Popular name for the shares of open-end management investment companies. Such shares represent ownership of a diversified portfolio of securities, which are professionally managed and which are redeemable at their net asset value. The prospectus of the mutual fund will detail the features of the fund.

The term also is used of any investment company security, but this usage is not common.

MUTUAL FUND CUSTODIAN

A commercial bank or trust company that holds in safekeeping the monies and securities owned by a mutual fund. The custodian generally, but not always, acts as the transfer agent and disbursing agent of the fund. To act as custodian, the bank must qualify under the provisions set forth in the Investment Company Act of 1940.

MYRA

Acronym for multiyear rescheduling agreement. MYRAs are documents created by financial center banks to rearrange and extend repayments of loans made to governments of countries unable to meet their current obligations. To avoid defaults, Poland, Mexico, Brazil, and Argentina sought relief from their debts in the form of lower current payments for longer time periods.

N

N

Fourteenth letter of the alphabet:
1. Used in parentheses in the newspaper tables of company earnings to designate that the principal market for the company's securities is the New York Stock Exchange; for example, (N).
2. Used, lowercase, in the stock transaction tables in the newspaper to designate that a stock is newly listed on an exchange.
3. Used, lowercase, in the U.S. government securities bid/offer tables to designate a note rather than a bond.

N/A
Initials representing "not available" or "not applicable." N/A is used to indicate that certain statistical facts (e.g., price, earnings, and the like) are not available or were not provided. It is also used to designate that a certain issue will not be offered publicly.

NABL
See NATIONAL ASSOCIATION OF BOND LAWYERS.

NAKED OPTION
Industry jargon for:
1. The writer of a call who does not own the underlying security, a convertible security, or a long call at a strike (execution) price equal to or lower than the strike price of the call that was written and that does not expire before the call that was written.
2. The writer of a put who is not short the underlying security, or who does not own a long put with a strike price equal to or higher than the strike price of the put that was written and that does not expire before the put that was written.

NAKED POSITION
Any security position, either long or short, that is not partially or completely hedged from market risk as prices fluctuate. For example, the writer of a call option is naked if he does not own the underlying security; he is partially hedged if he owns the underlying security, in that he cannot lose if the stock goes up, but he can lose if the stock goes down.

NAKED SHORTING
See GHOST SHORTING.

NAKED SHORT SALE
A quaint NASD expression for a short sale in which no security is borrowed to deliver to the purchaser. The expression is used of incidental intra-day trades (sales) with no backup inventory. The presumption is that the dealer will offset such short positions with purchases that cover and provide securities for delivery.

Otherwise, naked short selling does not fulfill the SEC and industry definitions of a short sale and may be legally or ethically improper.

NANCY REAGAN DEFENSE
The expression is patterned on the former First Lady's ad campaign against drugs. In effect, when an unwanted merger and acquisition suitor tries to take over a company, the proper defense is "Just say no."

NARROWING THE SPREAD

Action by a broker/dealer or a specialist whereby she bids higher or offers lower than the previous bid or offer, thus narrowing the spread between bids and offers.

Also called "closing a market."

NASAA

See NORTH AMERICAN SECURITIES ADMINISTRATORS ASSOCIATION.

NASD

See NATIONAL ASSOCIATION OF SECURITIES DEALERS, INC.

NASDAQ

Acronym for National Association of Securities Dealers Automated Quotations. It is a subscription computerized service, owned by the NASD. It displays, on an electronic screen, current quotes made by registered marketmakers in specific OTC securities.

See also LEVEL III, LEVEL II, and LEVEL I SERVICES.

NASDAQ OPTIONS AUTOMATED EXECUTION SYSTEM

Acronym: NOAES. A computer-assisted process designed to facilitate NASD-member trades in over-the-counter put and call options. By means of CRT terminals, members may automatically trade up to three contracts in specific option series if a marketmaker shows the best bid or offer. The transaction is executed and automatically compared between the parties. The transaction also is reported immediately to the OPRA (options ticker tape) system.

NASD FORM FR-1

A blanket certification form used by foreign broker/dealers and banks who want to subscribe to a hot issue in distribution but are not members of the syndicate. The form, when signed, attests to their understanding of the National Association of Securities Dealers' (NASD) rules on the allocation of hot issues and promises to abide by them.

NASDIM

Acronym for National Association of Securities Dealers and Investment Managers. This U.K. group oversees and regulates a significant number of securities firms and investment managers not subject to the jurisdiction of the International Stock Exchange of the United Kingdom and the Republic of Ireland. NASDIM is comparable to the NASD in the United States and is registered as an SRO under the 1986 Financial Services Bill.

NATIONAL ASSOCIATION OF BOND LAWYERS

Abbreviation: NABL. This is a professional group of law firms that serve as bond counsel to municipal issuers. They serve as a source of information to one another and as a lobby for the improvement of municipal securities laws.

NATIONAL ASSOCIATION OF SECURITIES DEALERS, INC. (NASD)

The NASD is a nonstock membership organization, registered with the SEC under the provisions of the Securities Exchange Act of 1934. Membership is limited to broker/dealers in securities, or securities underwriters, who have an office in the United States, who are not commercial banks, and who promise to abide by the rules and regulations of the association.

NATIONAL ASSOCIATION OF SECURITIES DEALERS AND INVESTMENT MANAGERS

See NASDIM.

THE NATIONAL COMPANIES AND SECURITIES COMMISSION

See NCSC.

NATIONAL CRIME INFORMATION CENTER (NCIC)

Computer information service, operated under authorization of the SEC, to which the theft or misplacement of securities must be reported. As such, the NCIC can be used to check the validity of ownership of securities offered for sale. For example, a person comes to a broker/dealer and wants to sell 2,000 shares of IBM. A check of the security and its certificate number through NCIC will determine if that certificate has been reported as stolen or misplaced.

NATIONAL FUTURES ASSOCIATION

Acronym: NFA. A commodities industry regulatory organization to which futures exchange members, commodity pool operators (CPOs), and commodity trading advisers (CTAs) must belong. NFA is responsible to the CFTC (Commodity Futures Trading Commission) for futures industry registrations, rule formulations, and recordkeeping examinations within member offices.

NATIONAL HOME LOANS

Acronym: NHL.
    See HOMES.

NATIONALLY RECOGNIZED MUNICIPAL SECURITIES INFORMATION REPOSITORY

See NRMSIR.

NATIONAL MARKET ADVISORY BOARD (NMAB)

A board of 15 persons appointed for terms of 2 to 5 years by the SEC. The board, mandated by the 1975 revisions of the 1934 Act, advises the SEC about the establishment, operation, and regulation of securities markets, especially on the subject of a "national market" for securities.

NATIONAL MARKET SYSTEM (NMS)

1. Congress, in the 1975 amendments to the Securities and Exchange Act of 1934, mandated a national market system. The amendments did not say how such a system was to be implemented; thus, the system is more theory than fact at present.

   In practice, the system envisions a nationwide electronic linkage of the various marketplaces for securities so all bid and asked prices are publicly displayed on a CRT so everyone has access to the best available prices.

2. The initials are also used of those NASDAQ-traded issues that meet certain trading requirements in terms of size of issue, shares outstanding, number of marketmakers, and so forth. NASDAQ/NMS securities are eligible for margin purchases.

NATIONAL PARTNERSHIP EXCHANGE

Acronym: NPE. This is a computer-based marketplace, located in St. Petersburg, Florida, for units of public limited partnerships.

Only SEC-registered partnerships are eligible for such secondary market trading.

NATIONAL QUOTATION BUREAU, INC. (NQB)

A subsidiary of Commerce Clearing House, Inc., that gathers bids and offers from marketmakers in over-the-counter (OTC) securities and disseminates them to subscribers. The service gives OTC equity security quotes on pink sheets and corporate bond quotes on yellow sheets. The pink and yellow sheets also identify the marketmakers. The service is printed each business day.

See also PINK SHEETS and YELLOW SHEETS.

NATIONAL SECURITIES CLEARING CORPORATION (NSCC)

Formed by the merger of the NASD, NYSE, and ASE clearing facilities, this organization receives trade information, validates it, and facilitates the delivery and receipt of money and securities for its members.

NATIONAL SECURITIES TRADING SYSTEM

See NSTS.

NATIONAL SECURITY TRADERS' ASSOCIATION

Acronym: NSTA. The lobbying arm of professional salespersons and traders who deal in over-the-counter securities. The association is composed of affiliated membership groups located in many places where brokers and dealers are centrally based. The association has approximately 4,600 members and they hold both instructional and social meetings.

NATURAL SELLER

Term used to identify the offerer of a security currently held in an investment portfolio. By definition, a natural seller is long, not short, the underlying security. The term is not used of proprietary or block trading accounts.

The term *natural*, used alone, often identifies a trade involving a natural seller and a contra party other than the member firm. Thus, the firm had no inventory risk. Example: That 100,000 share trade was a natural.

NAV

See NET ASSET VALUE.

NC

Abbreviation for noncallable. Often used on bond offering sheets to designate bonds that are noncallable.

See also NONCALLABLE.

NCC

1. The ticker symbol for National City Corporation, a large bank holding company listed on the New York Stock Exchange.
2. The common designation in the United States for Norsk Clearing Central, one of the two clearing corporations designed to process options transactions executed on the five exchanges located in Norway.

NCSC

Initials frequently used for the National Companies and Securities Commission. NCSC is the Australian counterpart of the SEC in the United States. The commission supervises the securities industry in Australia and insures the financial integrity of its marketplace.

NDFS

Acronym for next-day-funds settlement. This is the principal method used by the Depository Trust Co. (DTC) to satisfy member participant securities contracts. Payment is in the form of a paper check, which takes approximately 24 hours to clear at a Federal Reserve bank and to be available for use by the broker/dealer.

NEARBYS
In both futures and options markets, this expression signifies the months closest to expiration (options) or delivery (futures). For example, if it is October and the following futures contracts are trading: January, February, March, June, September, and December, in this context, January and February would be "nearbys."

NEAR MONEY
Accounting term used to describe noncash assets that can be quickly liquidated at a reasonable value. Near money items include marketable securities, government savings bonds, bank accounts, and the cash value of certain insurance policies.

In practice, accounts receivable are treated as near money in the computation of net quick assets and the acid-test ratio. Actually, such accounts are not near money because they must be factored; that is, sold at a discount, to produce ready cash.

NEAR MONTH
In commodities and futures trading, contracts that will expire (options) or be delivered (futures) in the next available trading month. For example, it is December 21, and call option contracts in ABC are available for January, February, and April expirations. The January contract is the "near month."

NEGATIVE CARRY
Term used if the percentage of return on a security is less than the interest charge paid for the money borrowed to buy the security. For example, a bond with a 12% return that was purchased with funds borrowed at 13% would have a negative carry.

NEGATIVE YIELD CURVE
Term used of fixed-income securities if interest rates for shorter-term securities are greater than rates for longer-term securities of the same class and rating. Term derives from the graph which depicts yields on the y-axis against times to maturity on the x-axis.

Also called "yield curve with a descending slope."

NEGOTIABLE
1. Any instrument that is readily transferable.
2. A security in registered format that has an assignment and power of substitution signed by the registered owner, either on the certificate or on an accompanying stock or bond power.
3. A price that is not firm and thus is subject to further clarification and discussion.

NEGOTIABLE CERTIFICATE OF DEPOSIT

A time deposit at a fixed rate of coupon interest. The issuer must redeem at maturity at the face value plus the stated interest rate. Holders can, however, resell the instrument in the secondary market at prevailing rates. To be negotiable, such certificates of deposit (CDs) must have face values of $100,000 or more, with $1 million and multiples thereof being most common. Maturities of less than one year are common, but there is no time limit and CDs of three to five years are also issued.

NEGOTIATED BID

Term used of an underwriting if the issuer and a single underwriting syndicate agree upon a price through discussion and mutual understanding. Most common stock underwritings are negotiated.

Negotiated bid is used in distinction to competitive bid. In a competitive bid, competing syndicates propose their price to the issuer. The issue is awarded to the syndicate with the highest bid. Competitive bids are common in municipal bond underwritings.

NELLIE MAE

See NEW ENGLAND EDUCATIONAL LOAN MARKETING CORPORATION.

NEO

Commonly used abbreviation for "nonequity options." NEOs are puts and calls on other underlying instruments (or investments) than stocks. For example, NEOs are currently being traded on foreign currencies, U.S. government notes and bonds, real estate debt issues, precious metals, and market indexes.

NET

1. As noun: dollar difference between proceeds of a sale compared to a purchaser's adjusted cost of acquisition. A negative number is a loss; positive, a gain.
2. As verb: the act of netting. Netting may be by individual transaction or by completed transactions for a specified time. For example, taxpayers must net all completed securities transactions for their tax year.

You will also see "net down" used to describe this process.

NET ASSETS

Bookkeeping term: the dollar difference between a corporation's assets and liabilities. Used in this sense, net assets also are called "net worth" or "stockholders' equity."

NET ASSET VALUE

Acronym: NAV. Used by investment companies to identify the net tangible asset value per share. Typically, the NAV forms the bid price in the quotation for an open-end management company. NAV also is used for closed-end management companies shares to determine the premium or discount reflected by the market price.

Calculation: value of portfolio securities minus management group fees and all other liabilities divided by the number of shares outstanding. NAV is calculated each business day, generally at the time that securities trading ceases on the NYSE.

NET BALANCE SYSTEM

This is a cashiering delivery system in which each firm's daily purchases and sales per issue are "netted" to arrive at a single delivery or receipt requirement. Thus, if Prudential-Bache sells 100,000 shares of IBM and buys 90,000 shares on a single market day, it has a net delivery requirement of 10,000 shares.

Under such a system, the clearing corporation notifies participant firms of its net requirements for that day. It also notifies the firm of the contra party to all trades.

The term is used in contradistinction to a trade-for-trade settlement system.

NET CAPITAL REQUIREMENT

Popular term for SEC Rule 15c3–1 that mandates the ratio of net capital; that is, cash and other assets readily turned into cash, and aggregate indebtedness, which is customer-related indebtedness that must be maintained by a broker/dealer.

The rule is complex, and various measurement standards can be used. In general, however, it can be said that aggregate indebtedness may not exceed net capital of a broker/dealer by more than 1500%.

NET CHANGE

Used in newspaper stock, bond, and mutual fund financial reports to designate the point difference between today's price and the price on the previous trading day for that security.

As a general rule, the net change represents the difference between closing prices on listed securities and the difference between bid prices on OTC securities.

NET CHG

See NET CHANGE.

NET CURRENT ASSETS

The dollar difference, if a positive number, between the current assets of a corporation and its current liabilities.

If current assets are divided by current liabilities, the resulting quotient is called the "current ratio." Thus, if a corporation has current assets of $5 and current liabilities of $2, its net current assets are $3 and its current ratio is 2½ to 1.

Also called "net working capital."

NET DOWN

Also: netdown. Used as a verb: term describes the process whereby a taxpayer offsets short-term gains against short-term losses, and long-term gains against long-term losses to achieve a final figure in both columns. If there is a net loss in one column and a net gain in the other, the client must net down once more for the final tax consequences.

Note: In some cases, tax advice is needed to determine what is, or is not, a capital loss.

NET INTEREST COST

Abbreviated: NIC. NIC is the basis for the awarding of competitive bond issues. Thus, the syndicate with the lowest NIC is typically awarded the issue.

There are different methods of computing the cost of interest to the issuer: NIC and TIC (true interest cost).

The NIC formula is:

$$\frac{\text{Total interest payments} + \text{Bond discount (or} - \text{Premium)}}{\text{Total bond years}}$$

In conjunction with municipal and corporate underwritings, NIC identifies the issuer's rate of interest expense over the life of its debt security. NIC often is computed as an interest rate for the average life of a bond issue.

NET LEASE

A long-term commercial property lease in which the tenant promises to pay: (1) a specific dollar amount to the landlord and (2) to all the incidental expenses connected with ownership, such as taxes, utility costs, repairs, and insurance. In effect, the landlord takes care only of the financing charges, if any, on the building itself. In return, the tenant has possession of the property for its use, and possible renewal privileges, tax-benefit adjustments, and—in some cases—property appreciation rights.

Often called "triple net lease."

NET LIQUID ASSETS

The dollar difference, if any, between a corporation's cash and readily marketable securities and its current liabilities. Thus, a corporation with $5 in cash and $5 in marketable securities and current liabilities of $7 has $3 in net liquid assets.

Net liquid assets is the strictest measurement of a corporation's ability of meet current debt obligations.

NET MARGINING

Term used in conjunction with the carrying of positions in futures and options on most commodities and options exchanges in the United States. If net margining is permitted, the carrying firm must provide margin or collateral based on the difference between long and short positions. Thus, if a carrying firm has 1,000 long calls and 1,300 short calls on the same underlying margin would be required only on the 300 net short contracts.

NET PROCEEDS

The actual dollars that a client receives from a completed sale of a security.

The net proceeds are the contract price minus the cost of the transaction plus any adjustments that must be made. For example, a client sells a security for $40, but there is a brokerage charge of $1, so the net proceeds are $39. However, if a client sold a call at $30 for a premium of $2 and the call were exercised, the client's net proceeds would be $32.

The term is important because it is the basis for tax gain/loss computations.

NET QUICK ASSETS

A more strict measurement of corporate liquidity; it starts by removing inventory from current assets. The remaining current assets are then compared to current liabilities. If current liabilities are subtracted from this number, the remainder is net quick assets. If this is divided by current liabilities, the quotient is the acid-test ratio. For example, if current assets minus inventory are $8 and the current liabilities are $5, the net quick assets are $3 and the acid-test ratio is 1.6 to 1.

NET SALES

Primary entry on the income statement of a corporation. Net sales represent the dollar value received for products and services minus any adjustments that must be made for refunds or returns.

NET SHARES MARKET

Term used of the trading of U.S. equity securities in European marketplaces. In Europe, most U.S. securities are traded in dealer markets.

Thus, the trades are made by banks and brokers as principals; that is, net of commissions.

NET TANGIBLE ASSETS PER SHARE

Most common formula: take total assets of a corporation and subtract any intangible assets on the balance sheet to get total tangible assets. Then, subtract all liabilities and the par value of preferred stock. Divide the remainder by the number of common shares outstanding to get net tangible assets per common share.

Also referred to as BOOK VALUE.

NET TRANSACTION

Term used of a securities transaction where no additional fee is levied on either the buyer or the seller. For example, an underwriter offers shares of a new issue at $31 net. The buyer will pay $31 and there will be no added charges.

NETWORK A

A subscription service provided by the Consolidated Tape Association. Network A gives successive round-lot transaction reports, as they are received, for New York Stock Exchange-listed securities regardless of the marketplace on which the transaction occurred. In practice, therefore, tape displays of NYSE-listed stocks may represent transactions on the NYSE, on any of the exchanges, or in the third market.

NETWORK B

A subscription service provided by the Consolidated Tape Association. Network B gives successive round-lot transaction reports, as they are received, for American Stock Exchange-listed securities regardless of the marketplace on which the transaction occurred. In practice, therefore, tape displays for ASE-listed stocks may represent transactions on the ASE, on any other exchange, or in the third market. Network B also shows transactions in issues listed exclusively on regional stock exchanges.

NETWORKING

Term used of a supporting system of information and service sharing among members of a group that have a common interest. Although nothing prevents networking within an individual firm, or by members of a specific group or department, the inference of the term is that the members of the group—who may otherwise be competitors—work together to share information and promote common interests.

Examples are too numerous to mention and are primarily exemplified by trade associations and by informal personal contacts between persons engaged in similar occupations.

NET WORKING CAPITAL
See NET CURRENT ASSETS.

NET WORTH
The dollar value by which assets exceed liabilities.

Also called "stockholders' equity" when used on corporate balance sheets.

NEUTRAL SPREAD
A vertical call spread with a long call at a lower price, and two short calls at a higher price. Thus, it is the same as a ratio write for the holder of the underlying shares.

Term is used when the market for the underlying shares is calm; that is, the underlying is trading in a fairly narrow range. Term is not used in other circumstances.

NEW ACCOUNT REPORT
Document required to be prepared, maintained, and updated by all broker/dealers who conduct business with customers. The new account form must contain essential information about the customer: the background, financial circumstances, and investment objectives of the customer.

NEW COLLAR FAMILY
Tongue-in-cheek expression for young investors who are part of a two-worker family. It is not uncommon for such persons to be employed in high-technology fields in a nonmanagement role; thus, they fall somewhere between "blue" and "white" collar status.

Their economic status is such that they can become emerging investors able to start a program of financial planning.

NEW ENGLAND EDUCATIONAL LOAN MARKETING CORPORATION
Nickname: Nellie Mae. A Massachusetts private, nonprofit corporation organized for the sole purpose of acquiring student loan notes incurred under the federal Higher Education Act of 1965.

Nellie Mae offers tax-exempt bonds to the public. The proceeds are used to purchase qualified education-related loans from eligible lenders. In this way, the lenders are made liquid, and they are in a position to make new student loans.

NEW HOUSING AUTHORITY BONDS
See PUBLIC HOUSING AUTHORITY BONDS.

NEW ISSUE
Popular term for any security offered for sale by the issuer. Technically, a new issue offers authorized but previously unissued shares. In practice, the term also encompasses the resale of Treasury shares.

NEW MONEY
Used if an issuer offers new bonds with a greater par value than the par value of bonds to be retired through a call or maturity. For example, a company issues bonds worth $12 million to refund bonds with a par value of $10 million.

NEW MONEY PREFERRED
Legal term for preferred stocks issued after October 1, 1942. New money preferred shares provide corporate holders with an 70% exclusion for cash dividends.

Old money preferred shares provide only a 60% exclusion of cash dividends to corporate holders.

NEW TIME
An International Stock Exchange of the United Kingdom and the Republic of Ireland term for a transaction (popularly called a "bargain" in the United Kingdom) completed on the last Thursday or Friday of an account period which, at the request of the buyer or seller, will be carried over for settlement in the following account period. In this way, the buyer/seller will have approximately 12 business days, rather than 1 or 2, to complete the contract.

The ISE total expression is "dealing on new time." It is negotiated and there is a slight charge, which is normally included in the price of the transaction.

NEW YORK CASH EXCHANGE
Acronym: NYCE. A network of commercial banks in the northeastern United States that is connected by computer to provide their customers with a common automated teller service. Customers of these banks may make account inquiries and cash withdrawals at any of the group's teller machines.

NEW YORK FUTURES EXCHANGE
The New York Futures Exchange is a wholly owned subsidiary of the New York Stock Exchange. The NYFE (pronounced knife) provides for

the trading of futures contracts in Treasury bills, notes, and bonds, and in GNMA debentures.

NEW YORK INTERBANK OFFERED RATE

Acronym: NIBOR. The interest rate at which U.S. financial center bank deposits trade in the U.S. marketplace. NIBOR is comparable to LIBOR (London Inter-Bank Offered Rate) and is often preferable because it is set in the same time frame and regulatory environment (principally, the reserve requirement) in which they operate.

NEW YORK MERCANTILE EXCHANGE (NYME)

A commodities exchange, located in New York City, on which futures contracts in certain metals, currencies, petroleum, and agricultural products are traded. Slang: New York Merc.

NEW YORK PLAN

An infrequently used method for issuing equipment trust certificates, which are serial debt obligations that a common carrier, such as an airline or railroad, issues to buy equipment. Basically, the issuing company acquires title to the equipment under a conditional bill of sale. As the serial maturities are retired, the issuer gradually assumes full title to the equipment.

See also PHILADELPHIA PLAN.

NEW YORK SECURITIES AUCTION CORPORATION

See NYSAC.

NEW YORK STOCK EXCHANGE (NYSE)

Acronym for New York Stock Exchange. Founded in 1792, the NYSE is a not-for-profit membership organization. It provides space and facilities for the trading of securities issued by many of America's largest and most prestigious corporations.

Often called the "Big Board," the NYSE is the largest of the nation's securities trading organizations for stocks. The dollar value of shares listed exceeds $1.25 trillion, a dollar value that represents over 60% of the top 5,000 publicly traded corporations in the United States.

NEW YORK STOCK EXCHANGE INDEX

A market measurement of the value change of an average share of common stock listed on the New York Stock Exchange.

The index is measured hourly and at the end of the trading day. The NYSE index is a composite measurement. It is divided into four categories: industrials, transportation, utilities, and finance companies. The index gives a value measurement because it takes into account the number of outstanding shares for the individual stocks. Average price change measurements also are provided to the news services.

Also called the "NYSE composite index."

NEW YORK STOCK EXCHANGE RULE 387
See RULE 387.

NEW YORK STOCK EXCHANGE RULE 405
See RULE 405.

NEW ZEALAND STOCK EXCHANGE
This exchange has four regional trading floors (Wellington, Auckland, Christchurch, and Invercargill). Trading is open from 9:30 to 11:00 A.M. and from 2:15 to 3:30 P.M. After-hour trading is permitted for 30 minutes following each half-day session. Regular way settlement is by delivery versus payment, which in many cases may take up to 30 days.

NFA
See NATIONAL FUTURES ASSOCIATION.

NG
Popularly used initials for: not good.

Although used of checks that are returned for insufficient funds, NG also is used popularly in the brokerage industry for defective or returned securities deliveries.

NH
See DRT and NOT HELD.

NHL
See HOMES.

NIBOR
See NEW YORK INTERBANK OFFERED RATE.

NIC
See NET INTEREST COST.

NICKEL
1. Popular identifier for the shares of INCO, a Canadian corporation formerly called International Nickel Company, Ltd.
2. Street slang for a movement, plus or minus, of five basis points (+/−.05%) in the yield of a debt security. Example: "Since yesterday, the bonds have moved down a nickel."

NICS

Acronym for Newly Industrialized Countries. Term used of four Asiatic countries, Singapore, Hong Kong, South Korea, and Taiwan, that developed into economic powerhouses in the 1970s and 1980s. Together with Japan, these countries represent the largest segment of the U.S. balance of payment deficit.

NIDS

Acronym for National Institutional Delivery System. NIDS is a central processing system for COD transactions by customers of broker/dealers in the United States. NIDS is operated by the Depository Trust Co. (DTC) and it confirms, affirms, and settles transactions via book entry between executing firms and their COD customers (or their agents or custodians).

NIF

See NOTE ISSUANCE FACILITIES.

NIFTY FIFTY

A term used of the top 50 stocks favored by institutional investors. The term was popular in the 1970s when, despite bear markets, these institutional favorites maintained their value.

You will also see the term *first tier* or *top tier* to designate these securities.

NIKKEI STOCK INDEX

An index of the price movement of 225 high-quality stocks traded in the Japanese marketplace (i.e., on the Tokyo Stock Exchange). It is widely followed by persons interested in the economic movements in Japan, and it is considered a barometer of domestic interest in Japanese equities.

The NIKKEI is also linked to redemption values of some international securities.

NIL-PAID SHARES

Term used in allotment letters in the United Kingdom to describe shares during the interim period between the announcement of the offering and the actual subscription date. During this period, the value of the shares can be both theoretical and the subject of supply/demand forces for the subscription rights. As a result, no money is required for the subscription until such time as the market value of the shares is determined.

NINE-BOND RULE

Popular term for the NYSE Rule 396 requiring that orders for nine listed bonds, or less, be sent to the floor to seek a market. In practice, it means the order must be left on the floor for an hour, or until the NYSE closes for the day—if such time is smaller. Customers may request the rule be waived, but the accepting member firm may, in this case, only execute agency orders for the bonds. Usually, the nine-bond rule works to the advantage of small investors in bonds.

1992

This is the year in which all tariffs in the European Economic Community (EEC) will be removed. As a result, members of the Common Market in Europe will be granted equal and free access to each other's markets. 1992 is used to designate a time of wide-ranging change in Europe.

In the United Kingdom, in compliance with the Financial Services Act of 1986, European financial services firms will be able to provide services in the United Kingdom if they provide suitable documentation of their compliance.

NIPPER

Slang for the shares of Northern Indiana Public Service Company. The nickname is derived from the NYSE stock ticker symbol: NI.

NITWIT

Slang for the common shares of Northwest Industries, Inc., now known as Farley Northwest Corp., a large conglomerate involved in consumer and industrial businesses. Term is derived from its former NYSE symbol: NWT.

NL

See NO LOAD.

NMAB

See NATIONAL MARKET ADVISORY BOARD.

NMS

See NATIONAL MARKET SYSTEM.

NNOTC

Official designation for a non-NASDAQ security. In other words, a NNOTC stock is a corporate equity that is publicly traded and is neither listed on an exchange nor traded on the NASDAQ system.

NNOTC stocks are often referred to as "Pink Sheet" issues and, under Schedule H of the NASD bylaws, are subject to special trade reporting requirements.

NO-ACTION LETTER
Often it is difficult to determine whether an activity is prohibited under the securities laws of the United States. In such a case, the party contemplating the action may write to the SEC for a specific opinion. A no-action letter from the SEC means that it will undertake neither civil nor criminal action if the activity occurs as indicated. No-action letters are specific to the inquirer and are applicable only to the circumstances outlined in the inquiry.

NOAES
See NASDAQ OPTIONS AUTOMATED EXECUTION SYSTEM.

NOBO LIST
NOBO is an abbreviation for "non-objective beneficial owner." This is a reference to SEC Rule 14b-1(c). Under this rule, an issuer has the right to demand of a nominee the names of actual beneficial owners of stocks, provided the owner does not object to such disclosure.

NO BRAINER
1. Trader's term of a customer transaction that can be completed quickly and completely. Also called, to use a basketball term, a "lay up."
2. A reference to an obvious market trend; that is, one that needs neither technical nor market analysis skill to discern.
3. Any investment procedure that is automatically applied without reference to fundamental or market conditions. For example, "Dollar-cost-averaging and constant dollar plans are no-brainers."

NOB SPREAD
Acronym for notes-over-bonds spread. A futures contract based on the relationship between the price of Treasury notes and the price of Treasury bonds. A change in the price spread impacts the shape of the yield curve and, it is believed, reflects investor confidence in the direction of the debt markets.

NO LOAD
Popular designation of those open-end investment companies that do not levy a sales charge. NL is commonly used in mutual fund columns in the financial section of newspapers.

In practice, no load means that both the bid and offer price of the fund are the same (i.e., the net asset value of the underlying shares).

NOLO CONTENDERE
Legal term, from the Latin: "I do not wish to contend (or contest) the action. . . ." Technically, it implies partial but not full guilt, and thus is usually the preliminary step to an out-of-court settlement.

NOM
1. The ticker symbol for Norbeau Mines, Inc., a Canadian company listed on the Toronto Stock Exchange.
2. The common designation in the United States for Norsk Opsjon-marked, one of two clearing corporations designed to process options transactions executed on the five exchanges located in Norway.

NOMINAL EXERCISE PRICE
The dollar value for a GNMA option contract found by multiplying the strike price times the unpaid principal balance on a GNMA certificate with an 8% stated rate of interest. For example, at a strike price of 65 and an unpaid principal balance of $98,000 on a certificate with an 8% coupon, the nominal exercise price is $63,700.

See also AGGREGATE EXERCISE PRICE.

NOMINAL QUOTATION
A bid and offer given by a broker as an estimate of the value of a security. The broker, however, is unwilling to trade at the prices given. NASD and other industry rules require that nominal quotations be clearly identified as such.

NOMINAL YIELD
The yield, stated as a percentage, on a fixed-income security that divides the annual payout in dollars by the par value of the security. Thus, the nominal yield on a bond that pays $110 per year in interest and that has a par value of $1,000 is 11%.

Also called the "coupon yield," although this term is inappropriate for preferred stock.

NOMINEE
1. The name inscribed on a stock/bond certificate if it is different from that of the beneficial owner.
2. Also: nominee name. Term is used to describe securities registered in the name of a partnership specifically formed to facilitate transfer or sale on behalf of the actual owner. Example, CEDE is a partnership

organized by the Depository Trust Company, Inc., to facilitate transfer of securities it holds for the actual owners.

Synonyms: in nominee name, in the name of a nominee, held by the nominee, and the like.

NONBORROWED RESERVES

A weekly statistical indicator issued by the Federal Reserve. It states the total of member bank reserves minus their borrowings through the discount window. As such, nonborrowed reserves is a factual dollar amount; it may or may not reflect the Federal Reserve's willingness to supply or absorb reserves from the commercial banking system.

We use the term *moral suasion* to indicate whether the Federal Reserve, through personal contact with its member banks, would like to see this number increase or decrease.

NONCALLABLE

A security, either equity or debt, that does not give the issuer the option of redeeming the security before the maturity date, in the case of bonds, or during the lifetime of the issue, in the case of preferred stock.

Most securities, even if callable, are noncallable for a period of years after issuance.

The absence of callability or the details of the call privilege are always stated at the time of issuance.

NONCLEARING MEMBER

A National Association of Securities Dealers member or an exchange member who does not maintain his or her own operations function; instead, the person uses the facilities of another member to make comparisons and to arrange for final settlement of contracts. The nonclearing member pays a contractual fee to the clearing member for these services.

NONCOMPETITIVE BIDS

Term used in conjunction with auctions for U.S. Treasury securities. Persons who wish to buy $1 million or less of Treasury bills, notes, or bonds may enter noncompetitive bids. Such bidders always receive an execution, and the price they will pay is the average of the prices paid by those competitive bidders whose bids are accepted by the Treasury.

Also called "noncompetitive tenders."

NONCUMULATIVE PREFERRED

A class of preferred stock that imposes no future obligation on the issuer if a dividend payment is omitted.

Noncumulative preferred stock is extremely rare. Almost all preferred issues with a stated dividend are cumulative.

NONDIVERSIFIED MANAGEMENT COMPANY

A management investment company that declares that it does not intend to be bound by the definition of a diversified company. This declaration, made to the SEC, also is included in its prospectus.

A nondiversified management company is not subject to the asset allocation limitations outlined in the Investment Company Act of 1940, but it loses the privileges accorded to registered and diversified management companies accorded by the Internal Revenue Code. In practice, therefore, it loses a tax exemption. This loss can be justified only by the prospect of extraordinary long-term capital gains.

NON-EQUITY OPTION

See NEO.

NONPURPOSE LOAN

A loan made, using collateralized securities, in which the borrower attests that the money will not be used to purchase, carry, or trade in securities subject to Federal Reserve Board credit regulations or limitations. Example: "I went to my bank to borrow $50,000. I brought along listed securities worth $80,000. My banker said that the bank could not lend the money unless I made it a nonpurpose loan." (Reason: A $50,000 loan on $80,000 of securities collateral exceeds the percentage amount permitted under Federal Reserve credit regulations if the money is to be used to buy securities.)

NONQUALIFYING ANNUITY

An annuity—either fixed, variable, or hybrid—that is not purchased in an IRS-approved pension plan. Because it is nonqualifying, it is purchased with aftertax dollars. Nonqualification, however, does not take away the tax sheltering of the growth of the original investment dollars, subject to the provisions of the Internal Revenue Code.

NONQUALIFYING STOCK OPTION

An option, granted by the issuing corporation, to purchase a fixed number of shares at a fixed price on or before a specified date. Such options are often granted to corporate executives. Because it is nonqualifying, the difference between the option price and the fair market value is considered as earned income in the tax year when the option is exercised. Thus, this difference is subject to withholding and income taxes.

NONRECOURSE LOAN
Used of direct participation programs. A limited partner borrows funds to partially finance his participation in the partnership and pledges as collateral his ownership in the venture. The lender, therefore, can attach the ownership but not other assets of the partnership. The advantage to the borrower is the leverage it provides.

Recourse loans that pledge the assets of the partnership itself can only be made by the general partner on behalf of all the partners.

NONRECURRING CHARGE
One-time income or expense entries on the income statement of a corporation.

Also called "extraordinary items," with the implication that there will be no similar entry in the future. For example, the sale of an asset, such as property, or the write-off of a loss are typical one-time nonrecurring income and charges.

NONREFUNDABLE
Provision of a bond indenture in which the issuer promises not to retire a bond issue by funds from a second bond issue. The provision may be permanent, or limited to a refunding at a future date, or to a refunding only if a new issue can be made at a fixed interest rate difference from the present issue. For example, an issuer of 14% bonds promises no refunding unless a subsequent issue can be made at 11% or less.

NONRESIDENT AFFIDAVIT
Term formerly used when opening a brokerage account. It refers to a form that attests that the account holder—an individual, joint, or partner—is not a resident of New York State. By definition, all corporations were residents.

This attestation exempted the owner from resident stock transfer taxes, although nonresident stock transfer taxes were applicable.

The stock transfer tax, while still on the books, is subject to a 100% rebate. Thus, no tax is paid and the form need not be supplied.

NON-RESIDENT ALIEN
See NRA (1).

NONRESIDENT-OWNED INVESTMENT CORPORATION
Acronym: NRO. Term used in Canada of a company whose shares and funded indebtedness are exclusively owned by nonresidents of Canada.

An NRO can qualify, if it meets certain other requirements concerning sources of revenue, for a preferential tax rate of 25% on taxable income.

Status as an NRO obviously encourages foreign investment in Canada.

NOOKIE
Sales and trading slang used to identify the common stock of UNC Resources, Inc., a company engaged in uranium mining and nuclear development. The company's former name was United Nuclear Corporation—hence, its nickname.

NO-PAR VALUE
An equity security which has no minimum dollar value assigned to each share. Instead, a stated value is assigned and used in the makeup of the corporate balance sheet.

Also called "no-par stock."

NO-REVIEW OFFERING
Slang for an accelerated public offering of securities under an S-16 registration statement.

Substantial-sized issuers, up-to-date in their SEC reports and with publicly held securities already outstanding, can file this registration statement, receive a no-review commentary from the SEC, and make an underwritten public offering within 48 to 72 hours (in most cases).

NORMAL EXERCISE OPTION
CBOE term for an option that may be exercised at any time prior to its expiration date. All CBOE options are normal exercise options within the limits set for the exercise of options of the same class during a period of five business days.

Antonym: limited exercise options. *Limited exercise options*, a British term, permits exercise only within the five business days preceding expiration.

NORMAL INVESTMENT PRACTICE
A norm used to justify the allocation of hot issue securities to the personal accounts of decision makers of institutional accounts. For example, if the senior trust officer of a bank has, over the past two years, made 10 purchases from the underwriter, with an average of $2,000 per issue, it would not be unethical to allocate $2,000 of a hot issue to her account. The exclusive purchase of hot issues does not justify a normal investment practice.

Also called "history of investment in the account."

NORMAL SCALE
Term used of the offering scale of new serial bonds in which the yield on closer maturities is lower than the yield on farther serial maturities or term bonds, or both.

Antonym: inverted scale.

NORMAL TRADING UNIT
The accepted minimum trading quantity for a purchase or sale. For equity securities, 100 shares is normal, although 10- or 25-share units exist, and some institutional traders now make markets with 500-share units.

Purchases and sales below the unit of trading are called "odd lots."

Bond market units may vary, but it is not uncommon for units to be 25 bonds for municipals, 100 bonds for governments, and 250 bonds for corporates.

Also called "normal unit of trading," also a "round lot."

NORSK CLEARING CENTRAL
See NCC (2).

NORSK OPSJONSMARKED
See NOM (2).

NORTH AMERICAN SECURITIES ADMINISTRATORS ASSOCIATION
Acronym: NASAA. A trade organization comprised of state securities administrators of the United States, Mexico, and the Canadian provinces. Purpose: to provide a medium for cooperation and coordination of state and international securities regulations.

NORTH/SOUTH OF . . .
Used of the direction of interest rates in relation to a well-known benchmark; for example, LIBOR. Rates are said to be going north of LIBOR when they are moving up, and south if they are declining. Other benchmarks might be the federal funds rate, the discount rate, or the 30-year T-bond rate.

NOTARIAL SECURITIES
This is the term used in the financial services industry for an issuer's securities if there is no transfer agent. Notarial securities typically arise if an issuer is bankrupt.

Since certificates cannot be immediately re-registered in the name of the new owner, such securities trade with a stock power attached. The name of the previous owner must be notarized on the stock power to constitute good delivery.

NOTE

A debt security with a relatively limited maturity, as opposed to a long-term bond. The expression "note" is commonly used of government securities with maturities of from 2 to 10 years.

Privately placed corporate debt securities and noncallable shorter-term debt securities are commonly called "notes."

Municipal notes may be very short term or they may have maturities up to 2, 3, or even 4 years.

In practice, a note is a debt security so-called by the issuer. No specific time limitations can be given as a universal rule.

NOTE ISSUANCE FACILITIES

Acronym: NIF. General term for the underwriting facilities associated with offerings of offshore Eurodollar notes and Eurodollar certificates of deposit.

Frequent synonym: revolving underwriting facilities.

NOTES-OVER-BONDS SPREAD

See NOB SPREAD.

NOT HELD (NH)

An instruction that may be added to a market order to buy or sell. It permits a floor broker, but not a specialist, to use time or price discretion for the effective execution of the order. Used principally for large orders.

Older practice was to use DRT (i.e., disregard tape).

Both NH and DRT mean that the customer will not hold the floor broker responsible if a better execution might have been possible.

NOTIFICATION

This is the simplest form of blue-sky registration for a public offering within a state. To commence the public offering of securities within a state that permits notification, the issuer need only notify the state's securities commissioner.

NOT RATED

1. Used of bonds and preferred stocks that are not rated by one of the national services. The designation is factual and implies neither the lack nor presence of credit risk.
2. Used in tombstones of debt issues, particularly municipals, to designate that a serial maturity is not being reoffered for sale.
3. Used as an abbreviation for nonrefundable.
   See also NONREFUNDABLE.

NOT TO PRESS
See NTP.

NOVATION
The substitution of one debt for another by the payment of a dollar difference. Many synonyms could be used: restructuring, postponing, and the like.

Here is a frequent example of novation: a GNMA forward contract is cancelled, another contract is substituted, and either the buyer or the seller makes a cash settlement to the other, depending on market conditions and the conditions of the new contract.

Novation is not considered to be a capital transaction by the Internal Revenue Service; therefore, gains are ordinary income gains and losses.

NOW ACCOUNT
Acronym for negotiable order of withdrawal. Term for a savings bank account that permits checking privileges. The depositor can earn interest on savings until such time as checks are presented for payment. In practice, therefore, NOW accounts are a combined savings and checking account.

NPE
See NATIONAL PARTNERSHIP EXCHANGE.

NQB
See NATIONAL QUOTATION BUREAU, INC.

NR
See NOT RATED.

NRA
1. Abbreviation for: nonresident alien; that is, an individual or institution with no permanent address or place of business in the United States. If such an individual or institution has an account with a U.S. broker/dealer, it must sign a Treasury Department affidavit (W-8) and thus be subject to certain withholding taxes on dividends and interest received (if the security is subject to such withholding).
2. Often used as NR in newspaper bond reporting columns if a security is not subject to withholding for NRAs.

NRMSIR
Pronounced: NURM-SUR.

Acronym for Nationally Recognized Municipal Securities Information Repository, a term created in conjunction with MSRB Rules G-36 and G-8.

Beginning in January 1990, all municipal issues of $1 million or more require an Official Statement (which is comparable to a prospectus).

To make sure that Official Statements are kept for records and proper owner referral, a copy is maintained by the underwriter and a copy is sent to an "information repository."

NSCC
See NATIONAL SECURITIES CLEARING CORPORATION.

NSE
Initials of the Nagoya Stock Exchange. NSE is the third largest of the Japanese exchanges (after Tokyo and Osaka) and like the others is a membership exchange with both regular and saitori members responsible for exchange activities.

See also SAITORI.

NSTA
See NATIONAL SECURITY TRADERS' ASSOCIATION.

NSTS
Acronym for National Securities Trading System. NSTS is an automated electronic execution system used by the Cincinnati Stock Exchange, and it is used to provide members with agency transactions of up to 1,099 shares at the best available ITS quote prices. Under the system, both market and limit agency orders are matched with contra agency orders at the same price before pairing them against dealer (principal) orders.

NTP
Acronym for not to press. These initials may be added as a qualifier on an execution by a jobber on the International Stock Exchange of the United Kingdom and the Republic of Ireland. They signify that the jobber (marketmaker) has sold short to complete the trade and does not want (nor expect) the buyer to press for delivery of the shares under threat of buy-in proceedings. The shares will be delivered in the normal course of business by a later purchase by the jobber.

NUCLEAR WAR
Corporate finance term for a situation where two or more companies compete for the acquisition of another corporation.

The expression reflects the fears of any nuclear confrontation: The situation is mutually destructive for all concerned.

NUMBER CRUNCHER
See RACCOON.

NUMBERS ONLY

Synonym for a nominal quotation. For example, in response to a request for a quote, a dealer responds 18–19, numbers only. The response does not obligate the dealer to make a transaction.

NYCE

See NEW YORK CASH EXCHANGE.

NYFE

See also NEW YORK FUTURES EXCHANGE.

NYME

Acronym for New York Mercantile Exchange. NYME provides a marketplace for the trading of futures contracts in several metals, currencies, petroleum, and agricultural by-products.

NYSAC

Acronym for New York Securities Auction Corporation. An alternative to market liquidity for certain inactive securities. Designed to permit subscribers to offer or bid weekly for issues with limited marketability, it is an attempt to derive realistic prices for infrequently traded bonds and stock. Included are issues in default, high-yield/low-quality (junk) bonds, and unusual-sized blocks of stock.

NYSE

See NEW YORK STOCK EXCHANGE.

O

O

Used in newspaper reports of a corporation's earnings to designate that the principal market for the corporation's securities is over the counter (OTC); for example, MCIC (O).

O –

See ZERO-MINUS TICK.

O +

See ZERO-PLUS TICK.

OARS

Acronym for Opening Automated Report Service. Computerized service subscribed to by specialists on the New York and the American stock exchanges to facilitate opening and reopening of the market for individual securities.

OATS

Acronym for Obligations Assimilables du Tresor, the treasury obligations of the French government. OATs are now available in the United States as ADRs, the first such ADRs created for a foreign debt issue. As such, the ADRs are denominated in U.S. dollars.

The underlying debt obligations are the 9.80s due 1/1/96 and the 8.50s due 6/1/97.

OB
See OR BETTER.

OBLIGATIONS ASSIMILABLES DU TRESOR
See OATS.

OBO
See ORDER BOOK OFFICIAL.

OCC
See OPTIONS CLEARING CORPORATION.

OCD
See OTHER CHECKABLE DEPOSITS.

OCO ORDER
See ONE-CANCELS-THE-OTHER ORDER.

OCT

Acronym for order confirmation transaction. OCT permits NASD members to directly negotiate OTC option transactions for more than three contracts, yet use the NOAES facility. Once contract terms have been agreed upon, the completed transaction can be entered into the NOAES system and will appear on the (OPRA options ticker tape) system.

ODD LOT

Specific name for exchange transactions that are for less than the unit of trading. For example, a trade for 90 shares if the unit of trading is 100 shares.

Technically, over-the-counter (OTC) transactions are negotiated; thus, there are no odd-lot transactions. In practice, OTC transactions below the units of trading are also called "odd-lot transactions"; but there is no standard odd-lot differential charged for purchases or sales. The trader, however, will change the bid for smaller sales, or change the offer for smaller purchases.

ODD-LOT THEORY

Hypothesis, on a theory of Garfield Drew, that one may predict a general market trend opposed to the trend of odd-lot transactions. Thus, if odd-lotters are buying, sell; if selling, buy.

The theory is without statistical validity and has no predictive value. For example, in the past 10 years, with big market drops in terms of total return versus inflation, odd-lot holders have been sellers on balance—the right thing to do. The theory is historical and has no present value.

OEX

Ticker symbol and common identifier of the Standard & Poor's 100 Index option traded on the CBOE. Both puts and calls are available at five point striking point intervals and with three months traded at any one time: the current month, the subsequent month, and the following month. Options are American style (as opposed to the S&P 500 Option) and thus may be exercised at any time during the life of the option. Settlement is in cash and is based on the deviation of the strike price from the index value times $100. Thus, if a call at 305 is exercised on a day when the closing price of the OEX option is 340, the writer would be forced to pay the holder $35 \times \$100$, or $3,500. The options are used extensively to hedge or moderate systematic market risk.

OFF BOARD

Although the term may be used of any over-the-counter transaction, the most prevalent usage is of a transaction in a listed security that is completed either in the OTC market or is completed within the member firm itself. For example, if a member firm receives a sell order for a listed security that is transacted OTC, or that it buys for its own account, the transaction is off board.

OFF-BUDGET AGENCY

A government-sponsored enterprise whose activities do not appear in the federal budget, although these agencies are within the discipline of the federal budget because of guarantees, both legal and moral. Typical of such off-budget agencies are: the U.S. Postal Service, the Student Loan Marketing Association, and the Federal Home Loan Mortgage Association.

OFFER

The price at which someone is willing to sell a security. In practice, the amount the offerer is willing to sell is a round lot of the security. On exchange transactions, the offer price is commonly combined with a size; that is, the number of shares so offered.

Also called "offer price."

Asked price is a common synonym for offer price.

OFFERING DATE

The date on which a security is first offered for sale to the public, although on bonds the dated date is technically the date from which accrued interest begins and may not be the same as the offering date.

See also DATED DATE.

OFFERING PRICE

The lowest price at which someone is willing to sell a round lot of a security.

Also called the "asked price."

See also OFFER.

OFFERING SCALE

The prices, expressed in points and decimal parts of a point or as eighths, or expressed as a yield to maturity, at which the underwriters will sell the individual serial maturities of a bond issue.

The expression is commonly used in municipal underwriting. For example, the 10s of 1992 are offered at par, while the 11s of 2002 are offered at 11.50 (i.e., at a discount to yield 11.50% to maturity).

Also called the "scale."

OFFER WANTED

Offer wanted (OW) is often entered in the pink or yellow sheets by a dealer who wants another dealer to make an offer for the security.

See also PINK SHEETS and YELLOW SHEETS.

OFF-FLOOR ORDER

General New York Stock Exchange term for an order that originates off the floor of the exchange. As a rule, off-floor orders take precedence over orders that originate on the floor. For example, a typical order from a member firm customer is an off-floor order, while an order from a competitive floor trader, who is on the floor at the time, is not.

OFFICE OF SUPERVISORY JURISDICTION (OSJ)

A National Association of Securities Dealers' term for an office, or a group of offices, supervised by a parent office of a member. The concept involves two ideas: the office of supervisory jurisdiction (1) must have a written set of procedures that is to be followed and (2) must be responsible for the ethical conduct of registered representatives within the OSJ. Every member of the NASD must have at least one office of supervisory jurisdiction.

OFFICIAL NOTICE OF SALE
An announcement by a municipal issuer that it is soliciting competitive bids for a forthcoming issue of municipal securities. The notice gives important facts about the issue: par value, conditions of the issue, and name of a municipal official who can be contacted for other information about the issue. Such notices appear in the *Daily Bond Buyer* under the heading, Official Notice of Sale.

OFFICIAL STATEMENT
Abbreviation: OS. This is the counterpart in the municipal securities industry of a prospectus in the corporate securities field.

Technically, municipals are exempt securities and need not register with the SEC. Issuers are, however, required to avoid "fraud and manipulation." To avoid any semblance of selling securities without making the full facts known to the buyer, many municipal issuers prepare an official statement, quite similar in appearance to a prospectus, for distribution to the initial purchasers.

OFFSET
General term for a transaction that:
1. Eliminates a commitment in a futures or forward contract by means of an equal and opposite transaction in an identical commodity or security. For example, a long contract for $1 million GNMA 9% of September 2003 can be offset by the sale of a forward contract for the same amount, coupon, and date.
2. Hedges, partially or fully, a present position in a security or commodity. For example, a client with a long-term paper profit in a security sells an equal number of shares short against the box.
   See also HEDGE and BOX.

OFFSHORE
As an adjective: to qualify a financial organization that is domiciled outside the United States and thus not regulated by U.S. securities laws. For example, a mutual fund, domiciled in the Bahamas, is an offshore fund. The fact that an organization is offshore does not mean that its securities may be legally sold within the United States. The designation is factual only. To legally sell securities within the United States, they must conform with U.S. laws.

OFF THE CURVE

The yield curve is a graph of the yields to maturity of various U.S. Treasury securities listed according to time to maturity.

Corporate debt securities are said to be "off the curve" if the Treasury yield curve is used as a benchmark in the pricing of the corporate debt securities.

OFF-THE-RUN ISSUE

Slang used by OTC marketmakers for equity securities that are not regularly included in the pink sheets.

Such securities are off the run because there is little trading or interest in the security. Thus, such securities do not merit the effort needed to update prices until an inquiry is received.

O'HARE SPREAD

Facetious floor term used on the Chicago trading floors—whether it be CBT, CME, or CBOE—to designate a spread that goes against a trader; thus, if the trader expects the spread to widen, it narrows, and vice versa.

The concept is simple: The trader is now out of capital and goes to O'Hare Airport to fly out of Chicago forever.

OID BOND

See ORIGINAL-ISSUE DISCOUNT BOND.

OIL PATCH

Broad description of those areas of the United States that are the principal locations for exploration, drilling, pumping, and refining petroleum products and their derivatives. Offshore drilling is also included in the designation. As a general rule, Texas, Louisiana, Oklahoma, California, and Alaska are considered U.S. oil patches.

The term is also used as the location of economic problems caused by a drop in petroleum prices and the effect on the purveyors of other services and property values in these areas. For example, "There has been a dramatic drop in housing prices in the Texas oil patch."

THE OLD LADY

Affectionate term in the United Kingdom for the Bank of England. The Bank of England has a place in the economy of Great Britain similar to that of the Federal Reserve in the United States. Thus, it acts as a central bank for the issuance of currency and as a regulator of credit and the money supply in the United Kingdom—although the Bank of England exercises much more moral suasion over credit than does the Fed.

Also called the "Old Lady of Threadneedle Street."

OLD MONEY PREFERRED

A designation given to preferred shares of domestic corporations. Preferred shares of domestic corporations issued before October 1, 1942, are—if held by another domestic corporation—eligible for a 60% exclusion of dividends from taxable income. Preferreds issued after that date are called "new money preferreds" and are eligible for an 70% exclusion if the holder is another domestic corporation.

Also called "old money."

OM

Acronym for Stockholm Options Market (Optionsmarknad). OM is a publicly owned trading institution overseen by the Swedish Bank Inspection Board (similar to the SEC in the United States).

Founded in 1985, OM trades in Swedish equity options, interest-rate options, Swedish OMX index options, and index forward options. Unlike U.S. options, *only* covered calls and puts are permitted to be written on stock options.

The index options or forwards may be settled for cash or for shares of a Swedish mutual fund.

ONE CANCELS THE OTHER ORDER (OCO)

Concept: A client enters an order for two transactions; if order A is transacted, order B must be cancelled.

Most member firms dealing with the public will not accept such an order.

Also called an "alternative order."

ONE DECISION STOCK

Term used of the selection of a "blue-chip" stock for permanent inclusion in one's portfolio. The concept is simple: Since there is no intention of selling, only a decision to buy need be made.

ONE-MAN PICTURE

A trader's description of a quotation that is obtained from only one marketmaker. This single source may represent a somewhat slanted view of the market; hence, it is a one-man picture.

ONE PERCENT BROKER

An agent who arranges for the borrowing and lending of securities between dealers and institutional investors. The fee for this service is 1% of the interest rate paid by the certificate lender for the receipt and use of the cash deposited by the borrower as collateral for the loan.

ONE SHARE, ONE VOTE RULE

Popular term for SEC Rule 19c-4. Effective July 7, 1988, no U.S. exchange or the NASD may list or provide quotations for any issuer that *reduces* the voting rights of existing shareholders. Thus, no-vote stock or less than equal could be issued, but no stock with "super voting rights."

Super voting right stock issued before July 7, 1988, is exempted. IPOs, secondaries, and securities issued to consummate a merger are also exempted, provided they have no greater vote than other common shares of the same issuer.

In 1990 the Supreme Court decreed this SEC rule to be unconstitutional.

ONE-SIDED MARKET

A trader who is willing to deal only on one side of the market (i.e., the trader is willing to buy or sell but not both).

Also known as a "one-way market."

ONE-WAY MARKET

See ONE-SIDED MARKET.

ON-FLOOR ORDER

General designation for an order originating on the floor or from the property owned by the exchange. This designation is to make sure that persons who are members cannot use their inside information of floor conditions to take advantage of buyers or sellers who do not have access to this information.

ONGOING BUYER OR ONGOING SELLER

Term to describe a buyer or seller who wishes to accumulate, if a buyer, or distribute, if a seller, by making many purchases or sales of a given security. Ongoing buying or selling, if done with limit or scale orders, will normally result in a better average price than a one-time order to buy or sell a large quantity of a security.

ONTARIO SECURITIES COMMISSION (OSC)

The OSC is the counterpart of the SEC in the Canadian province of Ontario. As such, the OSC has official jurisdiction over all securities-related registrations and the dealer and agent activities within its borders. In this role, the OSC also includes jurisdiction over the Toronto Stock Exchange (TSE), the largest of the Canadian exchanges.

ON THE CLOSE ORDER

A customer's order to buy or sell a specific amount of a stock on the NYSE as close as is practicable to the closing bell for trading. No assurance may be given that the order will receive the final price, nor that it will be capable of execution.

Generally abbreviated OTC on the order ticket.

ON THE HOOK ORDERS
See CAP ORDERS.

ON-THE-HOP
Trading room term for "immediately." Thus, to get the attention of another trader, a first trader may call: "Pick up XYZ broker on-the-hop."

ON THE OPENING ORDER
A customer's instruction to buy or sell a specific amount of a stock on the NYSE, but only as part of the initial transaction for that security on that market day. If the order cannot be executed in this fashion, the order is to be cancelled immediately.

Do not confuse the concept of "On the opening," which is a customer instruction, with the rule that all *market* orders received before the opening must be included in the opening transaction. Limit and stop orders need not be so included.

ON-THE-RUN ISSUES
Government securities trading term used to designate newly issued securities for which the firm intends to make a continuous market. The most popular on-the-run issues are newly issued governments and those with 5–7 year maturities.

OPD
Tape symbol designating a transaction that is:
1. Either the first transaction of the day in a stock whose opening was delayed beyond 10:30 EST.
2. Or, if used before 10:30, designates a transaction that represents a significant change from the previous day's close. Normally, this is 1 or more points for stocks selling below $20, or 2 or more points for stocks selling above $20.

OPEN
As adjective:
1. Used of syndicate members who will accept indications of interest, or of marketmakers who will accept bids or offers.
2. Used of security orders to buy or sell that are not yet executed or, more commonly, of good-till-cancelled orders.

OPEN BOX
See ACTIVE BOX.

OPEN-END MANAGEMENT COMPANY
A management investment company that issues new shares if people wish to buy them, and whose shares are redeemable whenever the present holders wish to tender them back to the management company.
Popularly called a "mutual fund."

OPEN-END MORTGAGE
A bond, with property as collateral, whose indenture permits further bond issues based on the same property. In the event of default, creditors for all issues made under an open-end mortgage have equal claim on the value of the asset.

OPENING AUTOMATED REPORT SERVICE
See OARS.

OPENING ONLY ORDER
See AT-THE-OPENING ORDER.

OPENING PURCHASE
A transaction that establishes or increases a customer's long position in an option series. For example, a customer, with no position in the ABC Jan 50 calls, buys five calls as an opening purchase.

OPENING SALE
A transaction that establishes or increases a customer's short position in an option series. For example, a customer, with no position in the LMN Apr 50 calls, writes five calls as an opening sale.
The expression *opening sale* is factual; it is used independently of the customer's position in the underlying security or option. Thus, an opening sale may be either covered or uncovered.

OPEN INTEREST
The aggregate number of exercisable contracts, for either an option series or a commodity future, that are currently existing on the records of a clearing corporation. An open interest of one means that there is a buyer and seller with the same contract specification. For example, a writer of an LMN Apr 50 call and a holder of an LMN Apr 50 call that has neither been exercised nor expired.

OPEN-MARKET OPERATIONS

Term used specifically of sales or purchases by the Federal Reserve Open Market Committee of securities in the secondary market. Such purchases or sales expand or contract the money supply.

Term also is used generically of the Fed's ability to make such transactions and thereby change monetary policy.

OPEN ON THE PRINT

Term used by a block positioner who takes the opposite side of the trade from an institutional client. The transaction will appear as completed on the consolidated tape, but the block positioner wants its sales force to know that they are to seek buyers or sellers to offset the resulting risk position. For example, a block positioner is short 10,000 shares because, on a purchase of 100,000 by an institutional client, the block positioner sold its inventory of 90,000 and went short 10,000 shares. The sales force will look for sellers of 10,000 shares so the firm can cover its short position.

OPEN ORDER

Technically, any unexecuted order to buy or sell a security. In practice, open order is used as a synonym for a good-till-cancelled order.

OPEN REPO

A repurchase agreement (repo or RP) without a specific date for the repurchase. Such repos are continued on a day-to-day basis. Either party may terminate the agreement at any time, and interest rates are negotiated as market conditions dictate.

OPEN 10 TRIN

A variation of the TRIN index as developed by Peter Eliades, the publisher of *Stockmarket Cycles,* a financial newsletter. This development incorporates 10-day moving average figures into the TRIN calculations, thereby tempering the volatile effect of a single good or bad day into the chart. The net technical effect, however, is the same: entries above one are bullish and entries below one are bearish.

OPERATING RATIO

Commonly accepted formula: cost of goods sold divided by revenues from sales. Thus, if a corporation receives $100,000 in revenues from sales and it costs $80,000 to produce and to sell the goods, its operating ratio is 80%.

The operating ratio, subtracted from 100%, gives the margin of profit ratio. Thus, a company with an operating ratio of 75% has a margin of profit ratio of 25%.

See EXPENSE RATIO.

OPERATIONS

General term for that function of a broker/dealer responsible for execution, clearance, and settlement of customer transactions and the recordkeeping of customer accounts.

Also called "operations department."

Industry slang normally refers to transacting, clearing, delivery, and settlement as the "street side," with customer recordkeeping as the "customer side" of individual transactions.

OPERATOR

1. The person who drills, completes, manages and, in general, oversees the production of oil or natural gas wells.
2. The person who inputs/outputs a computer or other form of electronic equipment.
3. A derisively used term for an overly aggressive salesperson, or a promoter of dubious investments, or who, in a work environment, is overly political and self-seeking, rather than a cooperator with the group.

OPINION SHOPPING

Under SEC rules, every issuer registered with the SEC must have an audit of its books by an independent public accountant. Should that accountant want to "qualify" its findings, management usually reserves to itself the right to seek another accountant for a "clean opinion."

The seeking of a second, more favorable, opinion is sarcastically called "opinion shopping."

OPM

See OPTIONS PRINCIPAL MEMBER.

OPPORTUNITY COST

Expression that compares current yields on a fixed number of dollars. For example, a customer can invest $10,000 at 10% with little risk of loss. Instead, the customer invests at 5% because the second investment, presents a better opportunity for substantial gain. The customer takes a known decrease in yield for the unknown opportunity to make substantial profits. The known decrease in yield is the opportunity cost.

OPPOSMS

Acronym for Options to Purchase or Sell Specified Mortgage Securities (pronounced: o–pahs'–ems). This packaged product was created by Merrill Lynch Mortgage Capital Corporation. In response to customer demand, Merrill Lynch creates conventional puts and calls on Ginnie Mae, Fannie Mae, and other mortgage-backed securities and customizes them by issue, coupon, exercise price, and expiration date to suit the needs of the client.

OPRA
Acronym for Options Price Reporting Authority. It is a subscription service that publicizes option transactions and quotations on a ticker tape or a CRT device.

OPTION
A privilege enabling the holder to take some market action in a fixed quantity of a security, at a fixed price within a specified time.

Calls, a privilege to buy, and *puts*, a privilege to sell, are the most common types of options. Corporations also grant options to buy stock to selected corporate executives.

Technically, rights, warrants, and convertibles also are options to buy.

OPTIONS AGREEMENT
An agreement by a customer of a member firm who opens an option account. The agreement normally contains three parts: (1) a verification by the customer of the financial information about the customer, (2) the receipt of the Options Clearing Corporation Disclosure Statement, and (3) an agreement to abide by exercise and position limits and the other rules and regulations of options trading.

Also called "option information form."

OPTION CYCLE
The expiration months normally used for the setting of option series trading. There are three cycles used for equity options:

JAJO — January, April, July, October.
FMAN — February, May, August, November.
MJSD — March, June, September, December.

When a company's options begin listed trading, the options are assigned to a cycle.

In practice, all listed equity options trade: the current month, the subsequent month, and the next two months in the cycle. Thus, a stock in the MJSD cycle, if it is before the June expiration date, would trade June, July (next month), September and December (next two months in the cycle).

Index, debt, and currency options trade continuous months.

OPTION HOLDER

A person who has purchased a put or call option and has not sold the option, nor exercised it while the option is still in effect.

OPTION MARGIN

The margin that the buyer of an option must put up, or the margin that a naked option writer must put up and maintain.

1. All long options require a one-time payment of the option premium in full.
2. Short uncovered equity options, if listed, require the premium plus 20% of the underlying if the option is in- or at-the-money.

    If out-of-the-money, the margin is the same, except that it is marked to the market and the out-of-the-money amount is subtracted. However, the minimum is the premium plus 10% of the underlying.

    The same requirements apply to narrow-based index options.
3. Broad-based index options use the same principle, but the initial amount is the premium plus 15% of the underlying. If marked to the market, the minimum is the premium plus 10%.
4. The margin on short straddles and combinations is the margin on the side with the greatest requirement (see #2) plus the premium on the other side.
5. The margin on vertical bullish call spreads and bearish put spreads is the net debit on the spread.

    On other vertical spreads, if the short option is uncovered, the margin is *either* the dollar difference between the strike prices, *or* the margin on the short "leg" (see #2)—whichever is less provided the short call expires at or after the long call.
6. Specific advice is needed on debt and currency options. Similarly, advice is needed on "strangles" (a short combination with the short call covered), or on "ratio writes."

OPTION PREMIUM

The dollar price, with further variations in 8ths or 16ths, per share paid by the holder of an option to the writer for the privilege given by the option. For example, a call on 100 shares for 3 months at $50 per share sells at a premium of $3. The purchaser of the option must pay the writer $300 for the privilege of holding the option.

Newspaper reports of the option premium are stated in dollars and fractions per share.

Also known simply as the "premium."

OPTIONS CLEARING CORPORATION

Corporation equally owned by the exchanges that handle option transactions. The OCC (1) issues and guarantees option transactions, (2) compares transactions and processes the money transactions, (3) maintains records, (4) assigns option exercises to the writers of options.

Of particular importance is the disclosure statement of the OCC, which outlines risks, establishes rules for the conduct of accounts, and sets the norms for ethical conduct in the handling of options accounts.

OPTION SERIES

A put or a call that has a specified exercise price and a specified expiration month. For example, a Monsanto January 50 call is an option series, as is an Eastman Kodak April 70 put.

Purchases and sales of listed options are always made by series: an investor cannot buy or sell a type or class of option—only a series of option—because the transaction requires another investor on the other side of the trade to make the offsetting sale or purchase.

OPTIONSMARKLARE

The name of the options exchange established in Finland to compete directly with the Stockholm Options Market (Optionsmarknad, or OM).

The Finnish exchange was organized by three banks, Kansallis, Osake, and Pankki (KOP), and will initially permit the trading of five call options and one index option on Finnish stocks.

OPTION SPREAD

A simultaneous long and short position in a class of option. Thus, a client who buys (holds) an XYZ Jan 50 call and who writes (sells) an XYZ Jan 60 call is said to have a "call spread."

Option spreads may be call spreads, put spreads, bearish (profitable if the market goes down), or bullish (profitable if the market goes up).

See also SPREAD POSITION.

OPTION SPREAD STRATEGY

Here is a schematic diagram of vertical bull and bear spreads:

	BULL SPREAD	BEAR SPREAD
Call *and* Put	Sell higher strike price	Buy higher strike price
	Buy lower strike price	Sell lower strike price

Bull spreads become profitable if the market for the underlying rises; bear spreads become profitable if the market falls.

Thus, the decision to put on a call or put spread will usually depend on whether the spread is put on a debit (all the client can lose) or put on at a credit (all the client can gain).

Call bull and bear spreads are "zero-sum games"; thus, what the bullish spreader gains the bearish spreader loses, and vice versa. The same is true of put bull and bear spreads.

For example, if a bullish call spreader buys a January 50 call at 3-1/2 and sells a January 60 call at 1, the net debit will be 2-1/2 for the bullish spreader and the net credit will be 2-1/2 for the bearish spreader. Both have a breakeven of 52-1/2. The bullish call spreader makes money above 52-1/2; the bearish spreader makes money below 52-1/2. On put spreads, the breakeven is the higher strike price minus the net credit or debit.

See also BULL SPREAD and BEAR SPREAD.

OPTIONS PRICE REPORTING AUTHORITY
See OPRA.

OPTIONS PRINCIPAL MEMBER (OPM)
An individual who has purchased from an exchange or from another member the right to buy and sell listed options on the floor of that exchange.

OPTIONS TO PURCHASE OR SELL SPECIFIED MORTGAGE SECURITIES
See OPPOSMS.

OPTION TENDER BONDS
Acronym: OTB. Term coined by Kidder Peabody & Company to identify certain variable- (floating-) rate tax-exempt bonds with a put option included in the indenture. The interest rate is reset semiannually. If the bondholder is dissatisfied with the newly set rate, the option permits the holder to tender the bonds at year end for the full principal amount plus accrued interest.

OPTION TRADING RIGHT HOLDER
Acronym: OTRH. A nonmember of the NYSE who has purchased a license from the exchange. The license permits floor access and trading privileges but only for use in listed NYSE index options.

OPTION WRITER
The seller of a put or a call. In exchange for the premium paid by the purchaser of the option, the writer grants the privilege to the buyer to demand performance: to buy from the writer in the case of a call, or to sell to the writer in the case of a put, in accord with the provisions of the option contract.

OR BETTER

Common abbreviation: OB. These words, sometimes written but always understood, form a supplemental instruction for all limit orders. In effect, the executing broker is instructed whenever possible to try to improve on the customer's limit price.

Generally, OB will be added to the order ticket when a buy limit order is entered above prevailing prices, or vice versa on a sell limit order. Thus, OB prevents confusion about the customer's intent to buy or sell.

ORD

British abbreviation for: ordinary shares.
See also ORDINARY SHARES.

ORDER BOOK OFFICIAL

Employees of the Pacific Stock Exchange who accept orders for options that are not capable of immediate execution. If and when such orders can be transacted, the OBO makes the trade, on an agency basis, and notifies the member firm that entered the order.

Employees with similar functions on the Chicago Board Options Exchange are called "board brokers."

ORDER CONFIRMATION TRANSACTION

See OCT.

ORDER DEPARTMENT/ROOM

Also known as: the order room or the wire room. A work area within a broker/dealer organization that is responsible for the routing of buy and sell instructions to the trading floors of the various stock exchanges. The order department also is responsible for the execution of over-the-counter transactions for customer and firm trading accounts.

ORDER SPLITTING

Term associated with the NASD's Small Order Execution System (SOES). SOES permits the automatic execution of up to 1,000 shares of stocks traded on the NASDAQ/NMS.

The concept is important because the NASD forbids members from splitting up customer orders into pieces small enough to be executed automatically by means of the SOES system. This is only fair: the market-makers are providing a service for small orders, not a method of breaking up blocks of buy-sell orders.

ORDER TICKET

The form, completed by a registered representative, that contains the customer's instructions to buy or sell plus the other qualifications imposed by the customer on the transaction. Federal law requires that customer instructions be entered on an order ticket and that the order tickets be maintained for a specified time.

ORDINARY SHARES
In British terminology, the equivalent of what is here called "common stock" (i.e., certificates representing residual ownership in a corporation).

ORIGINAL ISSUE DISCOUNT BOND
Technical designation given to an issue of bonds by the Internal Revenue Service. Once designated as OID, a bondholder must periodically adjust upward the cost of acquisition so that, if such a bond is held to maturity, there will be neither capital gain nor loss. The difference between purchase cost and adjusted cost is considered income. Professional tax advice is always needed because there is a difference in the tax treatment of government and corporate OIDs and municipal OIDs.

ORIGINAL MATURITY
Time difference between issue date and maturity date at the time a bond is issued. Thus, a bond issued in October 2002 that will be due in October 2022 has an original maturity of 20 years. Once issued, the remaining maturity shortens. It is customary to refer to the time remaining to maturity as the current maturity; thus, in October 2004, the bonds referred to above will be 18-year bonds.

ORIGINATION FEE
A service fee charged to the party that initiates the processing of a mortgage loan. Popularly known as "points," each point is 1% of the face value of the loan. Example: If the origination fee is 2 points (2%) on a loan of $100,000, the fee will be $2,000.

Current IRS rulings consider origination fees paid as interest; thus, the fee is a deductible item in the year paid.

ORIGINATOR
1. A nonfinancial corporation that is the issuer of a security.
2. A broker/dealer who, in a best-efforts underwriting, does not guarantee to purchase shares it is unable to sell.
3. An employee of a broker/dealer, investment advisor, or fiduciary, who creates an investment position either by developing a security with unique terms (e.g., CATS, MbearS) or by acting as an intermediary between an issuer and a customer.
4. Term commonly used of a bank or a savings and loan that was the original mortgagor of a pool of loans. When the pool of mortgages is

resold (e.g., in the form of Ginnie Mae pass-throughs), the bank is called the "originator" of the pool.
See also MORTGAGE POOL ORIGINATOR.

ORPHAN STOCK
Tongue-in-cheek expression for a company not covered by a research analyst. Hence, its story is never published, and its stock is never recommended. In general, the stock is neglected by investors who tend to follow recommendations made by research analysts.

ORPOS
Acronym for Office of Regulatory Policy, Oversight, and Supervision. ORPOS is a department within the Federal Home Loan Bank Board (Freddie Mac) responsible for establishing loan guidelines, investment policies, and underwriting criteria for member banks of that system.

OS
See OFFICIAL STATEMENT.

OSC
See ONTARIO SECURITIES COMMISSION.

OSE
Initials used for the Osaka Stock Exchange, the second largest exchange in Japan and a major participant in stock index market. In terms of national importance however, the OSE is a distant second to the Tokyo Stock Exchange.

OSJ
See OFFICE OF SUPERVISORY JURISDICTION.

OSLO STOCK EXCHANGE
This Norwegian stock exchange is all-electronic and relies heavily upon foreign activity for its existence. It is open on weekdays from 10 A.M. until 3 P.M. although over-the-counter activity may continue as long as there are contra parties willing to trade. Settlement is on the fourth business day after the trade date.

The Oslo Stock Exchange is the smallest of the Scandinavian exchanges.

OTB
See OPTION TENDER BONDS.

OTC
See OVER THE COUNTER.

OTC BULLETIN BOARD DISPLAY SERVICE
A NASD pilot program for making continuous markets in non-NASDAQ (NNOTC) securities. Through a NASD workstation or terminal, marketmakers in "Pink Sheet" qualified stocks can display their firm or subject quotations, or even one-sided or BW/OW indications. To differentiate these displays from regular NASDAQ displays the entering marketmaker precedes the alphabetical symbol with the numeric qualifier "3."

OTC MARGIN STOCK
Any stock, traded exclusively in the over-the-counter market, whose issuer meets certain qualifying criteria and, therefore, broker/dealers are permitted to extend credit on the purchase or short sale of such securities by Regulation T of the Federal Reserve banking system.

OTC OPTION
This is a call or put whose strike price, expiration, and premium are negotiated.
   Also called a "conventional option."

OTHER CHECKABLE DEPOSITS (OCD)
Federal Reserve Board terminology for one of the components used in the calculation of M1. Other checkable deposits consist of negotiable orders of withdrawal (NOW), automatic transfer service accounts at depository institutions, credit union share draft accounts, and demand deposits at mutual savings banks.

OTRH
See OPTION TRADING RIGHT HOLDER.

OUT FOR A BID
Terminology used when a dealer offers municipal bonds to a broker who, in turn, will solicit bids for the bonds. The broker's fee is contingent on the sale of the bonds. Usually the broker will solicit competing bids without revealing the underlying source of the offering.

OUT OF LINE
Term used of the price of a security, either a stock or a bond, that is substantially higher or lower than the price of similar securities trading in the marketplace.

494

The term may also be used of classes of securities; for example, the current yield on 20-year municipals is "out of line" with the traditional yield spread between municipals and Treasuries.

OUT OF THE MONEY
Industry term for any option whose exercise would result in a negative cash flow. Thus, a call at 50 would result in a negative cash flow if the underlying stock were at 49⅞ or below, and a put at 50 would result in a negative cash flow if the underlying stock were at 50⅛ or above.

Out of the money is always computed independently of premiums received and dividends that could be obtained by an exercise.

OUTRIGHT PURCHASES OR SALES
Expression that refers to net purchases or sales by the Federal Open Market Committee. Thus, the expression excludes buys or sells that may be partially offset by repurchase or reverse repurchase agreements.

OUT THE WINDOW
A slang expression used by investment bankers to designate the fact that a new issue sold rapidly and there are no more shares or bonds remaining.

The concept implies that the issue was priced correctly or even slightly below the price that would be indicated by the demand. Of itself, the term does not imply that the aftermarket price for the security caused it to be a "hot issue."

OVERALLOTING
Practice of investment bankers, if so permitted by the underwriting agreement, to sell more shares than are available for distribution. Shares so overalloted are being sold short by the syndicate in the hope that overeager buyers will resell the shares to the syndicate and thus the net short position will be covered at a profit. Normally, the percentage of shares, or of bonds, that may be overalloted is limited in the agreement among underwriters.

OVERBANKED
Slang for underwritings where the initial allotment to syndicate members exceeds the number of securities to be offered. Obviously, by the time the details of the underwriting are completed, participation will equal 100% of the offering. Some potential members will drop out; others will decrease their allotment; or, if too many members drop out, others will increase their allotments. Overbanking is common as the details of the underwriting are worked out.

OVERBOOKED

Slang for an underwriting where the indications of client interest exceed the number of securities available.

Although the term is technically applicable to registered offerings, it also is used of exempt offerings that are not subject to registration. In the latter case, however, the expression "oversubscribed" is more common.

OVERBOUGHT

Term used by technical analysts of the level of security or market prices if they believe that vigorous buying has left prices too high and thus prone to an imminent decline. In the jargon of technical analysts, it is a "gap"; that is, trading opens substantially above the close of the previous day, which is usually associated with an overbought condition. The term infers that a price rise was expected but prices rose too rapidly to be sustainable at present levels. Example: Following last week's sharp rise of 40 points, the market appears to be overbought.

Antonym: OVERSOLD.

OVERLAPPING DEBT

Term used of a municipal security that uses the same tax base as that of another municipality. The underlying concept is that the second municipality is basically a "subsidiary" of the first.

For example, a city—to facilitate administration and to depoliticize education—sets up a school district. The school district is authorized to issue bonds based on the *ad valorem* value of residential and commercial property. This is the same property that the city also uses to pay part of its debt service. Note that both the city and the school district *overlap* in their source of income. Ultimately, the city is responsible both for its debts and the debts of the school district. The debts of the school district may be said to overlap those of the city.

OVERNIGHT POSITION

Industry term used by broker/dealers to describe their inventory in a security at the end of the trading day. For example, a broker/dealer is said to have an overnight position in ABC of 500 shares if, at the end of the trading day, the dealer has purchased the shares but not yet sold them. This dealer has a long overnight position. However, another broker/dealer who has sold short 300 shares of ABC and had not yet repurchased them has a short overnight position.

OVERNIGHT REPO

A repurchase agreement with expiration set for the following business day. The interest rate associated with such short-term borrowings is lower than that for term or open repurchase agreements because the risk is lower.

In an overnight repo, the seller agrees to repurchase a security at an increment over the original purchase price. The agreement may require that the purchase be made at 100.00 and the repurchase at 100.04. Thus, .04% of a $1 million par value would be an overnight interest of $400. Annualized, $400 as overnight interest on $1 million is approximately 14.6%.

See also REPO.

OVERREACHING

An expression used to describe the unethical action of a broker/dealer who executes a transaction as principal at a price that is less favorable than the price that would have been obtained had the broker/dealer acted as an agent.

In the past, dealer markups (markdowns) were not included as a separate entry on customer confirmations; thus, they were to an extent "invisible." New SEC regulations require that dealer markups and brokerage commissions be "broken out" on customer confirmations, and overreaching is less prevalent.

OVERSELLING

Term denotes an unethical sales practice in the securities industry. It refers to the practice of marketing securities of only troubled issuers. Little notice is taken of the customer's needs. The special compensation paid to salespersons is important. The term surfaces in litigation, usually in a recession, when many of these troubled issuers often became insolvent.

TO OVERSHOOT

As a verb, transitive or intransitive, meaning to exceed a goal or objective. It is used frequently in both economics and securities research to describe the fact that an economic indicator, economic measurement, or a security price/yield exceeded an anticipated goal. For example, "In the Q3 1989, M-2 overshot the 3.4% growth anticipated by the Fed."

It is also used to explain why the forecasts of economists or analysts were incorrect.

Antonym: undershoot.

OVERSOLD

Term used by technical analysts who (1) expected a security to go down in value, but (2) it went down too fast. An oversold technical situation is often manifested by a "gap," or "selling climax," in which the opening price is substantially below the closing price or the low of the previous trading day. Technical analysts expect an oversold condition to be corrected by a rise in the price of the security.

OVER THE COUNTER

1. General term for any marketplace—or marketing method—that does not involve the use of a securities exchange. Common abbreviation: OTC. Example: Most new issues of securities are sold over the counter.
   See also NATIONAL ASSOCIATION OF SECURITIES DEALERS.
2. Term used by security analysts for pharmaceutical products that do not require a prescription.
   Both terms are used with and without hyphens.
3. The communications network linking dealers in securities who make transactions that are completed by telephone or telex rather than in a centralized marketplace.
   See also OTC MARGIN STOCK and OTC OPTION.

OVER THE WALL
See BROUGHT OVER THE WALL.

OVERTRADING
An NASD term for this situation: A dealer, who is also an underwriter, offers a client a higher price than is justified for a security if the customer will purchase a portion of a new issue. The spread on the new issue offsets the special price set for the client's shares. Thus, if a client is offered 1/2 point more than is justified, provided he buys a new issue with a spread of 1 point, the underwriter will come out ahead on the combined transactions.

OVERVALUED
A term used by fundamental analysts who feel that the present market price of a security, judged in terms of the company's earnings and the current price-earnings ratio, is not justified in terms of historical values given to the securities of that company. The analyst who gives a judgment of overvalued to a security expects the price of the security to drop in value.

OVERWRITING

1. The sale of a call or put option whose premium is considered overvalued in relation to the market price of the underlying stock. In effect, the contract is not likely to be exercised. The sale may be covered or uncovered.
2. Of index options: the sale by an institution of index options as a partial hedge of a diversified portfolio of stocks. The premium received enhances the return on the portfolio and provides some downside protection against a temporary market decline.

OW

Acronym for offer wanted. Designation used by securities dealers to advise other professionals that it wants to buy a specific issue and is willing to negotiate a reasonable trade price with prospective sellers.

OWL STOCK

Clever allusion used of an equity isue that has no active market; that is, the price advertisements for the stock feature an offer but no bid. Thus, when a customer who is long the stock calls up a broker for an immediate sale, the broker legitimately imitates the wise old owl: "Whooo tooo—whooo tooo?"

OXY

Industry slang for the shares of Occidental Petroleum Corporation, an international producer and marketer of crude oil. Term is derived from NYSE ticker symbol: OXY.

P

P

The sixteenth letter of the alphabet, used:
1. Lowercase in newspaper option transaction tables to designate a put; for example, ABC Jan 55 p.
2. Uppercase in newspaper reports of corporate earnings to designate that a security's principal marketplace is the Philadelphia Stock Exchange; for example, East Park Realty Trust (P).
3. As the fifth letter in NASDAQ/NMS listings to designate a convertible preferred; for example, Health Images 0% cv. pfd.: HIMGP.
4. Uppercase alone to designate the NYSE ticker symbol for Phillips Petroleum, a major producer and refiner of oil and related chemicals.

PA

Used in newspaper reports about a company's earnings to designate that the principal marketplace for the security is the Pacific Stock Exchange. Normally printed Pa.

PAC

Acronym for planned amortization class. (Also PACB: planned amortization class bonds.) PACs are associated with CMOs. CMOs are so established that earlier classes (tranches) generally have a pre-established maturity date with all of the prepayment risk transferred to the residual security. Thus, a mortgage pool with its interest payments and principal repayments are set up in four classes. All payments go first to retire class A, then class B, then class C securities; as a result, any prepayment risk is transferred to the PACs in class D.

PACB
See PAC.

PACE
Acronym for Philadelphia Stock Exchange Automated Communication and Execution System. This is an electronic linkage between the specialists on the PHLX and the Intermarket Trading System (ITS) and the Computer Assisted Execution System (CAES).

PACE permits the automatic execution of agency orders up to 599 shares at the best available price in the three marketplaces.

See also ITS and CAES.

PACIFIC OPTIONS EXCHANGE TRADING SYSTEM
See POETS.

PACIFIC STOCK EXCHANGE (PSE)
The Pacific Stock Exchange has trading floors located both in Los Angeles and San Francisco. The trading floors are interconnected electronically. The PSE trades in stocks listed on the exchange, in many securities traded on other exchanges, and in options listed on that exchange.

PAC-MAN DEFENSE
Named for the Atari video game, owned by Warner Communications Corporation, to designate a financial maneuver that is used to thwart an unfriendly merger. Under Pac-Man defense, the reluctant target tries to purchase control of the raider before the raider can exercise controlling influence over that party.

PACS
Acronym for Principal Appreciation Conversion Securities. This is a Smith Barney Harris Upham version of Goldman Sachs' GAINS.

See GAINS for a full explanation.

PAID-IN CAPITAL
The dollar difference between the aggregate par value of issued common shares of a corporation and the price at which they were sold. Paid-in capital is given on the balance sheet of the corporation. Normally, paid-in capital is adjusted downward if a corporation repurchases its own shares and places the repurchased shares in the treasury.

Also called "capital surplus."

PAINE WEBBER/GAS 100

An index of price performance of selected issues in world markets as determined by Paine Webber Corp. and Global Analysis Systems Corp.

PAINTING THE TAPE

Expression used if the speaker thinks that someone, or a group working in concert, is making transactions without a true change of beneficial ownership. The speaker has inferred from the flurry of transactions reported on the exchange tape that the transactions were made to give the impression (i.e., to paint the tape), of widespread activity in the stock—thereby causing others to buy or sell the security.

PAIRED SHARES

Normally, the common stock of two companies under common management sold as a unit. Usually, the certificates are printed back and front on the same piece of paper to facilitate transfer.

Also called "Siamese shares" or "stapled stock."

PAIR-OFF

1. Used as a synonym for "offset" in commodities markets; that is, the liquidation of a position by selling the same future month contract.
2. The technique used by exchange specialists to open the market. In a pair-off, orders to buy are so coupled to orders to sell that the specialist who knows whether there is a market balance can determine the proper price at which to open the market.
3. Terminology used in some program-type executions where the executing firm is held to its report. Thus, if there are errors resulting from DKs or QTs, the executing firm assumes such charges and "pairs them off" against the correct amounts.
4. Term used to describe this situation: a client has a long position in a security in one account, and a short position in the same security in another account. A pair-off occurs if the positions and money balances are combined in one account.
5. Term used in connection with the net settlement procedures used by the Depository Trust Co. (DTC), the National Securities Clearing Corp. (NSCC), and other such services. All purchases and sales in the same securities are aggregated daily and settled five business days later with a single delivery or a single check for the pair-off.

PALE BLUE CHIPS

A descriptive term sometimes used of a company whose stock is well on its way to becoming a "blue chip." Traders often refer to such stocks as "second tier" stocks.

PAMM

Acronym for performance appointment marketmaker. This is a CBOE term for an exchange member obliged to maintain two-sided markets in designated classes of CBOE-traded options. PAMMs must maintain quotes and must trade in illiquid as well as popular option series. PAMMs thereby provide market depth and supplement the activities of registered competitive marketmakers. In exchange for this service, PAMMs are accorded certain economic advantages by the CBOE.

P & I

Abbreviations for: principal and interest. The expression is often used by bond traders, salespersons, and institutional customers to describe the typical periodic payments made by issuers of bonds.

If the principal and interest are "stripped" from the bond and sold separately, thereby making them zero-coupons, you will see the expressions: "P only" and "I only."

P & L

An abbreviation for a profit and loss statement, which is a financial statement issued by a corporation to reflect its gross income and expenses and thus its profits or losses.

Also written P and L.

P & S

General industry term for the purchase and sale function of a broker/dealer. Although the function may include other aspects of the operations area, P & S normally is responsible for comparing and reconciling the terms of completed transactions to facilitate securities and money settlements.

Also written: P and S.

PANTY RAID

A colorful term used to describe a very low bid for a company made by a well-known corporate raider. Concept: The raider is trying "to steal the pants" off the company.

Such a low bid is often followed by a more reasonable bid for the company. For example, in early 1988, Donald Trump made a low bid of $23 per share for the Class A stock of Resorts International only to be followed by a successful bid by Merv Griffin of $36 for these shares.

PAPER

General industry term for shorter-term debt securities. Commercial paper is an obvious example, but bankers' acceptances and negotiable certificates of deposit often are included under the general term.

You also will see or hear the term *short-term paper* as a synonym for such debt securities.

Also used to designate any debt security of a corporation; for example, AJAX Corp. has both long- and short-term paper outstanding.

PAPER LOSS
An unrealized loss on a security position. Paper losses become realized losses only if a long security is sold or a short position is covered.

PAPER PROFIT
An unrealized gain on a security position. Paper profits become realized only if a long position is sold or a short position is covered.

Generally, there are no tax consequences on paper profits until the position is sold or covered. However, tax advice is needed on paper profits if one leg expires in one tax year and the other leg in another year.

See also UNREALIZED PROFITS.

PAPER TRADING
Hypothetical trading of securities (usually at closing prices and without commissions) often used in gaming situations or as part of a training program. Paper trading can be very helpful in teaching selection and timing techniques to market beginners.

PAPILSKY RULES
Named for the plaintiff in a civil suit brought against an investment adviser and the broker/dealer affiliate.

The suit resulted in certain rule modifications by the National Association of Securities Dealers (NASD) regarding securities taken in trade by an underwriter, selling concessions made in exchange for bona fide research services, and the allocation of new issues to related persons.

PAR
From the Latin: equal. Used in the securities industry to represent any security whose market or offering price is the same as its face value at the time of redemption. For example, a bond with a face value of $1,000, offered at par, can be purchased at $1,000.

PARALLEL LOANS
See BACK-TO-BACK LOANS.

PAR BOND
A bond that is offered at, or whose current market price is, 100% of its redemption value.

PAR CAP

Used of GNMA forward contracts if a seller must deliver securities with the same coupon rate as that designated in the contract. As a result, no adjustments are permitted if securities with other coupons are delivered.

PARI PASSU

Latin: from Vergil's *Aeneid*, to walk with equal stride, or lock-step. By attribution, to have equal ranking.

The word is used in conjunction with bankruptcy proceedings in the sense that all general creditors have equal ranking in their claim against the assets of the bankrupt corporation.

The term can also be used for any events that seem to be in lock-step; for example, the market is marching *pari passu* with the economy.

PARI PASSU BONDS

This term is used of two or more bonds by the same issuer that have an equal claim on the assets of the issuer in the event of default. The term is Latin and means "with equal stride," or "lock-step."

In practice, the expression tends to be limited to municipal securities because if corporate bonds have equal claim on assets they are called "open-end" mortgage bonds.

PARIS BOURSE

The largest exchange in France and the third largest in Europe.

There are two trading periods per day (9:30 A.M. to 11:00 A.M. and 12:30 P.M. to 2:30 P.M.) but electronic trading is permitted from 10:00 A.M. until 5:00 P.M. and informal trading is permitted until 6:00 P.M. All regular-way contracts require month-end settlement through the SICOVAM clearance system.

Deregulation through "le petit bang" (q.v.) mirrors many of the changes in the United States and the United Kingdom.

THE PARIS MARCH

Slang for a strategy in index options named after the swift, and infamous, German march on Paris in World War II.

The strategy centers on the day before expiration in certain index options. The concept is to sell stocks short while both buying and selling equity call options on the same stocks. The goal is to cause program-type traders into action. This should enhance the short stock positions and the short call options. When done in unison near the close of trading (remember there is no remaining time value), it produces sharp price movements in the indexes and underlying stocks. This, in turn, results in the "march" to describe the near panic of the arbitrageurs.

PARITY

1. The price, exclusive of commissions and taxes, at which the value of the underlying stock is the same as the value of a convertible exchangeable for such stock. For example, a bond convertible into 40 shares is selling at $880 when the stock is selling at $22.
2. In the options market, if the stock is selling at the same price as the option plus its premium it is in parity. For example, a stock sells at $42 when the premium on the 40 call is $2 ($42 = $40 + $2).
3. In the auction market, if the broker with priority has a fill and other brokers can complete all of the remaining order, they are on parity. They will flip a coin to determine which of them will trade with the contra party.

PARITY PRICE FOR AN OPTION

Term used if an option strike price plus the premium equals the market price of the underlying on a call (minus the premium on a put). For example, a stock is selling at $40\frac{1}{2}$ on a day when the premium on the 40 call is $\frac{1}{2}$ point $(40\frac{1}{2} = 40 + \frac{1}{2})$. In effect, the in-the-money option has no time value.

Although such situations are not rare, they are most common when an option is deep in-the-money and the time remaining to maturity is short.

PARKING

A term used to cover illegal practices. Parking occurs if:

1. A dealer sells a security to another dealer to reduce its net capital requirement. Later, when a customer is found, the dealer buys back the security at a price that repays the other dealer for his cost of carrying the security.
2. An employer's transferring the registration of an employee to another employer so, at a later date, the former employee can be rehired without the need for a new registration examination.

PARKING REGISTRATIONS

This term refers to a violation of procedures under NASD Rules of Fair Practice. Because the NASD permits part-time employment of registered representatives and principals by member broker/dealers the privilege can sometimes be abused by persons leaving the industry but who want to retain registration to avoid retesting requirements if they return more than two years later. With the improper cooperation of a member firm such persons are fictitiously carried and reported to the NASD as employed registrants in good standing.

PARTIAL DELIVERY
Industry expression for a delivery against a sale of less than the contract amount. For example, a selling broker of 1,000 shares delivers 500.

Also called a "partial."

PARTIALLY PAID BONDS
Term used to describe certain initial public offerings of dollar-denominated bonds sold to foreign investors. The name derives from the fact that the purchasers deposit only 20 to 30% of the cost and agree to pay the balance at some specified time in the future. Such payments are legal if they are completed outside the United States and thus away from the jurisdiction of the Federal Reserve Board's credit restrictions.

PARTICIPANT EXCHANGE AGREEMENT (PEA)
A contract between the option exchanges participating in the linkage of trading and clearance between European and American stock exchanges.

The first PEA was signed in 1987 and links the European Options Exchange and the American Stock Exchange. The PEA included essential information required for disclosure to persons dealing in Major Market Index (XMI) options.

PARTICIPATE BUT DO NOT INITIATE ORDER (PNI)
Instruction given on some very large orders to buy or sell. The instruction says, in effect, buy or sell, but do not initiate a new price—let market forces create the new price. Such instructions are given by institutional buyers or sellers that want to accumulate or distribute shares without disturbing the normal market forces, or by institutions that are not permitted by law to create an uptick, if buying, or a downtick, if selling.

PARTICIPATING INCENTIVE PREFERRED STOCK
Acronym: PIPS. An equity security issuable by a prospective takeover target. Its purpose is to deter the acquiror intent on 100% ownership because it is sold to, and provides voting power to, the business constituencies of the target company. It is designed to protect the financial interests of those constituencies. PIPS is convertible, participating, and nontransferrable.

PARTICIPATING PREFERRED
Preferred shares that offer a bonus dividend if, in any quarter, the dividend on common shares of the same issuer exceeds a stated dollar amount. Normally, any extra dividends declared by the company are shared equally by common and participating preferred shareholders.

Very few issues of participating preferred shares are outstanding.

PARTICIPATING TRUST

A type of unit investment trust that issues shares representing an interest in an underlying investment in a mutual fund.

Participating trusts are called "plan companies" and form the legal entity underlying a contractual-type mutual fund. Because some features come from the underlying mutual fund, and some from the plan company, investors in a fund through a participating trust receive two prospectuses: one for the plan company, one for the mutual fund shares.

PARTICIPATION CERTIFICATE (PC)

A security that represents an undivided interest in a pool of mortgages with the same interest rate and maturity date.

PARTLY PAID STOCK

The term is used in the United Kingdom to describe securities that are bought with a number of installment payments; thus, if the purchaser pays for an offering with a partial payment and the balance is due on specific future dates, it will be partially paid stock.

In this context, "stock" may be either stock or bonds. For example, the British government's bonds are properly called "stock," and this is a preferential financing technique used in their purchase.

PARTNERSHIP

An association of two or more individuals who pool their money and talent to conduct a business. If the individuals are personally responsible for the liabilities of the partnership, they are called "general partners." Individuals who contribute only money and who are not personally responsible for the liabilities of the partnership are called "limited partners."

PARTNERSHIP DEMOCRACY

An expression variously used in the context of a limited partnership.
1. A provision in the partnership agreement whereby the general partner(s) may exceed a limitation normally imposed upon the business agreement.
2. A provision in the partnership agreement whereby limited partners may, under certain circumstances, vote to discontinue the partnership, or may replace the general partner.

PART OF A ROUND LOT

See PRL.

PART-OR-NONE

A term associated with a best-efforts underwriting if a minimum sale of the offering is required. In effect, sales before the minimum is reached are held in abeyance (and the money in escrow). When the minimum is reached, these sales are confirmed, the offering is official, and the underwriting continues until it is completed.

If the minimum is not reached, the offering is cancelled and funds are refunded.

Similar in concept to a MINI-MAX offering.

PARTS
Acronym for periodically adjustable-rate trust securities. PARTS are a pass-through mortgage trust composed of municipal loans; thus, interest payments are exempt from federal taxes.

PARTS have a put feature and rates periodically are adjusted to reflect early calls and ordinary mortgage redemptions. In effect, interest rates may vary, but the holder, because of the put option, is protected against loss of principal.

PARTY IN INTEREST
Term used in the Employee Retirement Income Security Act (ERISA) to identify a person who provides a service to a pension or other employee benefit plan. Service includes investment advice to a retirement plan; it also includes broker/dealers who make purchases, sales, leases, underwriting, or credit transactions for or with a retirement plan.

PAR VALUE
Latin: equal (adjective); equal to (adverb).

Term used to state basic equality of securities of the same class.

When used of common stock, par is an identifier. For example: ABC Corporation issued stock with a par value of $10 per share. The par value is used to evaluate the stock on the balance sheet of the corporation. Stock splits will cause the par value to be adjusted to reflect the number of authorized shares following the split. A two-for-one split up will adjust the par value down by one half.

When used of preferred stock, par is the basic redemption value if the company chooses to retire the preferred stock. In practice, the company usually retires preferred stock at a premium over par value.

When used of bonds, par value is used as a synonym for the face value; that is, the dollar amount that the company must pay at the time of maturity to the holder of a bond.

Par is sometimes inaccurately used for parity. For example, a person buys a call on XYZ at 50 with a premium of 5. If XYZ is selling at 55, one may say that the call option is "at par."

See also FACE VALUE.

PASSED DIVIDEND

1. Used of the dividend on cumulative preferred shares if omitted by a corporation. Such passed dividends form an arrearage that must be paid before any dividends may be paid on common shares.
2. Used of an expected dividend on common shares that is not declared by the board of directors. There is no obligation to pay passed dividends on common shares.

PASSING THE PARCEL

A quaint and colorful trading expression from England. In effect, a broker/dealer purchased a block (parcel) of stock from an institutional customer. Before the news of the trade was disseminated, the broker/dealer sold it to another broker/dealer. Thus, the seller and the original purchaser are now "out of the loop," and the new purchaser has all of the risk.

Current SEAQ rules prohibit this practice without proper notification.

PASSIVE INCOME GENERATORS

See PIG.

PASS THE BOOK

Also known as "PASSING THE BOOK."

Term used by trading firms to describe 24-hour worldwide trading activity. For example, an international brokerage firm has offices in New York, Los Angeles, Honolulu, Tokyo, Singapore, Bahrain, and London. As the day progresses, the "book" (i.e., the firm's inventory and its control) is passed from office to office in a westward direction to be traded successively by the office listed above. In effect, customers can trade on a 24-hour basis by referring their orders to the appropriate trading office.

To be effective, passing the book requires a single financially responsible trading manager.

PASS-THROUGH SECURITY

A debt security that represents a fractional interest in a pool of mortgages. Abbreviation often is written P/T.

Payments on such securities, made monthly, are partially interest on unpaid principal balance and partially a repayment of principal.

Such securities are said to be "modified" if the originating mortgage bank partially reduces the interest rate on the underlying mortgages and uses the reduction as its fee for the pass-through service.

PAYDOWN

1. Used of a refunding of one debt by another if the new debt is smaller than the originally outstanding debt. Example: A company borrows $8 million to refund bonds with a face value of $10 million.
2. Used of Ginnie Mae modified pass-through pools if the experienced reduction in the unpaid principal balance is greater than the anticipated reduction. Example: a GNMA pool, after eight years, should have a factor of .8532456; its experienced factor is .7894321.

PAYING AGENT

The person designated in an indenture or bond resolution to make principal repayment and periodic interest payments for an issuer of debt securities.

Normally, one or more commercial banks will be the paying agent(s), although it is not uncommon for the treasurer of the issuer to also be designated as a paying agent.

Also called the "disbursing agent," although this term is more frequently used in connection with common stock dividends.

PAY-IN-KIND SECURITIES

See PIK.

PAYMENT DATE

Date on which a cash payment, either dividend or interest, will be made by an issuer.

See also DATE OF PAYMENT.

PAY-THROUGH BOND

This is a hybrid security with some characteristics of both mortgage bonds and pass-through certificates.

The issuer uses a pool of mortgages it owns (an asset) and, rather than turn them into pass-throughs (the sale of an asset), it uses them as collateral for further borrowing (thereby creating a bond and a liability for the issuer).

The interest received from the original mortgages is used to pay the holders of the pay-through bonds, while the principal payments are used to systematically retire the bonds.

PAY-UP

1. Used if a mutual fund manager, in exchange for research services, pays a larger commission than usual for the execution of portfolio trades. In effect, the fund is spared the expense of a separate research area.
2. Used if a customer, to acquire a very large block of a security, is willing to pay a price that is greater than the typical market price for the security.

3. In a bond swap, if the price of the purchase is greater then the proceeds of sale, the dollar difference is called a "pay up." Antonym: take out, if the proceeds of the sale exceeds the price of the purchase.
4. As verb: pay up. As adjective or noun: pay-up.

PBN
See PRIME BANK NOTES.

PBR
Used to designate the price/book value ratio in security analysis.

Although the term is not used in the United States—we use *market-to-book*—it is used extensively in Japan. In Japan, price to earnings is not particularly meaningful because a large amount of the assets of a typical Japanese company may be in the form of nonearning real estate. Yet, it represents a significant amount of the "value" of the company. Thus, in Japan the market value of stocks tends to represent the "liquidating" value of the company, rather than its earning power.

PBW
Older abbreviation for the Philadelphia, Baltimore, Washington Exchange. It is now called the "Philadelphia Stock Exchange" and its commonly accepted designation is PHLX.

PC
1. Used of a participation certificate; that is, a fractional interest in a pool of mortgages or real estate loans. The holder receives a monthly flow-through benefit of interest and principal repayment.
2. In securities trades, PC stands for "plus commission," which, in practice, means that commissions will be added to purchases and subtracted from sales for services rendered.

P-COAST
An identifier often used for the Pacific Stock Exchange. This exchange is located in California, has trading floors in Los Angeles and San Francisco, and is a registered national exchange.

PCT
See PERCENT.

P-DAY
U.K. terminology for Provisional Authorization Day. On that day in 1988, authorities granted temporary authorization to do financial business in the United Kingdom to certain entities while the details of the 1986 Financial Services Act were being implemented.

PEA
See PARTICIPANT EXCHANGE AGREEMENT.

PEACE DIVIDEND
General term used in fiscal policy for the shifting of priorities from defense expenditures to peacetime expenditures. Thus, in the United States, a peace dividend would see some of the funds in the $300 billion defense budget shifted to education, housing, and other needed consumer items. Generally, the peace dividend does not result in lowered taxes—although it did following World War II.

A PEARL
Allusion to a "gem" of an investment that is a lucky find, as is a pearl in an oyster.

The term is also used to designate the premier holding in a portfolio; for example, "That stock is the pearl of all of my holdings."

In both meanings, the term implies diligence, some luck, and a lot of patience.

A PEDESTRIAN PERFORMER
An expression used of a stock that achieves average performance both in its operations and in market performance.

In this context, "pedestrian" means commonplace; that is, a foot traveler, as opposed to a runner, a rider, or a "high" flier.

PEEK-A-BOO
U.K. slang for an unscheduled offering of new securities in the Euro-marketplace.

Because there are no filing requirements, the actual offering can take place shortly after the decision to bring the security to market. In such circumstances, the critical consideration is favorable market conditions, which as a window of opportunity may open and close quickly. Thus, the expression "peek-a-boo market conditions" is also used.

PEER REVIEW ORGANIZATION
See PRO.

PEE-WEE STOCKS
Slang for stocks above the "penny stock" category but decidedly below good quality and investment grade ("blue-chip") stocks.

They are considered second tier stocks and usually are the last to rise in bull markets and the first to fall in bear markets.

PEFCO
See PRIVATE EXPORT FUNDING CORPORATION.

PEGGING
Maintaining the offer price for a security by a bid at or slightly below that price.

When used of underwriting, pegging is legal. In other circumstances, pegging is a form of price manipulation and is illegal.

Also called "stabilization."

PEGGY
Industry nickname for the shares of Public Service Electric and Gas Company, a large utility operating in the state of New Jersey. The term is derived from the NYSE ticker symbol: PEG.

PENALTY PLAN
A term used by critics of contractual mutual funds. Reason: Because the purchaser has prepaid a large portion of the sales charge during early years of the contract, the purchaser will, in many cases, suffer a severe loss if the contract is not completed. Recent revisions of the Investment Company Act of 1940 have substantially reduced the penalties that will be suffered by an investor who discontinues a contractual plan.

PENALTY SYNDICATE BID
A stabilizing bid made by the manager of a syndicate, with the proviso that selling concessions will be withheld, and often a monetary penalty assessed, against those members of the account whose customers reoffer to the account manager securities just sold to them by members of the account.

PENNANT
Term used by technical analysts to describe a chart pattern for a security. The pattern roughly conforms to a triangle whose base is to the left of the chart and whose apex is to the right.

Pennant formations usually indicate a stock whose price may either rise or fall as the apex is reached; thus, no conclusive trend is indicated.

PENNANT FORMATION
See PENNANT and TRIANGLE FORMATION.

PENNY
Industry nickname for the shares of J. C. Penney, Inc., a large retail department store chain.

PENNY STOCK RULE
See SEC RULE 15c2-6.

PENNY STOCKS
Wall Street expression for relatively low-priced, highly speculative securities. Although the term implies securities priced at less than $1 per share, the term is not limited to such shares. Many member firms have special margin maintenance requirements for such shares and often limit purchases of such shares to unsolicited orders by clients.

PENSION PARACHUTE
Term used to describe the dedication of excess assets in a pension plan to the benefit of pension plan participants in the event of a change in control in the underlying corporation. Thus, the pension parachute serves to enhance the interests of the plan participants while at the same time serving as a "poison pill" in the event of a hostile takeover attempt.

PENSION REVERSION
The act of terminating an overfunded defined benefit pension plan and reclaiming the surplus assets. In practice, the plan is cancelled, the plan purchases fixed annuities to cover employee's entitled benefits, and the surplus is reclaimed by the corporation to become part of its assets. Usually, the cancellation of the defined benefit plan is accompanied by the substitution of a defined contribution plan for the continued benefit and retirement planning of the employees.

The courts have decided that plan termination is not covered by ERISA rules; thus, many firms with excess pension plan values have used this procedure.

PENTAPHILIA THEORY
One of the many theories ascribed to by technical analysts. In this case, the theory holds that the market always moves higher in calendar years ending in, or divisible by, five. Example: 1975, 1980, 1985. Thus, our next certain moves will be in 1990, 1995, 2000.

As with most of such technical theories, they are jocular.

PEOPLE PILL
A term used to describe a defensive strategy that may be used in the face of a hostile takeover attempt. Under a "people pill" defense, current management announces that, if the takeover is successful, the managers will resign *en masse* and thus leave the company directionless.

PEP

Acronym for program execution processing. An NYSE-endorsed plan designed to facilitate executions of orders in multiple issues entered simultaneously as part of an institutional investor's index-based portfolio program. PEP is tied into the exchange's Super-DOT program and, at the time of writing, may involve as many as 30,099 shares of certain stocks if such orders are entered before the opening.

PER

1. Acronym for Post Execution Reporting. PER is used on the American Stock Exchange and, through it, members can direct market, limit, and odd-lot orders to the specialists at the various posts. Details of the execution reports are made directly to the members without their physical attendance at the post.
2. Used outside the United States to designate the price-earnings ratio; in the United States, "P/E" is the more common expression.

   PER is numerically expressed as the quotient of the price per share divided by the earnings per common share; for example, 10, 12.5, or 15.

   Also called the "multiple."

P/E RATIO

See PRICE-EARNINGS RATIO.

PER CAPITA DEBT

Used by municipal bond analysts of general obligation bonds. Total bonded debt divided by the population of the municipality gives the per capita debt.

PERCENT

Also: per centum. Abbreviation: pct. A ratio stated as a part of the base 100, so capitalizations, dividend and interest yields, and other numbers may be directly compared. Example: There is currently a spread of 7% between the yields on stocks and bonds. Or, AJAX Corporation has a bond ratio in excess of 35%.

PERCS

Acronym for Preferred Equity–Redemption Cumulative Stock. This Morgan Stanley innovation was tailor-made for Avon Products, Inc., at a time when it was about to reduce its common dividend by 50%. Holders of common shares could exchange for PERCS and would retain their old dividend but from a preferred share. The exchange worked well. Sufficient common shareholders elected to receive PERCS and thereby took a lot of potential selling pressure off of the common when the payout crisis became known.

PERFORMANCE APPOINTMENT MARKETMAKER
See PAMM.

PERFORMANCE INDEXED PAPER
See PIP.

PERFORMANCE PLUS
A Shearson Lehman Brothers servicemark for a CD issued by a commercial bank (thus, amounts of $100,000 or below were FDIC insured). Under the "performance plus" concept, the CD holder had a choice: *either* a fixed rate of interest for the life of the CD, *or* a return based on the performance of the S&P index during the life of the instrument.

The "Performance Plus" CDs were sold by Shearson through its network of retail brokerage offices.

PERFORMANCE STOCK
A stock that is expected to rise in market value over the near or long term. Used as a synonym for a growth stock.

The term is not used of stocks chosen for income nor of stocks chosen for total return (i.e., a combination of steady income and some capital growth). Performance emphasizes capital growth.

PERIODICALLY ADJUSTABLE-RATE TRUST SECURITIES
See PARTS.

PERIODIC PAYMENT PLAN
Common expression for a contractual mutual fund. The investor, through a contract, agrees to make monthly or quarterly payments to the plan company; in return, the investor receives certain benefits from the plan company, usually plan completion insurance and certain asset withdrawal privileges, and certain benefits from the underlying fund, usually a sharing in a diversified portfolio of common stocks and reinvestment privileges.

Normally, periodic payment plans have a 10-year or 15-year accumulation program, with a contract life that is twice as long.

PERIODIC PURCHASE DEFERRED CONTRACT
Term used of annuity contracts, either fixed or variable, whereby the investor makes monthly or quarterly fixed-amount payments. The contract has not been annuitized, thus payout is deferred pending an election by the annuitant of the payout method desired.

PERLS

Acronym for Principal Exchange-Rate-Linked Securities. PERLS are a Morgan Stanley product designed for insurance companies seeking higher rates of return on foreign investments in exchange for controlled foreign currency risks.

The instrument is a debt security denominated in U.S. dollars and with interest paid in U.S. dollars, but the *repayment* of principal is linked to the performance of the U.S. versus the Australian dollar; thus, if the Australian dollar is stronger than the U.S. dollar at maturity, redemption will be at a premium.

Thus far, only Sallie Mae (Student Loan Marketing Association) with its strong credit rating and short-term repayment period (three years) has made a successful offering of PERLS.

PERMANENT MORTGAGE REIT

A form of real estate investment trust that lends long-term monies to builders and developers of commercial and residential projects. Such long-term loans often run up to 40 years.

PERPETUALS

A U.S. term for a debt issue without a maturity date. The Canadian Pacific 4s are an example and are the only such bond traded in the United States. The reason: the IRS has never ruled whether or not such interest payments are deductible before taxes; if the IRS was to make an adverse ruling, such securities would be construed as equity securities, because they are perpetual and have a fixed rate of return similar to a preferred stock.

In the United Kingdom, such securities are called "irredeemables." Irredeemables have no maturity date, but they are redeemable by the issuer at its option; in effect, they are similar to a callable preferred stock.

PERPETUAL WARRANT

A warrant to purchase a fixed number of common shares of a corporation at a fixed price that has no expiration date. For example, TriContinental Corporation, a closed-end management company, has perpetual warrants outstanding.

PERUVIAN BONDS

A derogatory term for a worthless security. The term originated in the 1930s when the government of Peru defaulted on its bonds and created great financial losses for retail and institutional investors.

PESO
The primary unit of currency in Spain and many other nations that were originally colonized by that nation, such as Mexico, Argentina, the Philippines.

PETS
Slang for "perpetual floating rate notes" innovated in 1986 by Citicorp. Many variations have since been created.

The core concept includes three ideas: (1) interest was pegged to LIBOR, (2) there was no specific maturity date on the bonds, and (3) the holder had a put option permitting redemption of the bond.

Later PETS have had some maturity date assigned thereby giving the issuer greater control on the open-endedness of the original concept.

PFD
See PREFERRED STOCK.

PFX OPTIONS
Any foreign currency option traded on the Philadelphia Stock Exchange.

PG
Acronym for parent guaranteed. Used in descriptions and statistical tables of certain debt securities that are issued by a subsidiary corporation and whose interest and principal payments are guaranteed by the parent corporation.

PHA BONDS
See PUBLIC HOUSING AUTHORITY BONDS.

PHANTOM INCOME
Income that must be reported as taxable income for the tax year that has no corresponding cash flow with which to pay the tax.

The term applies in certain limited partnership situations and particularly to zero-coupon bonds (except Series EE or nontaxable municipals) that are not held in a tax-sheltered account. The price of such zeros must be adjusted upward (accreted) each year according to the economic experience of the holder. This accreted amount is taxable on an annual basis, despite the fact that there is no cash flow to the customer.

PHANTOM SHELF
See CONVENIENCE SHELF.

PHANTOM STOCK PLAN
A work-compensation incentive given to officers of a corporation. Under this plan, future bonus compensations are tied to the dollar value increase of the company's common stock. Thus, the bonus compensation will be computed as though the officers held a fixed number of the underlying shares; hence, the word "phantom" and the term *phantom stock*.

PHIBRO ENERGY OIL TRUST
See SYNTHETIC OIL FIELD.

PHILADELPHIA PLAN
Used of equipment trust certificates wherein title to the leased equipment remains with the trustee until such time as all of the outstanding serial maturities for the issue are retired. At this time, title passes to the leasing issuer of the securities.
  See also NEW YORK PLAN.

PHILADELPHIA STOCK EXCHANGE
The commonly used acronym for the Philadelphia Stock Exchange is PHLX. The exchange, founded in 1790, provides a marketplace for many local issues and for designated security options, and it serves as an alternate marketplace for many securities traded on the New York or other exchanges.

PHILADELPHIA STOCK EXCHANGE AUTOMATED COMMUNICATION AND EXECUTION SYSTEM
See PACE.

PHLX
See PHILADELPHIA STOCK EXCHANGE.

PHYSICAL ACCESS MEMBER
An individual who, for a special fee paid annually, has purchased from the NYSE the right to use the trading floor facilities to buy and sell securities. Such a member has no voting privileges in exchange affairs and has no liquidation rights in the event of the exchange's dissolution.

PI
Acronym for principal and interest. Term used by bond traders in discussing the typical payments made by bond issuers to their creditors.

PICKUP
Term used of a swap of bonds with similar coupon rates and similar maturities at a basis price that is advantageous to the swapper. For exam-

ple, a client sells 8¹/₂% bonds of 2000 at a basis of 10.30% and buys 8¹/₂% bonds of 2001 at a basis of 10.70%. The client has picked up 40 basis points of yield.

Pickup implies that the monetary adjustment between the purchase and sale prices is relatively small.

See also PICKUP BONDS.

PICKUP BONDS
Term used of bonds with a relatively high coupon and a relatively short callable date. If interest rates drop, the issuer usually will call the bonds at their premium price. The investor, therefore, will receive a return that is higher than anticipated because of the premium received when the bond is called.

THE PICTURE
Term used to describe the prices at which a dealer, or a specialist acting as either a broker or a dealer, is willing to trade. Often, size indications are included in the picture.

The term is slang and may be used as a synonym for quote and size. For example, "What's the picture on ABC?" "It's 19¹/₂ to 20, 2,000 either way."

PIGGYBACK EXCEPTION
This is a colloquial term that stems from a 1984 amendment to SEC Rule 15c2-11.

The rule makes an important presumption. Generally, factual information must be filed with the SEC—and this rule continues in force. However, the amendment presumes that regular and frequent quotations in an actively traded market are an appropriate substitute for information. The SEC's point of view: The market will not trade if they sense any reticence by the company to provide up-to-date information, both positive and negative.

PIGGYBACKING
The term is used in the securities industry to describe the unethical practice whereby a salesman uses knowledge or market information provided by a customer to effect trades in his or her personal account. Using such tips provided by customers is considered an inherent conflict of interest and may violate securities laws.

PIGGYBACK REGISTRATION
Term used if an issuer making a primary distribution of securities permits holders of shares purchased privately to include their shares in the offering. Such offerings are combined primary/secondary distributions,

and the prospectus will disclose this fact and the names of the major sellers of securities previously purchased privately from the corporation.

PIGs

Acronym for passive income generators. The Tax Reform Act of 1986 originated the term *passive income and losses* to describe income that comes from business enterprises in which the customer has no substantial management control; for example, an interest in a limited partnership.

Many customers had limited partnership interests that provided passive losses. Such losses would have to be carried forward unless they could be offset by passive income. Hence the term: A limited partnership interest that provided sufficient passive income to offset such losses.

PIK

Acronym for pay-in-kind. PIK is used of securities in which the issuer has the option of paying interest in cash or in the form of other securities. The payment decision is totally at the option of the issuer.

Such PIK securities are typically debt obligations used in conjunction with an LBO. During the first few years, there will typically be either a PIK payout or no payout. Later, cash payments will begin as the company begins to manage the leveraged debt.

PIN

1. Acronym for personal identification number—a unique series of numbers assigned by the SEC to all public corporations registered with the commission under the '34 Act. This number is used when filing periodic SEC reports through the use of the EDGAR system.
2. Ticker symbol for Public Service Company of Indiana, a large utility listed for trading on the NYSE.

PINCs

Acronym for property income certificates. PINCs are permitted in the United Kingdom under the provisions of the 1986 Financial Services Act.

PINCs are real estate securities with two components:
1. Entitlement to a portion of the rental income from the underlying property.
2. A share in the property's management company created to control the property and collect the rental income.

PINK SHEET ISSUE

An equity security that is neither listed on a stock exchange nor traded on the NASDAQ quotation system.

Pink sheet issues include (but are not limited to) penny stocks, straight and variable preferreds, and ADRs. Trade activity by NASD members may be subject to special reporting requirements under Schedule H or the NASD's bylaws.

The "pink sheets" are published by the National Quotation Bureau, a subsidiary of the Commerce Clearing House, a large commercial printing concern.

PINK SHEETS

The National Quotation Bureau publishes each business day the list of securities being traded by over-the-counter market makers. Equity securities are published separately on long sheets colored pink; hence the name. Debt securities are published separately on long sheets colored yellow.

See also YELLOW SHEETS.

PIN-STRIPED PORK BELLIES

A somewhat derogatory term used for index futures contracts in stock market indexes. The term arose when such futures contracts were initially offered by the Chicago Mercantile Exchange (CME) because the contracts were traded in the pit next to the pit where contracts in pork bellies (bacon) were traded.

PIP

Acronym for Performance Indexed Paper. PIP is a Salomon Brothers product linked to the performance of the German mark. This is a commercial paper program where Salomon interposed itself between issuer and investor. The issuer is guaranteed a fixed interest-rate expense; the investor is guaranteed a rate that can vary according to fluctuations in the foreign currency to which it is linked.

If investor interest develops, this concept could be expanded to other underlying currencies.

THE PIPE

Term used of the information system designed to link all European stock exchanges in an attempt to get multiple listings of major European corporations. The plan will enable residents of participating countries to trade popular foreign stocks in their own currencies on their own exchanges.

PIPELINE

Word signifying all of the procedures in a typical underwriting except the actual public offering. Thus, securities that are being underwritten but not yet sold are said to be "in the pipeline."

The word also is used by mortgage bankers to describe mortgage contracts that have been negotiated but not yet closed.

PIPELINE THEORY

Tongue-in-cheek term used for an IRS taxation privilege accorded to regulated investment companies. Under this privilege, neither the net investment income from dividends and interest nor net capital gains is taxable to the investment company; instead, these distributions (even if reinvested) become the annual tax obligation of the fundholder.

At present, 98% of the net investment income must be distributed by the fund. There is no minimum distribution requirement on net capital gains, although in practice most investment companies distribute 100% of such gains.

Also called the "conduit theory."

See also CONDUIT THEORY.

PIPS

See also PARTICIPATING INCENTIVE PREFERRED STOCK.

PIR

Acronym for Professional Investor Report. PIR is a Dow Jones news service publication for traders and arbitrageurs. The service is by private wire and alerts viewers to rumors and information about issues undergoing unusual volume or price activity.

PIT BOSS

A member of the CBOE appointed by the exchange to assist regular floor officials. Although this is a junior position, a pit boss is nevertheless authorized to: (1) resolve disputes unrelated to rule violations; (2) oversee the quality and accuracy of quotation information, as well as opening and closing prices; and (3) act as a preliminary contact between trading crowds and the exchange's regulatory staff.

A PITCH

The International Stock Exchange of the United Kingdom and the Republic of Ireland term for the location of where a dealer (jobber) maintains a continuous market for specific stocks. In the United States, such locations are called "posts."

Physically, the pitch is one of the faces of the hexagonal booths that are located on the floor of the ISE.

PITI

Acronym for principal, interest, taxes, and insurance. Since PITI basically put the mortgage holder at risk, it is common to incorporate such factors into the contract associated with a mortgage loan when made by a bank. In this way, the principal remains fixed, but there are adjustments that can be made to raise the mortgage payments usually on an annual basis—so the lender is protected against increased taxes, mortgage insurance, and the like.

TO PLACE
Industry jargon for a distribution of securities to a buyer through a public or private sale.

PLACEMENT RATIO
The percentage of new municipal issues of $1 million or more that have come into syndication within the past week and have been sold. Thus, a placement ratio of 87% means that 87% of the dollar value of new municipal issues syndicated in the past week have been sold.

The *Daily Bond Buyer* compiles the placement ratio from municipal underwriters at the close of business each Thursday.

PLAIN VANILLA
Street lingo used to designate a simple solution to a problem. Most often used in conjunction with a corporate financing to signify that a security offering is routine and traditional and thus without gimmicks or special features to enhance or promote it.

PLAM
Acronym for price-level adjusted mortgages. This is a term developed by Housing and Urban Development (HUD) to help home buyers afford mortgages in the early years of their acquisition of a home. The interest level was pegged at 4% in 1988. The difference between the pegged rate and the market rate (e.g., 10%) is adjusted in one of two ways:
1. Monthly payments rise as the loan matures.
2. The difference is added to the principal amount due (negative amortization).

PLAN COMPANY
A sales organization registered with the SEC as a participating unit investment trust. The plan company sells contractual-type funds on behalf of the fund's underwriter.

Because the plan company's units and the shares of the underlying mutual fund are both registered with the SEC, the contractual plan purchaser will receive two prospectuses: one for the plan company, one for the mutual fund.

PLAN COMPLETION INSURANCE
Decreasing term life insurance sold at group rates to subscribers to a mutual fund contractual plan. If the planholder dies before the completed plan contract, the difference between the planholder's contributions and the plan amount is paid to the custodian bank. The bank, in turn, completes the plan with the insurance money and holds the share, together with share already purchased, for the decedent's estate.

PLANNED AMORTIZATION CLASS
See PAC.

PLASTIC BONDS
Nickname for asset-backed debt securities collateralized by accounts receivable arising from VISA and MasterCard charges.

Various names have been used for such asset-backed debt securities: Salomon Brothers calls them "CARDS," Citibank calls them "Citi-Credit Card Trusts."

PLATINUM PARACHUTE
An obvious takeoff based on the concept of a "golden parachute"—only better! The concept involves two ideas:
1. A payoff for an executive who loses his or her job because of a corporate merger on unfriendly acquisition.
2. The payoff is sufficiently large to assure the executives of a "safe landing" as they either retire or look for another position.

PLATO
Acronym for a computer-assisted instruction and testing procedure developed by the Control Data Corporation. Many industry regulatory examinations, including the branch office manager and the state blue-sky examinations, are taken at the Control Data Learning Centers on the PLATO system.

PLAYER
1. Any person who likes to speculate by the frequent purchase and sale of securities.
2. Any person who becomes involved in takeovers and LBO situations. For example, "The arbitrageurs are major players in the takeover game."

PLAYING THE MARKET
A loosely used term to designate someone who buys and sells stocks frequently; in effect, the person uses the stock market as a game.

The term originated in the mid-1920s when the stock market seemed to go only upward and buying and selling stocks became a game. Although the seriousness of investment risk has become more well known, the term is still used.

PLC

1. In the United Kingdom, an abbreviation for: public liability company; plc is analogous to "corporation" in the United States in that the owners have their liabilities limited to the money they have invested in the business enterprise.
2. The stock symbol for Placer Development, Ltd., a Canadian mining company listed on the American Stock Exchange.

PLUM

Slang for anything that is particularly desirable.

The term may be used as a noun. For example, "That investment is a plum." Or it may be used as an adjective. For example, "That is a plum job."

The word is derived from the delicious fruit of the same name.

PLUNGER

Descriptive name for a speculator who tends to concentrate his or her assets in single transactions; thus, a person who puts all investment capital in one speculative investment or makes a series of speculative investments involving all, or almost all, of investible assets is a plunger. An example: "Mr. Jones became a plunger and put all of his speculative money into long sugar futures."

+

See PLUS.

PLUS

Often written as a mathematical sign: +.

1. A fractional variation to designate a quote in 64ths; for example, 85.16+ means 85 and $33/64$ths of par. The numerator is 2 times 16 plus 1; 64 is the denominator.
2. A designator for a transaction above the previous regular-way transaction. Example: On the Quotron system, 45+ means that the last trade at 45 is higher than the previous trade.
3. In the stock column of the newspaper, a + in the change column means that the closing price of listed securities was higher by the stated amount over the previous day's close. For mutual funds and OTC securities, the change is measured from the previous day's bid price.

4. Used of the difference, if a positive number, between a closed-end investment company's offer price and the net asset value of the underlying share assets.

PLUS TICK

Expression signifying that a transaction in a listed security occurred at a price higher than the previous regular-way transaction in that security. Thus, 74+ means that the prior regular-way transaction in the security was at 73⅞ or below.

See also SHORT SALE and ZERO-PLUS TICK.

PLUS-TICK RULE

SEC rule requiring short sales of round lots of listed securities be made at a price that represents an advance over the last different regular-way price for that security on its principal exchange. Exception: If the last sale was itself an advance, a sale at the same price is a zero-plus tick and may be a legitimate short sale.

PMI

See PREMEMBERSHIP INTERVIEW.

PMP

See PRIMARY MARKET PROTECTION.

PN

See PROJECT NOTE.

PNI

See PARTICIPATE BUT DO NOT INITIATE ORDER.

POB

Acronym for Public Oversight Board. The POB is a division of the SEC Practice Section of the AICPA. This board is composed of distinguished individuals from outside the accounting profession. The POB monitors the audit activities of AICPA members and publishes statistical reports regarding them for public and SEC inspection.

PODM

Acronym for put option deutsche marks. PODM is a conventional option, European style, that permits the holder to deliver a fixed amount of German marks at a fixed price in terms of U.S. dollars on a predetermined date in the future.

POES

Acronym for public order exposure system. This is a soon-to-be-developed industry procedure to make sure that customer orders are not crossed in-house before they have an opportunity to get a better price in the public marketplace.

POETS

Acronym for Pacific Options Exchange Trading System. POETS is a program that encompasses order routing, automated execution, and market quote updates for equity options processed on the PSE. POETS is designed to handle quickly and efficiently retail-type orders and to compete effectively with other option exchanges. A by-product of the system: it facilitates trading by marketmakers and recordkeeping by exchange board brokers.

POINT

1. Used of equity securities: a $1 change in the market price, or the quote, of the underlying security. For example, an equity security that went up 2 points means that its price per share increased by $2.
2. Used of bonds: a change of 1% of the par value of the bond relative to its market price. Thus, if the market price of a bond with a par value of $5,000 went up 1 point, the market value change was $50.
3. Used of bond yields: 100 basis points equals 1%.
   See also BASIS POINT.

POINT AND FIGURE CHART

A method of plotting significant price changes in a security independently of time. On the graph, successive upward price changes are plotted on the same line with an X; if a price reversal occurs, successive downward prices are plotted on the same line with an O. Succeeding upward price movements, again using X, are plotted on the next line, and so on. The method will produce a trend in the stock's prices.

The method, because it abstracts from time, gives an insight into sentiment for the security; but it loses the momentum implied by a chart that measures price movements over time.

POINTS

See COMMITMENT FEE.

PO/IO

See IO/PO.

POISON PILL DEFENSE

Slang for a corporate finance tactic to defend against unfriendly takeovers. Generally, the "poison pill" is an issue of convertible preferred stock distributed as a stock dividend to current stockholders. The preferred stock is convertible into a number of common shares equal to or greater than the present number of outstanding shares. However, because of dividend adjustments, there is little incentive to convert unless there is a takeover. The takeover attempt, therefore, becomes its own poison because it will vastly increase the price that will have to be paid for the company.

POISON PUT

A quaint term for a provision in a bond indenture that permits the bondholder to tender the security to the issuer at par (or at a premium, as determined) if: (1) there is a hostile takeover proposal or (2) the bond is downgraded by a national rating service. It is presumed that this provision will discourage an unsolicited takeover.

POLICYHOLDER LOAN BONDS

See DEATH-BACKED BONDS.

POLISH DIVIDEND

See SCOTTISH DIVIDEND.

POLISHING THE ELEPHANT'S TOENAILS

Colorful British expression for work that is a waste of time and effort.

The term is most often used in the context of securities litigation in which lawyers (solicitors, in Britain) use an inordinate amount of time preparing a case and the time, in practice, does not seem justified in the results of the case.

POLITICAL STOCK

See ELECTION STOCK.

POM

1. NYSE ticker symbol for Potomac Electric Power, a large utility corporation serving the mid-Atlantic area of the United States.
2. See PUBLIC ORDER MEMBER.

PONZI SCHEME

Popular name for any scam that bilks people by promising high returns for money invested but that can only do so by using funds received from new investors to pay earlier depositors. The scheme is doomed to failure because its pyramid effect requires ever-increasing sums of money "borrowed from Peter to pay Paul." Charles Ponzi, after whom the scheme is named, cost investors millions of dollars with such fraudulent practices in the 1920s.

POOL
Commonly used expression if a group of debt instruments is gathered together and an undivided interest in the securities is represented by another security. Example: A bank issues mortgages on 50 homes with a $20,000 mortgage on each home. If the bank were to issue a security with a face value of $1 million, the security would represent a pool of mortgages.

See also MORTGAGE POOL.

POOLING OF INTEREST
Balance sheet term for the accounting procedure used if one corporation acquires another through merger or acquisition.

Principal concepts: (1) all assets and liabilities are merged; (2) if there is a difference between the cost of acquisition and the net tangible value of the acquired corporation, it is entered on the acquiring corporation's balance sheet as "goodwill." Present IRS rules permits this entry to be amortized over 40 years.

POPULARIZING
An NYSE term applied to certain promotional activities by exchange specialists in options on stock issues in which they make markets. These activities may be advertisements, market letters, sales literature, research reports, or buy-sell recommendations made to investors to trade in the overlying options.

PORCUPINE DEFENSE
Colorful name for a strategy designed to thwart a hostile takeover attempt. The metaphor arises from the fact that those who attack a porcupine often come out the worse for wear because they are stuck wearing its quills.

PORTAL
Acronym for Private Offerings, Resales, and Trading through Automated Linkages. This is an NASD term for the ability to trade private offerings using the automated quotation services of NASDAQ.

Such service is available only to sophisticated institutions, financially qualified investors (accredited persons), and to selected foreign investors. Thus, PORTAL gives some liquidity to what was in the past a highly illiquid market.

PORTFOLIO

Commonly accepted term for those assets of an individual or a legal person, such as a bank, trust company, pension or profit-sharing plan, or an investment company, which are invested in primary or secondary market securities. Generally, hard assets (e.g., gold, silver, art) and commodities are excluded from the term.

In the broadest sense, however, a person's portfolio is the sum of items of value which are (1) saleable and (2) needed for day-to-day use.

See also PRIMARY MARKET, SECONDARY MARKET, SECURITY.

PORTFOLIO INSURANCE

Generic term used to describe a kind of insurance of portfolio values by tracking a market index and the corresponding purchase/sale of index futures. Thus, portfolio insurance is a self-established hedging technique versus stock holdings. When the market declines by a predetermined amount, index futures are sold; when the market rises, index futures are bought. In effect, the portfolio manager has set up the situation whereby a loss in one instrument will be offset by gains in the other, thereby co-insuring the portfolio.

PORTFOLIO MANAGER

A person who makes day-to-day investment decisions for another.

Commonly, the term is used of investment managers for mutual fund, pension or profit-sharing plans, or bank-trust companies.

However, anyone who manages the assets of another and who invests these assets in things that have resale value can be called a "portfolio manager."

PORTFOLIO PUTS

A trading strategy used by some institutional portfolio managers as a successor to "portfolio insurance." With "insurance" the portfolio manager sells index futures contracts to hedge against a large, long security position. But, with portfolio puts, the institutional manager has a broker/dealer sell it an index put option (or futures contract), for a specific number of portfolio dollars in exchange for the immediate payment of a negotiated premium. Then, if the market declines, the portfolio manager receives payment from the broker/dealer which, in theory, should offset the loss in value for the stock holdings.

PORTFOLIO SYSTEM FOR INSTITUTIONAL TRADING

See POSIT.

POS

Acronym for Preliminary Official Statement. Both the Preliminary Official Statement and the Final Official Statement are similar in purpose to the Preliminary and Final Prospectuses on a registered offering. There are these principal differences: Municipal issuers need not publish either statement; and, in recent years, a number of municipal issuers have published a preliminary official statement but not a final official statement because of the size of these documents and the cost of publication. In this latter case, the principal underwriter (or dealer) is required to send a copy of the preliminary official statement (or summary thereof) to the original purchaser in lieu of the final official statement, as required in the rules of the MSRB.

POSIT

Acronym for Portfolio System for Institutional Trading. POSIT is an experimental computerized trading system that endeavors to trade entire portfolios between institutional investors without benefit of an intervening central marketplace.

In effect, the system functions as an exchange between subscribers. Overages in dollar amounts are executed by Jeffries & Co. in formal exchange transactions. The dollar proceeds would go to the firm with the larger portfolio value.

POSITION

1. As noun: the number of shares owned (long position) or owed (short position) by an individual or a dealer. A dealer's position is also called "inventory."
2. As verb: to acquire a net long or short inventory in a security. For example, "The dealer is trying to position the security."

POSITION BID (OFFER)

A bid (offer) made by a broker/dealer who is willing to buy (sell) a block of securities for his or her own account as an accommodation to an institutional customer. Generally, the bid (or offer) is slightly away from the market to provide the broker/dealer some protection against market risk, while the broker/dealer seeks to close out the resulting long or short position.

POSITION BUILDING

Term used of account executives as they endeavor to establish net long (shares owned) or net short (shares owed) positions in the portfolios of their clients.

Position building, although it increases both the risk of selection and the risk of timing, decreases the number of security issues that the account executives must follow. The offset, of course, is that they must follow fewer issues in depth; thus, advice to buy or sell can be more timely in terms of short-term profits.

POSITION LIMIT
Maximum number of option contracts that a customer, or a group of customers working in concert, may hold in the same underlying security. Currently, the maximum for some stock options is 8,000 contracts on the same side of the market. For example, long calls and short puts, or long puts and short calls.

The position limits on interest-rate options vary with the kind of underlying instrument.

POSITION RISK ADDITION
PRA is a process employed by English broker/dealers in the calculation of their net capital requirements. Unlike the U.S. procedure, which is based on a "haircut" of the current market price, British brokers must add a specified percentage to reflect the degree of potential risk maintained in the position. This addition is called "PRA."

POSITION TRADER
This is a term associated with "upstairs trading" by member firms for their own account. The persons who evaluate the potential risk/reward of the position and make the market decisions to buy or sell for the firm's proprietary security positions are called "position traders."

POSITIVE CARRY
Term that describes the use of borrowed funds to purchase interest-producing securities. If the income received is more than the income paid, there is a positive carry. For example, a person borrows money at 9% to buy bonds with a 10% coupon. Thus, the net gain is 1%.

POSITIVE YIELD CURVE
Term used to describe the yield versus time graph of securities of the same issuer, or of securities with a similar credit rating, in which longer-term securities have a higher yield than shorter-term securities. Thus, if 2-year Treasury bonds yield 8% and 4-year bonds yield 9% and 15-year bonds yield 11%, there is a positive yield curve.

Also called "yield curve with an ascending slope."

POST
Location on the floor of an exchange where specific securities are traded, and where, in most cases, the specialist is available to receive bids and offers or to give a quote for specific securities.

Also called "trading post."

POSTAL SERVICE
The successor corporation to the Post Office Department. It is a federal agency that issues debt securities to finance capital improvements and to cover deficits in operating expenses. The Postal Service pledges its own assets and revenues as collateral for these bonds, although the Postal Service could ask for and receive a U.S. government guarantee from the Secretary of the Treasury.

POST-DATED
1. Any document that is dated after the calendar date on which the agreement was signed.
2. A check, draft, or other transfer document that is dated at some future date. Although both the issuance and acceptance of a post-dated check, in many circumstances, may signal a credit problem, there is one exception. Bankers' acceptances are always post-dated checks. Any credit problem is quickly solved: the accepting bank's guaranteed performance on the loan.

POST EXECUTION REPORTING
See PER (1).

POSTING A LEVEL
Expression used by issuers of short-term paper as they endeavor to borrow money at the best possible rate.

Thus, commercial paper borrowers endeavor to find an interest rate, in comparison with U.S. T-bills, CDs, and LIBOR at which they can attract short-term capital. Once found, this standard, or level, becomes the norm at which other comparable borrowers will endeavor to attract short-term money during that time frame. The process of establishing a norm is called "posting a level."

POST 30
A numbered post on the floor of the New York Stock Exchange where relatively inactive listed preferred shares are traded. Bids and offers are entered in cabinets so contra brokers may have a market for trades. All of the stocks traded on Post 30 trade in round lots of 10-shares rather than 100-share units.

THE POT
Slang for that portion of the shares or bonds of a corporate issue returned to the account manager, as agent, for convenient sale to institutional buyers.

If sales are made from the pot, the members of the syndicate share in the spread in proportion to their takedown of the issue. Thus, on an issue of 1 million shares with 100,000 in the pot, a member of the account with a 10% participation (takedown) will share in 10% of the sales from the pot.

THE POT IS CLEAN
An announcement made by the manager of a syndicate to the account members that all the securities set aside for institutional sales have been sold.

POT LIABILITY
Term that refers to an underwriter's financial responsibility for unsold securities remaining in the pot when the syndicate price restrictions are lifted by the manager. Generally, each member of the syndicate is liable for unsold pot securities in direct proportion to its percentage commitment to the issuer.

POUND
As a general rule, this represents the primary unit of currency in Great Britain. Because other nations also use pound as a primary currency unit, the word is often used in a compound form: pound sterling.

POWER OF ATTORNEY
A signed document that empowers a second party to act on behalf of the signer.

If a brokerage account is managed by someone with power of attorney, it is important that it be specified whether the power of attorney account is general or limited. Persons with limited power of attorney may sell assets and reinvest the proceeds within the account. Persons with general power of attorney may deliver assets out of the account.

Brokerage accounts with limited power of attorney given to an employee of the brokerage firm are called "discretionary accounts."

PPM
See PRIVATE PLACEMENT MEMO.

PR
A commonly used abbreviation for preferred stock. The other commonly used abbreviations are PF and Pfd.

PRA
See POSITION RISK ADDITION.

PREARRANGED TRADING

An arrangement between two or more commodities exchange members to buy and sell between themselves at predetermined prices. Thus, their transactions are not at risk but are done for their own personal economic reasons. Usually such reasons pertain to taxes.

Prearranged trades violate industry rules and may be fraudulent.

PRECEDENCE

Exchange trading floor term. It signifies that a broker (e.g., a buyer), is permitted to buy before other brokers despite the fact that other buying brokers also could complete the transaction.

As a general rule, precedence is determined by the time a broker makes a bid, then by the size of the bid relative to the number of shares being offered at that price.

THE PREDATORS' BALL

The tongue-in-cheek name for an annual conference of junk bond (high-yield bond) issuers and buyers sponsored by the former Drexel Burnham Lambert, at one time the premier underwriter of such bonds. The macabre name for the conference was based on the fact that many of the attendees were directly involved in many of the mergers, acquisitions, LBOs, and hostile takeovers of the 1970s and 1980s.

PREEMPTIVE RIGHT

A privilege granted by the charter of some corporations to current common shareholders. It gives them the right to buy a portion of newly offered common shares that is proportional to their current common share holding. In this way, a common shareholder has the opportunity to preserve his or her proportional share of ownership in the corporation.

Because such newly offered shares are priced below the current market price, there is also a monetary incentive to subscribe to the new shares.

Most corporate charters do not grant a preemptive right to the shareholders.

PREFERENCE

Exchange floor term for who goes first in an auction impasse. For example, if two or more brokers, following an execution because of time priority, have orders that equal the remainder of the other side of the trade, they are on parity. Preference will be given to the broker who was the first to enter the group of brokers competing for a transaction (the crowd).

PREFERENCE INCOME
Certain income items (such as the excluded portion of capital gains and excess depreciation over straight-line) that are not included in the adjusted taxable income of an individual. If such excluded income items exceed a specified amount, the taxpayer is required to compute an alternate minimum tax. If the alternate minimum exceeds the tax found by using the tax schedules, this becomes the individual's tax for that year. Concept: To prevent wealthy individuals from paying a lower percentage tax than that paid by wage earners.

PREFERENCE SHARES
1. Often used as a synonym for any preferred shares.
2. Specifically used of preferred shares that give precedence to other preferred shares; thus, preference shares are junior in their claim on dividends and assets to other preferred shares of the same issuer.

PREFERRED DIVIDEND COVERAGE
The quotient found by dividing the net income after taxes of a corporation by the dollar amount of preferred dividends. Thus, if a corporation's net income is $10 million and annual preferred dividends are $1 million, the preferred dividend coverage is 10 to 1, or simply 10 times.

PREFERRED EQUITY—REDEMPTION CUMULATIVE STOCK
See PERCS.

PREFERRED PREFERRED
Slang often used with prior preferred stock (i.e., an issue of preferred stock that takes precedence over one or more issues or preferred stock of the same corporation). This precedence may be in terms of dividend payments or the claim on assets upon dissolution of the company.

PREFERRED STOCK (PFD)
A form of equity security that generally has a fixed annual dividend, a stated call price related to its par value, and has no voting right. Preferred stock has priority over common stock in the payment of dividends and in the distribution of assets if the company is dissolved. However, it is not a debt security and has no fixed maturity date.

PREFERRED STOCK RATIO
The ratio found by dividing the par value of outstanding preferred shares of a corporation by the total capitalization.

PRELIMINARY AGREEMENT
A temporary commitment between an issuing corporation and an underwriter drawn up prior to the effective date of the issuer's registration statement. The replacement of the preliminary agreement by a formal agreement hinges upon the underwriter's estimation of the success potential for the offering and the corporation's acceptance of the underwriter's terms and conditions.

THE PRE-MARKET
A British term for the active trading of proposed new issues before they are actually offered for public sale. The practice is condoned in the United Kingdom for nonexchange members, but it is fraught with financial risk.

In the United States, the practice is not permitted for securities "in registration," but it is similar in concept to the U.S. trading on a "when issued" basis of exempt securities before they are actually offered.

PREMEMBERSHIP INTERVIEW (PMI)
Under Schedule C of the NASD bylaws, an applicant for membership must be first interviewed by officials of the district office where the applicant's principal office will be located. Among the documents that the applicant must submit at this meeting are: a copy of its SEC BD Form (Broker/Dealer form), a copy of its written supervisory procedures, and a copy of its financial statements.

PREMIUM
1. The dollar amount by which the market price of a bond exceeds its par value. Used in a similar way if a preferred share's market price exceeds its face value.
2. A fee paid by a short seller to the lender of the security that is sold short.
   See also CALL PREMIUM.

PREMIUM BOND
A bond whose dollar price exceeds its par or face value.

PREMIUM RAID
British securities industry term to describe a quick purchase of a large percentage of a company's stock at prices above the prevailing market. Because there is little advance notice, and because the trade often is completed in 30 minutes or less, few public investors have a chance to sell their shares at these advantageous prices.

PREPAID CHARGE PLAN

Another name for a contractual mutual fund in which most of the total sales charge on the plan is paid in the first or in the early years of the plan.

See also FRONT-END LOAD and LOAD SPREAD OPTION.

PREPAID EXPENSE

The pro rata portion of a fully paid charge for a service if a portion of the service overlaps the end of a corporation's fiscal year. For example, a corporation pays a six-month premium for insurance in October. Its fiscal year ends in December. One half of the premium covers expenses for the first three months of the next year. This half of the premium will be listed on the corporation's balance sheet as an asset entitled prepaid expense.

PREPAYMENT

If a member firm pays a selling customer before the assigned settlement date, it is called a "prepayment."

PRER

This is an abbreviation for "pre-refunded," a municipal bond identifier for a debt security that is fully collateralized by U.S. Treasury issues. In effect, the outstanding municipal debt is guaranteed by a pool of funds equal to the debt and having a maturity that is the same as that of the municipal debt.

Other abbreviations are used for "pre-refunded," and occasionally the abbreviation ETM (escrowed to maturity) is similarly used.

Pre-refunded securities may have a maturity that is equal to the earliest call date of the original municipal issue.

PREREFUNDING

If an issuer borrows, through a second bond issue, funds for the future refunding of an outstanding bond that is not yet callable, it is called a "prerefunding." The outstanding issue that will be called at its earliest call date is said to be "prerefunded."

The borrowed funds for the refunding normally are invested in Treasuries that will mature at the earliest call date. For this reason, prerefunded bonds are normally rated AAA.

PRESALE ORDER

A buy order accepted by the manager of a municipal syndicate for a portion of the issue before the details of the offering are known.

Although such an order would be illegal for an offering under registration with the SEC, such orders are accepted for municipal securities because of their exemption.

PRESCRIBED RIGHT TO INCOME AND MAXIMUM EQUITY
See PRIME.

PRESENT VALUE OF A DOLLAR
The amount of money required right now to become a dollar at a time in the future at a given rate of compound interest over a given number of years. The formula is the reciprocal of the Future Value formula (q.v.). It is:

$$\frac{1}{(1 + R)^n}$$

Where n is the number of compounding periods, and R is the compounded rate of return.

Thus, to achieve $1 if money is invested at 7% over 5 years would require:

$$\$0.71298$$

PRESOLD ISSUE
An issue of municipals or governments that is completely sold before announcement is made of the price or coupon rate.

This would be an illegal practice on a registered corporate offering that requires a bona fide public offering. It is not illegal in the primary distribution of exempt securities.

PRESUMPTIVE UNDERWRITER
Term, by SEC interpretation, that describes any investor who acquires a relatively large amount of securities in a public offering with a view toward an early resale. In practice, the SEC has regarded anyone who purchases 10% or more of an offering and sells it within two years as a presumptive underwriter.

PRICE CHANGE
When used of an individual security, price change is the net rise or fall in the market value of the security.

When used of a group of securities, the average of the price changes. For example, if security A rises 1 point and security B falls 1 point, the average change is zero: $+1 - 1 = 0$.

PRICE-EARNING RATIO
Abbreviations: PE or PR. The ratio is formed by dividing the current market price of a company's shares by the current annual earnings per common share. Technically, the ratio is the quotient of this division.

Normally, the fraction is so rationalized that the denominator is 1. Thus, a common stock that is selling at $50 per share, and that has earnings per share of $5, has a PE of 10 to 1. Commonly, the shares are said to have a PE of 10, although technically this is a multiple of 10. The price is 10 times the earnings.

Synonym: multiple. Example: The stock is currently selling at a multiple of 9.

PRICE GAP
Term used by technical analysts if a security's daily range does not overlap the daily range on the previous market day. For example, yesterday's range for a stock was $38\frac{1}{2}$–39; today's range was $39\frac{1}{2}$–40. There was a gap of $\frac{1}{2}$ point between 39 and $39\frac{1}{2}$.

Price gaps are usually considered indications of an oversold or overbought condition, and a consolidation can be expected in most cases.

The term also is used if successive trades exceed the minimum trading variations. Thus, successive trades at 40, $39\frac{1}{2}$, 39 exceed the normal variation of $\frac{1}{8}$ and would be considered a gap.

PRICE IDEAS
See PRICE TALK.

PRICE-LEVEL ADJUSTED MORTGAGES
See PLAM.

PRICE RANGE
The high and low prices for a security over a defined time.
See also RANGE.

PRICE SPREAD
See VERTICAL SPREAD.

PRICE TALK
Term describing the preliminary discussions among underwriters about the range within which they will offer a negotiated issue or within which they will bid on a competitive issue.

Price talk is informal, with this exception: the preliminary prospectus of a corporate issue of common stock will state the maximum offering price if this is a first-time public sale of the security.

PRICE THOUGHTS
See PRICE TALK.

PRICEY
Industry slang for a bid that is underpriced, or an offer that is overpriced. For example, if the current market for a security is 35–36, a cus-

tomer who insists either on a bid at 32 or an offer at 39 is pricey—he is currently unrealistic about buying or selling the security.

PRICING
Securities industry term for the establishment of a value for the sale of a security. The term applies:
1. To the determination of the price at which a public offering will be made; for example, the pricing meeting.
2. To the determination of the value at which proprietary securities will—after the statutory "haircuts"—be carried in the determination of net worth of the broker/dealer.

PRIMARY DISTRIBUTION
Term used to describe a sale of new securities by an issuer.

In the case of bonds, all sales by an issuer are primary. In the case of stocks, the sale of authorized and previously unissued shares is primary. Thus, a resale of Treasury shares that were previously issued but which are resold is a secondary.

PRIMARY EARNINGS
The quotient from dividing a corporation's net income after taxes, minus preferred dividends, by the number of common shares currently outstanding.

See also FULLY DILUTED EARNINGS PER SHARE (if a company's outstanding shares will be changed by the conversion of convertible securities, or by the exercise of rights, warrants, or stock options granted to corporate executives).

PRIMARY MARKET
General term for any market for assets where the proceeds of the sale go to the issuer. As such, the term includes:
1. The underwriting of original issues of securities.
2. Government securities auctions.

It is also used of a principal marketplace for the trading of securities. These include:
3. Opening sales of option contracts and commodity futures contracts.
4. An exchange, or the OTC market, which is the principal market for a specific outstanding security.

PRIMARY MARKET PROTECTION (PMP)
This term refers to the protection that regional exchange specialists must provide to customers if they accept an order that is "away from the market." Generally, if a transaction occurs on the issue's primary exchange

(usually the NYSE) at the customer's price or better, the regional specialist must guarantee at least a partial execution of the limit order.

PRIME
Acronym for prescribed right to income and maximum equity (i.e., one of the two component parts of an Americus trust). The first Americus trust was established for the common shares of AT&T.

Holders of the PRIME component receive all dividend distributions plus any asset value of the trust up to a maximum of $75 per share when it is dissolved. Holders of the SCORE component receive the remainder of the capital value of the underlying shares.

See also SCORE.

PRIME BANK NOTES (PBN)
PBNs are debt obligations of good-quality bank holding companies associated with the major banks in the chief financial centers of the United States.

PRIME PAPER
Industry term for commercial paper that is given a rating of P by Moody's Investors Service.

The rating implies an investment grade security . The rating is further subdivided into:

P-1: Highest quality.
P-2: Higher quality.
P-3: High quality.
Ratings below P-3 are not prime paper.

PRIME RATE
A preferential rate of interest on short-term loans granted by commercial banks to their most credit-worthy customers. Theoretically, it is the lowest rate of interest for bank loans that are not backed by items of value pledged as collateral.

PRINCIPAL
1. The face amount of a debt security. The term is applicable even if the security is a zero-coupon bond.
2. Any person—including an individual investor, an institution, or a broker/dealer—who buys or sells a security for its own account and risk.
3. A person associated with an NASD broker/dealer who is actively engaged in that firm's securities or investment banking business. Such a person may be a sole proprietor, a partner, a corporate director, or a manager of an office of supervisory jurisdiction.

4. Any person who authorizes another—often in writing—to act as his or her agent in a transaction or a business. For example, "Tom Jones is principal in that power of attorney account."

See also PRINCIPAL AMOUNT (if term is related to an issue of debt securities).

PRINCIPAL AMOUNT
1. The face amount or par value of any debt security.
2. The face amount of a loan.

PRINCIPAL APPRECIATION CONVERSION SECURITIES
See PACS.

PRINCIPAL EXCHANGE-RATE-LINKED SECURITY
See PERLS.

PRINCIPAL ONLY/INTEREST ONLY
See IO/PO.

PRINCIPAL STOCKHOLDER
Generally, a stockholder who owns a large amount of a company's outstanding shares.

Specifically, under Section 12 of the Securities and Exchange Act of 1934, a person who holds 10% or more of the voting stock, including long calls on such stock, of a corporation registered with the SEC.

Also called a "control person" or "affiliated person."

PRINT
Slang expression for the records of securities transactions that appear on exchange tapes.

PRIORITY
Auction (trading) market term for the first member to bid or offer at the current highest bid or lowest offer. If a transaction occurs at that price, the contra broker must trade with the broker who has priority, regardless of the size of the bid or offer by the broker with priority.

In essence, therefore, in the auction market, the broker with priority always receives a full or partial execution if a trade occurs at that price.

PRIOR LIEN BOND
A debt security that gives priority to its holders over the claim of other bondholders.

The term is not used to distinguish secured bonds from unsecured bonds; for example, mortgage bonds as opposed to debentures. Instead, a prior lien bond would give priority to one secured bond over another.

Secured bonds with a prior lien over other secured bonds normally are issued by companies in financial difficulty and then only with the authorization of the holders of previously issued bonds who give their authorization to try to save the company.

PRIOR PREFERRED
The term identifies an issue of preferred stock that takes precedence over another issue of preferred stock in its claim on corporate assets in the event of dissolution of the company, or in its claim on earnings if dividends are declared.

PRIVATE EXPORT FUNDING CORPORATION
Acronym: PEFCO. A corporation that makes loans to foreign importers of goods and services of U.S. manufacture or origin. Its interest and principal repayment liabilities on borrowed money are guaranteed by the Export-Import Bank (Eximbank), which in turn is guaranteed by the full faith and credit of the United States.

PRIVATE MARKET VALUE
Often used as a synonym for liquidating value, as opposed to its value in a stock market.

The term became necessary because many LOBs are "asset plays" in which parts of a company will be resold in private negotiations with the owners of ongoing businesses. In effect, the advisability of the merger or LBO will be decided by the price at which the portions of the company can be resold in a private transaction.

PRIVATE OFFERINGS, RESALES, AND TRADING THROUGH AUTOMATED LINKAGES
See PORTAL.

PRIVATE PLACEMENT
A sale of securities to relatively few investors. As a general rule, the investors may not exceed 35 persons, although "accredited investors" are excluded from this number.

If a sale is truly private, the sale is an exempt transaction and need not be registered with the SEC.

See also ACCREDITED INVESTOR.

PRIVATE PLACEMENT MEMORANDUM
Initials: PPM. A PPM is similar to a prospectus for registered offerings in that it discloses the pertinent facts about the private placement. Remember: For a placement to qualify as "private," the purchasers must have sufficient information to make an informed decision. Such a memo would undoubtedly have pertinent information about the issuer, the limited or nonexistent marketability of the issue, and what is going to be done with the funds raised by the issue.

PRIVATISATION
An English term for the sale to the public of shares in what had previously been government-owned enterprises. In the 1980s, Margaret Thatcher's government sold shares in British Airways, British Telecommunications, British Gas, and British Petroleum.

In a similar fashion, the Japanese government sold shares in Japan Air Lines and in Nippon Telephone and Telegraph.

PRL
Exchange terminology for "part of a round lot."

The term is associated with the sale of a part of a round lot (odd lot) in conjunction with a round lot; for example, the sale of 225 shares involves two round lots of 100 shares plus part of a round lot (25 shares).

Such a designation is required on exchange-directed orders to point out that (1) the odd lot differential should not be charged and (2) that the odd lot (PRL) is to be transacted at the same price as the round lot(s).

PRO
Acronym for Peer Review Organization. A PRO is an SEC-recognized accounting firm with authority to examine other accounting firms that certify financial statements of publicly traded securities.

Under SEC Regulation S-X, the purpose of "peer review" is to make sure that the audit of such publicly traded firms comforms to generally accepted account standards (GAAS).

A body of three independent individuals oversees the work of the PRO.

PROBATE COURT
This is the juridical arm of local government given power over wills, intestacies, guardianships, adoptions, and—in some cases—incompetencies. Such courts are also known as "surrogate courts."

Judges of probate issue letters (often called "certificates") to executors, administrators, or guardians to complete certain financial actions. Examples: manage the assets of an incompetent, settle an estate, or guard the financial affairs of a minor.

PROCEEDS SALE
National Association of Securities Dealers' term describing a customer sale in the secondary market with the proceeds of the sale to be used for a purchase in the secondary market.

The NASD rule for proceeds sales says that the swap must be considered as one transaction and that the total sales charges or commissions must come under the 5% policy governing markups, markdowns, or commissions.

PRODUCTION RATE
The current coupon rate for issuance of pass-through securities of the Government National Mortgage Association (GNMA). It is an interest rate set 50 basis points ($\frac{1}{2}$%) below the prevailing FHA mortgage rate (i.e., the maximum interest rate at which the Federal Housing Administration will insure, and the Veterans Administration will guarantee, residential mortgages).

PROFESSIONAL INVESTOR REPORT
See PIR.

TO PROFILE A CUSTOMER
Expression used by sales and administrative personnel to describe the act of soliciting customer background information. Profiling results in the fulfillment of one of the basic requirements of financial service: to "know the customer." As a general rule, profiling is done by registered representatives (RRs) who alone among brokerage personnel are permitted to solicit buy and sell orders for securities.

PROFIT
Generally, a positive difference between the current market value of a security and the investor's purchase price.

Specifically, the net positive difference between the proceeds of a sale and the investor's adjusted cost of acquisition.

PROFIT AND LOSS STATEMENT
A financial statement, prepared at least once a year by a corporation, that lists the firm's income, expenses, and net profit or loss over the period covered by the statement.

PROFIT MARGIN
Subtract the cost of goods sold from net sales to obtain operating income. Divide operating income by net sales to find the profit margin. For example, a company sells goods worth $10; it cost $8 to make the goods; the operating income is $2. The $2 divided by $10 gives a profit margin of 20%.

Also called the "margin of profit," the "margin of profit ratio," or the "profit ratio."

See also MARGIN OF PROFIT.

PROFIT RATIO
See PROFIT MARGIN.

PROFIT TAKING
A commonly used expression to explain a sudden drop in the stock market following a long- or intermediate-term rise in the market.

As a matter of fact, the expression means that the pundits have no accurate reading of the cause for the drop. The drop may have been caused by selling—a reasonable cause for a drop—or by a lack of interest of buyers. Thus, the reader may substitute his or her own reason for the drop. In practice, the reason is unknown.

PRO FORMA
Latin: according to form or custom. In practice, the expression is used:
1. If a financial statement is currently unaudited but is sufficiently representative of the corporation's financial condition to be a reasonable and fair disclosure of the company's balance sheet.
2. If an action, done with due diligence and proper authorization, awaits only official approval. Example: The shareholders of a corporation have approved a stock split and application has been made for a charter revision. The application is pro forma because it will be approved.

PROGRAM EXECUTION PROCESSING
See PEP.

PROGRAM TRADING
A general term for any endeavor by a portfolio manager to replicate the movement of a popular index and to use this in the management of the account.

Usually program trading is accomplished by the use of a computer to (1) either measure the index or (2) to initiate trades—or both. Program trading may be a hedging (offset or position before the fact) technique, or an arbitrage (profit-capturing) technique.

There is currently much controversy about program trading and whether it inordinately increases market volatility.

PROGRESSIVE TAX
General term applied to any system of taxation where the tax bracket (marginal rate) increases as the dollar value of the tax base increases. In the United States, both income and estate taxes are progressive taxes.

Antonym: regressive tax, where the rate remains the same for all persons.

PROJECT NOTE (PN)
Short-term municipal security issued by local housing agencies as temporary financing during the building of public housing. They are normally redeemed by the permanent bonds that form the long-term financing for the buildings. Project notes carry a U.S. guarantee through the Department of Housing and Urban Development (HUD).

Abbreviated PN on municipal bond offering sheets published by dealers and by Standard & Poor's in its daily Blue List.

PROPORTIONATE SHARE OF ASSETS
The right of common stockholders to the residual assets of their corporation upon its dissolution. In practice, after all liabilities have been fully satisfied, and preferred stockholders have been provided for, the common stockholders divide the remaining assets, if any, among themselves.

PROPRIETARY
1. Securities and other assets of a broker/dealer as well as those of its principals that are pledged as capital contributed to the organization.
2. Anything owned by a proprietor.
3. A product or service covered by a patent or by a trade or service mark.
4. As an adjective in conjunction with an account: the broker's inventory—either long or short—used in securities trading.

PROPRIETORSHIP
A form of business organization comprised of one owner-person that is not incorporated. The owner has great flexibility in managing the business, but capital resources are often limited and personal financial liability for the debts of the organization is unlimited. Proprietors are self-employed and, as such, are eligible for Keogh account contributions.

PROSPECTUS
The printed summary of a registration statement filed with the SEC in conjunction with a public offering of nonexempt securities. The prospectus, which contains the material information about the offering of securities, must be given to the original purchasers of the security no later than the confirmation of their purchase.

PROTECTIVE COVENANTS
General term for agreements and promises of a municipality to protect purchasers of an issue of municipal securities. These agreements are in the bond resolution made when the security is issued.

Typical content of the covenant: a promise to service and repair the facility built with the borrowed funds, adequate insurance coverage, the maintenance of books and records, and the assessment of adequate rates or tolls to cover interest and the repayment of principal.

PROTECT PREFERRED
A new form of convertible preferred that sets a specific price that the common is to achieve by a certain target date. If the common fails to reach that price, there is a special dividend equal to the shortfall. The purpose of the security is to enhance shareholder value by giving predictability to the stock.

PROVISIONAL ALLOTMENT LETTER
In England: the means whereby corporations offer present shareholders the right to subscribe to additional shares before the general public is allowed to participate. The letter, therefore, is the English equivalent of a rights offering in the United States.

PROXY
A form whereby a person, who is eligible to vote about corporate matters, transmits his or her written instructions, or transfers to another the right to vote in place of the eligible voter. Normally, the corporate management transmits a form that is suited to the transmission of such voting instructions, but shareholders may request other forms of proxy if they wish to give special instructions. A proxy permits an eligible voter to vote without being present at the actual meeting.

PROXY DEPARTMENT
A work area in a broker/dealer cashiering function that distributes corporate publications, including financial reports, meeting notices, and voting information to the beneficial owners of shares held by that broker/dealer. Thus, the proxy department acts as an intermediary between the issuer and these beneficial owners and casts votes on their behalf according to the instructions received from these owners.

PROXY STATEMENT
A statement of material information that must be provided by management, or any other person, who solicits the proxies of corporate shareholders. Such statements must be filed with the SEC for examination prior to their distribution to stockholders.

PRUDENT MAN RULE

Rule contained in the laws of many states governing the investment activities of persons who act as fiduciaries, such as trustees, executors, and administrators.

In general, the rule precludes speculative activities by fiduciaries and legislates as a norm the kind of investment actions that a prudent man would use in the conduct of his own financial affairs.

See also LEGAL LIST.

PSA

See PUBLIC SECURITIES ASSOCIATION.

PSBR

Acronym for Public Sector Borrowing Requirement. PSBR is an important segment of the British budget. Because Britain has a socialized health program and other government-sponsored public benefits programs, PSBR is an important indicator of the United Kingdom's fiscal policy for the year.

PSDR

Acronym for Public Sector Debt Repayment. PSDR is an important segment of the British budget. PSDR gives an insight into the British government's ability and willingness to repay its annual public services debt, rather than refund it through further borrowings. Thus, together with PSBR, PSDR gives an insight into the net change in the public debt of Britain.

PSE

See PACIFIC STOCK EXCHANGE.

P/T

Abbreviation for pass-through, a form of mortgage-backed security in which holders of certificates receive monthly interest and principal repayments made by the underlying borrowers in those real estate loans.

PTA

Common abbreviation for peseta, the principal currency of Spain. All securities traded on Spanish stock exchanges are denominated or traded in pesetas.

Plural: Ptas.

THE PUBLIC

1. Used in opposition to market professionals, who are often called "market insiders."

2. Used derisively of the small investor who is considered to do exactly the opposite of the sophisticated investor by buying at the top, selling at the bottom. This concept is at the heart of what is called the "odd lot" theory: do the opposite of the public and you will invest smartly.
3. Used without "the" as an adjective in distinction to private; for example, the stock is now public, or the company went public with the information.
4. Used extensively as an adverb in such expressions as "publicly traded," "publicly known," and so on.

PUBLIC HOUSING AUTHORITY BONDS (PHA)

Technical name for longer-term municipal bonds used to finance the construction of public housing and which are guaranteed by the full faith and credit of the United States government.

PUBLIC LIABILITY COMPANY

See PLC.

PUBLICLY HELD

Technically, any corporation whose shares are freely transferrable. Specifically:
1. Under SEC definition, a corporation with assets of $1 million or more and 500 or more holders of any class of equity security. Such corporations are required to make periodic reports to the SEC.
2. Under New York Stock Exchange rules, a member corporation whose outstanding stock is owned by 100 or more persons, not including members, allied members, or employees of that member corporation.

PUBLIC OFFERING

General term for a sale of securities by an issuer or control persons.
Often called a "distribution."

PUBLIC OFFERING PRICE

The price asked (offer) at the original sale (primary distribution) of a company's securities to the public.
See also INVESTMENT BANKER, ISSUE PRICE and UNDERWRITER.

PUBLIC ORDER MEMBER

Acronym: POM. A POM is a participant in the British options market who is neither a marketmaker nor a member of the London Options Clearing House (LOCH). A POM (1) buys and sells English listed options on his own behalf or (2) as an agent on behalf of his clients. In order to do so, the POM must appoint a member of LOCH to act on its behalf.

PUBLIC OVERSIGHT BOARD
See POB.

PUBLIC SECURITIES ASSOCIATION
A trade association representing banks, dealers, and brokers who underwrite and trade municipals, governments, and federal agency securities.

PUBLIC UTILITY DISTRICT
See P.U.D.

PUBLIC UTILITY HOLDING COMPANY ACT OF 1935
The federal law requires SEC registration for all publicly owned holding companies engaged in the electric utility business or in the retail distribution of gas. The law also requires, in many circumstances, that public issues of such securities be the subject of competitive underwritings.

P.U.D.
A common abbreviation used in listings of municipal bonds for: public utility district. A P.U.D. is generally established as a quasi-governmental agency or authority within a municipality organized to provide citizens with water, gas, or electricity.

The initials (or the full expression) will also appear on the face of bond certificates, Official Statements, or tombstones accompanying bond issues of the P.U.D.

PUFFING
Term used to describe the act of bragging or exaggerating the qualities of an issue or the fortunes of the issuer. The noun form of the concept is "puffery."

Puffing, or puffery, in research publications, in sales literature, or in communications with clients is considered promissory and thus lacking in "truthfulness and good taste" as required by the NASD and NYSE rules for communicating with the public. As such, it may also violate federal securities laws.

PULLING IN THEIR HORNS
Term used of market professionals—although it can be used of any investor—when they take a defensive position in the marketplace. Such defensive positions may be the transference of risk through sales, or the hedging of positions through options or futures. For example, "Traders were pulling in their horns during the session by extensive profit taking. . . ."

The term was originally used when bullish sentiment was offset by bearish sentiment, but now the term can be used when any aggressive trading (long or short) is moderated by offsetting activities.

PULL THE PLUG
Colorful expression used to describe the dissemination of unfavorable information about a company, or the act of making a decision that adversely affects others. The analogy: removing the plug from a basin of water causes a vortex of water to rapidly go down the drain. For example, "The company's announcement that it was laying off workers in its Midwest plant quickly pulled the plug on speculative activity in the stock."

Pulling the plug usually results in an immediate lack of demand for a stock, coupled with a large amount of supply from sellers. Generally, there is a dramatic drop in the price of the underlying security.

PUMP AND DUMP OPERATION
Slang used by securities fraud prosecutors to describe the activity of "penny stock" promoters who "hype" low-priced or worthless stocks to investors by high-pressure tactics.

A "pump and dump" operation may result in large losses for gullible investors and huge profits for the promoters. SEC Rule 15c2-6 prohibits such fraudulent operations, and recent NASD rules also apply to "penny stock" promotions.

PUNT/PUNTER
1. Slang in the United Kingdom for a gambler or speculator. Thus, a punter is a handicapper; that is, one who takes the opposite side of a bet. For example, "Investors are anxious to buy LMN, but there are plenty of punters around to take their money."
2. Used as a verb to signify a delaying tactic. The analogy is with the game of football, where a punt transfers the ball to the opposing team at a worse field position. For example, "If you want a prediction of the market activity for that stock in this year, I'll have to punt."
3. Official currency of the Republic of Ireland.

PUPPY TAX
A colorful term for the turnover tax levied on transactions on the Stockholm Stock Exchange. The tax is a 0.30% levy on brokered transactions and is equally split between buyer and seller.

The term originated when the Swedish finance minister jocularly referred to the brokerage community in Sweden as "finance pups."

PURCHASE ACQUISITION
Term used if one company acquires another for cash, or for Treasury stock purchased within the last two years, and the cost exceeds the net tangible assets of the acquired corporation. In this case, the difference between the cost and the asset value is considered goodwill on the acquirer's balance sheet. The goodwill will be amortized against future revenues over a 40-year period.

PURCHASING POWER
Term used of client general accounts that contain excess margin or other credits in the special memorandum account (SMA). Purchasing power is the dollar amount of marginable securities that may be purchased, or sold short, without causing a margin call. For example, under current Regulation T 50% margin requirements, a client with an SMA entry of $1,000 could purchase marginable securities worth $2,000 without adding additional funds to the margin account.

PURE PLAY
Term that designates a speculation in the stock of a single company with the company, in turn, engaged in a single business. In effect, the speculator is "putting all his eggs in one basket." Hence, the term denotes concentration as opposed to diversification.

PURPOSE LOAN
Name of a loan, collateralized by securities, if the money borrowed will be used to purchase, carry, or trade in securities subject to Federal Reserve Board credit regulations and limitations.

PURPOSE STATEMENT
A form that must be completed by a borrower and filed with the lender if margin securities collateralize the loan. In the statement, the borrower lists the purpose of the loan and attests that the loan is not made to purchase, carry, or trade securities subject to Federal Reserve Board restrictions.

PUSSY
A colloquial and picturesque name for the shares of Pillsbury Company, derived from its NYSE ticker symbol: PSY.

PUT A LINE THROUGH IT
English expression for a transaction that is canceled by the mutual consent of both buyer and seller. Term is derived from those somewhat easier and more informal days when trades were jotted on a pad; putting a line through it, in effect, canceled the trade.

PUT BONDS
Also: putable bonds. A feature of some debt securities that enables the holder to redeem the bonds at face value according to a schedule set forth at the time of issuance. This optional feature will prevent loss—at the time the put option is operative—if there is a general rise in interest rates.

PUT INTO PLAY
Used of a company that currently is not, but which may become, the target of an acquisition. Companies are "put into play" by means of rumors, or by block purchases of slightly less than 5% of the outstanding shares. Thus, there is no SEC Rule 13-D filing as yet. The buyer or rumormonger hopes to get others, particularly arbitrageurs, to also buy large quantities of the company. Example: "There was a lot of activity in Harmon Cross stock. No one is taking credit for the move, but it looks as though someone is trying to put the company into play."

PUT ON
1. In the United Kingdom, the term is used when a customer has authorized a broker to act on his or her behalf. For example, "I had my broker put on a buy for me."
2. In the options market, the act of establishing an options spread; that is, the purchase and sale of options of the same class. For example, "The time seemed right to put on a bull spread on ABC."
3. To dissemble or to fake; for example, "His illness was a put on." By derivation in the securities industry, any fraud or deceit perpetrated against the contra party to a trade.

PUT OPTION
A privilege that permits the holder of the put option to sell to the writer of the option a fixed number of shares at a fixed price within a specified time.

PUT THROUGH
1. In the United States, as a verb: to complete or to effect. For example, "I was able to put through the buy order."
2. In the United Kingdom, the use of an intermediary on a loan. For example, "Jones and Co. acted as a put through on the loan from Smith & Co. to Reilly & Co."
3. The simultaneous sale and repurchase of the same security through the same broker on the same exchange. In the United Kingdom, this is permissible to establish a new price for the owner's portfolio. In the United States, such an activity is called a "wash sale" and is illegal.

PUT TO SELLER
Industry jargon for the exercise of a put option by the holder, thereby obligating the seller of the option to purchase the underlying shares.

PV
1. Common abbreviation for par value.
   See also PAR VALUE.
2. In mathematical formulas for the computation of yield to maturity, PV stands for present value.

PVT
Abbreviation: private. The abbreviation is generally followed by the word *placement* (i.e., a distribution of securities to a relatively small number of nonaccredited investors, and thus an offering that does not have an effective SEC registration statement).

PX
Often used as an abbreviation for price on offering sheets or other communications about securities.

TO PYRAMID
As used in the finance industry, to pyramid means to accumulate further holdings in a security by borrowing against the increasing paper profits of a position. For example, to use the buying power of a margin account to accumulate more shares of the original purchase is a form of pyramiding.

Pyramiding can be extremely successful if the underlying asset continues to rise in collateral value; but—like a house of cards—pyramiding can quickly become unprofitable if the underlying falls in value and the borrower is overextended and must be liquidated to reduce the loans.

The term is also used in real estate and commodities trading.

Q

Q
Seventeenth letter of the alphabet:
1. Used uppercase before the ticker symbol on Consolidated Tapes A and B to designate the stock of a company that is in bankruptcy and will be liquidated or reorganized.
2. Used as the fifth letter in the symbol of a NASDAQ/NMS stock to signify that the company is under the protection of federal bankruptcy laws. For example, WOWIQ is the symbol of World of Wonder, Inc., operating under Chapter 11 of the Federal Bankruptcy Code.

Q1, Q2, Q3, Q4

Used by security analysts and newspaper financial reports to designate the operating results of a company during successive three-month periods. Thus, Q1 means the first quarter of the fiscal year, Q2, the second quarter, and so on.

QIB

See QUALIFIED INSTITUTIONAL BUYER.

Q-RATIO

A measurement of a company's hidden assets in relation to its market value.

Q-ratios are particularly important in Japan where many assets—particularly real estate and stock ownership in subsidiaries and other companies—are carried at cost. Thus, traditional price earnings ratios in Japan are at an average of 50+ to 1 (with worldwide averages about 12 to 1) and seem to make the market overpriced. On a Q-ratio basis, however, if the hidden assets are factored into the consideration, the prices do not seem overinflated.

QT

1. Acronym for a questioned trade between brokers. A trade is questioned if one or more of the details of the trade (e.g., the details of amount and price of the contra broker) do not compare with the other broker's records.
2. Used commonly as an abbreviation in financial reports for the latest fiscal quarter.

Q-TIP TRUST

Industry jargon for a "qualified terminable interest" in a transfer of assets between spouses by means of a legal trust instrument. Under it, the grantor bequeaths income from the assets to the spouse, but upon that person's death, orders disposition of the property to one or more other parties.

QUACK

This seemingly derogatory term is part of the floor lingo on the exchanges. It designates a trade made at a quarter of a point. Thus, "Forty-four and a quack" means $44\frac{1}{4}$. It is used in the noisy environment of the floor to keep the trade from being confused with a trade at $44\frac{3}{4}$.

QUALIFICATION

1. The recognition by an SRO (q.v.) of registration status of an individual either through waiver or examination. For example, "John Jones

is recognized by the NASD as a registered representative," or "Peter Smith qualified for registration as a financial principal."
2. The act of registration of a particular security for sale under the blue-sky laws of an individual state.

QUALIFIED INSTITUTIONAL BUYER (QIB)
Term coined by the SEC in its Rule 144A. The definition set forth in that rule permits unlimited resales of unregistered securities by concerns meeting certain requirements. For example, many eligible insurance companies, investment companies, banks, and broker/dealers could subscribe to a "private placement" and resell it to another eligible institution at any time without violating SEC registration rules.

QUALIFIED LEGAL OPINION
A conditional opinion by bond counsel about a proposed municipal issue.

If the bond counsel has any reservations about the enabling legislation for the issue, its taxability/nontaxability under federal statutes, or the existence of prior restrictive covenants that would impede this issue, their opinion will be "qualified." If there is no question on these three points, the opinion will be "unqualified."

The terms are used exactly as they would be in ordinary parlance. For example, "The office party was an unqualified success," or "I have some qualifications about the feasibility of this plan."

QUALIFIED STOCK OPTION
Term describing a stock option granted before May 21, 1981. Under it, recipient could exercise the option at the less than market price of the security. If the security was then held three or more years, the entire profit was a long-term capital gain. If sold before three years, the difference between the exercise price and the fair market value at the time of exercise was an ordinary income gain and a tax preference item. Only the amount above the fair market value and the ultimate sale price was eligible for capital gains.

QUALIFYING ANNUITY
A fixed, variable, or hybrid annuity approved for inclusion in an IRS-approved pension, profit-sharing, Keogh, or IRA retirement plan. Qualification permits the inclusion of pretax dollars in the annuity and the deduction of these dollars from the planholder's taxable income for that year. In effect, therefore, the dollars are tax sheltered until they are withdrawn from the qualifying annuity. When withdrawn, all withdrawals are taxable as ordinary income in the year received.

QUALIFYING COUPON RATE

Used in conjunction with Ginnie Mae contracts, whether cash, forwards, or options, if GNMAs with coupon rates below the current production rate are deliverable against the contract. There is, of course, an adjustment in the aggregate exercise price that takes into account the lowered coupon rate on the certificates delivered. Thus, current production GNMAs may be delivered at par, but GNMAs with coupons 4% below current production could only be delivered at 80% of par.

QUALITATIVE ANALYSIS

Term used by security analysts to describe value judgments about a security that are based on nonfinancial information. Thus, a buy-sell judgment about a security that is based not on the balance sheet or income statement but on the status of labor relations, the quality of management, or the employee morale would be qualitative.

See also QUANTITATIVE ANALYSIS.

QUANT

A shortened expression for a market research technician who makes financial decisions only in terms of quantitative measurements. In practice, a synonym for a "number cruncher." The term is derogatory.

Effective securities research requires both quantitative and qualitative judgments about a company and its performance.

QUANTITATIVE ANALYSIS

Term of security analysts to describe value judgments about a security that are based on financial information contained in the balance sheet or income statement of a corporation and on financial trends within a particular industry. The term does not necessarily exclude the use of qualitative judgments in arriving at a buy-sell decision by the analyst. The term does imply, however, that incidental market price movements on a short-term basis are excluded from the measurement criteria.

QUESTIONED TRADE

See QT.

QUICK ASSET RATIO

A measurement of corporate liquidity that uses current assets minus inventory divided by current liabilities. Thus, if a corporation's current assets are $1 million and $300,000 represents inventory, its quick assets are $700,000. If its current liabilities are $600,000 its quick asset, or acid-test, ratio is 7/6, or 1.16+. Under this criterion of corporate liquidity, ratios in excess of 1 are considered adequate. However, very high quick asset ratios may not be desirable; they may indicate that a cash-rich corporation is a candidate for a takeover.

Also called the "acid-test ratio."

See also LIQUIDITY RATIO.

QUICK ASSETS

Commonly accepted term in financial statement analysis to mean current assets minus inventory. Thus, a corporation with current assets of $7 million and an inventory of $2.5 million has quick assets of $4.5 million.

Do not confuse quick assets, as computed above, with net quick assets. Net quick assets is defined as quick assets minus current liabilities.

QUID PRO QUO

Latin: one thing (*quid*) for (*pro*) another thing (*quo*).

The term is used extensively in the securities industry to describe any situation in which something of value is exchanged for another. The expression is not limited to sales for value received. It also is used if one party provides information or security research and the other party provides a trade that is profitable to the person providing the research.

QUIET PERIOD

Term used to describe the 90-day period between an issuer's initial public offering and the earliest time its underwriters may publish and distribute original research material about the company and its business.

The purpose of this SEC rule is to enable these securities to settle into investment portfolios (as opposed to trading accounts) based on the merits set forth in the prospectus. By legislating a quiet period, the SEC wants to make sure that investors are not swayed by dealers who may have a vested interest in the success of the offering and its secondary market.

QUOTATION

A statement of the highest bid and lowest offer for a security. Thus, a quote of $8\frac{1}{2}$ to 9 represents a bid of $8\frac{1}{2}$ per share to a seller, and an offer of 9 to a buyer.

Quotes, by industry rules, are presumed to be firm for the accepted round-lot of trading. Quotes that are not firm must be so designated.

On exchanges, quotes normally will be accompanied by size; thus, the quote represents both prices and amounts available at those prices.

Also called the "market."

QUOTE
See QUOTATION.

Q.V.
Latin: which see (*quod vide*).

R

R
Eighteenth letter of the alphabet, used:
1. Lowercase in older copies of stock option transaction tables to signify that no transactions took place in that market session in a given option series.
2. Uppercase as the fifth letter in a NASDAQ/NMS entry to designate a subscription right. For example, RABTR stood for Rabbit Software Corp. subscription rights. Such usage is limited to the life of the rights.
3. Uppercase as a single letter, R is the ticker symbol of Rothschild Holdings, Inc., the parent corporation of L. F. Rothschild, a prominent broker/dealer.

R + 1, etc.
A technical designation used by industry operations departments to designate "RECAP date plus 1." The enumeration continues: plus 2, plus 3, and so on.

This procedure is used to count the elapsed days since a broker/dealer submitted to the NSCC for a reconfirmation and repricing of a fail with a contra dealer member of the clearing corporation.

RABBI TRUST
Nickname for a retirement vehicle used to protect the financial benefits that have already accrued to present executives of a company bought out in a hostile takeover. Deferred compensation, for example, is corporation-funded but administered by an independent third party (a commercial bank or trust company) without fear that successor managements will default or appropriate the assets.

RACCOON
Slang expression for a number cruncher; that is, an analyst who does only quantitative research. The allusion is to the rings around the eyes of raccoons and the rings around the eyes that number crunchers get from endless hours in front of their computer screens.
See QUANT.

RACING THE TAPE
Jargon used to describe the unethical practice of transacting personal business in front of and because of a transaction about to be entered by a customer. Thus a registered representative buys in anticipation of a large buy order to be entered by a customer to profit from the activity caused by the customer's buy order. The same concept also applies to sales.

RACKETEER INFLUENCED AND CORRUPT ORGANIZATION ACT
See RICO.

RADAR ALERT
Industry jargon for the close monitoring of the market activity in a client's stock to determine whether an accumulation is taking place in advance of a hostile tender offer or takeover attempt. If this is perceived to be happening, corporate officials are immediately notified so they may take appropriate defensive actions.

RAES
Acronym for Retail Automatic Execution System. This is a computerized facility that expedites the execution of small orders in the Standard & Poor's Index Options traded on the CBOE. With RAES, customer orders for five or fewer contracts are immediately executed at a single price determined by prevailing bid-asked quotations.

RAIDER
1. Anyone who tries to buy control of a company's stock so he can install new management. Federal law places restrictions on raiders if they become control persons; that is, holders of 10% or more of a company's outstanding stock. The term *raider* is not generally used if the purchaser is buying stock as an investment.
2. Bear raider: a person who tries to sell a company's stock, either long or short, with the intent of repurchasing it at a lower price.

RAINMAKER
Slang for a big producer—either an RR or an investment banker—who brings new business to the broker/dealer. As such, the rainmaker brings profit to the firm and receives additional personal compensation.

RALLY
Industry term for a sharp rise in the price of a company's stock. It also can apply to a sharp rise in bonds or in preferred stock.

Rally does not necessarily imply a previous drop in security prices; thus, a rally can follow a long sideways movement.

In every case, the term implies a sudden rise in prices.

RAM
See REVERSE ANNUITY MORTGAGE.

RAMP
The U.K. equivalent of what in the United States is called a "corner." A ramp, or corner, arises when an individual, or group of individuals working in concert, control so much of a security or commodity that they, in effect, control the trade price.

Ramp, or corner, usually implies that individuals or groups provide the price control; if the price control is done by groups of governments, the word *cartel* is used.

RAMP UP FINANCING
British term for the use of convertible preferred shares as a form of capital financing. The concept centers on this: A shareholder starts with a senior security and, as the company prospers, the shareholder can convert and thus become a common shareholder of the company.

RAN
See REVENUE ANTICIPATION NOTE.

R&D
Acronym for research and development. R&D is an expense item found in the budgets of many corporations. It designates funds set aside from operating revenues to finance the discovery and introduction of new products, thereby ensuring the corporation's future economic well-being.

RANDOM WALK
A market philosophy that states there are no special techniques to outperform the market—just luck, and enough random selections. Theoretically, throwing darts at the listing of stocks in the financial pages of the newspaper will provide as much return as those who use complicated strategies.

This is obviously an oversimplification, but it has been shown that an increase in the number of random selections made of stocks does substantially reduce the standard deviation (the degree of risk) in terms of nonsystematic risk in a portfolio. To this extent, therefore, it does seem that portfolio diversification improves the chances for a random walker.

RANGE
Unless otherwise qualified, the term means the opening, the high, the low, and the close of a security for a specific trading session.

The term is variously used to give the high and low for a week, a month, or 52 weeks. Currently, newspapers tend to give the daily and 52-week ranges. Opening prices are often omitted from the range.

RANGE FORWARD CONTRACTS
A servicemark of Salomon Brothers used to identify certain foreign exchange agreements that combine features of futures and option contracts. Range forward contracts are structured to limit down-side currency risk while protecting up-side profit potentials. The customer chooses either end of a currency range and the expiration date of the contract. Salomon Brothers chooses the opposite end, based on market conditions and currency rate spreads. If the rate moves against the customer, the risk is limited to the lower end of the range. If the range at expiration is inside or above the range, the contract is exercised and the obligation offset at the spot exchange rate.

RATCHET COMPENSATION
An incentive compensation program whereby management receives additional remuneration in the form of salary, cash, stock options, and the like in terms of its ability to reach certain preset revenue or earnings figures for a year or other period.

The analogy is with a ratchet, which goes forward but not backward.

RATE COVENANT
Agreement incorporated into the bond resolution for a municipal revenue issue that promises to adjust rates for the use of the facility in such a way that revenues are sufficient to provide for maintenance and repair and for bond debt service. Thus, a rate covenant would not provide for a sinking fund or for expansion of the facility; but it would promise to repair, insure, and pay debt interest and principal repayment.

RATE OF RETURN
1. Of an investment: the annual cash flow divided by the replacement cost. Commonly called "current yield."
2. Of corporations: the annual net income, after preferred dividends, divided by the net common stockholder equity. Also called "return on investment," or "ROI."

If rate of return is not used as a synonym for current yield or return on investment, the user normally so qualifies the term that the reader knows the usage.

RATE REOPENER
Term used in conjunction with long-term financing so arranged that the interest rate is renegotiated and adjusted every three to five years over

the life of the loan. At the time of each reset period, the issuer generally has the option of terminating the loan at a small premium.

RATING
Judgment of creditworthiness of an issuer made by an accepted rating service, such as Standard & Poor's, Moody's, or Fitch.

The judgment, based on rater's investigation of the risk of default by the issuer, is stated in letters. Ratings of AAA, AA, A, and BBB (S&P) are considered investment grade. Ratings of BB or below have increasing risk of default. Similar ratings are given to preferred stocks.

Letter ratings for common stock pertain to firm's history of dividends and dividend coverage, but make no promise about future coverage.

RATIO BULL SPREAD
Term used to describe a call option spread position that is composed of one long call option and two short call options in the same underlying stock with the same expiration month.

It is called "ratio" because there are two short options and one long option. Technically, the strategy is neutral; but it is called "bull" because the long call has a lower strike price than the short calls.

RATIO SPREAD
A person who holds long calls on a security and who writes more short calls than can be covered by the long calls. Thus, a ratio spread can be 2 for 1 if a person owns 1 long call for each 2 calls written. Ratio spreads can be bearish or bullish; that is, profitable if the market goes down (bearish), or profitable if the market goes up (bullish).

RATIO WRITER
Commonly accepted term for a person who owns an underlying security and who writes more call option contracts than stock he owns. For example, a person who owns 300 shares of XYZ writes six calls on XYZ. The person has a 2 for 1 ratio write. The ratio writer has a middle-risk position between the writer of three covered calls and the writer of six naked (uncovered) calls.

RBA
See REPRESENTATIVE BID & ASKED PRICES.

RCMM
See REGISTERED COMPETITIVE MARKETMAKER.

RCT
See REGISTERED COMPETITIVE TRADER.

R-DAY
Term used by the Association of International Bond Dealers (AIBD) to designate April 3, 1989. On this day and following, it has been agreed that all international bond trades will be reported within 30 minutes following execution. The report will be made to the association, which—as a registered investment exchange (RIE) and recognized by the Securities Investment Board (SIB)—has been authorized to receive these reports.

REACH THROUGH
Slang for a broker's endeavor to enter a quotation in the Intermarket Trading System (ITS) that is worse than the best quotation already in the system for that issue. The endeavor to reach through is a form of carelessness on the part of the entering broker. The system will reject the new quotation.

READY MARKET
A market in which there exist bona fide bids and offers, reasonable liquidity, and prompt settlement for securities trades.

The term is important because it is used by the SEC in its net capital rule (15c3-1) to describe the value to be given to portfolio securities in measuring capital requirements. The value must be reasonably related to the last sale price in bona fide competitive markets.

READY TRANSFERABILITY
A feature of all publicly traded securities that gives shareholders the right to sell, give, or bequeath the security without prior consultation or consent of the corporation.

REAL ESTATE APPRECIATION NOTE
An obligation of a corporation that has pledged real estate as collateral for this loan. The loan is unique: it promises a fixed rate of interest plus a percentage of accrued appreciation of the underlying property. The percentage of appreciation often is payable annually from the fifth year until the maturity of the loan.

REAL ESTATE INVESTMENT TRUST (REIT)
A trust, modeled after the diversification feature of investment companies, that invests in a diversified portfolio of real estate holdings. Such trusts, if publicly owned, must be registered with the SEC under the '33 Act.

See also EQUITY REIT and MORTGAGE REIT.

REAL ESTATE MORTGAGE INVESTMENT CONDUIT
See REMIC.

REAL ESTATE MORTGAGE PRODUCT
See REMP.

REALIZED PROFITS AND LOSSES
Completed transactions for which the taxpayer must accept tax accountability. Most investors pay their security tax obligations on this basis; thus, there is no "taxable event" until long positions are sold or short positions covered at a profit or loss.

Not all gains or losses need be realized to cause a tax obligation. Tax advice is needed on certain forms of "phantom income," and on certain required "marks to the market" required by federal tax statutes on zero-coupon bonds and certain "spreads" in commodities.

REALLOWANCE
A term used in corporate underwritings if the syndicate permits National Association of Securities Dealers' members who are outside the syndicate to receive a sales commission for sales made to their customers. Thus, if the sales concession on a registered offering is 50 cents per share, a reallowance of 25 cents per share could be made to other NASD members who are granted shares for sale to their customers.

REALS
Composite term for Real Yield Securities. REALS are a Morgan Stanley innovation. Basically, the security is a debenture with a 2.75% coupon. However, this coupon is adjusted quarterly and pays at a rate keyed to the government's consumer price index. In effect, the debenture holder gets a quarterly payment, as opposed to a semiannual payment, that is inflation-adjusted to give a "real" return.

REAL YIELD SECURITIES
See REALS.

REBATE
1. A return of monies previously collected. Generally, such rebates are made to encourage sales. Example: In recent years, the automobile industry has engaged in extensive rebates.
2. A return of sales commission charges to the buyer or seller. Such rebates are legitimate if done by a principal; if done by an agent, they violate industry standards.
3. The term *rebate* also is used of directed payments to a third party. Example: A directed payment of part of an underwriting spread to another member of the syndicate could legitimately be called "a rebate" (although such usage is not common).

RECAPS
See RECONFIRMATION AND PRICING SERVICE.

RECEIVER
Technical term for the court-assigned person who sees to the details of a bankruptcy and thus effects either a liquidation for the benefit of bond and stockholders or oversees a corporate reorganization.

Full term: *receiver in bankruptcy.*

In practice, a receiver may or may not manage the corporation, but he is responsible for the control and preservation of the company's assets.

RECEIVER IN BANKRUPTCY
See RECEIVER.

RECEIVER'S CERTIFICATES
Short-term debt securities issued by a court-appointed receiver to effect a corporate reorganization or liquidation. These securities take priority over all other debts of the corporation, including taxes due and unpaid wages. Thus, they are very low risk because monies received from the liquidation of assets will be used first to pay off these securities.

RECEIVE VERSUS PAYMENT
Instruction often added to sell orders entered by institutional clients.

Concept: The buyer will pay in cash when the seller, or his agent, delivers the securities. The contract is, in effect, made COD (cash on delivery), or RAP (receive against payment). Such contracts are made to obtain immediately usable funds or because the seller is obligated, by law, to have either the security or its cash value.

It is important that both buyer and seller agree that there will be a transfer of securities for cash on the settlement date.

Also called "RVP Transaction."

RECESSION
Economic term used to describe a period of reduced economic activity. Generally, a recession is marked by two successive quarterly drops in the GNP; recessions usually are short lived, are marked by increased unemployment, increased business inventories, and increased short-term interest rates. Although the term is usually widespread within the economy, recessions also may mark decreased production in sectors of the economy. Example: The agricultural sector has gone through a four-year recession.

TO RECLAIM
As verb: the act of recovering money or a certificate after an irregularity is discovered in the settlement of a security contract.

RECLAMATION
As noun: the privilege of either party to a security contract to recover money or a security from the contra party if an irregularity has occurred in the settlement process. For example, a buyer finds that the certificate delivered in settlement for a contract has been stolen. The buyer may make a reclamation.

RECOGNIZED INVESTMENT EXCHANGE
See RIE.

RECONCILEMENT OF OUT-TRADE NOTICE
See ROTN.

RECONFIRMATION AND PRICING SERVICE
Popularly known as RECAPS, this is a security valuation service overseen by the National Securities Clearing Corporation (NSCC). Under this service, the NSCC marks members to the market for transactions that have been compared but not cleared on settlement date. In this way, there is financial integrity in all contracts, both cleared and as yet uncleared.

The service was originally set up for municipal bond contract fails but now includes fails in corporate securities as well.

RECORD DATE
Calendar date on which an issuer temporarily closes its register of holders to identify those holders who are eligible for a distribution of dividends, either cash or stock, interest or rights. The date is determined by the board of directors, and the register is closed at the end of business on that specified date.

RECOURSE
A financial term that describes the ability of a lender to hold the borrower of money responsible for losses in the event of a default in connection with that loan. Thus, the term *recourse loan* or *nonrecourse loan.*

Recourse loans are often taken out by limited partnerships (CDPP) to leverage the enterprise. In this event, the lender has recourse against the assets of the partnership (but not against the assets of the limited partners). In other situations, the recourse may be limited to a percentage of the assets.

RECOURSE LOAN

A financing arrangement frequently used in direct-participation programs (tax shelters) if the partnership borrows money to finance the business venture. In default, the lender has recourse not only against the assets pledged for the loan but also against the personal assets of the general partner.

REDEMPTION

Retirement of a security by repayment of the principal amount.

The term *redemption* also is used of bonds or preferred shares that are retired before the maturity date at a premium price. The retirement of mutual fund shares through redemption at the net asset value when tendered by the fundholder also is included in this concept.

REDEMPTION PRICE

The dollar price at which a security may be redeemed by an issuer prior to its maturity date.

Usually, for bonds or preferred shares, the redemption price will be set at a premium above the par or face value of the security. For example, a bond with a face value of $1,000 has a redemption price, if called, of $1,050.

RED HERRING

Industry jargon for: a preliminary prospectus. The name arises from the caveat, printed in red along the left border of the cover of the preliminary prospectus, warning the reader that the document does not contain all of the information about the issue and that some of the information may be changed before the final prospectus is issued.

Also called a "red herring prospectus."

REDISCOUNT

Term used if a member bank of the Federal Reserve System borrows funds from the Federal Reserve using eligible collateral which was, in turn, pledged to the bank by one of its borrowers. For example, a bank accepts collateral from a borrower. The bank is said to "rediscount" if it again pledges this collateral to the Fed for a loan.

REDS

See REFUNDING ESCROW DEPOSITS.

REDUCIBLE RATE BOND

A debt instrument for which the issuer has an option of lowering the interest rate as well as its call premium. Usually, bonds have a reducible rate only if the bond is subsequently collateralized by U.S. government securities through an advanced refunding and thus becomes triple-A rated. This characteristic is not common and when found marks certain municipal obligations.

REDUCTION OPTION LOAN
Acronym: ROL. ROLs are a form of mortgage financing in which the borrower is allowed a one-time opportunity during the second through the fifth year to match current mortgage interest rates. If elected, these new rates are fixed for the remainder of the mortgage. Usually the reduction is permitted only if rates have dropped more than 2% in any one year.

In effect, the mortgage holder is given an opportunity to take advantage of lower rates. Such an adjustment is cheaper than refinancing the mortgage.

REDUNDANT
Although the term is basically an adjective and means dull or repetitious or useless, in the United Kingdom the term is also used as a noun to signify someone who has been laid off from a job because of economic forces (as opposed to being fired for cause). For example, "Jim is redundant as a result of the merger of his firm with British Ford."

REFINANCING
Term used if an issuer sells new bonds and uses the proceeds to retire an existing issue. In this way, the issuer by borrowing at a lower rate can substantially reduce interest charges. Many outstanding bonds limit the circumstances under which they may be refinanced.

The terms *refinancing* and *refunding* are synonymous and may be used interchangeably.

REFUNDING
See REFINANCING. The two words are used as synonyms.

REFUNDING ESCROW DEPOSITS
Acronym: REDS. REDS are a First Boston innovation designed to enable municipal securities issuers to lock in future financing rates. The sale proceeds of these securities are invested in short-term Treasuries which, at maturity, are used to refund an earlier dated issue of a municipal security. At that time, these deposits will then represent ownership in the new tax-exempted refunding bonds.

REGIONAL INTERFACE ORGANIZATION
See RIO.

REGISTERED BOND
See REGISTERED SECURITY.

REGISTERED COMPANY
A corporation that has filed a registration statement with the SEC and is now obliged to file certain periodic reports, including annual and quarterly reports and periodic reports, of important matters that could influence stockholder activities.

REGISTERED COMPETITIVE MARKETMAKER (RCMM)
A member of the New York Stock Exchange who may initiate trades for a personal or firm account. Such members are expected, in addition, to make bids or offers—either voluntarily or as requested—that will contribute to the general maintenance of the market if there is an imbalance of buy or sell orders. Thus, these members augment the dealer function of exchange specialists.

REGISTERED COMPETITIVE TRADER (RCT)
A member of the New York Stock Exchange who may initiate trades for a personal or firm account. These members attempt to make a profit from short-term trading, but are required to follow the rules of the specialists. Thus, 75% of their transactions must be stablilizing. This means that they should not buy above the sale price of the previous transaction nor sell below it. In addition, their bid-offer may not take precedence over an order from a public customer of a member firm at the same price.

REGISTERED EQUITY MARKETMAKER (REMM)
American Stock Exchange term. Such ASE members perform a function similar to the registered competitive marketmaker on the NYSE. The ASE term is more restrictive, because both securities and options are traded on the ASE floor.
See also REGISTERED COMPETITIVE MARKETMAKER.

REGISTERED HOME OWNERSHIP SAVINGS PLAN
Acronym: RHOSP. A special type of savings account permitted in Canada. A person may deposit up to $1,000 annually of tax-deductible income (total $10,000) provided the money is eventually used to purchase residential property for personal use. Only one such plan is permitted during a person's lifetime.

REGISTERED OPTIONS PRINCIPAL (ROP)
A person engaged in the management of a broker/dealer's options business; that is, who supervises registered representatives and their con-

tacts with the investing public. ROPs must pass a qualifying examination.

REGISTERED OPTIONS REPRESENTATIVE (ROR)
An employee of a broker/dealer who engages in soliciting or accepting option business from the employer's customers. Such employees must apply for registration and must pass an examination to qualify for this position. Presently, the General Securities Examination qualifies a representative.

REGISTERED OPTIONS TRADER
American Stock Exchange term for an ASE specialist in one or more classes of options traded on that exchange. Such members are required to maintain a fair and orderly market in the classes of option assigned to them.

REGISTERED REPRESENTATIVE (RR)
An employee of a broker/dealer who is a member of the National Association of Securities Dealers (NASD), a broker/dealer or a bank/dealer who is a member of the Municipal Securities Rulemaking Board (MSRB), or a member firm of an exchange who makes customer contacts to buy or sell securities.

Qualification is by the regulatory General Securities Examination; in some cases, however, limited registration is available. As a general rule, persons who make buy-sell recommendations, who underwrite, and who sell investment advice for a fee must be registered as representatives.

REGISTERED REPRESENTATIVE RAPID RESPONSE PROGRAM
Acronym: RRRR. Also known as: 4R. This was a NYSE communications system that enabled salespersons in member firm offices to immediately quote execution prices to buying or selling customers without the need to wait for a trade confirmation from the exchange floor.

REGISTERED RETIREMENT SAVINGS PLAN
Acronym: RRSP. The Canadian equivalent of the Keogh plan. Under RRSP, an individual may deduct annually the lesser of $5,500 or 20% of taxable income and deposit it in a savings contract established by a bank, trust company, insurance company, or mutual fund. The maximum is $3,500 if the person also is covered by an employer-sponsored retirement plan. The plan money accumulates tax free, and at maturity

(when the subscriber is 60–71 years old) the money can be used to purchase an annuity or shares in a retirement income fund.

REGISTERED SECONDARY DISTRIBUTION
Term for a sale of securities by an owner under an effective registration with the SEC.

Generally such registered secondaries are made by a control person or other holder of restricted securities:
1. As part of a combined primary-secondary offering under a prospectus issued by the corporation.
2. As a "shelf registration"; that is, an offering by the owner using currently filed disclosure documents of the issuer as his disclosure document in the sale of the securities to the public.

REGISTERED SECURITY
1. Any certificate that has the name of the owner inscribed on the certificate. Example: A registered bond or a registered stock.
2. Any stock or bond or other security whose public sale was registered with the SEC at the time of sale, or that—excluding such initial registration—was subsequently sold publicly in conformity with SEC rules. Example: A security originally sold privately is subsequently included in a registered secondary or a public sale under SEC rule 144 or 145.

REGISTERED STOCK
See REGISTERED SECURITY.

REGISTRAR
In the securities industry, a person who:
1. Maintains the names and addresses of the security holders of an issuer.
2. Verifies that ownership transfers have been correctly effected; thus, no more new shares have been issued than have been properly cancelled.

Usually, a registrar is a commercial bank other than the transfer agent.

REGISTRATION FEE
A money fee charged by the SEC at the time that a public offering of securities is made.

See also SEC FEE.

REGISTRATION STATEMENT
Technical term for the documents filed with the SEC in conformity with the requirements of the Securities Act of 1933. The originally filed documents, before their final revision and amendments, are called the "preliminary registration statement." The amended registration statement with the final details of the publicly sold issue is called the "final registration statement."

REGLEMENT LIVRAISONS DE TITRES
See RELIT.

REGRESSIVE TAX
1. The opposite of a progressive tax; that is, a tax that decreases as the tax base increases. For example, if the tax on one gallon of gasoline were 10 cents and on two gallons of gasoline were 19 cents, the tax would be regressive.
2. Any tax that affects the poor as much or more than it does the rich. For example, the payroll tax (Social Security) affects all persons equally on the first $51,300 of wages (1990), but those who make over that amount pay a lower percentage of wages on their total earned income.

REGULAR SPECIALIST
A stock exchange member, so registered by the exchange, who is obliged to maintain a fair and orderly market in specific stocks. In this capacity, the specialist accepts orders from other members in these specific stocks and, as needed, buys and sells for his or her own account and risk. This latter function is highly regulated and is never in conflict or competition with public orders.

See also SPECIALIST.

REGULAR-WAY SETTLEMENT (RW)
Industry term for the normally accepted settlement date for secondary market transactions.

The generally accepted regular-way settlement is the fifth business day after the trade date. There are three exceptions: opening/closing transactions in listed options, round-lot transactions in government issues and money market securities settle the same or next business day.

REGULAR-WAY TRANSACTION
General term for the settlement date of a *secondary* market transaction unless other terms are negotiated.
1. In the United States, regular-way transactions in stocks, municipal, and corporate bonds is the fifth business day following the trade date in clearing house funds.

2. In the United States, transactions in money market securities, Treasuries, and agencies are on the next business day in "good money"; that is, federal funds. Listed options, by exchange rules, settle on the next business day; clearing house funds are acceptable.
3. Regular-way settlement on foreign exchanges is usually made by the "account period" (a fortnight in the United Kingdom), the end of the month, or on a specific day following the trade date.

In the United States, primary market transactions are generally made on a "when issued" basis.

REGULATED INVESTMENT COMPANY
Acronym: RIC. RIC is a tax code term. In general, a regulated investment company is eligible for a tax exemption as a corporation *if* it fulfills certain requirements. The tax is paid by the fundholder on an annual basis.

To qualify as a RIC, these are the principal requirements:
1. The fund must be registered with the SEC.
2. The fund must be "diversified."
3. The fund must be "domestic."
4. 90% of the fund's total income must come from dividends, interest, and capital gains (of which no more than 30% may be short term).
5. The fund must distribute at least 98% of its "net investment income."

The term *conduit theory* is used to describe this tax exemption.

REGULATION A
An SEC-authored adjunct to the Securities Act of 1933 that sets a limit to the value of securities that may be offered publicly under an abbreviated registration statement. At present, issuers may complete an offering under Reg A if the value of all securities issued in the previous 12 months does not exceed $1.5 million.

REGULATION D
A generic name for a series of SEC rules that describe the various ways in which an offering of securities may qualify as a "private placement."

One of the most important definitions given in Regulation D is that of "accredited investor"; that is, those institutional and individual investors who are not included in the upper limit of 35 persons to whom a private placement may be sold because of their sophistication or income/net worth qualification.

REGULATION G
Federal Reserve Board rule that governs the amount and type of credit that can be extended by anyone except broker/dealers or banks to customers who purchase, carry, or trade corporate securities.

REGULATION Q
Rule of the Federal Reserve Board that governs the rate of interest that banks may pay on time deposits. Deposits in excess of $100,000 and for more than 30 days are exempt from Reg Q. This exemption gives rise to negotiable certificates of deposit.

REGULATION T
Federal Reserve Board rule that governs the amount and type of credit that a broker/dealer may extend or maintain if customers purchase, carry, or trade corporate securities. The extension or maintenance of credit by a broker/dealer for a customer who purchases or trades in exempt securities is not covered by Regulation T.

Usually abbreviated as Reg T.

REG(ULATION) T CALL
This is a notice, mandated by the Federal Reserve Board, requesting a customer to deposit a specific amount of money following initiation of a securities transaction. The dollar amount will be the Reg T initial margin requirement minus funds available through the Special Memorandum Account.

A Reg T call must be satisfied by the seventh business day following the trade date, although industry rules require settlement by the fifth business day.

REG(ULATION) T EXCESS
A widely used term for the amount of credit a broker/dealer may extend to a margin account customer over and above the amount of credit already being utilized. The procedure for determining excess credit and the method of annotating it is set forth in Regulation T of the Federal Reserve Board.

REGULATION U
Rule of the Federal Reserve Board that governs the amount and type of credit that a bank may extend to a customer who purchases, carries, or trades in corporate securities.

REGULATION W
Federal Reserve Board rule that governs commercial credit; that is, it governs down payments, and loan maturities for such consumer items as automobiles, household appliances, and revolving charge accounts.

REGULATION X
A rule of the Federal Reserve Board that governs the amount and type of credit that can be obtained and accepted by someone who purchases, car-

ries, or trades in corporate securities. This rule regulates persons who need credit, as opposed to Regulations T, U, and G, which apply to persons who give credit.

REGULATORY FLEXIBILITY ACT
Acronym: RFA. RFA is a federal law that requires each governmental agency to consider, in the course of proposing substantive rules, the effect those rules will have on "small" entities. In this context, the law defines *small* as a business or organization that is independently owned and operated and not dominant in its field.

REHYPOTHECATION
Technical term for the act of repledging securities originally pledged (i.e., hypothecated) as collateral with a broker/dealer for margin account loans. Thus, if a broker/dealer takes securities left as collateral for margin loans and repledges them with a bank to obtain money to finance a customer's margin account, this repledging is called "rehypothecation."

REINTERMEDIATION
The flow of funds by the public from money market and debt securities into savings and time deposits within the banking system.

Reintermediation takes place after disintermediation has occurred. It is a return flow into the banking system as bank savings interest rates become higher than the interest on comparable debt securities.

REINVESTMENT RATE
1. The presumed rate of return that a fixed-income investor will receive if he is able to reinvest the cash flow from interest income at the same rate as that obtained when the security was purchased.
2. The actual rate at which the proceeds from the sale or maturity of a fixed-income investment can be reinvested.

REIT
See REAL ESTATE INVESTMENT TRUST.

REJECTION
Industry term if a buyer, or a buyer's broker, refuses to accept a security delivered in satisfaction of a trade.

RELATIONSHIP SHARES
It is common for Japanese companies to own substantial amounts of other companies to enhance the business relationships between the companies. Such shares are called "relationship shares"; and it is taken for granted that such shares will be held as a permanent investment and that they will never appear in the public market. It is said that such

shares show sincerity and respect; in practice, such shares seriously restrict the "float" and act as a barrier to uninvited takeovers.

RELATIVE VALUE
The comparative attractiveness of a security investment over another. The term may be used of one issue of securities over another of the same issuer based, for example, on call features, convertibility, or maturity, or it may be based on the valuation of securities of different issuers based on price, yield, liquidity, or risk.

RELEASE LETTER
Sent by the manager to the other participants in the syndicate, the letter contains final details of the offering, whether or not the offering will be advertised, the handling of the good faith deposit, the participation, and how the delivery of the certificates will be handled when they are ready for distribution. Normally, the expression is used of competitive bids for issues of bonds.

Also called the "syndicate account letter" and the "release-terms letter."

RELIEF SPECIALIST
Exchange term for a member affiliated with a regular specialist who is both trained and authorized to substitute for the regular specialist if this is necessary.

RELIT
Acronym for Reglement Livraisons de Titres. RELIT is an automatic clearing and settlement system featured exclusively on the Paris Bourse. This system formalizes trade comparisons and completes settlement procedures on the fifth business day following execution. RELIT is also linked directly to the bourse's central depository, SICOVAM.

RELUCTANT BID
Used in the United Kingdom in certain merger and acquisition situations to comply with London's City Code on Takeovers. Although the code is not a legal document, the panel policing it has great political clout. In effect, the code requires that anyone who acquires 30% or more of a public corporation to make a bid for the remainder of the shares. The bid (often reluctant!) must be at a price that is not less than the highest price paid in the marketplace during the previous 12 months.

REMARKETED PREFERRED STOCK (RP)
A form of equity security in which the dividend rate is set by a single sponsoring dealer every 7 or 49 days, as the case may be.

It differs from straight preferred where the issuer sets the rate, and from auction market preferred where the rate is set every 49 days by a disinterested trustee. Remarketed preferred carries a variable rate determined by a single dealer with a vested interest in the issuer based upon its own book of buy and sell orders for that issue.

Remarketed preferred has many varieties, including issues with enhanced credit ratings based on letters of credit from major banks.

See also RP.

REMEDIAL POISON PILL
An offshoot of the original poison pill concept that mandated purchase rights for shareholders if a hostile suitor acquired as little as 20% of a company.

The "remedial" poison pill contains the same purchase rights but, in addition, allows the prospective suitor to convene a stockholders' meeting with as little as 1% of the target company's stock. The suitor (bidder) must furnish an investment banker's "fairness opinion" and pay for one half of the cost of that meeting.

RÉMÉRÉ
Using French franc/French government bonds as collateral, this is a reverse repurchase agreement in which the customer buy-back is not assured in advance. Thus, it is a conditional agreement, but not an obligation, to repurchase the bonds.

REMIC
Acronym for real estate mortgage investment conduit. REMICs are vehicles for financing real estate mortgages through multiclass pass-through instruments. Unlike MBSs and CMOs, which generally pool mortgages of similar characteristics, REMICs permit the aggregation of multiclass mortgages to collateralize debt issued by corporations, partnerships, or trusts.

REMM
See REGISTERED EQUITY MARKETMAKER.

REMP
Acronym for real estate mortgage product. The term *REMP* is a generalization used to classify such investments as collateralized mortgage obligations (CMOs), real estate investment trusts (REITs), Ginnie Maes (GNMAs), midget, and other "pass-through" investments.

RENEGOTIABLE RATE MORTGAGE
See RRM.

REOPEN AN ISSUE
Used of government securities if the Treasury sells more of an issue that is already outstanding, with the same terms and conditions, at prevailing price levels. For example, rather than auction a new issue of notes with a new coupon rate, the Treasury reopens an older issue and sells notes with the same coupon priced to compete with current prices.

REOPENING
1. The resumption of trading in an exchange-listed security after trading was previously suspended on that market day. For example, "Trading in LMN was halted at 10:03 A.M.; the reopening did not occur until 3:30 P.M."
2. If an issuer offers debt securities at various times with the same terms as the original offering (i.e., maturity and coupon interest rate), each subsequent offering is called a "reopening." The term is most frequently used of government securities, both U.S. and U.K.

REORGANIZATION DEPARTMENT
Popular term for that portion of the cashiering function that handles the exchange of one security for another. For example, the execution of rights and warrants, conversions, tender offers, and exchanges of securities following mergers.

REPEAT PRICES OMITTED
Designation on the consolidated tapes. It means that the tape is late, and, to save time, only the first transaction in a series of trades for the same security is printed. Thus, under a repeat prices omitted situation, a series of transactions that would appear as:

        ABC
        54...2s...54...9s...54

appears as
        ABC
        54

REPO
See REPURCHASE AGREEMENT.

REPRESENTATIONS AND WARRANTIES
"Boilerplate" used in contracts to generalize the legal opinions and guarantees of performance that are given by attorneys or the signatories to the contract. Should these representations be false, or the signatories default in their performance, they must bear responsibility for the losses sustained by the contra party to the contract.

REPRESENTATIVE BID AND ASKED PRICES

Acronym: RBA. This was the old system used on NASDAQ Level I quotes. RBAs were median bid and median offer prices.

Today, Level I quotes represent the highest bid and lowest offer prices from the inside, or interdealer, market.

REPURCHASE AGREEMENT (RP)

An agreement between a buyer and seller to reverse a trade at a specified time at a specified price. Such an arrangement is illegal if nonexempt securities are involved. In the case of exempt securities, however, such agreements are frequently used by dealers in government and municipal securities to reduce the cost of carry. Thus, a government securities dealer can sell a security, with an agreement to repurchase at a fixed price, and thereby reduce his loan with his bank with the proceeds from the sale. The dealer pays a negotiated rate of interest to the buyer that makes it profitable to both parties.

REQUISITIONIST

English term for an individual or group that is intent on unseating the management of a public corporation. We would use the term *insurgent*.

RESCHEDULED LOANS

A euphemism for a loan renegotiated to forestall default and bankruptcy. Because bankruptcy is so expensive and presents problems both for debtor and creditor, it is often advisable to "reschedule" the loan. Thus, a 10% 14-year loan, with the consent of both parties, could be rescheduled into a 30-year 9% loan.

RESCIND

In general, to cancel a contract; thus, both parties are restored to the condition that existed before the contract.

Fraud, misrepresentation, lack of consent, failure to comply with the law, or inability of one party to make a binding contract give rise to the rescinding of the contract. Popular example: a minor contract; the contract is rescindible. Another example: a registered representative solicits an order to buy a security that is not qualified for sale in the state of buyer.

The act of rescinding, viewed from the buyer's or seller's options, is called "rescission."

RESERVE CITY BANK

A bank in the metropolitan area of a city where a Federal Reserve District Bank or one of its branches is located. For example, in the Fourth

Federal Reserve District, the district bank is in St. Louis; the branches are in Memphis and Little Rock. Member banks of the Fed within metro St. Louis, Memphis, and Little Rock are considered reserve city banks.

Principal concept: Reserve requirements for such city banks are slightly higher than the reserve requirement for rural banks outside these areas. Reason: Checking activity will normally be greater.

RESERVE REQUIREMENT

The money that a member bank of the Federal Reserve System must keep on deposit with the nearest Federal Reserve District Bank. Cash in the vault of the member bank is included in the computation of the reserve. The required reserve differs for demand deposits and for time deposits.

Principal concept: The requirement must be in cash; thus, there is no possibility of loss of principal value.

RESET BOND

Term for a debt whose rate of interest payment will be adjusted to keep the face value of the instrument at par. In practice, on specific dates the issuer must change the rate of interest paid; but only if there is a change in the obligor's credit worthiness, or a change in general rates in the economy.

RESIDUAL INTEREST BONDS

See RIBS.

RESIDUAL VALUE

1. A description of common stock. It is the residual value of a corporation after all debts are paid and preferred stockholders are satisfied.
2. In real estate finance: the difference between out-of-pocket cost for real estate and what is received for it upon disposal in 10, 20, or later years. The residual value also includes the net rentals during this period.

See INTERNAL RATE OF RETURN for a measurement of "yield" on real estate.

RESISTANCE LEVEL

If the historical chart pattern for a security establishes a price at which sellers will tend to sell, this price is called the "resistance level." For example, a security over a period has traded between 12 and 16. Almost every time the price rose to 16, the price declined. Technical analysts would conclude that 16 is the resistance level. A substantial rise of the security above 16 is called a "breakout."

RESPONDEAT SUPERIOR

Latin: let the superior reply.

Concept: A complaint is brought against a broker/dealer because of an action done by one of its employees. The principle of this term means that the superior is responsible for the proper and adequate supervision of his or her employees.

RESTRICTED ACCOUNT

A margin account in which the customer's equity (i.e., approximate dollar value of customer's holdings if the securities were liquidated and debt to broker repaid) is less than the current Federal Reserve Board initial percentage requirement. For example, customer holds securities worth $50,000 in a margin account and has a $30,000 debit balance. The customer's equity is $20,000. The Fed's initial percentage requirement on securities worth $50,000 is 50%, or $25,000. Because the customer's equity is only $20,000 this margin account is restricted.

RESTRICTED INTERNAL MEMO

Acronym: RIM. Technical term for a document prepared by a broker/dealer for dissemination only to its sales force. Usually a RIM is an educational marketing tool prepared for the salespersons who will distribute the issue. Because of regulatory restrictions, RIMs may not be sent to customers or other prospective buyers.

Such documents will always be headed "For Internal Use Only," and this restriction must be scrupulously maintained.

RESTRICTED LIST

A list, periodically updated, which broker/dealers provide to their sales personnel. The list gives the names of issuers and, in some cases, specific security issues, which may not be traded or which may be sold by customers only if the order to sell is unsolicited. Generally, the restriction arises from an upcoming public offering of securities that is currently in registration with the SEC.

RESTRICTIVE COVENANT

A term often applied to the indenture, or bond resolution, of a municipal security.

The term is descriptive—that is, it looks at the indenture in terms of actions that the municipality may not take.

RESTRICTIVE ENDORSEMENT

If the assignment on the reverse side of a registered certificate—or the stock/bond power that accompanies a certificate—designates a specific person, the endorsement is said to be "restrictive." This is true whether the person named is an individual or a corporation.

As a general rule, clients who mail assigned securities are recommended to make a restrictive endorsement—that is, to appoint the brokerage firm as their attorney for the transfer of the certificate.

RETAIL AUTOMATIC EXECUTION SYSTEM
See RAES.

RETAIL CD
Common expression for a bank certificate of deposit of $100,000 or less.

In general, such certificates are nonnegotiable, subject to penalty for early withdrawal, and covered by deposit insurance (FDIC).

The term is used in distinction to *jumbo CD* (more than $100,000). "Brokered CDs" are purchased by retail customers in amounts under $100,000 through a broker/dealer. Such brokered CDs are insured but are paid only simple interest.

RETAIL INVESTOR
Term used of individual investors as opposed to corporate or other institutional-type investors, such as banks, mutual funds, and pension funds. The distinction, however, is nonspecific in that most broker/dealers differentiate retail from institutional investors by the amount of revenue dollars generated from the accounts on an annual basis.

Accounts that generate a lower dollar amount of commission business are called "retail"; those with a higher dollar amount are called "institutional."

RETAIL PRICE INDEX
Acronym: RPI. RPI is a monthly index of consumer prices based on a weighted basket of food, clothing, and shelter in the United Kingdom. The RPI will show inflationary and deflationary trends in the British economy and is prepared by a governmental agency.

RETAIL REPO
A collateralized loan between a bank and a depositor—as opposed to the traditional repo between a broker/dealer and an institutional investor. In a retail repo, the bank is the borrower and the depositor is the lender. As with the traditional repo, it is a two-part transaction: the sale and the repurchase of the underlying collateral. The borrower pays interest for the use of the money upon termination of the loan.

RETAINED EARNINGS

Corporate balance sheet entry that shows the cumulative total of net earnings that were not distributed as dividends to stockholders.

Also called "earned surplus."

RETAINED EARNINGS STATEMENT

A financial statement that often accompanies the annual report of a corporation. It gives a detailed record of dividend disbursements made in the current year from net earnings together with a summary of previous dividend payments.

Often called the "accumulated retained earnings statement" because it explains, over time, the retained earnings entry on the corporate balance sheet.

RETENTION

That portion of an underwriter's takedown it may sell to its customers. Normally, the syndicate manager will hold back some of the takedown to facilitate both institutional sales and sales by members of the selling group. The remainder forms the retention for the individual member of the syndicate. For example, an individual syndicate member may have a takedown of 10,000 shares. The manager holds 2,000 shares for institutional sales and selling group members. The syndicate member's retention is 8,000 shares.

See also TAKEDOWN.

RETENTION REQUIREMENT

Term from Regulation T of the Federal Reserve Board regarding disposition of proceeds of a long sale in a restricted margin account. Prior to February 1982, the broker had to retain 70% of proceeds in the account, thus lowering customer's debt to broker; the remaining 30% could be withdrawn from the account by the customer. In February 1982, the retention requirement was lowered to 50% and customer is now allowed to withdraw the other 50% of the sale's proceeds.

RETIREMENT

Used of debt securities or preferred stock if the issuer redeems, calls for early redemption, or exchanges an entire issue of securities so the issue no longer is outstanding. Redemption at the face or par value, plus any interest or dividends due, is the most common method of retirement of an issue, although a call prior to maturity is not unusual.

RETRACTABLE LOAN

A debt security with a provision that enables the issuer to change the specified rate of interest periodically or at predetermined intervals.

Such retractable loans are made attractive to investors by granting them the right to redeem the security at par value if the newly changed rate of interest is not to their liking. In this way, the retractable bond becomes competitive to both the borrower and the lender.

RETREAD

Industry slang for a registered representative transferee from another broker/dealer. The term denotes some experience as a securities sales-person but not with the new employer. Some additional training is usu-ally required.

RETURN

See RATE OF RETURN.

RETURN OF CAPITAL

A distribution of cash by a corporation or a trust that does not arise from net income or retained earnings. Example: A utility distributes cash that represents depreciation on certain assets, or a unit investment trust distributes cash that represents the proceeds of the sale of portfolio securities.

A return of capital is not a taxable distribution; instead, recipient must lower the cost of acquisition of the security because part of the orig-inal purchase price was returned. Later capital gains or losses will be computed from this adjusted purchase price.

RETURN ON EQUITY

Measurement used in financial analysis to judge the percentage of re-turn on the equity capital employed in a business. Most common mea-surement: net income (before dividends) divided by stockholders' equity at the beginning of the firm's fiscal year.

The return on common equity is more specific. It uses net income mi-nus preferred dividends divided by stockholders' equity after excluding the par value of outstanding preferred shares.

Common abbreviation is ROE.

RETURN ON INVESTED CAPITAL

Measurement used in financial analysis to judge the rate of return on all sources of long-term capital. Most commonly used formula: add interest paid on bonds to net income after taxes. Divide this by the par value of long-term bonds plus total stockholders' equity; that is, by the total capi-talization of the company. The exact application of the formula may vary by industry classification of the company.

Common abbreviation is ROI.

REVALUATION

An official change in the value of one nation's currency in terms of another's. For example, it would be a revaluation if the United States, independently of market factors, were to state that the Irish punt were now worth $1.25, rather than $1.10 as previously determined.

As a general rule, revaluation infers an upward valuation of the foreign currency. Devaluation, a downward valuation.

REVENUE ANTICIPATION NOTE (RAN)

Short-term municipal note issued by a state or municipality in anticipation of revenues other than those received from income taxes, or from the proceeds of a bond issue, that will be sufficient to retire the debt. For example, a note issued in anticipation of sales tax revenues could properly be called a "revenue anticipation note."

A RAN is retired when the revenue is received.

REVENUE BOND

General term for a municipal security whose interest and principal will be paid from tolls, charges, rents, or other sources of income generated by the facility built with the money borrowed by the issue.

Almost any type of facility may be built with the proceeds of a revenue bond issue: bridges, airports, turnpikes, hospitals, dormitories, sports complexes—provided there is enabling legislation and the facility is used for the common good of the municipality.

REVENUE INDEXED MORTGAGE BOND

A real estate backed security in which interest payments can be augmented by a specified percentage of the issuer's earnings.

REVERSAL

Term used by technical analysts in their charting of security price movements if a primary or a major secondary price trend is countered by a substantial change from the trend. For example, if a security's trend has been from $15 to $12 per share, a sustained rise above $13 per share would indicate a reversal of the trend.

Reversals are indicative only if they are sustained. Short-term price changes may negate the indication of a reversal. For example, a stock that dropped from $15 to $12, and then rose to $13, may rise in price (the reversal) but also may soon drop back to $11.

REVERSE ANNUITY MORTGAGE (RAM)

Concept: An elderly property owner arranges to borrow against the collateral value of fully owned property. However, the annual payments will not deplete the value of the property during the person's lifetime. Thus, borrower can assure himself of constant income for his life and make provisions for disposal of the property's residual value after his death.

REVERSE A SWAP
Term used of a second transaction in bonds that reestablishes a client's original bond portfolio position. For example, a temporary change in the yield spread between Treasuries and AAA corporates makes it profitable to sell Treasuries and buy IBM bonds. When the yield spreads return to their historical relationship, the client reverses the swap by selling the IBM bonds and repurchasing the originally held Treasury bonds.

REVERSE BID
English terminology for a takeover attempt in which a listed company makes a bid to buy out the holders of a private concern. No approval is required of the public stockholders because it is felt that such an acquisition will add to the product line and profit of the public concern.

REVERSE CONVERSION
1. An exchange of a customer's call option for a put option. The exchange is effected by an accommodating put and call broker.
2. An arbitrage technique used by a broker/dealer to lock in an interest-rate profit in money market securities.

Both strategies employ a similar technique by the broker/ dealer: the short sale of the underlying security while, at the same time, buying a call and selling a put with an identical exercise price at or near the short sale price.

REVERSE DOLLAR ROLL
Term used of certain short-term trading practices in GNMA securities. In a reverse dollar roll, the holder of high coupon GNMA bonds sells them during a period of lower rates with the expressed agreement to reacquire them in about a month or so (a repurchase agreement). The buyer enjoys a higher than prevailing rate for the short period that he or she holds them.

REVERSE HEDGE
Term used of a customer who owns a common stock and sells short a convertible security that can be converted into the common stock. The customer is speculating that the premium over conversion parity will decline and the total position can be closed out at a profit. Technically, the

combined position is not a hedge, as it would be if the customer were long the convertible security and short the common stock.

REVERSE LBO
Media term for a public sale of a company after a leveraged buyout was used to take it private. Generally, the motivation for such a resale following a purchase is an anticipated profit if the shares are again sold to the public.

REVERSE REPO
See REVERSE REPURCHASE AGREEMENT.

REVERSE REPURCHASE AGREEMENT
A customer delivers securities to a broker/dealer, receives cash, and promises to repurchase the securities at a later date at a fixed price. The difference between the cash received by the customer and the repurchase price represents, in effect, interest for the use of the money received. Usually, only government, agency, or municipal securities are subject to repurchase and reverse repos. The Federal Reserve Banking System is a frequent user of reverse repurchase agreements to fine-tune the money supply.

REVERSE SPINS
SPINS are acronyms for Standard & Poor's 500 Index Notes. SPINS were originally offered by Salomon Brothers in 1986 and were a *call* option on a rise in the S&P index after August 20, 1986. Meantime, the holder got a 2% nominal rate of interest payable semiannually.

Reverse SPINS were the opposite: a *put* option on the S&P index after September 14, 1987, to run until the maturity of the notes on September 14, 1990.

As with the original offering, the holder—in a worst case scenario—got a 2% annual rate of interest plus a full return of principal.

REVERSE SPLIT
Term used if a corporation reduces the number of outstanding shares by increasing the par value of the shares. For example, a company changes the par value of its common shares from $5 to $10. Outstanding shares will be turned in and the owner will receive half as many new shares, but the shares will have double the par value of the original shares. Used by firms whose shares are selling at very low market prices; thus, there will be fewer shares with a higher market value.

Also called a "split-down."

REVERSE STRATEGY
See BACKSPREAD.

REVERSE YIELD GAP

A U.K. term for a yield curve on gilts where the return on those government securities is greater than the rate of return on U.K. equities. If investment return is commensurate with risk, such a reverse yield gap would mean that the risk on gilts is greater than the risk on equities—certainly an anomaly.

In this concept, *yield* means total return; generally, the interest yield on gilts is less than the dividend yield on equities.

REVOLVER

See REVOLVING LINE OF CREDIT.

REVOLVING LINE OF CREDIT

Term used in banking if a bank establishes a line of credit for a customer to be used when, as, and if needed. Often there is a commitment fee paid by the potential borrower.

Slang: a revolver.

REVOLVING UNDERWRITING FACILITIES

Acronym: RUF. Term is associated with medium- to long-term debt origination agreements between issuers of Eurodollar securities and investment banking consortia. Under these agreements, the underwriters offer three- to six-month obligations of the issuer at favorable short-term rates but are required to reoffer the notes again and again as preceding notes mature. The issuer pays the consortia a fee. The underwriters' risk is rate-related, and it varies with the difference between short and medium rates to long-term rates at the time of the initial agreement.

RFA

See REGULATORY FLEXIBILITY ACT.

RFP

See RULES OF FAIR PRACTICE.

RHOSP

See REGISTERED HOME OWNERSHIP SAVINGS PLAN.

RIBS

An acronym for Shearson Lehman's Residual Interest Bonds, a class of municipal security issued in conjunction with select auction variable-rate securities (SAVRS). The municipal issuer contracts to pay a fixed sum of tax-exempted interest semiannually split among two classes of debt securities holders, SAVRS and RIBS. The holders of SAVRS receive a variable amount, determined by Dutch auction (q.v.) every 35 days, while the holders of RIBS receive what is left over. Thus, if rates decline in the municipal market, the RIBS' holders benefit greatly. If rates increase, they suffer!

RIC
Common abbreviation for: registered investment company. A RIC is a corporation (or Massachusetts trust) registered with the SEC under the Investment Company Act of 1940 and subject to all of the regulations appropriate to investment companies.

Domestic investment companies are required to register if they are face-amount certificate companies, unit investment trusts, or management companies (either closed- or open-end management companies). Holding companies and other companies whose principal occupation is the management of corporations—as opposed to the management of money—are not permitted to register. Open-end management companies are popularly called "mutual funds."

RICH
Commonly used expression to describe either a price or a yield that, in the mind of the the commentator, is too high. Example: "IBM at 155 is too rich for my blood."

The term connotes the implied belief that the securities are overpriced, or the yield is too high, and that the price or yield will drop to more acceptable levels.

RICO
Acronym for Racketeer Influenced and Corrupt Organization Act. This is a federal law that makes it a crime for any person to participate in any enterprise engaged in certain defined racketeering activities, including securities fraud.

RIDING THE TAPE
The simplest form of technical analysis: speculators are buying stocks that are rising and selling stocks that are falling, and they are using the ticker tape to tell them when to do this.

An expanded form of this technique arises when speculators buy stocks that are "in vogue" and sell stocks that are falling out of vogue.

RIE
Acronym for Recognized Investment Exchange. In the United Kingdom, an RIE is any organized body that provides a market framework within which specific transactions can be effected.

An RIE, under the Financial Services Act of 1986, is expected to provide facilities whereby the market price of an investment may be established in an open and fair way. In and of itself, an RIE need not be a place (it could be electronic) nor need it be an SRO. Part of the concept of an RIE is the ability not only to establish a fair price but also to disseminate the price to users of the marketplace.

RIGGING THE MARKET
A slang expression for price manipulation. In practice, such manipulation occurs if buyers in concert push prices up, or sellers in concert push prices down—for their own benefit. In practice, neither direct buying nor selling is required; rumors will often cause the appropriate effect to occur.

The term is also used of *imputed* manipulation; thus, following the two October crashes (1987 and 1989) many small investors were convinced that market insiders and sophisticated money managers manipulated the market to the disadvantage of the small investor.

RIGHT OF ACCUMULATION
Privilege offered by most open-end investment companies to current fundholders. The privilege becomes operative if the value of current holdings in any, or all, of the funds managed by the fund manager exceeds established breakpoints for fund purchases. For example, a fund's breakpoint is $25,000. A fundholder's shares are worth $22,000. A further investment of $4,000 will exceed the $25,000 breakpoint, and the $4,000 is eligible for reduced sales charges.

The prospectus of a fund describes how the right of accumulation applies to that fund.

RIGHT OF RESCISSION
Contract cancellation privilege because the purchase was made in contravention of existing laws.

See also RESCIND.

RIGHT OF WAY
A land use privilege accorded by property owners to public utilities or transportation companies whereby these companies are enabled to serve the interests of the general public through the use of the land. Example: Property owners in Greene County granted a right of way to County Light & Power to erect transmission poles in the county.

RIGHTS OFFERING
A privilege granted by some corporations to current common shareholders whereby they can purchase a proportionate number of new shares, at a price that is lower than current market prices, before the public is allowed to purchase the shares.

Commonly called a "subscription," the rights offering is effected by delivering a prospectus and a security called "rights to present common shareholders." The shareholders may subscribe by delivering their rights and the required number of dollars to the company. Rights also may be resold if shareholder declines the rights offering.

RIM
See RESTRICTED INTERNAL MEMO.

RING
Term that describes the trading locations on most commodity exchanges and the location in the bond room of the New York Stock Exchange where commodities or bonds are bought and sold.

RIO
Acronym for Regional Interface Organization. RIO is used of a limited participant member of the Midwest Securities Trust Co. (MSTC). The sole purpose of this limited form of membership is to have transactions cleared by MSTC but ultimately settled (*flipped* is the slang term) at another clearing agency that is electronically linked with MSTC.

RISK
Common term for financial uncertainty. The term, if used alone, generally means capital risk; that is, the possibility that an asset will be sold at a price that is lower than the purchase price.

The term is often used in combination with other terms. Examples: inflationary risk, a change in the purchasing power of money; market risk, uncertainty due to price volatility or market illiquidity; interest-rate risk, a change in value because general interest rates rise.

RISK ARBITRAGE
General term for a long and short position taken in anticipation of, or upon the announcement of, a proposed merger. Normally, the speculator will buy shares of the company to be acquired and sell short the shares of the acquiring company on the speculation that the shares of the company to be acquired will go up, and the shares of the acquiring company will go down. The risk is that the merger will be cancelled. In this case, there can be substantial loss as the shares go back to original price levels.

RISKLESS TRANSACTION
NASD term for a broker/dealer who takes a position in a security only upon receipt of a firm order to buy entered by a customer.

Also called a "simultaneous transaction." For example, a broker/

dealer with no position in a security receives a firm order to buy 500 shares from a customer. Rather than make an agency transaction, the dealer buys 500 shares, marks it up, and sells to the customer.

Riskless transactions do not violate industry rules provided the markup conforms to industry standards. The use of a riskless transaction to conceal an excessive markup violates the accepted ethics of the NASD.

ROAD SHOW
An issuer's presentation, made either in person or by a representative, to sophisticated investors. It highlights the features of an upcoming issue and publicizes the strengths of the company.

Also called: DOG AND PONY SHOW.

ROBINSON CRUSOE WEEK
A colorful and literary allusion to the novel by Daniel Defoe and is used to refer to a very dull and listless market. The term originated in the United Kingdom, and to devotees of the novel it means a week that "is waiting for Friday"—Crusoe's manservant—and for the end of the listless week!

In the United Kingdom the term has the added connotation that the British market is waiting for economic news from the United States (much of which appears on a Thursday here), which will have a market effect on Friday in Britain.

ROCK & ROLL MARKET
An analogy to the music popularized in the 1960s and 1970s enjoyed by the younger generations at that time. The financial industry uses this term to refer to a marketplace characterized by high volatility. The expression is used to describe stock or bond markets, or both, if prices begin swinging sharply, either between transactions or from a previous close.

ROID
A slang abbreviation for the Polaroid Corporation, a large manufacturer of camera equipment and a developer of instant photography.

ROL
See REDUCTION OPTION LOAN.

ROLL DOWN
The closing of an option position and the immediate establishment of a new position with a lower strike (exercise) price.

See also ROLL UP.

ROLLER COASTER SWAP

Colorful expression for a transaction in which two parties exchange interest payments on identical principal amounts, and the principal amounts are self-amortizing. The self-amortizing effect may result from sinking fund payments or other scheduled payments. For example, two parties could exchange the same principal amount of GNMAs for sinking fund bonds; the yield may be the same but the paydown may vary. Thus, as with other interest-rate swaps, the liabilities could be fixed versus "floaters," or any combination thereof.

ROLL FORWARD

The closing of an option position and the reestablishment of another position with a longer time to expiration. Technically, if the new position has a higher/lower strike price, it is a roll up/down and forward.

See also ROLL UP.

ROLLING BIG BANG

A term used on the Amsterdam Stock Exchange to classify certain reforms adopted by the ASE to regain lost institutional business and to compete more effectively in international marketplaces. The term was coined to mimic the "big bang" that occurred when London's International Stock Exchange initiated its reforms on October 27, 1986.

ROLLING COVERED WRITE

A description of a continuous covered call writing program on an underlying position in the stock (or a convertible).

The concept is simple: Following a covered write (but before its expiration), the writer makes a closing purchase followed by another covered write on the same underlying security. Thus, the writer voids the previous obligation, gains a second (and third, and so on) premium, and extends the time of the obligation to deliver the underlying.

However, such a program of rolling covered writes is not a "gold mine"—it requires proper timing, avoidance of unprofitable commissions from turnovers, and monitoring of premiums received and paid.

ROLLING PUT

Term used of the put feature on certain bonds. At specified times in the future, the holder may put the bond to the issuer at par (or at a premium). However, if the bond is not put at the first available put date, the holder must wait for the second (or the third) date to put the bond. Thus, unless put at a specific date, the holder has only two recourses: sell in the market at prevailing prices, or wait until the next put date.

ROLLING STOCK
Industry term used by transportation companies to designate movable equipment. In practice, the term includes railroad engines, freight and passenger cars, trucks, container cars, and, often, airplanes.

ROLLOVER
In general, the reinvestment of funds. Specifically, the term is used if:
1. Funds from a maturing bond or other debt instrument are reinvested in a similar security.
2. Funds in one qualified pension fund are reinvested in another. For example, an IRA rollover.
3. A security is sold at a profit and the funds are used to establish a new position in the same security at a new cost basis.
   In practice, the term is not used if a capital loss or a negative cash flow is involved in the successive transactions.

ROLL UP
1. A tax-free exchange of a partnership interest for a proportionate share interest in a corporation. Because partnership interest was taxed annually, most of the cash flow from this exchange is considered a return of the owner's capital and is not subject to tax.
2. Used of options if an investor closes a current position and immediately establishes a position at a higher strike price. Often used even if the new, higher strike price has a longer period to expiration. Technically, this latter strategy is a roll up and forward.

ROLY POLY CERTIFICATES OF DEPOSIT
A series of consecutive six-month CDs issued as a package covering two or more years. Under the package, buyers (depositors) are obligated to purchase the same dollar amount of CDs as the previous CDs mature. These CDs may have a fixed rate, or a floating rate, depending on the status of interest rates.

ROP
See REGISTERED OPTIONS PRINCIPAL.

ROR
See REGISTERED OPTIONS REPRESENTATIVE.

ROSOKU-ASHI
A popular Japanese term for a way of charting price movements. The term in Japanese means *candle chart.*

Using graph paper, *price* is the vertical measurement; *time* is the horizontal measurement. Thus, time versus price will make a rectangle. If the price is upward, the rectangle will be left white; if price trend is downward, the rectangle is shaded.

In effect, it is easy to identify upward moving stocks from downward moving stocks. The time frame may be extended to cover longer periods.

In the following illustration, A is the high, B is the open, C is the close, and D is the low. C is the critical measurement, and, as a result, white blocks signify stocks that have risen (closed high) and shaded blocks signify stocks that have fallen (closed low).

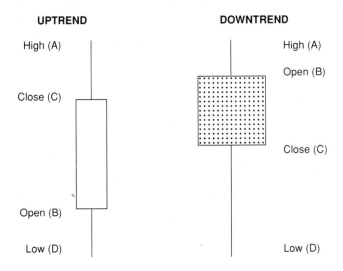

ROT
See REGISTERED OPTIONS TRADER.

ROTATION
See TRADING ROTATION.

ROTHSCHILD RULE
When asked about the secret of his financial success, the founder of the Rothschild dynasty is said to have replied: "Buy cheap, sell dear."

Obviously, such a secret is a tautology because one either bought cheap or one did not. As such, the saying became popular on Wall Street in the expression: "Buy low, sell high."

ROTN

Acronym for reconcilement of out-trade notice. ROTN is an abbreviation for a form submitted by clearing corporations to brokers involved in transactions that cannot be compared because of discrepancies in trade terms.

On trade plus one (T + 1), this notice of an out-trade is sent to the floor for reconciliation so an agreement can be reached by trade date about the terms of the trade.

ROUND LOT

Term used for the generally accepted unit of trading in a security.

For stocks, the generally accepted unit of trading is 100 shares, although there are 10-share units for some inactive stocks and a trend toward 500-share units in institutional markets. Listed bonds trade in $1,000 par value units, but OTC bond trading round lots vary greatly according to the security. For example, governments trade in round lots of $100,000; corporate bonds in round lots of $250,000; and Ginnie Maes and CDs in round lots of $1 million.

ROUNDTRIP

1. A purchase followed by a sale (or a sale followed by a purchase) of a security, commodity, or currency (*a*) during a relatively short period of time that (*b*) resulted in a net zero position in the underlying. For example, "The client did a roundtrip in March silver futures."
2. Before the time of commission negotiations (May 1, 1975), a reduced commission schedule for clients who bought and sold (or sold short and covered) within a relatively short period. Originally, this was 30 days; later, it was reduced to 14 days.

ROUND UP

1. Industry practice to achieve a normally used price variation. For example, a stock goes ex-dividend. The specialist will, if the dividend is not a multiple of $1/8$, round down to the next lower price that represents a multiple of $1/8$. A dividend of 60¢ will be rounded up to $5/8$, or $.625.
2. Customer instruction if a fixed dollar amount is invested. *Round up* means to buy a number of shares that leaves a debit in the account. The customer will pay the added amount. *Round down* means to leave a credit in customer's account by purchasing the closest share number under his deposit.

IRA and Keogh accounts should always be rounded down because the IRS does not permit debits in such accounts.

RP

1. A commonly used abbreviation for: repurchase agreement. Repurchase agreements are used by securities dealers to finance inventory. They are also used by the FOMC in its endeavor to fine-tune the economy.
2. An acronym for remarketed preferred stock (q.v.), originated by Merrill Lynch for its institutional and corporate customers.
   See also REPURCHASE AGREEMENT.

RPI

See RETAIL PRICE INDEX.

RR

See REGISTERED REPRESENTATIVE.

RRM

Acronym for renegotiable rate mortgage. This is a 20–30 year real estate loan. The rates, however, are fixed for only 3–5 years. At the end of each of these periods, the loan can be rolled over (renewed) at a new rate that is indexed to an average national mortgage rate determination. Although the rate cannot vary by more than 1–2% per year, over the life of the mortgage this may amount to an up/down fluctuation of 5% or more.

RRRR

See REGISTERED REPRESENTATIVE RAPID RESPONSE PROGRAM.

RRSP

See REGISTERED RETIREMENT SAVINGS PLAN.

RT

See REGISTERED COMPETITIVE TRADER.

RTC

1. NYSE ticker symbol of Rochester Telephone Company, a large communications company located in upper New York State.
2. The designator of the Resolution Trust Company, a legal entity established by Congress in 1989 to salvage failing thrift institutions in the United States. It is funded by the Treasury Department through the issuance of bonds.

RTD

Abbreviation for rated.
See also RATING.

RUF
See REVOLVING UNDERWRITING FACILITIES.

RULE OF NINETEEN (19)
A stock market theory that uses as a predictor of market direction the sum of the P-E ratio of the S&P 500 Index and the nation's inflation rate. If the sum is less than 19, the indicator is bullish; if the sum is greater than 19, the indicator is bearish. And, the greater the deviation from 19, the stronger the message.

RULE OF TWENTY (20)
A theory of stock market movements that holds that the annual rate of inflation in the United States plus the average price-earnings ratio of the Dow Jones industrial stocks should be equal to 20. In effect, as inflation goes up, the price-earnings ratio will go down.

RULE OF SEVENTY-TWO (72)
Rule of thumb to determine the answer to this question: Given a fixed rate of compound interest, how long will it take for my money to double? Formula: divide 72 by the fixed rate of compound interest. The quotient will be the number of years for the original investment to double. Example: At 9% compound interest—according to this rule-of-thumb formula—money will double in 8 years, and 72 divided by 9 is 8.

RULE 97
A NYSE rule that limits a member's proprietary activities in a stock on the same day after it has completed a block transaction to facilitate a customer's order.

RULE 387
Under this rule, the NYSE requires that COD/RVP transactions in DTC-eligible securities be confirmed, affirmed, and settled through the Institutional Delivery System (ID). Since most institutions use COD/RVP trades, compliance with this rule is very important for the efficient completion of such trades.

RULE 390
A famous NYSE rule that requires, with some exceptions, a member's execution of NYSE-listed securities only on the NYSE floor. Its principal exceptions have been used in connection with a domestic customer's transactions in Europe before the exchange opens and in Asia after the exchange closes.

RULE 405

A New York Stock Exchange rule requiring that member firms and registered representatives learn the essential facts about customers, their agents, and specific securities transactions entered either by the customer or the agent.

The rule requires that responsible brokerage professionals know or, if they do not know, ask for the pertinent facts about customers, their accounts, and their transactions. The rule is so written that a brokerage professional cannot use "I did not know" as an excuse for an improper or unsuitable transaction.

See also KNOW YOUR CUSTOMER.

RULE 535 SECURITIES

The International Stock Exchange of the United Kingdom and the Republic of Ireland rule that applies to the Unlisted Securities Market (USM) and certain exempted transactions for securities:
1. Principally traded outside the United Kingdom and Ireland.
2. Of small, local nonlisted companies that have been given permission to trade in the USM.
3. Of mineral exploration companies that have not been in existence long enough to qualify for listing.
4. Of suspended issuers, but only to cover shorts and to liquidate estates.

RULER STOCKS

Street slang for companies whose earnings growth seems to rise in a straight line year after year through good times and bad. The description is factual and does not indicate whether the results are from good management or good luck.

RULES OF FAIR PRACTICE (RFP)

National Association of Securities Dealers' rules that outline and often state in detail the norms of ethical conduct for members and for registered representatives.

The Rules of Fair Practice, in more or less detail, deal with fair treatment, fair prices, proper disclosure, and the avoidance of conflicts of interest in dealings with other members and with investors.

The rules incorporate both federal securities law and civil law in some cases, and accepted industry practice in others. In all cases, violations of the Rules of Fair Practice subject the violator to severe penalties, ranging from censure to fines to suspension and expulsion from the NASD. If the law is violated, civil and criminal penalties may also apply.

RUMP

Colorful English term for the remnant securities in a rights offering (or offering of warrants) that are not subscribed to by current stockholders. The "rump" is purchased by stand-by underwriters at prices that represent a bargain, compared to current market prices. The underwriter can then resell the securities to customers for a profit.

A RUN

Industry term for a marketmaker's current list of security offerings. In practice, the run for stocks includes bid-offer prices. For bonds, the run will usually include the par value of bonds offered with an offer price.

Government bills, notes, bonds, agencies, and money market securities may be represented by price ranges with actual prices given only after negotiation about dollar amount and method of settlement.

RUNDOWN

Popular term for the dollar amounts available and their prices on the remaining bonds in a municipal serial issue.

RUNNING AHEAD

Term used of the improper activity whereby a registered representative enters personal orders to buy-sell a security before customer orders are entered.

Most member firms have internal controls that prohibit or limit such orders. For example, Merrill Lynch has a 48-hour rule. If that firm issues a research report to buy-sell a security, its employees may not buy or sell that security for two business days (48 real hours). This time restriction on brokerage employees places the firm's customers at an advantage and excludes "running ahead."

RUNNING A SECURITY THROUGH THE POT

Term used if the manager of a syndicate recalls some of the shares or bonds taken down by syndicate and selling group members for retail sales and includes them in the pot devoted to institutional sales.

Central concept: Institutional sales seem to be going better than retail sales. If these securities can be sold to institutional investors, it will maintain the profitability of the syndicate and lessen the need to make a lot of retail sales to distribute all of the shares or bonds.

RUN-OFF

1. The execution and publication on the consolidated tape of transactions that occurred on the floor during the 30 seconds of the final bell.

2. Term used to describe a series of declining prices either in individual securities or the market in general during a relatively brief time. For example, "There was a run-off in the market this afternoon between 3:30 and 4:00 o'clock."

A RUN ON A BANK
Term used to describe a situation in which a substantial number of depositors, fearing a collapse of the bank, seek to withdraw their deposits at the same time.

RUSH WITHDRAWAL TRANSFER
See RWT.

THE RUSSELL 1,000
A stock market index developed by the Frank Russell Co., an investment advisor located in Tacoma, Washington. The index is composed of 1,000 of the largest equity-capitalized U.S. corporations in terms of market value. Because the smallest company in this index has a capitalization of about $250 million, the index has particular tracking appeal for large hedge funds and investment companies.

The Russell 2,000, on the other hand, is composed of 2,000 of the smaller publicly traded U.S. companies.

See also 2,000 SMALL STOCK INDEX.

THE RUSSELL 3,000
A stock market index developed by the Frank Russell Co., an investment advisor located in Tacoma, Washington. This market barometer is comprised of 3,000 of the largest U.S. companies in terms of market capitalization and represents about 98% of the U.S. equity market.

RUST BELT
A broad descriptive term used of the states of Pennsylvania, West Virginia, Ohio, Indiana, and Illinois. The allusion is to several facts: These states are the principal manufacturing states for iron in the United States; the factories in which the iron is fabricated are, in many cases, old and "rusty"; and the workers who manufacture iron and steel have suffered a number of economic hardships in recent years because their factories are noncompetitive.

RV
Acronym for recreational vehicle. Such RVs generally fall into three general categories: (1) travel trailers, (2) motor homes, (3) and van conversions.

There are several publicly traded stocks whose issuers manufacture such vehicles. Receivables for such RVs often form the collateral for asset-backed securities.

Many states place the initials RV prominently on the registration plates for such vehicles.

R.V.P. TRANSACTION
See RECEIVE VERSUS PAYMENT.

RW
See REGULAR-WAY SETTLEMENT.

RWT
These initials stand for: Rush Withdrawal Transfer. RWT is a special service provided by the DTC upon the request of member firm customers and the payment of a special fee. Through automation, a C.O.D. customer can obtain, upon payment of a $22.50 processing fee, urgent physical delivery of certificates purchased with clearinghouse funds.

S

S
Nineteenth letter of the alphabet, used:
1. On the consolidated tapes, a transaction in round lots of 100 shares; for example, 3s = 300 shares.
2. In older option newspaper tables, to signify that a specific series was not listed for trading.
3. In the stock table of the newspaper, following the name of the stock, to signify that within the past year there was a stock split or dividend that increased the number of shares by 20% or more; for example, Boeing s.
4. As the fifth letter in NASDAQ/NMS listings to signify shares of beneficial interest.
5. As the NYSE symbol for Sears, Roebuck & Co., a major U.S. retailer.

SABRES
Acronym for Share-Adjusted Broker-Remarketed Equity Securities. SABRES are a Smith Barney innovation designed to function like commercial paper, or medium-term notes, but is, in reality, a preferred stock. The stock is puttable to the issuer at par any time after a minimum 46-day holding period.

SAEF

Mnemonic for SEAQ Automated Execution Facility. SAEF is an off-shoot of SEAQ (Stock Exchange Automated Quotation) system of the International Stock Exchange in London.

SAEF will enter electronically and execute small buy and sell orders on the International Stock Exchange. It is modeled after the NYSE's DOT system. If successful, the SAEF system will be expanded to execute larger orders.

SAFE HARBOR

Financial term signifying that an action avoids legal or tax consequences. Implication: the action benefits the person doing the action.

SAFE HARBOR RULE

See SEC RULE 10b-18.

SAFEKEEPING

Protective measures that a broker/dealer must employ to protect customers' fully paid securities. Such measures involve proper segregation, identification, or other means of protection. Forbidden by federal securities laws are commingling of customer securities with the securities owned by the broker, improper repledging or lending of customer securities without the specific written permission of the customer, improper recordkeeping.

SAIF

See SAVINGS ASSOCIATION INSURANCE FUND.

SAITORI

Name given to a category of membership on the three major stock exchanges in Japan.

Saitori members act as intermediaries for regular members of the exchanges, in a manner similar to that of the $2 brokers on U.S. exchanges. They are not permitted to trade for personal or firm accounts, but they are permitted to report transactions electronically to securities firms and to news offices.

SALES CHARGE

The percentage fee charged by an open-end investment company, or by a unit investment trust, when shares or units are purchased. The fee is charged by the underwriter-sponsor of the fund and is shared by the underwriter and the dealer who makes the sale. Generally, the percentage fee decreases as the dollar value of the purchase increases. Funds that charge no fee are called "no-load funds."

See also SALES LOAD; NO LOAD; FRONT-END LOAD; LOAD SPREAD OPTION; LETTER OF INTENT; and RIGHT OF ACCUMULATION.

SALES LITERATURE
Any communication by a broker/dealer for distribution to customers or to the public that describes the services provided by the issuer of the sales literature. Such sales literature must be truthful and must accurately describe the services provided by the broker/dealer. Industry rules require that sales literature be approved by a person within the firm who is appointed to do so.

SALES LOAD
Commonly used term for the percentage sales charge on open-end investment company shares.
See also SALES CHARGE.

SALES WRAPPER
Term used of a broker/dealer's promotional material employed to accompany a prospectus. Technically, that material may only be a restatement of the information in the prospectus but, because it may be a more interesting synopsis, it is preferred by many firms marketing the new issue.

SALLIE MAE
See STUDENT LOAN MARKETING ASSOCIATION.

SALOMON–RUSSELL GLOBAL EQUITY INDEX
A joint effort by Salomon Brothers and the Frank Russell Company to gauge market performance of 1,572 equity securities traded in 23 different countries.
The base of the index represents approximately 81 percent of the capitalization of the participating marketplaces. The index is heavily skewed to the Russell 1,000 (q.v.) of important U.S. stocks because the index emphasizes liquidity and actively traded stocks in world markets.

SAM
Acronym for shared appreciation mortgage. It is a fixed-rate real estate loan in which the lender has an equity interest in the value appreciation that occurs during the life of the loan. Example: In return for a fixed-rate mortgage that is significantly lower than prevailing rates, a borrower stipulates that one third of any profit realized from a sale or property appreciation during the term of the mortgage will belong to the lender.

608

SAME-DAY SUBSTITUTION
The purchase and sale of marginable securities with the same dollar value on the same day in a margin account. If such a substitution is made, there is no margin call and there is no release to the special memorandum account (SMA). In practice, any decommitment (reduction of customer risk) coupled to a commitment (increase of customer risk) is considered a same-day substitution if the dollar value is the same. For example, a purchase and a long sale; a long sale and a short sale.

SAMMIE BEES
Sammie Bees are pooled Small Business Administration guaranteed loans that have been securitized as unit trust certificates. Commercial banks that make such loans organize them in pools of $1 million to $25 million. The pools, backed by the SBA, then are sold to institutional investors that seek higher-than-usual yields for prime-quality debts.

SAMURAI BOND
Slang for a debt security of a non-Japanese issuer denominated in Japanese yen. Such securities are not registered with the SEC for sale in the United States and, therefore, may not be offered to U.S. persons on an initial distribution.

S&L
See SAVINGS & LOAN ASSOCIATION.

S&P
See STANDARD & POOR'S; STANDARD & POOR'S INDEX; STANDARD & POOR'S RATING.

SANDWICH SPREAD
See BUTTERFLY SPREAD.

SANTA CLAUS RALLY
Jocular title for the anticipated year-end rally in the stock market. Historically, there has tended to be a year-end rally in anticipation of buying by institutions in early January as they receive pension fund contributions from employers.

SAO PAULO STOCK EXCHANGE
(Pronounced San Pau–loo, as in book.) The largest and most volatile of the South American stock exchanges. Most private sector securities in Brazil are traded there.

Trading is permitted between 9:30 A.M. and 1:00 P.M. on business days, with no after-hour trading permitted. Settlement is on the third business day following the trade date.

SAPCO
Acronym for single asset property company. A U.K. issuer whose sole asset collateralizing a security listed on the U.K. exchange is a single building (or a group of buildings consolidated to serve as a single asset). SAPCOs can now legitimately offer both equity and debt issues against such collateral.

SAR
See STOCK APPRECIATION RIGHTS.

SATURDAY NIGHT SPECIAL
This colorful merger and acquisition term is used to describe a quick and unexpected bid by a raider to acquire control of a company. A "Saturday night special" is designed to act fast, while the stock market is closed, to gain control before management can muster its defenses.

United Kingdom equivalent: dawn raid.

SAUCER FORMATION
Descriptive term for the graph of stock prices that approximates the shape of a saucer. If the rounded portion is on the bottom, which is the normal appearance of a saucer, the trend is considered upward. If the rounded portion is on the top, such as a saucer would appear that is upside down on a table, the trend is considered downward.

SAUCERS
Acronym for Sovereign Australian Currency Enhanced Securities. Saucers are a Bankers Trust Eurobond offering with a currency option attached. The issuer sells the bond but retains the right (an option) to redeem the bond in either U.S. or Australian funds. The option is selected just prior to the redemption date.

SAVINGS AND LOAN ASSOCIATION (S&L)
A national- or state-chartered institution that accepts savings deposits from individuals. The funds are invested in real estate mortgages and similar financial instruments. These institutions are similar to banks, but they provide fewer services than full-service commercial banks.

Savings and loan associations and savings banks are generally grouped in the popular term *thrifts* or *thrift institutions.*

SAVINGS ASSOCIATION INSURANCE FUND

An arm of the Federal Deposit Insurance Corporation (FDIC). SAIF was created under FIRREA (Financial Institutions Reform, Recovery, and Enforcement Act of 1989) to insure depositors' savings accounts, up to $100,000, at savings and loan institutions.

SAVINGS BANK

Generally, a state-chartered bank, organized as a stock or mutual company, that accepts both time and demand deposits. Deposits are invested in mortgages, real estate, government bonds, and other securities as permitted by the state banking commissioner.

SAVINGS DEPOSIT

An interest-bearing account with a banking institution from which money can normally be withdrawn without prior notice. Technically, banks can require 30 to 60 days' notice for withdrawals, but few banks have chosen to require such notice. Because the deposits are uncertain in duration, banks pay a lower rate of interest for savings deposits than they do for time deposits.

SAVRS

Acronym for Shearson Lehman's Select Auction Variable-Rate Securities, a class of municipal security issued in conjunction with residual interest bonds (RIBS). The municipal issuer contracts to pay a fixed sum of tax-exempted interest semiannually, split among two classes of debt securities holders, SAVRS and RIBS. The holders of SAVRS receive a variable amount, determined by Dutch auction every 35 days; while the holders of RIBS receive what is left over. Thus, if rates decline in the municipal market, the RIBS holders benefit with an increased portion of the residual interest. If rates increase, the RIBS holders suffer with a smaller portion of the interest pool. SAVRS have a prior claim to the available interest.

SAX

Acronym for Stockholm Automated Exchange. SAX is a fully automated trading system in Sweden's largest financial center. SAX is also fully compatible with trading systems in Copenhagen, Oslo, and Helsinki.

SAX was designed and installed by Tandem Computers (U.S.) and is linked by the Ericsson Information System so member brokers can trade from their offices, rather than be present on the floor of the exchange.

SAX is similar in function to SEAQ on the International Stock Exchange in London.

SB

Used in corporate and municipal bond calendars, these initials identify Salomon Brothers Inc a major underwriter of securities.

SBA

See SMALL BUSINESS ASSOCIATION.

SBI

Acronym for share of beneficial interest. Term often is used of an equity security that represents an undivided interest in a pool of debt securities.

SBO

Commonly used initials for: settlement balance order—a procedure now employed by the Mortgage Bond Service Clearing Corporation (MBSCC) to expedite deliveries in satisfaction of sales. This method pairs off each dealer's purchases and sales of mortgage pools by face-amount quantities. Because each pool is unique in its monthly prepayments of interest and principal, actual market values may vary by as much as 2.499%; a monetary dollar adjustment to account for these differences is processed by MBSCC each month, in the month after delivery.

SCA

See ALL SUBSEQUENT COUPONS ATTACHED.

SCALE

1. Interest rates payable for the chronological maturities of an issuer's serial debt securities.
2. A schedule of interest rate payable for time deposits of varying maturity dates. Example: The scale varies from 9.10% to 10.50% for maturities from six months to three years. The same concept applies to commercial paper if the issuer varies the interest rates according to time to maturity.
3. Used, at the time of the initial offering of bonds with serial maturity, to designate the number of bonds, the maturity date, the coupon rate of interest, and the offering price of one of the serial maturities.

The term also is used collectively of all of the bonds, their maturities, coupons, and prices for the entire issue.

SCALE ORDER

A single-order ticket that, in fact, contains multiple buy limit or sell limit orders at prices so staggered that the buyer or seller achieves an advantageous average price. For example, a buy limit order might contain the following instruction: "BUY 200 ABC 57, and 200 each half-point down. Total: 2,000 shares. The buyer wants a total position of 2,000 with an average price midway between 57 and 52½ per share."

Because of increased clerical work and the possibility of error, many member firms will not accept scale orders.

SCALPER
Slang for a marketmaker who places excessive markups, or markdowns, on transactions that involve minimum risk to himself. This activity violates the National Association of Securities Dealers' 5% guideline for fair prices and commissions.

SCALPING
An unethical practice, which may also be illegal, whereby an investment adviser or research analyst recommends a security for purchase after buying the security for a personal account. The subsequent purchases by persons who followed the recommendation pushes up the price of the security and permits the recommender to profit on the original purchase.

THE SCARLET LADY OF WALL STREET
Colorful nickname for the New York and Lake Erie Railroad, a major East Coast transportation system of the 19th century. The railroad was so called because of the many major stock manipulations during this era between Cornelius Vanderbilt and Daniel Drew. Many investors found themselves on the wrong side of the market and lost a great deal of money in these manipulations.

SCHEDULE C OF THE NASD BYLAWS
A section of the National Association of Securities Dealers (NASD) bylaws that contains the criteria which certain persons associated with a member must meet to be registered as a principal, financial principal, or representative.

SCHEDULE 13D
A Securities and Exchange Commission form that must be filed within 10 business days by anyone who acquires 5% or more of an equity security registered with the SEC under the Securities Exchange Act of 1934. Purpose: to disclose the method of acquisition of the shares and the purchaser's intentions in terms of management or control of the company.
See also SCHEDULE 13G.

SCHEDULE 13G

A short-form version of Schedule 13D. The short form is to be filed by a person who, at the end of a calendar year, owns 5% or more of an equity security of a company registered under Section 12 of the Securities Exchange Act of 1934. The short-form filing is permitted if the person acquired the securities in the ordinary course of business and if the owner does not intend to change or influence control of the company. Broker/dealers, banks, and investment companies are typical filers of Schedule 13G. It is due within 45 calendar days of year's end.

SCHULDSCHEIN

A securitized participation in a commercial loan offered by a German bank acting as private placement manager of an underwriting group. The initial certificate is issued in global form for the first 90 days and, even when available in definitive version thereafter, cannot be assigned to another owner more than three times before maturity.

SCIENTER

Latin: with knowledge, or knowingly. Used in cases of fraud. To gain a conviction under federal securities law, the Securities and Exchange Commission often must prove that the accused acted with knowledge.

SCIN

Acronym for self-cancelling installment note. A SCIN is an estate tax-savings technique for persons who do not expect to survive the minimum of 15 years required for a GRIT.

Under a SCIN, an asset is sold to an heir for an installment note with the proviso that the liability is cancelled upon the seller's death. The buyer pays a premium for the self-cancellation privilege and a market rate of interest for the installment notes. If the seller dies before the sale is completed, only the asset value above the installments already paid to that date are included in the estate.

SCORCHED EARTH TACTIC

A corporate defense tactic whereby an unwilling takeover target discourages bidders by selling off attractive assets or by entering into long-term contractual commitments. Thereby, the company makes itself less attractive to the buyer.

SCORE

Acronym for special claim on residual equity. One of the two component parts of an Americus trust. Holders of the SCORE component of the trust receive no dividends; instead, they receive any assets above a certain agreed-upon dollar value. Example: Holders of SCORE for the Americus trust on American Telephone & Telegraph shares will receive all assets above $75 per share when the trust is to be dissolved.

See also PRIME.

SCOREX SYSTEM
Acronym for Securities Communication, Order Routing, and Execution facility. This facility of the Pacific Stock Exchange enables members to automatically transmit and execute market orders up to 599 shares (300 on limit orders) at the best available price represented by all Intermarket Trading System (ITS) participants.

SCOTTISH DIVIDEND
Slang for a reverse split—that is, a split down so the shareholder owns fewer shares after the split than before.

Also known as: an Irish dividend or a Polish dividend.

SCR
Initials standing for: safe custody receipt. An SCR works in much the same way as an ADR; that is, the receipt for the security is bought and sold just as though it were the underlying security. Dividends on the underlying security are received through the custodian.

Unlike ADRs, where the actual certificates are held in the foreign branches of American banks, SCRs represent certificates held in safe-keeping by the U.K.'s Talisman system.

SCRIP
1. In the United States, it was not uncommon in the past for a corporation to issue partial shares, or scrip. Such scrip could be "rounded up" by the payment of a subscription fee, or the partial share could be sold in the marketplace. It is no longer a common practice.
2. In the United Kingdom, the term is *scrip issue* and is used when a corporation makes a stock split. A stock split, or capitalisation issue, results in more shares outstanding but no more capital in the treasury of the company.

See also CAPITALIZATION ISSUE.

SCRIPOPHILY
(Pronounced: scri–pop´-fily.) The hobby of collecting old stock and bond certificates. Such certificates have no value except for their rarity as collectors' items. Many, however, have great artistic interest because of engravings, coloration, or calligraphy.

S/D
1. When used on a customer confirmation, S/D stands for: settlement date.
2. When used in a description of municipal bonds, S/D stands for: school district.

SD
See STATUTORY DISQUALIFICATION.

SDFS
Acronym for same-day-funds settlement. SDFS is a method of settlement used by the DTC for certain securities transactions. Same-day funds are federal funds ("good money") and are paid—if both parties to the trade are properly collateralized—for transactions in U.S. government securities, short-term municipal notes, medium-term (commercial paper) notes, collateralized mortgage obligations (CMOs), auction-rate preferred issues, and certain other instruments.

Other DTC transactions are settled on the fifth business day following the trade date.

SDR
See SPECIAL DRAWING RIGHTS.

SDRT
Acronym for stamp duty reserve tax. SDRT is a levy imposed by the British government on transactions in equity securities in the United Kingdom. There is no duty if both the seller and buyer are domiciled outside the United Kingdom.

Technically, stamp duty is a re-registration tax paid on secondary transactions by the *purchaser;* thus, it is not unlike the SEC fee paid on exchange transactions in the United States by the *seller.*

SEAQ
Acronym for Stock Exchange Automated Quotations. This is the London Stock Exchange's version of NASDAQ. SEAQ permits marketmakers to give their quotes for 3,500 domestic (English) and international stocks. SEAQ entries are divided into alpha, beta, and gamma. *Alpha* stocks have firm quotes and require immediate reporting of trades. *Beta* stocks are firm, but do not require immediate reporting of trades. *Gamma* stocks are infrequently traded and quotations are subject, rather than firm.

SEAQ AUTOMATED EXECUTION FACILITY
See SAEF.

SEASONED

1. Descriptive term used of an issue that was distributed to a large number of holders and now trades frequently with good liquidity in the secondary market. For example, "With 30,000–40,000 shares trading each day, LMN is now a seasoned issue."
2. Used of Eurodebt issues that were originally issued for sale outside the United States and which were not registered with the SEC. If such an issue is actively traded for a period of time (i.e., "seasoned") it may be purchased by sophisticated U.S.-domiciled investors without violating U.S. securities laws.

The term is also used as a participial noun; for example, *seasoning*. "That issue needs a bit more seasoning before I would make a major investment in it."

SEASONED MORTGAGE

A real estate loan older than 30 months. Thus, a mortgage that has been outstanding 30 months or less is considered to be "unseasoned."

SEAT

Used as a synonym for a membership on a national securities exchange. For example, "John Jones purchased a seat on the Philadelphia Stock Exchange."

In recent years some of the exchanges have permitted members to lease seats to others; the person who leases the seat is permitted to perform the functions of a member.

SEATS

Acronym for Stock Exchange Automated Trading System. SEATS is an electronic trading system used to coordinate trading activity on the different marketplaces known collectively as the Australia Stock Exchange.

SEC

See SECURITIES AND EXCHANGE COMMISSION and SEC RULES.

SEC FEE

A statutory fee of one cent per $300, or fraction thereof, levied on the sale of equity securities registered on an exchange, no matter where the transaction takes place. Traditionally, the fee is paid by the seller. Principal exceptions: registered new issues, listed options, private placements, the exercise of a warrant or a right, conversion of a convertible security, or a sale as a result of a tender offer or exchange.

SECONDARY DISTRIBUTION

Generically, any sale of securities, whether by an effective registration or not, made by a selling holder of the bonds or stocks. More specifically, a method of selling a large block of securities to investors by a previous holder. Such distributions may be "spot secondaries," if their sale is not SEC registered, or "registered secondaries," if the sale is registered. Such sales are made at a net price, with all sales charges paid by the seller. Secondary distributions, although they are made over-the-counter, are normally announced on the exchange tape before the transaction, and buy limit orders on the specialist's book at or above the price of the distribution will be executed at the distribution price.

SECONDARY DOOMSDAY VALUE

For purposes of determining capital gains tax liability in the United Kingdom after April 6, 1982, all purchase transactions are adjusted to the English retail price index to establish a basis cost. Investors, therefore, are not penalized just because of inflation when they sell.

The dates of reference and the benchmarks are different, hence, "secondary."

SECONDARY FINANCING

Term used to identify borrowings that use loans subordinated to previous loans on the same collateral. Example: Second and subsequent mortgage bonds issued by corporations are forms of secondary financing.

SECONDARY MARKET

General term for the place where issued and outstanding securities are sold. The term includes both exchanges and the over-the-counter market. Distinguished from the primary market, which is the method of selling new issues so the proceeds of the sale go to the issuer.

SECONDHAND OPTION

See SPECIAL OPTION.

SECOND MARKET

Occasionally used to designate the over-the-counter (OTC) market. Concept: The exchanges are the first market; the OTC is the second market; those dealers in the OTC market who specialize in the trading of listed securities are the third market.

SECOND-ROUND FINANCING
Colorful term used to designate product development costs for a relatively new business concern.

These funds are generally provided by the same venture capital firm(s) that provided the original seed money for the new business. Invariably, such capital contributions are made in exchange for equity in the company.

SECPS
Acronym for Securities and Exchange Commission Practice Section. SECPS is a division of the AICPA.

SECPS is comprised of CPA firms that conduct almost 90% of the audits of publicly traded firms. Its goal is to make sure that those companies comply with the SEC's financial reporting requirements and procedures.

SEC REGULATIONS
See SEC RULES.

SEC RULES
The following rules of the Securities and Exchange Commission often are used in the jargon of the industry. The rules, with their numbers, are identified by the following entries. This identification is not meant to be an explanation of the rule. Many of these rules are so complex, and have further SEC and legal interpretations, that advice of counsel is needed.

The order of the SEC rules is by number, as opposed to the letter-by-letter order in the rest of this glossary.

SEC RULE 10a-1
The so-called plus-tick rule. This rule prohibits the short sale of securities registered on an exchange unless the sale, wherever made, is effected at a price that is above the last different regular-way transaction on the principal exchange where the security is traded. Thus, under this rule, a short sale of ABC common stock, following transactions at $19\frac{1}{2}$ and 19, could only be made at $19\frac{1}{8}$ or above.

See also ZERO-PLUS TICK.

SEC RULE 10b-2
This rule forbids anyone from soliciting purchase orders for a security on an exchange while involved in a distribution (i.e., a sale) of that same issue.

SEC RULE 10b-4

The rule forbids the short sale of securities in response to a tender offer. Thus, a person could not sell borrowed securities to a person making a tender offer to buy.

SEC RULE 10b-6

This rule prohibits issuers, underwriters, broker/dealers, or anyone with an interest in a distribution of securities from purchasing, or inducing anyone else to purchase, the issue prior to the start of the public offering.

Underwriters, however, may accept indications of interest in such issues from prospective buyers, but no sales may be made.

SEC RULE 10b-7

The rule sets the terms and conditions under which an underwriter may use a stabilizing bid to facilitate a distribution of securities.

SEC RULE 10b-8

This rule prohibits the manipulation of the open-market price for a security by persons involved in the distribution of that security through a rights offering.

SEC RULE 10b-10

This rule regulates the preparation and distribution of purchase or of sale confirmations by a broker/dealer to customers. The rule sets forth the minimum information required, the necessary disclosures required, and the frequency of such confirmations to customers.

SEC RULE 10b-13

The rule prohibits persons involved in an exchange or tender offer from making other purchases of the same security, either publicly or privately, until the tender offer has expired.

SEC RULE 10b-16

This rule, which is the security industry's response to the truth-in-lending law, requires broker/dealers who extend credit to customers (e.g., a margin-account customer) to provide complete information about the financing terms, conditions, and arrangements.

SEC RULE 10b-18

Also known as the "safe harbor" rule, this rule permits issuers and their affiliated accounts to repurchase their own common stock without charges of market manipulation. The rule sets forth the conditions under which such purchases may be made.

SEC RULE 11A

A series of paragraphs that govern the trading by exchange members for their own accounts.

SEC RULE 13D

This rule, which has subnumbers 1 through 7, require the filing of certain disclosures by anyone who acquires a beneficial ownership of 5% or more in any equity security registered with the SEC.

SEC RULE 13E

This rule, which has subnumbers 1 through 4, regulates the purchases by an issuer, or an affiliate of the issuer, of its own securities in the public marketplace.

SEC RULE 14A

This rule governs the preparation and distribution of proxy material to stockholders. It also sets forth the kind of information that must be included with the proxy statement, the supporting documents, the format, and the need for prior submission to the SEC of such material.

SEC RULE 15c2-1

This rule regulates the safekeeping of customers' securities left with a broker following their purchase in a margin account.

In substance, the rule prohibits commingling customers' securities with the broker's securities and prohibits the broker from hypothecating more of the securities than is justified by the customers' indebtedness to the broker.

SEC RULE 15c2-6

Popularly known as the "penny stock rule," this is an attempt by the SEC to cut down investor fraud in the marketing of low-priced securities. The rule establishes a suitability test, and a "cooling off" period for shares selling at less than $5 if the company has less than $2 million in tangible assets. There is an exemption for low-priced shares that are exchange-listed or NASDAQ-traded.

SEC RULE 15c2-11

This rule prohibits a broker/dealer from submitting quotations for publication in any quotation medium unless it has in its records such specific information about the issuer as would normally be required to make an intelligent investment decision. The rule outlines the kinds of information required.

In effect, the broker/dealer not only has to know its customers, it has to know its companies if it is to act as a marketmaker.

SEC RULE 15c3-1

The "net capital" rule governing the liquid capital that a broker/dealer must maintain in terms of his aggregate indebtedness to customers. The rule dictates the minimum net capital and the ratio of debt-to-equity capital of a broker/dealer; but from the viewpoint of a member firm customer, the most important aspect is the coverage that a broker/dealer's net capital provides for customer indebtedness.

Although other measurement criteria may be used, the rule of thumb is that customer-related indebtedness may not exceed net capital by more than 15 to 1.

SEC RULE 15c3-2

This rule governs the use of credit balances left with a broker/dealer by a customer, if the credit balance may be freely withdrawn. The rule requires a broker/dealer to notify customers that such credit balances may be withdrawn at any time. If the customer does not request the withdrawal of these balances, the broker/dealer may use the credit balance in the conduct of its ordinary course of business. The customer, of course, retains his or her right to the money left on deposit with the broker/dealer.

SEC RULE 15c3-3

This rule regulates the handling of fully paid securities and money on deposit with a broker/dealer. In substance, the rule requires the proper segregation of customer securities that are fully paid and requires that, at least weekly, money on deposit be deposited in a special account for the benefit of all customers of that broker/dealer.

SEC RULE 16a-1

This rule mandates that officers, directors, and principal stockholders (10% or more) must file reports of beneficial ownership of any equity security they hold in their company, if that issue is registered. The rule also requires that additional reports must be filed each time their previous position is increased or decreased.

SEC RULES 17a-3 and 17a-4

Rules that establish the recordkeeping and maintenance requirements of broker/dealers. The rules set forth the documents that must be prepared, maintained, and preserved for regulatory enquiries.

SEC RULE 17a-8

This rule parallels the Foreign Currency Transaction Reporting Act of 1970. Under this rule, broker/dealers must report to the U.S. Treasury or the IRS: (1) receipt or transfer of U.S. currency in excess of $10,000; (2)

the import or export of any country's currency in excess of $5,000; (3) a bank securities or other financial-type account in any foreign country in which a citizen or resident has an interest.

SEC RULE 17a-12
Rule that sets forth the filing requirements for broker/dealers who make markets in over-the-counter margin securities and who obtain preferential credit terms to finance these positions.

SEC RULE 17a-17
Rule that sets forth criteria by which broker/dealers can register with the SEC as block positioners and obtain preferential credit terms to finance their positions.

SEC RULE 17f-1
This rule requires that broker/dealers, banks, and transfer agents report promptly any knowledge of lost, stolen, counterfeit, or misplaced securities to a centralized computer service maintained for this purpose. This service, called the National Crime Information Center (NCIC), acts as a central clearing service for anyone who wishes to inquire about the report of a missing or stolen security.

SEC RULE 17f-2
Rule that necessitates the taking of fingerprints of virtually every employee, partner, or officer of a broker/dealer as a condition of affiliation with that concern. The fingerprints are then submitted to the Attorney General of the United States for identification and background validation.

SEC RULE 19b-3
Rule that forbids the fixing of commissions and floor brokerage rates by any national securities exchange.

SEC RULE 19c-3
This rule permits securities listed on an exchange after April 26, 1979, to be traded by exchange members on or off the exchange, as they see fit. Purpose: to establish an experiment for the widest possible market for listed securities.

SEC RULE 19c-4
See ONE SHARE, ONE VOTE RULE.

SEC RULE 134

Rule that defines the type of language that may be used by a dealer in conjunction with the sale of a registered offering. The rule provides a guideline for materials prepared about issuers, and it outlines information that is not deemed to be a prospectus subject to the stringent restrictions that apply prior to the effective date.

SEC RULE 144

In substance, this rule permits a holder of unregistered securities to make a public sale of such securities, without the need for a formal registration statement, if certain conditions are met. The rule is complex and legal advice is needed, but as a rule of thumb, sales that represent less than 1% of outstanding shares during a 90 day low value period will not require a formal registration with the SEC.

SEC RULE 145

This rule sets forth the conditions under which persons who receive securities as a result of a reclassification, merger, consolidation, or transfer of corporate assets may sell these securities without the need for an effective registration statement.

SEC RULE 147

Rule that defines the terms and conditions under which a resident issuer may make an intrastate public offering of a security without the need to register the sale with the SEC.

SEC RULE 156

This rule prohibits the issuance or use of false or misleading sales literature in conjunction with the sale of investment company securities.

SEC RULE 174

This rule lists the circumstances under which a dealer must continue to deliver a prospectus in connection with secondary market transactions in securities that were recently registered.

SEC RULE 254

This rule sets forth the dollar limitations on sales made under the provisions of Regulation A. At present, issuers may sell securities worth $1.5 million or less—using a short-form registration and providing buyers with an offering circular—without the need for a full and formal registration with the SEC.

SEC RULE 415
Rule pertaining to the public offering of securities by means of a shelf registration. Under this rule, qualified issuers may register an offering to be sold at prevailing market prices over the next two years.

SEC RULE 433
This rule outlines the conditions under which a dealer may use a preliminary (i.e., a "red herring") prospectus.

SECTOR
A term used to describe bonds of the same class with similar ratings, coupons, and maturities. For example, the Salomon AA utility bond index or the Daily Bond Buyer 20-bond and 11-bond indices are based on the concept of sector. The presumption is that bonds in the same sector will have similar price and yield movements.

SECULAR TRUST
Secular, from the Latin *saeculum*, meaning long term. A secular trust is a form of deferred compensation on which the tax rate is frozen at 28%. The amount deferred is immediately taxed at 28%, and the trust pays an annual tax of 28% on dividends and interest received and realized long-term capital gains. New funds can be deposited into the trust after the 28% tax is paid.

The trust is qualified under ERISA and is so established that it cannot be appropriated in the event of a hostile takeover. Because taxes are paid on a current basis, there is no further obligation when funds are distributed.

SECURED BOND
Term used of bonds if the issuer, in the bond indenture, has set aside certain identifiable assets as collateral for the prompt payment of interest and the repayment of the principal. In a default the bondholder, through the trustee, can lay claim to the asset. Generally, the asset has a greater value than the outstanding claim of the bondholder.

SECURED DEBT
As a general rule, this term is used as a synonym for secured bond.

SECURED LOAN
Any borrowing arrangement that is collateralized by marketable securities. Example: Margin loans advanced by broker/dealers to their customers are secured loans, because the securities purchased are held by the broker/dealer as collateral. In the event the borrower defaults, the holder of the securities can sell them to recover the money loaned.

SECURITIES ACT OF 1933

Federal law that requires adequate disclosure of the facts about new issues of securities sold to the public. The disclosure is made by the filing of a registration statement with the SEC and the delivery of a prospectus to the original purchaser. The law exempts many securities from such disclosure (exempt securities) and many transactions are not required to be registered. As a rule of thumb, however, public and interstate transactions of corporate securities come under the requirements of the Securities Act of 1933.

SECURITIES AND EXCHANGE COMMISSION

A federal agency, established by the Securities Exchange Act of 1934 as amended, that has five commissioners appointed by the President with the advice and consent of the Senate of the United States.

The powers of the commission include the interpretation, supervision, and enforcement of the securities laws of the United States. The commission has the authority to bring administrative proceedings against firms and persons registered with the SEC, but allegations of criminal violations of the law must be prosecuted by the Department of Justice.

SECURITIES & INVESTMENT BOARD

See SIB.

THE SECURITIES ASSOCIATION (TSA)

The Securities Association is the successor to the merged London Stock Exchange and the International Securities Regulatory Organization (ISRO). As a new SRO, the Securities Association will have administrative responsibility for the combined membership, including business authorizations and capital compliance oversight, under SIB rules.

THE SECURITIES DEALERS ASSOCIATION OF JAPAN

See JASD.

SECURITIES EXCHANGE ACT OF 1934

This law, which is a keystone in the regulation of securities markets, governs exchanges, over-the-counter markets, broker/dealers, the conduct of secondary markets, the extension of credit in the purchase and sale of securities, the conduct of corporate insiders, and principally the prohibition of fraud and manipulation in securities transactions.

This law also outlines the powers of the Securities and Exchange Commission to interpret, supervise, and enforce the securities laws of the United States. Enforcement includes all but the civil and criminal aspects of the Securities Exchange Act of 1934.

SECURITIES EXCHANGE OF THAILAND (SET)
Located in Bangkok, the SET is a prominent Asian exchange. Trading is conducted daily from 9:30 until 11:30 A.M., with settlement on the third business day after trade date.

SET is dominated by local banks and cement companies and there is a strict limitation on the extent of foreign ownership of companies listed on the exchange. In fact, share transfers are halted when this limit has been reached.

SECURITIES INDUSTRY ASSOCIATION (SIA)
It has two functions: to promote instruction of member employees and to lobby for the interest of the members of the association.

Many exchange member organizations and many NASD members belong to the SIA; to this extent, the SIA may be considered to be representative of the broker-dealers who buy and sell nonexempt securities.

SECURITIES INDUSTRY AUTOMATION CORPORATION (SIAC)
Owned by the New York and American stock exchanges, SIAC operates automated communication systems that support trading, surveillance, and market data for these exchanges. These data, in turn, are provided to the National Security Clearing Corporation (NSCC), the Consolidated Tape Association (CTA), the Consolidated Quotation System (CQS), and the Intermarket Trading System (ITS).

SECURITIES INDUSTRY COMMITTEE ON ARBITRATION
See SICA.

SECURITIES INFORMATION CORPORATION
Initials: SIC. SIC is a private firm that works under contract for the SEC to serve as a clearinghouse of information about lost, stolen, or missing securities. SEC Rule 17f-1 sets the provisions for compliance by broker/dealers and banks.

SECURITIES INVESTORS PROTECTION CORPORATION
A nonprofit corporation, under the provisions of the Securities Investors Protection Act of 1970, that will provide protection to customers of insured members in the event of the member's insolvency. The upper limit of protection is $500,000 per customer account. Of this amount, no more than $100,000 may represent cash left with the member.

SECURITIES LOAN
Term refers to the lending of stock or bond certificates to another broker/dealer principally for use in the completion of short sales. The borrowing broker/dealer must fully collateralize the loan of the certificates with

cash equal to the full market value of the certificates to protect the lending broker, or the broker's customer if the certificates, in turn, were borrowed from a customer.

Commonly called a "stock loan."

SECURITY

An instrument, usually freely transferable, that evidences ownership (stock) or creditorship (bond) in a corporation, a federal or state government, an agency thereof, or a legal trust. The courts also have included evidences of indirect ownership in the definition. For example, rights, warrants, options, and partnership participations.

The term also is used of property, whether a security or not, pledged as collateral for a loan. For example, an issuer of bonds pledged its plant and equipment as security for an issue of mortgage bonds.

SECURITY PURCHASE CONTRACT

Acronym: SPC. A unique security that is issued as a debt instrument and that changes into an equity security of the same issuer after a predetermined period. The changeover is mandatory at that time, although the holder may exchange for equity securities at an earlier date. In the early 1980s, some large banks used this financing technique to raise equity capital although it is technically a liability for the first 10 years.

SECURITY TRADERS' ASSOCIATION OF NEW YORK

See STANY.

SEDOL

Acronym for Stock Exchange Daily Official List. SEDOL is similar in concept to CUSIP in the United States. It is a seven-character number assigned to each of about 6,000 issues admitted to trading on London's International Stock Exchange. Thus, SEDOL is used as an identifier for comparing, clearing, and settling transactions made on the ISE floor.

SEED MONEY

Term used by venture capitalists for the initial expansion of new corporations. This may involve building a plant, further exploring a process of manufacturing, or initial marketing endeavors. In exchange for the seed money, the venture capitalists take an equity interest in the enterprise.

SEEK A MARKET

To try to get a transaction.

SEER

A prophet or oracle, thus a person with great foresight. The term is used in the financial industry to describe someone who makes accurate predictions about the market's movements. Many technical, market, and economic analysts have deserved reputations as "seers" and their suggestions are eagerly followed.

The term is similar in concept to *gnome*. Gnome, however, emphasizes the expertness of the person; seer emphasizes the predictive ability of the person.

SEE-WEE

Phonetic expansion of the NYSE ticker symbol CWE, Commonwealth Edison Corporation. It is used by floor traders to designate trades in the stock of that large electric utility that services the Chicago area.

SEGREGATED SECURITIES

Industry term for customer securities that must be kept in a separate place and which may not be used by the broker/dealer in the conduct of the firm's business. Fully paid securities in cash accounts and securities in margin accounts—over and above the amount needed to collateralize the client's debit balance with the broker—must be segregated.

Normal practice: segregate securities in a separate vault on the broker's premises or leave them on deposit with an industry depository (e.g., the Depository Trust Corporation).

SEGREGATION

The act of segregating (i.e., keeping separate) customer securities from securities owned by the broker in its proprietary accounts.

In practice, fully paid securities owned by customers and that portion of margin-account securities, over and above the amount required to collateralize the broker's loan to the client, are segregated in accordance with federal law. In no case may the broker hold more than 140% of the customer's debit balance in the form of collateral for the loan made in margin accounts.

Antonym for segregate: to commingle (i.e., to mix customer-owned securities and broker-owned securities and to use them in the conduct of business).

SEGREGATION ACCOUNT 100

This is a special account at the DTC for shares of communications and maritime issues held by members for foreign owners.

Because there are legal limitations on the extent of foreign ownership of most of these issues, DTC used to require registration of beneficial ownership and would not hold such certificates in street name. Now, such securities may be held in nominee name if they are put into this special account where foreign ownership is readily identified.

SEGREGATION OF INFORMATION PRINCIPLES
A popular term for the internal rules within member firms whereby confidential information obtained from issuers by investment banking and research employees is kept secret from sales and trading personnel who might be tempted to use it illegally.

The concept of such separation of information within the firm is also known by the colorful term *Chinese wall.*

SELECT AUCTION VARIABLE-RATE SECURITIES
See SAVRS.

SELECTED DEALER AGREEMENT
Official term for the selling group agreement used by the underwriting syndicate in the distribution of securities. The selected dealer agreement sets forth the rights and responsibilities of selling group members, particularly the obligation to market the securities only at the public offering price established by the syndicate.

SELF-CANCELLING INSTALLMENT NOTE
See SCIN.

SELF-LIQUIDATING ASSET PURCHASE
Acronym: SLAP. Term used in corporate finance to identify the purchase of a company with a large cash flow by means of newly issued debt. The idea is to retire the debt as quickly as possible with the cash flow. Thus, in a few years, the purchasers will own the asset free and clear; this, in turn, will enhance the value of the common stock of the company.

SELF-REGULATORY ORGANIZATION
See SRO.

SELF-SUPPORTING
Term used in the analysis of municipal securities if the revenues generated by a project are sufficient to pay the debt service without any additional revenues from another source. For example, "The bridge tolls make the revenue bonds self-supporting."

SELF TENDER
An offer by the issuing company to repurchase a specific number or percentage of its outstanding shares. Using cash or other assets in ex-

change for these shares, companies sometimes use this tactic to equal or to top the bid made by a corporate raider that is endeavoring to take over the company.

SELL
To transfer ownership for a monetary consideration. The term is used in conjunction with the disposition of specific quantities of stocks, bonds, or other financial assets.

TO SELL A BEAR
Colorful English expression for a short sale. The term originated in the 18th century when bear skins were actually traded. A person who sold skins before the bears were actually caught in anticipation of a drop in bear skin prices was said to "sell a bear." Thus, short sellers anticipate a drop in prices and are said to be "bearish."

SELL AT BEST
Instruction used by over-the-counter traders when using other broker/dealers to help them sell portions of a market order. In effect, the instruction directs the sale at the best available bid price.

SELLER'S MARKET
A market condition in which prospective demand so exceeds supply that potential sellers can dictate prices and sale terms on most transactions.
   Antonym: buyer's market.

SELLER'S OPTION
A securities contract that establishes the contract price for securities and, in the case of bonds, the amount of accrued interest to be paid by the buyer to the seller, but which permits the seller to deliver the securities to the office of the buyer at a later date, within the provisions of the contract. For example, a seller's option 60 establishes all of the details of the sale, but the seller may deliver the security to the buyer any time following the 7th calendar day up to and including the 60th calendar day following the trade.

SELLING AWAY
A euphemism for the illegal practice whereby registered representatives (RRs) conduct business that is not recorded on the books and records of the employing broker/dealer while utilizing the reputation and facilities of their employer.
   The private placement of securities and the sale of questionable tax shelters are examples of "selling away" that have been discovered in the past. Registered representatives are agents of the broker/dealer,

and the broker/dealer has a right to know and approve the business done by its employees.

SELLING CLIMAX
Term used by technical analysts of a downward price trend that is suddenly marked by an increase in volume and a dramatic price drop.

Generally, the selling climax is marked by a "gap" (i.e., a series of transactions with volume that are below previously established lows for the security).

Technical analysts consider a selling climax as an overreaction and use it to predict a rise in the security's value, at least to the point where the gap occurred.

SELLING CONCESSION
Industry term for the fee that will be paid to selling group members for each unit of the offering they sell. It is not unusual for the selling concession to be 50% or more of the underwriting spread on an issue. For example, bonds were purchased at $98^{1}/_{2}$ to be reoffered at par with a $^{3}/_{4}$-point concession. The gross underwriting spread is $15 ($1^{1}/_{2}$ points), and a selling group member who sells a bond will receive $7.50 ($^{3}/_{4}$ point).

SELLING DIVIDENDS
The unethical practice whereby a representative persuades a client to purchase investment company securities solely to obtain a soon-to-be-paid dividend. The practice is unfair because the dividend is already included in the net asset value for the fund; thus, the customer, in effect, is paying for the dividend with his own funds.

SELLING GROUP
Popular name for dealers who associate with the underwriting syndicate in the marketing of a distribution of securities. The selling group has no financial involvement in the distribution; instead, on an agency basis, it agrees to sell portions of the issue to its customers. If successful, selling group members receive a concession, or selling commission, for these sales.

SELLING THE CROWN JEWELS
Slang term used in corporate finance to describe a defense used by a takeover target opposed to a forced merger. Under it, the target company sells certain valuable assets to make it a less attractive takeover candidate.

See also SCORCHED EARTH TACTIC.

SELLING THE ORDER FLOW

A colorful expression that describes the handling of large institutional orders for securities. Thus, upon receipt of a block trade, a member firm will often shop the order with other customers to see if there is a contra order. This will facilitate the trade and lessen the risk to the broker/dealer if it must take the other side of the trade; or to the customer if a larger order is "dumped" on the auction market or on the third market (the over-the-counter market).

SELLING THE SPREAD

A term used in the options and futures marketplaces to describe the simultaneous *purchase* of a contract in a nearby month and the *sale* of a contract in a far out month. In options, if the strike price is the same, the far out month should have a larger premium than the nearby month and the person "selling the spread" receives a credit for the difference in the premiums. In the futures market, particularly if it is a "carrying charge market," there should also be a net credit.

SELL OUT

Industry term for the procedure whereby a broker/dealer liquidates client holdings that were purchased on behalf of the client but have not yet been paid by the client in accordance with the terms of the contract.

The term also is used if a buying broker fails to pay for securities bought from a selling broker. Sell outs are made at the best available market price, and the buyer is responsible for any financial loss suffered by the broker.

SELL-OUT PROCEDURE

The seller's remedy if the purchasing broker/dealer in a contract between two broker/dealers fails to accept and pay for the purchased securities without a legitimate reason for refusal. The selling broker/dealer can sell those securities at the best available market price without giving notice to the defaulting purchaser. The seller can also hold the buyer responsible for any financial loss resulting from his default.

Also called "close-out."

See also BUY-IN PROCEDURE.

SELL PLUS

Instruction sometimes used on a market order for exchange-traded securities. The instruction requests that the sale be made at a price higher than the last differently priced transaction in the security.

The instruction is used by selling clients who do not want to sell on downticks. The instruction is not used on orders to sell short; by federal law, such sales may not be made on downticks.

SELL SIGNAL

A term used by chartists. It means that the technical measurements of previous price movements indicate that this is the appropriate time to sell.

Generally, a sell signal occurs when the price of a security fails to break through a resistance level, or if the price breaks down through a previously established upward trend. Market volume is an important consideration.

SELL STOP ORDER

An instruction that may be placed on orders to be transacted on an exchange. The instruction tells the broker to sell at the market when and if there is a transaction at or below the stop price designated on the order. For example, Sell Long 500 ABC 27 STOP. When and if there is a transaction at 27 or below, the broker is instructed to sell 500 ABC at the market.

Also called a "stop-loss order." The American Stock Exchange permits such orders only if the customer also provides a limit price equal to the stop price. For example, Sell Long 500 LMN 29 STOP 29 LIMIT.

SELL THE BOOK

A seller's instruction: "Sell as many shares as you can at the prevailing best bid on the exchanges where the security trades."

The instruction includes sales at that price to broker/dealers in the crowd who are willing to accept the same price.

SENIOR REGISTERED OPTION PRINCIPAL

An officer or general partner specifically designated with overall authority and responsibility for customer options transactions and accounts.

The SROP may also be the CROP (the compliance registered option principal). In this latter capacity, the option principal has responsibility for advertising, sales literature, and training in option transactions for the member firm. In many firms, the SROP and the CROP are different persons.

SEP

See SIMPLIFIED EMPLOYEE PENSION PLAN.

SEPARATE ACCOUNT

Term used of variable annuities. Because the risk is borne by the investor in a variable annuity, the issuer may not commingle funds invested in the variable annuity with the general funds of the issuer; such funds are invested in a separate account. Although the separate account may contain individual securities, the most common investment is in a "market basket" of other securities having objectives similar to those set forth in the prospectus of the variable annuity.

SEPARATE CUSTOMER
Term used in conjunction with the protection offered under the Securities Investor Protection Corporation (SIPC). The maximum protection is by separate customer; thus, accounts that are bookkeeping formalities, such as cash, margin, and special bond account, are grouped as if they are in the name of the same customer. However, accounts with differing ownerships (e.g., an individual's account and a joint account with a spouse) are not grouped and are considered separate customer accounts for purposes of SIPC protection.

SEPON
Acronym for stock exchange pool nominees. SEPON is a common pot of securities on an issue-by-issue basis in which stock exchange members may have a specific interest as a partner participant, based on their daily trade activities.

SEPON is not unlike the DTC's use of a nominee pool, under the common nominee name of CEDE, in which member security interests are registered.

SEQUAL
A melding of the terms *SEAQ* and *QUALITY* transactions.

The program is still a pilot. The concept is to have an on-line computer matching system for trades in non-British equities. Under SEQUAL, within five minutes of the trade, the details are displayed within the system to the participants for comparison and confirmation. Once done, the trade is "locked in" and subject to settlement and transfer of the underlying securities.

SEQUENTIAL TRANSACTIONS
A flurry of trading activity in the same issue on a stock exchange. The transactions may be at the same or of varying prices. In the event of sequential transactions, the report on the ticker tape gives them in consecutive order by volume and price but without a repetition of the stock symbol. Example: Sequential transactions in Ford Motor Company common stock could appear on the ticker tape as:

F

5s 57.2s 57¹/₈.10s 57.45s 57

SERIAL BOND

An expression for a bond offering so issued that portions of the debt are redeemed each year.

Serial bonds always are identified as such, and the individual bond certificate designates the time of its maturity. Bonds that may be subject to premature redemption—either through a full or partial call or through the operation of a sinking fund—are not designated as serial bonds.

Serial bonds are a common form of municipal bond offerings.

SERIAL CATS

Evidences of ownership of the semiannual interest payment on a collection of U.S. Treasury notes or bonds. Because only one payment of cash will be received by the owner, serial cats are effectively zero-coupon bonds.

Evidences of ownership of the underlying bond, as opposed to the interest payments, are called "principal CATS."

See also CATS.

SERIES E BONDS

Government savings bonds issued from the time of World War II until December 31, 1979. They have been replaced with Series EE bonds. Outstanding Series E bonds continue to bear interest, but, by congressional action, bonds held for 40 years or more cease to bear interest, although these bonds may be exchanged for Series EE bonds or Series HH bonds.

SERIES EE BONDS

Nontransferable U.S. government bonds issued in denominations of $50 to $10,000. The bonds are purchased at 50% of their face value and mature at face value, although they continue to bear interest if held for a longer period. Since 1982, the interest rate has been pegged to a prestated percentage of the average interest rate on other Treasury securities and will vary accordingly.

No distribution of interest is made until the holder redeems the bonds. Holders may choose to pay income tax on the interest as it accrues, but most choose to pay the tax only when bonds are redeemed.

Commonly called "savings bonds."

See also SERIES HH BONDS.

SERIES H BONDS

These were non-marketable savings bonds sold by the U.S. Treasury until December 31, 1979 when they were replaced by Series HH bonds. The principal difference between the two issues is that the HH bond pays interest at a level rate throughout its lifetime while the H bond carried a balloon rate in its early years, levelling off later.

SERIES HH BONDS

Nontransferable U.S. government bonds that pay semiannual interest directly to the registered owner. Prior to 1982, Series HH bonds could be purchased directly. Now, these bonds are available only in exchange for Series EE bonds. The exchange is advantageous for holders of Series EE bonds because it continues the tax sheltering of the interest previously accrued, but not paid out, on the Series EE bonds until the newly acquired Series HH bonds are redeemed. However, current taxes are payable on the interest earned on the Series HH bonds acquired by exchange.

Commonly called "current-income bonds."

See also SERIES EE BONDS.

SERIES OF OPTION

A class of option on the same underlying security with same expiration date and same exercise (strike) price. Thus, the Merrill Lynch January 20 calls form a series of option. The IBM March 120 puts would form another series of option.

Currently, the newspaper listing of option transactions uses "r" if no trades in an option series occurred; an "s" if a series is not available for trading.

SERIES 7 REGISTERED

Industry term used to describe an employee of a member broker/dealer who has qualified to be a registered representative by passing an NYSE/NASD six-hour industry examination.

The term is also used of persons who previously qualified and thus were "grandfathered" and did not have to take the Series 7 examination. In certain circumstances, the NASD will consider waiving the exam for persons with extensive industry experience.

SERP

Acronym for supplemental executive retirement plan. SERPs are enhanced pension plans for key executives. Because of ERISA rules regarding "top-heavy" plans, they are usually not funded by company contributions; instead, they are funded by the employees themselves. On the other hand, they are not under the control of an acquiring group in case of an unfriendly merger.

SERVICING A MORTGAGE

The work responsibilities involved in loan analysis, bookkeeping, delinquency follow-up, and the preparation of financial statements for a pool of mortgages. When banks pool such mortgages and agree to service the mortgage, they charge a fee. This fee is subtracted from the mortgage payments made by the borrowers. The remainder of the payment is passed through to the lenders. This concept of a fee for servicing the mortgages lies beneath many mortgage-backed securities.

SES

Initials for: Stock Exchange of Singapore. Trading is conducted on three separate trading sessions on each working day, and settlement is on the fifth business day following the trade date. "Fails" are not condoned.

SESDAQ

Acronym for Stock Exchange of Singapore Dealing and Automated Quotation System. SESDAQ is similar to NASDAQ in the United States. Second tier stocks (i.e., those that do not qualify for listing on the SES) are traded through SESDAQ. In this way, SESDAQ acts as an adjunct to the floor trading on SES.

SET

See SECURITIES EXCHANGE OF THAILAND.

SET-ASIDE

An expression developed in the 1980s to describe the percentage of underwritten securities reserved for minority broker/dealer organizations. Set-asides are typically found in municipal issues where minority-run broker/dealers may have influence on the underlying issuers, but they are now beginning to show up in corporate underwritings, also.

SETTLE

Industry term for the completion of a securities transaction (i.e., a buyer pays for and a seller delivers the security purchased to the buyer).

In industry jargon, the term *clear* is commonly used as a synonym for *settle* if transactions between broker/dealers are being discussed. Thus, Broker A and B cleared the transaction, but Broker A and his customer settled the transaction.

SETTLEMENT BALANCE ORDER

See SBO.

SETTLEMENT DATE (S/D)

The date on which a securities contract, by prearranged agreement, must be cleared or settled.

In the primary market, only when-issued settlement is available; when the securities are available, a specific settlement date will be established.

In the secondary market, "regular-way settlement" is the normal contract: payment or delivery is due on the fifth business day after the trade date.

For listed options, regular-way settlement is the next business day, just as it is for government securities.

Contracts for same-day settlement (cash) or delayed-delivery settlement (seller's option) also may be negotiated in secondary market transactions.

Also called "delivery date."

SETTLEMENT DAY

The day on which payment and transfer of security requirements (if any) must be met.

1. In the United States, settlement day is based on trade date. In general, it is the fifth business day following trade date for secondary trades in stocks and bonds. The exceptions are governments, agencies, and listed options that settle on the business day following trade date.
2. In the United Kingdom, settlement day is based on the account period, a two-week period in which all trades are "netted." It is usually the seventh business day following the end of the account period.
3. In other countries, there are fixed days for settlement. The Italian exchanges are an apparent exception because long delays are the rule. Such delays seriously impede the efficient running of these exchanges.

SEVENTY PERCENT EXCLUSION

Commonly written: 70% exclusion.

Feature of the federal tax law that permits 70% of the cash dividends received by one domestic corporation from another domestic corporation to be excluded from taxable income. Taxes are paid at corporate rates on the remaining 30%.

Tax advice is needed because dividends from some domestic corporations are not eligible for the exclusion.

SEVERALLY AND JOINTLY

Used of underwritings where the syndicate members agree to purchase an issue and are both individually (severally) and as an account (jointly) responsible for the purchase price of the securities.

Such underwriting accounts are called "Eastern accounts" and are commonly used in the underwriting of municipal issues.

SEVERALLY BUT NOT JOINTLY
Used of underwritings where the syndicate members agree to individually purchase a specific portion of the issue (severally), but they are not responsible as a group (but not jointly) for unsold securities.

Commonly used in corporate underwritings. For example, Underwriters A and B make such an underwriting agreement. A sells his total takedown; B only sells two thirds of his. Underwriter A has no obligation for the securities unsold by B.

When used of municipal underwritings, the term *Western account* is used of this financial arrangement.

SF
See SINKING FUND.

SFN
See SWISS FRANC NOTE.

SGB EFFECT
A European term derived from the aborted attempt to take over the Societe General de Belgique in 1988. Because of the bad aftereffects, many companies have adopted antitakeover measures modeled after the "poison pill" measures in the United States.

SHADOW BOND
Name for a municipal security issued outside of the credit constraints of the underlying legal entity. Consequently, the creditability and the collateral securing that obligation are subject to question. Because of these unknown factors, such bonds carry interest premiums, in comparison to other municipal issues.

SHADOW CALENDAR
Industry slang for issues in registration with the SEC for which no approximate effective date is available. The backup in the processing of the registrations often is the result of a backlog of work at the commission or because of unsettled market conditions.

SHARE
A unit of ownership of a corporation. The basic proportion of such ownership is established by the corporate charter, which states the number of authorized shares that may be issued. However, the practical value of such ownership is a function of the number of issued shares. Thus, a cor-

poration with 10,000 authorized shares has only 5,000 issued shares. A person who owns 500 shares owns 10% of the company although, in theory, if the company issues the remaining authorized shares, he will own only 5% of the company.

SHARED APPRECIATION MORTGAGE
See SAM.

SHARE-ADJUSTED BROKER-REMARKETED EQUITY SECURITIES
See SABRES.

SHAREHOLDER
A person, or other legal entity, who owns either common or preferred stock of a corporation. Usually, evidence of ownership is in the form of a certificate, issued by the company, that describes the number of ownership units, or shares.

The term *shareholder* is not used of owners of nonstock or mutual corporations. For example, the NYSE is a nonstock corporation. The owners of the NYSE are its members; they are not called "shareholders."

SHAREHOLDERS' EQUITY
Used in financial statements to identify the net worth of a corporation (i.e., the residual value of a company after all liabilities are subtracted from all assets). The net worth is further subdivided into the par value of outstanding preferred and common shares, the paid-in capital (surplus), which represents what the owners paid above the par value when the shares were purchased from the company, and retained earnings (i.e., cumulative earnings not paid as cash or stock dividends).

Also called "stockholders' equity."

SHARE REPURCHASE PUTS
See #SHARPS#.

SHARK REPELLANT
Slang used in corporation finance to designate a change in a corporation's charter designed to make that company less attractive to persons seeking to acquire control.

SHARKWATCH SERVICE
A computerized information service offered by Georgeson & Co., a well-known proxy solicitor in the financial community. This service is able to detect unusual trading activity in an issuer's stock and, through careful analysis, determine the identity of someone who may be accumulating the stock in advance of a proxy contest or tender offer.

#SHARPS#

Acronym for share repurchase puts. This is a Merrill Lynch innovation designed to assure equal treatment of all shareholders and to discourage arbitrage activities. It is an alternate to corporate self-tender offers or large stock repurchase programs in that a put option is attached to shares that can be exercised by the holder at any time before expiration. By knowing in advance how many shares—and at what price—may be repurchased, the issuer has greater operating flexibility, and unfriendly corporate takeovers are discouraged.

SHEARSON LEHMAN WORLD INDEX

Shearson and Quantum Matrix work together in the preparation of this measurement of international market performance. This global index stresses total return, rather than simple price movements, of the selected issues.

SHELF DISTRIBUTION

A time-to-time public offering of an SEC-registered security at prevailing market prices by the issuer or an affiliated person over a two-year period. The offering may be made by the holder/issuer, or through an identified underwriter, in amounts aggregating the quantity set forth in the registration statement.

See also SHELF REGISTRATION STATEMENT.

SHELF REGISTRATION STATEMENT

This abbreviated registration statement, also known as Form S-3, permits corporations and affiliated persons to make offerings of identified securities at prevailing market prices over a two-year period. Example: A corporation files a shelf registration for $100 million of bonds. The corporation uses dips in interest rates to offer portions of the issue at various times over a two-year period.

SHELL COMPANY

Jargon for a corporation, usually without assets or a valid business operation, whose shares are offered for sale. Although such sales are not necessarily fraudulent, the value of the shares is questionable and are always high risk.

SHERIFF

Colorful term used to describe a CBOE member who is empowered to ensure the forced liquidation of a position at the request of a clearing member organization. If the equity of an options trader (or an options member organization) falls below the margin requirement of its clearing firm, that firm may immediately demand more collateral *or* the liquidation of established positions to reduce its financial exposure. Its surrogate, which is known as the "sheriff" or the "leg breaker," oversees completion of this liquidation.

SHERMAN ANTI-TRUST ACT
This act, which has been amended in some ways since its original passage in 1890, addresses the problem of cartels and monopolies and their impact on the country's economy. The law attempts to restrict business combinations that lessen competition or which manipulate prices of goods.

SHINGLE THEORY
SEC jargon used to describe the ethical responsibility applicable to brokers in connection with their registration. Under this concept, a broker implicitly promises to treat customers fairly when hanging out a "shingle"—that is, advertising that he or she is available to do business with the public.

SHINJINURI
Japanese term for a high risk or "go go" trader; that is, a free-wheeling speculator who plays with the most volatile issues in the market. Needless to say, when such persons are successful, they make huge sums of money; when wrong, the results are catastrophic.

SHOCK ABSORBERS
Colorful term for a number of temporary measures adopted by the securities and commodities marketplaces to avoid the disastrous volatility of October 19 and 20, 1987. Some of these measures include trading halts if certain indicators are up or down by a specified number of points; restrictions on the automatic trading systems (e.g., D.O.T.); the elimination of proprietary program trading; and limitation on the entry of orders marked "on the close."

Also called "circuit breakers."

SHOGUN SECURITIES
Colloquial term for dollar-denominated securities issued by U.S. corporations for exclusive distribution in Japan. Southern California Edison became the first U.S. issuer to overcome both the technical and legal barriers for the offering of such securities in Japan. This issue was distributed in 1985.

SHOP
1. As noun: the location of the office of a broker/dealer. For example, "His shop is very active these days."

2. As verb: the act of soliciting the highest bid or lowest offer for a security. For example, "We'll shop around for the best price."
See also SHOPPING THE STREET.

SHOPPING THE STREET
Colorful expression used to describe the practice of canvassing other dealers and marketmakers to determine the best bid/offer available before executing an order.

SHORT
Used of a transaction in a client security account that causes both a credit and an obligation of future performance. For example, a client sells a borrowed certificate. The client is short because there is a credit of the proceeds of the sale and the client is obligated to return the borrowed certificate. Or a client sells a call or put; there is a credit and the client is obligated to deliver (call) or purchase (put) a specific security.

The term *short* is not used if there is a credit but no future obligation. For example, a client sells a security owned. There is a credit but no future obligation. This is called a "long sale."

In commodity accounts, short is used of clients who obligate themselves to a future sale of the commodity.

SHORT AGAINST THE BOX
Descriptive term for an offsetting long and short position in the same security in a client account. For example, "The client is long 500 shares of Monsanto and short 500 shares."

The technique establishes a perfect hedge whereby the client can neither gain nor lose from that point onward. The technique can be used to transfer the tax consequences of the long position to a future tax year. It cannot be used to turn a short-term paper gain on the long security into a long-term gain because the short sale, if the long security was held one year or less, wipes out the holding period on the long security.

SHORT BOND
1. A bond sold short (i.e., sold and a borrowed certificate is used to complete delivery).
2. A bond, originally issued with a long maturity, whose remaining time to maturity is now relatively short. For example, a bond that was issued in 1967 with a 25-year maturity, in 1991, has only one year remaining to maturity.

SHORT COUPON
1. Used as a synonym for a short-term bond (i.e., a bond whose remaining time to maturity is relatively short).

2. Used of a new issue of bonds whose first coupon payment will be less than six months of interest. For example, a bond issue is dated March 1. The semiannual interest payments are scheduled for June–December 1. The first coupon will be short and will represent interest only for the three months between March 1 and June 1.

SHORT EXEMPT

Indication placed on certain short-sale orders sent to an exchange for execution. In practice, customer short-sale orders may be so designated if they are part of a bona fide arbitrage transaction. The designation informs the floor broker that the short sale need not be made on an uptick (i.e., the transaction is exempt from this regulation).

Member firm orders made to correct an error on the floor and specialist orders used to complete certain odd-lot buy transactions, also are short exempt.

SHORTFALL

1. Verb: the act of failing to meet a financial objective.
2. Noun: the amount by which a planned financial objective is not met. For example, "There is a shortfall of $10 million in the city's budget." Also, "The company will have a shortfall of 10% in meeting its marketing objectives."

SHORT HEDGE

Term for the strategy that fully or partially limits the downside risk of ownership. A short against the box provides a full hedge against downside risk. A short call against an established position provides a partial protection against downside risk. For example, a client long $1 million Ginnie Mae pass-throughs could provide a short hedge by selling 10 GNMA calls. If interest rates rise, both the GNMA pass-throughs and the calls will go down in value. Thus, the premium received when the calls were sold will partially protect the client from the drop in value of the GNMA pass-throughs.

The term also is used if a client reduces downside risk exposure by the use of commodity future or forward contracts.

SHORT INTEREST

The total short positions in listed securities. The short positions for individual member firms are provided to the exchanges. The exchanges, in turn, compile the total short positions and, about the 15th of each month, provide these figures to the news media.

Both the *New York Times* and *The Wall Street Journal* provide a representative listing of the securities with the largest short interest.

The short positions represent total shorts, and no differentiation is made between regular short sales and short positions against the box.

SHORT INTEREST THEORY

A theory that predicts an upward price movement in a security based on the total short positions in the security. Basic rule of thumb: if the short interest exceeds 1½ to 2 times the average daily volume in the security, it is predictive of a price rise.

In recent years, because many covered call writers deliver borrowed stock if exercised, technical analysts place less credence in the total short position in a security. Instead, these analysts look more closely at the short positions established by specialists as an indicator of possible price rise in the security.

Also called the "cushion theory."

SHORT LEG

Slang for the short option that forms part of a spread. For example, a client buys and sells a call to establish a call spread.

SHORT POSITION

1. Industry term for a client account in which completion of a sale was made by the delivery of a borrowed certificate. The client is said to have a short position because the client owes the security borrowed to the broker.
2. Industry term for a client account in which a client has written an option, either a put or a call, and has not yet made a closing purchase, has not been exercised, or the option has not expired.
3. Industry term for a client commodity account in which the client has contracted to sell the commodity at a future date for a fixed price.

SHORT SALE

Any sale that is completed by the delivery of a borrowed certificate. Short sales are made because the seller anticipates a decline in the price of a security.

Regular short sales (i.e., where the client has no other position in the security) are made to profit from a price decline.

Short sales against the box (i.e., where the client has an offsetting long position) are made to avoid a loss and to postpone the tax consequences of a long sale to a subsequent tax year.

See also SHORT AGAINST THE BOX.

SHORT-SHORT TEST

To qualify as a regulated investment company, the IRS requires that an investment company acquire no more than 30% of its gross income from the sale of securities held less than three months. This is to prevent short-term trading as a normal pattern of investing.

This prohibition and its measurement is called the "short-short" test or the "short 3" test.

SHORT-STOP ORDER
This is a multiple instruction order for stock exchanges. It requires a short sale at the market, but only if someone else first makes a transaction at or below the memorandum price (the "stop" portion of the order). The short sale, as usual, requires an uptick.

SHORT SWING
Term used in conjunction with profitable transactions made by directors, officers, and principal stockholders of publicly owned corporations within a period of six months. Such transactions may involve a purchase followed by a sale, or a sale followed by a repurchase, of securities of their corporation. The prohibition is made because of the presumption that they may be using inside information. Under federal securities law, such profits may be recoverable by the corporation.

SHORT TENDER
A person who accepts a tender offer by the delivery of securities that are borrowed. This practice is forbidden by SEC Rule 10b-4; only long securities can be tendered under this rule.

SHORT TERM
For purposes of capital gains considerations, a term of ownership of a security of 12 months or less.
See also LONG TERM.

SHORT-TERM DEBT
Debt securities with a relatively short time remaining to maturity. On corporation balance sheets, bonds with one year or less to maturity are listed among current liabilities.

In the analysis of corporations or municipalities, bonds with five or less years to maturity remaining are considered short term. The meaning of the term, therefore, depends on the context in which it is used.

SHORT-TERM GAIN
If a taxpayer purchases a capital asset and within one year or less sells it at a profit, the IRS considers the gain as short term. Two exceptions: profits on commodity futures contracts are short term, based on a holding period of six months or less; all profits on short sales are short term because it is a profit based on a sale followed by a purchase, rather than a purchase followed by a sale. Thus, the client has no holding period.

SHORT-TERM INDEXED LIABILITY TRANSACTIONS
Acronym: STILTS. STILTS are a form of commercial paper that gives the issuer the ability to convert this debt into more commercial paper at a guaranteed interest spread for a series of short-term rollover periods.

SHORT-TERM LOSS
If a taxpayer purchases a capital asset and within one year or less sells it at a loss, the IRS considers the loss to be short term. Two exceptions: losses on commodity futures contracts are measured on six months or less for short term, more than six months for long term. If a taxpayer hedges a long-term capital gain with a short sale against the box and, in covering the short position, suffers a capital loss, the loss is considered long term by the IRS.

SHORT-TERM TAX-EXEMPT PUT SECURITIES
A municipal security with a put option designed by Merrill Lynch. This feature enables the holder to sell the security back to Merrill Lynch during the limited lifetime of the security. The feature substantially limits the market risk to the holder if interest rates rise.
Acronym: STTEPS.

SHORT THEIR BOGEY
Quaint expression used by fixed-income portfolio managers.
The term means that the portfolio manager has portfolio maturities that are shorter than the fixed-income index on which their performance will be based. This will result in a better performance than the index only if the yield curve is inverted (short-term rates are higher than long-term rates); otherwise, it will result in a poorer performance for the portfolio.

SHORT 3 TEST
See SHORT-SHORT TEST.

SHOSHA
Japanese term for the giant trading houses; for example, Mitsubishi, Mitsui, C. Itoh, and Nichimen, which specialize in international export-import dealings as intermediaries for other Japanese industrial concerns and which, as a result, are the principal players in foreign exchange and foreign currency futures trading in Japan.

SHOW-IN BUYER/SELLER
Trading language used to designate a possible large buyer/seller in a particular security. Thus, the trader feels that if a contra party makes its presence known, the trader will be able to generate a large order.

SHOWSTOPPER
Corporate finance term used to describe litigation designed to thwart the takeover attempt of an unwelcome suitor.

SHS
This is a abbreviation for "shares," a synonym for a unit of ownership in a corporation, commonly called stock.

SIA
See SECURITIES INDUSTRY ASSOCIATION.

SIAC
See SECURITIES INDUSTRY AUTOMATION CORPORATION.

SIAMESE SHARES
See PAIRED SHARES.

SIB
Acronym for Securities and Investment Board. SIB is a quasi-governmental body established under the Financial Services Bill (1986) in Britain to oversee and regulate various forms of investments in the United Kingdom.

Although the SIB is, in many ways, similar in function to the SEC in the United States, SIB is more independent and less political.

SIC
See SECURITIES INFORMATION CORPORATION.

SICA
Acronym for Securities Industry Committee on Arbitration. This is a private body that establishes and monitors compliance with an arbitration code for individual complaint cases involving customers and securities firms.

SICAV
Acronym for Societes d'Investissement a Capital Variable. SICAV is one of two types of mutual funds found in France. SICAVs are organized as corporations and are required to invest a minimum of 30% of their assets in French bonds. The remaining 70% may be invested in other forms of securities, either French or international.

A variation on the SICAV: the "monory" (equity) SICAV has 30% in French bonds, 60% in French stocks, with remaining 10% in other investments.

SICOVAM
Acronym for Societe Interprofessionelle pour le Compensation des Valeurs Mobilieres. SICOVAM is similar in function to the DTC in the United States in that it holds certificates in nominee name so they can be cleared and transferred. SICOVAM was set up under French law and, in effect, has created a certificateless (book entry) society for French broker/dealers, banks, and other financial institutions. SICOVAM is also linked with many foreign clearing corporations so they may take part in the internationalization of the French securities markets.

SIDE-BY-SIDE TRADING
See INTEGRATED MARKETMAKING.

SIDE CAR RULE
Colorful name for Rule 80A of the NYSE. In effect, this rule governs the use of the DOT system in times of great market volatility. If the S&P 500 has declined 12 or more points (about 96 points on the DJIA), institutional orders of a program type are routed into a separate file for five minutes so individual customer orders may have time priority. After five minutes, the institutional orders are eligible for execution.

The term *express lane* is also used of the fact that individual orders are given precedence over institutional orders in this circumstance.

SIGHT DRAFT
Term describing an immediately negotiable instrument used to transfer money from a buyer to a seller. When this checklike document is signed by the buyer, it also identifies the paying agent, and the seller can deposit it for personal credit and use the money.

SIGNIFICANT ORDER IMBALANCE
A stock exchange term sometimes used if trading is halted because the market is demoralized; that is, there is a wide spread between bid and offer, or the bid side of the market has suddenly disappeared. As a rule of thumb, for example, a spread of 10% or 3 points, whichever is lower, between the bid and offer on stocks selling below 100 (10% or 5 points for stocks above 100) would be a "significant order imbalance."

This imbalance may apply either to the opening or the reopening of the market. In addition, trading may be halted because of pending news, and following the news there may be a "significant order imbalance."

SILENT PARTNER
Industry term for a limited partner in a direct participation program. The term is so used because limited partners have no vote in the management of the venture. For example, a partnership that will engage in

the development of oil wells has one general partner who will manage the venture and 30 limited partners who will contribute capital. The limited partners, because they have no voice in management, are silent partners.

SILENT SALES
Slang used to describe the secret sale of residential housing without notification of the municipality of the transfer of ownership, or notification of the original mortgagor. Such sales are illegal. They usually are motivated by the seller's desire to sell, or the buyer's inability to get either a new mortgage or unwillingness to pay new mortgage rates.

SILVER
Popular identifier of the shares of Insilco Corporation, formerly known as International Silver Company, a well-known manufacturer of silverware and related products.

SIMEX
Initials of the Singapore International Monetary Exchange, a prominent futures exchange in the Orient. SIMEX has futures contracts in foreign currencies and is linked with the Chicago Mercantile Exchange (CME). SIMEX also trades futures contracts in the popular Nikkei Index of Japanese stocks.

SIMPLE MAJORITY
The agreement by holders of more than 50% of the outstanding shares of a company in a vote conducted by the company. Under most circumstances, that minimum percentage is all that is required to elect directors, to ratify independent auditors, and to carry other amendments to the charter of the corporation.

SIMPLIFIED EMPLOYEE PENSION PLAN (SEP)
A hybrid that combines features of IRA and Keogh accounts. Under SEP, an employer may make contributions to the plan for employees who are 25 years or older and who have 3 or more years of employment. The contributions are vested, are not considered taxable income for the employees, and are tax-sheltered until withdrawn by the employee. Employees may upon termination roll over their vested interest into another IRA plan. Contribution by the employer may be linked to firm profits; thus, in practice, they become combined pension and profit-sharing plans.

SIMULTANEOUS TRANSACTION
See RISKLESS TRANSACTION.

SINC

A tongue-in-cheek term from the '80s to stand for: single income no children. This term describes a couple in which one person works and the other goes for an advanced professional degree; for example, MBA, JD, MD, and the like.

SINGLE ASSET PROPERTY COMPANY

See SAPCO.

SINGLE-PREMIUM LIFE INSURANCE

A form of whole or universal life that is marked by:
1. A one-time payment in full of all premiums.
2. A fixed death benefit.
3. Tax sheltering of the internal growth of the policy.
4. Some direction of investment values within the policy.
5. A minimum restriction on loans against the policy.

Most recent tax law changes have severely restricted policy loans before age 59½. Now, to be eligible for such policy loans, the premium must be paid over seven years.

SINGLE PROPERTY OWNERSHIP TRUST

See SPOT.

SINGLE-PURCHASE CONTRACT

Term used of an annuity, either fixed or variable, where the investor makes a lump-sum purchase. Such contracts, at the election of the investor, may provide immediate payout or future payout. Once the investor elects for the terms of the payout, the terms may not be changed.

SINKER

Industry slang for a bond with a sinking-fund provision.

SINKING FUND

A fund of money that a corporation must set aside annually to provide for the early retirement of portions of a bond issue or, occasionally, an issue of preferred stock. Generally, these funds are used to retire bonds in the year that the funds are set aside, although the bond indenture may provide for alternate bond redemption provisions. Sinking funds, if promised in the bond indenture, are obligatory on the issuing corporation.

Many municipal revenue issues also have sinking-fund provisions; these are not obligatory, however, unless the revenues are sufficient to maintain the facility and provide for debt service.

The abbreviation SF often is used by Moody's or Standard & Poor's bond guides in the brief description of a bond issue to designate that a sinking-fund provision is applicable.

SIPA

Acronym for Securities Investors Protection Act.

See also SECURITIES INVESTORS PROTECTION CORPORA-TION (for an explanation of the protection provided by the act).

SIPC

See SECURITIES INVESTORS PROTECTION CORPORATION.

SITUS

Acronym for System for Institutional Trading of Unregistered Securities. SITUS was a plan initiated by the American Stock Exchange to foster trading by foreigners and U.S. institutions of unregistered (with the SEC) securities of large, high-quality, foreign issuers. Such securities were originally issued outside the United States or in private placements. SITUS facilitates the trading of such securities without the need to register them in the United States. It has not been approved by the SEC.

SIZE

1. Industry term for the quantity of shares or bonds available for purchase or sale. For example, (1) in asking for an OTC quote, a dealer may designate that he wants a "quote-large" (i.e., for more than the unit of trading) or (2) in response to a request for a quote, a specialist may give both the quote and the size. Thus, a specialist could quote: "It's 19½ to 20, 11 by 13." There are 1100 shares to be bought at 19½; 1300 to be sold at 20.
2. Used in the expression "in size" or "available in size" to designate that large quantities are available for purchase. In practice, the term is not used of the buy side of the market.

SIZED OUT

Exchange floor terminology used to explain the inability of a broker to cross stock at a block trader's specified price. Sized out means that another broker is currently bidding or offering a larger quantity at the stated price.

See BLOCKED for the same idea when caused by a competitor's price.

TO SIZE OUT A BROKER

Term used in the auction market on exchange floors if a broker is trying to "cross" a block. The broker usually waits for another broker to trade in the crowd. This trade takes care of the broker with time *priority*. Now the broker with the "cross" can freeze out the other brokers because his or her order is the largest. This floor rule is termed *precedence;* that is, getting an execution by virtue of the size of the order.

SIZE THE BOOK
Term used by block trading organizations when they effect block trades on the floor. In effect, the floor broker asks not for a quote and size but asks to get an insight into the size of limit orders above (if buying) or below (if selling) the current quote. In this way, the floor broker can ascertain the quantity and price at which the block can be effected. The block, if executed, must include all limit orders capable of execution at the transaction price. Thus, if the lowest offer is 75 and the block trade (a buy) is made at 75¼ everyone whose shares are taken will get 75¼.

SJ (SUBJECT)
Initials sometimes used to qualify a quotation for a security as subject—that is, subject to further discussion and qualification about price and volume.

SK
Initials occasionally used to designate safekeeping: security measures that a broker/dealer must employ to protect customers' fully paid securities.
    See also SAFEKEEPING.

SKELETON
See INVESTMENT SKELETON.

SKID
Floor traders' nickname for the shares of Standard Oil of California. The nickname is a play on the NYSE ticker symbol for the stock: SD.

SKIP-DAY SETTLEMENT
A negotiated settlement that calls for delivery and payment on the second business day following the trade date. Although such settlement may be called for in transactions for T-bills and bankers' acceptances, it is the usual method of trading commercial paper. Reason: Dealers are willing to break up commercial paper into smaller lots to suit investor needs, and they want the chance to market the remainder of the "piece" to other investors.

SKIPPIES
A play on the acronym: school kids with income and purchasing power. Skippies are an important marketing force. Not only do they spend (and

often invest) their own money, it is estimated that they influence 40–60% of the fashion buying in their families.

SL
1. Common abbreviation for: sell.
2. As used on order instructions: an abbreviation for sell long; that is, the customer is selling securities owned by the customer and the customer intends to deliver those securities.
3. Used in corporate and municipal bond calendars, these initials identify Shearson Lehman Corp., a major underwriter of securities.

SLAM DUNK
From basketball: an unopposed and forceful score. By analogy in mergers and acquisitions: an unopposed corporate takeover.

SLAP
See SELF-LIQUIDATING ASSET PURCHASE.

SLD
Abbreviation for: sold sale. This designation follows the symbol for a security on the consolidated tape if, for any reason, the report of the transaction is out of time sequence.

See also OPD.

SLD LAST SALE
Designation on the consolidated tape placed after the symbol for the security. The designation, which means sold last sale, signifies that the price designated is significantly higher or lower than the preceding transaction in that issue.

As a rule of thumb, the designation is used if the current price is one or more points away from a previous transaction of $19^7/8$ or below, or two or more points away from a previous transaction of 20 or above.

SLEAZE BAG
See DIRT BAG.

SLEEPER
Slang for an investment opportunity that has been overlooked by public and professional investors. Example: The return to more conservative accounting procedures has understated the value of LMN Corporation. At this time, and at this price, it must be considered a sleeper.

THE SLEEPING LEVEL

Colorful expression often used when giving financial advice, particularly if the person is already invested. If there is a drop in the market, the investor is counseled to sell a sufficient amount of his or her holdings so he or she may sleep quietly at night. This is the investor's mental level of comfort.

The expression is also used before the investment. For example, "Mr. Jones, 100 shares of this stock should not disturb your sleeping level."

SLGS

Acronym for State and Local Government Series. SLGS is pronounced "slugs."

SLGS are private offerings of U.S. government securities to municipalities that enable them to pre-refund their outstanding debt in compliance with IRS and Treasury Department regulations. Such issues are often labeled PRE-REF or ETM (Escrowed to Maturity) on dealer offering sheets.

SLIPPAGE

Metaphor from the science of mechanics where it means the loss of work because of inefficiencies in a system.

1. In the United States, a shortfall in projected revenues or sales from a predetermined plan. For example, "The company's sales caused a slippage in anticipated earnings."
2. In the United Kingdom, the consumption of available capital faster than anticipated. Thus, it may be difficult to obtain further capital from investors. For example, "Eagle Industry's plant was not completed with the proceeds of its initial public offering. This slippage may make it difficult to successfully offer a second block of stock."

SLOB

1. Slang expression used by salespersons and traders for the common stock of Schlumberger, Ltd. The jargon is derived from the NYSE ticker symbol for the stock: SLB.
2. Acronym for secured lease obligation bonds. SLOBs are the modern-day equivalent of mortgage bonds; that is, a bond secured by specific real property.

In effect, the proceeds of a bond issue are used to build a utility plant. The plant is then leased to the utility with lease payments equal to the bond debt service over the life of the bond (interest and principal). If there is a default, the bondholders become general creditors for the amount above the resale value of the plant.

SLUGS

See SLGS and DEFEASANCE.

SMA

See SPECIAL MEMORANDUM ACCOUNT.

SMALL BUSINESS ADMINISTRATION

A government agency. It provides small businesses with loans and management assistance. Monies borrowed by the SBA through bond issues are guaranteed by the full faith and credit of the U.S. government. Interest received from SBA securities is subject to federal income tax but not to state or local taxation.

SMALL ORDER EXECUTION SYSTEM

Acronym: SOES. An NASD system used to automate customer OTC orders for 1,000 shares (or less) of certain eligible issues (five NASDAQ marketmakers or more) to the marketmaker with the best price. This is an immediate transaction and trade terms are automatically routed to the clearing corporation for on-line comparison between the two members.

SMALL SAVER CERTIFICATE

A time deposit savings account in a bank or thrift institution in which the money pledged remains there for at least 30 months. The money so pledged may be as little as $100. The rate of interest paid is pegged to the average yield of U.S. Treasury securities of comparable maturity. The privilege was rescinded by subsequent tax law.

SMART MONEY

Term ascribed to those investors who seem to do the right things at the right time.

Smart money, for example, appears to be able to profit both from good markets (they are long) and bad markets (they are short).

The term is also used of individual investment decisions. For example, "At this time and with this yield curve, the smart money is in one to two-year CDs."

Needless to say, the term is also used as a substitute for the proverbial *they*. For example, "They say that . . .." becomes "Smart money says. . . ." This latter usage may not be suitable or ethical.

SMB

Used on municipal and corporate bond calendars to identify Smith Barney, Harris Upham & Co., a major underwriter of securities.

SMM

See SUPPLEMENTAL MARKETMAKER.

SMMEA

Common abbreviation for Secondary Mortgage Market Enhancement Act of 1984. SMMEA encourages access by home buyers to capital market financing. For example, it places highly rated mortgage-backed securities on a par with government agency securities in terms of several, otherwise restrictive, regulatory requirements. Thus, mortgage-backed securities are exempted from the seven-day settlement rule for purchases under Regulation T of the Federal Reserve. (MBS settlements are generally on one day per month.)

SMO

Slang for the GNMA Collateralized Mortgage Obligations issued by Salomon Brothers Mortgage Securities, Inc.

Pronounced: shmow, to rhyme with show.

SNAKE

Nickname for an agreement between leading European nations to allow their currencies to float freely in the open market, intervening only if certain parameters are exceeded. The term derives from the days when their currencies were pegged to the U.S. dollar and a graph of their value fluctuations resembled the configuration of a snake.

Also, any graph whose configuration resembles the movement of a snake.

SNIF

Acronym for short-term note issuance facility. A term formerly used in international financing to describe ongoing placements of 1 to 5-year Eurodebt instruments.

SNIF has been replaced by RUF: revolving underwriting facilities.

SNOWBALLING

Generally used as a verbal noun (a gerund) to mean:
1. The establishment of a market trend that induces an ever-increasing number of investors to trade on the same side of the market. For example, "The program trades in the early afternoon caused snowballing as the market slid continuously downward."
2. The incessant triggering of stop orders from the specialist's book as one set of trades sets off others. For example, "Snowballing increased as the buy stops at $59\frac{1}{2}$ caused a wave of short selling."

SNUGGING
Nautical term: to haul in and tighten sails in preparation for a storm.

Thus, as a metaphor, when the Federal Reserve, the agency responsible for the control of credit in the economy, tightens credit either through raising the interest rate or lowering available credit. For example, "The Federal Reserve anticipates a rise in inflation and as a result is snugging available credit."

SOCIALISM
1. State ownership of the means of production, especially heavy manufacturing, utilities, and transportation.
2. An economic system in which the state provides, through heavy taxation, medical and old-age care for all citizens regardless of need.
3. In Marxist theory, a transition stage between capitalism and communism. It is a transition stage and is an imperfect application of collectivist principles.

SOCIÉTÉ INTERPROFESSIONALLE POUR LA COMPENSATION DES VALEURS MOBILIERES.
See SICOVAM.

SOCIETES d'INVESTISSEMENT A CAPITAL VARIABLE
See SICAV.

SOCIETY FOR THE PROMOTION OF INSIDER TRADING
See SPIT.

SOCIETY FOR WORLDWIDE INTERBANK FINANCIAL TELECOMMUNICATIONS
See SWIFT.

SOES
See SMALL ORDER EXECUTION SYSTEM.

SOES-ED
Pronounced "so–sed." From SOES, the NASD's Small Order Execution System.

SOES automatically executes many orders to buy-sell for 1,000 shares (or less) against available firm quotes made by marketmakers on the NASDAQ system. Thus, if a marketmaker is *slow* in changing its quotes on the NASDAQ system, the marketmaker may get an execution at a price that it really does not want. For example, a complaint by one marketmaker to another: "I was SOES-ed on my last trade in ABCD; I received $57\frac{1}{4}$ instead of $57\frac{1}{2}$, and thus I lost $250."

SOFE
Acronym for Swedish Options and Futures Exchange. Located in Stockholm, SOFE is the principal exchange in Sweden for the trading of SX 16 (Swedish Index) and the SX 16 (Swedish Index Futures) contracts.

SOFFEX
Acronym for Swiss Options and Financial Futures Exchange. SOFFEX was founded by the Zurich, Geneva, and Basel exchanges and five major Swiss banks.

SOFFEX will trade options on 14 Swiss companies and will also trade futures contracts for interest rates on Swiss government bonds.

SOFT BULLET ASSET-BACKED SECURITY
A debt obligation collateralized only by credit card receivables. Thus, there is no other guarantee of performance on the bond except the principal amount received from the credit card debtors.

SOFT CURRENCY
Used in opposition to "hard currency"; that is, any currency backed, to some extent, by gold, a substantial trade balance, a large and steady GNP, or by realistic purchasing power.

"Soft currency," on the other hand, has no backing in gold, or has an unrealistic exchange rate in terms of actual buying power. The Chinese yuan, the Russian ruble, Argentina's austral, Brazil's crusado, and Israel's shekel are classic examples of soft currencies.

Soft currencies usually mark "closed economic systems" or countries with a severe flight of capital because of uncontrolled inflation. Countries with severe soft currency problems tend to be marked with large "black markets."

SOFT DOLLARS
Jargon for a method of payment by means of directed underwriting credits and commissions from portfolio transactions. This payment for research and other brokerage services takes the place of payment in "hard dollars" (i.e., dollars that are a direct payment from the portfolio manager). For example, "The computerized analysis of your portfolio will cost $3,000 hard dollars, or $10,000 soft dollars."

SOFT FOR NET
Colorful U.K. term for what in the United States are called "soft dollars"; that is, the customer pays the broker in "hard commission dollars" and the brokerage firm bears the cost of research services to that customer. This is what is known as "soft dollars."

In the United Kingdom, the practice is acceptable for all broker/dealers except marketmakers.

SOFTING
English jargon for the practice of paying in "soft dollars." For example, a broker/dealer with excess computer time does research and provides computer services to an institutional money manager. The institutional money manager indirectly pays for the services by directing commission business to the broker/dealer. The institution pays in "hard dollars"; the broker/dealer rebates part of the commission/markup in "soft dollars" (the services rendered for no apparent payment).

SOFT MARKET
Description of a market for stocks or bonds that has very little demand. As a result, even slight selling pressure will cause prices to drop.

SOFT PUT
A special arrangement between a purchaser and an underwriter of an issue enabling the buyer to sell the security back to the underwriter (a) at a prearranged price, (b) within a specific time period, (c) but usually only on specific dates within the effective period. An example of the latter could be on the date when the issuer will reset the rate on a "floater."

The issuer is not involved in this transaction because it is not a party to the guarantee.

SOGO SHOSHAS
Japanese term for those trading firms that are prominent in the futures markets. The term literally means "conglomerates."

The role of the sogo shoshas on the Japanese commodities exchanges was similar to that of the "locals" who trade for their own accounts on U.S. commodities exchanges. In recent years, negotiated commissions and decreased liquidity on the Japanese exchanges have reduced the importance of the sogo shoshas.

SOKAIYA
Japanese term for a person who tries to extort money from public corporations by a threat to disrupt their stockholders' meeting. Such gangsterism is not condoned by public officials but it is a recognized way of corporate life in Japan.

SOLD
Past participle of the verb *to sell*. Sold is used to accept a bid, and thereby completes a transaction. For example, a broker/dealer (or a specialist) bids 59½ for 1,000 shares. By saying "sold" the contra broker accepts

the bid and contracts to deliver 1,000 shares at 59½ to the broker/dealer.

SOLD LAST SALE
See SLD LAST SALE.

SOLD SALE (SLD)
Identified by the letters SLD following a security's ticker symbol this term describes a transaction reported on the Consolidated Tape System out of its proper sequence.

SOLD TO YOU
This is part of industry jargon used by over-the-counter traders when they reconfirm that their offer has been accepted by the contrarader. For example, the buying trader, "We buy 200 Pabst at 27." The selling trader, "We confirm, we sold to you 200 Pabst at 27."

SOL SPREAD
A term used in the futures markets in the United Kingdom. A SOL spread involves the purchase of short-term gilt futures and the sale of long-term gilt futures. The strategy will be profitable if the spread narrows because the yield curve flattens.

SONYMA
Pronounced Sonnie-Mae.
Acronym for State of New York Mortgage Agency.
See also STATE OF NEW YORK MORTGAGE AGENCY.

SOP
In older literature, the abbreviation for the SEC's Statement of Policy.
The SOP governed the advertising and merchandising of investment company securities. The SOP was rescinded in 1980 but its terms have been incorporated into various NASD rules.

SOUR BOND
Slang for a debt issue that is in default on its interest or principal payments. Such a bond has a very low rating and will be deeply discounted in the marketplace; in effect, it has gone "sour."

SOUTH KOREA STOCK EXCHANGE
South Korea is one of the "Asian Tigers" that has prospered in recent years. This growth has been manifested in the value of its industrial stocks, and it has caused the role of the South Korea Stock Exchange to

expand. At present, foreign investors are not permitted direct access to Korean markets; this will change, however, in 1991.

There are two scheduled trading sessions on weekdays and a half-day session on Saturdays. Settlement is on the third business day following the trade.

SOVEREIGN AUSTRALIAN CURRENCY ENHANCED SECURITIES
See SAUCERS.

SOVEREIGN ISSUE
A security issued and backed by the guarantee of an ongoing government. Most offerings of governmental bodies, particularly those in Western Europe and Canada, are exempted from SEC registration requirements in the United States. Those issues also qualify for extensions of credit in the United States under Regulation T.

SOVEREIGN RISK
The risk faced by an investor who invests funds in a foreign country. The risk refers to possible changes in currency values and changes in governments and laws that may be disadvantageous to the investor.

SOX 'N STOCKS
Tongue-in-cheek term used of Dean Witter Reynolds, a large U.S. broker/dealer, because the firm is owned by Sears, Roebuck & Co., the largest retailer in the country.

SOYD
See SUM-OF-THE-YEARS' DIGITS.

SOYLAND BONDS
Quaint term for the debt securities of Soyland Power Cooperative, Inc. The debt of this rural electric utility cooperative is actually placed into trusts deposited with and serviced by the National Rural Utilities Cooperative Finance Corporation, a not-for-profit organization founded to facilitate financings for farmland power requirements. Its guarantees for repayment of principal and interest are, in turn, guaranteed by the U.S. government.

SPACE ARBITRAGE
Slang term for the nearly simultaneous profitable purchase and sale of the same, or substantially identical, securities based on price differentials prevailing in different marketplaces.

The term is more specific than arbitrage, which may, in practice, include space arbitrage or arbitrages on the same exchange or marketplace.

SPAGHETTI OPTIONS
A facetious term used of the proliferation of option products introduced by the various exchanges. The allusion is a bit farfetched: like cooked spaghetti thrown against a wall, some will stick (and these options will be successful) while others drop to the floor, dry out, and become useless.

SPAN
Acronym for Spread Adjusted Note. A Merrill Lynch debt product providing for semiannual changes in interest payments. But this will take place only at that time, if there is a change in that issuer's yield spread over a comparable U.S. Treasury note. Thus, this debt security is sensitive to movements in the yield curve and not to changes in the level of general rates in the economy.

SPANISH BOLSA
Common name for the Madrid Stock Exchange. Trading is by open outcry during the hours of 10 A.M. and 1 P.M., with negotiated trading for the next three hours. Settlement is made on the Wednesday after the week in which the trade was made.

SPC
See SECURITY PURCHASE CONTRACT.

SPECIAL AGREEMENT TRANSACTION
An infrequent form of transaction on the Tokyo Stock Exchange that permits settlement within 14 days of the trade. Its original purpose was as a convenience for investors in remote areas of Japan. With the advent of securities depositories and book-entry re-registration, such trades are now outmoded.

SPECIAL ARBITRAGE ACCOUNT
A form of margin account in which a customer may receive advantageous credit terms if he purchases a security and, at about the same time, either (1) sells it in a different market or (2) sells an equal security in the same or a different market to take advantage of a difference in prices. For example, in a special arbitrage account, a client buys 5,000 ABC in market A at $21 per share and at the same time sells 5,000 ABC in market B at $21.50 per share.

SPECIAL ASSESSMENT BOND

A form of municipal general obligation bond so named because there is a special tax, or assessment, paid by users of the facility. The tax is sufficient to pay the bond debt service. Used for the construction of streets, curbs, sewers, water, and other public utilities.

SPECIAL BID

A bid made by a New York Stock Exchange member, publicized on the tape, for a block of stock at a fixed price. The buying member pays all transaction costs, including a special commission to the contra broker. Special bids are seldom used.

SPECIAL BID/ASKED QUOTE

A Japanese market term that is used when there is an imbalance of buy-sell orders. The special quote is used (higher bid *or* lower offer) to attract contra parties into the marketplace and thereby eliminate the imbalance. The special quote may change every five minutes, either higher or lower, until supply and demand are again in balance.

SPECIAL BOND ACCOUNT

A form of margin account with a broker/dealer in which a customer may purchase, carry, or trade on advantageous credit terms: (1) U.S. government, government-guaranteed, or municipal securities; (2) nonconvertible corporate bonds listed on an exchange; (3) many nonconvertible corporate bonds that are unlisted but meet special qualifications published by the Federal Reserve.

The broker/dealer may set its own initial margin requirement, but customers are governed by the margin maintenance requirements set by the exchanges and the National Association of Securities Dealers (NASD).

SPECIAL CASH ACCOUNT

Technical term for what is popularly called a "cash account." In such accounts, brokerage clients may purchase or sell long any security. Delivery of securities sold and payment for securities purchased must be made promptly and, in any event, be within seven business days following the trade date.

The special cash account does not permit the broker to maintain a creditor/debtor relationship with the customer, although debits of less than $500 do not require that the broker buy in or sell out the account. Regulation T gives the client seven business days following the trade date; industry rules require payment by the fifth business day following the trade.

SPECIAL CLAIM ON RESIDUAL EQUITY
See SCORE.

SPECIAL COMMODITY ACCOUNT
This is the title of an account at a broker/dealer in which a customer can effect and finance transactions in commodities and commodities futures contracts.

SPECIAL CONVERTIBLE DEBT SECURITY ACCOUNT
A form of margin account in which a customer may finance the purchase or short sale of debt securities that are (1) convertible into a margin stock or (2) carry a warrant or right to subscribe to a margin stock.

Convertible preferred stocks are carried in the client's general margin account.

SPECIAL DEAL
An improper practice, prohibited in the National Association of Securities Dealers' Rules of Fair Practice, whereby an underwriter of investment company securities pays or gives anything of material value, other than the selling concessions granted in the prospectus, to an employee of another dealer in concurrence with the sale of the fund's shares. The NASD defines material value as something worth more than $50 in a one-year period.

SPECIAL DRAWING RIGHTS (SDR)
Special drawing rights are used to settle international trade imbalances between governments. The special drawing rights, which are adjusted about once a year to represent changes in trading patterns between nations, are a statistically weighted composite of currencies of the world's leading trading nations. They are, in effect, a kind of money used between governments through bookkeeping transfers in the international banking system.

Sometimes called "paper gold."

SPECIAL INSURANCE PREMIUM FUNDING ACCOUNT
This is the title of an account at a broker/dealer in which a customer can finance the premiums needed to purchase a life insurance policy with the equity in shares of a registered investment company purchased in conjunction with the policy.

SPECIALIST
A member of a national securities exchange registered by that exchange to maintain an orderly market in selected securities traded on that exchange. In fulfilling this function, specialists normally act as (1) brokers in opening

the market and in the prompt execution of orders left with them by other members and (2) as dealers in buying or selling for their own account, to give market depth and reasonable price continuity in their specialty stock, and by taking the other side of all odd-lot transactions.

SPECIALIST'S ACCOUNT
The title of an account at a broker/dealer in which stock exchange specialists and marketmakers in listed options can obtain advantageous credit to finance their dealer inventories. The special credit privileges do not extend to their long-term investment holdings.

SPECIALIST'S BOOK
Popular name for the recordkeeping device used by specialists to record orders left with them by other members. In some cases, the book is a loose-leaf notebook; in others, the actual order tickets are time-stamped and arranged by price or, in more modern instances, a computer bank will record customer buy or sell orders and the number of shares and the conditions or prices at which the orders are to be executed.

SPECIALIST UNIT
A group of three or more fully qualified specialists who work together to maintain an orderly market in specific stocks listed on an exchange. The units may be an association, a partnership, or a corporation.

SPECIALIZED COMPANY
See SPECIALIZED MUTUAL FUND.

SPECIALIZED MUTUAL FUND
Popular term for a mutual fund that concentrates its investments in a particular industry or a specific geographic area. Examples are the Energy Fund, the Chemical Fund, the Merrill Lynch Pacific Fund.

SPECIAL MEMORANDUM ACCOUNT (SMA)
The SMA is an ancillary bookkeeping record used in conjunction with a client's margin account. In the account are noted excess margin, dividends and interest received, deposits of cash, and a portion of the proceeds of long sales. In this way, the SMA becomes a line of credit that may be extended by the broker to the customer for cash withdrawals, withdrawals of securities, or the purchase of additional securities without the need to deposit further margin into the account.

Formerly known as the "special miscellaneous account."

SPECIAL MONEY TRUST
See TOKKIN FUND.

SPECIAL OFFERING

Term designating a method of selling a large block by a NYSE member for its own or a customer's account. The offering, which is made on the consolidated tape, is for a specific number of shares at a fixed price. The seller pays all transaction charges, including a special commission to the buying brokers.

SPECIAL OMNIBUS ACCOUNT

Title of an account with one broker/dealer opened by another broker/dealer who is registered with the SEC. In this account, the second broker/dealer can transact for its customers without disclosing the names of the customers.

SPECIAL OPTION

Term used of a conventional (OTC) put or call option with some remaining lifetime that is offered for resale by a broker/dealer or a customer in a secondary market transaction.

Also known as a "secondhand option."

SPECIAL QUOTE

Tokyo Stock Exchange terminology reflecting the existence of an imbalance of orders. The Special Quote is used, higher (buy) or lower (sell) to attract contra orders into the marketplace and eliminate the imbalance. It may change, upward or downward, every five minutes until supply and demand are again in balance.

SPECIAL SITUATION

Industry jargon for a security that appears to be undervalued in price and which, because of a one-time event, seems due for a rise in price. The one-time event could be a change in management, a change in the fortunes of the industry or the company, a new product, or a tax-loss carryover that will improve the fortunes of the company.

SPECIAL TAX BOND

A class of municipal revenue bonds so called because the bond debt service will be paid by an excise tax on certain luxury items, principally gasoline, liquor, or tobacco products.

SPECTAIL DEALER

Pun on speculator and retail. Slang for a broker/dealer who handles some retail client accounts but who seems to devote more time to speculative trading positions in its own account.

SPECULATION

Latin: *speculare,* to watch or to examine closely. In industry usage, the assumption of high risk, often without regard to current income or to the preservation of principal, to achieve large capital gains. As a general rule, the shorter the time in which one endeavors to achieve the desired capital gains, the more speculative the investment.

SPECULATOR

One who speculates.
See also SPECULATION.

SPEL–BOND

Acronym for Stock Performance–Exchange Linked Bond. This bond was introduced by Mitsui & Co. (USA) as a Euromarket debt instrument. The key feature is that the redemption value at maturity is linked to the *upward* movement of the NYSE's Composite Index. Thus, holders will receive a premium if the index value is greater on maturity date than it was on issue date. For this reason, many call these bonds "bull bonds."

SPEQ

Acronym for Specialist Performance Evaluation Questionnaire. This is a NYSE document used to screen specialists. The questionnaire is given to floor brokers who, it is felt, have most to do with specialists. SPEQ asks floor brokers to truthfully answer questions about specialists. SPEQ is used to appoint, retain, and improve the performance of specialists.

SPIKE

Any significant aberration in the typical performance of a company or its securities, such as a sudden rise in the price of a stock followed by a just as sudden fall or a rise in corporate earnings in one quarter followed by a fall in the next.

Although the term ordinarily is used as a noun (e.g., there was a spike), there are many examples of its use as a verb. Example: The earnings of LMN spiked between 1984 and 1986.

SPIN-OFF

A distribution of stock made to shareholders by a parent company of shares in a subsidiary. The subsidiary thereby becomes an independent corporate entity. For example, Company A is the parent company of Company B. Company A spins off Company B by distributing its shares, on a pro rata basis, to its shareholders of record. Company B is now independently owned by the persons who own the shares distributed to them.

SPINS

Acronym for Standard & Poor's 500 Index Subordinated Notes. SPINS was a Salomon Brothers product that gave subscribers a four-year call option on the S&P Index, with settlement made in cash on maturity date. Investors received a nominal rate of periodic interest, but at maturity were entitled to the par value amount of difference between the SPIN value at issuance and the SPIN value at maturity. (The August 1986 unit exchange ratio was 3.75 per $1,000 bond.)

In effect, this product assumed features of debt, equity, and options marketplaces.

SPIRS

Acronym for Standard & Poor's Index Receipts. The American Stock Exchange's alternative to Index Participations (IP). Specifically identified as a security (and not a futures instrument) it is a trust portfolio of Standard & Poor's stocks with no maturity (expiration) date. Patterned after the Toronto Stock Exchange's Index Participations (TIPs) they are scheduled for quarterly pass-through dividends and regular trade-settlement delivery features.

SPIT

Acronym for Society for the Promotion of Insider Trading. While it may seem to be a facetious organization, in actuality it is a legitimate society in New Zealand. There, insider trading is not illegal, and market participants are accustomed to ferreting out inside information to use in their trading.

SPLIT

1. It identifies a board-authorized recapitulation for an issuer in which more shares will be distributed to shareholders (split up); or fewer shares will be mandated to consolidate outstanding capital (split down). A split requires stockholder approval.
2. It reflects a difference of opinion between two major credit agencies about the financial outlook for holders of an issuer's debt instrument. For example, Moody's may rate a particular bond as an "A" while Standard & Poor's rates it as a "BBB."
See also SPLIT UP and SPLIT DOWN.

SPLIT COUPON BONDS

A euphemism for a debt instrument that begins life as a zero-coupon security and, at a specified date in the future, starts paying a fixed interest rate as set forth in the indenture. This was a popular form of debt offered in the late 1980s on behalf of corporate and municipal issuers.

SPLIT DOWN

This amendment of the corporation's charter decreases the number of authorized shares and increases their par value proportionately. For example,

Before: 2 million shares authorized at a par value of $5.

After: 1 million shares authorized at a par value of $10.

Split downs often are used by corporations whose shares are low-priced. The split down will decrease the number of shares and increase the market price.

Also called a "reverse split."

SPLIT OFFERING

Term describing a public sale of a debt issue that is comprised of both serial maturity bonds and large-term maturity bonds of the same issuer. For example, an issue that is comprised of $40 million serial maturity bonds maturing between 1990 and 2000 and $100 million in term bonds maturing in 2007.

Split offerings are common in the issuance of municipal revenue bonds and some general obligation issues.

SPLIT RATING

The situation that results if one major bond rating service gives a higher or lower rating than another bond rating service to the same issue. Example: Moody's may rate a bond Aa but Standard & Poor's rates it A.

Split ratings are not uncommon for nonconvertible debt securities. They are usual for convertible securities because Moody's generally rates convertibles one grade below nonconvertible securities.

SPLIT-TERM REVERSE MORTGAGE

Such mortgages provide monthly loans using the borrower's home as collateral. It is like a fixed-term reverse mortgage in concept, but the split-term permits longer time periods, and also permits lump-sum loans in addition to periodic loans. Both forms of reverse mortgages defer repayment until the borrower moves or dies.

SPLIT TRUST

The U.K. equivalent of what in the United States is known as a "dual fund" (investment company). Such dual funds arise when an investment company's share capital is divided into two classes: income shares that get all dividends, and capital shares that get all capital gains. Thus, the income shares reflect the dividends from all of the capital, while the capital shares reflect all of the gains (losses) from all of the capital.

SPLIT UP

This amendment of the corporation's charter increases the number of authorized shares and decreases the par value proportionately. For example,

Before: 1 million shares authorized at a par value of $6.

After: 3 million shares authorized at a par value of $2.

Split ups often are used by corporations whose shares are highly priced, usually $80, $100, or more per share. The split up will increase the number of shares available and decrease the market price.

Also simply called a "stock split" because it is the most common split used by corporations.

SPONSOR

For investment company securities, the sponsor is the same as the underwriter.

The terms *distributor* and *wholesaler* also are used synonymously with the term *sponsor*.

SPONSORED SPINOFF

See SPONSORED SPINOUT.

SPONSORED SPINOUT

The concept is this: A company establishes a new company for the exploitation of a new and specific business opportunity. While the new company is owned (and often managed) by the parent company, it is not uncommon for additional shares to be offered to new investors to increase capital. Although it may be looked at as a conglomerate, there is a "corporate shield" that protects the parent from the debts of the spinoff.

Also called "sponsored spinoff."

SPONSORSHIP

Term used to describe the active support of a specific stock issue by one or more interested professional investors.

These professional investors may be large institutions or broker/dealers with well-known research capabilities. Example: Among its sponsorship, that stock numbers Merrill Lynch and the Vanguard Funds.

SPOOK

Verbalized slang identifier of the Standard & Poor's index options and futures contracts traded on major option and commodity exchanges.

The word play derived from the original S&P 500 Index Option and its symbol: SPX. In practice, the term is used not only of the S&P 500 Index Option but also of the S&P 100 Index Option (OEX) and the futures contracts. All are jocularly called "spook contracts."

SPOT
Acronym for single property ownership trust. In the United Kingdom, SPOT is the issuer of unit investment trust shares whose sole underlying asset is a single property generating rental income and prospective gains.

In this regard, SPOT is similar to a SAPCO. The principal difference: SPOT owns *and* manages the property and thus provides shareowners with steady rental income.

SPOT COMMODITY
Industry jargon for commodity transactions that will result in actual physical delivery of the commodity, as opposed to a transaction for future delivery.

Futures contracts that are due to expire in the current month often are called "spot commodities."

SPOT LOAN
A mortgage granted on a case-by-case basis on single-family housing as opposed, for example, to a commitment to finance an entire housing project.

SPOT MARKET
Industry jargon for trades in commodities either for immediate delivery (the same or the next business day) or for trades in futures contracts that will expire this month.

SPOT MONTH
Industry jargon for the current month if a previously traded futures contract will become deliverable during the month.

SPOT PRICE
Industry jargon for the current price of a physical commodity, either agricultural, mineral, or a government security.

SPOT RATE
See SPOT PRICE.

SPOT SECONDARY
Term designating a secondary offering of a stock or a bond that is being sold without an effective registration statement.

SPOUSAL IRA
An individual retirement account opened in the name of a nonworking spouse. Under the IRS rules, the total annual amount that may be contributed is $2,250. This amount may be divided in any way the spouses see fit, provided no more than $2,000 is contributed to either party's account.

Whether or not the contribution is tax deductible depends on the income of the spouses and whether or not the working spouse is covered by another qualified plan.

SPOUSAL REMAINDER TRUST
A pool of assets created under a legal agreement. Ownership of the assets passes to a spouse after a fixed number of years. In the interim, income from the assets is dedicated to the welfare of a third party, usually a child (or children).

Tax advice is needed both for inter vivos and testamentary trusts because of tax law changes.

SPRAYING THE MARKET
Slang in the exchange community for the DOT (Designated Order Turnaround) system and its ability to enter at almost the same time orders for many securities; in effect, the orders are "sprayed" all over the market.

Although such spraying by DOT facilitates arbitrage in program trading situations, or permits the sale (or purchase) of a "market basket" of securities, it is blamed for unusual activity and volatility.

See also CIRCUIT BREAKER and SIDE-CAR RULE as partial remedies for such activity in the marketplace.

SPREAD
In the securities industry:
1. The difference between the bid and offer price for a security. For example, a security is bid 18, offered 19. The spread is 1 point.
2. The difference between the proceeds to the issuer and the public offering price on an underwriting. For example, The syndicate bought the bonds at 98½ and reoffered them at par. The spread is 1½ points.
3. In listed option trading: a purchase and sale of options of the same class. For example, "Buy an Eastman Kodak January 85 call, sell an Eastman Kodak January 95 call."
4. The difference between yields on various fixed-income securities.

SPREAD ADJUSTED NOTE
See SPAN.

SPREAD BANKER
Common expression for a commercial banker, or in some cases an investment banker, who attempts wherever possible to match the maturities of its own borrowings to those of loans extended. In this way, it can profit from the spread in the rate at which it borrows and lends money.
  See also MATCHED BOOK.

SPREADING
Used of option trading if a customer buys and sells options of the same class in an endeavor to profit from price change movements in the underlying stock and thus profit in the value of the premiums for the options. Spreads limit profits by limiting risk.

The term also is used of commodity contracts that partially offset risk in the hope of limited reward.

See also BEAR SPREAD; BULL SPREAD; CALENDAR SPREAD; VERTICAL SPREAD.

SPREAD LOAD
Term used of contractual-type mutual funds if the principal portion of the sales charge is paid over the first four years of the contract, with the remainder of the sales charge paid in equal installments over the remainder of the contract. Under current law, the maximum charge for sales may not exceed 20% of any year's contributions to the fund, and the total of the first four years' charges may not exceed 64% of one year's contributions. In practice, therefore, the sales charge will average 16% per year for the first four years. The advantages or disadvantages of the prepayment of fund sales charges should be weighed against the benefits provided by the plan.

SPREAD OPTION
When used of conventional (OTC) options, a spread option is a long put and a long call with the same expiration time but with different exercise prices. Thus, it is the equivalent of a long combination in listed options. This gives rise to confusion, so the reader must note the context in which the term is used.

SPREAD ORDER
Used of orders for listed options if the client is endeavoring to put on a spread. Because there is much volatility in option premiums, due to the price movement of the underlying stock, spread orders usually designate the series desired and the net debit or credit to the customer. It is

the net debit or credit that determines the client's strategy. Example: with ABC at 48, a client enters this spread order:

Buy 10 ABC Jan 45 calls
Sell 10 ABC Oct 40 calls
Net debit 3¼ points

The floor brokers will execute the spread if they can do so at a net debit of 3¼ points per contract.

SPREAD POSITION
Term used to describe the status of a client account in listed options if the client has both long and short options of the same class on the underlying security. For example, a client has the following option positions:

long 15 LMN Jan 55 calls
short 15 LMN Apr 50 calls

The client has a spread position in LMN options.
  See also OPTION SPREAD.

SPREADS
Acronym for Spread Protected Debt Security. A Morgan Stanley servicemark of a technique used to market the Transcontinental Gas Pipeline 8¹/₈s of 1/15/97. The security had a put feature enabling a one-time redemption two years after issue date if the issue was not trading at least at 132¹/₂ basis points above the U.S. Treasury 7¹/₄s of 11/15/96. In effect, as the name suggests, the bond is guaranteed a spread over Treasuries two years after issue date.

SPREAD SWAP
An arrangement, generally illegal if nonexempt securities are involved, between a customer and an underwriter of an upcoming issue of debt securities. It is an agreement to purchase a customer's securities in exchange for the new security at a fixed difference in price or yield that is determined before the new issue's registration statement becomes effective.

  This is not illegal if it is done after the registration statement becomes effective if the price is related to the market for both securities.

SPX
Identifier and ticker symbol for the Standard & Poor's 500 Index class of option traded on the CBOE. Settlement is made in cash and is dependent on the closing price of the S&P 500 Index on the day before expiration. As an European-style option, the SPX may only be exercised on the day before expiration.

A SQUARE TRANSACTION

Term used of a transaction in stocks/bonds where the broker/dealer buys and sells an equal amount. In effect, the broker/dealer takes no risk position subject to market volatility.

Also called a "natural."

SQUAWK BOX

An internal telephonic system used by many broker/dealers to provide two-way interoffice communication.

Such systems provide a means for marketing and other timely information to be communicated to the branch offices, and for branch office personnel to ask relevant questions.

Also called a "bitch box" because some of the questions are basically comments about home office shortcomings.

SQUEEZE OUT

Term used of a merger/acquisition technique that tends to discriminate against most stockholders in the acquired corporation. Under a "squeeze out," a soliciting group with 10% or more of the corporation gains effective control of a corporation through an offer of cash and junk bonds to the remaining stockholders. Using the company's assets to secure the debt, it—in effect—converts the company's stockholders to creditors of questionable status while assuming absolute control of management.

SRO

1. In the United States, the term means: self-regulatory organization. An SRO is a national securities exchange, a registered securities association, or a registered clearing agency that oversees and regulates the conduct of its members. SROs derive their authority from the SEC.
2. In the United Kingdom, an SRO is: self-regulating organisation. They are empowered under the Financial Services Bill of 1986 to oversee and regulate members of authorized trade associations that choose to register with them. There are many SROs in the United Kingdom, all subject to oversight by the Securities and Investments Board (SIB).

SROP

See SENIOR REGISTERED OPTION PRINCIPAL.

S
S

Used on the consolidated tape, usually in a vertical configuration, to designate two things: (1) a security trades in 10-share units and (2) that the number of units represented on the tape is not in round-lots, instead

it represents the total transaction in shares. For example, the consolidated tape displays the following transaction:

$$\text{UEP Pr}$$
$$30\overset{\text{s}}{\text{s}}\,97$$

Meaning: there was a sale of 30 shares of Union Electric Power preferred shares at $97 per share.

SSAP 15

The term means: stipulated standards of accounting practice—and the
abbreviation stands for procedures used to calculate taxes on corporate
income in the United Kingdom.

Although similar in concept to the Financial Accounting Standards
Board (FASB) in the United States, the practices in the United Kingdom
are more flexible. This often results in two companies with similar earnings having divergent tax consequences and thus different price-
earnings ratios in securities analysis.

$\dfrac{\text{S}}{\text{T}}$

Used on the consolidated tape, usually in a vertical configuration, to
designate that an execution on the floor was at a guaranteed price (i.e., it
was "stopped" by the specialist or by another member). For example,
the consolidated tape shows:

$$\text{MER} \qquad \qquad \text{S}$$
$$6\text{s}\ldots 62\ldots 2\text{s}\ldots 62\overline{\text{T}}$$

Meaning: There was a sale of 600 Merrill Lynch at 62, and that sale
caused the specialist to also trade 200 MER at the price of 62 that was
guaranteed to another floor broker.

STABILIZATION

The act of so pegging a price for a security with a bid that the price will
not drop below the bid price. Stabilization, which normally is illegal,
may be used in conjunction with a registered offering. Thus, the syndicate that is offering shares at $31 may stabilize the price with a bid at
$31 or $30⅞ or $30¾. Stabilizing bids always are identified as such.

SEC Rule 10b-7 gives the guidelines for stabilizing bids.

STABILIZE

Term frequently used by market technicians to designate that a previous trend (up or down) has reversed itself, either temporarily or per-
manently.

STAG

In British parlance, someone who subscribes to a net issue anticipating an immediate resale at a premium price. We have no similar word in the United States. However, an issue which should sell at an immediate premium is called a "hot issue" here.

STAGGERED BOARD

Term used to describe a corporate board of directors whose terms of office are so arranged that shareholders do not vote for an entire slate in any one year. Staggered boards often can be used to stymie a takeover attempt because new owners can only change a portion of the board in any one year.

STAGS

Acronym for Sterling Transferable Accruing Government Securities. This is the British equivalent of CATS and TIGRs. In effect, STAGS are zero-coupon bonds based on gilts—that is, sterling-denominated English Treasury bonds.

STAIRS

Acronym for Stepped Tax-Exempt Appreciation and Income Realization Securities. This is a Salomon Brothers version of the GAINS initiated by Goldman Sachs.

See GAINS for a detailed description.

STAKE-OUT INVESTMENT

Term used in conjunction with the purchase by one bank holding company of the convertible, nonvoting preferred stock of another bank holding company.

Concept: Present federal or state laws may prevent interstate banking; but if those laws are modified or repealed, the holder can convert the preferred into common stock. Thus, it has staked out its claim on the other bank.

STALE BULL/BEAR

Slang expression for an investor with a long-term long (or short) position in a stock. Thus, a "stale bull" is someone who has held a long position for a long time. The time period is relative. The opposite is true of a "stale bear."

STALE QUOTE

Term often used of a quote for a derivative product (an option or a future) that has remained unchanged while the price of the underlying has changed. Thus, if the premium for a short term 50 call remained at 3 while the price of the underlying had gone from 50½ to 51, the quote on the call would be considered "stale."

STAMP DUTY
An English tax on equity securities payable by a person transferring ownership in a British company. The stamp duty is payable only if the transfer occurs in the United Kingdom.

Purchase and sales made during the same account period are not subject to tax. Transfer of an ADR is similarly exempt from tax because the re-registration takes place outside the United Kingdom.

STAMP DUTY RESERVE TAX
See SDRT.

STANDARD & POOR'S
A leading registered investment adviser that specializes in financial reports. The Standard & Poor's manuals, its stock and bond guides, and its Blue List (book), which gives daily municipal bond offerings by dealers, are common publications sponsored by S&P.

In addition, the S&P Index of 500 Stocks is followed by many investors.

See also STANDARD & POOR'S INDEX.

STANDARD & POOR'S 500 INDEX SUBORDINATED NOTES
See SPINS.

STANDARD & POOR'S INDEX
A measurement of the value movement of 500 widely held common stocks. The index reflects the number of shares outstanding for each of the individual companies. It is considered as a measurement of average stock market performance and thus is used as a norm of above or below average price volatility of other securities. It is based on the price of the stocks times the number of outstanding shares; thus, it is capitalization weighted.

The 500 stocks represent 400 industrial, 20 transportation, 40 public utility, and 40 financial companies. These 500 companies are quite large and they represent over 70% of the dollar value of the top 5,000 companies whose stocks are publicly held.

Also called the "S&P Index."

STANDARD & POOR'S INDEX RECEIPTS
See SPIRS.

STANDARD & POOR'S RATING

A rating of credit risk assigned by Standard & Poor's to corporate and municipal bonds. The higher the rating, the lower the risk of default in the payment of interest and in the repayment of principal. The top four ratings, AAA, AA, A, and BBB, with their subdivisions, are considered investment grade and suitable for trust accounts and investments by fiduciaries. Bonds rated BB, B, and below are considered to be increasingly speculative.

STANDARD DEVIATION

Statistical term that designates the deviation (on average) of two thirds of the samples from the mean of the sample. Also abbreviated S/D.

To illustrate, during the past 60 years, the average annual compounded return on the 500 stocks of the S&P Index is +12.1%. The standard deviation, however, is +/- 21.2%. Thus, two thirds of the time, a random selection of *one* stock will fall between - 9% and +33%.

Standard deviation gives an insight into the unpredictability of a financial event, and thus an insight into the risk inherent in the choice. To lower this statistical risk of selection, the use of diversification within the portfolio is recommended. With eight or nine stocks in the portfolio the S/D is lowered to +/- 8%.

STANDARD MARGIN

1. Used in the futures industry to designate the good faith deposit required when a customer initiates purchase or sale positions. The good faith deposit differs by commodity and whether or not the customer is a commercial or speculative account. The margin is released when the customer closes the position.
2. Sometimes used in the securities industry to designate the initial margin required by the Federal Board or the NYSE when a customer buys or sells short a security.

STANDBY

See GNMA STANDBY.

STANDBY FEE

1. Used in investment banking of the fee paid to an underwriter who is willing to purchase any shares remaining from a rights offering to current shareholders.
2. A fee paid by the originator (issuer) of Ginnie Mae securities to selected institutional investors. The fee enables the originator to deliver the securities to the investors at a fixed price. In effect, the fee, which ranges from 1/4 to 1 1/4% of the face amount, gives the originator a put option on the securities it is about to issue.

STANDBY UNDERWRITER

Term used of an investment banker who agrees to purchase any shares that remain unsubscribed after they are offered to current shareholders through a rights offering. The investment banker is paid a fee to provide this service, and any unsubscribed shares are purchased by the investment banker at a price below the subscription price.

STANDING ROOM ONLY

Nickname for the common shares of Southland Royalty Company, a company engaged in oil and gas exploration. The nickname is derived from the NYSE ticker symbol: SRO.

STANDSTILL AGREEMENT

A corporate finance term that describes the contract between an issuer and the holder of a significant block of stock in that company. The holder, for example, agrees not to acquire more shares, nor to dispose of shares presently held, without prior consent of the issuer. Thus, the holder agrees to stand still.

STANY

Acronym for Security Traders' Association of New York. STANY is a membership group that meets for social, instructional, and lobbying purposes and is composed of persons in the New York City area who trade securities. STANY is affiliated with NSTA (National Security Trader's Association.

STAPLED STOCK

See PAIRED SHARES.

STAR

1. Acronym for Short-Term Auction Rate, a money market preferred stock issued by the Lincoln National Corporation. As with most such issues, the rate is reset each 49 days and has a put feature.
2. Euphemism for a successful investment. Generally, a "star" is one whose profits are such that they repay all prior losses.
   Also called a "gem" or a "pearl" (q.v.).

STATED PERCENTAGE ORDER

This is an order for a significant quantity of a listed stock. The instruction is to buy or sell in such a way that the amount constitutes a specified percentage of the total market volume in that security. In this way, the order will not upset the equilibrium that marks the normal price movements in the security.

STATED RATE AUCTION PREFERRED STOCK
See STRAPS.

STATED VALUE
A bookkeeping value assigned by the corporation to no-par stock. For example, a company has no-par stock outstanding. It assigned a stated value of $2 per share. Its balance sheet will appear:

Common stock: 1,000,000
shares outstanding at
$2 stated value. . . . $2,000,000

STATEMENT OF ACCOUNT
Term describing the periodic reports by broker/dealers to their customers that summarize account balances and list securities transactions. Federal law requires that statements of account be sent quarterly to all customers who transacted or who have a debit or credit balance or a net security position with the broker. In practice, statements are sent monthly if there was a transaction in the account or if there are option positions.

STATE OF NEW YORK MORTGAGE AGENCY (SONYMA)
A political subdivision of New York State empowered to liquify private banks, thus enabling them to provide residential housing loans within the state.

STATEMENT OF POLICY
See SOP.

STATUTE OF LIMITATIONS
The provision in every law that fixes the time parameters within which parties must take judicial action. After the time has elapsed, enforcement is barred.

Under the securities laws of the United States, the statute of limitations is usually three years for civil actions. It may be longer for criminal actions. Legal advice should be sought.

STATUTORY DISQUALIFICATION
Often abbreviated as SD, this is a list of offenses set forth in the Securities and Exchange Act of 1934 that would prohibit someone from qualifying as an associated person of a broker/dealer.

The NYSE and the NASD have adopted similar provisions in their rules or bylaws to disqualify persons from membership.

STATUTORY UNDERWRITER

Federal law defines an underwriter as a person who purchases a security from an issuer for purpose of resale. The term *statutory underwriter* describes a person who performs such an action, albeit inadvertently, and thereby subjects himself to the penalties of the law for those who sell unregistered securities. Example: A registered representative fails to exercise proper diligence in the sale of securities by a control person. The representative and his firm could be penalized, as a statutory underwriter, for violations of the Securities Act of 1933.

STATUTORY VOTING

A procedure, outlined in a corporations charter, whereby shareholders may cast one vote for, or one vote against, each of the candidates on the slate of candidates proposed for the board of directors. Shareholders, however, may not concentrate their vote (number of shares times number of candidates) on any one of the candidates. End result: holders of 50–67% of a corporation's shares will control the election of the board of directors. Most corporations provide for statutory voting.

See also CUMULATIVE VOTING.

STEEL-COLLAR WORKER

Tongue-in-cheek term that reflects the increased presence of automation in manufacturing. The "steel" refers to metal robots that replace human workers in many automated industries.

STEENTH

Abbreviation for one sixteenth. Commonly used to designate bids or offers quoted in 16ths. For securities quoted in dollars, a steenth is $6\frac{1}{4}$ cents per share; if a security is quoted in bond points, a steenth is $.625 ($62\frac{1}{2}$ cents) per $1,000 of face value. Popular usage: "It's quoted a quarter to a steenth." Meaning: the bid is one quarter ($\frac{1}{4}$), the offer is $\frac{1}{16}$th higher ($\frac{5}{16}$). The quote could also be 4 to 5 steenths (i.e., $\frac{4}{16}$ bid and $\frac{5}{16}$ offered).

STEENTHING

A questionable practice whereby a floor broker undercuts another order by the minimal amount and, after getting an execution, claims parity for a larger amount with the order that formerly had a time priority at that price. This practice is often possible in stock option contracts—although ethically inappropriate—because of exchange rules regarding priority, parity, and precedence in verbal bids and offers.

STEP-DOWN FLOATING-RATE NOTE
A three- to five-year security with a changeable interest-rate payment pegged periodically to the prevailing commercial paper rate *plus* a declining adjustment in interest for each year of life. Thus, the rate may be the competitive commercial paper rate plus 0.25% the first year, 0.20% the second year, and so forth.

STEPPED-COUPON SECURITIES
A debt security in which all bonds pay the same interest rate each year. However, that rate is set to rise periodically on a pre-established schedule.

Some municipal securities have been issued with this characteristic.

STEPPED TAX-EXEMPT APPRECIATION AND INCOME REALIZATION SECURITIES
See STAIRS.

STERLING SECURITY
A corporation's debt securities that are issued in the United Kingdom or, if issued outside the United Kingdom, are denominated in pounds sterling.

STERLING TRANSFERABLE ACCRUING GOVERNMENT SECURITIES
See STAGS.

STICKERS
Industry jargon for prospectus supplements. Such supplements may be required because material information has changed between the time of the printing of the prospectus and the time of the actual offering of the security. Such information may be printed on small "stickers" that are appended to the prospectus.

The term is not used of "supplemental information" that often accompanies the prospectuses of investment company shares. Because such securities are in constant registration and information changes, many mutual funds print a standard prospectus and a supplement of additional information. Both are sent to customers. The supplement is periodically updated.

STICKY DEAL
Industry jargon for an underwriting that will be difficult to market. The difficulty may arise from market conditions, the company, or economic factors. For example, "At $45 per share, this could be a sticky deal." Ba-

sic idea: The underwriter is measuring its risk against the risk the investor will assume.

STIF

Acronym for short-term issuance facility. This practice has also been succeeded by RUF: revolving underwriter facility.

See also SNIF.

STIF FUND

Acronym for short-term investment fund. Industry term for any pool of money invested in money market instruments, generally with maturities up to 90 days. The popular money market mutual funds are STIF funds.

In practice, the term is not used frequently. *Money market fund*, however, is a well-known and widely used term.

STILTS

See SHORT-TERM INDEXED LIABILITY TRANSACTIONS.

STK

This is a sometimes used abbreviation for stock, an equity security issued by a corporation.

STOCK

Term used of an investment represented by an ownership certificate. For example, "I own stock in ABC corporation," or "We own 200 shares of stock."

Basic meaning: Any capital contribution to a business venture. For example, "I own livestock"; "I've got to restock my shelves"; "I've got to take stock of my investments"; and, from long ago, "public stock" (the name for the first public bond issue of the United States).

In practice, therefore, as a noun the word *stock* means a transferable evidence of ownership of a corporation; but in other contexts, stock may mean a debt or an action.

STOCK AHEAD

Trading floor expression. "Stock ahead" would be relayed to a registered representative who asks about the status of a client's unexecuted limit order. Meaning: There were other executions at the client's limit price, but the client's order was not executed because other brokers had prior limit orders at the same price. For example, "If the best bid for a stock was $18, and your client's bid for 100 represented the 28th of 36 round-lot bids for the stock at that price, transactions for 1,500 shares at $18 would execute many orders but would not execute your client's order." If you asked about your client's order, the response would be, "Stock ahead."

STOCK APPRECIATION RIGHTS

Acronym: SAR. Privileges that are sometimes accorded to officers and directors of publicly owned corporations as a form of special compensation. SARs represent the right to receive a financial benefit based on a specific number of shares granted to the affiliate's account with the company. The difference is often that between the market value of shares on the day the right is granted and the day on which it is exercised. In this way, it is an *artificial option* in which the employee neither pays money nor can lose money.

STOCK/BOND CERTIFICATE

The actual piece of paper that evidences ownership in a corporation.

Industry standards prescribe paper quality, engraving, and other obstacles to forgery.

The term *bond certificate* also is used.

Antonym: book entry. In this case, there is no certificate, and journal entries are used to transfer ownership.

STOCK BUSINESS

Term used in municipal bond underwriting if a dealer or a dealer bank buys part of a municipal issue for a personal account to make short-term profits by a later resale of the bonds.

Also used in the expression "going for stock" to designate that part of an underwriting was bought by members of the account for future bond sales.

STOCK CLEANING

Name of an innovative financing technique used by the Algemene Bank Nederland (ABN) in its takeover of Exchange Bancorp in Chicago. ABN placed privately 9.4 million ordinary shares with *no* dividend in 1989 in exchange for 7.5 million ordinary shares entitled to a 1989 dividend (in effect, making a stock dividend before the fact). ABN then sold the shares entitled to a dividend publicly on a worldwide basis. The net result was an immediate increase in bank equity with no outlay of new funds in 1989.

STOCK DIVIDEND

A distribution of additional shares to current shareholders made by the issuing corporation in lieu of a cash dividend. The distribution, which requires approval of the board of directors but not the shareholders, conserves cash within the corporation. The shares, which normally come from authorized but unissued shares, are bought with retained earnings. The distribution is not a taxable event for the recipients until the shares are sold.

STOCK EXCHANGE AUTOMATED QUOTATIONS
See SEAQ.

STOCK EXCHANGE AUTOMATED TRADING SYSTEM
See SEATS.

STOCK EXCHANGE DAILY OFFICIAL LIST
See SEDOL.

STOCK EXCHANGE OF SINGAPORE
See SES.

STOCK EXCHANGE POOL NOMINEES
See SEPON.

STOCK FUTURES 50
This is a futures contract traded on the Osaka Stock Exchange (OSE). It is an equity-related futures contract indexed to the component issues. Unlike most such contracts, it settles not for cash but for physical delivery of the underlying package of its 50 component stocks.

STOCKHOLDER
A person, either real or legal, with a proprietary participation in a corporation. This interest, in most cases, is represented by a certificate that, in the case of public corporations, is freely transferrable.

STOCKHOLDERS' EQUITY
See SHAREHOLDERS' EQUITY.

STOCKHOLM STOCK EXCHANGE
This bourse is located in the capital of Sweden and is the largest bourse in Scandinavia.

Trading hours are from 10:00 A.M. until 2:30 P.M. without any restrictions on after-hour trading. Settlement is on the fifth business day following trade date.

There is an onerous transfer tax on Swedish shares; for this reason most international companies buy shares outside Sweden. Leading Swedish companies are also listed in London and New York.

STOCK INDEX FUTURE
This is an obligation to make or take a cash settlement, during a specific month in the future, based on the price movements that occur in the specific stock index underlying the contract. The most common stock indexes used for these contracts are Value Line, S&P, NYSE, and Dow Jones.

STOCK JOCKEY
Colorful expression for a registered representative (RR) who generates a significant amount of commission dollars from the short-term trading of customers' accounts. Such activities often take place in accounts over which the RR has discretionary authorization.

As a general rule, the term is pejorative.

STOCK LIST
A function of each of the registered exchanges that examines the eligibility of companies for listing on that exchange, the possibility of unlisted trading, and whether a listed security should be delisted from trading.

Also called the "stock list department."

STOCK LOAN BUSINESS
A service industry, or part of a broker/dealer's business, that endeavors to make a profit from the lending of securities, or charges a fee to bring lenders and borrowers of securities together.

Such fees usually are based on the value of the securities borrowed, although in some cases, if interest rates are very high, the lender will be charged for the free use of the money obtained when the securities are loaned.

STOCK LOAN DEPARTMENT
A work area of a member firm that is involved in the lending and borrowing of securities. Securities are borrowed to complete short sales or to complete transactions if the broker's client is a seller and has failed to deliver the sold security.

STOCK PERFORMANCE EXCHANGE-LINKED BOND
See SPEL-BOND.

STOCK POWER
A form of assignment and power of substitution used in the sale and transfer of securities. The form, which is a separate piece of paper, duplicates the transfer form on the back of registered securities. If signed, witnessed, and guaranteed by a member firm or a commercial bank and attached to a stock or registered bond certificate, it will be accepted by

the transfer agent and the certificate will be registered in the name of the new owner.

Also called a "stock/bond power."

STOCK RECORD
This function monitors the movement of all securities, both stocks and bonds, within the firm. The stock record department identifies by name the securities it controls and the owners and audits on a day-to-day basis the location of these securities.

Also called the "stock record department" in many firms.

STOCK RECORD BREAK
The term is used of any out-of-balance situation in a firm's recordkeeping of securities that are its responsibility. In effect, there is a position debit without a corresponding credit—or vice versa. Such "breaks" must be reconciled quickly, because the older they are the more difficult they are to reconcile; in addition, such "breaks" can have an adverse effect on the member's capital requirements.

Also called a "break."

STOCK SPLIT-UP
See STOCK DIVIDEND.

STOCKWATCH AUTOMATED TRACKING SYSTEM
See SWAT.

STOP-LIMIT ORDER
An instruction on a stop order to buy or sell. If there is a transaction at the stop price or higher (buy stop limit), or at the stop price or lower (sell stop limit), the customer wants to buy or sell at the designated limit price given on the order. For example, Buy 400 LMN 52 STOP 53 LIMIT. Explanation: The customer wants a limit order entered at 53 as soon as there is a transaction at 52 or above.

The American Stock Exchange permits such orders only if the stop and limit prices are the same.

STOP ORDER
An instruction by a customer on an order to buy or sell. The instruction requests that a market order to buy or sell be executed once a given transaction price is attained in the security. For example, Buy 800 ABC 28 STOP. Any transaction at 28 or above elects (activates) the stop and the order now becomes a market order to buy at the best available price.

Stop orders may not be entered for over-the-counter transactions.

Also called a "suspended market order" because the execution is suspended until a transaction in the public market elects the order.

STOP-OUT PRICE
Term used of Treasury security auctions. It is the lowest price accepted in the auction. This price plus the highest price are used to determine the average price. Noncompetitive purchasers—$1 million or less for T-bills, T-notes, and T-bonds—pay the average of the competitive bidder prices.

STOP OUT RATE
Slang for the lowest rate of interest the Federal Reserve will accept from a nonbank dealer on repurchase agreements. In effect, the Federal Reserve is buying securities from nonbank dealers, providing cash for up to 15 days, and presuming that the nonbank dealers will deposit these funds into the banking system. In this way, the Federal Reserve is indirectly providing funds to the banking system.

See also REVERSE REPO.

STOPPED OUT
Industry jargon used on an exchange floor if a customer's order is executed at the stopped (guaranteed) price given by a specialist or other member. For example, a broker with a market order to buy is guaranteed a price of $53 per share. If the next transaction is at $53 per share, that also is the price that the broker's client will receive. The client has been stopped out. His transaction will appear on the tape with the symbol ST following the price.

STOPPED STOCK
Term used to describe the guarantee that a specialist or other member gives to a broker with a public order to buy or sell. The guarantee of a specific price or better permits the broker to seek a better price without the fear of missing the market. For example, a broker with a market order to buy is stopped at 52 by a specialist. This means that the broker will not pay more than 52 for the stock.

STORY BONDS
Debt securities of corporate issuers rumored to be takeover targets. Unlike the stocks of these companies, however, which usually go up in value, the debt securities of these issuers usually decline because the takeover will usually raise the amount of debt and lower the quality of other outstanding bonds.

STORY STOCKS

Slang term for any stock whose market value is more dependent on a story (either real or fictitious) than on its balance sheet figures.

At the end of bull markets, story stocks abound as the market looks for a favorite; thus, an abundance of story stocks often presages a downturn in the market.

In the 1980s, the term was also applied to companies about whom there was a rumored takeover or a financial restructuring.

STOX IN A BOX

Slang for a form of illegal price manipulation. Such manipulation may occur during the original distribution of a "penny stock." The scam involves a partial withholding of the original offering by the underwriter, thereby lowering the supply. Later, when the artificially lowered supply causes the price to rise, the underwriter carefully releases the "stox in a box" at inflated values.

STRADDLE

When used of listed stock options, a straddle may be either long or short. A *long straddle* is a long call and a long put on the same underlying security at the same exercise price and the same expiration month. For example, 1 long ABC Jan 50 call and 1 long ABC Jan 50 put. A *short straddle* is a short call and a short put on the same security at the same exercise price and the same expiration month.

When used of commodity positions, a straddle is a purchase of a commodity future with an expiration in one month, and the sale of a commodity future with an expiration in another month.

STRAIGHT BOND

Any bond that is not convertible into another security.

STRAIGHT-LINE DEPRECIATION

A conservative accounting procedure that apportions a corporation's cost of a qualified asset over its useful lifetime in equal annual amounts. The amount to be depreciated is the cost minus the estimated scrap value at the end of useful life. The annual amount of depreciation is subtracted from fixed assets on the balance sheet and from operating income on the income statement. Because depreciation is part of the cost of doing business, it reduces the company's tax liability.

See also CASH FLOW.

STRANGLE

Slang for a long call and a long put on the same underlying security when both options are out of the money. Example: When the underlying is at 85, a long call at 95 and a long put at 80 would be a "strangle."

To be profitable, a strangle requires a highly volatile movement in underlying security. In the example given above, there would have to be a minimum swing of 15 points for both long options, at one time or another, to be "in the money."

STRAP

A form of conventional option that couples one put and two calls on the same security at the same exercise price with the same expiration date. The premium is less than it would be if the options were purchased separately.

The term is not used of listed options; instead this would be a long straddle and a long call.

STRAPS

Acronym for Stated Rate Auction Preferred Stock. STRAPS are a Goldman Sachs' innovation made to appeal to investors in both fixed and variable rate preferred shares. Investors in STRAPS are entitled to the 70% "dividend received" exclusion for corporate investors. Dividend payments are at a fixed rate for five years and at a variable rate thereafter.

STRATEGY

1. Any defined plan for profiting from investments or groups of investments; thus, dollar cost averaging or diversification, or both, may be called "strategies."
2. A synonym for asset allocation. In this sense, the asset allocation may be recommended for all of a firm's customers; for example, "At present, our strategy is based on a portfolio of 65% stocks and 35% bonds."
3. The approach to investing that is specific to a customer. For example, "Mr. Jones, at your age and with your investment objectives, your main strategy should center on capital preservation for income."

Although *strategy* and *tactic* are often used interchangeably, strategy tends to be longer-term and tactics shorter-term in scope.

THE STREET

Popular term for Wall Street and the surrounding financial area. In recent years, the term has included all elements of the financial community, no matter where located. For example, "Here's what I hear on the Street."

STREET NAME

Popular term for a security registered in the name of a broker/dealer. For example, "The security is in street name." Securities owned by the broker/dealer are in street name, and securities owned by customers that have been deposited with the broker/dealer normally are registered in the name of the broker/dealer to facilitate transfer when the security is sold.

Customer-owned securities in street name are said to have the broker/dealer as the nominee and the customer as the beneficial owner (i.e., the owner of the security and all of the rights pertaining thereto).

STREET SIDE

Term that describes the relationship between buying and selling firms in a securities transaction made on behalf of their customers. Such transactions must be cleared and settled. In the typical member organization, the cashiering function handles the street side of the transaction.

Antonym: customer side—that is, the bookkeeping of the monetary relationship between the firm and its customers. The margin function handles the customer side.

In practice, "street side" is used both as a noun and an adjective.

STRIKE PRICE

Popular name for the exercise price of a put or call option.

Also called "striking price."

STRIKING PRICE

See STRIKE PRICE.

STRIP

A form of conventional option that couples one call and two puts on the same security at the same exercise price with the same expiration date. The premium is less than it would be if the options were purchased separately.

The term is not used of listed options; instead this would be a long straddle and a long put.

STRIPPED BONDS

These are debt instruments placed in escrow. Then, evidences of ownership in either the bond principal or the interest payments are sold separately.

Stripped bonds give rise to TIGRs, CATS, COUGARs.

Term also used: *stripped coupons*.

See PRIME and SCORE for a similar concept in terms of equity securities.

STRIPS
Acronym for Separate Trading of Registered Interest and Principal of Securities. An innovation by the U.S. Treasury to sell principal and interest payments separately on certain selected government issues.

All STRIPS are book entry only.

STRIPS have substantially lowered the number of CATS, TIGRs, and COUGARs issued.

STRONG HANDS
Industry term for investors who are likely to hold for the long term.

Originally, the term was used to mean institutional investors; that is, persons with sufficient funds that they are not forced to sell in down markets.

With the advent of program trading and the increased turnover of institutional portfolios (40% of the ownership versus 80+% of the trading), the term is no longer centered on long-term holding.

STRUCTURING DEPOSITS
An SEC euphemism for the deposit of cash (or cash equivalents) into customer accounts in amounts just short of $10,000. By doing this, the reporting requirement to the Treasury Department is avoided.

The Treasury Department requires notification of all transactions in cash, or cash equivalents, in amounts of $10,000 or more to prevent the illegal "laundering" of money. "Structuring" occurs when the amounts are purposely kept below $10,000 to avoid the reporting requirements.

STTEPS
See SHORT-TERM TAX-EXEMPT PUT SECURITIES.

STUB STOCK
Street slang for small amounts of publicly held stock left outstanding after a reorganization, tender, or merger.

Often, because of the large amount of debt assumed by the company, the actual net worth of the stock is negative. In this case, the value of the stock, if any, may be quite volatile.

STUDENT LOAN MARKETING ASSOCIATION
Nicknamed "Sallie Mae," this government-sponsored private corporation purchases, holds, services, and sells student loans made by banks and other institutions to qualified students of colleges, universities, and vocational schools.

Bonds issued by Sallie Mae are backed by the full faith and credit of the U.S. government.

STUF
Acronym for short-term underwriting facility. See SNIF and RUF (revolving underwriting facilities).

SUBCHAPTER M
That section of the Internal Revenue Code that sets forth the conditions under which investment companies and real estate investment trusts may distribute income, whether from dividends, interest, or capital gains, to their shareholders without incurring a federal tax liability for the company or trust.

See also CONDUIT THEORY.

SUBCHAPTER S
See SUBCHAPTER S CORPORATION.

SUBCHAPTER S CORPORATION
A relatively small corporation that qualifies and chooses to be taxed as a partnership under Subchapter S of the Internal Revenue Code. Under this option, taxable income and certain liabilities of the corporation flow through to the individual proprietors as part of their tax reports.

SUBJECT
Term used of a quote made by a dealer, whether a bid or an offer or both, that must be reviewed before a final decision to buy or sell is made. Examples: (1) all orders received by underwriting syndicates are subject to prior sale; thus, they are subject until confirmed; (2) requests for quotes made in excess of the common unit of trading will be given as subject until the dealer has more information about the trade.

Common industry practice requires that dealers identify quotes given as "subject" if further negotiation of the details of the contract is required.

SUBJECT MARKET
A quotation on which a broker/dealer is unable to trade until he confirms the acceptability of the bid and asked prices with the party he represents.

SUBJECT QUOTE
Industry term for a bid or offer, or both, that requires further negotiation before a firm quotation will be made by a dealer.

See also SUBJECT.

SUBORDINATED

Latin: *subordinare,* to be below. Term used of debt securities if the bondholder not only gives precedence to secured creditors but also to general creditors of the issuer. For example, an issuer has outstanding mortgage bonds and has accepted deposits from customers. The issuer then sells subordinated debentures. Holders of the subordinated debentures will receive payment after all other creditors are paid. However, they will be paid before the corporate owners are paid.

SUBPOENA

Also: sub poena. (Pronounced: s'peeny.) A document issued by a court that requires an action by the person who is served to provide information (duces tecum) or to appear in person at a judicial proceeding.

Failure to comply with the terms of the subpoena may result in punishment, either civil or criminal.

SUBPOENA DUCES TECUM

Latin: under penalty of law (I order you) to bring with you. . . . In effect, this court order requires that the recipient produce such records as are pertinent to a trial. Such orders may also be issued by the SEC in its investigation of violations, or allegations thereof, of the securities laws of the United States.

SUBSCRIPTION PRIVILEGE

This privilege allows a common shareholder to buy, on a pro rata basis, newly issued shares at a favorable price before the shares are offered to the general public. The privilege also may extend to an issue of convertible bonds or preferred stock. The privilege normally has a fixed period within which it must be exercised; the time usually is 30 to 60 days.

The evidence of the subscription privilege is known as a "subscription right."

Also known as "preemptive right."

SUBSCRIPTION RATIO

The company-established number of subscription rights needed by a shareholder to subscribe to a single share, or to a convertible bond, under the subscription privilege.

SUBSCRIPTION RIGHT

A security that evidences the number of rights granted to a shareholder on the occasion of a subscription to new common shares or new convertible securities. The practice is to issue one right for each common share held. The common shareholder may buy one new share, as determined by the subscription ratio, by sending the rights and the required dollar price to the company. For example, the subscription ratio is 4 rights for each new share; the subscription price is $40 per share. A stockholder who receives 40 rights may purchase 10 new shares if he sends the 40 rights and $400 to the company.

Subscription rights may be sold to other persons who wish to subscribe to new shares.

SUBSCRIPTION WARRANT

A security normally given in conjunction with the purchase of another security. For example, a bond or a preferred stock that permits the holder to buy one or more common shares of the issuing corporation at a fixed price for a designated time.

Subscription warrants are similar to subscription rights with these exceptions: they are generally valid for longer periods and, at the time they are granted, the subscription price is higher than the current market price for the common stock. Thus, immediate exercise will not be profitable for the recipient.

Also known as a "warrant."

SUBSTANTIALLY SIMILAR

Legal tax term used in connection with comparisons of debt instruments. The AICPA Audit and Accounting Guide defines it as a liability in which:

1. The obligors are the same (excluding sovereign nations, government sponsored entities and central banks).
2. Risks and rights of debtholders are identical in form and type.
3. The securities have identical interest rates.
4. The securities have identical maturities.
5. The securities have identical unpaid principal amounts.

SUBSTANTIVE INTEREST

Adjective often used in connection with the term *interest* or the term *matter* to designate a proposed corporate activity that will affect shareholders or facts that will influence investor decisions. For example, "The next annual meeting of the XYZ Corporation will propose matters of substantive interest to investors."

The term is legal; most unsophisticated persons would use the term *important* in its place.

SUBSTITUTION

1. The sale of one security and the purchase of another in a client account.
2. The withdrawal of one security from a client margin account and the deposit of a second security to collateralize the client's debit balance.

3. The action of an attorney whereby he permits a second attorney to exercise his function in the process of securities transfers. For example, a client provided his broker with a signed stock power that also permits power of substitution.

SUCKER RALLY
Slang for a general rise in prices in the midst of a bear market. It is often characterized by falling volume along with rising prices.

So called because sophisticated investors do not buy at such times, only "suckers" who are lured into the situation for illusory quick profits.

SUGGING
English slang for "selling under the guise of. . . ."

This practice is of questionable ethics and suggests that customer purchases are solicited on the occasion of a forthcoming research report. The concept is this: Buy now on the rumor and have an immediate profit when the actual printed report is published.

Perhaps from the Scottish "soughing" (pronounced "suffing"), meaning to spread a rumor.

SUITABILITY
A broad industry term that signifies that a firm, or registered representative, recommendation is appropriate in terms of the customer's investment objectives, financial capabilities, and other portfolio holdings.

The term *suitable* is used not because a recommended investment is the "best" but because—all things considered—it is not inappropriate. Often customer "risk tolerance" is the best determinant of suitability.

All SROs have arbitration facilities for customers who consider that they have been given unsuitable recommendations. As with many financial decisions, there are some wrong answers but many right answers.

SUMMARY COMPLAINT PROCEEDINGS
Under the National Association of Securities Dealers' (NASD's) Code of Procedure, the district business conduct committees may permit the respondent in a trade practice complaint to plead guilty to relatively minor infractions of the association's Rules of Fair Practice. Under such summary complaint proceedings, the respondent waives the right of appeal; but the maximum penalty is censure and a fine of $1,000.

SUM-OF-THE-YEARS'-DIGITS (SOYD)
An acceptable accounting method of accelerated depreciation. In it, the annual depreciation is found as follows: (1) determine the amount to be depreciated; (2) add the ordinal numbers of the years of useful life (e.g., 5

years is 1+2+3+4+5+15); (3) multiply the amount to be depreciated by the reverse of the ordinal year (e.g., first year is 5, second year is 4), and divide by the sum of the years.

To illustrate: if $15,000 is to be depreciated over 5 years, the depreciation in year 2 would be:

$$\$15{,}000 \times \frac{4}{15} = \$4{,}000$$

SUNDRY ASSET
Balance sheet entry used for an item of value owned by a corporation that will be held for a relatively long time but not used in the day-to-day operation of the corporation and thus does not fit neatly into current or fixed assets. For example, raw or undeveloped land or an investment in another company could be listed under sundry assets.

As a general rule, such intangibles as good will and prepaid expenses are not listed under sundry assets; instead, a separate entry is made on the balance sheet for such items of value.

SUNRISE INDUSTRY
Broad term used to describe businesses engaged in promising areas of the economy. At the present time, companies engaged in high technology, genetic engineering, pharmaceuticals, and waste disposal, for example, are considered to be in "sunrise industries."

SUNSET INDUSTRY
Broad term to describe businesses engaged in mature areas of the economy that are declining and may be phased out by rising technology. At the present time, coal mining, steel production, heavy machinery, commercial railroading, and automotive manufacturing are suffering a decline.

SUNSET PROVISION
Slang for a feature incorporated into a law that, unless positively reinstated by legislature, will expire at a specified future date. For example, the new tax law provides for the limited tax exemption of dividends from utility stocks reinvested in new shares of the same issuer under a sunset provision that expired in tax year 1985.

SUNSHINE LAW
Colorful expression that describes the public's right of access to the meetings and records of certain governmental agencies involved in investigatory, reporting, and rulemaking processes.

Most activities of the SEC and the Commodities Futures Trading Commission (CFTC) are subject to sunshine laws.

SUNSHINE TRADER
Street slang for a "fair weather" marketmaker. In other words, a broker/dealer who is willing to make an active two-sided market in those stocks that are going up in price. When the price starts to fall, the broker/dealer is unwilling to continue marketmaking activities.

SUNSHINE TRADING
Slang for the execution of large trades in the public marketplace made with prior notification to interested prospective customers. The practice is somewhat suspect because it is felt that the advance notice could frighten away contra parties to the transaction.

SUPER BOWL OMEN
A somewhat lighthearted market indicator used by forecasters. Concept: If the winner of the Super Bowl is from the old National Football League, the stock market will rise during that year. If the winner is from the old American Football League, the market will decline.

SUPER DOT
An NYSE automated order processing and trade reporting system that enables the prompt entry and execution of limited price orders. Super DOT can execute orders up to 30,099 shares if these are received before the opening of the market.

The Super DOT system has been greatly expanded in recent years.

SUPERMAJORITY
A stockholder vote in which 80% or more of the outstanding shares are voted in favor of a motion.

To thwart takeover attempts, some companies have written a requirement for a supermajority into their corporate charters in certain corporate decisions.

SUPER NOW ACCOUNT
This is an expanded version of the NOW (negotiable order of withdrawal) account. Under the Super NOW account, depositors with a minimum balance of $2,500 are permitted unlimited checking privileges and are paid prevailing money market rates, rather than the minimum interest rates.

SUPER PO
See SUPER PRINCIPAL ONLY BOND.

701

SUPER PRINCIPAL ONLY BOND

Term used of a collateralized mortgage obligation (CMO) stripped of its interest payments but inclusive of a planned amortization class (PAC) or a targeted amortization class (TAC).

These latter features lead to a disadvantageous impact on the residual class of securities in a CMO if interest rates change significantly. Such a Super PO is more volatile than ordinary POs in the face of interest-rate changes.

SUPERRESTRICTED ACCOUNT

Term formerly applied to margin accounts that were margined at less than 30% of the market value of the securities in the account. The term *superrestricted* was dropped from Regulation T in February 1982.

SUPERSHARES

Written "SuperShares." Name given to an investment trust that provides interested parties with a chance to participate in market trends without using portfolio "insurance."

Subscribers' monies are divided into two mutual fund pools: money market issues and stock portfolios. Holders can swap their interests into a trust issuing equity index units. The units, listed on the NYSE, can then be broken into four types of SuperShares, each with a different objective:
1. Downside Protection (falling market).
2. Indexed Income (slight falling market).
3. Money Market Income (flat market).
4. Upside Appreciation (surging rising market).

SUPERSINKER

Slang for debt securities that will be retired faster than would normally be expected by the use of sinking fund deposits. For example, a bond issue that uses a sinking fund to retire a debt in 3–5 years, rather than the usual 15–20 years, would be an example of a "supersinker."

SUPERVISORY ANALYST

Designation applied by the NYSE to an employee or principal of a member firm who qualifies to review and approve research reports designed for public distribution. Qualification is achieved through a special NYSE examination.

SUPER VOTING RIGHT

Management-accorded privilege permitting a select class of shareholders a greater voice in corporation management than another class of common stocks. Before the SEC implemented its "one share—one vote" rule, the use of a "time-phased" super voting right was a popular defense against a hostile takeover.

Under the "time-phased" concept, when an unwanted suitor acquired a specific percentage of stock, a new class of voting stock was initiated for earlier shareholders. This stock carried a greater voice in corporate affairs, thereby discouraging the prospective predator.

SUPPLEMENTAL EXECUTIVE RETIREMENT PLAN
See SERP.

SUPPLEMENTAL MARKETMAKER (SMM)
A category of member of the CBOE authorized to assist lead marketmakers (LMMs) in expediting the opening rotation in OEX Index options.

The SMM is appointed on a week-to-week basis by the exchange's Market Performance Committee. The SMM is required to accept previously agreed-to portions of customer order imbalances in specific OEX Index series. The SMM works closely with the LMM in specific series of OEX options.

SUPPLY-SIDE ECONOMICS
See THE LAFFER CURVE.

SUPPLY-SIDERS
A school of economic thought that holds that a cut in tax rates plus a concomitant cut in government spending is the best way to stimulate the economy. The central concept is based on the idea that, by giving people increased amounts to spend, more jobs will be created and the economy will expand. This, in turn, will provide more income for the government for needed social programs.

SUPPORTING
This term describes the practice of buying stock at prices to prevent a decline in value and thus discourage the exercise of put options. The practice may be manipulative and in violation of federal securities laws.

SUPPORT LEVEL
Based on the previous trading history of a security, this is the price level at which buyers have tended to purchase a security in volume, and thus have overcome the downward pressure from sellers. For example, "On five occasions in the past year, when the price of ABC has dropped to 35 or so, the price has consistently risen." A technical analyst would consider 35 as the support level.

SURPLUS INSURANCE
Term used in conjunction with the management of pension fund assets. The concept: The manager uses arbitrage and stock and index futures but only to hedge the amount whereby assets exceed expected benefit obligations. In effect, it is a form of portfolio insurance, but only with the balance sheet surplus of the pension fund.

SURROGATE COURT
See PROBATE COURT.

SURROGATE COURT CERTIFICATE
A judicial document issued by a surrogate court that recognizes the authority of someone to settle the estate of a deceased person. Such a certificate, dated within the past six months, must accompany requests for transfer of title of securities registered in the name of a decedent.

SUSHI BONDS
Obligations of Japanese entities issued and denominated in Eurodollars. By treaty, such instruments do not count against the limits on holdings of foreign securities imposed on some Japanese financial institutions.

SUSPENSE ACCOUNT
A record maintained by a broker/dealer for money or security balance differences until such time as they are reconciled.

SWAG THEORY
Acronym for scientific wild ass guess. This facetious vulgarism is part of the lingo of the Street. The term is a take-off of WAG theory (q.v.).

Typical usage could be as follows: "People are talking of a drop in interest rates, but I don't see it happening. According to the SWAG theory, when that happens, one really should go into short-term debt instruments."

SWAP
Industry jargon for the sale of one security and the purchase of another. The term, which basically describes a substitution, tends to be used with a qualifying phrase that describes the reason for the swap. For example, the client made a maturity swap, or a quality swap (higher rated for lower-rated bonds), or a yield swap (a higher yield for lower-yielding bonds), and so on.

SWAP FUND
See EXCHANGE-TYPE COMPANY.

704

SWAP ORDER
Instruction from a customer to sell one security and purchase another on the same day. As a general rule, the instruction is absolute and has no contingent conditions. Most member firms will not accept a swap order unless it can be executed in full within the member firm. For example, a swap of one unit investment trust for another. Instead, the firm will require two orders: one to sell and, when executed, another order to buy.

SWAP RATE
In foreign exchange markets, the swap rate is the difference between a currency's immediate (spot) price and its contract price in futures trading.

SWAPTION
A combination of "swap" and "option"; that is, an option on a swap transaction. A swaption gives the purchaser the right, but not the obligation, to enter into an interest-rate swap at a preset rate within a specified time.

The swaption writer assumes the obligation of providing the swap, but the writer can hedge the risk through certain offsetting transactions.

The swaption purchaser pays a premium to the writer for the privilege.

SWAT
Acronym for StockWatch Automated Tracking System. SWAT is an NASD computer program designed to identify abnormal trading patterns for OTC; that is, NASDAQ-traded securities. The program sets performance parameters; that is, price and volume figures. Activities that substantially exceed those parameters are investigated.

SWEEPING THE STREET
The term is used in conjunction with corporate takeovers and signifies that the person endeavoring to take over acquires large blocks of stock in a relatively short time period before the knowledge of the takeover is generally known. In this way, the initiator gets most of the stock before his or her intentions are known and the price of the stock becomes exorbitant.

SWEETENER
Industry slang for an issue of securities that adds a special feature to induce the purchase of the security. Thus, the addition of convertibility to an issue of bonds or preferreds, or a subscription right that permits

the purchase of shares at a price below the current market price, would be considered as sweeteners.

SWIFT
Acronym for Society for Worldwide Interbank Financial Telecommunications. SWIFT is a European version of CHIPS in the United States. SWIFT is a telex system between most European banks to facilitate customer transfer of deposit funds among the banks and of financial information.

SWING LINE
Slang for a demand line of credit extended by a bank to a customer. Under a swing line, the customer may borrow a fixed sum of money each day, as needed.

SWINGS
Acronym for sterling warrants into gilt-edged stocks. SWINGS are customized options to buy or sell a specific British government security; for example, a warrant to buy (a call), or a warrant to sell (a put) a specific gilt (the $8^{3}/_{4}$s of 1997, for example) during a specific period.

Although such warrants may be for longer periods, generally they are for one year or less.

SWISS FRANC
The primary unit of currency in Switzerland. The franc is divided into 100 centimes, or rappen.

The Swiss franc is a major "hard currency" and is actively traded in the spot, forward, futures, and options markets.

You also will see the term *Swissy* as a slang expression for the Swiss franc.

SWISS FRANC NOTE
Acronym: SFN. A Eurodebt security denominated in Swiss francs. The usual maturity is 5–10 years. Generally, an SFN is issued in the form of a global note held by a Swiss bank that arranges the loan for the entire life of the borrowing.

SWISSY
A slang expression for the Swiss Franc, the primary unit of currency in Switzerland.

SWITCHING
1. Used as a synonym for a swap; that is, a sale of one security and the purchase of another.

706

2. The substitution of one security for another as collateral in a margin account. This substitution may be effected by the physical substitution of one security for another, or the sale of one and the purchase of another.
3. A salesman's recommendation that a customer sell one mutual fund (for which a sales charge has been paid) and the purchase of a second fund with a second sales charge. This practice is also called "twisting" or "churning."
4. In the currency markets, the purchase of a spot currency contract together with its sale in the forward market.

SWITCH ORDER
Often used synonymously for a contingent order. For example, Sell 500 ABC at 55; when sold, BUY 1000 LMN at 27.

SWOON STOCK
A term associated with illiquid OTC equity markets. For example, at the first sign of bad news, or even a rumor, the bid for the stock disappears and its price collapses. In effect, the price swoons, or faints away. It would not be unusual for such a stock to lose 50% of its resale price in one day because there are no bidders.

SX INDEX OPTION
A put/call option based on an index of the 16 largest company stocks traded in Sweden. It is a European-style option traded on the Stockholm Stock Exchange.

SYNDICATE
Industry term for the group of investment bankers who guarantee the issuer its money by purchasing the securities and, in turn, agree to reoffer the securities at a fixed price to the public.

The term *account* often is used synonymously.

The term *syndicate* is also used of groups of investment bankers who bid for a competitive issue but who are not successful. The term is not used of broker/dealers who act as agents of the issuer or as agents of the underwriters (e.g., members of the selling group).

SYNDICATE ACCOUNT LETTER
The financial status of a syndicate. The syndicate letter, sent by the syndicate manager before the underwriting, describes the conditions under which the syndicate will operate. For corporate offerings, this agreement is a formal document called the "agreement among underwriters." After the underwriting, the syndicate account letter releases the members of the syndicate from the terms of the agreement and permits

syndicate members to make sales at prices different from the established public offering price. In every case, there will be a final financial report to members of the syndicate.

SYNDICATE CONTROL NUMBERS
Unlike U.S. underwritings where syndicate members are bound to make a fixed-price offering, European syndicates are not so bound. They must follow the manager's instructions, and sometimes those price limitations are surreptitiously broken. If the European syndicate manager can force all initial clearing through a single entity (e.g., CEDEL) and record distributed certificate numbers, it can control the offering prices at which syndicate members sell the security.

SYNDICATE MANAGER
Term applied to the leading underwriter in an account. The manager organizes the syndicate, forms a selling group when needed, allocates member participation, confirms subject orders received by the account, makes stabilizing transactions, and provides the final financial accounting for the account. If an underwriting is negotiated, the manager normally receives a fee for his services. It is common in competitive underwritings to have co-managers for the account (i.e., more than one manager).

SYNERGY
From the Greek: *syn*, meaning together, and *ergon*, meaning work; that is, working together.

In recent years, the term has become a "buzzword" for increased harmony and efficiency, often through a merger of companies or forces. For example, "The merger of A and B has given the combined company a synergy in its assault on market share." Or, "The addition of our new marketing department has given advertising a synergy it did not have before."

SYNTHETIC DEBT
Nickname for debt securities that arise when a broker/dealer strips interest payments from principal payments. By so doing, the broker/dealer hopes to satisfy the needs of different customers at a greater profit than if it had sold the debt as one piece.

In effect, the debt becomes two zero-coupon bonds with the dealer responsible for directing payments to the two parties.

SYNTHETIC MORTGAGE AGREEMENT
A one to five-year contractual commitment between a customer and a broker/dealer in which the customer receives the cash flow from a GNMA security with a specific coupon and maturity date. In return, the

708

customer pays the broker/dealer the prevailing LIBOR interest rate plus a negotiated spread. At the end of the period, the customer can choose to buy the GNMA security or walk away from the deal by paying the difference between the GNMA values on a current and forward basis. In effect, the agreement is simply a financing procedure with an interest in a mortgage-backed security.

SYNTHETIC OIL FIELD
Term used of a Salomon Brothers investment vehicle for trading in units with a claim on the future delivery price of light oil in Cushing, Oklahoma. Officially called the "Phibro Energy Oil Trust," its assets consist of 40 forward contracts held by the Phibro Energy Co. to deliver the oil over the 10-year life of the trust. A complicated formula determines the price at each delivery date, but, for simplicity sake, the amount to be delivered increases as oil prices rise in the marketplace.

SYNTHETIC PUT
Also known as: synthetic put option. An over-the-counter put option issued by a broker/dealer to accommodate a customer's request for a put option. The expression "synthetic" and the need for this type of contract arose in the period between 1977 and 1980 when, due to a moratorium imposed by the SEC, there was a large disparity between the number of call options available and the number of put options.

SYSTEM FOR INSTITUTIONAL TRADING OF UNREGISTERED SECURITIES
See SITUS.

T

T
The twentieth letter of the alphabet, used:
1. Uppercase alone to designate the NYSE ticker symbol for American Telephone & Telegraph Company, Inc., the largest communications company in the U.S.
2. Uppercase in parentheses (T), after the name of the company in the newspaper report of corporate sales and earnings to designate that the primary marketplace for the company's securities is the Toronto Stock Exchange.

T + 1, T + 2, ETC.
T stands for trade date. Thus, T + 1 means the business day following the trade date; so with T + 2, T + 3, and so forth.

In practice, the term is used of the sequence of events leading from the trade to settlement. Thus, T + 1 is comparison day; T + 2 confirmation of the trade (and an endeavor to clear up DKs); and T + 5 is settlement date.

The expression is in constant use in operations and in the clearing of securities.

TAA
See TACTICAL ASSET ALLOCATION.

TAB
See TAX ANTICIPATION BILL.

TAC
Acronym for targeted amortization class. TACs are associated with collateralized mortgage obligations (CMOs) and, specifically, the class of CMOs to which the risk of prepayment of principal is transferred. Usually the TACs are the last and second to last of the classes to mature, with earlier classes having relatively stable maturities.

TACTIC
A short-term military maneuver designed for a specific objective. In general, a tactic is part of an overall strategy.

Thus, in the financial services industry, a tactic is part of an overall strategy to achieve the customer's financial objectives. For example, "Mr. Smith, we have discussed your overall strategy of capital growth. I would suggest two tactics that will help you achieve this goal. We will recommend (1) stocks with a low market-to-book ratio and (2) stocks with low price-to-earnings ratios. In this way, your portfolio will be value-oriented and should produce long-term capital growth."

TACTICAL ASSET ALLOCATION
Often abbreviated TAA. Term coined by institutional portfolio managers to describe changes in investment strategies based upon their view of the upcoming market. The term refers to the percentage allocation of assets; that is, the amount of the portfolio in cash, in bonds, or in equities. In anticipation of a downswing in the equities markets, the manager may opt to have more assets in the form of cash and short-term bonds.

TAG ENDS
Slang: means that only small amounts of an offering of debt securities are available from the syndicate. The remainder of the issue has been sold.

710

TAIL

1. In a U.S. Treasury auction: the difference between the average bid and the lowest bid price accepted.
2. In a competitive underwriting: the decimals that follow the point bid. Example: In a bid of 98.7542 for a bond, .7542 is the tail. There is no limit on the number of decimals that can be used.
3. In Ginnie Mae terminology: a certificate that, when issued, does not bear a round-dollar face value. Example: A certificate with an original face value of $52,431.56.

See also GNMA and GOVERNMENT NATIONAL MORTGAGE ASSOCIATION.

TAILGATING

Slang: a registered representative, following the purchase of a security for a customer's account, purchases the security for a personal account. Practice is questionable if the customer gave the impression that he had special reliable information and the registered representative not only buys but also recommends the security to others.

TAIWAN STOCK EXCHANGE

Located in Taipei, the capital of Formosa (Latin: beautiful; Chinese: Taiwan), this exchange is one of the smallest and one of the most active of the world's exchanges. Trading is from 9:00 A.M. until noon six days a week. Physical settlements are made on the third business day following the trade date. Foreigners may not deal directly on the exchange, but they may transact through a Taiwanese nominee.

TAKE

Term used by dealers and exchange members to indicate that, as buyers, they are accepting another dealer's or member's offering price, thereby completing a transaction.

TAKE A POSITION

Action whereby a dealer or a customer establishes a net inventory, either long or short, in a security. For example, the dealer sold 10,000 shares, thereby taking a net short position of 2,500 shares.

The term also can imply that the position was taken as a longer-term investment. For example, the Williams brothers took a major position in the stock of the ABC company.

TAKE DOWN

1. As one word: takedown is the dollar discount given by the manager of a municipal syndicate to syndicate members when they take bonds

from the account. Example: The bonds have a public offering price of 100 and the syndicate member's takedown price is 98.75.

2. As two words: take down is used in corporate underwritings to signify the number of shares or bonds for which a syndicate member is financially responsible. Example: Member A's take down is 150 bonds.

TAKE OFF

1. Verb: to begin flight; thus, by metaphor, a strong rise in the market or in the price of an individual stock. For example, "At 11:00 A.M. the market took off."
2. In the United Kingdom, the cancellation of an order previously given to a broker to execute.
3. In the United States, the removal of a print from the consolidated tape. This may be done only if buyer and seller agree and a floor official concurs.

TAKE OUT

1. Slang: for the dollar amount an investor removes from an account if he sells one security and purchases another at a lower cost.
2. A trader's bid for the remainder of a seller's holdings that she has been selling piecemeal. Purpose: to remove overhanging supply from the marketplace.
3. Also called a "backup bid" if a Ginnie Mae dealer offers to finance a mortgage banker's loans offered for sale at a GNMA auction. The dealer gets the right to repurchase them later at a specified price.

TAKEOVER

The acquisition of one company by another. The takeover may be accomplished with cash, with securities, or by a combination of the two.

Takeovers may be friendly or unfriendly.

As a rule, mergers cause both companies to survive. Acquisitions, or takeovers, cause the company acquired to go out of business, although its component parts become operating entities—in most cases—of the new corporation.

TAKEOVER ACTIVITY

A term used to generally describe a market where stock trading appears to be marked with a large number of buyouts, mergers, tender offers, hostile offers, consolidations, and other actions that accompany mergers and acquisitions. For example, "Volume today was 150 million, of which a third seemed to be takeover activity."

If this activity marks a long time period, a common synonym is "mergermania."

TAKING A BATH

Slang for the loss of a significant sum of money either by an individual or by groups of investors. For example, "Investors in ABC took a bath today when the company announced negative earnings for the quarter."

The word is of unknown origin and is informal, but it may arise from the days of piracy. When ships were overtaken, the crew was often set adrift or forced into the water to prevent pursuit.

TAKING A VIEW

A colorful English expression for predicting the near and future prospects of interest rates, yields, and securities prices. In the United States, we would tend to use the word "forecasting."

TAKING PROFITS

See PROFIT TAKING.

TAKING THEIR TEMPERATURE

Expression used by broker/dealers in discussing how a SRO may react to a proposed change in operating or market procedures. It is also used by SROs in debating about rule submission proposals to the SEC. In both cases it merely questions whether the higher regulatory body will be receptive to those changes.

TALISMAN

Acronym for Transfer Accounting Lodgement for Investors, Stock Management for jobbers. TALISMAN is an International Stock Exchange (in London) procedure similar in function to the DTC (Depository Trust Co.) or CNN (Continuous Net Settlement) in the United States.

All ISE transactions are settled through TALISMAN by physical delivery, although book-entry balances are established each day for jobbers (specialists). Actual money settlements are made approximately every two weeks according to the account period.

TAMRA

Acronym for Technical and Miscellaneous Revenue Act of 1988. This act was passed by Congress to correct certain technical errors in previous tax laws.

TAMRA requires that losses and gains on foreign currency options and futures be considered ordinary income or ordinary income losses. It also decrees that the wash sale rule apply to options and futures as well as to the underlying securities. Interest on Series EE savings bonds, currently tax sheltered, is also tax free in most cases if used for educational purposes.

TAN
See TAX ANTICIPATION NOTE.

TANDEM PLAN
Arrangement whereby GNMA (Ginnie Mae) buys selected mortgages above their market value and concurrently uses FNMA (Fannie Mae) to sell them in the secondary market to minimize the loss. GNMA, in effect, is subsidizing selected housing projects with a minimum cash outlay.

See also GOVERNMENT NATIONAL MORTGAGE ASSOCIATION (GNMA) and FEDERAL NATIONAL MORTGAGE ASSOCIATION (FNMA).

TANDEM SPREAD
Term for a strategy that resembles a spread, but involves the purchase of one security and the short sale of another. Concept: There is a historical price relationship between the two securities. If the spread between the prices widens, the investor will have a gain; if the spread narrows, the investor will have a loss.

TAN-ITSU-YAKUJO
See ITAYOSE TRADING.

TAPE DANCING
Slang used by block traders of equity securities who sometimes accommodate institutional sellers by paying 1/8 or 1/4 over the last sale and then levy a larger-than-usual commission. The effect is twofold: (1) the block trader receives increased commission revenues to cushion possible trading losses, and (2) the print on the consolidated tape makes it appear that an anxious buyer is in the market to acquire stock. This can lure eager speculators.

THE TAPE IS LATE
Industry expression used when the consolidated tape is reporting transactions one or more minutes after they take place on the floor. Although the tape can run faster, it will be too fast for the human eye, so the tape is programmed to use no more than 900 characters per minute.

The consolidated tape often adjusts for lateness by having digits deleted from the prints. Usually the price digits are deleted first; then, if the tape continues late, the volume digits are deleted.

TAPE RACING
Unethical practice of transacting personal business in an issue with prior knowledge of and before executing a customer's large order in that

security. This ploy attempts to profit from the price momentum generated by execution of the customer's order.

TAPE-WORM
A term used of boardroom habitués; that is, persons who sit hour by hour mesmerized by the activity of the tape, philosophical comments on the market, and who in actuality do very little trading.

The term originated in the days when there was an optical projection of the actual tape, or a mechanical reproduction of the tape in brokerage offices. Today most stockbrokers have such price information electronically reproduced at their workstations.

TAP ISSUE
An offering of securities with the same terms and conditions, albeit at different prices, as a previous issue of bonds. The issuer, in effect, is tapping the same market as with the previous issue. U.S. Treasury notes occasionally are tap issues.

See also REOPEN AN ISSUE.

THE TAP SYSTEM
Metaphor for the system whereby the British government distributes Gilts. The Bank of England, as marketing agent for the government, sells Gilts little by little as the government directs. In effect, the Bank of England can turn off or on the supply of Gilts whenever it thinks the time is right. Hence the metaphor "tap."

TARGET
1. A corporation that is the object of a takeover attempt is said to be the "target."
2. Slang expression for the common stock of Tenneco, a major pipeline, shipbuilder, and manufacturer. The nickname is derived from its NYSE symbol: TGT.

TARGET COMPANY
A company whose shares are being secretly acquired by someone who intends to gain control. No public announcement is made until the purchaser reaches the 5% level of outstanding stock; at that time the purchaser must file the information with the SEC. Term also is used once the information becomes public.

TARGET LETTER
A written communication to an individual from the Securities and Exchange Commission, advising that person of an SEC investigation in progress that may lead to a charge and subsequent indictment for fed-

eral securities law violations. A recipient of this letter is advised to retain personal counsel to defend against this allegation and expedite the adjudication process.

TARGETED AMORTIZATION CLASS
See TAC.

TARGETED INDEX MATRIX
Abbreviated: TIM. TIM is a Salomon Brothers' customized bond index of selected debt securities. TIM is designed for bond portfolio managers who want to track certain duration/quality parameters.

The matrix starts with Salomon's Broad Investment Grade Bond Index of mortgage/corporate issues. It then adds other statistics for bond duration so it, in effect, becomes a multitracking vehicle to meet the specialized needs of various portfolio managers.

TARS
Acronym for Trade Acceptance and Reconciliation Service. This is an NASD-supported computer system in which uncompared trade problems in over-the-counter executions can be quickly resolved. Ultimately, TARS will provide on-line reporting of trade data for the immediate comparison of contracts.

TAT
See TEMPORARY AGENT TRANSFER PROGRAM.

TAURUS
Acronym for Transfer and Automated Registration of Uncertified Stock. TAURUS was developed by London's International Stock Exchange to computerize the process of transferring share ownership for securities organizations and their customers. TAURUS is an offshoot of the TALISMAN system (q.v.).

TAX AND LOAN ACCOUNT
Demand deposits owned by the U.S. government at commercial banks. The depositors are corporations or persons who owe Social Security payments or withheld taxes from employees' income. Banks may use these deposits, subject to reserve requirements, until such time as the U.S. government withdraws them.

TAX ANTICIPATION BILL (TAB)
Treasury bill periodically issued by the U.S. government to raise money in anticipation of the quarterly payments of corporate taxes.

Special feature: The bills, which mature several days to a week after the due date for corporation income taxes, will be accepted at face value on tax due date if a corporation uses the bills to pay its quarterly taxes. The corporation, in effect, receives a few extra days of interest and is thereby motivated to purchase the bills.

TAX ANTICIPATION NOTE (TAN)
Short-term municipal security issued to raise money for the interim financing of municipal expenses. The TAN will be paid off with taxes received from taxpayers and corporations.

Used extensively by cities and other municipalities to provide a reasonably level income for salaries and other expense items that will be offset by income taxes due annually or quarterly.

TAX EQUITY AND FISCAL RESPONSIBILITY ACT
Acronym: TEFRA. A U.S. law designed to increase federal revenues through targeted levies and reform measures designed to improve taxpayer compliance. Among features having an impact on the securities industry are the requirement for a 20% withholding of interest and dividend payments under certain circumstances, sale transaction reporting of customer orders, and owner registration of debt obligations.

TAX-EXEMPT DEFERRED INTEREST SECURITIES
See TEDIS.

TAX-EXEMPT DIVIDEND SERVICE
See TEDS.

TAX-EXEMPT ESOP NOTE SECURITIES
See TEENS.

TAX-EXEMPT SECURITY
General name for municipal securities. Reason for name: The interest income received from most municipal securities is exempt from federal taxation—although it is not necessarily exempt from state or local taxation.

The term is not used of securities that pay interest income subject to federal taxation but which is exempt from state or local taxation. For example, the interest income paid by U.S. government securities is exempt from state and local taxes but not from federal taxation.

TAX-LOSS CARRY-FORWARD
Dollar amount of a net capital loss, in excess of the $3,000 annual deduction permitted on a tax form for such losses, that may be carried into the next, and subsequent, tax years. Such losses, which retain their identity

as short- or long-term capital losses, are included in the capital computations for gains or losses on the purchase and sale of assets in the next tax year. There is no time limit for the carry-over of tax losses for an individual taxpayer.

TAX ROLLOVER
See ROLLOVER, SECTION #2.

TAX SELLING
1. Any sale of securities made to realize a capital loss.
   See also WASH SALE and PAINTING THE TAPE.
2. A euphemism used by technical analysts to explain a market drop just before a payment date or accounting date for federal tax liabilities. Example: It is not uncommon for tax selling to occur late in a calendar year.

TAX SHELTER
General term, inappropriately used, that describes an investment of aftertax dollars that will provide the investor with current deductions based on depreciation of an asset, or a tax credit based on the investment tax credit or on the depletion allowance.

The term also implies a possible capital gain with preferential tax treatment.

Technically, the term *tax-advantaged investment* is appropriate. Specifically, a tax shelter is an investment that keeps current income untaxed until it is used. For example, Keogh and IRA accounts, which permit deductions from current income, are tax sheltered.

TAX STRADDLE
General term for a strategy whereby a client with a realized short-term capital gain could take offsetting positions in commodity futures contracts. Purpose: Take a short-term loss in the same tax year as the realized short-term gain—thus, no tax on the net position—but get a long-term gain in the next tax year on the remaining position. The Economic Recovery Tax Act (1981) requires that the remaining position be considered a completed transaction (i.e., marked to the market for tax computations). As a result, tax straddles are no longer an effective strategy for negating a gain in one tax year and postponing it to the next.

TAX UMBRELLA
Term to describe prior and current losses sustained by a corporation. Concept: Such losses may be carried forward to shelter future profits of the corporation.

TAX WAIVER
A written consent of a decedent's state of domicile stating: (1) that state inheritance taxes have been paid or (2) that it will forgo immediate payment of such taxes. As a general rule, no re-registration of securities registered in the name of a decedent can be made without such a tax waiver.

TBA MARKET
Acronym for: to be announced. Used in the jargon of the GNMA market if settlement for a future contract in GNMAs can be satisfied by presently existing certificates at a price that subsequently will be decided.

T-BILL
See TREASURY BILL.

T-BOND
See TREASURY BOND.

TBRs
Treasury Bond Receipts, a proprietary product of Shearson Lehman Corp. similar in nature to Merrill Lynch's TIGRs and Salomon Brothers' CATS. In effect, TBRs are stripped Treasuries that become zero-coupon bonds.

TCO
See TRANS-CANADA OPTION.

T/D
See TRADE DATE.

T-DAB
Acronym for Treasury Debt Automated Bill recording system. T-DAB was originated in 1978 to maintain the ownership records of T-bill holders when "book entry" became prevalent. The system has been superceded by TREASURY DIRECT (q.v.).

TEAR SHEET
Slang for individual stock comments published by Standard & Poor's. Term arises because S&P publishes stock reports in a loose-leaf binder. Many brokers, in response to customer requests, tear these sheets from the binder and send them to customers.

TEASER RATE
Used in conjunction with adjustable-rate mortgages (ARMs), the teaser rate is a particularly low rate of initial interest used to attract mortgage

loans. The teaser rate may be valid for a year or two but then it returns to usual ARM rates. Generally, usual ARM rates have a cap and a floor and an annual maximum/minimum change. It is not uncommon for ARMs to feature balloon maturities.

TECHNICAL ANALYSIS
A method of predicting stock price movements over a short term— generally, four to six weeks. The prediction is based on current stock price trends and relationship of the present trend to prior trends, and it presumes trading volume will corroborate the trend. Technical analysts use charts of price movement to predict future price movements.

Technical analysis is an endeavor to predict investor psychology; as such, it has all the shortcomings of statistical sciences, such as sociology, economics, and statistics.

TECHNICAL POSITION
The term is used to designate the net positions, long or short, of dealers and marketmakers in specified securities.

Technical positions are short term and, as such, can dramatically effect supply and demand—hence price—in the marketplace.

TECHNICAL SIGN
A movement in the price of a security which, if accompanied by normal volume of trading, indicates a short-term trend in the price.

TEDDY-BEAR PAT
Merger and acquisition jargon for the initial contact by a raider to a target issuer. The "teddy-bear" pat may be a seemingly innocent letter or telephone call designed to frighten management into submission. If the raider is given no encouragement, the raider can back off without further publicity.

See also CASUAL PASS.

TEDIS
Acronym for Tax-Exempt Deferred Interest Securities. (Pronounced: teddies.) This is a Kidder Peabody counterpart of GAINS initiated by Goldman Sachs.

See also GAINS.

TEDS
Acronym for Tax-Exempt Dividend Service. This is a DTC service whereby eligible holders of Canadian securities on deposit with the DTC can receive dividend and interest payments without deduction for the Canadian withholding tax.

Revenue Canada (its IRS) has approved this program and Canadian transfer agents can make unrestricted payments to the DTC nominee.

TED SPREAD
Term used of the interest rate difference between U.S. T-bills and Eurodollar futures contracts.

The spread reflects the price difference between these two instruments and thus is reflective of credit concerns in the United States and Europe. The spread tends to widen as interest rates rise and to narrow as they fall.

A TEENIE
Trading slang for $1/16$ of a point (0.0625 cent). Sixteenths are used in option trading for options selling below $3, for subscription rights, and occasionally for short-term municipals.

Popularly called a "steenth."

TEENS
Acronym for Tax-Exempt ESOP Note Securities. TEENS are a Salomon Brothers debt product designed to provide eligible investors with a 50% tax exemption for interest received. It is a seven-year note that evidences a loan taken out by a corporation from a bank, insurance company, finance company, thrift institution, or mutual fund—all of whom would be eligible to receive tax-preferenced interest income (50% exemption) if the loan proceeds are used to finance a contribution to the issuer's employee stock option plan (ESOP). The corporation lends the proceeds to the plan's trustee who, in turn, uses the proceeds to purchase shares in the company for immediate deposit into the plan. Since the employer's ESOP contribution is also tax deductible, both the issuer of the note and the lender receive tax benefits.

TEE WAY
Jargon used to identify Trans World Corporation, a major airline. The nickname is derived from the NYSE symbol: TWA.

TEFRA
See TAX EQUITY AND FISCAL RESPONSIBILITY ACT.

TEL AVIV STOCK EXCHANGE
Israel's largest exchange for stocks and bonds, but a relatively inactive exchange. The government strictly regulates all activity on the exchange. Sessions are held from Sunday to Thursday from 10:30 A.M. to 3:30 P.M. Settlement is for the business day following trade date.

TELEPHONE BOOTHS

Exchange and industry term for the communication facilities maintained by member firms. In practice, the booths are located on exchange floors. They permit the firm and its employees to receive orders to buy or sell securities, to return the details of executed orders, and to retain records of unexecuted orders. Also, incoming orders may be routed for possible execution to the firm's employees (floor brokers) or to other members ($2 brokers or specialists).

TELESCOPING

An alternate term for a *reverse split*. A reverse split is used by a corporation if there are many shares outstanding and the market price of the shares is relatively low. Thus, a company with 100 million shares outstanding with a market price of $3 could cause a reverse split so there would only be 10 million shares outstanding. If the shares are selling at a reasonable multiple to earnings, such a reverse split could cause the new shares to sell at or about $30 per share.

TEMPORARY AGENT TRANSFER PROGRAM

Acronym: TAT. A program created by the North American Securities Administrators Association (NASAA) to expedite the transfer of agent registrations between broker/dealers using the NASD's Central Registration Depository (CRD). TAT grants temporary registration to salespersons before the submission of new U-4 forms providing a termination notice, U-5 form, has been filed by the former employer and the termination was not "for cause."

TEMPORARY RESTRAINING ORDER

Popularly initialed as TRO.

TROs are a court-issued document that prohibits the continuation of a specified activity, which is deemed to be harmful, until an investigation and due process of law are completed. Thus, the owner of property builds a fence across a road because he contends that there is no "easement." A person who has been using that road for 20 years contends that there is an easement. A court could grant a temporary restraining order against the fence until the matter is properly adjudicated.

TEMPORARY SPECIALIST

An exchange member appointed temporarily to take over the duties of a specialist for a limited time. The temporary specialist has the same obligations and financial responsibilities as the regular specialist.

TENANT

In the securities industry, a part owner of a security. Accounts with tenants are called "joint accounts" and are variously designated on the certificates and on the brokerage records of the account.

See also TENANTS BY THE ENTIRETIES; TENANTS IN COMMON; JOINT TENANTS WITH RIGHTS OF SURVIVORSHIP.

TENANTS BY THE ENTIRETIES

A form of joint ownership used in several of the states as the equivalent of joint tenants with right of survivorship, except that it is limited to married couples.

Often abbreviated ATBE on registered securities and brokerage account records.

TENANTS IN COMMON

A form of joint ownership of property whereby the portion owned by a decedent passes to his or her estate for probate rather than to the possession of the other party, or parties, to the account.

Often abbreviated TIC or TEN COM on registered security certificates and brokerage account records.

TENBAGGER

Common term used by security analysts to describe the multiple of return they expect on a particular stock. Thus, a "tenbagger" anticipates a 10-fold return on invested capital; a twentybagger, a 20-fold return; and so forth.

Analogy with baseball to measure the number of bases a hit produces: a one-bagger, two-bagger, and so forth.

10b-5 LETTER

Named after the SEC rule, such a letter is used by lawyers in conjunction with a municipal underwriting. A 10b-5 Letter is written by a municipal issuer to a prospective underwriter. It attests to the authenticity of the information presented and further promises the issuer will not employ any manipulative devices in the sale of the security.

TEN. BY ENT.

See JOINT TENANTS BY THE ENTIRETIES.

TENDER

1. To submit a formal bid for a security. Example: to tender a bid in a Treasury offering of bills, notes, or bonds.

2. To submit a security in response to an offer to buy at a fixed price. Example: When ABC made an offer to buy the security at $29 per share, the client tendered his shares.

TENDER OFFER
Public announcement of intent to acquire, at a fixed price, any or all of the securities of a company. Notice of the announcement first must be filed with the SEC. The acquisition also may be by exchange rather than by a cash offer. Used often in the takeover of another corporation.

TENDER OPTION PUT SECURITY
Acronym: TOPS. A municipal security that carries a short-term put option enabling the holder the right to redeem it at par. This feature, during the life of the put, effectively turns the long-term obligation into a short-term trading instrument. The title TOPS was created by Paine Webber for certain municipal securities that it underwrites.

TEN. IN COM.
See JOINT TENANTS IN COMMON.

TENNESSEE VALLEY AUTHORITY (TVA)
U.S. government agency, established in 1933, to develop the Tennessee River and the area surrounding it. Both power and development and nonpower activities are financed through the sale of bonds and notes.

As agency securities, they may be bought and sold through government securities dealers.

TENOR
A word occasionally used as a synonym for "maturity" when referring to the age of a debt security. Example: "That bond is not an alto, it's a tenor."

TEN PERCENT GUIDELINE
Term used in the analysis of municipal debt issues. A rule of thumb: total bonded debt of a municipality should not exceed 10% of the market value of real estate within the municipality.

10-UP RULE
Popular name for an option exchange requirement imposed on specialists and registered option traders whereby they must be in a position to bid or offer at least 10 contracts on either side of the market on the exchange marketmaking computer screen. Generally, the 10-up rule applies only to the near month—although individual exchanges may require the 10-up rule to apply to other series' expiration months. The rule is intended to provide both depth and liquidity to options markets.

TERM BOND

Generally, a longer-term bond with a single maturity date. The expression does not exclude the possibility of an early call or the application of a sinking fund.

In the municipal securities industry, the expression is used of longer-term maturities, in opposition to shorter-term maturities that will be redeemed serially.

Most corporate and U.S. government bonds are term bonds.

TERM CERTIFICATES OF TIME DEPOSIT

General expression for certificates of deposit with maturities from two to five years. Normally, interest is paid semiannually.

TERM FEDERAL FUNDS

Excess reserves of commercial banks loaned at a negotiated rate of interest for longer periods than the customary overnight basis.

TERM LOAN

Loan made by a commercial bank for a defined period. For example, a loan made for a period of 90 days, or three to five years.

TERM REPO

A repurchase agreement that has a longer life span than the normal overnight agreement.

TERMS

Acronym for Top Efficiency Reliable Maturity Securities. TERMS are a Salomon Brothers innovation in the special mortgage-backed securities market. TERMS are issued by thrift institutions and protect an investor against premature call of the bond.

If the thrift institution becomes insolvent, the trustee promises to sell the mortgage collateral and replace it with Treasury securities. In effect, the mortgage-backed security is "defeased" instead of redeemed.

TESTAMENTARY TRUST

Legal document that empowers a person or an organization to administer assets for the benefit of one or more persons. The document becomes operative upon the death of the person who establishes the trust.

TESTATE

Legal term for someone who died and left a valid will to direct the disposition of the assets in the estate.

Antonym: intestate.

TEXAS HEDGE

A tongue-in-cheek expression based on the traditional optimism that is associated with Texans. Thus, in a bull market, a "Texas hedge" means that a speculator buys everything before it becomes more highly priced—instead of hedging current holding against a possible drop in prices.

TEXAS PREMIUM

A term used to describe the extra interest offered by relatively insolvent savings and loans to lure added deposits in the wake of the drop in real estate prices in Texas and in other states in the "oil patch" (q.v.).

The drop in real estate prices went hand in glove with the drop in oil prices. For example, "You can get 8% CDs in the East but you can get a Texas premium in the Southwest where CDs are earning 9.5%."

THEORETICAL VALUE

Any evaluation that is based only on mathematical computation and which does not take into account market factors that may affect its worth. Used frequently of rights once a company announces a subscription but before the rights have been distributed to shareholders of record. Accepted computation of theoretical value of a right:

$$\frac{\text{Market price} - \text{Subscription price}}{\begin{array}{c}1 + \text{Number of rights required to} \\ \text{subscribe to 1 new share}\end{array}}$$

THETA

An options analyst's term used to describe the change in premium for an option versus the change in the number of days to expiration. Thus, as the time to expiration shortens, one would expect the time value to shrink toward zero for out-of-the-money options, and toward the intrinsic value for options that are in-the-money.

Do not confuse with DELTA, which is the differential calculus for the difference in the premium compared to the difference in the price of the underlying. DELTA tends toward "one" as the option approaches expiration; THETA tends toward "zero" as time expires.

THIN MARKET

Slang for a lack of liquidity for a security. In effect, there are few buyers and sellers at current price levels.

THIRD MARKET

Commonly used expression for over-the-counter dealers who specialize in the buying and selling of listed securities. Also used of transactions made by or with such dealers.

Third-market transactions in NYSE- and ASE-listed securities are reported on the consolidated tapes of those exchanges.

THIRD-PARTY ACCOUNT

Brokerage account carried and operated in the name of a person other than the owner. Example: Bill Jones carries and manages a brokerage account in his name that is actually the account of his brother-in-law. Such accounts are forbidden by industry regulation.

Do not confuse with power-of-attorney accounts, which are managed by a third party but which are owned and are held in the name of the person who gave such authorization.

THIRD-PARTY CHECK

A check payable to someone other than the current holder. For example, a check payable to Bill Smith and endorsed by him that is now held by Tom Jones. Normally, brokers will not accept such checks, even if endorsed by Tom Jones, in payment for security purchases.

THIRD-PARTY GIVE-UP

A *give-up* is the term used to describe a trade by member firm A for a customer of member firm B (or a customer of another office of member firm A). In effect, the *executing* firm is required to share part of its commission (mark up/mark down) with another firm.

If the other firm is outside the trading loop (i.e., a third party being rewarded for research and other services), the present term is used.

A "third-party give-up" must conform to federal, industry, and NASD rules.

THIRD-PARTY REPO

A dealer's collateralized financing transaction with a customer of a commercial bank, using that bank as an intermediary and guarantor of the loan. In general, the dealer pledges U.S. government securities, receives somewhat less than their current market value, and pays a negotiated rate of interest for the money borrowed, based on the amount borrowed and the time of the loan.

THIRD WORLD COUNTRY

A euphemism for any nation that is not one of the 10-or-so developed countries, nor a member of the Eastern European/Communist bloc. Thus, a country whose average per capita income is substantially below the average of either of these two blocs.

The term may be pejorative; thus, in one recounting, Mexico could be considered a "Third World" country in that it does not fit into either category. On the other hand, Mexico's per capita income is too high to be considered a "Third World" country.

See also LESS-DEVELOPED COUNTRIES.

THIRTY-DAY VISIBLE SUPPLY
Calendar of new municipal securities, both negotiated and competitive, that will come to market within the next 30 days. Published each Thursday by the *Daily Bond Buyer*.

Also called "visible supply."

THREE-HANDED DEAL
Slang in municipal security underwriting: the issue will combine serial maturities with two term maturities. Four-handed and five-handed deals expand the number of term issues accordingly.

THREE-LEGGED BOX SPREAD
In betting, a box is a four-position or nine-position bet that cannot be without a winner (although the net result may be a slight loss).

Thus, a "three-legged box spread" has three of the four positions needed to "box" the market, but one position is missing. Here is a "three-legged box":

Long October 40 call   Short October 40 put
Long November 45 put

The short November 45 call is missing to "complete the box."

THREE-STEP-AND-STUMBLE RULE
"Invented" by Edson Gould, this "rule" is a sort of axiom in technical analysis.

Simply stated, this rule says: There will be a major market decline if the Fed raises the discount rate three times in a row.

See also TWO-TUMBLE-AND-JUMP RULE.

THREE-WAY TICKET
Term used in the days before negotiable commissions.

In the days of fixed commissions, institutional customers could reward firms for good research (whose block handling capabilities were deficient) by directing orders to members of regional exchanges with the proviso that parts of the commission be directed to one or more other firms.

The practice did not altogether die with negotiable commissions.

THRIFT INSTITUTION
Expression, used singly or collectively, to describe a savings bank, a savings and loan association, or a credit union.

Also called "thrifts."

THROUGH-PUT
A Spanish term used to describe an "off-Bolsa" transaction. We would call it an "OTC trade."

Under Spanish law, a large trade done outside exchange trading hours can be done by a registered broker and not reported.

THROWAWAY BID/OFFER
A bid or offer that is nominal only and is not intended to give a price at which transactions can be made. Such bids and offers are approximate and must be identified as such.

THUNDERING HERD
Nickname for Merrill Lynch & Co. Used because of the size of the firm and the number of sales personnel it has registered.

TIC
See TRUE INTEREST COST.

TICK
1. The minimum variation that may occur in the trading of particular securities. Thus, stocks, corporate bonds, and most options trade in variations of $1/8$. Municipal bonds trade in minimum variations of $1/16$ (usually $1/8$). Governments and agencies trade in $1/32$, although trades in $1/64$ are also permitted. The term is not used of bonds that trade in basis points (yield to maturity).
2. Any report of a transaction. An allusion to the old ticker tapes.
3. The relative value of a transaction in terms of the previous transaction; thus, up-tick, down-tick, plus-tick, minus-tick, zero-plus tick, zero-minus tick.

TICKER
Commonly used expression for the mechanism, whether mechanical or electronic, that displays successive security transactions, their prices, and often the volume of the trades.

TICKER SYMBOL
The designation in letters used for individual security issues. Because these designations are previously agreed upon, they can be used to relay orders to buy or sell the specific security and to relay completed transaction information.

TICKET
1. In the United Kingdom, slang for the authorization to work in the financial services business. For example, to be associated as a jobber (specialist) or as a broker/dealer associated with one of the SROs.
2. The written form of buy/sell instructions received from the customer. For example, "To enter a ticket."
3. The authorization to enter and take a regulatory examination.
4. Any investment suggestion that patently fits the needs or objective of a customer. For example, "That's the ticket."

TICKETS IN THE DRAWER
The practice of hiding losing trade tickets from the management of the firm so the firm cannot hedge itself against loss.

This unethical practice can severely compromise the net capital requirements of the member firm.

TIDAL WAVE PURCHASE
A corporate finance term that describes a cash-rich corporate raider's open market purchase of the stock in a target company. The metaphor implies that the purchase is of a controlling interest made in a short time—hence, the target is overwhelmed (better: inundated) by the raider.

TIE GAUGE THEORY
This jocular stock market indicator was developed by the well-known technical market analyst, Alan Shaw. In effect, the width of men's ties predicts the direction of the stock market: wide ties, lower stock prices; narrow ties, higher stock prices.

TIE-IN SALE
An unethical prearranged trade between a member firm and a customer, or vice versa. For example, if a member firm were to allocate shares of a new issue to a customer *on the proviso that* the customer buy even more shares in the aftermarket, it would be a "tie-in sale." The prohibition arises because such a tie-in is basically unethical and manipulative of the price of the stock.

TIER
Popular designation of a class or group of securities. The term has no official standing. For example, "We are seeing a lot of activity these days in second, rather than first, tier companies."

See also BRACKET.

TIF

A customer-signed form authorizing the delivery of assets and money balances from one firm to another. The initials stand for Transfer Initiation Form and, as prescribed by the New York Stock Exchange, contain space for an authorized signature and for a listing of securities and approximate money balance for a specific account. The receiving firm will deliver it to the losing firm and expect delivery in a short time thereafter.

TIFFANY LIST

Slang for the issuers of the highest-quality commercial paper.

TIFFE

Acronym for Tokyo International Financial Futures Exchange. TIFFE is a new exchange. It is similar in function to LIFFE in England. At the time of its inception, TIFFE traded three contracts: a three-month Eurodollar, a three-month Euroyen, and a yen/dollar currency future.

TIGHT BID/OFFER

A quotation with a spread (difference) equal to the minimum trading variation. Thus, if the minimum variation were $1/8$th point, a tight bid (offer) would be one where the spread was $1/8$th point.

TIGHT MARKET

General description of an active, highly competitive market characterized by narrow spreads between bid and offer prices.

Also used of the market for an individual security or class of security. For example, "There is a tight market for the five-year Treasury notes with spreads of $1/8$ and $1/16$ prevailing."

TIGHT MONEY

An economic situation, often orchestrated by the Federal Reserve, in which the money supply is lowered and interest rates begin to rise. Thus, credit is difficult to obtain and businesses are faced with bankruptcy and unemployment begins to rise.

The shape of the yield curve often is inverted—that is, short-term rates are higher than long-term rates. It is possible, however, for all rates to be high.

TIGR

Acronym for Treasury Investment Growth Receipt. (Pronounced as the animal: tiger.) This Merrill Lynch product comes in two forms: serial TIGRs and principal TIGRs. Both arise from "stripping" a Treasury bond of its coupons. Ownership interests are sold in individual coupons (serial) or the stripped bond (principal), and the holder receives a single distribution of cash at a specified time in the future. TIGRs are similar in concept and operation to CATS and COUGARS.

TIM
See TARGETED INDEX MATRIX.

TIME DEPOSIT
Term for a bank deposit in which funds are pledged for a fixed time, usually at a fixed rate of interest. Chief concept: The bank can refuse the early withdrawal of the funds or impose a penalty for such a withdrawal.

Often used as a synonym for a savings account, although the expression "time deposit" is a broader term.

TIME DRAFT
Industry term for a post-dated instrument that transfers money from a buyer to a seller. Because the instrument is post-dated, the seller will not have the use of the money until the date specified. Used in distinction from a sight draft, which is payable as soon as it is received.

TIMES FIXED CHARGES EARNED
Term used by security analysts to describe the coverage of bond interest and, after taxes, of preferred stock dividends provided by the income of a corporation.

Also called "fixed-charge coverage."
See also FIXED-CHARGE COVERAGE.

TIME SPREAD
See CALENDAR SPREAD.

TIME VALUE PREMIUM
Term designating that portion of an option premium over and above the intrinsic value of an in-the-money option. For example, a call at 50 has a premium of 5. If the underlying stock is at 52, the call has an intrinsic value of 2, and the time value is 3.

Also called the "net premium." If an option is at- or out-of-the-money, the total premium is the time value, and no adjustment is made for the amount the option is out-of-the-money.

TIN
Acronym for taxpayer identification number.

TIN is a nine-digit numerical identifier assigned to all U.S. persons employed in the United States. For individuals, the numbers are arranged XXX-XX-XXXX. For corporations, trusts, and other legal entities, the numbers are arranged XX-XXXXXXX.

TIN PARACHUTE
An extension of the "golden parachute" usually reserved for senior management. Under this antitakeover measure, not only senior management but also middle management gets a cash payment (often equal to 2½ times annual compensation) in the event of an unfriendly takeover.

TINT
Acronym for Treasury interest payment. TINTs are the interest components associated with a stripped government security.

The term is used in conjunction with the reconstruction of the original stripped Treasury bond. To do this, both the principal (corpus of the bond) and the TINTs must be so "reassembled" that all components of the original bond are accounted for.

TIP
Slang for: a recommendation to buy, sell long, or sell short that is supposedly based on qualified information, often unknown to the investing public. Of itself, the term is neutral; the context will determine if the implication of inside information is given.

TIPPEE
Slang for the recipient of inside information.

TIPS
Acronym for Toronto Stock Exchange Index Participations. A trust instrument whose value is based on an index of 35 selected Canadian stocks. Listed on the exchange, the instrument has no maturity date and entails regular-way settlement procedures.

TIR
See TRANSFER INITIATION REQUEST.

TITLE X and TITLE XI BONDS
Title X and Title XI refers to sections of the Merchant Marine Act of 1936 that provide for the construction of airplanes (X) and ships (XI) financed and guaranteed by the full faith and credit of the United States. In the event of default, holders of the bonds purchased in compliance with this law would receive the full amount of principal and unpaid interest. The purpose of these government-guaranteed loans is to promote international commerce for the United States.

TOCOM

Acronym for Tokyo Commodity Exchange for Industry. TOCOM is the largest of the Japanese exchanges for the trading of metal futures.

TOEHOLD PURCHASE

Slang for the purchase of less than 5% of the outstanding stock of a company prior to the public disclosure to the SEC that the purchaser owns 5% or more of the shares.

TOHKI

Japanese word for speculation. The term has bad connotations for individual Japanese investors and, as a result, the government prohibits retail-type market participants from engaging in the practice.

TOKKIN FUND

A tokkin is a separate legal entity in Japan whereby corporate funds may be invested and yet kept separate from the corporation for tax and holding period purposes. For example, if Hitachi were to deposit a sum of money with a special money trust, it could give investment instructions and remain the beneficiary of the growth and income from the trust. Japanese regulations require that the identity of the beneficiary be revealed to the executing broker when these funds are invested.

Also called "special money trust."

TOKYO INTERNATIONAL FINANCIAL FUTURES EXCHANGE

See TIFFE.

TOM AND JERRYS

Slang for securities issued by Deutsche Bank and whose redemption values are linked to the performance of the FAZ Index over a five-year period. These securities are also nicknamed "bull bonds and bear bonds" because they offer investors a way to speculate on future price trends in German stocks.

TOMBSTONE

Slang for the newspaper advertisement of a public distribution of securities. The advertisement, which may be made before or after the fact, is basically a public relations event for the underwriting syndicate.

Called a "tombstone" because the announcement is factual and refers the reader to the prospectus, the offering circular, or the official statement for details of the issue.

TOM-NEXT
Jargon from the Eurodollar and foreign exchange markets for a transaction that will be settled on the next business day. The expression comes from "tomorrow next."

TOOTHLESS NOTES
Term used of an installment sale contract that has no penalty should the buyer of the securities defer or default on the promised payment.

TOP
1. As used by technical analysts, this noun means a price level through which an issue will not trade without encountering significant selling by other owners. Example: "We anticipate a top at 32."
2. As a verb: top means that a security has reached a relatively high price and (usually) has backed off. It is anticipated that some time will elapse before that level will be reached again. Example: LMN topped at 32, backed off to 29, and is now in a period of consolidation.

TOP EFFICIENCY RELIABLE MATURITY SECURITIES
See TERMS.

TOPIC
Acronym for Teletex of Price Information by Computer. TOPIC is a videotex information system developed by the ISE that provides business information on a timely basis. It is a subscription service providing up-to-the-minute price information on U.K. equities, options, gilts, and selected international issues, and on other business news.

The service can be effected by linkage with any IBM PC terminal.

TOPIX
Acronym for Tokyo Stock Price Index. TOPIX is a measure of performance of selected Japanese stocks traded on that exchange. Futures contracts are based on TOPIX.

TOP MANAGEMENT
General term for the highest ranking officers in a corporation. In terms of corporate titles, the chief executive officer, the president, the chairman, and the executive vice presidents are considered top management. In practice, senior vice presidents, the treasurer, the corporate secretary, and the corporate counsel may be top management.

TOPPING A BID
Term used if someone makes a bid higher than the then-prevailing bid. In effect, topping a bid means to improve the market.

TOPPING OUT
A market technician's term to signify the apparent final rising value for a security (or market in general). In and of itself, "topping out" does not imply a decline in the stock. The stock may go sideways before it goes higher, or lower. The term *consolidate* is used if the technician feels that a sideways movement will be followed by higher prices; the term *stabilize* is used if the sideways movement will be followed by a reversal of the upward trend. A market technician, for example, could say: "LMN is in a near-term topping pattern. We anticipate that the stock will plateau during its distribution phase. After that we expect a consolidation to even higher market values."

TOPPY
Slang for a market situation in which a security, or the market in general, has achieved its resistance level, either former or anticipated, and is now expected to decline. Example: The market at 2952 is rather toppy.

TOPS
1. See TRIPLE OPTION PREFERRED STOCK.
2. See TENDER OPTION PUT SECURITY.

TOP-UPS
A U.K. term for the issuance of debt securities with a significant number of warrants attached. The warrants are detachable soon after issuance and, if exercised, would greatly expand the number of shares an unwelcome suitor would have to purchase in a takeover attempt. Thus, "top-ups" are intended to protect the company from a hostile takeover.

TORONTO STOCK EXCHANGE
Acronym: TSE. Common newspaper abbreviation: T or (T).

The TSE is a major exchange, subject to the regulatory jurisdiction of the Ontario Securities Commission, located in Toronto, Ontario. The TSE provides trading facilities for many lesser-known Canadian mining companies as well as for most larger and more popular companies doing business in Canada. Stocks of American companies doing business in Canada also are traded on the TSE.

TORONTO STOCK EXCHANGE 300 COMPOSITE INDEX
An index of 300 actively traded stocks listed on the Toronto Stock Exchange. It is also called the "TSE 300" and is the basis for a futures contract.

TORONTO STOCK EXCHANGE INDEX PARTICIPATIONS
See TIPS.

TOTAL CAPITALIZATION
Redundancy for the capitalization of a corporation (i.e., the aggregate of fixed debt with a maturity of one year or more, the par value of outstanding preferred stock plus the par value of common stock, the paid-in surplus, and the retained earnings).

TOTAL COST
The out-of-pocket cost of a security purchase. It includes the contract purchase price, the commission, if any, and—depending on the context—the accrued interest.

The term should not be confused with "basis" (i.e., the cost of acquisition that is used to compute profit or loss for tax purposes).

Many investment situations require an adjustment of total cost to find the basis for tax computations. For example, a client purchased a municipal bond at 103 and held it to maturity. His total cost is $1,030 plus accrued interest; his basis is $1,000 because he is required to amortize the $30 premium over the life of the investment.

TOTAL RETURN
Mathematical consideration of yield that factors in both current cash flow from the investment and an ultimate capital gain or loss in terms of invested dollars.

Called "yield to maturity" on bonds if the current cash flow is reinvested at the same rate.

Most popular usage: an equity investment that sacrifices some current yield—and thus reduces fully taxable income—for an ultimate capital gain that receives preferential tax treatment.

Also called "total rate of return."

TOTAL VOLUME
Aggregate number of shares traded not only on the principal exchange but also on other marketplaces. For example, if ABC has trades for 100,000 shares on the ASE, but 25,000 shares trade on the other exchanges and on NASDAQ, the total volume is 125,000 shares.

TO THE BUCK
Slang expression used by traders in the U.S. government securities market. Term designates the offer side of a quote if the bid side is close to the offer and the offer is a round point. For example, the quote is $96^{28}/_{32}$ bid, 97 offered. Traders would quote "28 to the buck." The person who requested the quote would know that it means $96^{28}/_{32}$ bid, 97 offered.

THE TOUCH
Colorful English term for the marketmaker's spread. Thus, if the quote were 275 p. bid and 285 p. offered, the "touch" would be 10 p.

TOUT
1. Slang for any highly biased recommendation to buy or sell a particular security. Example: "LMN is being touted all over the Street."
2. The term also is used in a derogatory sense: of a particular registered representative who endeavors to buy or sell a particular security and thus generate commissions without regard to the financial circumstances and objectives of the customer. In this sense, tout and "churn" are close in meaning.

TPOD
Acronym for trade processing and operations department. (Pronounced: tee–pod.) A work area within a typical broker/dealer organization that is responsible for the processing of transactions, including all the steps between order execution and the monetary settlement of contracts.

TRADE
1. As noun: a synonym for a transaction. For example; the trade took place at 28½.
2. As verb: used generically to signify any investment action that results in a buy-sell transaction. For example; "We traded it at 54."
   Used specifically to designate the actions of a person whose business involves the buying and selling of securities. For example: "Bill trades securities in the over-the-counter market." In this latter sense, the verb may be used of the principal and his agent.
3. As verb: used to designate the act of frequent buying or selling of securities. For example, "I do not want to trade; I want to invest." To trade is not pejorative, but it implies frequent buying and selling.

TRADE ACCEPTANCE AND RECONCILIATION SERVICE
See TARS.

TRADE DATE (T/D)
The calendar day on which a securities transaction occurred. The designation is factual and is readily identifiable. For example, the trade date was September 29.
   Do not confuse trade date with settlement date: the date payment and delivery are due; or with dated date: the calendar date from which accrued interest will be computed on new issues of bonds.

TRADE-FOR-TRADE SETTLEMENT SYSTEM
A method of cashiering, clearing, and delivery whereby settlement is arranged between buyer and seller on a separately identifiable basis. This method is slow and cumbersome and generally inefficient.

Industry usage is toward a "net settlement" system, or the use of an intermediary, such as DTC, to effect trade settlements.

TRADER
Term for a person or organization who:
1. Buys and sells securities for personal profit. For example, "Bill is a trader in securities."
2. Completes transactions in securities for an employer. For example, "Mary is a trader for Salomon Brothers."

TRADES
Acronym for Treasury Reserve Automated Debt Entry System. TRADES is a computerized program of recordkeeping for government obligations designed to eliminate certificates. The identities of the beneficial owners are preserved by means of computerized third-party commercial accounts maintained on the books of a District Federal Reserve Bank. The system can accommodate a large volume of trades, such as that generated by bank and nonbank government securities dealers.

TRADES ON TOP OF
Slang used of debt instruments whose yield differential is very small or nonexistent. In effect, both instruments afford investors approximately the same basis point yield, and one investment is not preferred over the other. Example: This bond trades on top of the other—there is really no advantage of the one over the other.

TRADE THROUGH
Term used if an exchange member executes a transaction on the floor if a more advantageous price is available through the Intermarket Trading System (ITS). Thus, a trade on exchange A at 58 when exchange B was offering the same stock at 57 would be an example of a trade-through. Such trades are unethical unless the volume of the trade is such that it is to the customer's advantage to complete the entire transaction on the floor at one price.

TRADING AUTHORIZATION
Industry term for the document whereby the owner of an account gives power of attorney to an employee of a broker/dealer to make buy-sell transactions for the client.

TRADING DIVIDENDS
The act of buying/selling equity securities by a corporation to increase the number of annual dividends subject to the 70% exclusion of dividend income from corporate taxation.

Trading dividends is possible because the IRS requires only a 46-day holding period for a corporate holder to be eligible for the preferential exclusion privilege.

In practice, trading dividends is highly sophisticated because most corporate preferred securities tend to be priced in such a way that both seller and buyer share the advantages of the 70% dividend exclusion for corporate holders.

TRADING DOWN
The sale of portfolio securities and the purchase of securities with higher risk or lower-quality ratings. Example: The sale of investment-grade securities and the purchase of speculative securities.

Trading down generally is undertaken to increase yield or capital gains. Price volatility and increased annual income will compensate, it is thought, for the increased risk.

TRADING ON A SHOESTRING
1. A trader who uses little personal capital in day-to-day trading activities. Such a trader uses borrowed capital to leverage his position.
2. Any customer who trades with little margin.

TRADING ON THE EQUITY
Term describing the issuance of funded debt by a corporation. For example, a corporation, with equity of $5 million, issues bonds having a face value of $2 million. The corporation is "trading on the equity" in that the interest on the bonds, as a percent, may be less than the percent return on total capital ($7 million). Thus, the corporation is leveraging its total investment.

Trading on the equity increases the risk of bankruptcy because the fixed-interest charges on debt may exceed the return on total capital.

See also LEVERAGE.

TRADING ON THE PERIMETER
Term used when there is very active trading at a post on the floor of an exchange. Because the specialist cannot handle all of the trades, some trades are completed on the periphery of the crowd. In some cases, such trades are not known to the specialist and are not included in the volume figures for the day. Although such trades are "ex lex," they conform to the spirit of the law and generally are not a source of trading abuse.

TRADING PAPER
Used as a noun (paper) and an adjective (trading) to designate highly negotiable, short-term certificates of deposits. Concept: Trading paper is a highly desirable investment for corporate funds until more attractive investment opportunities arise. And, if none arise, they are safe until they mature.

TRADING PATTERN
Generally, a trading pattern is two parallel lines on a stock-trend chart that enclose all transaction prices for that stock over a certain period. The slope of these lines indicates the general trend of that stock.

TRADING POST
Industry term for specific locations on exchange floors where individual securities are traded. Chief concept: Exchange-listed securities are not traded at random on exchange floors; instead, there is a designated location, and a designated specialist, for the orderly maintenance of the market in listed securities. About 100 stocks are traded at each of the 20 NYSE posts.

TRADING RING
Designated area on the floor of the NYSE where exchange-completed trades in listed bonds must occur. Recently, this area was transferred from the old bond room of the NYSE and now is included in the same trading room as the New York Futures Exchange.

TRADING ROTATION
Procedure used to open trading in the various series of options for individual securities and for the various months in commodity futures contracts. After the rotation is completed, trading in the individual contracts may continue. This differs dramatically from the single execution price for the first trade in other listed securities on exchanges.

TRADING THROUGH THE FUND'S RATE
Term used of a debt security if its yield to maturity is less than the federal fund's rate. The federal fund's rate, which is particularly sensitive to interest-rate changes, is basically a market rate that changes with supply and demand for excess reserves. Trading through the fund's rate often is a leading indicator of a change in Federal Reserve monetary policy.

TRADING TO TOTAL VOLUME (TTV)
A criterion used to judge the specialist's willingness to provide liquidity and, thus, an orderly succession of prices.

In practice, the specialist's buy-sell activities as a dealer are divided by twice the reported share volume to give the ratio of trading to total volume. Reason for doubling stock volume: The specialist can act only as a buyer or a seller on an individual transaction.

TRADING UNIT
Popular name for a round lot.
See also UNIT OF TRADING.

TRADING UP
The sale of portfolio securities and the purchase of securities with higher ratings. Example: The sale of speculative securities and the purchase of investment grade securities.

Trading up generally is undertaken to better the quality of a portfolio and to reduce risk.

If done periodically to give a good impression, trading up is called "window dressing." Mutual funds often window dress shortly before they must make their semiannual reports to stockholders.

TRADING VARIATION
Minimum permissible price variation between trades if a subsequent trade does not occur at same price as the previous trade. On stock exchanges, the usual trading variation is $1/8$ point. Exception: Options with premiums below $3 per share may trade in minimum variations of $1/16$ point. Corporate and municipal bonds generally trade in variations of $1/8$. Government notes and bonds generally trade in minimum variations of $1/32$, although shorter-term bonds may trade in variations of $1/64$.

TRAFFIC TICKET RULE
Term associated with NYSE Rule 476. Under this rule, the NYSE has power to obtain summary judgments against members or their employees for relatively minor and undeniable offenses. This avoids long adjudication or even litigation. Under this rule, the exchange may levy (and the member accept) fines of $25,000 to $100,000.

TRANCH
Term used to describe two or more debt security offerings by the same foreign issuer at the same time. Example: Notes and bonds with differing interest rates and maturities. Tranches are issued to customize the issuer's capital needs and, in many cases, to conform to peculiar local requirements. Such issues are very popular in the Euromoney and capital markets.

TRANCHE FUNDING
Term associated with private financings and corporate buyouts. For example, the newly reorganized company secures additional capital for future investment, but the timing and amount of this future financing is determined prior to the takeover.

TRANCHETTE
Term used in the United Kingdom to describe the sale of additional gilts by the Bank of England with the same maturity and interest rate as an already outstanding issue.

In the United States, this procedure is called "reopening a Treasury issue."

TRANSACTION
Used synonymously for a trade (i.e., a completed agreement between a buyer and a seller).

Generally, the term means that a buyer accepts a risk and the seller removes a risk. In options, in commodities, and in the description of a person who is short, distinguish between *opening transaction* (one which places the investor at risk) and *closing transaction* (one which results in a net zero position; i.e., the person is no longer at risk).

TRANS-CANADA OPTION
Acronym: TCO. A put or call privilege traded on the Montreal or the Toronto stock exchanges for which the underlying stock is a corporation domiciled in Canada. An affiliate of the Options Clearing Corporation is the issuer of the privilege and the recordkeeper of all exchange-traded transactions.

TRANS-CANADA OPTIONS, INC.
A Canadian corporation, registered with the Securities and Exchange Commission in the United States. It is organized as an issuer of options traded on the Montreal and Toronto stock exchanges. In all instances, the underlying is the common stock of a Canadian corporation whose shares may be traded both in Canada and the United States.

TRANSFER AGENT
An institution, which generally is a commercial bank but may be the issuer itself, responsible for the cancellation of certificates that are sold, gifted, or bequeathed and the reissuance of new certificates to the new owner. The transfer is effected by cancellation of the old certificate and the issuance of new certificates in the name of the new owner.

TRANSFER AND SHIP
Instruction by the owner of a security to a brokerage firm holding the security to have it registered in his name and to send it to his address on the broker's new account form. Such instruction may be given at the purchase, or at any future time, if the security is fully paid. Separate instructions are required if the owner wishes the security registered in the name of another person. For example, to give the security to another person.

TRANSFER INITIATION FORM
See TIF.

TRANSFER INITIATION REQUEST
Acronym: TIR. This is a document issued by the National Securities Clearing Corporation (NSCC). It authorizes the transfer of a customer's assets (securities and money) from one member's account to another.

See also AUTOMATED CUSTOMER ACCOUNT TRANSFER SERVICE.

TRANSFER TAX
A tax levied by the states of Florida and New York on transactions in equity securities that are actually executed within those states, regardless of the residence of buyer or seller. The New York tax is currently subject to a 100% rebate.

TRANSLATION RISK
A colorful and descriptive term for the risk of currency exchange and the value of assets on the balance sheet of international companies. Thus, Royal Dutch, a Netherlands company, publishes its balance sheet in Dutch florins, despite the fact that its assets are distributed throughout its worldwide production and marketing network.

As the value of world currencies change, the "risk of translation" is great because some assets may go up and some down.

TRAPPER
An old slang and derogatory description for a registered representative. The term originated in the early 30s when securities business was slow and industry salespersons supposedly had to trap customers to survive.

TRAX
Code name for a trade comparison and confirmation system developed by the Association of International Bond Dealers (AIBD) to facilitate the matching and subsequent settlements of Eurodollar securities. TRAX provides members with an almost on-line comparison system for trading.

TREASURIES
General name for all negotiable debt securities of the U.S. government.

TREASURY BILL (T-BILL)
General name for short-term debt obligations of the U.S. government that (1) will mature within one year and that (2) are issued at a discount from their face value. T-bills are used primarily to give a level income to Uncle Sam.

Minimum denomination: $10,000 plus variations of $5,000. Format: book-entry only. Primary market price determination: competitive auction, unless the amount is less than $1 million. Secondary market: extremely liquid, active market featuring same-day or next-day settlement.

Many foreign governments issue similar short-term debt securities.

Special tax considerations apply if T-bills are sold before maturity and the sale price exceeds the ratable value based on a straight-line accretion from purchase price to face value.

TREASURY-BILL AUCTION
An auction, conducted weekly by the U.S. Treasury, in which persons desiring to purchase more than $1 million of short-term government obligations may enter competitive bids at a discount from the face value.

Noncompetitive bidders ($1 million or less) are awarded bills at the average discount paid by competitive bidders.

See also TREASURY BILL.

TREASURY BOND (T-BOND)
Longer-term debt security of the U.S. government. Maturity: more than 10 years from issue date. Minimum denomination: $1,000 and multiples thereof. Format: bearer, registered, or book-entry. Interest: paid semi-annually. Primary market price determination: by an auction unless tender is for $1 million or less. Secondary market: active, highly liquid market priced in points and 32ds with same-day or next-day settlement available.

Treasury bonds frequently are callable five years before term maturity.

TREASURY BOND RECEIPTS
See TBRs.

TREASURY CERTIFICATES
Short-term U.S. government debt securities formerly issued with maturities of six months to one year. The securities no longer are issued pub-

licly, although they occasionally are issued to facilitate transfers from the Federal Reserve to banks.

Also called "certificates of indebtedness."

See also CERTIFICATES OF INDEBTEDNESS.

TREASURY DIRECT

A book-entry securities system that permits private investors to maintain perfected interests in U.S. Treasury issues directly on the records of the Bureau of the Public Debt.

TREASURY DIRECT is the successor to T-DAB for Treasury securities issued after July 1, 1986.

TREASURY INVESTMENT GROWTH RECEIPT

See TIGR.

TREASURY NOTE

Popularly called "T-note." T-notes are intermediate-term (2, 4, 5, 7, and 10-year maturities) issued by the U.S. Treasury to finance government expenditures. T-notes are available in book-entry or registered format. Interest is paid semiannually. T-notes are noncallable and generally have minimum denominations of $1,000.

There are active secondary markets for T-notes, and prices are generally given both in points and 32nds and as yield to maturity (basis price).

Owners who are nonresident aliens are not subject to withholding on most recent issues of T-notes.

TREASURY RECEIPTS

Acronym: TRs. These receipts, created by the First Boston Corporation, are similar to TIGRs, CATS, and COUGARs. They are stripped Treasury bonds and are, in effect, zero-coupon Treasury securities.

TREASURY RESERVE AUTOMATED DEBT ENTRY SYSTEM

See TRADES.

TREASURY STOCK

Stock, formerly outstanding, reacquired by the issuing corporation, usually by repurchase. Such stock may subsequently be resold, or it may be retired (i.e., by stockholder vote it is removed from the number of authorized shares). The number of shares of stock in the treasury normally is designated on the balance sheet of the corporation. While held in the treasury, such stock receives no dividends, either cash or stock, and has no voting privilege.

TREND

An up or down movement in the market price of a security, or for the market in general, over an extended time period. Generally, a consistent movement for six or more months, or longer, is called a "primary trend."

Movements in the opposite direction to the primary trend are called "secondary trends."

The term also is used of the direction, up or down, of yields on classes of fixed-income securities.

TRENDLINE

A straight line drawn to connect top or bottom prices in an established price trend of a security. Generally, a straight line is used beneath prices if the trend is upward; above the prices, if the trend is downward.

Technical analysts use the trendline to estimate when a trend reversal has occurred. For example, if the general trend has been consistently downward from $40 to $30 per share, the trendline will connect the $40 with the $30 price, and a substantial movement of the price above $30 is considered a sign of a trend reversal.

TRIANGLE FORMATION

Term of technical analysts to describe the historical pattern of stock price movements that, in general, could be described as a triangle—with the base at left and the apex at right when looking at a chart of the stock's price movements. For example, a stock went from $50 to $30, up to $45, down to $35, and now to $40 per share.

Also called, depending on the degree of geometric symmetry of the pattern, a "flag," "coil," "wedge," or "pennant" formation.

A TRIGGER

1. Any event that is the occasion for a second event. For example, a trade at or through a stop price "triggers" the stop and the order becomes a market order. In this sense, *activate* and *elect* are synonyms for triggers.
2. In corporation finance, a "poison pill" tactic whereby the acquisition of a set percentage of a company's stock automatically causes certain changes to take place in other outstanding shares. For example, the other outstanding shares are given subscription rights for many new shares at bargain prices. Thus, the acquisition "triggered" the changes in the other shares.

TRIN

Popular name for a short-term trading index developed by Richard Arms, a journalist at *Barron's* in 1967.

Find the quotient of advancing issues divided by declining issues on the NYSE. Then, find the quotient of advancing volume on the NYSE. Finally, divide the first number by the second to find the TRIN (*Tra*ding *In*dex). TRIN numbers above one are bullish; below one are bearish.

TRIPLE EXEMPTION
Term used to describe a municipal bond providing interest income to a holder that is exempt from federal, state, and local taxation.

As a general rule, interest income from bonds issued within the state in which the holder-taxpayer is a resident has a triple exemption.

The term *triple tax exempt,* as a feature for any holder, regardless of the state of residence, normally is reserved for municipal bonds issued by the Commonwealth of Puerto Rico or by the District of Columbia because this feature is provided in the federal tax law.

TRIPLE MARY
Colloquial name for the shares of Minnesota Mining & Manufacturing Co., a large producer of cellophane tapes, audio/video products, and industrial abrasives. The nickname is derived from the NYSE ticker tape symbol: MMM.

See also MMM.

TRIPLE NET LEASE
Term used of a rental arrangement if the renting person pays a fixed sum to the renter and is responsible for the upkeep, utilities, and insurance on the property. In effect, the renter receives a fixed sum of income without any concern for these other expense items.

TRIPLE OPTION PREFERRED STOCK
Acronym: TOPS. A type of preferred stock that permits the holder, on a quarterly basis, to tender the stock back to the issuer and to receive, subject to the issuer's preference, either: (1) common stock valued at the preferred's par value, (2) a debt security valued at the preferred's par value, or (3) cash. The dividend rate on TOPS also is reset quarterly, based on some preset formula.

TRIPLE WITCHING HOUR
Slang for the final hour of trading immediately before the expiration for equity, index options, and index option futures contracts. The triple witching hour occurs quarterly (four times a year). There is voluminous trading as arbitrageurs and traders unwind their positions—often resulting in sharp price swings in these contracts and in the underlying common stocks.

TRO

See TEMPORARY RESTRAINING ORDER.

TRs

See TREASURY RECEIPTS.

TRUE INTEREST COST

Abbreviation: TIC. This is a municipality's calculation of its real interest cost to issue debt. TIC considers, on a semiannual basis, the time value of proceeds received versus the obligation to pay creditors both interest and principal.

TIC, also called "Canadian Interest Cost," is an alternative method to NIC (q.v.) for the awarding of competitive bond issues.

TRUF

Acronym for transferable underwriting facility. Term is used in Eurosecurity financing if one banker is able to transfer capital raising commitments to an issuer to another bank or broker/dealer.

TRUST

As noun: a legal instrument whereby a person or organization administers assets and their use for the benefit of one or more designated persons. For example, John Jones placed the assets in trust, to be administered by the First National Bank, for the benefit of his wife.

TRUSTEE

The person, or organization, administering a trust in accord with the specific instructions of the person who established the trust. Legal advice is needed for the establishment of a trust, and securities industry personnel dealing with a trustee should have evidence of the trust, its legality, and the restrictions on the activities of the trustee.

TRUST INDENTURE ACT OF 1939

Federal legislation that requires nonexempt issues of corporate debt securities with a face amount of $1 million or more to be issued under an indenture (deed of trust).

The indenture must specify the amount of debt, date of maturity, interest rate, and method of disbursement; also it must appoint a trustee, usually a bank, to safeguard the interests of bondholders. Generally, the registration statement and prospectus of corporate debt issues highlight main points of the trust indenture for the bondholder.

TRUTH-IN-ISSUANCE ACT

Descriptive explanation of the Securities Act of 1933, which requires disclosure of the material facts about new issues of nonexempt securities offered for public sale.

There are severe penalties, both civil and criminal, for persons who fail to register such public sales or who fail to include the material facts, or omit material facts, from the registration statement and prospectus for such issues.

Also called the "Truth-in-Securities Act."

TRUTH-IN-LENDING RULE

Federal law that requires a lender to specify the terms of the loan and its conditions to the borrower. SEC Rule 10b-16 instructs broker/dealers how they are to implement the provisions of the law.

TSE

1. Toronto Stock Exchange. The largest of the Canadian stock exchanges for the trading of stocks and options. The TSE is linked electronically to stock exchanges in the United States.
2. Tokyo Stock Exchange. The largest of the stock exchanges in the Orient and the originator of 80% of all securities trades in Japan.

TSE 300

See TORONTO STOCK EXCHANGE 300 COMPOSITE INDEX.

TSY

Common abbreviation for any of the negotiable forms of Treasury securities: bills, notes, or bonds. It is not used of Series EE bonds.

For example, on an order ticket: Buy 300M TSY 9s of '99. Translation: Buy $300,000 (face value) of the U.S. Treasury notes/bonds with 9% coupons that will mature in 1999.

TTV

See TRADING TO TOTAL VOLUME.

TUNNELS

See CYLINDERS.

TURKEY

Slang: a poor and unsuccessful performance. Used of the security that loses money for investors or of an offering of securities that loses money for the underwriters.

TURNAROUND

1. Of a corporation: a change for the better in the company's financial affairs.
2. Of a security: a change from a declining price trend to an upward price trend.
3. Of an investor's strategies: a change from one position to another, especially if it is marked by short-term trading.

The expression *day trading* is more commonly used, although the word does not exclude a change of investment objectives. For example, "Bill did a turnaround from income to growth as an investment objective."

TURNING A CORNER

1. Any decisive move in a person's life.
2. Used of persons and corporations who have survived a crisis and for whom the future looks prosperous. For example, "Ajax has had a number of poor marketing years, but it seems that in 1990 they have turned a corner and are back on track."

TVA

See TENNESSEE VALLEY AUTHORITY.

12b-1 FUND

Number of a paragraph in the Investment Company Act of 1940.

Under paragraph 12b-1, a mutual fund—if properly registered with the SEC—may charge certain costs against the income of the fund if these costs are to be used for advertising, certain general corporate purposes, and for distribution fees to reward securities salespersons. As a result, the expense ratios of such 12b-1 funds are generally higher than the expense ratios of other funds.

Generally, 12b-1 funds have no up-front sales charge, but most have a "deferred contingent sales charge" if the client prematurely redeems shares of the fund.

The prospectus will explain both features of 12b-1 funds.

TWENTY-DAY PERIOD

Industry term for the statutory waiting period between the filing of a registration statement with the SEC and the normal issuance of an effective date—the date on which a public sale may be made. The 20 days may be extended by the SEC if it requires more time for a full examination of the registration statement; or, upon request, it may shorten the 20-day period.

Often called the "cooling," or "cooling-off," period.

TWENTY-FIVE PERCENT RULE
Rule-of-thumb measurement in municipal bond analysis. In general, a municipality's bonded debt should not exceed 25% of its annual budget.

TWENTY-PERCENT CUSHION RULE
Rule-of-thumb measurement in the analysis of municipal revenue bonds. In general, the revenue of a facility built with bonds should exceed by 20% the budget for operations and maintenance and debt service. Reason: The 20% is a cushion for unexpected expenses.

TWINS
A Salomon Brothers product. The product is a six-month warrant that entitles the holder to purchase $1,000 face value of the U.S. Treasury $7^3/8$s of May 1996 at a discounted price. The discounted price is based on an index of U.S. dollar versus German deutschemark values. In effect, the warrant will appeal to investors who consider that the U.S. dollar will fall in value versus the DM during the life of the warrant.

TWISTING
Alternate name for "churning," especially if it involves the persuasion of a customer to change from one mutual fund to another with an additional sales charge.

   Also called "switching."

TWO-DOLLAR BROKER
Jargon for an exchange member who, acting as a broker's broker, transacts orders for member firms when their regular brokers are too busy, are ill, or are on vacation. Term arises from formerly charged fee of $2 per 100 shares in the transaction. Fee is now negotiable.

TWOFER
Slang for one long call at a lower exercise price and two short calls at a higher exercise price, all having the same expiration date. Equivalent, in terms of risk, to a two-for-one ratio write.

   See also RATIO WRITE.

TWO-HANDED DEAL
Colloquial expression for an underwriting in which two broker/dealers are comanaging the forthcoming distribution of securities. Example: Salomon Brothers and Merrill Lynch arranged a two-handed deal for $1 billion of State of California Bonds.

TWO-TUMBLE-AND-JUMP RULE

"Invented" by Norman Fosback in 1973 it is the opposite side theory of Edson Gould's "Three-Step-and-Stumble Rule."

Simply stated, the Rule says: There will be a major stock market rally if the Fed drops the Discount Rate two times in a row.

See also THREE-STEP-AND-STUMBLE RULE.

200-DAY MOVING AVERAGE

A popular technical indicator that moderates, over time, wide market swings on a daily, weekly, or monthly basis. Concept: Instead of charting daily, or even weekly, price movements, chart an average of the previous 200 days. The chart is made daily; each day, the average is based on today's price plus the prior 199 days. Thus, each day the price farthest away is so eliminated that only 200 prices are averaged.

Proponents contend that this method gives a better indication of trend. Other technicians follow 20- , 30- , 50- , and 100-day moving averages.

TWO-SIDED MARKET

This is a quotation for a security that gives both a bid and asked price.

With the exception of the market for municipal bonds, most American securities markets are two-sided and this is considered the ethical standard for dealers. The municipal market, with more than 1 million issues outstanding, does not find it practical to give both a bid and offer at all times.

Synonym: two-way market.

TWO-SIDED PICTURE

Jargon for an OTC marketmaker in NASDAQ securities who accepts orders to buy and sell at prices equal to (or slightly away from) the current market. For example, "We have a two-sided picture in Apple Computers" means that the marketmaker is showing bids and offers at those prices.

THE 2,000 SMALL STOCK INDEX

A barometer of stock market performance developed by Frank Russell Co., an investment advisor in Tacoma, Washington.

It is part of The Russell 3,000. The 1,000 stock index contains about 90% of the dollar value of the top 3,000 publicly traded stocks in the United States. The 2,000 stock index of small stocks contains about 10% of the dollar value of the 3,000 stock index. The 2,000 small stock index is particularly useful at the end of bull and the beginning of bear markets when such stocks show unusual activity.

Also called "The Russell 2,000."

TWO-TIER PRICING

This term, used in conjunction with a contemplated takeover, identifies the acquisition of controlling persons' stock at higher prices than that paid to other shareholders in a tender offer.

The practice is morally, if not legally, questionable and is in litigation in several courts in the United States.

TWO-WAY MARKET

See TWO-SIDED MARKET.

TYPE OF OPTION

Generic term for any option privilege. For example, by type, options are puts and calls. Specifically, *puts* are a class of option (i.e., the right to sell at a fixed price), *calls* are a second class of option (i.e., the right to buy at a fixed price).

U

U

Twenty-first letter of the alphabet, used:
1. Uppercase as the fifth letter in a NASDAQ/NMS symbol to designate an issue of units; that is, stock and some other distribution. For example, MOVYU is the symbol of New Star Entertainment units. Each unit is two shares of common plus a warrant to purchase a half share.
2. NYSE symbol for U.S. Air Group.

U-4

A uniform application form used by industry regulators to register security agents, representatives, and principals. When completed, the form provides the exchanges, the NASD, and the states with information about the educational, legal, and business and personal history of applicants for registration.

See also U-5.

U-5

A uniform notification document whereby securities industry employers can notify the exchanges, the NASD, and the states to terminate the registration of agents, representatives, and principals no longer associated with them.

UCC

See UNIFORM COMMERCIAL CODE.

UGMA
See UNIFORM GIFT TO MINORS ACT.

U.K. PROGRAMME TRADE
Unlike program trading in the United States, the U.K. Programme Trade is a package of securities that is offered to competing firms for their proprietary accounts. At the time it is offered in a blind auction, the competitors do not know the component stocks, only the package value based on their last trade price. The winner of the auction is speculating on its ability to reoffer the stocks at a price equal or greater than its last sale price.

U.K. STOCK EXCHANGE
A commonly used identifier for the International Stock Exchange of the United Kingdom and the Republic of Ireland. Before the "big bang" of October 27, 1986, this exchange was known as the London Stock Exchange.

UKULELE
A nickname for the common shares of Union Carbide Corporation, a diversified manufacturer of chemicals. The nickname is derived from the NYSE ticker symbol: UK.

ULTRA VIRES
Latin: beyond the powers of . . . .

Also: ultra vires act(ion). A corporate activity that is not illegal (contra vires) but that is beyond the specific powers granted in the corporate charter. Such actions may be rescinded to the detriment of the other party to the contract.

For this reason, corporate accounts are subject to close scrutiny. Corporate counsel, the director of compliance, or the manager of new accounts will—if there is any doubt—require a copy of the corporation's charter before certain security and commodity contracts are permitted.

UMBRELLA AGENCY
Term used in connection with a proposed government regulator to be appointed with jurisdiction over banks doing a securities business. Predicated on the repeal of the Glass-Steagall Act, such a regulator will have a limited lifetime; that is, until a transition period elapses, at which time jurisdiction would be accorded exclusively to the SEC.

UMBRELLA DESIGNATION
The NASD's description of a tagline, attached to the official name of a member to identify that member's market specialty, or to promote its

recognition. Thus, "ABC Corporation—Professional Marketmakers in Mortgage Securities" illustrates the official name plus the tagline.

UMBRELLA FUND
Name used for open-ended investment companies, domiciled outside the United Kingdom, that offer separate participations in one investment family's securities. Each fund is dedicated to a different specific objective and may encompass several currencies. Subscription is available to any or several of the subfunds, and exchanges can be made quickly, easily, and cheaply.

UNBUNDLED UNITS
Term applied to an idea sponsored by Shearson Lehman Corp. to discourage hostile takeovers. In exchange for their voting shares, the corporation would give the shareholders units composed of a 30-year bond, a preferred share(s), and an equity participation certificate (in effect, a warrant). Thus, in response to the issuer's tender offer, the holder of common stock would receive a package (the unit) of three different nonvoting securities, each with its own market value.

AN UNCLE SPOT
American slang for the amount of money an investor is willing to lose either on a particular issue or in the market in general.

The derivation seems to arise from street fighting terminology where one opponent tries to get the other to say "uncle"; that is, "I give up." The dollar amount is the point where the investor cries "uncle."

UNCOLLECTED FUNDS
Financial euphemism for a customer's check that has "bounced."

UNCOVERED OPTION
Term describes the status of an opening sale of an option if the writer does not have a corresponding position in the underlying stock (long position in the case of a short call; short position in the case of a short put) or the client does not have a long option that protects the short position.

Also known as a "naked option."

UNDERBANKED
Industry slang for a proposed underwriting if the investment banker is finding it difficult to attract other members into the syndicate to share the risk of the underwriting.

UNDERBOOKED
Industry slang for a proposed underwriting for which there is limited interest on the part of the investing public, as shown by the small indications of interest received by the members of the syndicate.

UNDERCAPITALIZED
Term used of any business that has inadequate funds to conduct its day-to-day business. In and of itself, this term is neutral; it simply means a shortage of short-term funds.

Firms that are undercapitalized must increase permanent capital, either by issuing stock or through debt securities.

UNDERCUTTING AN OFFERING
Attempting to sell securities at a price that is lower than the best prevailing offer.

UNDERLYING DEBT
Used in municipal finance to describe the liabilities of lower municipalities for which the residents of a higher municipality have some responsibilities. For example, county residents have some liability for the general obligations of cities and towns within their county's jurisdiction. The county can be said to have underlying debt.

UNDERLYING SECURITY
1. The stock subject to purchase (a call) or to sale (a put) if the holder of an option chooses to exercise the option.
2. The common stock that a corporation must deliver to a person who chooses to exercise a stock option, to subscribe to a rights offering, to exercise a warrant, or to convert a security that is convertible.

UNDER REFERENCE
In the United Kingdom, the expression used by a marketmaker when the marketmaker is unwilling to make a firm bid or offer. In effect, it is the counterpart of the "subject" quote in the United States. It is usually given because the trader must contact a principal for authorization to trade at a specific price or over a specific quantity.

UNDERVALUED
A judgment about the current market price of a security. The judgment states, in effect, that current corporate earnings, or market trends, or industry price-earnings ratios should justify a higher price for the security.

UNDERWATER OPTION
Slang for an option whose exercise is uneconomical. Although such an option is out of the money, the connotation is that the option is very deep out of the money. For example, an executive was granted a stock option exercisable at $28 per share. The stock is now selling at $19 per share. That would be an "underwater option."

UNDERWRITE
General term for the process whereby investment bankers purchase a new issue of securities from the issuer and resell the security to the investing public. The term implies that the investment banker is at risk between the time of purchase and resale.

The term also is used more loosely of some security distributions where the investment banker acts as the agent of the issuer and has no financial risk. For example: A best-efforts underwriting.

UNDERWRITER
General industry term for a person who facilitates the public sale of securities by an issuer.
1. Used as a synonym for an investment banker.
2. Used of the sponsor, also called the "wholesaler," of investment company securities.

Specifically, an underwriter is any person who purchases securities from an issuer for purposes of resale.

UNDERWRITERS' AGREEMENT
The contract between an underwriting syndicate and the issuer, or seller, of a security. The agreement sets forth the terms of the issue, the amount of money guaranteed, the fixed public offering price, and the details of final settlement of the account.

Also called the "purchase agreement."

UNDERWRITERS' RETENTION
See RETENTION.

UNDERWRITING GROUP
The investment bankers who make a contractual agreement among themselves and with the issuer of securities to buy and distribute a block of securities.

Used generically of the group before the final agreements are signed, or of groups that do not win a competitive bid.

Also called a "syndicate."

UNDERWRITING RECAPTURE

Used of a broker/dealer who is a member of a syndicate or selling group and who, in turn, sells part of the underwriting to an institutional portfolio that it manages or controls. If the broker/dealer passes the securities along to the institution at its cost, the institution, in effect, recaptures the underwriting compensation because it acquires the securities below the public offering price. This practice violates NASD rules prohibiting rebates to nonmembers.

UNDERWRITING SPREAD

The dollar difference, often stated in points per share or bond, between the price paid to the issuer by the syndicate and the price at which the securities are offered to the public. For example, if a syndicate buys shares from the issuer at $19 and sells the shares to the public at $20, the underwriting spread is $1.

UNDIVIDED ACCOUNT

See EASTERN ACCOUNT.

UNENCUMBERED

Term used of an asset that is fully owned and has no lien or other creditor claim against it. Securities in a client's cash account are unencumbered. So also is an asset that was previously used as collateral but the outstanding debt has been paid in full. The asset is now unencumbered.

UNIFIED CREDIT

Term used to describe the once-in-a-lifetime credit that may be applied against an individual's gift or estate taxes. Tax advice is needed.

UNIFIED MORTGAGE BOND

See CONSOLIDATED MORTGAGE BOND.

UNIFORM COMMERCIAL CODE

Acronym: UCC. This is a nationwide set of statutes designed to standardize commercial customs, usages, and procedures of trade associations in transactions between its members.

The State of Louisiana does not conform to the UCC, and there are some local modifications.

UNIFORM GIFT TO MINORS ACT

Law, standard in form in all states, whereby someone of legal age can serve as a custodian for a minor's assets. The law provides for a simplified procedure without extensive paperwork or cost.

Also used in the securities industry as a qualifier to describe securities purchased or sold under the provisions of this law, or accounts conducted for such purposes. For example, "I opened a UGMA account for my son."

UNIFORM PRACTICE CODE (UPC)

Rules and procedures established by the National Association of Securities Dealers (NASD) to regulate the business details of executing, clearing, and settling over-the-counter transactions in nonexempt securities. For example, the time of settlement, good delivery, ex-dates, and other transactional details.

Within the 11 districts of the NASD, the Uniform Practice Committees settle disputes at the local level and interpret the Uniform Practice Code.

UNIFORM SECURITIES AGENT STATE LAW EXAMINATION

At the present time, approximately 28 states require a specific examination of persons who wish to become registered representatives or principals as securities agents in those states. The exam (designated Series 63 by the NASD, which administers it) can be taken on the PLATO system provided by the Control Data Corporation or at local testing centers.

States that do not require the USASLE exam accept the Series 7 General Securities Representative Examination as their qualification for registration.

UNIFORM TRANSFER TO MINORS ACT

See UTMA.

UNISSUED STOCK

Term describing that portion of a corporation's authorized common or preferred shares that has never been exchanged for money, goods, or services. The term does not include treasury shares.

The board of directors may sell unissued shares. One exception: if a corporation has outstanding stock options, convertibles, rights, or warrants, the appropriate number of unissued shares needed to satisfy their exercise must be set aside (i.e., escrowed) until these options expire.

UNIT (UT)

1. Term used to describe securities sold as a "package." For example, a company offers two common shares and one convertible preferred share as a unit.

   Bonds and warrants are frequent unit offerings.

2. Term describing a group of exchange specialists who are responsible for maintaining a fair and orderly market in a specific number of securities.

Exchange rules require that specialist units maintain a common set of business records, although the form of business enterprise (corporation, partnership, association) is not predetermined.

UNITED ACCOUNT
See EASTERN ACCOUNT.

UNITED STATES GOVERNMENT SECURITIES
Generic name for the nonnegotiable and the negotiable securities of the United States. Series EE and HH bonds are nonnegotiable and may only be redeemed by the U.S. government. Treasury bills, notes, and bonds are negotiable and enjoy an active secondary market.

The U.S. government also issues certificates of indebtedness for interbank and interagency transfers of funds. These certificates are not publicly issued.

UNIT INVESTMENT TRUST (UIT)
A trust, registered under the Investment Company Act of 1940, that may take two forms:
1. A *fixed trust:* the most popular form. Such trusts assemble a portfolio of securities. Units are sold which represent an undivided interest in the underlying portfolio. Unit holders receive a proportional share of net income and, as underlying securities are sold or mature, a return of principal.
2. A *participating trust:* the legal form for contractual-type mutual fund agreements. The unit holder receives benefits both from the trust and the underlying mutual fund.

   All unit investment trusts are redeemable securities.

   Also called a "unit trust."

UITs are redeemable securities. They may increase or decrease in resale market value.

The term *bond fund* also is used of such unit investment trusts.

UNIT OF TRADING
Commonly accepted minimum quantity for which transaction contracts are made in exchange marketplaces. Term also is used of over-the-counter quotes and markets. Also called a "round lot."

Units of trading:
1. Stocks: 100 shares, although smaller units often are set.
2. Corporate bonds: 250 bonds is typical. Exchange transactions: 1 bond.
3. Municipals: 25 bonds is typical.
4. Governments and agencies: 50 bonds is typical.

Transactions less than the unit of trading are called "odd lots." See also DIFFERENTIAL.

UNIT PRICE DEMAND ADJUSTABLE TAX-EXEMPT SECURITIES
See UPDATES.

UNIT STOCK INVESTMENT TRUST
See USIT.

UNIVERSE OF SECURITIES
A general term for a group of issues having a common thread, or similar characteristics or business.

Similar in meaning to sector or industry.

UNLIMITED TAX BOND
Municipal securities term for an issue secured by the issuer's pledge of tax collections that can be levied upon constituents. In effect, the issuer may levy any rate in any amount needed to service the debt.

Antonym: limited tax bond.

As a general rule, unlimited tax bonds are issued only by states. Cities and other municipalities generally have limited taxing power.

UNLISTED SECURITIES MARKET
Popular abbreviation: USM.

The USM is an offshoot of the International Stock Exchange designed to meet the capital needs of young, small, growing companies in the United Kingdom. The USM provides offerings of these issues with a form of trading legitimacy in the English marketplace. The USM subjects them to exchange scrutiny, examination, and regulation normally afforded companies admitted to full trading privileges on the ISE.

UNLISTED SECURITY
Any security that has not been admitted to trading privileges on an exchange.

In general, equity securities that have not been qualified for trading on an exchange are called "over-the-counter" securities.

Also called "unlisted stocks" or "unlisted bonds."

UNLISTED TRADING
With the permission of the SEC, a security may be traded on an exchange without an application by the corporation for listing.

UNLISTED TRADING PRIVILEGES (UTP)

A request by a regional exchange to the SEC to permit it to allow the trading of shares of a particular issuer even though the issuer has not requested such trading nor has it signed a listing agreement.

The NYSE does not permit unlisted trading, and the ASE has not permitted it since 1933.

UNREALIZED PROFIT

See PAPER PROFIT.

UNREALIZED PROFIT AND LOSS

Also known as "paper" profit and losses. Thus, these represent capital transactions that are not yet completed by a sale, or, in the case of short sales, by a short cover. In most cases, for taxpayers who use the cash basis, there are no tax consequences for unrealized profits and losses. Certain commodity and option spread positions, however, must be "marked to the market" at year-end. Tax advice is needed. Tax advice is also needed for taxpayers, particularly corporations, who use accrual methods of computing tax responsibilities.

UNSEASONED SECURITY

1. Any security that is new to the marketplace and that has not yet been subjected to the forces of supply and demand.
2. An unregistered security. Example: A Eurosecurity that is sold outside the United States. Such securities may not be resold within the United States unless they are seasoned. Seasoning is a matter of fact. As a general rule, Eurodebt securities may not be sold within the United States within the first 90 days of their public offering and completed distribution.

UNSECURED DEBIT

Brokerage industry term for any customer debit that is not properly collateralized.

Unsecured debits may result from a sudden drop in market value of a customer's margin account, a maintenance call for securities or commodities that has not yet been met, uncollected funds (a bounced check), and, after settlement date, customer failures to pay or deliver. In a word, the broker/dealer is at risk because of a customer action.

UNSECURED DEBT

A bond that has no specific collateral backing. The good faith and credit rating of the issuer back the bond.

Such bonds are typically called "debentures," although shorter-term debt issues often are called "commercial paper" or "notes."

TO UNWIND A TRADE

1. To reverse a previously established transaction: a purchase is unwound by a sale; a short sale, by a short cover.
2. To cover a transaction made in error. Example: A broker/dealer makes a sale but the client actually entered an order to buy. The broker/dealer is short the security sold—this will have to be unwound to rectify the situation. The client's buy order is unexecuted. This, too, will have to be rectified.

UP

1. Preceded by a number (e.g., 10,000 up): used to signify that there is a bid (offer) for 10,000 or more shares or units.
2. Followed by a number, such as up $2^1/2$: used to signify the dollar value of a market price increase.
3. In general, any increase in market value or yield.

UP-AND-OUT OPTION

A form of conventional over-the-counter put option. The option holder has the privilege of selling a fixed number of shares at a fixed price for a fixed time. However, if the underlying shares rise above a predetermined price, the option is cancelled. Thus, if the price goes up, the option is out.

UPC

See UNIFORM PRACTICE CODE.

UPDATES

Acronym for Unit Price Demand Adjustable Tax-Exempt Securities. UPDATES are variable-rate municipal securities with a put feature developed and sold by Merrill Lynch.

The variable rate is reset daily; interest is paid monthly. Holders have the right to redeem the security at face value; but this privilege may be exercised only once a month, or once a week, depending on the indenture of the individual securities.

UP DELTA

See DELTA.

UP FRONT PAYMENT

1. Any money exchanged before a deal is settled.
2. In municipal bond terminology, a synonym for the good faith deposit given by the underwriter to the issuer for a scheduled underwriting.

3. In the underwriting of Ginnie Maes, a commitment fee paid by a borrower to a mortgage banker for assurance of a future loan.

UPSTAIRS MARKET
Industry term for the in-house trading facilities of a broker/dealer, whereby transactions for listed securities are completed within the broker/dealer's firm and are not transmitted to the exchange floor. For example, a broker/dealer gets an order to sell 5,000 XYZ. The broker/dealer, rather than send the order to the exchange floor, finds a mutual fund that wants to buy 5,000 XYZ at a negotiated price.

UPTICK
See PLUS TICK.

UPTREND
A generally upward movement in the price of a security.
See also TRENDLINE.

UR
Acronym for under review. Often used on corporate and municipal calendars if one or more of the bond rating services continues to have the issue under review and has not yet assigned a bond rating.

USABLE BONDS
Term used of a debenture issued as a unit with a detachable warrant. The warrant enables the holder to use the bond, at face value, to subscribe to common stock in lieu of cash at the price set forth in the initial offer.
In practice, the original bond often is issued at a discount from face. Thus, the unit represents a cheap call on the underlying.

USASLE
See UNIFORM SECURITIES AGENT STATE LAW EXAMINATION.

USIT
Acronym for Unit Stock Investment Trust. USIT is a trademark for the Americus trust. The initial Americus trust involved common shares of American Telephone & Telegraph before the breakup.
Americus trusts are available for the common shares of Exxon, General Motors, IBM, and other widely held common shares.
See PRIME and SCORE for a further explanation of the operations of the trust.

USM

See UNLISTED SECURITIES MARKET.

U.S. TERMS

In foreign currency transactions, the number of U.S. dollars needed to purchase one unit of a foreign currency. Example: If British pounds are offered at .6222, it means that:

$$\frac{\$1.00}{.6222} = \$1.6071$$

dollars will be required to buy one British pound. $1.6071 is a British pound stated in U.S. terms. And $.4204 could be a deutsche mark or Swiss franc in U.S. terms.

USURY

1. In general, the lending of money at interest. This meaning has become obsolete, although it is used commonly in older documents.
2. The lending of money at higher rates of interest than that allowed by prevailing state law. Conformity to state usury laws is an important consideration for broker/dealers in the conduct of client margin accounts.

UT

A frequently used abbreviation for: unit.
See UNIT.

UTMA

Acronym for Uniform Transfer to Minors Act. UTMA is similar to UGMA (q.v.) and is common to all 50 states. There are two major differences, however: UGMA permits gifts of cash and securities; UTMA extends the gifts to real estate, paintings, royalties, and patents. UTMA also prohibits the minor from gaining control of the assets until 21 years of age (25 in California).

Under UTMA, custodial assets may be held in a nominee's name.

UTP

1. Acronym for unlisted trading privileges. Under SEC rules, an exchange may apply for permission to trade an issuer's securities on its premises even though the issuer has never requested nor filed papers for such privileges. Few stocks, but most bonds, are traded under UTP.
2. NYSE ticker symbol for Utah Power & Light, a prominent utility company in this western state.

V

V

Twenty-second letter of the alphabet, used:

1. As the fifth letter in a NASDAQ/NMS symbol to denote an issue that has recently paid a stock dividend, been through a reorganization, or distributed additional shares. For example, Smith-Collins Pharmaceutical Co., after a 1–8 reverse split, was symboled CUREV.
2. Uppercase with a j (example: Vj) in front of NYSE and ASE listed stocks to denote that the parent company has filed for bankruptcy.
3. Alone uppercase as the NYSE ticker symbol for Irving Bank (now merged with Bank of New York Company).

VALUE CHANGE

Used only of groups of securities to indicate price changes of the individual securities weighted to represent the number of shares outstanding. For example, security A has 1 million shares outstanding and it goes up $1 per share; the same day, security B, which has 2 million shares outstanding, goes down 50 cents. Change up: +1 million. Change down: −1 million. The net value change of the two securities was zero.

Measurements of value change for a group of securities weighted to represent outstanding shares are called "indices," or "indexes."

VALUE DATE

Used synonymously with settlement date for Eurodollar and foreign currency transactions.

Generally, value date is the second business day after the trade date on spot transactions.

On forward trades, it is a negotiated date in the future.

VALUE LINE COMPOSITE INDEX

A market indicator originated by Value Line, Inc., a SEC-registered investment advisor founded by the late Arnold Bernhard. The Value Line Index measures approximately 1,700 stocks traded on the NYSE, ASE, and NASDAQ/NMS and uses an equal weighting system rather than a straight price or capitalization weighting.

The index is widely followed and is the benchmark for a futures contract traded on the Kansas City Board of Trade and an index option contract on the Philadelphia Stock Exchange.

VAMPIRE STOCK

Tongue-in-cheek description of a rumored takeover stock. The stock is so called because the rumor cannot be traced, or even stopped, until someone—such as a well-known raider—"spikes" it through the heart with a formal tender offer or a denial.

VARIABLE ANNUITY
A life insurance investment contract, purchased either lump-sum or by installments, that features an investment in an underlying portfolio of debt and equity securities. Because these securities are in a separate account and are not guaranteed from principal loss by the insurance company, their value and the income they derive may vary. Holders who annuitize their contracts may select different payout plans, but the amount paid out will vary with the value of the separate account.

VARIABLE COUPON RENEWABLE NOTE
See VCR.

VARIABLE-RATE DEMAND OBLIGATION
See VRDO.

VARIABLE-RATE MORTGAGE (VRM)
A 20-.to 30-year amortizing loan made on real estate. The interest rate is not fixed. Instead, the rate is adjusted every six months according to a prestated interest rate norm. As a general rule, the rate may not vary more than $1/2\%$ in any year, nor more than $2^1/2\%$ over the life of the mortgage. Because the mortgage is amortizing, the monthly payments made by the mortgagee will vary with the changes in the interest rate.

VARIABLE RATIO WRITING
An option writing technique whereby a holder of the underlying shares writes more calls than he has round lots to cover the short options. For example, a person with three round lots of ABC writes six calls. He has a 2-for-1 ratio write. The strategy accepts a middling risk position between that of the naked call writer and the covered call writer.

More commonly used term: *ratio write.*

VARIATION MARGIN
Term used most often in the futures industry to describe mark-to-the-market deposits required to supplement and collateralize open future contract commitments. In effect, both parties to the contract are properly secured on a day-to-day basis.

VAT
Acronym for value added tax. VAT is popular in Europe and the United Kingdom as a form of national sales tax. VAT is levied upon most goods

and services, based upon incremental increases in value at each stage of manufacture, distribution, or usage.

In the United Kingdom, VAT is also levied on commissions on securities transactions payable through inter-firm marketmakers, but not on orders placed with an in-house marketmaker.

VAULT CASH

Cash on hand in the vault of a bank. Concept: Member banks of the Federal Reserve System are required to maintain a statutory reserve (i.e., a specified percentage of time and demand deposits that they have accepted). This statutory reserve may take two forms: (1) money on deposit with the Federal Reserve and (2) cash in the vault of the bank. The latter is called "vault cash."

Neither 1 nor 2 is subject to capital risk; hence, they are truly a reserve against the deposits made by the clients of the bank.

VCR

Acronym for Variable Coupon Renewable Note. VCRs are a Goldman Sachs innovation designed to appeal to money market mutual funds. VCRs are a one-year note issued by a top-quality industrial company. The note is automatically renewable at the end of each quarter (91 days). The VCR is priced to float at 75 basis points above T-bills.

VCRs are putable (upon nine-month notice and a reduced yield).

VEGA

An analyst's expression used to describe the volatility of an equity issue. Specifically, vega measures the relationship between a stock's market price and the option premium it commands in the marketplace. In effect, vega is the inverse of DELTA.

VELDA SUE

Acronym for Venture Enhancement & Loan Development Administration for Smaller Undercapitalized Enterprises. Velda Sue is a U.S. government agency created to promote the funding of small businesses in the United States. It purchases and pools small business loans made by banks, securitizes them (in the same way as GNMA and FHLMC), and sells the security to large institutions as investments.

VELOCITY OF MONEY

Economic term that identifies the turnover of money in terms of expenditures for goods and services. Example: If the money supply were $500 billion and the gross national product were $3 trillion, the velocity of money would be 6: GNP divided by money supply equals velocity of money. Needless to say, this concept is fine-tuned by using the various money components, such as Ml, M2, and the like.

Also called the "velocity of circulation."

VENDOR PLACINGS
A somewhat inequitable British corporate finance technique used by some companies to acquire other companies. Recognizing that some shareholders may not want stock for their stock, the acquirer may intervene by placing such tendered stock with institutional holders in exchange for cash. It is inequitable in that all of the acquirer's shareholders do not get the same right to purchase new shares and maintain a proportionate interest in the company.

VENTURE CAPITAL
Industry term for an investment in a new, untried business venture with all of the financial risks inherent in such an enterprise.

Companies specializing in such in vestments are called "venture capital companies" and, as part of their compensation for such investments, usually demand a large portion of the equity ownership. Thus, if the risky enterprise prospers, they will be richly rewarded.

VENTURE ENHANCEMENT & LOAN DEVELOPMENT ADMINISTRATION FOR SMALLER UNDERCAPITALIZED ENTERPRISES
See VELDA SUE.

VERTICAL COMBINATION
See VERTICAL MERGER.

VERTICAL LINE CHARTING
Chart of a stock's price movement that uses a vertical line to represent the high and the low, with a horizontal line to represent the closing price. Line may be used of daily, weekly, monthly, or average prices over a period. As the information is charted, a trend may appear that will give indication of appropriate timing for purchase or sale of the security.

The completed chart also is called a "bar chart."

VERTICAL MERGER
A merger of businesses controlling various stages of production for a single product. Example: A merger of a paper mill with an ink producer and a newspaper publisher would be a vertical merger. The petroleum in-

dustry has many vertical mergers in that exploration, refining, and distribution often are combined.

Also called "vertical combination."

Antonym: a conglomerate—that is, a merger of businesses in disparate fields.

VERTICAL SPREAD

An option strategy whereby a client has long and short options of the same class, with the same expiration month, but with different strike prices. For example, long a July 60 put and short a July 50 put.

Also called a "price," or "money," spread.

See also BULL SPREAD and BEAR SPREAD.

V FORMATION

Description of a vertical line chart if the stock price pattern has the configuration of the letter V (bullish), or an inverted V (bearish).

Also called "V bottom" or "V top."

VI

Used lowercase in the stock or bond tables in the newspaper to designate that the corporation is undergoing reorganization under the bankruptcy laws of the United States.

VIENNA STOCK EXCHANGE

One of Europe's smallest stock exchanges. Trading is conducted each weekday from 11 A.M. until 1 P.M., with no after-hour activity permitted.

Settlements are scheduled for the second Monday following each full business week, either in cash or by means of a special weekly clearing system known as *arrangement*.

VIP

Acronym for Value of Index Participation contracts. VIPs are the CBOE counterpart of the PHLX's Cash Index Participations (CIPs).

VIPs are a type of security whose value is tied to the performance of either of two stock indexes created by the CBOE. Like the CIP and the EIP (AMEX), holders of this issue receive a proportionate share of the dividends paid to holders of the underlying stocks in the index.

However, unlike the other two products, naked (short) sellers can eliminate their liability (at the index value) by paying a small fee at cash-out time. That fee is paid to holders of the VIP as an extra dividend. They are now the subject of a court-issued injunction because of their similarity to futures contracts.

VISIBLE SUPPLY
The dollar value of municipal bonds that will come to market during the ensuing month. The value includes both competitive and noncompetitive issues.

Also called the "30-day visible supply" or the "calendar."

The visible supply gives underwriters an insight into the competitive risk they face from upcoming issues; thus, the underwriters of a marginal, small BBB-rated issue must so plan the offering that it does not compete head-on with a succession of AAA and AA offerings.

See also THIRTY-DAY VISIBLE SUPPLY.

VOCON
Abbreviation for: voluntary contribution.

Many participants in some employer-funded qualified pension plans are permitted to make voluntary contributions of aftertax dollars into such plans. Although the dollar contributions are aftertax, the internal growth of the contributed dollars is tax sheltered. This provides the principal benefit of VOCON contributions.

Following the Tax Reform Act of 1986, persons who are otherwise covered by qualified plans and who make above certain statutory amounts ($35K single, $50K married filing jointly) may not make $2,000 annual IRA contributions that are similar in function to VOCON contributions.

VOIDABLE
A transaction that can be annulled at a later date because, at the time of the transaction, it did not conform to the law. For example, a contract made by a minor.

See also RESCIND.

VOLATILE
Description of a stock, or a bond, or a market in general, whose price is subject to wide, rapid fluctuations.

VOLATILITY
Relative measure of a security's price movement during a specific time.
See also VOLATILITY RATIO.

VOLATILITY RATIO
Measurement of relative price movement of a security during a specific time. Normal measurement: subtract the low for the year from the high for the year. Divide the remainder by the low for the year to obtain the

percentage of volatility for the year. For example, the yearly range for a stock is 50 high, 30 low. The difference is 20 points. Divide 20 by 30 to get a volatility ratio of 2 to 3, or 66%.

VOLUME
The number of shares or bonds traded during a specific time. For example, the daily volume or the weekly volume.

Normally, volume figures are given for the principal marketplace for the security, although a wider base of measurement can be used.

Also used of total stock or bond trading. For example, 12 million shares were traded yesterday on the ASE.

VOLUME DELETED
Announcement on the consolidated tape that only symbols and prices will be given, unless the transaction is for 5,000 or more shares. Normally done when the tape is two or more minutes late in its reporting of securities transactions.

VOLUNTARY ACCUMULATION PLAN
Name for an informal and flexible program whereby a mutual fund owner, at various times and with varying amounts of money, may continue to purchase shares of the fund.

Also called an "open account."

VOLUNTARY ASSOCIATION
A membership organization that is not incorporated. However, there is continuing existence of the business enterprise. Membership in the organization is similar to membership in a partnership in that there is unlimited financial responsibility in the case of insolvency of the organization. For example, the NYSE was a voluntary association until 1971 when it became a not-for-profit corporation.

VOLUNTARY UNDERWRITER
Legal designation of an individual, partnership, or corporation that purchases a security from the issuer or an affiliated person and offers the security for public sale under an effective registration statement.

Antonym: statutory underwriter (i.e., a person who inadvertently becomes an underwriter because he purchases securities that are not registered and resells them publicly).

VOTING TRUST CERTIFICATE (VTC)
A registered certificate, issued by a bank under a trust agreement, to evidence the delivery of common shares into a voting trust. The certifi-

cate can be sold or transferred and has all the rights of ownership except the right to vote. This right is retained by the trust.

VTCs often arise when a company is in financial difficulties, or in proxy contests, and wants to so concentrate voting power that rapid changes in company management can be made as needed. Normally, voting trusts have a defined lifetime (e.g., five or seven years).

VRDO
Acronym for variable-rate demand obligation. VRDO is the generic name for a Shearson Lehman Corp. product similar to municipal commercial paper. VRDOs are tax-exempted debt whose interest rate is re-set daily and which can be put back to the underwriter or municipality at par value if the rate is unacceptable to the holder.

VRM
See VARIABLE-RATE MORTGAGE.

VSP
Abbreviation for: versus purchase. When followed by a calendar date on an order instruction to sell, or on a broker's confirmation, these initials identify the security being sold. Example: VSP 10-26-84 will identify the client's sale of securities acquired on October 26, 1984. Required in many cases because, if no designation is made by the client, the IRS requires that securities sales be considered as made on a first-in, first-out basis.

VTC
See VOTING TRUST CERTIFICATE.

VULTURE CAPITALIST
English euphemism for someone who contributes "seed money" to a new business but takes out so much in the early stages that the business is unable to succeed. In effect, a vulture capitalist is a venture capitalist with too little patience.

VULTURE FUNDS
A colorful name for organized pools of money assembled to purchase commercial real estate at sharply distressed prices. At the bottoms of business cycles (i.e., during recessions), such properties often are available at bargain prices and purchasers can profit tremendously as the economy recovers. Money for these purchases usually is funded by insurance companies, pension funds, and other well-capitalized institutional investors.

W

W
Twenty-third letter of the alphabet, used:
1. As the fifth letter in a NASDAQ/NMS symbol to signify a warrant. For example, LUVSW stood for Southwest Airlines warrants, a security enabling the holder to buy common stock at $35 per share through 6/25/90.
2. Alone uppercase as the NYSE symbol for Westvaco Corp., a large manufacturer of paper products.

WABO/WASO
Acronym for we are buyers (sellers) of. . . . Used by securities dealers in the United Kingdom as the heading for lists of securities that they are interested in buying (WABO), or are interested in selling (WASO). These lists are often circulated to salespersons and to other dealers prior to the opening of the market.

WAC
In real estate finance, this is the abbreviation for "weighted average coupon," the significant interest percentage applicable to a pass-through mortgage pool.

TO WAFFLE
From the Scottish dialect, "to speak equivocally." Thus, in practice, the act of changing one's opinion or to be indecisive. In the financial industry, the actions of someone who is ambivalent about investing, or who fails to take a firm stance in the management of a portfolio.

WAG THEORY
Facetious market theory, which sounds pretentious, but, in reality, stands for "wild-ass guess."
    See SWAG for a further explanation and example.

WAITER
The British equivalent of floor clerks on U.S. stock exchanges. On the International Stock Exchange, the waiters assist brokers in communicating messages, market information, and execution reports to member firms.

WAIVER BY CONDUCT DOCTRINE
Term used by U.S. regulators in their endeavor to obtain cooperation of foreign officials in the prosecution of persons violating U.S. securities laws from a foreign location. In effect, U.S. regulators endeavor to show

that the activity mutually violates the laws of both countries; in this way, they are able to get help from foreign governments. Otherwise, foreign laws often block international enquiries and conceal identities of persons acting to violate U.S. securities laws.

WAIVING THE MARKET
A regulatory term used to describe this action: A market arbitrageur, who is long stock and short an index future, sells the stock in an endeavor to lower its price and thereby profit on the futures contract. Such an action has quasi-manipulative overtones because it can make both sides of the arbitrage profitable to the detriment of public investors.

WALK-AWAY MERGER
In some mergers, there is often a built-in time delay because of needed approvals from regulators. Because of this, there may be a drop in the price of the acquirer's stock (which is going to be used in part to pay for the merger). Thus, there is usually a stipulation in the consolidation agreement that permits the acquired company to cancel; that is, to "walk away" from the merger if the acquiring company's stock falls below a predetermined price level.

WALKING DEAD
Stock market slang for an issue that does not react favorably to good news. In fact, such issues often do not react to any news—including the environment of a predominantly bullish market.

THE WALL
1. Verb phrase: going to the wall, or went to the wall. Used to signify a failure, or a defeat, for a corporation. For example, "They went to the wall because of the failure of their most recent marketing campaign."
2. Used in the expression "Chinese wall"; that is, the lack of communication of inside business information between the finance department of a broker/dealer (who have the information) and the sales and trading areas of the same firm (who do not have the information).

WALLFLOWER
A person who because of unpopularity or shyness remains without companionship at a party or dance. Thus, by metaphor, a stock, or indeed an entire industry, that is out of favor at the present time in the eyes of professional investors and portfolio managers. This unpopularity may be due to economic conditions or to lack of publicity about the company. For this reason, the role of the public relations expert for corporations has expanded dramatically in recent years.

WALLPAPER

As used in the securities industry, the term is derogatory and means a worthless certificate, either stock or bond. The inference is that the company became bankrupt and that no market exists for the security.

Do not confuse with the hobby of collecting old cancelled stock and bond certificates. Although these certificates have no stock or bond market value, they may have a great market value as collectors' items because of rarity or calligraphy.

See SCRIPOPHILY.

WAM

Acronym for weighted average maturity pools. In the pricing of securitized real estate pools, both MBSs and CMOs, it is possible that there will be a premature paydown of unpaid principal balance. Thus, the average life may be less than the stated time to maturity. For this reason, it is the custom to price such securities in terms of their estimated weighted average maturity. It is not unusual that such prices be stated as a yield, as a dollar price plus 32nds, or as a number of basis points above Treasuries of similar anticipated maturity.

WAR BABY

See WAR BRIDE.

WAR BRIDE

Also known as a "war baby," this is a reference to a company that was placed on an unusual footing because of its close connection to the government's war efforts in World War II. Such companies were immersed in defense contracting—hence the allusion—and many still are. General Dynamics, Raytheon, and Lockheed were "war brides"—and they still are to a great extent.

WAR CHEST

A picturesque term used in corporate circles to designate a fund of money set aside by a company to defend itself against a hostile tender offer. These funds are set aside to pay for legal fees and other costs deemed essential to preserve the company's independence.

WAREHOUSING

See PARKING.

WARM

Acronym for weighted average remaining maturity. The acronym has the same meaning as WAM (q.v.).

WARRANT
See SUBSCRIPTION WARRANT.

WARRANTS INTO NEGOTIABLE GOVERNMENT SECURITIES
See WINGS.

WART
Acronym for weighted average remaining term. It has the same meaning as WAM (q.v.).

WARTS
Acronym for warrants to buy Treasury securities. Initiated by Goldman Sachs, these are privileges to buy a fixed amount of a specific government issue at a fixed price from GS. The life of the warrant is generally six months to a year. Large amounts can be purchased under such warrants; thus, they appeal to speculators and portfolio managers who want to hedge large debt positions.

WASHINGTON METROPOLITAN AREA TRANSIT AUTHORITY (WMATA)
A government-assisted municipal agency created by Maryland, Virginia, and the District of Columbia to finance and operate mass transit facilities in the metropolitan District of Columbia. There is a federal guarantee on the bonds.

Interest income is subject to federal taxation and also may be subject to state and local taxation.

WASH-METS
Industry slang for the bonds of the Washington Metropolitan Transit Authority.

WASH SALE
1. A sale resulting in a disallowed capital loss because the seller purchased the same, or a substantially identical, security within 30 days prior to or 30 days after the sale at a loss. Tax advice is needed. (IRS definition.)
2. Popular name of the manipulative practice of buying and selling similar amounts of a security—at the same price through the same broker/dealer without a true change of beneficial ownership—to give the impression of trading activity. (SEC definition.)
See also PAINTING THE TAPE.

WASTING ASSET

1. Any asset that expires worthless at a particular time in the future; for example, a right, warrant, or option.
2. In particular, a long option; that is, the right but not the obligation to buy (call) or sell (put) a specified underlying. The specified underlying may be a stock, bond, currency, or index.

Because the option expires worthless at a specified time in the future, there is a "bias against its profitable exercise," and, therefore, long options are considered highly speculative and suitable only for speculative investors.

WATCHDOG (ON WALL STREET)

Tongue-in-cheek term for the Securities and Exchange Commission (SEC), the principal regulator of the securities industry in the United States.

WATCH LIST

Industry term for a security that is under surveillance to avoid illegal or unethical practices. A security may be on the watch list because of wide swings in price, a sudden flurry of buying or selling, or because a broker/dealer is about to underwrite the security and employee transactions in that security are not allowed. A watch list may be initiated by a broker/dealer or by an exchange or other self-regulating organization.

WATERED STOCK

Term for the practice of issuing additional shares of stock to represent the same amount of capital. For example, shares that are donated to corporate officers without an offsetting inflow of cash to the corporation's balance sheet.

Also called "diluting the shares."

WD

See WHEN DISTRIBUTED.

WEAK HANDS

Wall Street term for investors who are easily frightened into selling by bad news about a company or the market, or who—in the first adverse financial fortunes in their private life—sell to provide adequate funds for day-to-day budgeting.

Also called "weak sisters."

Antonym: strong hands (q.v.).

WEAK SISTERS

See WEAK HANDS.

WEDGE FORMATION
Alternate designation of the chart pattern termed a *coil, pennant,* or *triangle.*

Also called a "wedge formation."

See also TRIANGLE FORMATION.

WEE-WEE TRANSACTIONS
See WHEN-ISSUED, WHEN-ISSUED TRANSACTIONS.

WEIGHTED AVERAGE COUPON
See WAC.

WEIGHTED AVERAGE MATURITY POOLS
See WAM.

WELLS SUBMISSION
A written procedure that enables the subject of an SEC investigation to provide the commission with personal comments and opinions in an endeavor to persuade the SEC to discontinue the case under consideration.

WE OFFER RETAIL
See WOR.

WESTERN ACCOUNT
Term describing a corporate underwriting agreement in which syndicate members sign a contract with the issuer as a group but limit their individual liability to the specific quantity of shares or bonds that they individually underwrite.

In practice, the term often is used of corporate underwritings, although it is infrequently used of municipal underwritings that have similar responsibility features.

Also called a "divided account."

See also EASTERN ACCOUNT.

WE THE PEOPLE
This nickname, taken from the first three words of the Preamble of the Constitution of the United States, often is applied to Merrill Lynch & Company, the nation's largest brokerage firm. It also is the title of the company newspaper of Merrill Lynch.

W FORMATION
Term used to describe the appearance of the chart pattern of a security's price movement if, in general, it is similar to the letter w, either rightside up, or upside down.

See also DOUBLE BOTTOM and DOUBLE TOP.

WG

Initials used on corporate calendars, particularly if Canadian securities are being underwritten, to identify Wood Gundy, Inc., a major underwriter of securities.

WHEN DISTRIBUTED (WD)

Transactions made on the proviso that the contract is valid when, as, and if the underlying securities are distributed. For example, a company has proposed to distribute shares in a subsidiary, or shares of another corporation, subject to stockholder approval. Shares that may be distributed often will begin trading on a when-distributed basis.

See also WHEN ISSUED.

WHEN ISSUED (WI)

Technically: when, as and if issued.

1. A trade in U.S. Treasury bills after the auction is announced, but before the auction is actually held. After the auction, but before settlement, these bills trade on a when-issued basis.
2. Used to designate a trade settlement date that subsequently will be determined. Used extensively of the primary market for bonds, and occasionally for stocks. Example: The bond traded today but when-issued settlement will be in three weeks.

See also WHEN DISTRIBUTED.

WHEN-ISSUED, WHEN-ISSUED TRANSACTION

This is a trade in U.S. Treasury bills after the Treasury announces a forthcoming auction of those bills, but before the auction is actually held. After the auction, but before settlement, those bills trade on a regular when-issued basis.

WHIPSAW

Slang for the financial effect of a rapid upward price movement followed by a rapid downward price movement if a person is exposed to risk on both the up and down sides.

Usually used as a past participle: whipsawed. For example, "Writers of short straddles in ABC were whipsawed as the price shot up and then dropped like a rock."

WHISKEY

Popular nickname used by salespersons and floor traders for the common stock of Joseph Seagram & Sons, Ltd., a Canadian company listed on the NYSE.

The nickname is derived from the fact that Seagram's principal products are distilled spirits. Interestingly, the NYSE ticker symbol for Seagrams is VO, which also happens to be the name of one of its most popular brands of Canadian whiskey.

WHISPER STOCK
Descriptive term for a stock of a company that is rumored to be "in play"; that is, a company being purchased by arbitrageurs and speculators because they believe that the company will soon be the object of a friendly or hostile takeover. The allusion is to the fact that the name of the stock is "whispered" as though it were inside information; in fact, there is often more rumor than fact in the situation.

WHISTLE BLOWER
Term used in reference to the Insider Trading and Securities Fraud Enforcement Act of 1988. Thus, a whistle blower is anyone who informs the SEC about violators of the law. What is more, informants with facts or evidence, or both, of an illegal market transaction based on insider nonpublic information may be eligible for a bounty for their service to the country.

WHITE CHIPS
Colorful term for young, growing companies that are on their way to becoming "blue chips" as they mature and have stable earnings and markets.

WHITE-COLLAR WORKER
Generally accepted term for an administrative worker or a lower-level manager of a company. The allusion is to the uniform of accepted office wear: jacket, white shirt, and tie.

As a general rule, middle and upper management are so called and the term *blue-collar worker* is not used of them.

Antonym: BLUE-COLLAR WORKER.

See also STEEL-COLLAR WORKER.

WHITE KNIGHT
Slang for a person or corporation who saves a corporation from an unfriendly takeover by, in turn, taking over the corporation.

WHITEMAIL
The opposite of "greenmail" whereby a company is forced to buy out a potential raider at above-the-market prices just to get rid of the raider.

In whitemail, the company sells sizeable amounts of new stock to a preferred customer at below-market prices to perpetuate existing management. This "protection" makes a takeover quite difficult because the raider has to buy a large amount of extra stock, often at inflated prices.

WHITE-SHOE FIRM
Tongue-in-cheek expression for a broker/dealer that does not get involved in hostile relationships; that is, for or against clients. The origin of the term is uncertain: it may go back to college fraternity unwritten rules that a "brother" would do nothing to jeopardize social relationships with another "brother"; or it may mean that the broker/dealer would not get its shoes dirty in a fight between companies.

WHITE SQUIRE
A corporate finance term for someone who protects companies from corporate raiders. For example, there are some public relations firms that warn companies of unusual activity in company stock.

Do not confuse with "white knight"; that is, someone who comes to the rescue of a company *after* an unwelcome suitor appears on the scene. The "squire" acts *before* the raid is public.

WHITE'S RATING
A system of classifying municipal bonds developed by White's Tax-Exempt Bond Rating Service. The system is based on municipal trading markets, rather than on the credit rating of the underlying issuer. The classification, available on a subscription basis, endeavors to give an insight into appropriate yields for specific municipal securities.

WHOLE LOAN
Jargon for an unpooled, individual residential mortgage that is not part of a mortgage pool used to back a pass-through or a participation certificate.

WHOLESALER
1. Used as a synonym for the underwriter-sponsor of a mutual fund.
2. A broker/dealer who is eligible for discounts and selling concessions in his transactions with other broker/dealers.

WHOOPS
Nickname for securities of the Washington Public Power Supply System (WPPS). Term is important because of the large dollar volume of such securities (over $7 billion in 1982), the controversy over nuclear power, and a partial U.S. government guarantee of portions of this issue.

WI
See WHEN ISSUED.

WICKY

Slang for Warner Communications, a company engaged in the entertainment industry, derived from its NYSE stock symbol: WCI.

WIDE OPEN

Industry slang for an upcoming underwriting that has shares or bonds available for additional syndication because the present members of the syndicate have not subscribed fully to the available securities. The situation may exist because there are too few participants in the syndicate or because a lack of indications of interest has caused some prior participants to withdraw from the account.

See also UNDERBANKED.

WIDGET

1. The plastic tube used to hold messages and other information that are transported from place to place on the NYSE floor by its pneumatic tube system.
2. Term, used jocularly, of an item manufactured by a hypothetical corporation. For example, "Today, I want to talk about XYZ Corporation. Let's say that they make widgets. . . ."

WIDOW-AND-ORPHAN STOCK

A colorful term for a blue-chip investment that has both steady (or rising) prices and a steady (or rising) dividend.

The analogy is to the fact that widows and orphans are persons who are least able to stand a surprise. Thus, this stock is as steady as a rock in good times and bad.

WIGGLEY

Slang for Washington Gas Light Company, a major utility in the Northwest United States, derived from its NYSE stock symbol: WGI.

WILDCAT WELL

A speculative drilling venture for oil or gas in unproven territory—that is, in a location in which such products have not been found previously.

The term is used extensively in conjunction with direct participation programs.

WILSHIRE 5,000

The cumulative dollar value of the common stock of 5,000 publicly traded companies listed on the NYSE and ASE or traded on NASDAQ/NMS.

The index was created by Wilshire Associates, a Los Angeles-based SEC-registered investment advisor. The index, in effect, represents the trend in value (capitalization times price) of the 5,000 most widely traded stocks in the United States. At the time of writing (early 1990), the value of the Wilshire Index was approximately $3.25 trillion—with a "t."

WINDFALL
Used in the financial sense to describe a sudden and unexpected gain. For example, the sudden rise in world oil prices caused a windfall for well owners. Also used as an adjective. For example, Congress is proposing a windfall profit tax.

WINDOW
A time within which a person may do an action without additional cost or other adverse effects. Example: By signing a letter of intent, a mutual fund purchaser has a 13-month window within which to purchase a sufficient dollar amount of the fund to achieve the reduced sales charge for larger purchases.

WINDOW DRESSING
Slang for the portfolio adjustments made by the managers of portfolios at the end of the quarter so their printed reports to participants (mutual funds need only make semiannual reports) will include well-known investment-grade securities.

In effect, the managers are "dressing up" their reports for popular consumption. Losers, in the meantime, were sold off, and "blue chips" were put in the portfolio to dress it up.

See also TRADING UP.

WINDOWS
In the plural, the term does not allude to a recognized time frame for an investment opportunity; instead, it describes the periodic deposits of money into an insurance company's GIC for a qualified pension plan over an agreed upon number of years. Specified times for payments into these investment contracts of one to five years are called "windows."

WINDOW SETTLEMENT
Term used to describe the physical delivery against settlement of securities with the contra broker of the trade.

Term is descriptive: most broker/dealers have a specific location, usually a window, at which selling brokers can deliver securities and receive payment by check for the delivery.

In practice, window settlement is uncommon; most security transactions are cleared through continuous net settlement by a recognized depository. For example, they deal through SIAC, the Securities Industry

Association Clearing (Corporation), or through the facilities of the Depository Trust Company.

WINDOW TICKET
Industry term for a stamped receipt issued by a transfer agent to a broker/dealer for securities left with the agent for re-registration.

The term goes back to the old days when messengers physically delivered securities to banking windows and accepted receipts. Much of this work is now handled through depositories and is greatly simplified.

WINGGING
1. In the United Kingdom, a slang expression for doing something unethical or unprofessional in the financial industry. For example, "I feel that he is wingging the rules on suitability of customer recommendations."
2. Also in the United Kingdom, a constant complainer; that is, someone who blames his lack of financial success on outside manipulators of market prices.

WINGS
Acronym for warrants into negotiable government securities. Salomon Brothers' term for the option to buy a fixed number of Treasury notes at a fixed price for delivery at a future date. The immediate cash outlay is minimal. Used to hedge fixed-income portfolios, to establish a future price, or, in the case of foreign investors, to reduce foreign exchange risk.

WIRE HOUSE
1. Used factually of an exchange member firm that maintains a communication network linking its own branch offices or its own offices and those of other nonclearing members.
2. Used descriptively of any large member firm. Also used collectively. For example, "Most of the wire houses are competing for the few retail clients that remain."

WIRE ROOM
An operating area or function within a broker/dealer that is responsible for the transmission of customer orders, by changing them into floor tickets, so the orders may be executed in the appropriate marketplace.

Also called the "order room," or, more popularly, "wire and order."

WITHERING WITHDRAWAL PENALTY
Term used of no-load mutual funds, including 12b-1 funds, that have a diminishing fee for the early redemption of fund shares. The typical early redemption fee, known technically as a *contingent deferred sales*

charge, usually disappears in about four to five years after purchase of the fund shares; thus, it may be 5% the first year, 4% in the second year, and so on.

Some no-load funds charge a flat redemption fee; that is, a fee that does not diminish over time.

WITHHELD ORDER

NASD term descriptive of the practice of failing to enter a customer's mutual fund order in a timely fashion in an endeavor to outguess the market.

The withholding of orders violates industry rules.

WITHHOLDING

1. Action by a disbursing agent whereby a statutory portion of dividends and interest paid by a domestic corporation to holders who are nonresident aliens is withheld in payment of U.S. taxes. Under present tax laws, the practice applies to all distribution to U.S. citizens and resident aliens after July 1983.
2. Action by a broker/dealer whereby portions of the securities in an offering are sold to employees and members of their immediate family. The Rules of Fair Practice prohibit such actions if a hot issue is involved.

See also FREERIDING (1).

WITHHOLDING TAX AT THE SOURCE

Requirement of domestic issuers to withhold a portion of dividends and interest from nonresident aliens and foreign corporations in payment for the U.S. tax on these distributions. The percentage to be withheld is generally 30%, but the percentage often is reduced, or eliminated, depending on the tax treaty in effect between the United States and the alien's country of domicile.

WITH OR WITHOUT A SALE (WOW)

Instruction on an odd-lot limit order. Meaning: use an effective sale in the round-lot market or the quote for the stock, whichever comes first, to make this transaction. May be used for odd-lot buy or sell limit orders. The price to the customer must conform to his limit.

Not used of odd-lot market orders. Here, the customer may use buy on offer, or sell on bid, if he does not want to wait for an effective sale.

WITHOUT AN OFFER/BID

Expression often used to complete a one-sided quote. For example, a dealer may quote a security as 15 bid without an offer. Meaning: the dealer is willing to buy the security at 15, but the dealer is unwilling to sell—either because he does not have the security or is unwilling to sell short.

WITH PREJUDICE
Used in legal settlements if the parties to the original action are prohibited from reinitiating litigation on the same matter. In effect, the case is closed.

Antonym: without prejudice. The case may be reopened in the future.

Both terms also are used in popular parlance to signify the same concepts.

WITH RIGHTS OF SURVIVORSHIP
A form of joint account that permits assets in the account to pass to the ownership of the remaining party if one party dies. Often abbreviated JTWROS, or W/R/O/S.

See also JOINT TENANTS WITH RIGHTS OF SURVIVORSHIP.

WI WI TRANSACTION
See WHEN-ISSUED, WHEN-ISSUED TRANSACTION.

WMATA
See WASHINGTON METROPOLITAN AREA TRANSIT AUTHORITY.

WOLF PACK
Slang in corporate finance concerning some corporate mergers. It is best described as one investor purchasing a large position in a public company, then signaling others to follow suit by publicizing that company's vulnerability to potential takeover.

WONDER STOCK
Expression for a stock of a company that is involved in an exciting new technology and that, as a result, is expected to soar in price. Currently, stocks involved in AIDS research, pollution control, certain areas of high technology, robotics, and advanced communications are considered to be wonder stocks.

WOODEN TICKET
Slang for the unethical practice of confirming the execution of an order to a customer without actually doing so. The practice is deceptive and, in effect, the broker/dealer is relying on a change in the market price so the actual transaction, when later made, will provide the broker/dealer with a larger profit.

WOOLWORTH FIVES & TENS

Traders' reference to U.S. Treasury issues with 5- and 10-year maturities. Such bonds and notes are usually benchmarks for the pricing of other bonds in terms of yield spread. The designation is made to Woolworth's because that store was originally known as Woolworth's 5 and 10 Cent Store—a high-volume, lower-priced retailer.

WOR

Acronym for we offer retail; that is, at a net price to the buyer because all transaction costs are borne by the seller.

WORKING CAPITAL

General term for the remainder obtained if current liabilities are subtracted from current assets of a corporation.

Also called "net working capital."

See also NET CURRENT ASSETS.

WORKING CAPITAL RATIO

See CURRENT RATIO.

WORKING CONTROL

The ability to dictate corporate policy by a person, or persons, who have less than 50% ownership of a corporation. Persons with more than 50% ownership always have control of a company. In practice, because of the dispersion of shares among many holders, minority holders often may be able to effectively control the corporation.

WORKING INTEREST

In direct participation programs, this term refers to an investor's financial interest in a partnership that is drilling and maintaining oil and gas wells. Working interest is not synonymous with equity, because working interest may include large sums of borrowed money through recourse and nonrecourse loans.

The term also is used of other tax-sheltered ventures, such as limited partnerships created for real estate, cattle and horse breeding, movie production, and certain farming ventures.

WORKING ORDER

An instruction to buy or sell a significant quantity of a stock. "Working" means that the execution is to be effected slowly and carefully on a piecemeal basis and thus not unduly change the market price level of the stock.

WORKOUT MARKET

A range of prices within which a broker/dealer feels that a transaction may be made. For example, a client wants to sell a block of stock. He asks a broker/dealer for an approximation of the sale price. The response: "I feel that it is 20 to 22, workout." The broker/dealer's estimation is that the block can be sold somewhere between $20 and $22 per share.

WORLD BANK

1. The International Bank for Reconstruction and Development, abbreviation IBRD. A multinational bank created to promote economic development in countries that are members of the organization. IBRD provides loans for construction projects and technical assistance in those member countries.
2. The debt securities issued by the World Bank, the popular name for the International Bank for Reconstruction and Development.

WORLD GOVERNMENT BOND INDEX

A Salomon Brothers product designed to track the price performance of government securities in nine different international markets. Two government bonds (Japan and the United States) account for approximately three fourths of the index; the remaining countries are Great Britain, West Germany, France, Canada, the Netherlands, Australia, and Switzerland.

WOW ORDER

See WITH OR WITHOUT A SALE.

WRAP ACCOUNT

Term used of a customer's special brokerage account at a large diversified firm. The broker/dealer chooses a money manager for the customer, pays the money manager from the customer's assets, and executes the orders authorized by the investment advisor.

An annual fee is charged for the service. At year-end the broker/dealer is to monitor the performance of the advisor and report to the customer.

WRAPAROUND ANNUITY

An annuity contract that provides a tax shelter from dividends, interest, and capital appreciation, but in which the subscriber designates the specific securities upon which the security will be funded. The insurance company assumes no principal risk until such time as the contract is annuitized.

Also called an "investment annuity."

790

WRAPAROUND MORTGAGE

A mortgage loan built around two components: an assumable mortgage from the previous seller and a new loan from the carrying bank. The recipient of the wraparound mortgage has a lower average rate of interest than would be available if the entire mortgage amount were covered by one interest rate.

WRINKLE

Slang: a feature of a security that may be advantageous to the holder. For example, a company offers to exchange outstanding 11% bonds with new 10% bonds with this wrinkle: The holder may tender the bonds at par five years from the day of the exchange. Obviously, this feature would be profitable to the holder if, five years from now, interest rates were substantially in excess of 10%. He could redeem at par and reinvest at higher interest rates. Meanwhile, the company has saved 1% of its interest costs each year.

WRITE OUT

Exchange floor slang if a specialist decides, within exchange rules, to trade with an order that is on his book. Rule: specialist must summon broker who entered order. This broker writes the order, with the specialist as other side of the trade, and thus broker earns the commission for the completed trade. Broker's client will, in turn, trade with the specialist using normal industry channels to complete transaction. There is no additional charge to client for this procedure.

WRITER

Common term for the person who sells an option contract, thereby obligating himself to the performance agreed upon in the contract: to sell (if a call was written), to buy (if a put was written).

WRIT OF CERTIORARI

Legal writ issued by an appeals court to a lower court if it decides to hear an appeal. The term means that the lower court is to deliver the relevant trial or proceeding records to the appeals court. (Latin: to be informed.)

In practice, therefore, to appeal a court decision, one of the parties applies for a writ of certiorari. If the appeals court is willing to accept the appeal, it issues the writ to the original court.

W/R/O/S

Acronym for (joint tenants) with rights of survivorship. A form of joint tenancy in which ownership passes to the other tenant(s) upon the death of one of the tenants. Probate thus is avoided.

WT

Used on the exchange tape and in other industry literature as an abbreviation for a warrant.

See also SUBSCRIPTION WARRANT.

X

X

The twenty-fourth letter of the alphabet, used:

1. In the newspaper tables to designate a security that is trading ex-dividend.
2. On the Quotron system to differentiate the number of shares bid and offered. For example, 10 × 11 signifies that 1,000 shares are bid at the prevailing quote and 1,100 shares are offered.

XCH

Used of a transaction between broker/dealers that will be completed outside the regular clearing facilities. The term means: ex-clearing house.

XD

Abbreviation for: ex-dividend (i.e., the buyer of the security will not receive the next payable dividend).

Y

Y

The twenty-fifth letter of the alphabet, used:

1. As the generally accepted symbol for the Japanese yen. Generally, the Y is written with two horizontal lines through its downstroke; for example, ¥.
2. As the fifth letter in NASDAQ/NMS symbols if the underlying is an American Depository Receipt. For example, Fisons ADRs has the symbol FISNY.
3. Used alone uppercase as the NYSE symbol for Allegheny Corporation, a large title insurer and financial conglomerate.

¥

The symbol for yen, the primary currency of Japan.

See also YEN.

YACKER
Term associated with high-pressure salespersons in a "boiler room" operation. Although there are few such boiler rooms around today, the counterpart is the high-pressure "penny stock" sales organization. The "yacker" is the front person who engages the prospective customer in idle chatter to determine if the prospect is interested; one or more salespersons may then take over for the actual sale (or follow-up sale).

YANKEE BOND
Industry slang for a bond of a foreign issuer that is denominated in dollars and that has been registered for sale in the United States.

A YARD
Slang used in foreign currency transactions to signify "one billion." For example, "It is not unusual for large international money center banks to lay off 20 yards of currency transactions a day."

YB
NYSE specialist code name for "omnibus dealer accounts." It is a single contra party designation given up to floor brokers by specialists in lieu of a multitude of actual names on the opposite side of a particular transaction. Thus, in an active market, the specialist can give up YB as an omnibus designator, rather than take the time to designate each of the names. Eventually, the names will have to be given up for confirmation and clearing purposes, either to the contra broker or to the clearinghouse.

YBTO
Short identifier for: Yield-Based Treasury Option, an index listed on the CBOE that is European-style and cash settled.

    The excise price of this instrument is based upon the annualized yield to maturity of the underlying Treasury obligations.

YCA
See YIELD CURVE AGREEMENT.

YCAN
Acronym for Yield Curve Adjustable Note. YCANs are a Morgan Stanley product first employed by Sallie Mae as a five-year obligation whose interest-rate payments were keyed to LIBOR rates and reset semiannually until maturity.

YEARLING
Colloquial name in the United Kingdom for a bond with one year to maturity. Originally the term came from the weekly offering by English coun-

cils (governmental agencies not unlike our states and political subdivisions) under the auspices of the U.K. Treasury and the Bank of England.

Yearlings are issued in bearer form in the name of the individual councils. Their interest rate is set in common by the U.K. Treasury as dictated by current money market rates.

THE YEAR OF THE JUBILEE
A biblical theory of economics. Thus, there is a long wave cycle of approximately 50 years. The excesses of previous years will be "purged" by a depression, and then a new business cycle—one of prosperity—will begin and will last for another "jubilee"; that is, about 50 years.

See also KONDRATIEFF CYCLE for a similar long-term wave or cycle.

YELLOW COLOR THEORY
A lighthearted market indicator. It presumes that when the popularity of the color yellow is on the rise in clothing, packaging, and home decor the stock market is on the rise. When yellow falls out of popularity, the stock market will fall.

YELLOW SHEETS
A listing, published each business day by the National Quotation Bureau, of unlisted corporate bonds and their marketmakers. So called for the color of the paper on which the listing is made.

YEN
The primary currency in Japan. The yen is a major "hard" currency and is extensively traded in the spot, forward, futures, and options markets.

Symbol: ¥.

YEN BOND
A bond, originally issued outside the United States, that is denominated in Japanese yen. Such bonds are not registered for sale in the United States, although after the bond is "seasoned" (traded for a reasonable period outside the United States) it may become eligible for trading here.

YIELD
General term for the percentage return on a security investment. Although the context often will qualify the term, investors should be careful to use the term with a qualifier so the precise meaning is clear. For example, nominal (coupon) yield, current yield, yield to maturity, or yield to average life, and so on.

Often called "rate of return."

See also DIVIDEND.

YIELD ADVANTAGE
Term describing the difference, if any, between current yield on a convertible security and current yield on the underlying common stock. For example, a convertible preferred has a current yield of 7% and the current yield on the common stock is 4¹/₂%. The yield advantage is 2¹/₂%.

Added insight: The percentage premium over conversion parity paid on the convertible divided by the yield advantage will give the number of years to repay the premium paid for the convertible. For example, a premium of 8% over parity will be repaid in four years if the yield advantage is 2%.

YIELD-BASED TREASURY OPTION
See YBTO.

YIELD CURVE
General term for the graph depicting yields on the *y*-axis, and time to maturity on the *x*-axis, for fixed-income securities of the same class (e.g., corporates, utilities, governments, municipalities, and so on). Yield curves may be ascending (long-term bonds yield more than short-term bonds); descending (short-term bonds yield more than long-term bonds); or flat (both yield approximately the same).

A knowledge of the configuration of the yield curve and its trend is essential to intelligent fixed-income investing.

YIELD CURVE ADJUSTABLE NOTE
See YCAN.

YIELD CURVE AGREEMENT
Popular abbreviation: YCA. YCAs are arrangements between large investment banking firms and large institutional customers whereby the customer, on a semiannual basis, pays six-month LIBOR rates and receives in return the 10-year Treasury note yield minus 50 basis points. Thus, over the 10-year life of the YCA, the customer receives money every six months if the spread between LIBOR and 10-year T-notes is wider than 50 basis points.

The term *large* is important: only large investment bankers can take the risk and only large institutional customers have the sophistication to make such an agreement.

YIELD CURVE NOTES
Term associated with certain issues of medium-term Student Loan Marketing Association securities. The interest rate on these notes maturing after 1990 is pegged to the LIBOR rate and will rise or fall semiannually as that benchmark rate reflects current interest-rate trends.

YIELD EQUIVALENCE
Term used in the completion of GNMA contracts: spot, forward, or option.

In effect, yield equivalence permits a seller to deliver various GNMA securities—each one, after all, represents a different pool—so the buyer gets the agreed-upon yield. This is accomplished by so adjusting the contract purchase price that the yield is maintained. For example, a contract to deliver a 12% GNMA at 90 may be effected by delivering a 10% GNMA at 77, if the yield will be 13.21% on either security.

See also YIELD MAINTENANCE CONTRACT.

YIELD GAP
U.K. term for the average rate of return on gilts in relation to the yield on U.K. equities. Theoretically, the yield gap should be a function of risk, with the riskier equity investments yielding more than the blue-chip gilts.

Note: In this expression, the term *yield* when used of equities means *total return;* that is, a combination of growth and dividend income.

YIELD MAINTENANCE CONTRACT
Trading in GNMA securities permits the basic contract to center on yield. Thus, a contract may be settled with the specific rate designated in the contract, or with other rates, provided the yield to the buyer is that agreed upon. This will require a price adjustment if securities with differing rates are delivered against the contract.

YIELD TO AVERAGE LIFE
Term used by money market funds—and often by dealers in unit investment trusts—to designate the simple interest that a new investor will receive, based on present cash flow and the average life of the securities in the portfolio. The yield is an estimate and presumes no portfolio changes.

Term should not be confused with the *yield to average life* used of GNMA securities. In this case, the yield is the anticipated compound rate of return and presumes the reinvestment of the cash flows as received.

YIELD TO MATURITY (YTM)
A measurement of the compound rate of return that an investor in a bond with a maturity of more than one year will receive if: (1) he holds the security to maturity and (2) he reinvests all cash flows at the same market rate of interest.

YTM is an approximation and presumes a flat yield curve. However, it is used extensively in comparing fixed-income investments, in making fixed-income portfolio decisions, and in financial planning if an investor does not want to spend investment income but, instead, is looking for an increase in net worth.

The YTM is greater than current yield when the bond is selling at a discount, less when it is selling at a premium.

YIELD TRADING
See BASIS TRADING.

YMCA
Acronym for young married career-oriented accentuators. Tongue-in-cheek term for the group of college and business school graduates who descended on Wall Street and the investment banking industry during the bull market of the 80s intent on making it rich in a hurry. The allusion is to men of the YMCA (Young Men's Christian Association) who generally have loftier ideals.

YTM
See YIELD TO MATURITY.

YUPPIES
See DINKs.

Z

Z
Twenty-sixth and last letter of the alphabet, used:
1. In stock volume listings to designate that the number is to be multiplied by 10 and not by 100. Thus, z55 is 550 shares traded, not 5,500.
2. In mutual fund listings to designate that the fund did not provide bid-asked prices by press time.
3. As the fifth letter in NASDAQ/NMS listings to designate closed-end investment company shares, or "limited partnership" interests. For example, TPLPZ stands for Teeco Properties, LP.
4. Alone uppercase as the NYSE symbol for F. W. Woolworth Co., a major retailer in the United States.

ZAITECH
A Japanese term that aggregates the concept of "zaimer" (financial) and high technology; thus, ZAITECH.

It refers to the growing number of Japanese companies that have turned from manufacturing or product distribution to an investment of surplus funds into a multitude of financial instruments. Needless to say, the officials of these companies need superior financial sophistication to function profitably outside their original areas of expertise.

ZARABA TRADING
The method of trading that is used in the first session (9 to 11 A.M.) on the principal Japanese exchanges.

Zaraba trading is fast-paced. The auction system used is similar to the auction trading on the principal exchanges in the United States.

Z-BOND
Z-bonds are the residual tranche (class) of CMOs. As the last part of a serialized mortgage obligation, the interest payable is not immediately distributed. Instead, it accrues and is added to principal. Then, at the time of redemption or maturity (whichever comes first), the holder is told how much of the final distribution is interest and how much is principal.

Also known as an "accrual bond."

ZERIAL BOND
Slang to designate a zero-coupon bond that is issued in serial form. Stripped Treasury bonds are classic examples of "zerials."

See also MONEY MULTIPLIER SECURITY.

ZERO COUPON
Descriptive term for a debt security that (1) is issued at a discount from its face value, (2) matures at face value in more than one year, and (3) promises no other cash flow than the payment of the face value at maturity. The security may or may not be redeemable prior to maturity, depending on the indenture.

The difference between purchase price and the adjusted cost of acquisition, over time, is interest income. Tax advice is needed for the computation of the annual accretion of the adjusted cost of acquisition.

In general, zero coupon corporate bonds should be purchased by individual investors only in tax-sheltered accounts.

ZEROES
Popular designation for zero-coupon bonds (q.v.).

ZERO-MINUS TICK
Designation of a transaction price for a security that is (1) the same as the previous round-lot price, but (2) the previous round-lot price was lower than the next prior price. For example, transactions occur at:

21.....20.....20

The last transaction at 20 was made on a zero-minus tick. It was at the same price as the previous transaction, but both transactions were lower than the prior transaction at 21.

ZERO-PLUS TICK
Designation of a transaction price for a security that is (1) the same as the previous round-lot price, but (2) the previous round-lot price was higher than the next prior price. For example, transactions occur at:

$$30......31.......31$$

The last transaction at 31 was made on a zero-plus tick. It was at the same price as the previous transaction, but both transactions were higher than the prior price of 31.

Short sales may be made only on a plus tick or a zero-plus tick.

ZETA RISK
The prospective additional loss at each future contract price interval caused by a change in product volatility.

ZOMBIE BONDS
Slang expression for the debt obligations of near-bankrupt thrift institutions. Because no one knows whether or not these institutions will default, their debt sells at near-bankruptcy levels.

ZOMBIES
Nickname given to insolvent savings and loans that continue to function under the conservatorship of the FDIC. In effect, they are technically "brain dead" (hence the term *zombie*) institutions awaiting final congressional decision on whether they will be saved or scuttled.

ZURICH STOCK EXCHANGE
The exchange is actually the Zurich, Geneva, and Basle exchanges linked together by computerized quotations.

There is one daily trading session—from 10:30 A.M. until 1:30 P.M.—although after-hour trading is not prohibited. Settlement is made on the third business day after trade date by means of the Swiss Interbank Clearing System.

Eventually, trading on the exchange will be completely electronic.